prae/sens

Singularia Vindobonensia

herausgegeben von
Christian Gastgeber und Elisabeth Klecker

Band 6

Christian Gastgeber, Elisabeth Klecker (Hgg.)

Johannes Sambucus
János Zsámboki
Ján Sambucus
(1531–1584)

Philologe, Sammler und Historiograph
am Habsburgerhof

Praesens Verlag

Gedruckt mit Förderung durch

Kulturabteilung der Stadt Wien, Wissenschafts- und Forschungsförderung (Magistratsabteilung 7)

Umschlagbild:
Ioannes Sambucus, Emblemata et aliquot nummi antiqui operis. Antverpiae: ex officina Christophori Plantini 1566, p. 193, Emblem VIRTUTEM HONOR SEQUITUR (Farbbild)
(Wien, Universitätsbibliothek I 125.521)
Ioannes Sambucus, Emblemata cum aliquot nummis antiqui operis. Antverpiae: ex officina Christophori Plantini 1564, Vorsatzblatt[v] mit Widmung an Kaiser Maximilian II. vom 26. September 1564 und Titelblatt (Hintergrundbilder)
(Wien, Österreichische Nationalbibliothek 74.W.95)

Bibliografische Information der Deutschen Bibliothek
Die Deutsche Bibliothek verzeichnet diese Publikation in der Deutschen Nationalbibliografie; detaillierte bibliografische Daten sind im Internet unter <http://dnb.ddb.de> abrufbar.

ISBN: 978-3-7069-0968-6

© Praesens Verlag
http://www.praesens.at
Wien 2018

Alle Rechte vorbehalten. Rechteinhaber, die nicht ermittelt werden konnten, werden gebeten, sich an den Verlag zu wenden.

Neue Forschungen zu Johannes Sambucus

Vorwort

ELISABETH KLECKER (Wien)

Abb. 1: Gedenktafel für Johannes Sambucus
(Wien 1, Singerstraße 3)

Prosimus quibus est copia forte minor.
USUS LIBRI, NON LECTIO PRUDENTES FACIT. Sambucus, Emblemata 1564, 60f.

Im Gegensatz zu anderen bedeutenden Wiener Humanisten, Conrad Celtis (1459–1508), Johannes Cuspinianus (1473–1529) und Wolfgang Lazius (1517–1565), hat sich das Epitaph des Johannes Sambucus (1531–1584) nicht erhalten: Die im Besitz der Freiherrn Geyer von Osterburg befindliche Schlosskirche Inzersdorf, ein Zentrum des Protestantismus[1], wo Sambucus als Lutheraner seine letzte Ruhestätte gefunden hatte, fiel 1817 einem Brand zum Opfer; die Reste des im Zweiten Weltkrieg zerstörten alten Schlosses wichen 1965 einer Wohnhausanlage[2].

Auch Sambucus' Stadthaus (Innere Stadt, Singerstraße 3) besteht nicht mehr, am Nachfolgebau wurde zum 400. Todestag 1984 eine Gedenktafel mit seinem Porträt angebracht (Abb. 1)[3]. Zumindest durch diese ist Sambucus also im heutigen Stadtraum präsent, nachdem die drei oben genannten älteren Humanisten bereits Ende des 19. Jahrhunderts durch Straßennamen

---

[1] Rudolf LEEB, „Europa niemals kannte ein größere Kommun ..." Die evangelischen Pfarrzentren für Wien außerhalb der Stadtmauern in der Reformationszeit. In: Rudolf Leeb, Walter Öhlinger, Karl Vocelka (Hgg.), Brennen für den Glauben. Wien nach Luther. 413. Sonderausstellung des Wien Museums, 16. Februar bis 14. Mai 2017. Wien 2017, 182–197; hier 187–191.

[2] Ein Grabepigramm zitieren Otto Aicher, Theatrum Funebre [...] Extructum à Dodone Richea B. Salisburgi: sumpt. & typis Joannis Baptistae Mayr 1673, Bd. 2, 394 und wohl nach ihm David Czwittinger, Specimen Hungariae literatae [...]. Francofurti et Lipsiae: Jod. Guil. Kohlesius 1711, 329f. Der Historiker der Wiener Universität, Jakob Locher, lokalisiert das von ihm ebenfalls wörtlich wiedergegebene Epigramm in St. Stephan (Wien, Universitätsarchiv, B 141/II/L, pag. 340). Nach Auskunft von Andreas Zajic / Österreichische Akademie der Wissenschaften, Institut für Mittelalterforschung könnte entweder nur der metrische Teil der Inschrift (die komplett Namen, Sterbedatum und Stiftung durch die Witwe genannt haben muss) nach der Schließung der Schlosskirche nach Wien verbracht worden sein oder Locher für ein rein literarisches Grabepigramm St. Stephan als üblichen Begräbnisort für Angehörige der Universität (wie es Sambucus freilich nicht war) vermutet haben.

[3] Signiert Kamenyeczky 1984; Vorbild war das Porträt in Veterum aliquot ac recentium medicorum philosophorumque Icones. Ex bibliotheca Ioannis Sambuci [...]. Antverpiae: ex officina Christophori Plantini 1574, Nr. 67. – Auch von Sambucus' Landgut in Mannersdorf am Leithagebirge scheint sich nichts erhalten zu haben: Walpurga ANTL-WEISER, Mannersdorf am Leithagebirge. Stadtgeschichte. Mannersdorf [1994].

Vorwort

geehrt worden waren[4]. Gemeinsam mit diesen hatte er jedoch schon 300 Jahre zuvor ein Denkmal erhalten: Die Inschrift, die Peter Lambeck (1628–1680) 1663 für die von ihm neugeordnete Hofbibliothek verfasste und in sein monumentales Werk *Commentarii Augustissimae bibliothecae Caesareae* einfügte, erinnert an den Zuwachs der kaiserlichen Büchersammlung durch die Bibliotheken der Wiener Humanisten (Abb. 2)[5].

Sambucus' überragende Bedeutung für die Hofbibliothek (und damit für die heutige Österreichische Nationalbibliothek) ist mit dieser Inschrift freilich nur unzureichend beschrieben, wird jedoch für deren griechischen Handschriftenbestand von Lambeck immer wieder gewürdigt[6]. Und es ist in der Tat seine Handschriftensammlung mit den aus ihr hervorgegangenen Ausgaben, die Sambucus schon vor dem großen Aufschwung von Humanismusforschung und Neolatinistik im letzten Drittel des 20. Jahrhunderts das Interesse der Wissenschaft, insbesondere der Byzantinistik, gesichert hat[7].

So widmet sich der vorliegende Band der *Singularia Vindobonensia* einem Gelehrten, der in der Wiener Forschung schon lange kein Unbekannter ist, aktuell aber auf internationaler Ebene geradezu eine Renaissance erlebt: In den Jahren 2005 und 2009 erschienen umfangreiche Monographien[8], 2014 wurden die Paratexte seiner bzw. von ihm angeregter Publikationen zusammen mit einer Darstellung seiner philologischen Arbeitsweise ediert[9].

---

[4] Celtesgasse: 19. Bezirk (Döbling), Salmannsdorf (Beschluss 18. Juli 1894); Spießhammergasse: 12. Bezirk (Meidling), Untermeidling (Beschluss 1894); Laziusstraße: 23. Bezirk (Liesing), Inzersdorf (Beschluss im Gemeinderatsausschuss für Kultur 7. Oktober 1982). Für den Hinweis sei Herbert Bannert gedankt.

[5] Zum Übergang von Sambucus' Büchersammlung an die Hofbibliothek neuerdings: Noémi VISKOLCZ, The fate of Johannes Sambucus' library. *Hungarian Studies* 30 (2016), 155–166.

[6] Zu Lambecks Beschäftigung mit Sambucus vgl. den Beitrag von Christian Gastgeber in diesem Band.

[7] Zu verweisen ist vor allem auf Arbeiten von Hans Gerstinger (1885–1971). Vgl. Herbert HUNGER, Hans Gerstinger. *Almanach der Österreichischen Akademie der Wissenschaften* 121 (1971 [1972]), 353–368.

[8] Arnoud VISSER, *Joannes Sambucus and the Learned Image. The Use of the Emblem in Late Renaissance Humanism*. Leiden 2005 (Brill's Studies in Intellectual History 128); Gábor ALMÁSI, *The Uses of Humanism. Andreas Dudith (1533–1589), Johannes Sambucus (1531–1584), and the East Central European Republic of Letters*. Leiden 2009 (Brill's Studies in Intellectual History 185).

[9] Gábor ALMÁSI, Gábor Farkas KISS, *Humanistes du bassin des Carpates. II: Johannes Sambucus*. Turnhout 2014 (Europa humanistica 14).

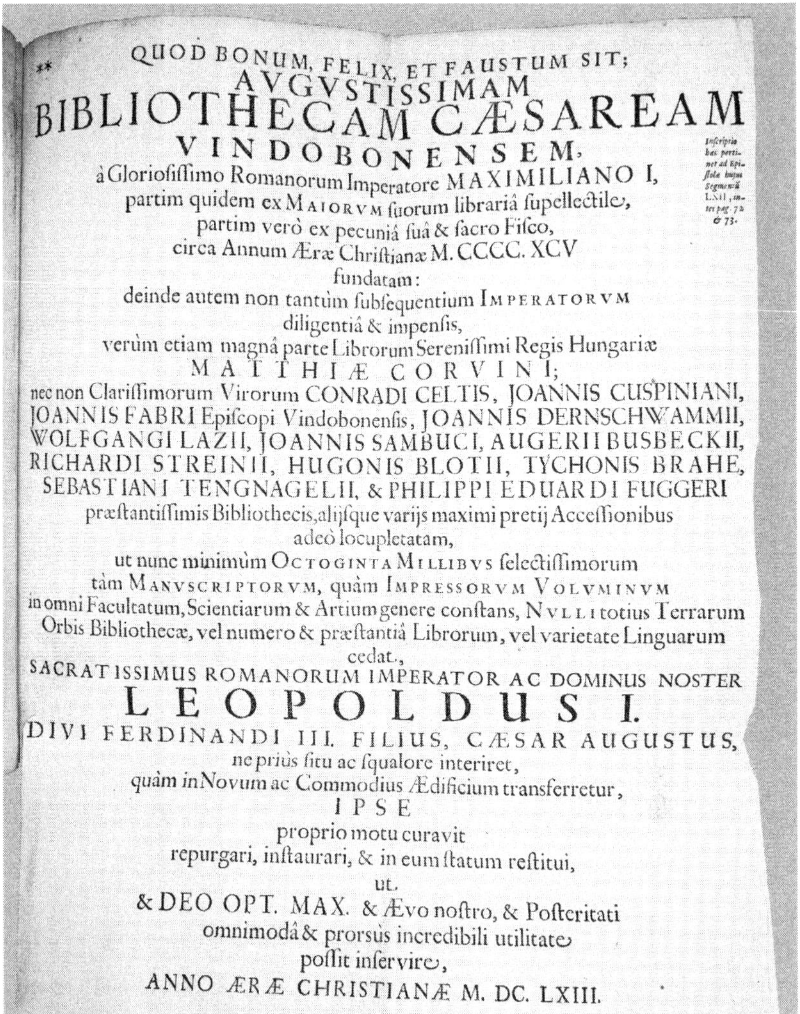
** QUOD BONUM, FELIX, ET FAUSTUM SIT;
AVGVSTISSIMAM
BIBLIOTHECAM CÆSAREAM
VINDOBONENSEM,
à Gloriosissimo Romanorum Imperatore MAXIMILIANO I,
partim quidem ex MAIORVM suorum librariâ supellectile,
partim verò ex pecuniâ suâ & sacro Fisco,
circa Annum Æræ Christianæ M. CCCC. XCV
fundatam:
deinde autem non tantùm subsequentium IMPERATORVM
diligentiâ & impensis,
verùm etiam magnâ parte Librorum Serenissimi Regis Hungariæ
MATTHIÆ CORVINI;
nec non Clarissimorum Virorum CONRADI CELTIS, JOANNIS CUSPINIANI,
JOANNIS FABRI Episcopi Vindobonensis, JOANNIS DERNSCHWAMMII,
WOLFGANGI LAZII, JOANNIS SAMBUCI, AUGERII BUSBECKII,
RICHARDI STREINII, HUGONIS BLOTII, TYCHONIS BRAHE,
SEBASTIANI TENGNAGELII, & PHILIPPI EDUARDI FUGGERI
præstantissimis Bibliothecis, alijsque varijs maximi pretij Accessionibus
adeò locupletatam,
ut nunc minimùm OCTOGINTA MILLIBVS selectissimorum
tàm MANVSCRIPTORVM, quàm IMPRESSORVM VOLVMINVM
in omni Facultatum, Scientiarum & Artium genere constans, NVLLI totius Terrarum
Orbis Bibliothecæ, vel numero & præstantiâ Librorum, vel varietate Linguarum
cedat,
SACRATISSIMUS ROMANORUM IMPERATOR AC DOMINUS NOSTER
LEOPOLDUS I.
DIVI FERDINANDI III. FILIUS, CÆSAR AUGUSTUS,
ne priùs situ ac squalore interiret,
quàm in Novum ac Commodius Ædificium transferretur,
IPSE
proprio motu curavit
repurgari, instaurari, & in eum statum restitui,
ut
& DEO OPT. MAX. & Ævo nostro, & Posteritati
omnimodâ & prorsùs incredibili utilitate
possit inservire,
ANNO ÆRÆ CHRISTIANÆ M. DC. LXIII.

Inscriptio haec pertinet ad Epistolæ huius Segmentũ LXII, inter pag. 72 & 73.

Abb. 2: Peter Lambeck, Inschrift der Hofbibliothek.
Commentarii Augustissimae bibliothecae Caesareae. Bd. I. Wien 1665,
Falttafel zwischen S. 72 und 73
(Wien, Universitätsbibliothek II 256.737)

Hinter diesem intensivierten Interesse stehen nicht nur die Bücherschätze einer facettenreichen Persönlichkeit, sondern auch rezente Umbrüche politischer und technologischer Natur: Die wiedergegebene Möglichkeit grenzüberschreitenden Forschens und Kooperierens erlaubt es nach langer Unterbrechung, der europäischen Dimension dieses Gelehrtenlebens, wie sie sich in Reisen und einem weitgespannten Briefnetzwerk zeigt, gerecht zu werden, damit auch die „Funktionen des Humanismus" nachzuverfolgen. Dazu sind in den letzten Jahren mit der Digitalisierung großer Bibliotheksbestände und der Einrichtung einschlägiger Internetportale, wie *Emblematica online*[10], günstige Bedingungen für die Bearbeitung von Sambucus' erfolgreichstem Werk, den *Emblemata*, geschaffen worden[11].

Als im September 2011 in Kooperation mit dem Balassi Institut / Collegium Hungaricum Wien ein Sambucus gewidmetes Workshop veranstaltet wurde, sollte diese neue Forschungssituation fruchtbar gemacht werden: für Sambucus als Handschriftensammler, Herausgeber und Inspirator von Ersteditionen, aber auch für die weniger beachtete Seite seines Wirkens, seine eigenen Werke, die abgesehen von den *Emblemata* von der bisherigen Forschung vernachlässigt wurden. Mit den verschriftlichten Referaten von 2011 und mehreren zusätzlich eingeholten Beiträgen will der nun vorliegende Band gleichsam vom Verdikt des Karl Gottlieb Windisch (1725–1793), Sambucus sei „geschickter" gewesen, „andern die Wissenschaften beyzubringen, als selbst etwas Wichtiges [...] auszuarbeiten"[12], zurückfinden zur ausgewogenen Beurteilung durch Nikolaus Reusner (1545–1602), der im Elogium der *Icones virorum literis illustrium* Sambucus' eigene Werke gleichberechtigt neben Sammel- und Editionstätigkeit gestellt hatte[13]:

---

[10] Angesiedelt an der University of Illinois, Urbana-Champaign <http://emblematica.grainger.illinois.edu/> (5. 4. 2017).

[11] Darüberhinaus dokumentiert die von Werner Wilhem Schnabel / Friedrich Alexander-Universität Erlangen-Nürnberg, Departement Germanistik und Komparatistik betreute Datenbank *Repertorium alborum amicorum* (RAA) <http://www.raa.phil. uni-erlangen.de/> (10. 7. 2017) die weitverbreitete Rezeption der *Emblemata* als Stammbuch.

[12] Ungrisches Magazin I, 423. Lesetext und Digitalisat sind zugänglich über das von Andrea Seidler / Universität Wien, Institut für Europäische und Vergleichende Sprach- und Literaturwissenschaft geleitete Projekt *Hungarus Digitalis. Digitale Quellenedition – Königreich Ungarn* <http://www.univie.ac.at/hungdigi/foswiki/bin/view.cgi/DigiHung> (10. 7. 2017).

[13] Icones sive imagines virorum literis illustrium ex secunda recognitione Nicolai Reusneri. Argentorati: curante Bernhardo Iobino 1590, 394–399; 395.

Maximam gloriam cum propriis scriptis elucubrandis tum autoribus veteribus recolligendis et quasi e mortuis excitandis adeptus.

Reusner, *Icones* 1590, 395

So lassen mehrere Beiträge eine Wechselwirkung zwischen Sammeln und Erschließen des Überlieferten und seiner eigenen literarischen Produktion erkennen und zeigen, wie die von Hans Gerstinger, von 1931 bis 1934 Vorstand der Handschriften- und Papyrussammlung der Österreichischen Nationalbibliothek, etablierte Tradition der Sambucusforschung in Hinblick auf Aktualisierung und Instrumentalisierung weitergeführt werden kann: Sambucus' Beitrag zur Diskussion um die Konstantinische Schenkung zeichnet sich durch die Auswertung eines besonderen Überlieferungszeugen aus (GASTGEBER), und eine im Unterschied zu den *Emblemata* wenig beachtete Publikation, die *Arcus triumphales*, basiert nicht zuletzt auf Sambucus numismatischen und antiquarischen Kenntnissen (KLECKER). Dass aber auch Windischs positives Urteil über Sambucus' Editionstätigkeit vertieft werden kann, zeigen eine Untersuchung seiner Janus Pannonius-Ausgabe (MAYER) sowie der ausführlichste Beitrag, der die Einleitung der bereits genannten Edition von Paratexten in aktualisierter englischer Fassung vorlegt (ALMÁSI – KISS).

Dem Literaten Sambucus widmet sich in seiner Heimat die Klassische Philologie bzw. Neolatinistik, die an der Comenius-Universität in Bratislava sowie an der *Universitas Tyrnaviensis* in seiner Geburtsstadt Trnava gut etabliert ist und sein Andenken im Namen der seit 2005 erscheinenden wissenschaftlichen Zeitschrift *Sambucus* hochhält[14]. Untersuchungen zum Dialog *De imitatione Ciceroniana* geben auch Anlass zu einem Rückblick auf die schwierige Situation der Humanismusforschung in der einstigen Tschechoslowakei (ŠKOVIERA; LÁBAJ). In Wien haben langjährige Forschungen zur Habsburger-Panegyrik den Blick auf Sambucus als Verfasser (und Herausgeber) von Lobgedichten gelenkt: Die Kenntnis von Texttraditionen ermöglicht es, in sorgfältiger Analyse die politischen Implikationen von Intertextualität offenzulegen (AMANN-BUBENIK). Auf die *Emblemata* sollte in einem Sambucus gewidmeten Band freilich nicht ganz verzichtet werden (BANNERT; ERDÖS).

---

[14] *Sambucus. Práce z klasickej filológie, latinskej medievalistiky a neolatinistiky* [Arbeiten aus Klassischer Philologie, lateinischer Mediävistik und Neolatinistik] herausgegeben von Daniel Škoviera und Nicol Sipekiová.

Besonders glücklich hat es sich gefügt, dass mehrere Wiener Forschungsprojekte, ohne auf ihn zu zielen, zu Sambucus führten und gleichsam als unerwartete ‚Nebenprodukte' Ergebnisse für den Humanisten erbrachten. Auch wenn in Wien das Erbe des Handschriftensammlers Sambucus seit jeher geschätzt wird, überrascht es doch, welches Gespür er bei seinen Ankäufen bewies – und so der modernen Palimpsestforschung Material liefert (GRUSKOVÁ). Die Neuordnung des Buchbestandes des Wiener Dominikanerkonvents hat nicht nur Einträge in Sambucus' Bibliothekskatalog durch das Auffinden der Buchobjekte bestätigt, sondern unsere Kenntnis seiner Sammlung noch darüber hinaus erweitert (REISNER). Schließlich ist eines jener Werke der griechischen Literatur, die ihre Wirkung einer Ausgabe *ex bibliotheca Sambuci* verdanken, die *Dionysiaka* des Nonnos von Panopolis, Gegenstand eines gräzistischen Forschungsprojekts am Institut für Klassische Philologie, Mittel- und Neulatein der Universität Wien. Die an Sambucus gerichtete Widmungsepistel der *editio princeps*, die hier mit deutscher Übersetzung vorgelegt wird, bringt bis heute diskutierte Positionen der Nonnosforschung zur Sprache (BANNERT).

Wenn damit die fächerübergreifende Bedeutung des Humanisten dokumentiert ist und sich der im Einleitungsbeitrag eröffnete europäische Horizont (PÁLFFY) in der Herkunft der Autoren spiegelt, so scheint noch in der modernen Forschung Sambucus' Absichtserklärung im Emblem *USUS LIBRI, NON LECTIO PRUDENTES FACIT* (Abb. 3) zu wirken: Mit den eigenen Bücherschätzen anderen zu nützen.

I. SAMBVCI
Vsus libri, non lectio prudentes facit.
Ad Fuluium Vrsinum suum.

NON *doceo semper, non est cur sæpè reuisas,*
  Lectorum memorem pagina nostra facit.
P *ossidet ingentem numerum qui vendit auarus,*
  Doctior at nunquam bibliopola fuit.
P *erpetuò si nos verses, relegasq́, seuerus,*
  Si non vtaris, contineasúe memor:
N *unquam proficies, perijt labor, atque lucerna.*
  O fficij hoc nostri vt te moneamus erat.
I *d quoniam rectè noras doctißime Fului,*
  Imprimis veteres te erudiere libri.
H *orum tu numerum insignem rarumq́, tueris,*
  Ingenio multos restituisq́, libros.
I *d quoque delectat Sambucum, & tota vetustas:*
  Prosimus quibus est copia forte minor.

Abb. 3: *USUS LIBRI, NON LECTIO PRUDENTES FACIT.*
Sambucus, Emblemata et aliquot nummi antiqui operis. Antverpiae: ex officina Christophori Plantini 1566, 56
(Wien, Universitätsbibliothek I 125.521)

Aus einer königlichen Freistadt Ungarns in die kaiserliche Residenzstadt Wien

Das Königreich Ungarn in der Zeit des Johannes Sambucus

GÉZA PÁLFFY (Budapest)

Abb. 1: Johannes Sambucus, Ungarnkarte. Wien: Caspar Stainhofer 1566
(Budapest, Országos Széchényi Könyvtár, Sammlung Alte Drucke, Apponyi M.130)

1. EINLEITUNG:

DAS LEBEN DES JOHANNES SAMBUCUS ALS MODELL ZUR GESCHICHTE UNGARNS
IM 16. JAHRHUNDERT

Johannes Sambucus (ung. János Zsámboky) ist bis zum heutigen Tage der berühmteste aus Ungarn stammende Gelehrte und Humanist des 16. Jahrhunderts. Den Namen des Hofhistoriographen und kaiserlichen Arztes machten in erster Linie seine bedeutende Tätigkeit als Philologe und Verleger sowie seine berühmte Bücher- und Handschriftensammlung weltweit bekannt[1]: Mit diesem Schaffen befassen sich die Beiträge des vorliegenden Bandes eingehend. Sein Leben, seine Laufbahn und sein Wirken sind zugleich hervorragend auch dafür geeignet, um mit ihrer Hilfe einzelne Hauptphänomene der Geschichte des Königreichs Ungarn und darüber hinaus sogar teilweise die der Geschichte Mitteleuropas im 16. Jahrhundert nachzuvollziehen. Sambucus lebte nämlich gerade in den mehr als fünfzig Jahren, die die Geschichte der Donau-Region Europas für einen langen Zeitraum umgeschrieben haben.

Bereits Geburts- und Todesdatum von Sambucus kennzeichnen diese entscheidenden Veränderungen recht gut. Er erblickte im Jahre 1531, also zwischen zwei großen Feldzügen von Sultan Süleyman dem Prächtigen gegen Wien (1529 und 1532) in einer nordwestungarischen königlichen Freistadt, in Tyrnau (ung. Nagyszombat, heute Trnava in der Slowakei), das Licht der Welt. Als er 1584 starb, hatte er wiederum schon zwei Jahrzehnte lang dauerhaft in jenem Wien gelebt und gewirkt, das durch die Übersiedlung von

---

[1] An dieser Stelle können nur Monographien verzeichnet werden: Pál GULYÁS, *Bibliotheca Joannis Sambuci. Sámboky János könyvtára.* Budapest 1941; Hans GERSTINGER, *Die Briefe des Johannes Sambucus (Zsámboky) 1554–1584.* Wien 1968 (Österreichische Akademie der Wissenschaften, Philologisch-Historische Klasse. Sitzungsberichte 255); Anton VANTUCH, *Ján Sambucus. Život a dielo renesančného učenca.* Bratislava 1975; Eleonore NOVOTNY, *Johannes Sambucus (1531–1584). Leben und Werk.* Wien: Phil. Diss. (masch.) 1975; Arnoud VISSER, *Joannes Sambucus and the Learned Image. The Use of the Emblem in Late-Renaissance Humanism.* Leiden 2005; Gábor ALMÁSI, *The Uses of Humanism. Johannes Sambucus (1534–1584), Andreas Dudith (1533–1589), and the Republic of Letters in East Central Europe.* Leiden, Boston 2009 (Brill's Studies in Intellectual History 185).

Aus einer königlichen Freistadt Ungarns

Kaiser Rudolf II. (1583) nach Prag gerade in jenen Jahren seine Rolle als kaiserliche Residenz- und Reichshauptstadt verlor. Und obwohl sich das Leben des humanistischen Gelehrten und die Lage der Stadt Wien in diesem halben Jahrhundert stark änderten, traf dies noch mehr auf das Königreich Ungarn zu. Die folgende Studie verfolgt diese Metamorphosen anhand des Lebens, der Funktionen und der Werke von Sambucus, also durch ein besonderes Objektiv – und tut dies in der Hoffnung, darauf hinzuweisen, dass die entscheidenden Wendungen in der Geschichte Ungarns nicht nur Leben und Karriere von Sambucus, sondern auch das gesamte Schicksal Wiens und Mitteleuropas von Grund auf bestimmten.

2. DIE OSMANISCHE EROBERUNG IM KARPATENBECKEN:

DAS ENDE EINER ALTEN EUROPÄISCHEN MITTELMACHT

Eine der größten Veränderungen in der Geschichte Mitteleuropas im 16. Jahrhundert trat durch die osmanische Eroberung ein[2]. Die Niederlage bei Mohács 1526 führte den ungarischen spätmittelalterlichen Staat in die Zerstörung[3]; dadurch, dass seine Hauptstadt (Ofen/Buda) 1541 in osmanische Hand geriet, sowie durch die weiteren, bis 1566 andauernden osmanischen Eroberungen (1543: Gran/Esztergom, Stuhlweißenburg/Székesfehérvár, Fünfkirchen/Pécs; 1552: das Banat und der östliche Teil von Slawonien; 1555: Fülek, heute Fiľakovo in der Slowakei; 1566: Gyula/Jula und Szigetvár/Siget) ist sein Territorium dreigeteilt worden. Lediglich die Festung von Erlau/Eger sowie Siget konnten 1552 bzw. 1556 die osmanischen Truppen aufhalten. Während das Königreich Ungarn mit seinem immer weiter schrumpfenden Territorium unter die Regierung König Ferdinands I. (1526–1564) gelangte, wurden die mittleren Gebiete des mittelalterlichen Staates zum Bestandteil des Os-

---

[2] Mit weiterer reicher Literatur: Zygmunt ABRAHAMOWICZ u. a. (Hgg.), *Die Türkenkriege in der historischen Forschung*. Wien 1983 (*Forschungen und Beiträge zur Wiener Stadtgeschichte* 13).
[3] Jenő GYALÓKAY, Die Schlacht bei Mohács. *Ungarische Jahrbücher* 6 (1927), 228–257; Ferenc SZAKÁLY, The 1526 Mohács Disaster. *The New Hungarian Quarterly* 18 (1977), 43–63; DERS., A mohácsi csata [Die Schlacht bei Mohács]. Budapest ³1981 (*Sorsdöntő történelmi napok* 2); Géza PERJÉS, *The Fall of the Medieval Kingdom of Hungary. Mohács 1526 – Buda 1541*. New York 1989 (*War and Society in East Central Europe* XXVI; *Atlantic Studies on Society in Change* 56; *East European Monographs* CCLV); János B. SZABÓ, Ferenc TÓTH, *Mohács (1526). Soliman le Magnifique prend pied en Europe centrale*. Paris 2009.

manischen Reiches, und in den östlichen Gebieten entstand ein schrittweise in die türkische Interessensphäre gerückter neuer Staat, das Fürstentum Siebenbürgen.

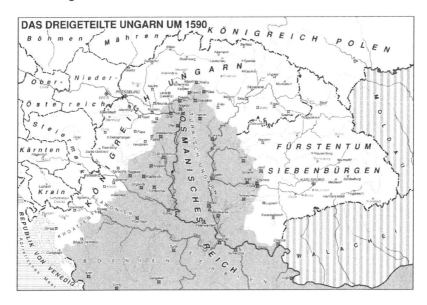

Abb. 2: Das dreigeteilte Ungarn im 16. Jahrhundert

Damit gehörte die entscheidende Rolle des ungarisch-kroatischen Staatsbündnisses, das im Spätmittelalter zu den führenden Mittelmächten des Kontinents zählte, in Europa – und das ist kein Irrtum! – ein für allemal der Vergangenheit an[4]. Sein Territorium reduzierte sich von 325.000 Quadratkilometern (es war somit kaum kleiner als das der heutigen Bundesrepublik Deutschland) auf etwa 120.000 Quadratkilometer, und zwar genau in den mehr als zwei Jahrzehnten, als Sambucus seine lange europäische Peregrinatio bewältigte[5]. Die langfristige Bedeutung dieser Verände-

---

[4] Géza PÁLFFY, *The Kingdom of Hungary and the Habsburg Monarchy in the Sixteenth Century.* New York 2009 (*East European Monographs* DCCXXXV; *CHSP Hungarian Studies Series* 18), 17–23 und 35–37.
[5] ALMÁSI (s. Anm. 1), 146–150.

rungen ist an der Tatsache gut zu erkennen, dass die territoriale und politische Einheit des einstigen ungarischen Staates zunächst nach dem Frieden von Passarowitz teilweise im Jahre 1718[6], vollständig jedoch erst 1867 nach dem österreichisch-ungarischen Ausgleich mit der Wiederinkorporierung Siebenbürgens wiederhergestellt wurde.

Diese entscheidenden Veränderungen spürte Sambucus zum einen auch an der eigenen Haut, zum anderen verewigte er sie teilweise auch in seinen Arbeiten. Eine von ihnen symbolisiert bereits sein Familienname plausibel. Obwohl über die Herkunft seiner Familie bis heute diskutiert wird[7], ist es meines Erachtens kaum in Zweifel zu ziehen, dass unter *oppidum Zamboc*, das in der Einleitung seiner Ausgabe von Plautus' Komödien 1566 in Antwerpen erwähnt wird, der etwa 30 km von Ofen entfernt liegende Marktflecken Zsámbék zu verstehen ist, der bereits 1467 über die entsprechenden Privilegien verfügte und in der Form *SAMBOK* auf der Ungarnkarte von Sambucus 1566 zu sehen ist[8]. Von hier aus übersiedelte sein Vater (Peter) wegen der osmanischen Eroberung nach Tyrnau, das zu einem der wichtigsten Nester ungarischer Bürger wurde, die aus Marktflecken auf türkisch besetzten Gebieten geflohen waren[9]. Seine Mutter stammte aus Kroatien, darauf verweist zumindest ihr Familienname Horváth, und wir wissen, dass sich die vor den türkischen Angriffen geflohenen Kroaten in so hoher An-

---

[6] Neuerdings Charles W. INGRAO, Nikola SAMARDŽIĆ, Jovan PEŠALJ (Hgg.), *The Peace of Passarowitz, 1718*. West Lafayette, Ind. 2011.
[7] Vgl. ALMÁSI (s. Anm. 1), 146, 4. Anm.
[8] M. Accii Plauti Comoediae Viginti, olim a Joachimo Camerario emendatae [...] opera et diligentia Joannis Sambuci Tirnaviensis Pannonii. Antwerpiae: Christopher Plantin 1566, A2ᵛ [Petrus Sambucus] *avitis sedibus ac bonis, quae ad oppidum Zamboc, ac ipsam Budam sita errant, eiectus*. Zur Ungarnkarte Tibor SZATHMÁRY, *Descriptio Hungariae. Magyarország és Erdély nyomtatott térképei 1477–1600* [Gedruckte Karten Ungarns und Siebenbürgens 1477–1600]. Fusignano 1987, 153f., Nr. 66.
[9] Lajos GECSÉNYI, Handelsbeziehungen zwischen Ungarn und den süddeutschen Städten am Anfang der Frühen Neuzeit. In: Herbert W. Wurster, Manfred Treml, Richard Loibl (Hgg.), *Bayern – Ungarn Tausend Jahre. Aufsätze zur Bayerischen Landesausstellung 2001. Vorträge der Tagung „Bayern und Ungarn im Mittelalter und in der frühen Neuzeit" in Passau 15. bis 18. Oktober 2000*. Passau, Regensburg 2001, 121–136; József BESSENYEI, *Menekültek... A kereskedelem helyzete Magyarországon 1526 után, Bornemisza Tamás és a budai menekültek működésének tükrében* [Flüchtlinge... Die Lage des Handels in Ungarn nach 1526 anhand der Tätigkeit von Thomas Bornemisza und der Flüchtlinge aus Ofen/Buda]. Miskolc, Budapest 2007, insbes. 47–49.

zahl in Westungarn und in Niederösterreich bis ins Marchfeld nahe Pressburg (ung. Pozsony, heute Bratislava in der Slowakei) und Tyrnau ansiedelten, dass sie bis heute etwa sechs Prozent der Bevölkerung des Burgenlandes ausmachen[10].
Paradoxerweise hing der Aufstieg von Sambucus mit der osmanischen Eroberung zusammen. Einerseits konnte 1542 sein Vater, weil er die neue Situation Ungarns nach dem Verlust der Hauptstadt Ofen (1541) sowie das Interesse seines Sohnes erkannte, bereits die Entscheidung für dessen Laufbahn als Intellektueller treffen, andererseits standen schon die ersten Dienste des jungen Gelehrten für die Habsburger im Zusammenhang mit den Türkenkriegen. Bis zum Herbst 1553 stellte Sambucus im Auftrag von König Ferdinand I. die lateinische Beschreibung der ruhmreichen Standhaftigkeit der Verteidiger der Festung von Erlau im Vorjahr (die hauptsächlich auf der ungarischen Chronik von Sebastian Tinódi basierte[11]) sowie die Erzählung über die erfolgreiche Verteidigung von Siget 1556 zusammen. Beide Arbeiten erschienen 1558 in der von ihm herausgegeben *Epitome rerum Ungaricarum* des humanistischen Geschichtsschreibers Petrus Ransanus[12]. Von der zwangsläufigen Dreiteilung Ungarns zeugte zugleich die im Jahre des Falles von Siget (1566) in Wien herausgegebene Landkarte von Siebenbürgen, während er Ende 1572 eine selbständige Karte der kroatisch-slawonischen Gebiete (*Illyricum*), d. h. der einstigen Heimat der Ahnen seiner Mutter, drucken ließ[13], die sich wegen der osmanischen Eroberung allmählich vereinigten[14].

---

[10] Josef BREU, *Die Kroatensiedlung im Burgenland und in den anschließenden Gebieten*. Wien 1970; sowie Géza PÁLFFY, Miljenko PANDŽIĆ, Felix TOBLER, *Ausgewählte Dokumente zur Migration der Burgenländischen Kroaten im 16. Jahrhundert / Odabrani dokumenti o seobi Gradišćanskih Hrvata u 16. stoljeću*. Eisenstadt / Željezno 1999.

[11] István SUGÁR, Ferenc SZAKÁLY (Hgg.), *Tinódi Sebestyén: Krónika*. Budapest 1984 (*Bibliotheca Historica* ohne Nr.).

[12] Petrus Ransanus, Epitome rerum Ungaricarum velut per Indices descripta [...] Opera Ioannis Sambuci, Tirnaviensis, Pan. Viennae Austriae: excudebat Raphael Hofhalter 1558.

[13] Siebenbürgen, 1566: SZATHMÁRY (s. Anm. 8), 155–156, Nr. 67, Illyrien, 1572: Luciano LAGO, Claudio ROSSIT (Hgg.), *Descriptio Histriae. La penisola Istriana in alcuni momenti significativi della sua tradizione cartografica sino a tutto il secolo XVIII*. Trieste 1981 (*Collana degli atti del Centro di ricerche storiche – Rovigno* 5), 120f., Nr. LVIII, bzw. *Descriptio Croatiae. Hrvatske zemlje na geografskim kartama od najstarijih vremena do pojave prvih topografskih karata*. Tekst Mirko MARKOVIĆ. Zagreb 1993, 75.

[14] PÁLFFY (s. Anm. 4), 50–51, bzw. DERS., Hrvatska i Slavonija u sklopu Ugarske Kraljevine u 16.–17. stoljeću (s posebnim osvrtom na političke, vojne i društvene odnose) [Kroatien

Ungeachtet all dessen vertraute der gelehrte Humanist – ähnlich wie die ungarische politische Elite und die Habsburgerherrscher – darauf, dass die einstige territoriale Einheit des ungarischen Staates früher oder später wiederhergestellt werden könne. Eindeutig signalisieren dies die 1566 und 1571 in Wien erschienenen Ungarn-Landkarten, die anhand der Korrektur der Landkarte von Lazarus Secretarius aus dem Jahre 1528 und jener des kaiserlichen Hofhistoriographen Wolfgang Lazius aus dem Jahre 1556 entstanden und den vollständigen ungarischen Staat im Mittelalter darstellten[15]. Den Wert der Ersteren zeigt, dass sie bereits ab Oktober 1566 in der Ratsstube der Wiener Hofkammer für den alltäglichen Gebrauch vorlag[16] und Sambucus auf der Letzteren das damalige ungarische Staatswappen in die Mitte der von den Osmanen besetzten Gebiete setzte.

Die Pflege der glorreichen Vergangenheit der ungarischen Mittelmacht im Spätmittelalter und die Sehnsucht nach ihr wurden auch dadurch symbolisiert, dass Sambucus – neben der bereits erwähnten Arbeit von Ransanus – 1568 die bis dahin vollständigste Ausgabe der Geschichte Ungarns von Antonio Bonfini (*Rerum Ungaricarum decades*), dem italienischen Geschichtsschreiber von König Matthias Corvinus (1458–1490), erstellte[17]. Mehr noch: Als er 1572 die berühmte ungarische adelige Gewohnheitsrechtssammlung, Stephan Werbőczys *Tripartitum*[18] in Wien erneut heraus-

---

und Slavonien im Verband des ungarischen Königreichs im 16.–17. Jahrhundert (mit besonderer Berücksichtigung der politischen, militärischen und gesellschaftlichen Beziehungen)]. In: Milan Kruhek et al. (Hgg.) *Hrvatsko-madarski odnosi 1102.–1918. Zbornik radova* [Kroatisch-ungarische Beziehungen 1102–1918. Studiensammlung]. Zagreb 2004 (*Biblioteka Hrvatska povijesnica* Posebna izdanja), 113–123.

[15] SZATHMÁRY (Anm. 8), 71–76, Nr. 25, 115–118, Nr. 44, 153–154, Nr. 66 und 171–172, Nr. 75.

[16] „Die Hungerisch Mappa, so die herrn in der ratstuben haben, belangen." Wien, Österreichisches Staatsarchiv, Hofkammerarchiv, Gedenkbücher, Österreichische Reihe Bd. 99 (1565–67), fol. 97ʳ (26. Okt. 1566).

[17] Antonii Bonfinii rerum Ungaricarum decades quatuor, cum dimidia [...] Ioan. Sambuci Tirnaviensis, Cas. Maiest. Historici, etc. opera ac studio [...]. Basileae: ex Officina Oporiniana 1568.

[18] János M. BAK, Péter BANYÓ, Martyn RADY (Hgg.), *The Customary Law of the Renowned Kingdom of Hungary. A Work in Three Parts Rendered by Stephen Werbőczy* (The „Tripartitum") / *Tripartitum opus iuris consuetudinarii inclyti regni Hungariae per Stephanum de Werbewcz editum*. Idyllwild CA, Budapest 2006 (*The Laws of the Medieval Kingdom of Hungary / Decreta regni mediaevalis Hungariae*, Series I, 1000–1526, vol. 5).

gab[19], führte er auf deren Titelblatt neben den Habsburger- und Jagiellonenherrschern des 15. und 16. Jahrhunderts das Porträt von Matthias Corvinus sowie die ihm bekannten Wappen der unter den Anspruchstiteln der Titulatur der ungarischen Könige auch nach 1526 genannten Länder Dalmatien, Bosnien, Serbien, Bulgarien usw. an (Abb. 3)[20]. Sambucus hat damit insgesamt sowohl durch seine Landkarten als auch durch seine Werke die Tradition des Reiches der Stephanskrone, also einer alten europäischen Mittelmacht gepflegt, und zwar auch dann, als diese in Wirklichkeit 60 Prozent ihrer Gebiete verloren hatte und zum Bestandteil eines neuen zusammengesetzten Staates in Mitteleuropa geworden war[21].

3. INNERHALB EINER NEUEN MONARCHIE:

VOM OFNER KÖNIGSHOF DER JAGIELLONEN AN DEN WIENER KAISERHOF DER HABSBURGER

Die andere langfristig wirkende und im Leben von Sambucus eingetretene Veränderung in der Geschichte des Königreichs Ungarn war der Anschluss an die neu entstandene Habsburgermonarchie, die von 1556/58 an bereits aus dem Heiligen Römischen Reich, den Ländern der Ungarischen und der Böhmischen Krone sowie aus den österreichischen Erbländern bestand[22]. Als Folge davon haben sich die Führung und Verwaltung des verbliebenen ungarischen Staates von Grund auf umgestaltet. Die Rolle von Ofen, das 1541 in türkische Hand gelangt war, wurde nämlich von keiner neuen ungarischen königlichen Hauptstadt, sondern von der jenseits der Grenzen Ungarns liegenden Residenzstadt der Monarchie (Wien) und dem neuen Schauplatz der Reichstage und der Königskrönungen (Pressburg) gemeinsam übernommen. Anders formuliert bekam der verbleibende ungarische

---

[19] Tripartitum opus iuris consuetudinarii, Inclyti Regni Hungariae. Per Spectabilem et Magnificum Dom. Stephanum De Werbewcz, Personalis presentiae Regiae Maiestatis olim Locumtenentem, accuratissime editum. Quarta Editio, cum Praefatione et Indice Ioan: Sambuci. Viennae Austriae: typis Blasii Eberi 1572.
[20] PÁLFFY (s. Anm. 4), 59, und fig. 2.
[21] Ebd. 50.
[22] Thomas WINKELBAUER, *Ständefreiheit und Fürstenmacht. Länder und Untertanen des Hauses Habsburg im konfessionellen Zeitalter.* 2 Bde. Wien 2003 (Österreichische Geschichte 1522–1699), passim; PÁLFFY (s. Anm. 4), insbes. 53–69.

Staat statt der früheren einen Hauptstadt nunmehr zwei Hauptstädte: Pressburg, das als „innenpolitische Hauptstadt" zu betrachten war und Wien, den Sitz der Residenz des Herrschers und der zentralen Verwaltung. Diese Situation wurde am Ende des Lebens von Sambucus dadurch weiter kompliziert, dass der Hof und die zentralen Regierungsorgane während der Herrschaft von Kaiser Rudolf II. für ein gutes Vierteljahrhundert nach Prag übersiedelten[23], während Wien und dem hier verbleibenden Erzherzog Ernst in der Führung des ungarischen Königreiches weiterhin eine wichtige Rolle zukam[24].

Davor jedoch, in der Mitte des 16. Jahrhunderts, musste der gelehrte Humanist – im Gegensatz zu seinen Vorgängern in Ungarn im 15. Jahrhundert – nicht mehr am Ofner Königshof[25], sondern am Wiener Kaiserhof auf seine Rechnung kommen[26]. Und obwohl er selbst dies mehr oder weniger erfolgreich verwirklichte, stellten sich einer erfolgreichen Integration der

---

[23] Neuerdings vgl. Jaroslava HAUSENBLASOVÁ, *Der Hof Kaiser Rudolfs II. Eine Edition der Hofstaatsverzeichnisse 1576–1612.* Prag 2002 (*Fontes historiae artium* 9).

[24] PÁLFFY (s. Anm. 4), 69; 81f.

[25] Zum königlichen Hof in Ofen im ausgehenden Mittelalter siehe József FÓGEL, *II. Ulászló udvartartása (1490–1516)* [Der Hofstaat von König Wladislaw II. (1490–1516)]. Budapest 1913; DERS., *II. Lajos udvartartása (1516–1526)* [Der Hofstaat von König Ludwig II. 1516–1526]. Budapest 1917; Andres KUBINYI, Der königliche Hof als Integrationszentrum Ungarns von der Mitte des 15. bis zum ersten Drittel des 16. Jahrhunderts und sein Einfluss auf die städtische Entwicklung Budas. In: Evamaria Engel, Karen Lambrecht, Hanna Nogossek (Hgg.), *Metropolen im Wandel. Zentralität in Ostmitteleuropa an der Wende vom Mittelalter zur Neuzeit.* Berlin 1995 (*Forschungen zur Geschichte und Kultur des östlichen Mitteleuropa* ohne Nr.), 145–162.

[26] Zum Wiener Hof unter Ferdinand I.: Christiane THOMAS, Wien als Residenz unter Kaiser Ferdinand I. *Jahrbuch des Vereins für Geschichte der Stadt Wien* 49 (1993), 101–117; Karl VOCELKA, ‚Du bist di port und zir alzeit, befestigung der christenheit' – Wien zwischen Grenzfestung und Residenzstadt im späten Mittelalter und in der frühen Neuzeit. In: Engel, Lambrecht, Nogossek (s. Anm. 25), 263–276; Volker PRESS, The Imperial Court of the Habsburgs. From Maximilian I to Ferdinand III, 1493–1567. In: Ronald G. Asch, Adolf M. Birke (Hgg.), *Princes, Patronage, and the Nobility. The Court at the Beginning of the Modern Age ca. 1450–1650.* London, Oxford 1991 (*Studies of the German Historical Institute London* ohne Nr.), 289–312; Jeroen DUINDAM, The Court of the Austrian Habsburgs. Locus of a Composite Heritage. *Mitteilungen der Residenzen-Kommission der Akademie der Wissenschaften zu Göttingen* 8/2 (1998), 24–58; DERS., *Vienna and Versailles. The Courts of Europe's Dynastic Rivals, 1550–1780.* Cambridge 2003; Ferdinand OPLL, Ferdinand I. und seine Stadt Wien. Versuch einer Neubewertung des Verhältnisses zwischen Herrscher und Stadt. *Jahrbuch des Vereins für Geschichte der Stadt Wien* 61 (2005), 73–98.

Angehörigen der ungarischen politischen Elite am Wiener Hof bis hin zum Zerfall der Österreichisch-Ungarischen Monarchie 1918 gewaltige Hindernisse entgegen[27]. Die wichtigsten Fragen Ungarns (die auswärtigen Angelegenheiten, das Militär- und das Finanzwesen) wurden nämlich von der Zeit an, da sich Sambucus in Wien niederließ, jahrhundertelang von der Kaiserstadt aus gesteuert. Darauf konnte die politische und militärische Führung der Habsburgermonarchie im Interesse der Verteidigung und der Versorgung Mitteleuropas nicht verzichten – auf diesen Punkt komme ich noch zurück.

Sambucus war sich natürlich über diese entscheidenden Veränderungen im Klaren, hing doch sein Aufstieg zum großen Teil davon ab, ob er in der Lage sein würde, in der Hauptstadt der Monarchie, bzw. in der kaiserlichen Hofhaltung den Posten eines Hofdieners zu erlangen, der einem gelehrten Philologen entspricht. Das war jedoch keine leichte Aufgabe. Davon zeugt die Tatsache, dass er zunächst keinen Posten in der Wiener Hofhaltung der Habsburger, sondern einen unwirklichen, nominell gewordenen Posten eines ungarischen königlichen Hofdieners erhielt. Ferdinand I. nahm ihn nämlich Ende 1557 unter die so genannten *aulae regiae familiares* mit einer Jahresbesoldung von zunächst 50, vom Frühjahr 1558 an bereits von 100 ungarischem Gulden (angewiesen durch die Ungarische Kammer aus Pressburg) auf[28], vermutlich war das in erster Linie seiner erwähnten Schilderung der Belagerung von Erlau 1552 zu verdanken. Einen Titel dieser Art erhielten in jenen Jahrzehnten – das ist zu betonen! – die Anhänger des Herrschers in Ungarn, denen damit ihre Dienste als Beamter, Intellektueller oder in der Wirtschaft honoriert wurden[29]. Den ungarischen Titular-Hofposten, der mit einer bis zum Tode gewährten Provision einherging, blieb dann bis zum 19. Jahrhundert erhalten und bot den Habsburgerherrschern die Möglichkeit, auch Vertreter des ungarischen Mitteladels und des Bürgertums in jene privilegierte Gruppe zu integrieren, die das Königreich Ungarn zusammen mit der Hofburg regierte.

---

[27] Gabriella ERDÉLYI, Diskurs über die ungarische Statthalterei. Gesichtspunkte zur Untersuchung des Verhältnisses zwischen Ferdinand I. und der ungarischen politischen Elite. *Mitteilungen des Österreichischen Staatsarchivs* 48 (2000), 93–126; Géza PÁLFFY, Der Wiener Hof und die ungarischen Stände im 16. Jahrhundert. *Mitteilungen des Instituts für Österreichische Geschichtsforschung* 109 (2001), 346–381.

[28] ALMÁSI (s. Anm. 1), 150–152.

[29] PÁLFFY (s. Anm. 4), 75.

Und obwohl Sambucus sein Studium in Europa und seine Rundreise zur Sammlung von Büchern und Kodizes bald fortsetzte, unternahm er anschließend alles dafür, dass sein virtueller ungarischer königlicher Hofdiener-Titel am Wiener Kaiserhof zu einem wirklichen Hofdienerposten wurde. Diesem Zweck diente von 1558 bis 1566 jede typisch humanistische Geste des Gelehrten in erster Linie an den Thronfolger Erzherzog Maximilian: Der bereits erwähnte, ihm gewidmete Ransanus-Band 1558 bzw. die ihm zugesandten, sehr wertvollen Kodizes[30], dann das in Versen verfasste Flugblatt über die Pressburger Krönung Maximilians 1563[31] sowie das 1564 als Neujahrsgeschenk ebenfalls ihm gewidmete berühmte Buch der *Emblemata*[32]. Danach folgten 1565 die zum Ableben Kaiser Ferdinands I. verfasste *Oratio*, 1566 die Genealogie der Habsburgerdynastie[33] sowie die Herausgabe der bereits ebenfalls erwähnten Landkarten Ungarns und Siebenbürgens. Sambucus' Sehnsucht nach dem Wiener Kaiserhof und später seine erfolgreiche Integration dort symbolisiert auf der Ungarnkarte nichts anderes besser, als das traditionelle Wappen des Königreichs Ungarn auf dem zweiköpfigen Kaiseradler (s. die Karte auf S. 16, Abb. 1).

Mit seinen Widmungen, Geschenken und Arbeiten erreichte Sambucus letztlich sein Ziel. Im Sommer des folgenden Jahres nach seiner Niederlassung 1564 in Wien verstarb der kaiserliche Hofhistoriograph Wolfgang Lazius, dessen Posten er in der ersten Hälfte 1566 erwerben konnte[34]. Aus einer königlichen Freistadt Ungarns kommend wurde er zum bezahlten Mitglied der Wiener kaiserlichen Hofhaltung mit einem Jahresgehalt von 100 Talern, das ihm neben seiner weiterhin von Pressburg aus angewiesenen Provision als *aulae regiae familiaris* zustand. Darüber hinaus war er ab 1567 bereits *aulicus medicus titularius* und *comes palatinus* und ein Jahr später sogar kaiserlicher Rat[35].

---

[30] ALMÁSI (s. Anm. 1), 153.
[31] Zuzana LUDIKOVÁ, Zsámboky János röplapja Miksa magyar királlyá koronázásáról [Flugschrift von Johannes Sambucus über die ungarische Krönung Maximilians (II.)]. *Századok* [Jahrhunderte] 143 (2009), 974–980.
[32] VISSER (s. Anm. 1).
[33] ALMÁSI (s. Anm. 1), 161–162.
[34] Ebd. 166.
[35] Ebd. 166–167.

Obwohl Letztere für Sambucus lediglich Titel bedeuteten, d. h. mit keinen weiteren finanziellen Zuwendungen einhergingen, festigten sie seine Position am Habsburgerhof erheblich, ähnlich wie die führenden Persönlichkeiten der Monarchie auch die Wichtigkeit des Königreichs Ungarn nicht in Abrede stellten. Zum einen lag das Territorium des ungarischen Staates – wie die folgende Tabelle beweist[36] – auch in seinem recht gestutzten Zustand über dem der österreichischen Erbländer und war etwa so groß wie das der Länder der Böhmischen Krone.

	Königreich Ungarn	österreichische Erbländer	Länder der Böhmischen Krone
Fläche in km²	ca. 120.000	110.000	125.000
Einwohnerzahl	1,800.000	2,390.000	2,950.000
Jahreseinkommen (rheinische Gulden)	ca. 800.000	ca. 800–900.000	ca. 700.000

Das Königreich Ungarn, die österreichischen Erbländer und die Länder der Böhmischen Krone in der zweiten Hälfte des 16. Jahrhunderts im Vergleich

Zum anderen lieferten die Einkünfte des Königreichs Ungarn nach den gleichen Daten zu den Dienstzeiten von Sambucus in Wien etwa ein Drittel der Einnahmen des mitteleuropäischen Habsburgerstaates[37], obwohl sein Territorium durch Türkenkriege ständig verwüstet wurde. Zum dritten zeigte auch jene Tatsache das Gewicht der mittelalterlichen ungarischen Mittelmacht, dass Ungarn in der Titulatur der Habsburgerherrscher nach dem Heiligen Römischen Reich auf den zweiten Platz vorrückte und damit sowohl das Königreich Böhmen als auch die österreichischen Länder über-

---

[36] PÁLFFY (s. Anm. 4), 52, Tab. 4.
[37] István KENYERES, Die Finanzen des Königreichs Ungarn in der zweiten Hälfte des 16. Jahrhunderts. In: Friedrich Edelmayer, Maximilian Lanzinner, Peter Rauscher (Hgg.), *Finanzen und Herrschaft. Materielle Grundlagen fürstlicher Politik in den habsburgischen Ländern und im Heiligen Römischen Reich im 16. Jahrhundert*. München, Wien 2003 (Veröffentlichungen des Instituts für Österreichische Geschichtsforschung 38), 84–122; hier 92–94; DERS., Die Einkünfte und Reformen der Finanzverwaltung Ferdinands I. in Ungarn. In: Martina Fuchs, Teréz Oborni, Gábor Ujváry (Hgg.), *Kaiser Ferdinand I. Ein mitteleuropäischer Herrscher*. Münster 2005 (Geschichte in der Epoche Karls V. 5), 111–146; hier 116–122.

holte.³⁸ Schließlich zeugte davon auch die von Sambucus mit Gedichten geehrte Wiener Trauerzeremonie von Kaiser Ferdinand im August 1565: Die Rangordnung der Ländergruppen der Habsburgermonarchie kam nämlich deutlich durch die Machtinsignien auf der Trauergerüst zum Ausdruck. Während die Reichsinsignien den vornehmsten mittleren Platz einnahmen, wurden die ungarischen Insignien vor ihnen auf dem zweiten Platz, die böhmischen Machtsymbole hingegen hinten, an dritter Stelle platziert³⁹. All diese Anzeichen wiesen auch für die Teilnehmer der Zeremonie eindeutig darauf hin, dass das Königreich Ungarn zum vornehmen (zweiten) Land der mitteleuropäischen Habsburgermonarchie geworden war.

4. VERTEIDIGUNG UND VERSORGUNG DER HABSBURGERLÄNDER:

BOLLWERK UND SPEISEKAMMER MITTELEUROPAS

Ungarn war nicht nur aus politischer, diplomatischer und finanzieller, sondern auch aus militärischer Sicht von grundlegender Bedeutung sowohl für die Monarchie als auch für Wien. Der Fortbestand der bis zur Mitte des 16. Jahrhunderts entstandenen neuen Habsburgermacht hing nämlich in nicht geringem Maße von der Zukunft des zum Kriegsschauplatz gewordenen Königreichs Ungarn ab⁴⁰. Geriet doch auch die Residenzstadt Wien nach dem Fall von Ofen 1541 in wirklich große Gefahr, denn sie lag kaum 200 Kilometer vom 1543 gefallenen Gran entfernt. Die Sicherheit der Monarchie wurde also von der in Ungarn auszubauenden Grenzverteidigung bestimmt. Auf diese Weise wurden Organisation und Finanzierung der neuen Türkenabwehr im 16. Jahrhundert zu einer der wichtigsten Aufgaben der politischen und militärischen Führung der Habsburger. Trotz erheblicher Schwierigkei-

---

³⁸ PÁLFFY (s. Anm. 4), 59, und Fig. 2.
³⁹ Géza PÁLFFY, Kaiserbegräbnisse in der Habsburgermonarchie – Königskrönungen in Ungarn. Ungarische Herrschaftssymbole in der Herrschaftsrepräsentation der Habsburger im 16. Jahrhundert. *Frühneuzeit-Info* 19/1 (2008), 41–66; hier 47 und Abb. 7; bzw. DERS., Ungarn in der Habsburgermonarchie. Ungarische Herrschaftszeichen an der Wiener Begräbniszeremonie Ferdinands I. 1565. In: Martin Scheutz, Vlasta Valeš (Hgg.), *Wien und seine WienerInnen. Ein historischer Streifzug durch Wien über Jahrhunderte. Festschrift Karl Vocelka zum 60. Geburtstag.* Wien, Köln, Weimar 2008, 29–46; hier insbes. 36, Abb. 1.
⁴⁰ Géza PÁLFFY, Bollwerk und Speisekammer Mitteleuropas (1526–1711). In: Ernő Marosi (Hg.), *Auf der Bühne Europas. Der tausendjährige Beitrag Ungarns zur Idee der Europäischen Gemeinschaft.* Budapest 2009, 100–124; hier 106–112.

ten wurde sie bis zum Lebensende von Sambucus durch den finanziellen Zusammenschluss der österreichischen, der deutschen, der böhmischen und ungarischen Länder der Habsburger sowie durch die enge Zusammenarbeit zwischen dem Wiener Hofkriegsrat und den ungarischen Ständen erfolgreich realisiert, während in diesem Rahmen auch Wien selbst zu einer Festungsstadt ausgebaut wurde[41]. Dieser bedeutende Zusammenschluss garantierte den Fortbestand und die friedliche Entwicklung Mitteleuropas auf lange Sicht.

In Kenntnis dieser Fakten ist verständlich, dass die Frage der Türkengefahr und -abwehr auch in den Werken des ungarischstämmigen kaiserlichen Hofhistoriographen große Beachtung fand. Neben den erwähnten Beschreibungen der erfolgreichen Verteidigung von Erlau (1552) und Siget (1556) verfasste Sambucus auch die Geschichte des Falles von Temesvar 1552. Außerdem verewigte er den erfolgreichen Feldzug des namhaften deutschen Feldherren Lazarus Freiherr von Schwendi Anfang 1565 in Oberungarn, der die Eroberung der Festung Tokaj (am Theiß-Ufer) und des östlichen Landesteiles vom siebenbürgischen Fürsten Johann Sigismund und damit einen beträchtlichen Zuwachs des Gebietes des Königreichs mit sich brachte[42]. Beide Arbeiten erschienen in der Basler Ausgabe von Bonfinis Geschichte Ungarns 1568[43] und brachten Sambucus beträchtliche Anerkennung. Daneben betonte auch seine zum Ableben Kaiser Ferdinands geschriebene Trauerrede nachdrücklich die Verdienste des Herrschers beim Ausbau der neuen Türkenabwehr[44].

---

[41] Géza PÁLFFY, The Origins and Development of the Border Defence System against the Ottoman Empire in Hungary (Up to the Early Eighteenth Century). In: Géza Dávid, Pál Fodor (Hgg.), Ottomans, Hungarians, and Habsburgs in Central Europe. The Military Confines in the Era of the Ottoman Conquest. Leiden 2000 (The Ottoman Empire and its Heritage, Politics, Society and Economy 20), 3–69; DERS., Türkenabwehr, Grenzsoldatentum und die Militarisierung der Gesellschaft in Ungarn in der Frühen Neuzeit. Historisches Jahrbuch 123 (2003), 111–148; DERS., Der Preis für die Verteidigung der Habsburgermonarchie. Die Kosten der Türkenabwehr in der zweiten Hälfte des 16. Jahrhunderts. In: Edelmayer, Lanzinner, Rauscher (s. Anm. 37), 20–44.

[42] Wilhelm JANKO, Lazarus Freiherr von Schwendi, oberster Feldhauptmann und Rath Kaiser Maximilian's II. Wien 1871 und neuerdings Géza PÁLFFY, Un penseur militaire alsacien dans la Hongrie au XVIe siècle: Lazare baron von Schwendi (1522–1583). In: Hervé Coutau-Bégarie, Ferenc Tóth (Hgg.), La pensée militaire hongroise à travers les siècles. Paris 2011 (Bibliothèque Stratégique), 41–59.

[43] BONFINI (s. Anm. 17).

[44] ALMÁSI (s. Anm. 1), 161f.

Letztlich spielte Ungarn auch in wirtschaftlicher Hinsicht eine Schlüsselrolle für die Monarchie und die Residenzstadt Wien. Anders formuliert: Das Territorium des mittelalterlichen ungarischen Staates wurde im 16. Jahrhundert zur Speisekammer Mitteleuropas, denn es versorgte die Habsburgerländer, deren Bevölkerung wuchs und daher einen immer größeren Fleischbedarf hatte, jährlich mit Zehntausenden Rindern und Schafen sowie Rohstoffen (Haut, Talg, Honig, Wachs usw.)[45]. Wie wichtig das alles war, wird daran deutlich, dass sowohl in Wien als auch auf den österreichisch-deutschen Gebieten der Monarchie schwere Versorgungsengpässe auftraten, wenn der Nachschub an Rindern wegen eines größeren Türkenfeldzuges, einer Tierepidemie oder schlechten Wetters ins Stocken geriet. Über all das waren sich auch die führenden Vertreter der Wiener Hofkammer im Klaren. Davon zeugt, dass es bis Mitte des Jahrhunderts zum Ausbau eines neuen Grenzzollsystems kam[46], während die wirtschaftlichen Interessen oft auch über den politisch-militärischen Entscheidungen standen. Schon seit den 1540er-Jahren gab es ständig Bestrebungen, den ungarischen und serbischen Ochsenhändlern, die aus den türkischen Gebieten kamen und oft auch spionierten, den Zutritt zur Kaiserstadt zu verwehren. Ein solches Verbot ließ sich jedoch nie durchsetzen[47]. All das hatte schließlich langfristige Folgen: Bis zum zweiten Drittel des Jahrhunderts hatte Wien nicht nur die regionalpolitische, sondern auch die wirtschaftliche Rolle von Ofen vor 1526 mit Erfolg übernommen und diese über mehrere Jahrhunderte bewahrt – wie dies teilweise auch in südöstlicher Richtung auf Belgrad (Griechisch Weißenburg) zutraf[48].

Über diese wichtige Rolle seiner Heimat war sich auch Sambucus völlig im Klaren. Einerseits war sein Vater als Richter in Tyrnau ein alltäglicher Beteiligter am Lebendviehhandel Richtung Westen, andererseits war seine Gattin Christina Egerer die Tochter eines betuchten Wiener Kaufmannes, der schon wegen seiner Pressburger Abstammung gute Beziehungen zu

---

[45] PÁLFFY (s. Anm. 40), 112–116.
[46] Lajos GECSÉNYI, Handel und Handelspolitik im Königreich Ungarn zur Zeit der Herrschaft Ferdinands I. In: Fuchs, Oborni, Ujváry (s. Anm. 37), 147–151.
[47] Vgl. Lajos GECSÉNYI, Zur Geschichte des Wiener Ungarnhandels im 16. Jahrhundert. In: Beiträge zur Landeskunde des burgenländisch-westungarischen Raumes. Festschrift für Harald Prickler zum 60. Geburtstag. Eisenstadt 1994, 149–172, sowie GECSÉNYI (s. Anm. 9).
[48] Antal MOLNÁR, Struggle for the Chapel of Belgrade (1612–1643). Trade and Catholic Church in Ottoman Hungary. Acta Orientalia 60/1 (2007), 73–134; PÁLFFY (s. Anm. 4), 149.

Handelsleuten in Ungarn pflegte[49]. Letztlich hinterließ Sambucus selbst der Nachwelt ein Zeichen, das anschaulicher als alles andere die besondere Situation vor Augen führte, dass auf den von Türken besetzten ungarischen Gebieten gezüchtete Graurinder einen erheblichen Teil der Fleischversorgung im damaligen Mitteleuropa sicherten. Auf seiner 1571 erschienenen neueren Ungarnkarte hatte er nämlich auf dem Gebiet zwischen Donau und Theiß sowie bei der Stadt Debrecen Rinderherden eingezeichnet[50]. Da der namhafte niederländische Kartograph Abraham Ortelius etwas später diese Landkarte weitere Male herausgab, wusste bald ganz Europa von Ungarns Rolle als Speisekammer[51].

5. DIE BLÜTEZEIT DES HUMANISMUS UND DER UNGAR(LÄND)ISCHEN KULTUR

Das gesamte wissenschaftliche Schaffen von Sambucus war auch dafür ein beredtes Zeichen, dass es dem Wiener Kaiserhof ebenfalls gelungen war, die Rolle des spätmittelalterlichen Ofner Königshofes – zumindest in Hinblick auf die Unterstützung der Humanisten – in erheblichem Maße zu übernehmen. Das gelang natürlich ebenwenig vollständig wie in Politik und Wirtschaft, wo – wie man sehen konnte – in erster Linie Wien und Pressburg bzw. Wien und Belgrad das Erbe gemeinsam unter sich aufteilten.

Es traf verständlicherweise besonders auf die ungarischsprachige Kultur zu, an deren Pflege zu dieser Zeit viele erfolgreich arbeiteten: die gebildeten Beamten der Ungarischen Hofkanzlei in der Kaiserstadt[52] genauso wie Mitglieder der Hofhaltung der Erzbischöfe von Gran in Pressburg und Tyrnau, zu denen (vor allem zu Nikolaus Oláh und Anton Verancsics) Sambucus enge Beziehungen unterhielt[53]. Währenddessen übernahmen dabei die Resi-

---

[49] ALMÁSI (s. Anm. 1), 167.
[50] SZATHMÁRY (s. Anm. 8), 171, Nr. 75.
[51] Ebd. 165–166, Nr. 73/A–B; Robert W. KARROW, *Bio-Bibliographies of the Cartographers of Abraham Ortelius, 1570. Based on Leo Bagrow's A. Ortelii Catalogus Cartographorum*. Chicago 1993 (*Mapmakers of the Sixteenth Century and Their Maps*).
[52] István FAZEKAS, A Magyar Udvari Kancellária leltára 1577-ből [Das Inventar der Ungarischen Hofkanzlei von 1577]. *Fons (Forráskutatás és Történeti Segédtudományok)* [Fons: Quellenforschung und historische Hilfswissenschaften, Budapest] 9/1–3 (2002), 227–247.
[53] István FAZEKAS, Oláh Miklós esztergomi érsek udvara (1553–1568) [Der Hof des Erzbischofs zu Gran, Nikolaus Oláh (1553–1568)]. In: Nóra G. Etényi, Ildikó Horn (Hgg.), *Idővel paloták...*

denzen der ungarischen Aristokraten (zu Sambucus' Lebzeiten in erster Linie die Höfe der Nádasdys in Sárvár/Scharwar, der Perényis in Sárospatak in Ostungarn, der Batthyánys in Güssing und die der Zrínyis in Tschakaturn, heute Čakovec, Kroatien) sowie der fürstliche Hof in Siebenbürgen einen recht entscheidenden Anteil. In diesen kulturellen Werkstätten arbeiteten katholische wie protestantische Humanisten daran, dass die zweite Hälfte des 16. Jahrhunderts trotz der ständigen Kriegszustände zu einer neuzeitlichen Blütezeit der ungarischen und ungarischsprachigen Kultur und Bildung werden konnte[54]. Dazu trug freilich auch das Schaffen von Sambucus entscheidend bei.

Von einer vielfältigen Weiterführung des Kulturerbes des Ofner Königshofes und einer goldenen Zeit der Bildung und Kultur im dreigeteilten Ungarn zeugen zahlreiche Faktoren. Erstens ist dies vielleicht am plausibelsten daran zu erkennen, dass gleichzeitig mit der Wiener Ausgabe von Sambucus' *Tripartitum* in Latein (1572) dessen ungarische Übersetzung zunächst in der Stadt Debrecen an der türkischen Grenze (1565), später im siebenbürgischen Klausenburg (1571) erschien, während die kroatische Übersetzung auf der Murinsel bald von dem ungarisch-kroatischen zweisprachigen Magnaten Georg Zrínyi (kroat. Juraj Zrinski) verlegt wurde (1574)[55], der beim Trauerzug von Kaiser Ferdinand im August 1565 in Wien die Fahne des Königreichs

---

Magyar udvari kultúra a 16–17. Században. [Palais im Lauf der Zeit ... Ungarische Hofkultur im 16. und 17. Jahrhundert]. Budapest 2005, 343–360; Zsófia GÁL-MLAKÁR, Adatok Verancsics Antal udvarának történetéhez [Angaben zur Geschichte des Hofes von Anton Verancsics]. *Fons (Forráskutatás és Történeti Segédtudományok)* [Fons: Quellenforschung und historische Hilfswissenschaften] 14/2 (2007), 279–337.

[54] Katalin PÉTER, *Papok és nemesek. Magyar művelődéstörténeti tanulmányok a reformációval kezdődő másfél évszázadból* [Priester und Adelige. Ungarische kulturgeschichtliche Studien aus dem Einundhalbjahrhundert nach dem Anfang der Reformation in Ungarn]. Budapest 1995 (*A Ráday Gyűjtemény tanulmányai* 8); Géza PÁLFFY, *A tizenhatodik század története* [Geschichte Ungarns im 16. Jahrhundert]. Budapest 2000 (*Magyar századok* 6), 218–222, 237–240; neuerdings István MONOK, *A művelt arisztokrata. A magyarországi főnemesség olvasmányai a XVI–XVII. században* [Der gebildete Aristokrat. Das Lesen der Hochadeligen in Ungarn im 16. und 17. Jahrhundert]. Budapest, Eger 2012 (*Kulturális örökség*).

[55] Nataša ŠTEFANEC, *Heretik Njegova Veličanstva: povijest o Jurju IV. Zrinskom i njegovu rodu* [Der Ketzer seiner Majestät. Geschichte Georgs IV. Zrínyi und seines Geschlechts]. Zagreb 2001 (*Homines, tempora, loci*), 231f.

Ungarn trug⁵⁶. Wenn man hinzufügt, dass der Drucker der Ausgabe von Debrecen und der Murinsel der gleiche Raphael Hofhalter war, der an der von Sambucus herausgegebenen Ungarn-Geschichte von Ransanus mitwirkte, dann spricht das für sich.

Zweitens lief die Peregrinatio zu den führenden Universitäten Europas (Wien, Wittenberg, Ingolstadt, Straßburg, Paris, Padua, Bologna usw.) trotz der Dreiteilung des mittelalterlichen ungarischen Staates aus jedem seiner drei Gebiete genauso weiter, wie auch Sambucus selbst diese durchwanderte[57]. Drittens kann es zwar nur für einen symbolhaften Zufall gehalten werden, doch das erste in Ungarn gedruckte und vollständig ungarischsprachige Buch, das *Neue Testament* von Johannes Sylvester kam genau in dem Jahr am Hof von Thomas Nádasdy in Sárvár/Scharwar heraus[58], als der Sultan Süleyman Ofen eingenommen hatte. Viertens ist auch die ungarische Literatursprache in der zweiten Hälfte des 16. Jahrhunderts entstanden, genau in jener Periode, als im Königreich Ungarn Bücher in der Sprache einer jeden Ethnie veröffentlicht wurden[59].

All das zeigt einwandfrei auf: Die Musen schwiegen auch in Ungarn nicht, das zu einer Grenzregion zweier Großmächte geworden war. So hat im April 1573 Nicasius Ellebodius, einer der bekannten Aristoteles-Experten Europas, der sowohl in Sambucus' Geburtsstadt Tyrnau als auch in Padua unterrichtete, an Gian Vincenzo Pinelli, einen bekannten humanistischen Gelehrter und Büchersammler, nicht zufällig geschrieben: Wenn Gott diesem Lande Frieden beschert, dann wird es zu einer der bestgeeigneten Stätten werden, um wissenschaftliche Pläne zu realisieren[60].

---

[56] PÁLFFY, Kaiserbegräbnisse (s. Anm. 39), 44: Abb. 1, und 52; PÁLFFY, Ungarische Herrschaftszeichen (s. Anm. 39), 42f., Abb. 2.

[57] Mit weiterer Literatur Márta FATA, Gyula KURUCZ, Anton SCHINDLING (Hgg.), *Peregrinato Hungarica. Studenten aus Ungarn an deutschen und österreichischen Hochschulen vom 16. bis zum 20. Jahrhundert*. Stuttgart 2006 (Contubernium. Tübinger Beiträge zur Universitäts- und Wissenschaftsgeschichte 64).

[58] Gedeon BORSA et al. (Hgg.), *Régi Magyar Nyomtatványok* [Alte ungarische Drucke]. Bd. I. Budapest 1971, Nr. 49.

[59] Ebd. passim; PÉTER (s. Anm. 54), 87–90, 95–97.

[60] Tibor KLANICZAY, Nicasius Ellebodius és poétikája [Nicasius Ellebodius und seine Poetik]. *Irodalomtörténeti Közlemények* [Literaturgeschichtliche Mitteilungen] 75/1–2 (1971), 24–34; hier 29; vgl. DERS., Contributi alle relazioni padovane degli umanisti d'Ungheria. Nicasio Ellebodio e la sua attività filologica. In: Vittorio Branca (Hg.), *Venezia e Ungheria nel Rinascimento*. Firenze 1973, 317–333.

6. FAZIT:

EIN HUMANIST AUS UNGARN ZUR ZEIT DER METAMORPHOSE MITTELEUROPAS

Johannes Sambucus' Leben und Aufstieg wurden von Grund auf durch jene Veränderungen bestimmt, die die Landkarte Mitteleuropas und damit auch die des Königreichs Ungarn im 16. Jahrhundert auf den Gebieten der Politik, der Macht, der Wirtschaft und der Kultur radikal, mit Auswirkungen bis heute umgestaltet haben. Die Laufbahn und das Wirken des namhaften humanistischen Gelehrten war zugleich ein besonderer Spiegel dieser Veränderungen, der hervorragend zeigte, wie Wien – das zum Zentrum der während der Herrschaft von Kaiser und König Ferdinand I. neu entstandenen Habsburgermonarchie, zur Residenz-, Reichshaupt- und Festungsstadt geworden war – in den über fünfzig Jahren nach der Schlacht bei Mohács 1526 die bis dahin in Mitteleuropa gespielte politische und wirtschaftliche, ja zum Teil sogar kulturelle Rolle der Hauptstadt der spätmittelalterlichen ungarischen Mittelmacht Ofen in erheblichem Maße übernehmen konnte. Da ein Teil dieser teilweise bereits unumkehrbaren Veränderungen mit bedeutenden ungarischen Ereignissen zusammenhing, symbolisiert daher die Laufbahn von Johannes Sambucus auch sehr wohl, dass man die Geschichte Mitteleuropas nicht ohne die gründliche Kenntnis der Historie des Königreichs Ungarn verstehen kann. Die Erforschung des Wirkens des berühmten kaiserlichen Hofhistoriographen bietet daher eine ausgezeichnete Möglichkeit dafür, dass Historiker, Literatur- und Kulturhistoriker aus den Ländern Mitteleuropas auf seinen Spuren in einer noch engeren Zusammenarbeit als bisher bei der Erschließung und dem Kennenlernen der gemeinsamen Geschichte tätig werden.

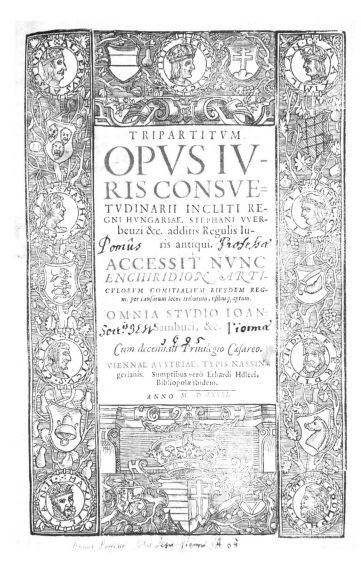

Abb. 3: Tripartitum opus iuris consuetudinarii [...] regni Hungariae [...] studio Ioannis Sambuci. Viennae Austriae: typis Nassingerianis, sumptibus Erhardi Hilleri 1581 (Wien, Universitätsbibliothek II 57.452)

In search of Sambucus

His philology, publications and friends

GÁBOR ALMÁSI (Budapest)
GÁBOR FARKAS KISS (Budapest)

SERENISSIMO ATQ.
ILLVSTRISS. PRINCIPI,
CAROLO ARCHIDVCI AV-
STRIAE, DVCI BVRGVNDIAE,
COMITI TYROLIS &c. DOMINO
SVO CLEMENTISSIMO.

Vt in veterum scriptis resti-
tuendis, atque producendis
operam suam ponunt, nō minus ij de hominum genere,
vsibusq;, quàm si ex ingenio
quiddam elucubrarint, mereri videntur.
Quanto enim difficiliùs in alienis, quàm
propriis est versari, & quò maior est auctoritas, rerúque veterum monumentis scien-
tia, quàm nostrorum comprehensa: hoc
gratiam ab omnibus bonis inire, laudemq;
asportare maioré qui illis eruendis, ac eme-
dandis, vt vulgò sint noti, occupantur, iu-
stissimè debent. Vt enim quę terra nascun-
tur, et animalia, quotidie vim nōnihil amittere videntur; ita hominum quoque inge-
nia & operas diminui, nec tam esse liberas,
& excellentes vel ad res nouas inuestigan-
das, vel explicādas obscuras, inq; vsum ad-

A 2 du-

Dedication to Archduke Karl, Diogenes Laertios, De vita philosophorum libri X. Antverpiae: ex officina Christophori Plantini 1566
(Vienna, University library I 161.822)

Johannes Sambucus[1] (1531–1584) was described by his contemporaries using a variety of epithets, including poet, historian, doctor, philosopher, antiquarian, book collector and political councillor[2]. While the word 'philologist' (which was rarely used at that time) does not feature in this list, Sambucus's early followers were keen to emphasise his contributions to publishing: "He won the highest glory in universal Christianity both through his own writings and the collection of old authors, whom, as it were, he brought back from the dead", claimed the historian and emblem writer Nicolaus Reusner[3]. Another historian, Jacques Auguste de Thou, lent similar emphasis to Sambucus's publishing activity, and later biographers never failed to provide long lists of works associated with his name. Thus Sambucus was often praised as a collector and publisher of manuscripts and books, while his philological activity was rarely extolled. At the heart of this paper is a presentation of Sambucus as philologist, bearing in mind that philology should not be, and at the time was not, divorced from other associated cultural practices such as the search for manuscripts and books, the building up of private libraries, or cultivating networks of likeminded friends, patrons and publishers.

The long list of epithets generally attached to Sambucus's name (and to which others could easily be added) should be seen as an indication of the complexity of Renaissance patronage networks and of the intellectual and

---

[1] In Hungarian, Johannes Sambucus is known as Zsámboky János. His Hungarian and German correspondence was signed Sambuky, Samboky or Samboki (Janos), the initial "S" probably being pronounced as the French "J". For the correspondence, see Anton VANTUCH, Die Sambucusbriefe im Kreisarchiv von Trnava. *Österreichische Akademie der Wissenschaften. Philologische-Historische Klasse. Sitzungsberichte* 255 (1968), 329–353. The present study is an updated English version of our introduction to the edition of Sambucus's paratexts of his philological publications: Gábor ALMÁSI, Gábor Farkas KISS, *Humanistes du bassin des Carpates II. Johannes Sambucus.* Turnhout 2014, v–lxxiv. Our research was supported by the MTA Lendület research grant, and by the OTKA research grant n. 104316.

[2] On Sambucus's image among his contemporaries see Gábor ALMÁSI, *The Uses of Humanism. Andreas Dudith (1533–1589), Johannes Sambucus (1531–1584), and the East Central European Republic of Letters.* Leiden 2009, 199–200.

[3] *Maximam gloriam cum propriis scriptis elucubrandis, tum auctoribus veteribus recolligendis, & quasi a mortuis excitandis adeptus in orbe Christiano universo.* Nicolaus Reusner, Icones sive imagines virorum literis illustrium. Argentorati: Bernardus Iobinus 1590, 395.

social models that many Renaissance 'humanists' were trying to unite and realise. The ideal of the universal intellectual, the polymath in the style of Leon Battista Alberti (which long outlived Renaissance humanism), was also an inspiration in Renaissance Hungary and attracted some members of the social elite. Sambucus was not a member of the social elite, although he became a nobleman through the merits of his father at the age of 18[4]. Noble rank certainly meant higher status but not necessarily identification with all aristocratic habits and attractions. As we will see, Sambucus's prestige was based more on his wide learning, the resulting social contacts, his close relationship with the imperial court and his proximity to the emperor himself than on noble rank. Nevertheless, the fact remains that the imperial historian Sambucus, as a noble courtier of the Holy Roman Emperor, was faced with a number of social expectations that most 16th-century philologist-publishers would never experience. These expectations mostly concerned habits (ways of socialising) and presentation (ways of dressing, living or getting around), and not necessarily concrete expectations with respect to his job as a historian. These latter expectations (perhaps not unrelated to his noble title) were unusually relaxed, especially when compared with the job description of later imperial historians. In fact, Sambucus's contribution as a historian is negligible: the title 'imperial historian' was just one of the titles, albeit the most important one, that he managed to procure through both luck and good strategies. It should be noted here that there were only a very few similar court titles that allowed time for leisured intellectual activity. Sambucus the 'historian' was thus never hindered by his imperial titles from pursuing other activities. On the contrary, such titles only lent him greater prestige in his tasks as antiquarian, publisher, editor, poet, mapmaker and physician. Among these activities, without doubt what inspired Sambucus the most was collecting and publishing – the central themes of his correspondence[5].

---

[4] Anton VANTUCH, Nové dokumenty k životu a dielu Jána Sambuca. *Historické Štúdie* 13 (1968), 243–255.
[5] Hans GERSTINGER, *Die Briefe des Johannes Sambucus (Zsámboky) 1554–1584*. Graz, Wien 1968 (*Österreichische Akademie der Wissenschaften. Philologisch-Historische Klasse. Sitzungsberichte* 255), 7–324 (also see Vantuch's edition, n. 1, which is a continuation of Gerstinger's). Although Gerstinger collected most available letters written by Sambucus, he ignored the letters addressed to him and the letters that appeared as dedications. Sambucus's more

HOW TO BECOME A COURTLY SAVANT:

SAMBUCUS'S CAREER IN VIENNA

Johannes Sambucus was born in the peaceful, prosperous and ethnically mixed small town of Trnava, in north-western Hungary[6]. In his publications he not only mentions his native region (Pannonia) but also proudly praises his hometown Tyrnavia[7]. His Hungarian father, Petrus, owned three houses there and was twice mayor[8]. Johannes was the first member of the family to receive thorough schooling, mostly through the generous support of his father. His 22-year academic tour, which commenced at the age of 11 at the University of Vienna, was exceptional even by 16th-century standards. Dating from his contact with the little-known Greek scholar and geographer Georg Rithaymer[9] in Vienna, the central concern in his studies appears to have

---

comprehensive correspondence (with the dedications) numbers over 340 items, whereas the Gerstinger–Vantuch edition has 193 pieces.

[6] On Sambucus's life see recently ALMÁSI (n. 2), 145–238; Arnoud VISSER, *Joannes Sambucus and the Learned Image. The Use of the Emblem in Late-Renaissance Humanism.* Leiden 2005, 1–48; Anton VANTUCH, *Ján Sambucus. Život a dielo renesančného učenca.* Bratislava 1975. Also see the edition of the paratexts of Sambucus's philological publications: ALMÁSI, KISS (n. 1). Useful studies on Sambucus go back to as early as the end of the eighteenth century. See Karl Gottlieb Windisch, Biographie. Lebensbeschreibung des Johann Sambucus. *Allergnädigistprivilegierte Anzeiger* 6 (1776), 174–176, 183–184, 191–192, 205–208; idem, Beitrag zur Lebensgeschichte des Johannes Sambucus. *Ungrisches Magazin* 4 (1781), 414–423 and 10 (1787), 498–499; János ILLÉSY, Zsámboky János történetírójáról [About the historian János Zsámboky]. *Századok* 34 (1899), 524–532; Hans GERSTINGER, Johannes Sambucus als Handschriftensammler. In: *Festschrift der Nationalbibliothek in Wien zur Feier des 200jährigen Bestehens des Gebäudes.* Vienna 1926, 260–290; Stephan / Istvan BÁLINT-NAGY, Der weltberühmte Historicus Johannes Sambucus (1531–1584) als Arzt. *Sudhoffs Archiv für Geschichte der Medizin* 24 (1931), 150–174; Endre BACH, *Un humaniste hongrois en France. Jean Sambucus et ses relations littéraires (1551–1584).* Szeged 1932; Imre VÁRADY, Relazioni di Giovanni Zsámboky coll'umanesimo italiano. *Corvina* 15 (1935), 3–54; Pál GULYÁS, *Bibliotheca Joannis Sambuci. Sámboky János könyvtára.* Budapest 1941, 7–118; Imre TÉGLÁSY, A nyelv- és irodalomelmélet kezdetei Magyarországon *(Sylvester Jánostól Zsámboky Jánosig)* [The origins of linguistic and literary theory in Hungary from János Sylvester to János Zsámboky]. Budapest 1988 *(Humanizmus és Reformáció 15),* 65–186.

[7] Emblemata cum aliquot nummis antiqui operis. Antverpiae: ex officina Christophori Plantini 1564, 167.

[8] The origins of Sambucus's mother are uncertain. She may have come from the nationally mixed or Slovak family of Ivan Horváth Petransky. VANTUCH (n. 6), 243.

[9] See his Greek poem *In Geographicum librum Georgii Rithameri, praeceptoris olim sui* in: J. Sambucus, Δημηγορίαι hoc est conciones aliquot. Basileae: ex officina Ioannis Oporini

become Greek. Sambucus's itinerary in the early 1540s is less clear. He probably remained in Vienna until 1545, when he enrolled at the University of Wittenberg but apparently missed the lectures of Melanchthon[10]. The following summer the Schmalkaldic War forced students to leave the city, and Sambucus returned to Vienna only to continue his studies at the Catholic University of Ingolstadt in 1548[11]. Here, his masters were the rhetoric professor and Ciceronian expert Veit Amerbach, and the mathematician, cosmographer and philologist Petrus Apianus. After a shorter stay in the Strasbourg Academy, where he published the *Dialogues* of Lucian[12]. in 1550 he arrived in Paris, making the acquaintance of the professors of Greek at the Collège Royal: Jean Dorat (future royal poet); Adrien Turnèbe, one of the most significant contemporary French philologists; Petrus Ramus, the new holder of the Royal Chair of Philosophy; Pascal Duhamel, the mathematician; and other Parisian humanists such as Denis Lambin. In Paris, Sambucus delivered a longer oration in which he argued that children should study prose before poetry, and he finally became master of philosophy in 1552. In the same year, his second publication already appeared with Oporinus in

---

1552, 94f.. About Georg Rithaymer (Rithamer), see Christian GASTGEBER, Griechischhumanismus an der Wiener Universität: Der erste Professor Linguae Graecae Georg Rithaymer. *Graecolatina et Orientalia* 33–34 (Bratislava 2012), 83–110.

[10] Cf. GERSTINGER (n. 6), 261–266; VANTUCH, *Ján Sambucus* (n. 6), 47–75; and ALMÁSI (n. 2), 146. The theory of an earlier visit in Camerarius's Leipzig (maintained in all major biographies, also in ALMÁSI, n. 2, 145) needs revision, since the only indication for it is the poem addressed to Camerarius in Johannes Sambucus, Poemata quaedam. Patavii: Gratiosus Perchacinus excudebat 1555, 29ᵛ, in which he claims to have once carried a letter from Vienna to Camerarius (whereas there is no poem addressed to Camerarius in his Δημηγορίαι, n. 9, which is the most informative on his former teachers). Apparently, the first letter exchanged between the two dates back to late 1566, early 1567. See Joachim Camerarius [Sr.], Epistolarum libri quinque posteriores. Nunc primum a filiis [...] editae. Francofurti: ex officina Paltheniana 1595, 408–410; see also Sambucus's impersonal emblem addressed to Camerarius: Sambucus (n. 7), 187.

[11] Cf. his unknown work listed in his self-bibliography: Tabellae dialecticae in usum Hefflmari. Viennae: [n. d.] 1547, in: Catalogus librorum quos Ioan. Sambucus vel suos typis edidit, vel bibliothecae aliena pignora prodidit, vel praecipue adhuc divulganda prae manibus habet. Viennae: [n. d.] 1583). Republished by Gedeon BORSA, James E. WALSH, Eine gedruckte Selbstbibliographie von Johannes Sambucus. *Magyar Könyvszemle* 85 (1965), 127–133 (the reprint is between p. 128–129).

[12] ΛΟΥΚΙΑΝΟΥ ΣΑΜΟΣΑΤΕΩΣ Διάλογοι οὐράνιοι, ἐνάλιοι καὶ νεκρικοί. Luciani Samosatensis Dialogi coelestes, marini et inferni. Argentorati: apud Vuolfium Cephaleaum 1550.

Basel[13]. After interrupting his studies to return home to seek a new source of financing, he continued his study tour in Italy from 1553 as a tutor to George Bona, nephew of Hungary's Archbishop Nicolaus Olahus. For practical reasons, as he explained in a poem dedicated to his former master Veit Amerbach, he decided to study medicine[14]:

> Phoebo me, ac medicis dedi colendum:
> Donec quid magis accidat venustum
> Et meo placet simul palato
> Consultum hoc studio tamen propinquis
> Et meae cuperem bonae saluti.
>
> *Poemata quaedam* 1555, 30ᵛ–31ʳ

I have devoted myself to medicine, to the service of Phoebus Apollo, until something more elegant comes along, which also pleases my taste. By this study, however, I wish to help my dear ones and my own good health.

In 1555, he received the grade of licentiate but continued his studies within and outside the university halls of Padua, Bologna and other Italian cities. He continued working as a tutor and touring Italy before finally achieving what he had been longing for: he became a member of the imperial court as *aulae familiaris* in 1558. Having won the patronage of Emperor Ferdinand he turned to his first-born son, King and Archduke Maximilian – allegedly the most keen to acquire new antiquities and books – who took him under his protection. This new position left Sambucus free of concrete responsibilities, and he apparently interpreted it as a means of continuing his travels and his bookhunting activities, which had already commenced in Paris in 1551–52[15]. He was soon back in Italy and France, travelling from southern Italy up to the North, the centre of humanist printers and woodcutters: the Netherlands. The massive collection of manuscripts that he built up during these years is truly admirable, especially taking into consideration his restricted financial resources (as a courtier and tutor). In addi-

---

[13] Sambucus (n. 9).
[14] Sambucus (n. 10), 30–31. The translation is by VISSER (n. 6), 27.
[15] Sambucus's first registered manuscript – according to GERSTINGER (n. 6), 291 – contained 22 dialogues by Plato and was bought in Paris in 1551. This interpretation, and Maximilian's encouragement, are reflected in the letters of 1561 and 1563: GERSTINGER (n. 5), 61; and Imre TÉGLÁSY, Conrad Gesner és magyar barátai [Conrad Gesner and his Hungarian friends]. *Orvostörténeti Közlemények* 112 (1985), 195–209.

tion to acquiring old codices and antique coins and publishing some original works (such as a dialogue on Ciceronianism), he also developed personal relationships with Europe's intellectual elite. There can be no better proof of his wide learning, prestigious relationships, and humanist talents and taste than Plantin's beautiful *Emblemata*, which made his name famous and which were a significant means of self-promotion at court[16].

The *Emblemata* were a central product of his life (as expressed by Sambucus's portrait "*aetatis XXXIII*", preceding the first emblem addressed to Maximilian II), and the publication coincided exactly with his final settlement in Vienna. After 22 years of almost continuous peregrination, Sambucus – already a man of repute – finally returned to the imperial capital already in possession of the best part of his final book collection. His stunning 'museum' (as he called it) became as much of a tourist attraction in Vienna as a repository for later publications[17]. Sambucus's manuscript collection (finally sold to the Habsburg Emperor) – including more than 600 codices, the majority in Greek – was probably the greatest private collection in Northern Europe at the time[18]. It was also an immense motivation for the later imperial librarian Hugo Blotius, who came to Sambucus's support when, under the pressure of continuous financial crisis, he decided to sell the majority of his collection to the emperor:

> Non dubito, quin, si manuscripti Ioannis Sambuci libri accesserint et cultura deinceps mediocris adhibita fuerit, regis Galliae bibliothecam, in qua 400 tantum manuscripta volumina esse dicuntur, sit superata et illam summi pontificis

---

[16] See VISSER (n. 6).
[17] ALMÁSI (n. 2), 178–183.
[18] Gerstinger identified 497 codices (384 Greek and 113 Latin codices) once pertaining to Sambucus now kept in the National Library of Vienna (Österreichische Nationalbibliothek / ÖNB), while more recently a former researcher of the ÖNB, István Németh, could name another 88 titles (see Appendix 2 in ALMÁSI, KISS, n. 1, 245), all of them in the library. Gerstinger then listed six volumes kept in other libraries outside the ÖNB, and added nine lost codices to the list. We can add to these lists five more codices: cod. Vindob. hist. gr. 36, the cod. Lat. 249 in the National Library of Budapest, the ms. 159 of the University Library of Groningen, the ms. VLQ 62 of the University Library of Leiden and the lost manuscript of Théodore II Doukas Lascaris's *De communicatione naturali libri VI*. (We thank Kees Teszelszky for the indication of the Dutch manuscripts.) This makes altogether 590 known codices once in Sambucus's possession. On the printed volumes, see GULYÁS (n. 6). His printed book collection of 3.327 volumes (according to the catalogue published by Gulyás) was also among the greatest in Europe.

Vaticanam proxime adaequatura. Erunt enim in hac Caesareae Maiestatis Vestrae bibliotheca volumina Graeca tantum et antiqua plus quam mille, quorum plurima nusquam extant excusa. Eam ego quoque quotidie novorum et rarorum atque undique conquisitorum tam scriptorum quam librorum accessione illustrare conabor. In Italia Sambucum imitatus multa passim rara, singularia et lectu iucundissima utilissimaque scripta corrogavi.

I do not doubt, Blotius wrote to the emperor, that in procuring the manuscript books of Johannes Sambucus, Your collection, even with little care, will supersede the library of the French king, where 400 manuscripts are said to be kept, and almost equal the pontifical collection of the Vatican. The number of the ancient Greek manuscripts in Your Majesty's imperial library should reach 1,000, several of which have never been published. I will then adorn the collection day by day, purchasing new and rare manuscripts and books from everywhere. Imitating Sambucus, I have already collected several rare, unique, most useful and entertaining manuscripts from all over Italy.[19]

The programme of restoring, correcting and publishing classical manuscripts started already in the Netherlands in 1564, the first books coming out with Plantin in 1565 and 1566. Soon Sambucus's fame as an editor and collector reached to 'beyonds' far and wide, with more and more learned men[20]. While Sambucus's books flowed from the presses, his gestures towards Emperor Maximilian II (1564–1576), in the form of gift copies, poems, orations and other occasional writings, were generously compensated: his salary (paid by the imperial and Hungarian chambers) was raised to around 430 talers, and he was granted every title imaginable[21]. His 1567 marriage contract with a wealthy patrician girl was already signed as follows: "Philosophus und medicus Kayserlicher Maiestatis Historicus und Pfalzgraf oder comes Palatinus."[22] It is characteristic of his poise that, at the time the contract was signed, the title of comes Palatinus (often distributed to foreigners as well) had not yet been given to him: he would only apply

---

[19] Jahrbuch der Kunsthistorischen Sammlungen des allerhöchsten Kaiserhauses 7 (1888), no. 4663 (dated 30 May 1578).
[20] Sambucus voiced his programme in several places, for example in the dedication of Diogenes Laertius, De vita philosophorum libri X. Antverpiae: ex officina Christophori Plantini 1566, 3–6.
[21] ALMÁSI (n. 2), 157–171.
[22] Hans LIEBL, Der Heiratskontrakt des Johannes Sambucus. Unsere Heimat 6 (1946–1948), 183–184.

for it a month later[23]. Settling down as a family man, and becoming the father of two daughters and a son, Sambucus was fully integrated into the court and city life of Vienna. After just a few years he already owned two houses in the city and a manor house close to the Hungarian border[24].

Sambucus's career peaked early. In around 1569 he received yet another honorary title (consiliarius aulae), and in 1573 he was given a final salary rise. What followed was stagnation, or degeneration, in prestige, social relations and wealth. Sambucus (like so many of his peers at court) was soon to become painfully aware of the unpredictability of employment at the imperial court. Salaries were habitually in arrears, and without good contacts at court (and some good luck), regular reimbursement could not be expected. In other words, an employee could never relax or be absent, since social contacts required continuous care and manoeuvring. By the early 1570s, Sambucus had lost a number of influential patrons at court – Sigismund Seld († 1565), Siegmund von Herberstein († 1566), Mark Sinckmoser († 1569) and Johann Ulrich Zasius († 1570) – and he apparently had difficulties acquiring new patrons. This contributed greatly to his defeat in his famous rivalry with the newcomer Hugo Blotius for the newly established position of imperial librarian in 1575[25]. Sambucus had already been attempting to solve his financial problems by selling a good part of his collection to the emperor. The transaction was made a few years later (with Blotius's backing, as mentioned above), but the purchase money was never paid to him in its entirety[26]. The selling of a cherished collection, put together with so much mastery and effort, is surprising. On the one hand, Sambucus's financial crisis must have been profound. On the other, the deal reveals his sense of pragmatism and his entrepreneurial spirit. Sambucus knew that his collection would survive for posterity and would continue to bear his name; he knew it would remain close at hand and at his disposal; and he also knew that it would bring him a sum of money equivalent to 10 years' salary. This

---

[23] ALMÁSI (n. 2), 167–168.
[24] Ibid. 180–181.
[25] Ibid. 186–190. On Blotius see Paola MOLINO, *L'impero di carta. Storia di una biblioteca e di un bibliotecario (Vienna, 1575–1608)*. Roma 2017 (PhD thesis, European University Institute, Florence 2011).
[26] ALMÁSI (n. 2), 193–196.

puts his gesture into perspective: Sambucus's collection was not the only one integrated into the imperial library during these years.

Sambucus's last years at court were spent in a period of change. With Maximilian's death in 1576, the politics of religious *via media* were lost for good and the Counter-Reformation began with tragic speed in Vienna. Despite being a Lutheran, Sambucus retained his position, trying to survive and avoid fines such as that levied on him for having his child baptised by Protestant priests[27]. Although he was a titular doctor of the court, licensed to treat courtiers (despite the lack of a medical decree), and despite being mentioned in later documents among the university professors, there is no documentation in the sources of either teaching, or treating patients. Sambucus's prestige was doubtless too great at court for him to give lectures for bad money at a provincial university, which became a hotbed of religious tensions after 1576, or to deal with anything more than the occasional aristocratic patient.

SAMBUCUS APUD EXTEROS:

HIS INTERNATIONAL NETWORK

Sambucus's international network of friends and colleagues can best be reconstructed using his surviving correspondence (which he cared little to preserve) and the many dedications attached to emblems in the various editions of the *Emblemata*[28]. The latter method must be regarded as rather inaccurate, despite the author's reassuring comment in the foreword that the numerous dedications were not inserted out of ambition:

> Quod vero aliqua clarissimorum virorum nomina addiderim, non ambitiose factum putes: nec enim hos novi solum, qui omnem adhuc aetatem apud exteros traduxi, sed ut pro meritis, memoriaque et opinione de me publice, scriptisque eorum testata, gratiam hac saltem occasione aliquam haberem, id vero spectavi [...]
>
> *Emblemata* 1564, A2ᵛ

---

[27] Friedrich Tillmez (ed.), Conspectus historiae Universitatis Viennensis ex actis, veteribusque documentis ab anno 1565. ad annum 1701. deductae. 3 vols. Viennae: Schwendimann 1722–1725, vol. 1, 46. Cf. Gábor ALMÁSI, Paola MOLINO, Nikodemismus und Konfessionalisierung am Hof Maximilians II. *Frühneuzeit-Info* 22 (2011), 112–128.

[28] Dedicatees are summarised in tables by VISSER (n. 6), 267–271.

Do not think if I have added some names of well-known men, it was out of ambition. For I have not only known these persons, having lived all my life among people of the world, but sincerely meant to use the opportunity to show at least some gratitude and commemorate their services, and the good opinion of me they expressed in public and in their writings.[29]

If we ignore the *Emblemata* and base our conclusions entirely on the correspondence that has been preserved, we run the risk of neglecting all those relationships from which there are no surviving letters. As a result, long-distance international contacts might well appear dominant. In fact, apart from the imperial doctor Johannes Crato von Krafftheim, who was apparently among Sambucus's best Viennese friends[30], we know hardly anything about Sambucus's relationships with Viennese intellectuals such as the Greek scholar Georg Tanner or the mathematician-astronomer Paulus Fabritius (who were both apparently his friends), or with intellectuals in Hungary like Miklós Istvánffi (his former student); Giovanni Michele Bruto (the future historian of Prince Stephen Báthory), whom Sambucus knew from Italy or France; Zsigmond Gyalui Torda (a translator of Euripides, to whom he dedicated an emblem and upon whose death he put together a lost volume of epitaphs); or the poet, botanist and physician Georgius Purkircher, who wrote an *epithalamium* upon his marriage[31]. On the other hand, additional information on local contacts is not always encouraging. In the correspondence of the Flemish philologist Nicasius Ellebodius (who found refuge in Pozsony/Pressburg/Bratislava having returned to Hungary after a decade-long Italian sojourn), the impression given is of Sambucus as a haughty person, although this may easily be a reflection of Ellebodius's own prejudices and feeling of social inferiority[32]. There is also a suspicious silence concerning

---

[29] The translation is from VISSER (n. 6), 114.
[30] On Crato, see Johann F. U. GILLET, *Crato von Crafftheim und seine Freunde. Ein Beitrag zur Kirchengeschichte*. Frankfurt am Main 1860; Howard LOUTHAN, *The Quest for Compromise. Peacemakers in Counter-Reformation Vienna*. Cambridge 1997, 85–105.
[31] ALMÁSI (n. 2), 70 and passim.
[32] Ellebodius's correspondence is preserved in Milan, BA, D 196 inf. We are grateful to Zsuzsanna Maurer for letting us consult her transcriptions. See, especially, the letter of 14 May 1571, in *ibid.* fol. 1^v and 13 February 1575, *ibid.* fol. 85^r. Although Ellebodius often relied on Sambucus's services (he consulted him on philological and other scholarly questions, received all sorts of information, bought books from him, used his library and postal connections etc.), there was apparently little trust between the two of them.

Sambucus's relationships with the famous learned diplomat Ogier Ghiselin de Busbecq (Busbequius)[33], the imperial antiquarian Jacopo Strada[34], not to mention Hugo Blotius, but we should not forget that these people were serious rivals of Sambucus at court.

Among the most important foreign contacts in Sambucus's network are Piero Vettori in Florence and Theodor Zwinger in Basel, who remained in regular touch with him for over 24 years. Both men reflect significant aspects of his character and interests. Besides being one of the most respected 16th-century philologists, Vettori represented a model of humanism that was hard to follow but the most engaging. Coming from an old and famously erudite Florentine family, he was already in his mature years when he categorically turned his back on the power games of Rome and the internal politics of Florence and decided to dedicate himself entirely to learning[35]. Zwinger, on the other hand, was a many-sided professionalist who combined a profound interest in methodology with encyclopaedic ambitions. He was born into a family of burghers with a number of ties to Basel's thriving intellectual life, and he secured his existence through marriage, university teaching and medical practice[36].

---

[33] The famous episode between Sambucus and Busbecq concerned Sambucus's attempt to sell his library. It was Busbecq who was sent to evaluate Sambucus's library, but when he finally arrived it was almost dusk. Sambucus commented incisively that "perhaps he prefers to get his codices sold to the emperor rather than to recommend mine." Letter to Crato von Crafftheim of 20 November 1573: GERSTINGER (n. 5), 150.

[34] On Strada, see Dirk J. JANSEN, The Instruments of Patronage. Jacopo Strada at the Court of Maximilian II: a case-study. In: Friedrich Edelmayer, Alfred Kohler (eds.), *Kaiser Maximilian II.: Kultur und Politik im 16. Jahrhundert*. Vienna 1992, 182–201; LOUTHAN (n. 30), 24–48; Vittorio MARCHIS, Luisa DOLZA (eds.), *L'Album fiorentino dei 'Disegni artificiali' raccolti da Jacopo e Ottavio Strada* con saggi introduttivi di Thomas DaCosta Kaufmann and Dirk Jacob Jansen. Florence 2002.

[35] For Vettori, see Angelo Maria Bandini (ed.), Clarorum Italorum et Germanorum epistolae ad Petrum Victorium Florentinum. 2 vols. Florence 1758–1760; Lucia CESARINI MARTINELLI, Pier Vettori e gli umanisti tedeschi. In: Giancarlo Garfagnini (ed.), *Firenze e la Toscana dei Medici nell'Europa del '500*. Vol. 2: *Musica e spettacolo; Scienze dell'uomo e della natura*. Florence 1983, 707–726; Salvatore LO RE, Piero Vettori e la natione todesca a Siena: irenismo e inquisizione al tempo di Francesco de' Medici. *Bollettino della Societa di studi valdesi* 123 (2006), 52–92; IDEM, Tra filologia e politica: una medaglione di Piero Vettori (1532–1543). *Rinascimento* 45 (2006), 247–305. Also n. 112 below.

[36] On Zwinger, see Carlos GILLY, Zwischen Erfahrung und Spekulation. Theodor Zwinger und die religiöse und kulturelle Krise seiner Zeit, I–II. *Basler Zeitschrift für Geschichte und Alter-*

Sambucus's enduring connections were almost all direct personal acquaintances. While Zwinger was a fellow student in Padua, Sambucus met Vettori during his travels in Italy. The two men reflect two of the major directions of Sambucus's network: Italy and Switzerland. In Italy he kept in closest touch with Vettori's Roman friend Fulvio Orsini, the Venetian Paolo Manuzio and his son Aldo, and their friend, the famous Ciceronian Marcus Antonius Muretus in Rome. He communicated with the Vatican librarian Guglielmo Sirleto and with other humanists like Gian Vincenzo Pinelli, Carlo Sigonio, and Bacio Valori[37]. In Switzerland, Sambucus had a good relationship with the great Basel publisher Johannes Oporinus (Zwinger's uncle); the proofreader-publisher Eusebius Episcopius; the oriental historian Johannes Leunclavius (Löwenklau), who – as we shall see – resided for many years in Basel and became the most diligent editor of his manuscripts; the celebrated humanist publisher Henricus Stephanus in Geneva; the naturalist and bibliographer Conrad Gesner; and his follower Josias Simmler in Zurich[38]. North of Switzerland, his most trusted contacts were Joachim Camerarius senior and junior. A Hellenist professor at Leipzig University, Camerarius Sr., one of Melanchthon's closest friends, was clearly a central figure in 16th-century Greek and Latin philology. In fact, the title page of the mature Sambucus's Plautus edition claims to do no less than supersede Camerarius's edition, among others, by the addition of more than 200 lines (see below). Camerarius, as a model humanist, apparently had a great influence on Sambucus from an early age, becoming a significant contact after Sambucus's settlement in Vienna[39]. His son Joachim Jr., another fellow-student of Padua, worked as a

---

tumskunde 77 (1977), 57–139 and 79 (1979), 125–225; Paola MOLINO, Alle origini della Methodus Apodemica di Theodor Zwinger: la collaborazione di Hugo Blotius, fra empirismo ed universalismo. *Codices Manuscripti. Zeitschrift für Handschriftenkunde* 56–57 (2006), 43–67.

[37] Besides the letters published in GERSTINGER (n. 5), there is an unpublished letter written to Marcus Antonius Muretus in Rome (Vatican Library, Lat. 6946, fol. 36–37). His communication with Pinelli is mentioned by Nicasius Ellebodius in a letter to Pinelli in Milan (Bibl. Ambr., D 196 inf. 69ʳ).

[38] The correspondence with Simmler (1560, 1567–68) has not yet been published. It is preserved in the Simmler Sammlung of the Zurich Zentralbibliothek.

[39] Cf. note 10 above. More recently on Camerarius Sr., see Stephan KUNKLER, *Zwischen Humanismus und Reformation. Der Humanist Joachim Camerarius (1500–1574) im Wechselspiel von pädagogischen Pathos und theologischen Ethos*. Hildesheim 2000; Rainer KÖSSLING, Günther WARTENBERG (eds.), *Joachim Camerarius*. Tübingen 2003; Joachim HAMM, Joachim Camerarius d. Ä. *Frühe Neuzeit in Deutschland 1520–1620. Literaturwissenschaftliches Verfasserlexikon* I

doctor and naturalist in Nuremberg, where he owned a large botanical garden[40]. Sambucus had several other renowned German contacts in various places, but none of these friendships appears to have acquired the importance of his relationship with the Camerarius family[41]. The Netherlander friends, who represent the fourth direction of Sambucus's network, appear to be more significant. The more long-lasting of these relationships were with his trusted publisher Christophe Plantin and the great cartographer, geographer and antiquarian Abraham Ortelius[42]. Another important Netherlander friend was Carolus Clusius who Sambucus knew from his early student years from Wittenberg and Strasbourg, and who later moved to Vienna for many years[43]. Curiously, no letters between them survived in Clusius's Leiden collection, although there are a few indications that they remained friends until death. It was Clusius who started collecting epigrams written on Sambucus's death, among others by Joachim Camerarius Jr., Piero Vettori, the Dutch humanists Janus Dousa Sr., Janus Lernutius and Justus Lipsius, the German poets Paulus Melissus Schede and Johannes Posthius, and the Silesian doctor Peter Monau[44].

(2011), 425–438; and the forthcoming papers of the conference Camerarius Polyhistor (Würzburg, 2015).

[40] Franz RIMMER, *Joachim Camerarius II., ein Botaniker des 16. Jahrhundert*. St. Pölten 1888 and Svenja WENNING, *Joachim II. Camerarius (1534–1598). Eine Studie über sein Leben, seine Werke und seine Briefwechsel*. Duisburg 2015.

[41] However, his early friendship with Petrus Lotichius Secundus was surely more intimate than his relationship to the Camerarii. See ALMÁSI (n. 2), 211–212. Among other German friends we find Johann Löwenklau, Nicolaus Reusner, Georg Cassander, Johannes Sturm, Konrad Dasypodius, Fridericus Sylburgius, Nicodemus Frischlin and Henricus Porsius.

[42] There was apparently also an intimate friendship between Sambucus and the Flemish wandering humanist Carolus Utenhovius (Karl van Utenhove). See Utenhovius's letter in ÖNB, cod. 9736, fol. 7–10, and a poem of Sambucus to Utenhovius (fol. 26^r–27^v, published in GERSTINGER, n. 5, 53–54). A letter from Plantin from 1583 was published by Hans GERSTINGER, *Ein gelehrter Briefwechsel zwischen Wien und den Niederlanden aus dem Zeitalter des Humanismus. Deutsches Vaterland* 6–7 (1922), 8–14. Republished in: Maurice VAN DURME (ed.), *Supplément à la Correspondance de Christophe Plantin*. Antwerp 1955, 203–204.

[43] Clusius gave Sambucus a book (Johann Schöner, Tabulae astronomicae. Nuremberg 1536) in Paris in 1561. GERSTINGER (n. 6), 349; Friedrich W. T. HUNGER, *Charles de l'Escluse. Nederlandsch Kruidkundige 1526–1609*. The Hague 1942, 2, 17–19. On Clusius see Florike EGMOND, *The world of Carolus Clusius: Natural history in the making, 1550–1610*. London 2010.

[44] Sambucus was presumably in contact with all of these literati, although in the case of Dousa, Lernutius and Schede, documents have apparently not survived. See ALMÁSI (n. 2), 75.

This brief overview of Sambucus's network is necessarily incomplete and provides only a skeleton of his humanist relationships, omitting all those with whom he had less profound or enduring relationships or those that are simply absent from his extant correspondence. Nevertheless, it does prove what the *Emblemata* attempted to document: that is, Sambucus's prestigious place in the Republic of Letters. Sambucus's trusted contacts were mostly philologists, poets, collectors, antiquarians, naturalists and publishers. They were *the* 'humanists', dedicated almost exclusively to learned practices related to antiquity. Apart from a few open-minded Italian Catholics, they were either Lutherans or Calvinists. On the whole, they were people who rarely addressed openly religious, moral or philosophical issues (with the possible exception of Lipsius) but happily exchanged ideas about literature, books and science. They were German, Italian, Dutch, Hungarian, Austrian and French, although the latter – despite the several years that Sambucus spent in France – remain curiously absent from Sambucus's surviving correspondence[45]. They were exclusively men. Like Sambucus, the majority had middle-class origins and (with a few exceptions) enjoyed good social and economic circumstances similar to those of the Hungarian humanist. The socially inferior and younger savants appear to be underrepresented in his correspondence, although – as we shall see – they are dominant in Sambucus's publication projects. In other words, in Sambucus's enduring intellectual relationships, age, social status and prestige were of some importance, while in his 'working relationships' they mattered little.

---

[45] On Sambucus's sojourn in France, see BACH (n. 6).

FROM MANUSCRIPT TO PRINT:

SAMBUCUS'S PUBLISHING AGENDA

When Sambucus finally settled in Vienna after 22 years of academic wandering he had already made a name for himself in the Republic of Letters. Striking proof of this was the *Emblemata*, then in the process of being printed in Antwerp. As illustrated in the emblem *Fidei canum exemplum*, Sambucus had been touring Europe and was returning to Vienna on horseback with a sword at his side, accompanied by his faithful dogs Bombo and Madel. What the emblem did not show was the caravan of books and manuscripts that Sambucus had collected in the preceding 12 years, the final destination of which was likewise Vienna. While earlier, Sambucus's modest fame was based primarily on personal contacts established with Europe's leading humanists (although we might also mention the few – mostly pedagogical – publications he already had in hand and the loose contact he had managed to formalise with the imperial court in 1558), in later years his reputation was to be preserved and increased through an intense publication campaign (soon backed by a far more prestigious standing and connections at court). Such a publication campaign could not have been realised without a good library in the vicinity, and there was apparently none better than Sambucus's private collection, filled with valuable codices and rarities, many of which had been selected with potential publication in mind. As Arnoud Visser has justly asserted, "together with the contacts at court, the library constituted Sambucus's most important asset within the Republic of Letters."[46]

When Sambucus was made *aulae familiaris* in 1558 without much in the way of prior merits[47], his excuse for staying away from Vienna was to perform antiquarian services for the court – that is, to collect valuable manuscripts. Although the collection was meant to be private, Sambucus never failed to stress its public uses. This is illustrated by a letter he sent to Conrad Gessner at the beginning of 1560 with an appendix of rare Greek manuscripts in his possession – items he had forgotten to list in his previous, "hastily written" letter – "which I collected for the common good at vast

---

[46] VISSER (n. 6), 52.
[47] On the circumstances of his nomination see ALMÁSI (n. 2), 147–152.

expense and not without ingenuity and diligence"[48]. In the same letter he mentioned to Gessner that Archduke Maximilian, influenced by the example of private men and by encouragement from his side, now revealed great enthusiasm for all antiquities but especially old books. In other words, the patron of his activity abroad as a collector was Emperor Ferdinand's heir, the person who had once also intensively supported the collecting activity of the erudite, committed Protestant councillor and diplomat Caspar Nidbruck[49]. Three years later, in a letter from Naples, Sambucus once again explained to Maximilian his reasons for staying away from court:

> Meminit enim Tua Maiestas, quanto animi ardore, qua cupiditate studeam patriae totique orbi terrarum, imprimis vero Christi rebus prodesse; quod ego coram T(uam) M(aiestatem) pluribus verbis et vero exemplis testatus sum, ac T(ua) M(aiestas) benignissime atque clementissime voluntatem meam comprobavit. Ea re velut calcari vehementius incitatus denuo Galliam Italiam et alias regiones peragravi, ut libros graecos et latinos locupletes et idoneos cum humanitatis et religionis testes colligerem atque eis vel corrigendis vel edendis ad communem utilitatem ac T(uae) M(aiestatis) nomen celebrandum iuste uterer.
>
> Certainly, Your Majesty remembers my zeal and desire to be of value to the fatherland, the entire world, and, most of all, to the cause of Christ. I have given evidence of this personally in concrete examples and testimony, and Your Majesty most kind-heartedly and gently approved of my intentions. Spurred by this, I returned to France, Italy and other regions of the world even more motivated to collect Latin and Greek books that are rich in content, *testimonies of both humanity and religion*. Through correcting or editing them I would justly utilise them for the common good and for the celebration of Your Majesty's name.[50]

This was already a full-blown publication project, which changed little during the rest of Sambucus's life and which had already been initiated in the year of the last stop of his travels, in the Netherlands. The question remains as to how much the actual publications would fit into this Chris-

---

[48] [...] *quos maximis sumptibus, et non sine ingenio ac industria coëgi ad communem utilitatem.* Letter of 18 January 1560. Published in TÉGLÁSY (n. 15), n. 45. The original is kept in Zurich, Zentralbibliothek, Sammlung Hottinger, Ms. F. 61, fol. 98ʳ⁻ᵛ.

[49] On Caspar/Kaspar (von) Ni(e)dbruck (1525–1557), see Robert HOLTZMANN, *ADB* 52, 621–629; Viktor BIBL, Nidbruck und Tanner. *Archiv für Österreichische Geschichte* 85 (1898), 379–423. On Fabritius, see Joseph Ritter von ASCHBACH, *Geschichte der Wiener Universität.* Vol. 3: *Die Wiener Universität und ihre Gelehrten 1520–1565.* Vienna 1888, 187–193.

[50] [Our italics.] Dated 18 January 1563, in GERSTINGER (n. 5), 61.

tian humanist framework, one of the principal aims of which was the cause of Christ. To be sure, Sambucus was an avid collector of early Christian and Byzantine works, but this also corresponded to the way in which Renaissance humanism – with an unceasing accent on Greek textual heritage – developed in the sixteenth century[51].

Two years later, already back in Vienna, the Hungarian humanist publicly advertised his publication agenda in the dedication of Diogenes Laertius's *Lives and Opinions of Eminent Philosophers*, in which he addressed the targeted patron of the work, Archduke Karl, Emperor Maximilian's brother (see more below):

> Equidem, Serenissime Princeps Carole, cum ingenium post tot annorum studia, sumptus, peregrinationes, imbecillius mihi advertam, quam ut meo, ut aiunt, Marte aliquid excellens posterisque dignum efficere queam, sumpsi mihi eam provinciam, in qua diligentia proficere aliquando possim, atque ne otio pecudum more vitam transegisse dicar, improbitate laborum consequi. Quare in veterum scriptis, quorum cognitio pura sanaque et utilis est, corrigendis, eque tenebris in lucem proferendis libenter versor; in idque potissimum librorum supellex mihi conquisita est, quam non facile magnis thesauris commutarim. Libenter enim quod per ingenium ac vires possum, cum omnibus communico, nec qui latuerunt, eruditorum patiar labores fieri negligentia obscuriores, nec ab eis edendis typographos ulla gratia expetenda, minus exigenda deterrere aut morari unquam soleo: sat mercedis mihi publica est utilitas, cetera linquo avaris, modo sint patroni, qui conatus impressorum promoveant, ut ad Graecos praesertim excudendos sint faciliores.
>
> Diogenes Laertius 1566, A2ᵛ–A3ʳ

---

[51] On the reception of the Greek Church Fathers in 15th- and 16th-century humanism, besides the fundamental work of Charles TRINKAUS, *In Our Image and Likeness*. Chicago 1970, see Irena BACKUS, *Lectures humanistes de Basile de Césarée: traductions latines, 1439–1618*. Paris 1990, and the studies in EADEM (ed.), *The reception of Church Fathers in the West: from the Carolingians to the Maurists*. 2 vols. Leiden 1996; Leif GRANE, Alfred SCHINDLER, Markus WRIEDT (eds.), *Auctoritas Patrum: Contributions on the Reception of the Church Fathers in the 15th and 16th Centuries*. Mainz 1993; IDEM (eds.), *Auctoritas patrum II: neue Beiträge zur Rezeption der Kirchenväter im 15. und 16. Jahrhundert*. Mainz 1993; Mariarosa CORTESI (ed.), *I Padri sotto il torchio: le edizioni dell'antichità cristiana nei secoli 15.–16. Atti del Convegno di studi*. Bottai 2002. However, recent research has concentrated on the role of the *auctoritas patrum* in the context of Catholic and Protestant religious debates, while a thorough examination of the importance of Byzantine tradition from a less confessionally bound, erudite humanist point of view is still lacking.

Indeed, Your Princely Highness Karl, to avoid less uplifting things and in order to be able to do something excellent and worthy for posterity, which is also in my power, and relying on my innate capacities and the study of so many years, and all the travel and expenses, I have chosen a path in which I could slowly make some progress with diligence so that people would not accuse me of passing my life in idleness like a sheep, achieving results with improbity. Therefore, I gladly occupy myself with correcting as well as bringing antique texts from darkness to light, the knowledge of which is honest, healthy and useful. I have collected for this reason a treasury of best books, which I would not easily exchange for any gold. But as far as my talents and force allow me I happily make them public not to let them lay hidden and allow the work of erudite men to become even more obscure through neglect. I do not deter or defer typographers from publishing these works by asking for remuneration, since I will be duly rewarded by public utility, and I leave the rest to the greedy. We only need patrons who promote these publishing enterprises, making in particular the printing of Greek texts easier.[52]

The programme of publishing valuable (especially Greek) manuscripts from his private library, making public what had been primarily privately collected at great effort and expense (especially considering the young Sambucus's very moderate wealth) may sound familiar to historians of 16th-century humanism. However, it was a unique programme as much because of the size and value of Sambucus's collection as for the predominance of Greek manuscripts it contained. More importantly, it was unique in the sense that internationally famous private collectors would very rarely dedicate themselves to actual philological and publishing work. A collector on Sambucus's level would not have been a person of leisure but at the same time would rarely have been someone engaged in the type of humanist practices planned by the Pannonian humanist. Among the great private collectors in Sambucus's wider environment, the only exception was Fulvio Orsini, the librarian of the Farnese in Rome, who actually published the results of his philological and antiquarian efforts[53]. The bibliophiles of inter-

---

[52] Laertius (n. 20), A2^v–A3^r (our translation).
[53] On Orsini's antiquarian and philological efforts, which are partly parallel to those of Sambucus, see Pierre DE NOLHAC, *La bibliothèque de Fulvio Orsini. Contributions à l'histoire des collections d'Italie et à l'étude de la Renaissance.* Paris 1887, and Giuseppina A. CELLINI, *Il contributo di Fulvio Orsini alla ricerca antiquaria.* Rome 2004 (*Atti della Accademia Nazionale dei Lincei. Classe di scienze morali, storiche e filologiche. Memorie* s. IX, 18).

national fame around Sambucus – including the Parisian treasurer-general Jean Grolier (to whom Sambucus dedicated the images of his precious antique coins attached as an appendix to the *Emblemata*); the collector and maecenas Thomas Rehdiger a member of Breslau's most famous patrician families; and the imperial diplomat Ogier Ghislain de Busbecq (who would similarly sell his tiny but precious collection to Emperor Rudolf), not to mention Anton Fugger (whose son Sambucus had been tutoring in Padua) – while being lovers of old books, had largely different attitudes to intellectual labour[54]. On the other hand, nor did Sambucus conform to the type of the 16th-century philologist finding employment in the publishing house of one of the great humanist publishers, such as, for example, Sigismundus Gelenius, the in-house philologist of Frobenius, or the less famous but talented Hellenist Friedrich Sylburg, who worked for many years for the Wechel Press[55]. Although Sambucus did not fit into this group of hard-working philologists, nor did he fit into the group of rich patrons, a point that will be further developed below.

---

[54] For Jean Grolier, see Antoine J. V. LE ROUX DE LINCY, *Recherches sur Jean Grolier, sur sa vie et sa bibliothèque, suivis d'un catalogue des livres qui lui ont appartenu*. Paris 1866; Anthony HOBSON, *Renaissance Book Collecting: Jean Grolier and Diego Hurtado de Mendoza, Their Books and Bindings*. Cambridge 1999, 3–70; for Thomas Rehdiger, see Albrecht WACHLER, *Thomas Rehdiger und seine Büchersammlung in Breslau*. Breslau 1828, 18–19; Hans-Jürgen VON WITZENDORFF-REHDIGER, Die Rehdiger in Breslau. *Jahrbuch der Schlesischen Friedrich-Wilhelms-Universität zu Breslau* 2 (1957), 93–106; for Ogier Ghislain de Busbecq, see Zweder VON MARTELS, *Augerius Gislenius Busbequius: leven en werk van de keizerlijke gezant aan het hof van Süleyman de Grote: een biografische, literaire en historische studie met editie van onuitgegeven teksten*. Groningen 1989; IDEM, On his Majesty's Service. Augerius Busbequius, Courtier and Diplomat of Maximilian II. In: Friedrich Edelmayer, Alfred Kohler (eds.), *Kaiser Maximilian II.: Kultur und Politik im 16. Jahrhundert*. Vienna 1992, 169–181, and Ogier Ghislain de Busbecq, *Les lettres turques*. Ed. Dominique ARRAGHI, Paris 2010; for Anton Fugger, see Götz VON PÖLNITZ, Hermann KELLENBENZ, *Anton Fugger, 1555–1560*. Tübingen 1986.

[55] On Sylburg, see Johann Georg Jung, *Vita Friderici Sylburgii, Wetterani Hassi, polyhistoris quondam magni*. Berleburgi: apud Joh. Jacob. Haugium 1745; Karl PREISENDANZ, Aus Friedrich Sylburgs Heidelberger Zeit. *Neue Heidelberger Jahrbücher* N.F. (1937), 56–77; Antonio RIGO, Saracenica di Friedrich Sylburg (1595): una raccolta di opere bizantine contro l'Islâm, In: Mariarosa Cortesi (ed.), *I Padri sotto il torchio: le edizioni dell'antichità cristiana nei secoli 15.–16.: atti del Convegno di studi*. Bottai 2002, 289–310. On the Wechel Press, see the classical study by Robert EVANS, *The Wechel Presses: Humanism and Calvinism in Central Europe: 1572–1627*. Oxford 1975 (*Past and Present.* Supplement 2).

When Sambucus openly launched his publication project in the dedication to Diogenes Laertius, where he also mentioned a few forthcoming titles, he already had some items on his list of publications. In fact, he had started quite early, and the date of his settling in Vienna did not mark the beginning of a new project but the continuation of an old one in a new direction. According to his 1583 one-sheet printed bibliography, his first work was a certain *Tabellae dialecticae in usum Hefflmari* (either unpublished or lost), which was probably some teaching material that the 16-year-old Sambucus had prepared for a private student[56]. It was only a year later that Sambucus translated two speeches by Xenophon into Latin during the winter break at the University of Ingolstadt[57]. As stated in the preface to the work, he chose to translate these speeches because he realised that the translation by Francesco Filelfo was too far from the original work. In a letter to the reader, Sambucus's rhetoric professor Veit Amerbach stated that although the translations were not spotless they could be placed before the works of Francesco Filelfo and Willibald Pirckheimer, who often disregarded the original meaning of Xenophon's text. Although Amerbach claimed that he preferred not to encourage the publication of stylistic exercises prepared by students, the exceptionally diligent Sambucus, who was still not sufficiently passionate about liberal studies, needed some encouragement. Amerbach's well-placed exhortation had a lasting impact. At the age of 19, Sambucus – who had just become a nobleman – already had another publication in the press, a bilingual edition of Lucian's dialogues[58]. Alongside the translations of a few of the dialogues he attached synopses and explanatory Latin poems that were frequently republished in the sixteenth and early seventeenth centuries. Until 1558, Sambucus continued translating short Greek texts. These included a first Latin translation of Pseudo-Libanius's tract on letter writing, and of two short orations by a 13th- and an 8th-century Byzantine author, although these latter two were already first editions published from his own manuscript collection, even if only in translation[59]. Meanwhile, Sambucus's other humanist interests and

---

[56] BORSA, WALSH (n. 11), 130.
[57] Sambucus, n. 9.
[58] Lucianus (n. 12).
[59] [Ps.-]Libanius, Epistolarum conscribendarum methodus. Basileae: per Ioannem Oporinum 1552; Nilus Cabasilas, Oratio ad Deum. Patavii: [Grazioso Perchacino] 1555; Hippolytus

ambitions had also gained some publicity: his first volume of poetry was attached to his Xenophon translations, and in 1555 he published an independent volume of poetry, the *Poemata*[60]. Nor did he neglect Hungarian humanism and history, publishing works by Pietro Ranzano and Janus Pannonius[61]. Next to the popular *Emblemata*, Sambucus's most important original work, the *De imitatione Ciceroniana dialogi tres*, was written similarly during the long years spent in Italy but was published for the first time only in Paris in 1561 (and republished in Antwerp in 1563)[62]. This work fitted well into the tradition of humanist discourses on the appropriate way of imitation, and although it offered little original thought it was not without influence: Sambucus's insistence on the importance of thought and content over wordiness and questions of expression was admitted to be "eye-opening" by Gabriel Harvey[63]. These books were soon followed by two paraphrases, one on Cicero's *Somnium Scipionis* and another on Horace's *Ars poetica*[64]. Many of these works can be considered pedagogical: either they were Greek texts that were often translated as school exercises (such as the works of Lucian and Xenophon), or they aimed at helping the students embellish their Latin style and composition (such as the works on Cicero or Horace). Sambucus also authored many occasional works as well as some shorter historical pieces[65].

It is thus obvious that, after the publication of the *Emblemata* (1564) and his settling in Vienna, Sambucus's attention was completely reoriented.

Thebanus, De ortu, et cognatione Virginis Mariae libellus. Patavii: Gratiosus Perchacinus excudebat 1556; [Ps.-]Plato, Dialogi duo Platonis. Viennae: Michael Zimmermann 1558.

[60] Sambucus (n. 10). On Sambucus the poet, see ALMÁSI (n. 2), 210–215.

[61] [Ps.-]Plato (n. 59); Janus Pannonius, Lusus quidam et epigrammata nunc primum inventa et excusa. Patavii: [no date] 1559.

[62] The work has been analysed in TÉGLÁSY (n. 6), 65–185. Also see Daniel Škoviera's and Iván Lábaj's papers in the present volume; and Judit VÁSÁRHELYI, Két XVI. századi magyarországi ciceroniánus. *Irodalomtörténeti Közlemények* 82 (1978), 273–285.

[63] Harold S. WILSON, *Gabriel Harvey's 'Ciceronianus'*. Trans. Clarence A. FORBES. Lincoln 1945, 69. Cited by Brian VICKERS, The myth of Francis Bacon's 'anti-humanism'. In: Jill Kraye, Martin Stone (eds.), *Humanism in Early Modern Philosophy*. London, New York 2000, 135–158, at 144.

[64] Johannes Sambucus, De imitatione a Cicerone petenda dialogi tres, nunc recogniti et aucti. Eiusdem Somnium Scipionis luculenta paraphrasi. Antverpiae: excudebat Libertus Malcotius 1563; Johannes Sambucus, Ars poetica Horatii et in eam paraphrasis. Antverpiae: ex officina Christophori Plantini 1564.

[65] For a bibliography see ALMÁSI, KISS (n. 1), 239–244 (Appendix 1).

The works published under his hands after 1565 were of a different character and importance: Petronius and Lucretius in 1565, Aristaenetus, Diogenes Laertius and Plautus in 1566, Janus Pannonius, Demetrius Phalerus, Theophylactus and Gregorius Nyssenus in 1567–1568 – to mention only the first three very productive years[66]. The change in Sambucus's publishing orientation is also noticeable in the first lines of the Diogenes Laertius dedication, developing Erasmus's ideas on editorial Herculean labours:

> Qui in veterum scriptis restituendis atque producendis operam suam ponunt, non minus ii de hominum genere usibusque, quam si ex ingenio quiddam elucubrarint, mereri videntur. Quanto enim difficilius in alienis, quam propriis est versari, et quo maior est auctoritas rerumque veterum monumentis scientia, quam nostrorum comprehensa, hoc gratiam ab omnibus bonis inire laudemque asportare maiorem, qui illis eruendis ac emendandis, ut vulgo sint noti, occupantur, iustissime debent.
>
> Diogenes Laertius 1566, 3
>
> Those who expend their efforts on the restoration and publication of antique texts seem to serve mankind and its everyday needs no less than if they had composed something original. Seeing how much more difficult it is to deal with the work of others than with our own, and how much greater authority the study of antique works has than that of the moderns, all good men should justly be full of praise for and grateful to those engaged in digging up and emending antique texts in order to make them popularly known.[67]

However, it will also become obvious that this series of publications differed not only from those of the earlier period but also from those of the years that followed. The year 1567 appears to be another turning point both in Sambucus's life and in the way he continued to function as a philologist publisher. It was in this year that Sambucus finally stabilised his posi-

---

[66] Petronius Arbiter, Satyrici fragmenta, restitua et aucta. Antverpiae: ex officina Christophori Plantini 1565; T. Lucretius Carus, De rerum natura libri sex. Antverpiae: ex officina Christophori Plantini 1565; Aristaenetus, Ἀρισταινέτου Ἐπιστολαὶ ἐρωτικαί. Antverpiae: ex officina Christophori Plantini 1566; Laertius (n. 20); T. M. Plautus, Comoediae viginti. Antverpiae: ex officina Christophori Plantini 1566; Janus Pannonius, Eranemus nunc repertus. Viennae: Stainhofer 1567; [Ps.-]Demetrius Phalereus, De epistolis doctrina. Antverpiae: ex officina Christophori Plantini 1567; Theophylactus Bulgariae Archiepiscopus, Explicationes in Acta Apostolorum. Coloniae: apud haeredes Arnoldi Birckmanni 1567; Gregorius Nyssenus et al., De occursu Domini nostri Iesu Christi quinque diversorum scriptorum orationes. Coloniae: apud haeredes Arnoldi Birckmanni 1568.

[67] Laertius (n. 20), 3 (our translation). Cf. Erasmus, Adagia 3, 1,1.

tion in Vienna through a good marriage into a merchant family and through the acquisition of the titles *comes palatinus* and *medicus aulicus* (he had already received the title of imperial historian a year earlier). This was also the year when Sambucus stopped doing direct philological work on the texts he "published" – with the exception of a few such as Janus Pannonius (1569) or Vegetius (1574)[68]. Most of the future editions that come out of Sambucus's library (*ex bibliotheca Sambuci*) were prepared for publication by others (and as we shall see, not even the publications of the first text editions were fully Sambucus's work). It is this feature of Sambucus's philological activity that appears the most intriguing, meriting further investigations and explanations. It was this same question that the astute historian Jacques Auguste de Thou raised in his succinct summary of Sambucus's life[69]:

> [...] cuius ea fuit in veteribus libris colligendis diligentia, liberalitas in publicandis, vt principibus viris, qui hac re laudem consecuti sunt, quamuis in dispari fortuna, aequari debeat, quod Nonus Dionysiacων scriptor, Aristaenetus, Eunapius, Hesychius Illustrius, alij eius beneficio editi abunde testantur, alioqui aliena quam sua industria clarior.
>
> *Historiae sui temporis* 1609, 2, 4, 644

In collecting old books and in generously providing for their publication he should be considered as equal (although not in his fortune) with the greatest men who made their name through these occupations. This is amply proven by the editions of Nonnus, the author of the *Dionysiaca*, of Aristaenetus, Eunapius, Hesychius Illustrius and others, which were published with his support; in any case, *he became famous less by his own diligence than by others*. (Italics added.)

This is clearly a problematic evaluation of Sambucus's literary activity, which requires further clarification. The question of what we should claim as Sambucus's works is indeed a difficult one. In order to see more clearly and to have a more balanced judgement we need to return to the sources

---

[68] Iani Pannonii [...] illius antiquis vatibus comparandi, recentioribus certe anteponendi, quae uspiam reperiri adhuc potuerunt, omnia. Opera Ioannis Sambuci Cons. et Hist. Caes. Vienna: Stainhofer 1569; P. Flavius Vegetius Renatus, Mulomedicina. Basileae: Perna 1574.

[69] Jacques Auguste de Thou, Historiae sui temporis. Parisiis: apud Ambrosium et Hieronymum Drovart 1609, pars 2, tom. 4, 644. Apart from his negative comments, Thou closely followed Gesner. See Conradus Gesnerus, Iosias Simmlerus, Bibliotheca instituta et collecta. Zurich: Froschoverus 1583, 493.

and see how Sambucus himself viewed his own activity. As a starting point, we can look at Sambucus's choice of words to describe the different aspects of publishing and editorial activity.

In 1566, Sambucus gave a brief account of his recent achievements in a letter to Paolo Manuzio, the former Venetian humanist publisher elevated to the office of papal typographer[70]. He claimed to have published (*edidi*) a collection of emblems, to have explained (*illustravi*) Horace's *Ars poetica*, and to be preparing (*edo*) the first edition of Eunapius and Ps.-Hesychius, adding that he had "corrected (*correxi*) Diogenes Laertius, Plautus and Petronius."[71] Although he does not clearly define the differences between these editorial activities anywhere in his works, Sambucus's choice of words does not seem to be arbitrary: he claims to have edited (*editio, edere*) the *Emblemata*, the result of his own intellectual efforts; and to be about to publish the text of Eunapius and Ps.-Hesychius, which had not previously been printed[72]. In all three cases, Sambucus uses the word *editio* coherently, by which he means to offer a previously unknown work to the public. At the same time, he uses the word *illustratio* to describe his explanatory notes on the *Ars*

---

[70] For Manuzio, see Anne Jacobson SCHUTTE, The Lettere Volgari and the Crisis of Evangelism in Italy. *Renaissance Quarterly* 28 (1975), 639–677; Francesco BARBERI, *Paolo Manuzio e la stamperia del popolo romano (1561–1570): con documenti inediti*. Rome 1942 (^{2}1985); Paul F. GRENDLER, The Adages of Paolo Manuzio. Erasmus and the Roman Censors. In: James V. Mehl (ed.), *In laudem Caroli. Renaissance and Reformation Studies for Charles G. Nauert*. Kirksville 1998, 1–21; H. George FLETCHER, Paulus Manutius in aedibus populi romani. The campaigne for Rome. In: David S. Zeidberg (ed.), *Aldus Manutius and Renaissance Culture. Essays in Memory of Franklin D. Murphy*. Florence 1998, 287–321, and Tiziana STERZA, Paolo Manuzio editore a Venezia (1533–1561). *Quaderni di ACME* 61 (2008), 123–167.

[71] *Dum a vobis absum, praeter numismatum opus edidi Emblematum ludos, Horatii Poeticam illustravi, Laertium, Plautum, Petronium correxi, Eunapium cum Illustrio et alia edo, omnia ex officina Plantini.* GERSTINGER (n. 5), 72. Compare the similar letter written to Pompilius Amasaeus on 13 January 1567: *Ego septem authores δυσευρήτους περὶ σχημάτων collegi, illustravi παρεκβολαῖς δημηγορίας Xenophonis, Laërtium correxi, Eunapii philosophi et Illustrii poëtae sub praelo sunt Antverpiae ac nisi civile hoc calamitosumque ob religionis novae opinionem bellum in Belgicis arderet, iam absoluta fuissent omnia.* Parma, Bibl. Palatina, Ms Parma 1019, fasc. IX, fol. 13^r.

[72] Both text were published by Hadrianus Junius: Εὐναπίου τοῦ Σαρδιανοῦ Βίοι φιλοσόφων καὶ σοφιστῶν. E bibliotheca Ioan. Sambuci Pannonii Tirnaviensis. Antverpiae: ex officina Christophori Plantini 1568; [Ps.-]Hesychius Milesius, Ἡσυχίου Μιλησίου Ἰλλουστρίου περὶ τῶν ἐν παιδείᾳ διαλαμψάντων σοφῶν. Ex bibliotheca Ioannis Sambuci Pannonii Tirnaviensis. Antverpiae: ex officina Christophori Plantini 1572.

poetica, as in this commentary he did not deal with the constitution and correction of the text; his sole aim was to prepare interpretative and rhetorical comments on the poetic teachings of Horace. Thus, strictly speaking, by *editio* he meant only the first publication of any text, while the term *illustratio* referred to commentary. It is only with respect to the third category of texts, which he defines as having been corrected (*correxi*), that the philologist executes the painstaking work of textual emendations. Although in modern usage philological work is generally considered to be tantamount to textual corrections and the constitution of the text, for both Sambucus and the philologists of his age this activity seems to have been clearly separated both from publishing a new text and from commenting on an already published source[73]. In his account of his activities to Manuzio, Sambucus clearly indicates by his use of the term *correxi* that he has applied textual criticism only to three works: those of Diogenes Laertius, Plautus and Petronius.

Sambucus's consistent use of contemporary philological terminology can be double-checked against the printed bibliography that he issued towards the end of his life[74]. The terms *editio*, *illustratio* and *correctio* (or *emendatio*) always have a clear and distinct meaning and refer to different phases of editorial work. Nowhere in his bibliography does Sambucus ever confuse the concept of *editio*, by which he means creating the possibility (for himself or for others) of getting a work published, with that of *correctio* or *emendatio*, which refer to the concentrated efforts of the philologist on textual criticism. However, the same editions that he described to Manuzio – plus the edition of Lucretius – are referred to in his bibliography using the words "he partly corrected"[75]

---

[73] Sambucus's philological vocabulary fully complies with contemporary humanist usage. See Silvia RIZZO, *Il lessico filologico degli umanisti*. Rome 1973, 265–275; 319–323.

[74] BORSA, WALSH (n. 11).

[75] *Plautum, Laërtium, Petronium, Lucretium partim emendavit.* It is possible that the qualification "partly" refers only to Lucretius, which was edited by Hubertus Giphanius from the annotated book supplied by Sambucus (see below, note 245).

translation[76]	commentary	first edition of a previously unpublished text	augmented version	textual criticism
vertit[77] interpretatus	artificii notatione illustravit[78] illustravit[79] artificio distinxit[80]	edidit[81] produxit[82] protulit[83] collegit ediditque[84] extulit[85] vulgo legi curavit[86] edendum curavit[87]	auxit[88] aucta[89] cum suo auctario[90]	correxit[91] emendavit[92] purgavit[93] emaculatum edidit[94] recognovit[95] emendatiora edidit[96]

[76] When supplying the bibliographical data for these publications, we follow the corrections made by BORSA, WALSH (n. 11).

[77] *Conciones Xenophontis, post aliorum vertit* (n. 9); *Platonis Axioch: Alcibiad. vertit, interpretatus* (n. 59); *Libanium et alios de ep[isto]lis formandis libellos vertit:* (n. 59); *Nili precationes, Hipolyti Thebani de ortu Mariae vertit libellum* (n. 59).

[78] *Luciani opera scholis [sic], artificii notatione illustravit* (n. 12).

[79] *Horatii Poëticam, & Somnium Scipionis, paraphrasibus, & scholiis illustravit* (n. 64).

[80] *Conciones Xenophontis [...] artificio distinxit* (n. 9).

[81] *Carminum suorum velut pammetron edidit* (n. 10); *In Hippocratem lectiones antiquas edidit Zuingerus cum Hippocrate* (Hippocrates, Viginti duo commentarii. Basileae: Episcopius 1579); *Palladium in defract: Hyppocra. per Iunium Crassum edidit* (Palladius et al., Medici Antiqui Graeci. Basileae: Perna 1581).

[82] *Petri Ranzani Epitomen rerum Ungaricarum cum suo auctario primus produxit* (n. 61).

[83] *Ioannis Stobaei Eclogas physicas protulit* (n. 264).

[84] *Gregorii Nazanzeni flosculos salutares collegit, ediditque* (Gregorius Nazanzenus, Sententiae et regulae vitae. Antverpiae: ex officina Christophori Plantini 1568).

[85] *Basilicorum summam extulit, per Leonclaium* (LX librorum Βασιλικῶν. Basileae: Episcopius 1575).

[86] *Constantini Ducis naturalium libros, e graeco latinos, per Auberium vulgo legi curavit* (n. 276).

[87] *Rerum Hispanicarum tom. tertium edendum cum praefatione sua curavit* (Alvarus Gomecius, De rebus gestis a Francisco Ximenio Cisnerio. Francofurti: And. Wechel 1581.

[88] *Caesarum effigies cum historiis emendavit, auxitve* (Johannes Hutichius, Romanorum principum effigies. Argentorati: Köpfel 1552); *Consuetudines Ungariae iterum correxit, auxit* (n. 224).

[89] *Emblemata aucta, & quintum recusa* (Emblemata. Antverpiae: ex officina Christophori Plantini 1564–1576); *Iani Pannonii opera iterum emendatiora dimidioque aucta edidit* (n. 68).

[90] *Petri Ranzani Epitomen rerum Ungaricarum cum suo auctario primus produxit* (n. 75).

[91] *Homeri opera correxit, novis indicibus expediit. Argent. 1552*: referring to Köpfel's editions of the *Iliad* and the *Odyssey* (Argentorati: Köpfel 1550); *Vegetii Mulomedicinam correxit, purgavit*: Vegetius (n. 68); *Consuetudines Ungariae iterum correxit, auxit* (n. 81).

[92] *Caess: effigies cum historiis emendavit, auxitve* (n. 81); *Plautum, Laërtium, Petronium, Lucretium partim emendavit* (Antverpiae: ex officina Christophori Plantini 1565–1566).

[93] *Vegetii Mulomedicinam correxit, purgavit* (n. 84).

[94] See n. 90.

[95] *Aegynatem totum recognovit* (never published).

As these documents testify, Sambucus had a clear idea of the different roles he played in the publishing process: editions referred to by the words *correxit* or *emendavit* were subject to his own textual corrections. A thorough analysis of these will be carried out in the next chapter, further illuminating Sambucus's philological methodology and his actual concept of textual criticism. Sambucus was fairly consistent in differentiating these works from those *editiones* where he simply presented the manuscript to other philologists or to a publishing house to produce an *editio princeps*. However, this is not to deny that in some cases he clearly exaggerated the depth and extent of his work on a text. A case in point is the edition of Plotinus, about which he claimed in the bibliography that "he has edited Plotinus for the first time, which he himself has corrected."[97] The first edition of the *Enneads* was indeed published from a manuscript of Sambucus, and it was probably his own initiative to have the Greek text printed, since the scholarly community still knew the work only in Marsilio Ficino's widely available Latin translation. In a letter of 13 April 1577 he mentioned his intention to bring out Plotinus to his friend, the imperial physician Johannes Crato: "I have sent Plotinus, emended and collated with the edition of Ficino, to Perna [the printer] who was asking for it." Only a day later, on 14 April 1577, he wrote to Theodor Zwinger that he wished the manuscript of Plotinus that he was sending to Perna could be collated with the edition of Ficino: "I am sending the Greek Plotinus to Perna, a nicely corrected and rare manuscript, and I wish it to be collated with Ficino's translation."[98] Evidently, Sambucus could more easily overstate the extent of his collaboration on this edition to Johannes Crato than to Zwinger, who was working in Basel, the same city as Pietro Perna[99]. In fact, Sambucus's work was largely limited

---

[96] *Iani Pannonii opera iterum emendatiora dimidioque aucta edidit* (n. 82).
[97] *Plotinum à se emaculatum graecè primus edidit per Pernam.* BORSA, WALSH (n. 11), 128–129.
[98] See GERSTINGER (n. 5), 212–213: *Misi Plotini codicem Graecum emendatum et collatum ad Ficini editionem Pernae flagitanti. Mitto Pernae Graecum Plotinum, optime correctum et rarum Codicem, quem cum Ficini Versione collatum velim.*
[99] Pietro Perna, a former Dominican monk who converted to Protestantism, opened a prolific printing press after leaving Italy and getting married in Basel. Perna's willingness to print the Greek text of Plotinus might be explained by his longstanding interest in medical, magical and Neoplatonic sources. He had already published Ficino's Latin translation of Plotinus in 1559. See Leandro PERINI, *La vita e tempi di Pietro Perna*. Rome 2002, 161–169.

to sending his manuscript to Perna[100], which the Basel printer duly acknowledged in his preface, although it was only one of the four manuscripts that he used[101].

In explaining the many *editiones* on Sambucus's list of publications and the parallel lack of *correctiones* – that is, his failure to expend greater effort on the textual emendation of works meant for publication after 1567 – we need to bear in mind that one of the greatest strengths of his library, amassed mostly in Italy, was the relatively large number of never before published manuscripts. Obviously, these texts were considered to be the greatest treasures of a library, as the owner could allow or deny access to these manuscripts to other scholars. At the same time, the publication of texts that were known to exist only in a single manuscript brought both fame to the library and suggested the generosity and magnificence of their owner. It should come as no surprise that the private owner of a manuscript library with a large number of unpublished texts was interested in getting at least some of these sources printed, as this raised the prestige of both the library and the owner, whose name could either be mentioned in the introductory paratexts or directly on the title page. In Sambucus's case, the "*Ex bibliotheca Sambuci*" inscription on the title pages of his *editiones* became a kind of trademark of the Sambucus publishing institution, to which the Hungarian humanist would often allude when speaking of himself in the third person or referring to his *musaeum*. If Sambucus failed to contribute to the textual emendation of many of the works published from his library we should neither ignore that the extent of the publishing campaign he had in mind could hardly be realised without the help of assistants, nor disregard the apparent fact that within the broadly interpreted Republic of Letters the social importance of the act of getting an unpublished work into

---

[100] In fact, Sambucus's notes appear on three folios of the manuscript (now ÖNB, cod. phil. gr. 102, fol. 108ʳ, 177ᵛ, 184ᵛ), as noted by: Paul HENRY, *Études Plotiniennes*. Vol. 2. *Les manuscrits des Ennéades*. Paris, Bruxelles 1948 (*Museum Lessianum, Section philosophique* 21), 271. Sambucus seems to have collated – at least partially – the Greek text of his manuscript with the Latin translation of Ficino.

[101] Plotinus, Operum omnium philosophicorum libri LIV. Basileae: Perna 1580, α4ʳ. The manuscript returned from Perna almost exactly four years later (fol. 3ʳ: *Remissus a prelo Pernae 15. Apr. 1580.*). On Perna's edition and its sources, see HENRY (n. 93), 295–317. The preface of Perna is edited by PERINI (n. 99), 361–366.

print was considerably greater than the philological care invested into the work in question. On the extent of Sambucus's publication scheme, the best document is his bibliography, where the list of planned editions (28 in total) occupies the same amount of room on the page as those he had already published. In this light, it is less surprising that some unpublished texts in the bibliography were even offered freely to anyone willing to publish them[102]:

> Greg. Corinthii, Ioan. Syceliotae, Glycaei, Dyaraeti comment. in Hermog. qui volet, facile communicabit.
>
> The commentaries of Gregory of Corinth, John of Sicily, Glycaeus and Georgius Diairetes on [the rhetoric of] Hermogenes can easily be published by anyone who is willing to do so.

This policy would often appear to contemporaries as exceptional generosity, even if they were well aware that the rhetoric of serving the public good matched Sambucus's personal carving for fame. Sambucus's correspondents and the authors of dedications in the publications coming from his library would repeatedly emphasise his selfless concern for the interests of the scholarly community[103].

However, there are two more explanations for why Sambucus left the editing work to others in so many cases: one concerns his philological attitude, while the other has to do with Vienna's marginal location. If Sambucus refrained from editing manuscripts that were appearing for the first time (*editiones principes*), he was both in line with the editing practices of the age and loyal to his own philological principles. An illustration of this is the way in

---

[102] BORSA, WALSH (n. 11), 128–129. The generous offer concerned the contents of the manuscripts ÖNB, cod. phil. gr. 15 and 16. He bought the first manuscript in Florence in 1576. Cf. Herbert HUNGER, *Katalog der griechischen Handschriften der Österreichischen Nationalbibliothek.* Bd. I: *Codices historici, codices philosophici et philologici.* Vienna 1961, 147–148.

[103] Among the many places, see, for example, Leunclavius's dedication in Antonius Bonfinius, *Symposion trimeron sive pudicitia coniugali et virginitate dialogi III* [ed. Johannes Leunclavius]. Basileae: ex officina Oporiniana 1572, †6ᵛ: *Equidem si libere profiteri, quod sentio, debeo: facis tu profecto perbenigne, qui libros utiles studio tuo perquisitos et aere non exiguo coemptos non apud te privatim abditos esse pateris, sed liberali manu cum omnibus lubens communicas. Debebunt hoc nomine tibi tam litterae, quam litterati omnes ubique terrarum neque beneficia tua praedicare desinent, qui non elabores ipse tantum Apolline digna, sed etiam aliis ad usum publicum elucubranda suppedites et urgere non cesses, ut in iis velut extrudendis nequaquam segnes sese praebeant.* Cf. Joachim Camerarius [Sr.], *Libellus gnomologicus.* Lipsiae: [Voegelin?] 1569, 23–24.

which Aristaenetus's *Love epistles* were published by Plantin in 1566[104]. As the title lines state, the work came from Sambucus's library and Plantin's publishing house, but the name of the actual editor is not given[105]. The manuscript once owned by Sambucus is still the most important and only intact copy of the text (now preserved in the Österreichische Nationalbibliothek – henceforth ÖNB –, cod. phil. gr. 310)[106]. According to a note in the manuscript, Sambucus bought this codex in 1561, probably in southern Italy, and he delivered it to Plantin in Antwerp in 1564. Plantin returned it on 3 June 1566, according to another note in the same manuscript[107]. The paratexts of the edition reveal further details of the publication process: the imperial privilege (for a period of six years) was issued in Brussels on 17 March 1564, while the dedication to Baron Philipp von Winnerberg is dated 13 July 1565. Here Sambucus extols the virtues of Aristaenetus exhaustively but does not say a word about the principles of the edition. This was because the manuscript had been with Plantin for more than a year by then, and it was Plantin's assistant Frans Raphelengius who prepared the edition from the manuscript itself, as one of Plantin's cost-accounting notes reveals[108].

As we shall see, the basic rule of preparing an *editio* for Sambucus was to retain all the readings of the manuscript source and to make an exact transcription instead of an emended edition. This approach to editing clas-

---

[104] Aristaenetus, n. 66.
[105] Sambucus originally intended to have Philo's *De virtutibus* published together with Aristaenetus's epistles. However, Plantin realised that Philo's text had already been edited, and from a better manuscript than the one owned by Sambucus. He consequently decided not to print it, despite the fact that the text had already been composed. See Leon VOET, *The Plantin Press (1555–1589). A Bibliography of the Works printed and published by Christopher Plantin at Antwerp and Leiden*, 6 vols. Amsterdam 1980–1983, vol. I, 194.
[106] The two other existing manuscript sources have been copied from his text. On the origins and fate of this manuscript, seen by John Lascaris in Apulia in 1492, cf. Aristaenetus, *Epistularum libri II*, ed. Otto Mazal. Stuttgart 1971. On the authorship of the two epigrams at the end of the volume, see André JACOB, Une épigramme de Palaganus d'Otrante dans l'Aristénète de Vienne et le problème de l'Odyssée de Heidelberg. *Rivista di studi bizantini e neoellenici* n. s. 25 (1988), 185–203.
[107] Otto MAZAL, Die Textausgaben der Briefsammlung des Aristainetos. *Gutenberg-Jahrbuch* 1968, 206–212.
[108] VOET (n. 105). First editions were usually printed from a single manuscript copy, which was usually destroyed in the process of preparation for typesetting and split into quires. Luckily, the manuscript of Sambucus survived this process, probably because of its uniqueness. Cf. Alphonse DAIN, *Les manuscrits*. Paris ³1975, 160–161.

sical sources suited both his aims and his personal situation. In order to reach wider humanist audiences, Sambucus had to turn to international publishing and trading centres (such as Antwerp, Basel, Cologne and Frankfurt), which were far from Vienna, his home and the setting for his career at court. Publishing Greek and Latin authors for an international humanist audience in Vienna was out of question: the imperial city did not have a publishing house that could easily reach the targeted public and that had adequate typographical experience and highly skilled typesetters and correctors[109]. Such publishing houses existed in only a very few cities in Europe, and Sambucus had contacts with most of them. Bearing in mind the slow communication channels, a constant exchange of proofs and textual corrections between the printing shop and the philologist would have been awkward, if not impossible. Thus Sambucus's choice to have the codices published as they were was not only a demonstration of his faithfulness to manuscript sources or an indication of the greater prestige of *editio* (the publication itself) over *correctio* (the arduous process of emendation): it was also a rational decision based on the limited possibilities for communication and the extent of Sambucus's publication agenda.

However, none of this explains the fading pace of Sambucus's publications in the last decade of his life and the curious lack of any transmitted work after 1576 (disregarding Plotinus). The reason was surely not Sambucus's idleness or lack of interest, since he never stopped complaining in his correspondence about publications or projects that were obstructed at some point or other[110]. His bibliography, printed only a year before his death, was also motivated by his evident frustration over the number of failed or unfinished projects.

---

[109] Unfortunately, the history of Viennese publishing houses in this period (just like the history of Viennese censorship) is still unstudied. The work of Michael Denis (*Wiens Buchdruckergeschicht bis 1560*. Vienna 1782) finishes just before our period.

[110] These are exhausively analysed in Hans GERSTINGER, Zusammenfassung. In: GERSTINGER (n. 5), 285–318.

UNFINISHED PROJECTS

As mentioned above, Sambucus refers to 28 ongoing publishing projects in his bibliography at the end of his life[111]. Although many of these projects were apparently no more than passing whims, in certain cases his intentions were serious – as, for example, the publication of Aristotle's work, for which he claimed to have collected some 60 manuscripts and laboured incessantly for many nights[112]. He accumulated a great number of variant readings and corrections on Hippocrates's work from two manuscripts and a printed book on the margins of a printed edition in around 1561[113], which

---

[111] BORSA, WALSH (n. 11).
[112] For all dates concerning Sambucus's edition of Aristotle, see GERSTINGER (n. 5), 286–289. His first conjectures concerning the *Historia animalium* and the *De generatione animalium* appear in a letter to Vettori in 1568. GERSTINGER (n. 5), 91. He seems to have sent his corrections to the Episcopius press in Basel in an annotated printed copy of Aristotle (probably the one referred to in the said letter to Vettori: Aristoteles, Opera [...] omnia. Basileae: Bebel, Isengrin 1550) in 1574, and waited for their publication impatiently until his death. In spite of his efforts to find a cooperating financial partner for the project (first in Henricus Stephanus, then in Andreas Wechel, and his heir, Jean Aubry), and despite the fact that Episcopius paid 32 thalers to him for his labours, the edition was never realised, either because of the lack of public interest in Greek philosophical texts, or because of the unfinished state of his work, as was the case with Plotinus. In a letter, Sambucus blamed the delay on the uninterested German audience: *Pollicetur se quidem impressurum, sed temporibus commodioribus, quo philosophicae hae disputationes in Germanis refrixerint minusque vendabiles sint* (GERSTINGER, n. 5, 237). Unfortunately, the copy with the manuscript notes of Sambucus cannot be traced. Similarly, the plan for publishing Georgius Trapezuntius' Latin translation of Aristotle's works on natural history was never carried out, and the manuscript remained with Episcopius (GERSTINGER, n. 5, 306).
[113] Petrus Lambecius saw this annotated edition (probably the one printed by Aldus in Venice in 1526) in the imperial library: *obiter significem extare in Aug. Bibliotheca Caesarea Hippocratis Opera, Venetiis typis Aldi Manutii anno 1526 graece in folio edita, quibus Joannes Sambucus, anno 1561, incredibili cura ac studio in margine codicis Aldini adiunxit aliquot mille varias lectiones manuscriptas ex pervetusto quodam codice manuscripto Tarentino et ex alio quodam codice manuscripto Fontemblensi, necnon ex exemplari quodam excuso quidem, sed plurimis locis Romae correcto.* Petrus Lambecius, Commentariorum de augustissima Bibliotheca Caesarea Vindobonensi liber sextus. Viennae: Cosmerovius 1674, 154. Sambucus's notes were finally used by Stephan Mack: Hippocrates, Opera omnia, cum variis lectionibus [...] partim depromptis ex Cornarii et Sambuci codd. in Caesar. Vindobonensi Bibliotheca hactenus asservatis et ineditis [...], 2 vols. Ed. Stephanus Mackius. Vienna 1743. As André Rivier has established, Sambucus's manuscript from Fontaineblue was BNF gr. 2255. André RIVIER, *Recherches sur la tradition manuscrite du traité hippocratique "De morbo sacro".* Bern 1962, 163–166.

he duly sent Zwinger with some later additions in the hope of publication[114]. In 1568, he collated his own two codices of Quintilian against each other and another two manuscript sources, which he wanted to publish once Aristotle appeared in print[115]. However, these projects were never realised, chiefly due to a lack of interest from publishers, and probably due to lack of time on Sambucus's part. The most significant and notable among the failed projects was the plan to restore the text of Dioscorides, in which Sambucus invested great philological and organisational efforts[116]. The Dioscorides project was locally motivated, the imperial court having been the main sponsor of Pietro Andrea Mattioli's best selling edition of Dioscorides's *De materia medica*, with which Sambucus aimed to compete, and it was also in Vienna that five Dioscorides manuscripts landed from the collection of Busbecq and his learned botanist companion William Quackelbeen, among them the beautifully illuminated ancient "Vienna Dioscorides"[117]. Consulting more than seven codices (including his own manuscript), several of which were sent to him from Italy, as well as several printed editions, Sambucus was truly ambitious in the edition of Dioscorides[118]. His contribution would have been as much textual as aesthetic (with new planned illustrations) and botanical (adding to Dioscorides's work on herbs – already a botanical encyclopaedia of 900 plants – more than 100 new plants that were prom-

---

[114] GERSTINGER (n. 5), 307–309.
[115] See GERSTINGER (n. 5), 87. His manuscripts (ÖNB, cod. lat. 30, lat. 3101.) contain his marginal annotations and corrections.
[116] See Gerstinger's excellent summary (as in note 110), 297–302. Cf. Alain TOUWAIDE, Sambucus' project for a critical edition of Dioscorides, De materia medica. In: *Proceedings of the 40 International Congress on the History of Medicine, August 26–30, 2006.* Budapest 2006, vol. 2, 639–644.
[117] On Quackelbeen, see Joseph E. OPSOMER, Un botaniste trop peu connu: William Quackelbeen (1527–1561). *Bulletin de la Société royale de botanique de Belgique* 93 (1961), 113–130. On cod. med. gr. 1, see Hans GERSTINGER (ed.), *Dioscurides: Codex Vindobonensis med. Gr. 1 der Österreichischen Nationalbibliothek.* 5 vols. Graz 1965–1970.
[118] See the letter to Fulvio Orsino of 8 December 1575. We do not know whether he had access to all codices of Busbecq or how he counted Vettori's manuscript, sent to him from Florence (med. gr. 14), which contains in its margins a collation of three manuscripts. However, he did not stop working on Dioscorides and twice sent Henri Estienne new materials (GERSTINGER, n. 5, 234 and 259). The letter to Camerarius of 1578 (*ibid.*, 234) suggests that Sambucus gained access to a new codex from Rome and fragments from Florence most probably from Orsino. Sambucus's collations can be found in his fully annotated Greek edition (Paris 1549) in Vienna, ÖNB, shelfmark *J.69.141.

In search of Sambucus

ised to him by Johannes Crato)[119]. The project appeared so appealing that initially he demanded an honorary amount of just 300–500 florins from the eventual typographer[120]. However, printing Dioscorides demanded huge investments and few publishers were willing to compete with Mattioli's popular edition. Eventually, the project was embraced by Henri Estienne, a humanist publisher with an astute eye for the commercial imperatives of quality publishing (and not different in this respect from Plantin or Perna). Although Sambucus complained that Estienne was greedy (or, in other words, that he wanted to make the project lucrative), it was surely more than financial considerations that made the publisher cautious. With Sambucus's collations and annotations in hand (which the frustrated Pannonian humanist once even considered publishing separately), Estienne felt little nearer the desired end[121]. For a new edition he needed an expert philologist who was ready to go through the text once more, make a new Latin translation and prepare it for print[122]. This person he found in the learned doctor and botanist Jean-Antoine Sarasin, whom he put into contact with Sambucus[123]. Sarasin was, however, extremely slow, and neither seemed ready to hurry: Dioscorides soon became his life project. Although his 'book proposal' was sent to Sambucus as early as the end of the 1570s (with a promise to have Sambucus's collations printed on the inner margins and to insert his notes at the end), the book was ready only 20 years later, in the year of Sarasin's death[124]. By this time, the French botanist had far outdone the deceased

---

[119] See Sambucus's letter to Vettori of 13 September 1570, in GERSTINGER (n. 5), 112–113.

[120] GERSTINGER (n. 110), 299.

[121] In fact, the gap between Sambucus's annotated copy held now in Vienna (see above) and the annotations realised by Sarasin is huge. If this copy was the one sent to Estienne (which is unsure), its application to the text edition needed real intellectual efforts and further investigations. (Compared to the copy *J.69.141 the French doctor's notes were short, selectively made remarks, often containing new additions, etc.)

[122] See the letter to Zwinger of 12 March 1576 in GERSTINGER (n. 5), 192; and to Johannes Crato of 8 March 1577 (ibid., 210–211): *Nil prorsus ab Henrico. Sed facit suo more; ubi aliquid extorsit, proprium esse vult et captat fere sordidus et avarius ex nugis lucellum etc.* Cf. GERSTINGER (n. 110), 300.

[123] See Sarasin's undated letter in ÖNB, cod. Lat. 9736, fol. 23ʳ–24ᵛ, partly transcribed in GERSTINGER (n. 110), 301.

[124] Πεδακίου Διοσκορίδου τοῦ Ἀναζαρβέως τὰ Σωζόμενα Ἅπαντα. *Pedacii Dioscoridis Anazarbaei Opera quae extant omnia. Ex nova interpretatione Jani Antonii Saraceni Lugdunaei, Medici.* Francofurti: Wechel 1598. Sarasin remained rather reticent about the

master, thoroughly consulting even more manuscripts, providing a new translation, and attaching to the text 140 folio pages of commentaries testifying to his massive philological and botanical knowledge. Sambucus's numerous collations (on the inner margins) and notes were included but paled in significance when compared to Sarasin's own contribution. Sambucus's three and a half pages of notes on pages 141 to 144 of the *Scholia* were preceded by an introduction, once more paying tribute to the Hungarian scholar and stressing his efforts and generosity while not hiding the editor's opinion of Sambucus's notes:

> Occurrent, fateor, haud ita pauca, quae ut mihi ita et tibi fortasse merito suspectiora aut veritati dudumque receptae medicorum opinioni minus consentanea videbuntur: attamen malui, qualicunque erant, iudicio tuo subiicere, quam temere nimiumve audacter quicquam immutare. Tuum erit, quicquid id est, aequi bonique consulere hominemque literariae Reipublicae quandiu vixit iuvandae quam studiosissimum pro tua prudentia excusare: quippe cui, ceu aulicum vitam agenti, quum alia quam medica saepenumero tractanda essent, ad amussim singula expendere non ita licuerit.

> There will be, I confess, not a few places [in the notes] that will perhaps appear to you [the Reader] (just as they did to me) suspicious or contrary to the long-received opinion of doctors. Nevertheless, no matter how they appear, I preferred to leave it to your judgement than to change rashly or far too confidently any of their parts. It will be up to you, whatever the matter, to form a lenient opinion of and prudently excuse this man, who, as long as he lived, wished to support as zealously as possible the Republic of Letters, and who could obviously not afford to focus meticulously on details since he lived the life of a courtier, hence often needed to engage in matters other than medicine.[125]

Another characteristic project was the publication of a huge collection of Greek and Latin letters by Manuel Chrysoloras, Basilius Bessarion and Maximus Planudes, and 600 letters by Church Fathers[126]. Part of the letters

---

role of Sambucus in the preparations leading to this edition, and consequently, Olivier Reverdin, who – not knowing their epistolary exchange – examined only the 1598 edition, completely minimised the contribution of the Hungarian humanist. Cf. Olivier REVERDIN, Exposé, en forme de causerie, sur le Dioscoride de Jean-Antoine Sarasin. In: Hellmut Flashar (ed.), *Médicine et morale dans l'antiquité*. Geneva 1997 (*Entretiens sur l'Antiquité classique* 43), 365–381, esp. 374–376.

[125] Dioscorides (n. 124), 141.
[126] See BORSA, WALSH (n. 11), 128–129.

(mostly those by Chrysoloras) were entrusted to Joachim Camerarius the Elder following his visit to Vienna, where he was enchanted by Sambucus's library[127]. The letters from the Church Fathers (Saint Gregory, Gregory of Nyssa, Chrysostom and others) were sent to Plantin[128]. When Camerarius died in 1574 and the letters by Chrysoloras were still not published, Sambucus made sure that they came into the hands of Bonaventura Vulcanius, one of the leading Greek scholars of the Low Countries[129], who was requested to publish them. However, Vulcanius did not publish Chrysoloras's letters (because of their mixed arguments and style, as he later explained to Plantin[130]), nor were the manuscripts sent back to Vienna. When Sambucus got tired of waiting for Vulcanius, he asked Lipsius for help in getting hold of his manuscripts, since his Hungarian friend Andreas Dudith intended to translate them into Latin[131]. In fact, after Sambucus's death Dudith eagerly enquired about the future of these letters, although there is no indication that he was ever asked to translate them, or indeed ever thought of doing so[132].

---

[127] Sambucus also lent Camerarius his manuscript of Palladius's *Epistolae de Indiae gentibus*, which he published in his *Libellus Gnomologicus* (n. 103). Also see Camerarius the Elder's undated Greek letter to Sambucus in Camerarius (n. 10), 412. Cf. Gerstinger (n. 110), 294–295; and Almási (n. 2), 219.

[128] See the letter to Nicasius Ellebodius of 26 March 1573, in Milan, Biblioteca Ambrosiana, D 196 inf., fol. 126^{r-v}. Cf. the end of the dedication to Busbecq: [Ps.-]Hesychius Milesius (n. 72), 5.

[129] On Vulcanius, see Alfons DEWITTE, Bonaventura Vulcanius en de Officina Plantiniana (1573–1600). In: Marcus de Schepper, Francine de Nave (eds.), *Ex officina Plantiniana: studia in memoriam Christophori Plantini (ca. 1520–1589)*. Antwerp 1989, 591–597; and Harm Jan VAN DAM, The Blacksmith and the Nightingale: Relations between Bonaventura Vulcanius and Daniel Heinsius. In: Dirk Sacré, Jan Papy (eds.), *Syntagmatia: Essays on Neo-Latin Literature in Honour of Monique Mund-Dopchie and Gilbert Tournoy*. Leuven 2009, 557–568.

[130] See Plantin's letter to Sambucus of 18 May 1583, as in note 42.

[131] See his letter to Lipsius of 1 May 1582 in Tom DENEIRE, Jeanine DE LANDTSHEER, Lipsiana in the Waller Manuscript Collection: In Particular an Unknown Letter from Johannes Sambucus (1582) and a Letter to Janus Dousa (1583) reconsidered. *Humanistica Lovaniensia* 57 (2008), 209–226, here 219.

[132] See his letter to Sylburgius of 25 February 1585: *Scripserat mihi se nescio cui typographo excudendum dedisse veterum patrum, ut vocantur, Graecorum epistolas supra 800, tum alios quosdam libros manu scriptos. Rogo te, ut de his epistolis, quid factum fuerit, me doceas, ut sciam an eas bonus aliquis in lucem emittere velit. Sum enim harum rerum et similium perquam studiosus.* Pierre COSTIL, *André Dudith humaniste Hongrois (1533–1589). Sa vie, son œuvre et ses manuscrits grecs*. Paris 1935, 447.

Space does not allow further investigation of Sambucus's failed projects, which are one of the central themes of his late correspondence. In any case, they are indicative of the extent of his publishing agenda and of the way he worked as a humanist book collector: relying strongly on his own, finite, repository of manuscripts, on long-distance relationships, and on the help of philologist assistants.

CORRECTIO OR *EMENDATIO*:

SAMBUCUS'S PHILOLOGICAL WORK

As already stated, most of Sambucus's *editiones* were prepared for publication by philologists who lived near to the place of printing. It was these philologist 'friends' (presented below) who transcribed, translated and emended the texts sent to them directly or indirectly by Sambucus. Only the editions that he marked with the word *correxit* or *emendavit* (his Plautus, Petronius or Vegetius) came closer to meeting the expectations that 16th-century philological practice generally suggested. In what follows we will study this group of Sambucus's publications and analyse his philological contribution.

It is well known that, by the mid-16th century, textual corrections had been grouped into two major categories: emendations based on an existing manuscript reading, as distinguished from invented, excogitated conjectures (*emendatio ope codicum* and *ope ingenii*). Already at the end of the 15th century, Poliziano expressed his discontent with textual corrections that were not backed by any sound, trustworthy manuscript variants, and in the *Miscellanea*, his major philological work, his argument repeatedly returned to the differentiation between the vulgate edition or manuscript – that is, the one accessible to everyone (*exemplaria quae sunt in manibus*) – and the unique 'very old codex' (*codex pervetustus, vetustissimus*) that Poliziano could get hold of[133].

---

[133] Sebastiano TIMPANARO, *The genesis of Lachmann's method*. Transl. Glenn W. MOST. Chicago 2005, 46. See also Jill KRAYE, Cicero, Stoicism and textual criticism: Poliziano on katorthoma. *Rinascimento* 23 (1983), 79–110; Anthony GRAFTON, *Joseph Scaliger: A Study in the History of Classical Scholarship*. 2 vols. Oxford 1983–1993, vol. 1, 9–100; John D'AMICO, *Theory and Practice in Renaissance Textual Criticism: Beatus Rhenanus between Conjecture and History*. Berkeley 1988; and Pierre PETITMANGIN, La terminologie philologique de Beatus Rhenanus. In: James S. Hirstein (ed.), *Beatus Rhenanus (1485–1547). Lecteur et éditeur des textes anciens*. Actes du Colloque International tenu à Strasbourg et à Sélestat du 13 au 15

The humanist philologist stands apart from his public not by his overwhelming knowledge and his original, ingenuous emendations, but because of his privileged access to a manuscript that is not known to other readers. Around the middle of the 16th century, the Florentine Piero Vettori (1499–1585) was one of the most valiant defenders of the priority of manuscript tradition over inventive textual conjectures[134]. Similarly to Poliziano, Vettori arrived at the conclusion that the philologist had to systematically prefer the variants of the better manuscript instead of selecting individual readings from various manuscripts. Furthermore, he realised that it is not always the more ancient manuscript source that preserved the better textual variant, but that more recent copies may transmit ancient, authentic readings, and philologists had to rank their manuscript sources according to the quality of their entire text, not their age. The role of conjectural criticism is negligible in Vettori's work compared to the importance that he attributed to the variants of ancient manuscripts. He seems to have considered conjecture to be a tool of premature and temporary judgment rather than a final solution to textual problems[135].

novembre 1998. Turnhout 2000, 195–222; Gábor KECSKEMÉTI, A humanista filológiai hagyomány és Magyarország [The humanist philological tradition and Hungary]. In: Gábor Kecskeméti, Réka Tasi (Eds.), *Filológia és textológia a régi magyar irodalomban*. Miskolc 2012, 13–51, and IDEM, Philological Activities of Early Modern Hungarian and Transylvanian Humanists. In: Rhoda Schnur et al. (ed.), *Acta conventus neo-Latini Budapestinensis: Proceedings of the Thirteenth International Congress of Neo-Latin Studies*, Budapest, 6–12 August 2006. Tempe 2010 (Medieval and Renaissance Texts and Studies 386), 343–351.

[134] GRAFTON (n. 133), 46–70. See also Antonietta PORRO, Pier Vettori: editore di testi greci. La 'Poetica' di Aristotele. *Italia medioevale e umanistica* 26 (1983), 307–358; R. MOUREN, Un professeur de grec et ses élèves: Piero Vettori (1499–1585). *Lettere italiane* 59 (2007), 473–506, and Raphaële MOUREN, *Biographie et éloges funèbres de Piero Vettori. Entre rhétorique et histoire.* Paris 2015. The collection of Vettori's letters is now housed in the British Library and cataloged in Cecil ROTH, I carteggi volgari di Piero Vettori nel British Museum. *Rivista storica degli archivi toscani* 1,7 (fasc. 3) (1929), 1–34. On his connections to Carlo Sigonio, see William MCCUAIG, *Carlo Sigonio. The Changing World of the late Renaissance.* Princeton 1989, 50–60.

[135] In the *Variae lectiones* of Vettori, the discussion of a philological crux and its conjectural solution is often ended with the remark that only a better manuscript source can provide a final solution to the problem See for example Petrus Victorius, Variarum lectionum libri XXV. Lugduni: Temporal 1554, 90 (6, 7); 323 (18, 9); 472 (25, 9). When he edited the *De lingua latina* of Varro from a single old manuscript of the Biblioteca di San Marco in Venice, Vettori took great pains to reproduce the mistakes of the manuscript as well: *Petrus Victorius ac Iacobus Diacetius contulimus cum vetusto codice ex Divi Marci Bibliotheca*

Sambucus was a great admirer of the elderly Vettori: the Florentine master was already over 60 years old when he addressed his first letter to Sambucus in 1559. It was followed by a constant exchange of letters and ideas that continued until the death of Sambucus[136]. It is clear from their correspondence that Sambucus considered the Florentine patrician as his master in philology, and that Vettori was one of the few friends whom Sambucus wanted to impress with his philological skills, as indicated by the list of emendations that he appended to two of his letters to Vettori[137]. The textual corrections directed at Vettori are essentially in line with the concept of philology propagated by the Italian master: there is only one single conjecture (a minor correction: ἄρθρων for ἀνθρώπων) among the 11 emendations listed by Sambucus, while most of them are interpretations of passages or corrections made on the basis of his own "old manuscripts".

The epistolary exchange between Sambucus and Vettori intensified after 1565, around the time when Sambucus was publishing his editions of Diogenes Laertius, Petronius and Plautus. On one occasion he even mentions the *Variae lectiones*, the most important philological work of Vettori, with a wish to see its second volume published[138]. Sambucus consciously follows Vettori's commitment to the "very ancient manuscripts" (*vetustissimi codices*) both in his letters, and, as we shall see, in his editions. The abbreviation "V. C." (vetus codex) occurs throughout his epistolary, becoming the focal point of his philological work. In a letter to Vettori, Sambucus reproaches those critics in particular who are ready to censure a great scholar because of one single syllable, without ever having held an old manuscript in their hands[139].

---

literis longobardis exarato, tanta diligentia sive potius morosa observatione ut vel quae in eo corrupte legebantur in hunc transtulerimus. Cited by Élie BORZA, Venise, Rome et Florence: Quatre exemples d'éditions de Sophocle en Italie au XVIe siècle. *L'information littéraire* 54 (2002), 13–22, here 21.

[136] At present, we know altogether 28 letters. See GERSTINGER (n. 5).

[137] GERSTINGER (n. 5), 90–91. *Veteres codices* in the possession of Sambucus are mentioned recurrently in the corrections 3, 5, 7. See also HANS GERSTINGER, Joannes Sambucus als Philologe. *Wiener Studien* 79 (1966), 551–556.

[138] *Secundum lectionum tomum discupio videre.* GERSTINGER (n. 5), 89.

[139] *Multi hodie tuo praecipue exemplo id genus scriptionis arripuere sive potius corrupere, qui levissime summis viris ob syllabulam infesti esse caeperunt, cum ex aliis audita (!) coniecturisque*

Annotations to Caesar

One telling illustration is Sambucus's philological notes in Fulvio Orsini's 1574 edition of Caesar's works[140]. Although the name of Sambucus appears on the title page, he contributed only a two-page list of emendations to Orsini's edition of Caesar, published at the very end of the volume[141]. The nature of Sambucus's notes is fully in line with his theoretical considerations: he suggested a total of 68 corrections to the text of the *Commentaries*, of which 58 were variant readings from one or several 'old manuscripts'. While Fulvio Orsini had already tried to identify clearly the manuscripts and editions that he was using for the collation of the text, while preparing a short list of sigla to his notes[142], Sambucus remained unclear on what manuscript sources exactly he was referring to – whether just quoting an 'old manuscript', or claiming it as his own, "rather old" codex (*meus quidam satis vetus codex*). Sambucus's notes abound in references to the superiority of the readings of old manuscripts ("the old variant is more appropriate", "it is clearer" – *vetus lectio aptior, planior*), whereas he turns to conjecture on only six occasions, and even these are rather corrections of simple typographical mistakes rather than inventive speculations on the text (e.g. *conversaretur* for *conservaretur*, *tutum montem* or *totum montem*, *plerique* or *pleraque*, *impediebatur* for *integebatur*). Sambucus displayed his profound knowledge of antiquities in only four cases (out of 68) when he combined manuscript readings with short philological explanations and clarified passages of Caesar quoting Livy, Varro or Herodianus[143].

---

eorum, qui nullos viderunt Veteres Codices, sua vestiunt. GERSTINGER (n. 5), 89 (1 Sept. 1568). On the broad meaning of the concept of "vetus codex", see RIZZO (n. 73), 147–168.

[140] C. Julius Caesar, Commentarii, novis emendationibus illustrati, eiusdem librorum qui desiderantur fragmenta. Ex bibliotheca Fulvii Ursini Romani, scholia Aldi Manutii, Pauli f. Aldi, N. Ioannis Sambuci spicilegia. Antverpiae: ex officina Christophori Plantini 1574, unnumbered folio.

[141] Ibid., D7^v–D8^r.

[142] Ibid., K8^v. In fact, Orsini's practice to equate manuscripts with their printed version (e. g. *C – Gryphij, minimae formae, qui ex vetusto admodum exemplari est excusus Lugduni*) justifies Sambucus's method of text editing. In this sense, the printed transcription of an old manuscript corresponds to our modern notion of facsimile, and technically it was the only feasible method to reproduce a manuscript in its integrity.

[143] For instance, in one case he supported the reading of his old manuscript, which left out the numeral (on *Bell. Gall.* 3, 26 *illi ut erat imperatum eductis quatuor cohortibus*) by claiming

Among these more nuanced philological questions, the most revealing example is Sambucus's treatment of the issue of the use of body paint by Britons, a textual problem that tormented several scholars in the 16th century, including Piero Vettori, Adrian Turnèbe and François Hotman. In a passage of the *Gallic Wars*, Caesar described the Britons as painting their bodies in order to have a fearsome appearance in battle. The material used for dyeing, and the resulting colour of the paint, were referred to in manuscripts with great variations:

> *Omnes vero se Britanni vitro inficiunt, quod caeruleum efficit colorem, atque hoc horridiores sunt in pugna aspect*
>
> Caesar, bell. Gall. 5, 14, 2
>
> All the Britons, indeed, dye themselves with woad, which produces a bluish colour, and thereby have a more terrible appearance in battle.

The dye used by the ancient Celts appears in modern editions normally as *vitrum* ("woad") and was corrected and interpreted either as *luteum* ("egg yolk"), *lutea* ("chrysocolla"), *nitrum* ("soda") or *glastum* ("woad"). Pietro Vettori argued for *luteum* at this place, claiming that this was the proper Latin name of the herb called *chrysocolla* in Greek. Significantly, he supported his opinion by adding that the textual variant *ultro*, which is found in old manuscripts (*vetusta exemplaria*), is a graphically distorted misreading of the original *luteo*. Later on, this meaningless *ultro* would be exchanged for the vulgar, Gallic name of the herb, *glastum*. Thus Vettori explains the mistake by returning to the readings of ancient manuscripts and reconstructing a hypothetical deterioration of the text, through which an inferior, vernacular word infiltrated the *Commentaries* of Caesar, otherwise written in immaculate Latin[144].

Turnèbe (1512–1565), probably the most erudite French philologist of his age[145], opted for *vitrum*[146], as he supposed that the older manuscript

---

that Caesar often does not disclose the exact number of armies (*numero caret et hoc frequens est Caesaris*, D7ᵛ).

[144] Petrus Victorius, Variarum lectionum libri XXXVIII. Florentiae: apud Junctas 1582, 219 (19, 3). To support his claims, Vettori refers to the Latin translation of Dioscorides by Marcello Virgilio, who already identified *luteum* as the Latin word for *chrysocolla* in his Pedacius Dioscorides Anazarbeus, De medica materia libri sex, interprete Marcello Virgilio secretario Florentino, cum eiusdem annotationibus, nuperque diligentissime excusi. Florentiae: apud Junctas 1518.

[145] On his life, see John LEWIS, *Adrien Turnèbe, 1512–1565: a Humanist Observed*. Geneva 1998.

version, *ultro*, must be a scribal mistake derived not from *luteum*, as Vettori speculated, but from *vitrum*, a word which generally means glass in Latin, but to which he reconstructed its supposed original meaning, the plant woad. Turnèbe used a wide range of botanical and poetic texts to prove his point, where either *vitrum* was written indeed in Renaissance copies, or could have been written, if the meaning of this word had not been forgotten. However, he did not refer to any manuscripts that would have reinforced his findings. This creative philological practice elicited the severe judgment of the austere Vettori, who scolded Turnèbe for having invented too many conjectures instead of searching for ancient manuscripts[147]. François Hotman, the French Protestant jurist (1524–1590)[148] added one more hypothesis to the already considerable array of possibilities when he derived the incriminated *ultro* from the otherwise unaccounted *lutro*, which he explained from the Greek λύτρον, a plant used for blue dyeing[149].

In Sambucus's annotations on Caesar, this is the only case where he based a textual correction without manuscript evidence on a parallel passage from another author. Sambucus remained succinct also on this issue. Trying to resolve the thorny question of the body paint of Britons he referred to a parallel from the Greek historian Herodian without quoting it, although it had very little relevance to the question of the dye[150]. Sambucus instead simply suggested that the correct reading is *lutum*, yellow-weed, and he changed the word blue (*caeruleus*) in the following sentence to yellow

---

[146] Adrianus Turnebus, Adversariorum libri triginta. Paris 1580, vol. I, 193–195 (6, 17).

[147] Vettori reproached Adrien Turnèbe in his *Variae lectiones*: *Quod vero excogitavit Adrianus Turnebus [...] magis remotum perspicitur a vestigiis veteris lectionis, et ut arbitror, falsum et explodendum est. Vtinam autem hic vir, sane doctus ac multae lectionis, non tam cupidus undique fuisset omnia emendandi: melius nobis, melius existimatione suae consuluisset.* (Cited by BORZA, as in note 135, 21.)

[148] On François Hotman, see Rodolphe DARESTE, François Hotman, sa vie et sa correspondance. *Revue Historique* 2 (1876), 1–59.

[149] Franciscus Hotmanus, In Caesaris Commentaria notae. In: C. Julii Caesaris De bello Gallico commentarii VII cum scholiis Francisci Hotomani, Fulvii Ursini, Aldi Manutii. Lugduni: apud Bartholomaeum Vincentium 1574, (new page numbering) 28.

[150] Herodian 3, 14 describes the custom of body painting custom among the Britons, but he does not mention the colour of the paint: "They tattoo their bodies with coloured designs and drawings of all kinds of animals; for this reason they do not wear clothes, which would conceal the decorations on their bodies." (*History of the Roman Empire*. Transl. by Eduard C. ECHOLS. Berkeley Los Angeles 1961).

(*cerinus*) accordingly[151]. His impulsive way of exposing his opinion in this case ("but the reading has to be *yellow-weed*") and his lack of detailed argumentation appear to be against existing philological etiquette and the cautious and prudent manner in which some contemporary philologists discussed the same passage. On the other hand, it is significant that, by opting for *lutum*, he chooses the version closest to the opinion of his friend Vettori and remains close to his argument based on the superiority of the readings of old manuscripts.

In sum, Sambucus's desire to preserve important manuscript readings dominated his willingness to put down anything by conjecture, and this will be a major motif in all his 'corrected' editions, as we shall see. Nevertheless, his notes on Caesar are only perfunctory, and his very few original conjectures are badly argued. Sambucus seems to have committed himself to rigorous philological work with ancient texts only in the editions of Plautus, Diogenes Laertius, Petronius and Vegetius (disregarding unpublished texts such as Dioscorides). We will therefore examine these editions in detail in the following pages.

Diogenes Laertius, *Lives of the Philosophers*

In his edition of the *Lives of the Philosophers* of Diogenes Laertius[152], Sambucus actually republished the Latin translation of Ambrogio Traversari rather than the original Greek text, to which he appended Greek textual variants in the margins from an unknown manuscript. Traversari, who prepared his translation in around 1423, was working on the basis of a vulgate version of the *Lives*, and his translation was further transformed after its first publication in 1472 by Benedetto Brognolo (Prunulus), who altered some wording at the request of Francesco Filelfo in his 1475 edition[153], The *editio princeps* of the Greek text was printed only in 1533 in Basel by Froben, similarly

---

[151] *Britanni luteo inficiunt: varie torquet eruditos haec scriptura: sed luto est legendum, hancque consuetudinem illorum egregie confirmat de Severo Herodianus in tertio. Pro Caeruleum tamen lego Cerineum et cerinum, hoc est luteum.* Caesar (n. 140), D8ʳ.

[152] Laertius (n. 20).

[153] On the textual history of Diogenes Laertius in the Renaissance, see Denis KNOEPFLER, *La vie de Ménédème d'Érétrie de Diogène Laërce. Contribution à l'histoire et à la critique du texte des Vies des philosophes*. Basel 1991, 21–78, here 22.

based on one single manuscript of the vulgate tradition, which originally belonged to Bohuslaus Lobkowitz von Hassenstein[154],

The edition of Sambucus, or more precisely his marginal notes, is the first to introduce the readings of the better manuscripts and to bring the text closer to the three best manuscript witnesses known today. Nevertheless, Sambucus did not correct the Latin translation of Traversari in a thousand places, as promised on the title page ("corrected in more than a thousand places from trustworthy and ancient Greek manuscripts" – *plus quam mille in locis restituti ex fide dignis vetustis exemplaribus Graecis*) but limited his efforts to listing the Greek variants in the margins[155]. It is certain that he did not use his own copy of Diogenes that is still preserved today, as it is a twin manuscript of the Lobkowitz copy containing the vulgate text, which served as the basis of the first edition by Froben[156]. All the variants are quoted from a single manuscript – considered lost today – except for one place, where he cites otherwise unidentified Roman and Venetian manuscripts[157]. The *vetus codex* of Sambucus might have been a copy of one of the three most important manuscripts known today, the Parisinus[158], thus it was a good choice and an important contribution to the improvement of the text. Importantly, some precious variants have been added from the excerpts of Diogenes Laertius attributed to Hesychius, whose edition and translation were prepared by Hadrianus Junius two years later from a manuscript provided by Sambucus.

---

[154] Giuseppina DONZELLI, De Diogenis Laertii editione quae princeps vocatur. *Maia* 10 (1958), 317–323. Cf. Kamil BOLDAN, Emma URBÁNKOVÁ, *Rekonstrukce knihovny Bohuslava Hasištejnského z Lobkovic. Katalog inkunábulí roudnické lobkovické knihovny.* Prague 2009.

[155] KNOEPFLER (n. 153), 51.

[156] Ibid. 51–53. His own manuscript (marked as K in modern editions) is now ÖNB, cod. hist. gr. 59, a twin copy of the Lobkowitz manuscript (Nelahozeves, Lobkowitz library, VI Fc 38). See also Tiziana DORANDI, *Laertiana: Capitoli sulla tradizione manoscritta e sulla storia del testo.* Berlin 2009, 30–31.

[157] Laertius (n. 20), 289.

[158] The Parisinus (P, BNF gr. 1759) manuscript was still in Rome in Sambucus's day, in the Palazzo Strozzi, from where it arrived in Paris after 1560. He might have used two early apographa of the Parisinus (Q=Par. gr. 1758 or W=Vat. gr. 140, or perhaps Co=Istambul, Seraglio 80), but we cannot rule out his use of the Parisinus itself, either still in Rome or more probably later in Paris. In any case, making his notes before settling in Vienna could partly explain the curious way of presenting Greek corrections in a Latin translation. For a detailed discussion, see KNOEPFLER (n. 153), 53.

LAERTII
DIOGENIS
DE VITA ET MO-
RIBVS PHILO-
SOPHORVM
LIBRI X.

PLVS quàm mille in locis reſtituti,& emendati ex fide dignis vetuſtis exemplaribus Græcis, vt inde Græcum exemplum etiam poſſit reſtitui;opera IOANNIS SAM-
BVCI Tirnauienſis Pannonij.

Cum Indice locupletiſsimo.

ANTVERPIAE,
Ex officina Chriſtophori Plantini,
cIↄ Iↄ LXVI.
CVM PRIVILEGIO.

Diogenes Laertios, De vita philosophorum libri X.
Antverpiae: ex officina Christophori Plantini 1566
(Vienna, University library I 161.822)

Sambucus's mixed edition (Latin translation with Greek variants) did not garner universal support from contemporary philologists. Although Henri Estienne did not attack his Hungarian friend publicly, he did not name him anywhere in the paratexts of his volume. We can only guess the reason for this reticence, especially in the light of his dedication to their common friend, Johannes Crato: Estienne was unsatisfied both with the number of manuscript witnesses surveyed[159], and with the correctness of the Latin text of Traversari[160]. This might explain why he almost completely neglected Sambucus's marginal notes in his own edition, although they belonged to a superior tradition than the manuscript that Estienne and his friends had examined[161]. Despite the fact that the edition of Estienne was based on the collation of several manuscripts and that he invested far greater efforts into its textual criticism, the manuscripts that he selected for his work belonged to the vulgate family, and were thus of lesser value. Since it lacked a survey of the manuscript tradition and since the exact sources of variants were not identified, Sambucus's work was easily dismissed and neglected in later editions; its importance surfaced only with the coming of age of Lachmannian philology and the systematic reconstruction of the stemma[162].

---

[159] Stephanus prided himself on having collated several manuscripts, so that he would not include all of them in his apparatus: *Quum superior Diogenis Laertii editio, quae Basilea prodierat, cum variis exemplaribus antiquis collata partim a me, partim ab aliis fuisset, eaque collatio magnum variarum lectionum numerum nobis dedisset, quarum pleraeque meliores essent iis, quas editio illa habebat, nonnullae eiusmodi essent ut utrae utris anteponi deberent,* [...] *consilium hoc a me initum fuit,* [...] *ut quae aperte potiores forent iis, quas editio illa attulerat, istarum loco in istum contextum reciperentur.* See Diogenes Laertius, De vitis, dogmatis et apophthegmatis eorum, qui in philosophia claruerunt. Genevae: H. Stephanus 1570, (part 2, new numeration), 1. Stephanus dedicated his edition to their common friend, Johannes Crato. See also ALMÁSI (n. 2), 225.

[160] In his dedication to Crato, Estienne provides a list of simple Latin abbreviations (*io* for *ideo*, *qq* for *quamquam*), which seem to have been misinterpreted in previous editions of the translation of Traversari.

[161] Estienne discussed the textual problems in his annotations printed with new page numbering after the Greek text, although he stopped two-thirds of the way through the text at page 314 ("I did not have time to continue" – *ulterius pergere non vacavit,* p. 36). I could find only one, rather negative reference to Sambucus's edition among them (*At in editione Latina quae meam proxime praecessit, legitur* ἄνθρωπος, ὦ φιλόσοφος, *quae lectio stare nullo modo potest*).

[162] Keimpe Algra rightly emphasises in his review of Knoepfler's book (n. 153) that Sambucus's choice of an important manuscript cannot unequivocally be considered a

Petronius, *Satyricon*

The fragmentary text of the *Satyricon* of Petronius has posed serious problems for philologists since the 15th century. The first editions, like the *editio princeps* from 1483 (Milan), and the later prints of 1500 (Leipzig), 1508 (Leipzig), 1517 (Vienna)[163], published only parts of the 'shorter extracts' from the *Satyricon*, even though a great number of medieval and humanistic manuscripts transmitted the text of the 'shorter extracts' in its integrity (class O of manuscripts). Sambucus must have realised this deficiency when he compared the text in his own manuscript (ÖNB, cod. 3198)[164] with the 1520 Paris edition, which still followed the text of the *editio princeps*. Sambucus's manuscript belonged to the family of the widespread humanistic vulgate manuscripts of the *Satyricon*, which started circulating after Poggio Bracciolini had discovered the 'shorter extracts' in England in around 1420[165]. As the Paris edition was yet another reprint of a selection of the 'shorter extracts' belonging to another branch of the same family, Sambucus did no more than blend the readings from the two sources belonging to the same family rather arbitrarily, either noting the variants of his *vetus*

---

philological merit: without the recension of the entire transmission later philologists had no reason to follow either Sambucus's variants, or any better readings from 'ancient manuscripts' (e. g. Aldobrandini's text, published in 1594), as the choice between the readings of two or more 'old manuscripts' remained just as arbitrary as the conjectural emendations. Thus, precious manuscript witnesses could easily be disregarded later. Cf. Keimpe ALGRA, Denis Knoepfler, La vie de Ménédème d'Érétrie de Diogène Laërce (review). *Mnemosyne* 50 (1997), 359–365; 362.

[163] The latter edition is dedicated to Stephan Werbőczy, palatine of Hungary, whose *Customary Law of the Kingdom of Hungary* (Tripartitum) Sambucus republished twice (cf. n. 88).

[164] Cod. 3198 is a humanistic miscellany. A part of it was written by Niccolò Fonzio in Florence. Albinia C. DE LA MARE, *The Handwriting of Italian Humanists.* Oxford 1973, vol. I.1, 133, n. 84. See also Ida MAIER, *Les Manuscrits d'Ange Politien. Catalogue descriptif avec 19 documents inédits en appendice.* Geneva 1965, 327–328 (about the seven epitaphs on Theodore of Gaza contained in the manuscript).

[165] Konrad MÜLLER, Textüberlieferung. In: Petronius, Satyrica. Ed. Konrad Müller, Wilhelm Ehlers. Munich 1983, 381–448, here 389. The 'shorter extracts' of Petronius were rather widely known in the 15th century, Albinia de la Mare could identify 14 manuscripts of this version: Albinia C. DE LA MARE, The Return of Petronius to Italy. In: *Medieval Learning and Literature.* Essays presented to Richard William Hunt. Oxford 1976, 220–254, for Sambucus's ms. see p. 223. See also Gareth L. SCHMELING, Johanna H. STUCKEY, *A Bibliography of Petronius.* Leiden 1977, 1–9.

codex on the margins, or inserting them into the text itself[166]. Nevertheless, Sambucus seems to have proceeded prudently in emendating the vulgate text: he added his variants to the main text only if they were clearly superior, while in ambiguous cases he simply noted them on the margins[167]. He applied conjectural criticism more often here than in any other edition of his, but he repeatedly called attention to these places: "we write it by conjecture" (*a coniectura ducti scribimus*)[168]. Next to the variants of his *vetus codex* he added some other marginal variants marked by the letter "f.", which are probably identical to the readings that were provided to him by Theodor Poelmann, Plantin's collaborator, and Hadrianus Junius[169].

Unlike Sambucus's Diogenes Laertius, the *Satyricon* had a major impact on the forthcoming editions of Petronius, which is considered in a rather negative light by modern textual criticism: when the 'longer extracts' (manuscript L) surfaced a few years later, its editors (Tornaesius, 1575 and Pierre Pithou, 1577) used Sambucus's easily available edition as their starting point and compared (and sometimes emended) the readings of manuscript L to the far inferior and more interpolated text given by the Hungar-

---

[166] Sambucus's edition mixes the readings of an α manuscript of the vulgate tradition with the Paris edition belonging to the ξ class of the same family, and he does so, in the words of Konrad Müller, "mit wenig Sorgfalt". See MÜLLER (n. 165), 389.

[167] E. g. p. 17: he corrected the vulgate *furtivis oculis* with his manuscript's *furtivis osculis*.

[168] See p. 10, 16, 20, 21, 24, 25, 29, 34, 37, 38, 40, 49, 50, 53, 55. At one place (*Sat.* 88, 6), Sambucus conjectured *vino scortisque demersi paratas quidem artes avemus cognoscere* for the vulgate *audemus*. This conjecture was duly scolded and ridiculed by Jan Dousa in his *Praecidaneorum libri III*. Although he did not name Sambucus (at another place he favours his editions over French ones), he was rather harsh on this point because it proved that the originator of this conjecture had no idea about the old, Plautine meaning of the verb *audere* ('to wish' instead of the common 'to dare'): *In pervulgatis hoc loco, audemus, antea lectitabatur, quo magis subit admirari eorum hominum audaciam, ne imperitiam dicam, qui principes illud avemus commutare insisterunt [...] Sed hoc beat saltem, quod ita coniectura ductum de ingenio (quo supra Sicambrum praeditus) ipsus se restituisse inficias non eat. Nam (ita me Deus amet) a blattariis Codicibus male metuebam miser. Quos ille, quoties videtur, perpetuos auctores habet [...]*. See Jan Dousa [Sr.], Pro Satyrico Petronii Arbitri viri consularis praecidaneorum libri tres. Lugduni Batavorum: ex officina Ioannis Paetsii 1583, 104.

[169] See Sambucus's dedication to János Liszthy, in: Petronius Arbiter (n. 66), A2ʳ. Theodor Poelmann (Pulmann, Pulmannus) (1512–1581) was a Dutch philologist collaborating with Plantin. See S. Surdèl's article in the forthcoming Dutch volume of the series *Europa Humanistica*. We would like to thank Steven Surdèl for having sent us his biographical article before publication.

ian humanist[170]. Nevertheless, they had no reason not to do so: the best available text of Petronius was that of Sambucus between 1565 and 1575, and – as we have seen above – most Renaissance editions were prepared by collating one or more manuscripts with a recent printed edition.

Plautus: *Comedies*

Similarly to the case of Petronius, Sambucus's edition of Plautus was the result of his work with a single manuscript, from which he published his variant readings. The *Comedies* of Plautus had recently been edited in the groundbreaking edition of Joachim Camerarius (Basel: Johann Herwagen, 1552)[171], who had access to two early (11th–12th-century) manuscripts: the *Codex vetus Camerarii* (today Vat. Pal. lat. 1615, B), which contains the second best text of the entire collection of Plautine plays (matched only by the Milan palimpsest discovered in 1815); and the *Codex decurtatus* (Heidelberg: Pal. 1613, C)[172]. Despite these early manuscript witnesses, Plautus's *Comedies* were – and still are – some of the most debated and least safely correctable ancient literary texts. It is little wonder that most of Sambucus's humanist contemporaries tried their hand at understanding the versification of Plautus's dramas, the earliest surviving Roman literary works, and tried to restore its interpolations, lacunae and storylines in multiple versions. It was during these years precisely that Turnèbe collated an im-

---

[170] Mildred DASCHBACH, *Sambucus and the Text of Petronius*. PhD Diss., University of Pittsburgh 1931. On the editions of Tornaesius and Pithou, see also Anthony GRAFTON, Petronius and Neo-Latin Satire: The Reception of the Cena. *Journal of the Warburg and Courtauld Institutes* 53 (1990), 237–249, here 242–243.

[171] After a long process of partial editions, this became his final recension of the text. See Friedrich RITSCHL, Über die Kritik des Plautus. Eine bibliographische Untersuchung. In: idem, *Kleine philologische Schriften*. Bd. 2. *Zu Plautus und lateinischer Sprachkunde*. Leipzig 1868, 95–99.

[172] See Friedrich RITSCHL, Bio-bibliographisches zu Camerarius' Plautusstudien. In: idem, *Kleine philologische Schriften*. Bd. 3: *Zur Römischen Literatur*. Leipzig 1877, 67–119; Richard J. TARRANT, Plautus. In: Leighton D. Reynolds (ed.), *Texts and Transmission. A Survey of the Latin Classics*. Oxford 1983. 302–307; on Camerarius's summaries and his moral judgment of Plautus, see Ekkehard STÄRK, Camerarius' Plautus. In: Kössling, Wartenberg (n. 39), 235–248.

portant old (and now lost) manuscript of the *Comedies* (T), close to the archetype, which he quoted now and again in his *Adversaria*[173],

Sambucus tried to enter the company of the saviours of Plautus by editing the variants that he found in his own *vetus codex*. Nevertheless, this codex was not as old as it seemed at first sight. It is well known that the entire corpus of the Plautine *Comedies* surfaced only after Nicolaus Cusanus discovered the first manuscript containing all 20 plays in 1429 (the later Codex Ursinianus: Vat. lat. 3870). This single codex became the origin of all other copies and printed editions until the edition of Camerarius[174], and this *Itala recensio* was the only one accessible to Italian humanists. Sambucus's manuscript (ÖNB, cod. 3168, W) bore the colophon date 1243, which would have predated the discovery of Cusanus by around two centuries. Nevertheless, as demonstrated by Friedrich Ritschl, this manuscript belongs equally to the *Itala recensio*, the copies of the Codex Ursinianus, and as a result it cannot be earlier than Cusanus's discovery[175]. In fact, one 'C' has been scratched out from the dating of the copy, and another one badly written by a scribe, thus the manuscript received a much earlier dating in its colophon (MCCCCXLIII > MCCXLIII)[176]. Rita Cappelletto was able to prove recently that the entire manuscript was annotated by the young Giovanni Pontano, and the text itself was copied before 1458[177]. Later on, the manu-

---

[173] See the excellent analysis of Gaia CLEMENTI, *La filologia plautina negli Adversaria di Adrien Turnèbe*. Alessandria 2009.

[174] In fact, the *Codex vetus Camerarii* was already known to Camerarius's master, Veit Werler, who lectured on Plautus at Leipzig University at the beginning of the century. See Friedrich RITSCHL, Zur Geschichte der classischen Philologie. I. Veit Werler als Leipziger Docent und die Leipziger Plautusstudien im Anfang des sechzehnten Jahrhunderts. In: idem, *Kleine philologische Schriften*. Bd. 5: *Vermischtes*. Leipzig 1879, 40–92.

[175] Friedrich RITSCHL (n. 171), 114–116.

[176] Rita CAPPELLETTO, *La 'Lectura Plauti' del Pontano, con edizione delle postille del cod. Vindob. Lat. 3168 e osservazioni sull' 'Itala recensio'*, ed. by M. Apa. Urbino 1989, 24–26. Cappelletto considers the entire colophon an unauthentic later addition to the text, which has nothing to do with the actual date of the manuscript. Thus, the forger's first intention was to write "MCCCXLIII", from which a C was erased later.

[177] See Rita CAPPELLETTO, Un Plauto autografo del Pontano (e l' 'Itala recensio'). In: *Materiali e discussioni per l'analisi die testi classici* 14 (1985), 209–236; superseded by EADEM (n. 176), especially p. 24–26 and 46; and Liliana Monti SABIA, La mano di Giovanni Pontano in due Livii della Biblioteca Nazionale di Napoli (mss. ex. Vind. lat. 33. et IV. C. 20.). *Italia medioevale e umanistica* 39 (1996), 180–185.

script was inherited by two members of the Accademia Pontaniana, Marcantonio Epicuro and Antonio Feltro, and after the death of the latter it was passed to a Neapolitan antiquarian bookseller, who may have manipulated the dates before selling the manuscript to Sambucus in 1562[178]. Sambucus made a collation of his copy, most probably with the edition of Camerarius, in the summer of 1565, and he sent his variants to Plantin, which he also noted in his manuscript[179].

The title page of the Plantin edition promised remarkable achievements[180]: the text was supplemented with more than 200 verses[181] that Sambucus found missing in the edition of Camerarius, coming from old manuscripts (*plusquam CC versibus ex Veteribus Codicibus additis*), so the plays got back some of their former shine (*nitori restitutae*). The dedication to Christophe Plantin, dated one day before finishing the collation, is more of a private letter than a typical dedicatory epistle. Sambucus does not mention the book itself at all. Instead, he speaks of his "various observations on Plautus from old manuscripts, and especially from his own, which once belonged to Giovanni Pontano." Once again, he confined himself to simply adding variants to the margins (originally perhaps on a copy of Camerarius's edition), leaving it to the reader to decide on the right ones, as he wanted to refrain from prescribing the correct reading[182]. He wholly abstained from any conjecture, arguing that the main reason for doing so was not theoretical but rather the recent death of his father (adding a moving eulogy that matched the personal tone of his letter) and the urging of Plantin motivated him to finish his work. Thus the edition appeared with the readings of Sambucus's (not so) 'old manuscript' on the margins, and with the lines missing from Camerarius's edition inserted in the main text in italics. Plantin arranged for three im-

---

[178] Besides CAPPELLETTO (n. 176) see also Cesare QUESTA, Pontano, Panormita, il. Vindob. lat. 3168. e l'Itala recensio. In: idem, *Parerga Plautina. Struttura e tradizione manoscritta delle commedie*. Urbino 1985, 232–242.

[179] ÖNB, cod. 3168, fol. 1ʳ: *Finivi collationem exemplarium ego Ioannes Sambucus Viennae ad editionem Plantini 24 Augusti* σὺν θεῷ *1565*.

[180] M. Accii Plauti Comoediae viginti olim a Joachimo Camerario emendatae nunc vero plusquam CC versibus qui passim desiderabantur, ex VV. CC. additis, suo quodammodo nitori restitutae; opera et diligentia Joannis Sambuci Tirnauiensis Pannonii (cf. n. 66).

[181] The dedicatory epistle mentions already "almost three hundred verses" (A2ʳ).

[182] We may surmise that the dedicatory epistle was in fact an accompanying letter that Sambucus sent together with the annotated volume of Camerarius to Plantin.

portant additions: Carolus Langius's manuscript collation (marked by 'L.' if it coincided with Sambucus's text, otherwise printed as an appendix); Hadrianus Junius's notes on the text (mostly conjectural); and textual variants taken from Adrian Turnèbe's recently published *Adversaria*, the reading of the famous lost manuscript T[183]. The organisation of the notes was somewhat awkward, with Langius's notes distributed between the margins and the appendix of the volume, which Plantin blamed "on the lack of space in the margins" (*quod ora libri eas non caperet*). As Luigi Battezzato has pointed out, "[t]his is as close as we get to the admission, by a scholarly printer, that an apparatus criticus was typographically impossible."[184] The multiplicity of textual variants and notes would have required a different layout of the page, while Plantin left the usual page arrangement (main text and variant readings with asterisk) unchanged. By giving prominence to the readings of Sambucus's codex, he immediately distinguished the rank of the manuscript witnesses as well.

The greatest achievement of this edition was of course to add more than 200 new lines to the *Comedies*. Friedrich Ritschl, who put Sambucus's claims to the test, found that in fact he had only added 149 lines according to the format of his edition, equal to 86 (partly) new Plautine verses[185]. Despite the negative view of Ritschl[186], it must be acknowledged that it was Sambucus who first called attention to the large number of missing verses that were abandoned by Camerarius because he considered them spurious (e. g. 37 verses of the second, variant ending of the *Poenulus*); because of their obscenity (*Pseud*. IV 7, 85); because the text was corrupt and scarcely understandable (44 verses in the *Casina* and one in the argument of the *Mercator*); or simply by mistake (*Poenulus* III, 1, 72-74). Strangely, Camerar-

---

[183] *Annotationes Ioachimi Camerarii, quae quidem ad lectionum veritatem constituendam faciunt* (763–806); *Antiquae lectiones Caroli Langii, ex Plauti tribus exemplaribus manuscriptis* (807–839); readings from the *Adversaria* of Turnèbe (840–843); Hadrianus Junius's notes (844–847; mostly conjecture of others, e. g. Erasmus, or his own, on the basis of Nonius Marcellus and versification).

[184] Luigi BATTEZZATO, Renaissance Philology: Johannes Livineius (1546–1599) and the Birth of the Apparatus Criticus. In: Christopher Ligota, Jean-Louis Quantin (eds.), *History of Scholarship*. Oxford 2006, 75–111; here 105–106.

[185] RITSCHL (n. 171), 114–115.

[186] Ritschl claims that Sambucus could have added even more lines: e. g. he overlooked *Most*. III, 1, 45, added by Celio Secundo Curione in 1568; cf. RITSCHL (n. 171), 116.

ius did not even mention these omissions in his annotations, although these lines were present in his manuscripts.

The most surprising of all these omissions is the second, variant ending of the *Poenulus*, about which Camerarius remains completely silent[187]. As they were present not only in Camerarius's manuscripts but also in the entire *Itala recensio*, they had been published before in numerous earlier editions[188]. Nevertheless, the German humanist's text was so influential that earlier editions fell into disuse, and even learned contemporaries attributed the restoration of the missing parts of the *Comedies* to Sambucus. As Lipsius noted in his *Antiquarum lectionum libri* (5, 13): "This scene was added by the famous Sambucus to the end of the Plautine *Poenulus*, but I have also found them written in the Vatican manuscripts."[189]

Although Lipsius thought there was good reason to doubt the authenticity of these verses, since he also found them in the Vatican manuscripts he thought them worthy of publication, correcting some 'monstrous' errors in the text (*monstra aliquot lectionum*). The antiquity of this double ending was later reinforced by the Ambrosian palimpsest. Thus Sambucus rightly supposed their publication to be an important contribution to Plautine scholarship, and he remained far closer to the idea of *emendatio ope codicum* than any of his predecessors.

For Sambucus, the importance of preserving the manuscript readings overcame any possible moral scruples concerning the text. The pun on

---

[187] Cf. M. Accius Plautus, Comoediae XX, diligente cura et singulari studio Ioachimi Camerarii [...] editae. Basel: Hervagius ²1558, 687–688. Variant endings to a number of ancient comedies survive, and modern scholarship is still much divided about their genuiness. See e. g. Otto ZWIERLEIN, Lesarten-Varianz und Zweitfassung. Von Homer bis zu Fabio Chigi's Pompeius. In: idem, *Lucubrationes Philologae*. Bd. 2. *Antike und Mittelalter*. Berlin 2004, 18–19. Zwierlein supposes that the second variant, published by Sambucus, is the authentic ending.

[188] See e. g. M. Accius Plautus, Comoediae XX. Strassburg: Johann Grüninger 1508, Dd6ʳ⁻ᵛ.

[189] *Quam scaenam clarissimus Sambucus Plautinae Poenulo a fine addit, eam in Vaticanis libris et ipse perscriptam repperi.* Justus Lipsius, Opera. Leiden: Horatius Cardon 1613, vol. 1, 510–511. In the footsteps of Camerarius, Lambinus omits the entire scene without saying a word about it in his 1576 edition. See M. Accius Plautus, [Comoediae] Ex fide atque auctoritate complurium librorum manuscriptorum opera Dionysii Lambini. Paris: Ioannes Macaeus 1576, 887.

male homosexuality (*Pseud.* IV 7, 85)[190], which might have seriously troubled Joachim Camerarius and later led Denis Lambin to exclaim "Spare our ears!"[191], does not seem to have worried Sambucus at all, and his choice of texts (including Plautus, Lucretius and Petronius) suggests that the worldview exposed in the ancient texts had no bearing whatsoever on his publication agenda, which spread from the obscene Petronius and the pagan Lucretius to Byzantine Church Fathers. The Hungarian humanist's text of Plautus was not superseded until the edition of Denis Lambin in 1576.

Vegetius, *Mulomedicina*

Vegetius's *Mulomedicina* is a late antique, technical text dealing with veterinary medicine, thus it is full of rare words and textological problems. The first edition was published as late as 1528 by Johannes Fabri in Basel, based on the collation and combination of two manuscripts, an older and a more recent one, neither of which could be identified by modern scholarship[192], Unfortunately, Fabri – to whom the task of publication was entrusted by Count Hermann von Neuenahr, the owner of one or both manuscripts – did not distinguish between the readings of the two codices, although his edition preserves important witnesses of the earliest family of the manuscripts (SCLW). Nevertheless, the published text contained serious deficiencies, as noted by Conrad Gessner, a prominent reader of the *Mulomedicina* in the 16th century[193]. Sambucus's endeavour to publish a new edition was therefore welcomed by students of ancient veterinary medicine. He sent his edition of the *Mulomedicina* to Theodor Zwinger on May 17, 1570, together with a letter[194]. Once again, he emphasised to Zwinger that he had not added any annotations or conjectures (*sine tamen* ἐπιλόγῳ *seu*

---

[190] "Does the sword of a soldier match your sheath?" (*Conveniebatne in vaginam tuam machaera militis?*), asks the pimp Ballio of the male slave Harpax.

[191] *Conveniebatne: obscaenum, per machaeram militis partem militis virilem significat. Per vaginam servi podicem, sit honos auribus.* M. Accius Plautus, [Comoediae] ed. Lambinus (n. 189), 827.

[192] Vincenzo ORTOLEVA, *La tradizione manoscritta della 'Mulomedicina' di Publio Vegezio Renato*. Catania 1996.

[193] Conrad Gesner, Historiae animalium liber I. de quadrupedis viviparis. Zurich: Froschauer 1551, 41. This passage was noted in a copy (Munich, BSB 4. A. lat. b. 690.) of Sambucus's edition by an erudite reader.

[194] GERSTINGER (n. 5), 106–107.

ἐπικρίσει *vel meis coniecturis*) and strictly adhered to the readings offered by the two manuscripts that he had noted in the margins (*duobus manuscriptis adhibitis varietatem adnotavi*). He suggested that the printer should either publish his variants as marginal notes, or insert them in the text in those places where that variant was clearly superior, or publish them at the end of the book[195]. Thus it was most probably a copy of the *editio princeps* of Fabri, annotated by Sambucus, which he sent to Basel[196]. The edition was finally published by Perna in 1574 in Basel[197], and the title page promised the collation of three manuscripts (*tribus vetustissimus codicibus varietate adiecta*). The printer Perna seems to have chosen the simplest method of publishing: the main text of Fabri remained unchanged, and Sambucus's variant readings appeared in the margins, in fact reproducing as it was the entire volume that Sambucus sent him.

It seems, however, that Sambucus's marginal annotations were based on a single manuscript, his own, and that he may have counted Fabri's edition and the source of his edition as the two other manuscripts[198]. All the annotations appearing in the margins are derived from the manuscript now housed in the ÖNB (cod. 115; V)[199]. As this manuscript contains a significantly altered, 'epitomised' version of the *Mulomedicina*, Sambucus had to transcribe many readings, which he did rather carelessly[200]. After a

---

[195] *Poterit Typographus vel textum pristinum sequi, et varietatem in margine addere, vel inserere quae manifesta saniora excusis tuo iudicio videbuntur, vel ad extremum libri [...] reicere.*

[196] Ortolani argues for the existence of an intermediary manuscript, but actually there is little evidence to support this possibility. Cf. ORTOLEVA (n. 192), 124.

[197] Perna specialised in printing medical and alchemical texts, and he was one of the major editors of Paracelsian texts in the 16th century. See PERINI (n. 99), 149–160. See also Wilhelm KÜHLMANN, Joachim TELLE (eds.), *Corpus Paracelsisticum: Dokumente frühneuzeitlicher Naturphilosophie in Deutschland*. Bd. 2: *Der Frühparacelsismus*. Tübingen 2004, 746–747.

[198] For details, see ORTOLEVA (n. 192), 121–124. Lommatzsch arrived at a similar conclusion: P. Vegetius Renatus, Digestorum artis mulomedicinae libri. Ed. Ernst LOMMATZSCH. Leipzig 1903, iv–v.

[199] A nicely illuminated 15th-century Italian manuscript, see Hermann J. HERMANN, *Die Handschriften und Inkunabeln der italienischen Renaissance*. Bd. 1: *Oberitalien: Genua, Lombardei, Emilia, Romagna*. Leipzig: 1930, table LI. For a short description, see ORTOLEVA (n. 192), 13.

[200] Of course, we must bear in mind that we do not possess the copy that he transmitted to Zwinger and Perna. The inaccuracies in his edition might well be due to the process of typesetting. It is obvious from Sambucus's letters urging the publication of the volume that he did not receive proofs of any kind. Cf. GERSTINGER (n. 5), 140–141, 146–149, 155–157. On the other hand, we still do not know enough about the standards of

cursory check of the first five leaves of the second book of the *Mulomedicina* (ÖNB, cod. 115, fol. 46ᵛ–51ʳ), one can say that he omitted around one-fifth of the variant readings offered by his source. Some of these are insignificant variations[201], but some are more important and would alter the meaning of the text significantly[202]. In one case, it seems certain that the typesetter had trouble reading the annotations of Sambucus, as he printed 'ex' instead of 'Re.', the common abbreviation for "prescription"[203]. Although the corrections were based on a single manuscript, the editor had no regard for orthographic variants[204]. Sambucus's most important mistake, which cannot be explained away by the process of typesetting, is the omission of the prologue of the fourth (now third) book, which was missing from Fabri's edition but present at least partially in his own manuscript[205]. In sum, the case of Sambucus's *Mulomedicina* shows clearly his commitment to 'old readings' against conjecture, but also his superficiality and inconsistency, which cannot be fully excused by pointing at the physical distance between the philologist and the printing press and the lack of personal surveillance of the process of printing.

---

scientific exactness in 16th-century philology: a good illustration is the history of the variants of the *codex Turnebi* of Plautus, where the inconsistent collation of texts by humanists caused many difficulties for modern researchers. Cf. CLEMENTI (n. 173).

[201] Although he sometimes noted the omission even of an 'et', the following variants were disregarded in his annotations (the edited text collated with the manuscript): *itaque: igitur* (fol. 46ᵛ); *animantium: animalium* (fol. 47ʳ); *enim:* – (fol. 47ᵛ); *effugere velit: velit effugere; iecinoris: iecoris; gyrabit: girat* (fol. 48ᵛ); *et tarde: tarde; oporteri: oportet; diem tertiam: diem tertium; auferetur: auferatur; penitus nihil: nihil penitus* (fol. 49ʳ); *accipiet: accipiat*, etc.

[202] E. g. *labore: langore* (fol. 46ᵛ); *curas etiam quarum: curas ex quarum* (47ʳ); *corrupti sanguinis: corrupti sanguinis virus* (fol. 48ʳ), *sentiens: sentit* (fol. 48ᵛ); *minus etiam: nec bene; valetudines: valetudinis capitis; opus est autem: est autem necessaria* (fol. 49ʳ), etc. In the case of head diseases in animals, the specification of the head (*valetudinis capitis*) is very important, as otherwise the entire prescription would refer to all kinds of animal diseases.

[203] The manuscript has Re[cipe] *pulveris nitri folia, raphani* [...] (fol. 49ʳ) instead of the marginal note's agrammatical *Ex pulveris nitri, folia raphani*. It is hardly imaginable that the Hungarian humanist, who had significant medical training, would commit such a serious mistake.

[204] E. g. *hybbernalibus/hibernalibus, obtinet/optinet, cum/quum, valetudo/valitudo, quoties/quotiens, subcreuerit/succreuerit, pigrum/pugrum*, etc.

[205] ORTOLEVA (n. 192), 114–115, 125, note 53.

Humanistic texts:
Pietro Ransano, Janus Pannonius, Bonfini's Decades,
and the Customary Law of Hungary

Sambucus was not only an editor of classical texts. He also published four major editions of humanistic sources: an epitomised history of Hungary (1558) by Pietro Ranzano, originally commissioned by Queen Beatrice of Naples (1457–1508)[206]; the collected poems of the most important humanistic poet of Hungary Janus Pannonius (in 1559, and in a greatly enlarged version in 1569)[207]; the *Decades*, the fundamental – although unfinished – Renaissance history of Hungary by Antonio Bonfini (1568)[208]; and the *Customary Law of Hungary* (*Opus Tripartitum*), an important legal compilation by István Werbőczy. Sambucus, closely connected to the Hungarian secular and ecclesiastical aristocracy from his youth and later as a court historiographer, obviously participated in the publication of texts that served to benefit his country and promote its European reputation. The prefaces of these books often gave emphasis to the fact that the major motivation for their publication was patriotic. Significantly, when he cited the preface to the earlier edition of Beatus Rhenanus in his own edition, he quietly corrected the German humanist, who claimed that Janus Pannonius – together with Erasmus – was German[209]. He devoted great efforts to acquiring manuscripts of the humanistic heritage of Hungary and lamented over the loss of the *Annales* of Janus Pannonius, an epic poem on Hungarian history, which was perhaps never written[210]. When he found the previously unpublished

---

[206] Petrus Ransanus, Epitome rerum Ungaricarum. Vienna: Raphael Hofhalter 1558.
[207] Janus Pannonius 1559 (n. 61). Idem, Quae uspiam reperiri adhuc potuerunt omnia (n. 68).
[208] Antonius Bonfinius, Decades quatuor cum dimidia. Basel: Johannes Oporinus 1568. It was republished by the Wechel Press in Frankfurt am Main in 1581. Furthermore, he helped Leunclavius publish another text of Bonfini from his library: Bonfinius (n. 103).
[209] István BORZSÁK, Sambucus Janus-kiadásai. In: Tibor Kardos, Sándor V. Kovács (eds.), *Janus Pannonius. Tanulmányok* [J. P. Studies]. Budapest 1974, 548–549, and István BORZSÁK, Die Janus Pannonius Ausgaben des Johannes Sambucus. *Acta Antiqua Academiae Scientiarum Hungaricae* 21 (1973), 361–374.
[210] Cf. Csaba CSAPODI, Janus Pannonius elveszett 'Annales patriae'-ja. *Irodalomtörténeti Közlemények* 89 (1985), 472–479.

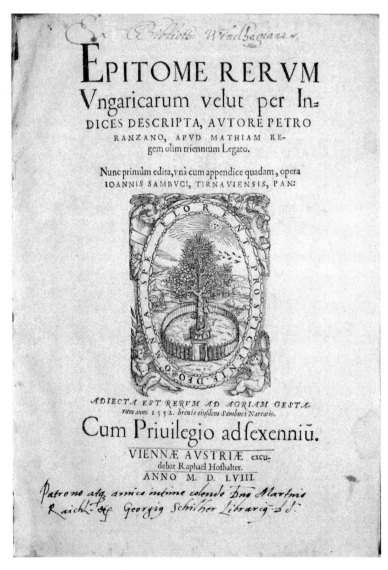

Petrus Ranzanus, Epitome rerum Ungaricarum.
Viennae Austriae: excudebat Raphael Hofhalter 1566
(Vienna, University library II 251.737)

Eranemus ("The contest of winds") of Janus Pannonius in a Florentine manuscript, he immediately printed it, appended to his own rhymed summary of the series of the Kings of Hungary (*Reges Ungariae ab anno Christi*, 1567), which demonstrates how closely he associated his duties as a historian with disseminating the written heritage of Hungary to the European public, especially if it was expressed following the norms of Renaissance literary style[211].

Sambucus's publications of humanistic texts are not easily comparable to his classical editions. Firstly, there is always a patriotic motive behind the projects dealing with the past of the country, sometimes coupled with practical considerations, as in the case of the *Customary Law of Hungary*, which was one of the books most often reprinted in early modern Hungary. Furthermore, the *vetus codex*, which was of central importance in his concept of philological work, obviously played a negligible role in the publication of these almost contemporary texts. It was not the *vetus codex* but the owner of the manuscript and the patron of the publication who added to the prestige of the book, such as Ferenc Révay, Ferenc Forgách, Antonius Verantius or János Liszthy, who belonged to the aristocracy of the country. Sambucus's choice of printers is a telling indication of the different audiences that he was targeting with these publications: while the classical editions had been published in the printing and book trade centres of early modern Europe (Basel and Antwerp), he selected the internationally less accessible Viennese presses for Janus Pannonius and the *Customary Law of Hungary*, which were aimed at a local readership[212].

The difficulties of printing from a distant country have been mentioned above, but no other edition illustrates better the difficulties of publishing distantly than the troubled history of the edition of Antonio Bonfini's *Rerum Ungaricarum Decades*. Bonfini, the court historian of King Matthias Corvinus and his successor Vladislaus II, suffered a stroke in 1497 and died in 1502 before he could bring his history of the Kingdom of Hungary to an end[213]. The partial or fragmentary texts of the *Decades* started to circulate in several

---

[211] Despite the wide range of Sambucus's publishing efforts, we do not find any medieval historical documents or chronicles among the publications prepared or organised by him.

[212] His edition of Bonfini with Oporinus forms an exception in this aspect, and we may surmise that the book was aimed at an international audience.

[213] See Péter KULCSÁR, *Bonfini magyar történetének forrásai és keletkezése* [The sources and creation of the Hungarian history of Bonfini]. Budapest 1973.

manuscripts from the beginning of the 16th century[214], and the Transylvanian Martin Brenner published the first three *Decades* in 1543, followed by a Hungarian paraphrase of the fourth decade by Caspar Heltai in 1565. As Bonfini was writing under the rule of King Matthias Corvinus and Vladislaus II, he could freely air his anti-Habsburg and anti-Austrian sentiments in several passages of his historical work, adding malicious remarks about the bad morals of Frederic III and the lewdness of Viennese women. Attempts made to publish a fuller *Decades* were also halted by worries about Bonfini's strong anti-Austrian tone in the last part of the work. This did not concern Sambucus, who took the trouble to arrange for the printing of the unpublished fourth and the unfinished fifth *Decades*, which he received from the noble Révay family and Ferenc Forgách[215]. It must also have been due to the political sensitivity of the subjects treated in the last books of the *Decades* (the military success of Matthias against Austria and the defeat of Frederic III) that the Basel printer Joannes Oporinus insisted on obtaining an imperial privilege in support of the volume, which was finally arranged for by Sambucus and two employees of the Imperial Chancellery on 8 February 1568[216].

The edition finally appeared in March 1568, apparently somewhat rushed, and Sambucus probably had not enough time for proofs or any kind of corrections. To aggravate matters further, the printing was transferred by Oporinus to a subcontractor[217]:

> In Bonfinii impressione multa mala mihi praeter animi sententiam acciderunt, adeo male excusus est. nam quod domi nostrae fieri non potuit, tota editio et magna pars per alios facta est, qui fidelem tamen operam ipsi quoque pollicebantur, multa negligentius quam vellem, curata sunt. [...] Haec excusare ut necesse habeo, ita alio tempore me diligentiorem fore polliceor.

---

[214] Péter KULCSÁR, Bonfini kéziratok [Manuscripts of Bonfini]. *Magyar Könyvszemle* 111 (1995), 213–237, here 224–225.

[215] Cf. ALMÁSI (n. 2), 172–175 and Antonius de Bonfinis, Rerum Ungaricarum Decades. Ed. Iosephus FÓGEL, Béla IVÁNYI, Ladislaus JUHÁSZ. Leipzig 1936, xxi–xxv.

[216] Cf. GERSTINGER (n. 5), 85 and 94. Contrary to what is stated by Bernhard (Jan-Andrea BERNHARD, *Konsolidierung des reformierten Bekenntnisses im Reich der Stephanskrone*. Göttingen 2015, 262), Sambucus did not write a preface to Bonfini's *Decades* in 1551, and did not publish it in Christoph Mylius' *De scribenda universitatis rerum historia* (Basel 1551). An extract from his preface was published only in the second, extended edition of Mylius' work in 1579 (644–650).

[217] Basel, 31 March 1568. GERSTINGER (n. 5), 94.

> Many things happened while printing Bonfini, which were not according to my will, and it is printed rather badly; as the entire edition could not be issued by our publishing house, a large part of it was printed by others, who promised a diligent work to us, but many things have been treated more carelessly than I wished [...] I think it is necessary to excuse myself for this, but I will be more careful next time.

The book finally reached Hungary in the early summer of 1568: the Hungarian bishop János Listhius, Sambucus's close friend and mentor, noted 10 June in his copy, which he immediately filled with critical remarks[218]. Sambucus must have been embarrassed in front of his Hungarian friends, and his dissatisfaction must have been tremendous, as the printer had to apologise once more: "I wish that you liked the printing more than I do. But one has to abide by what one cannot change."[219] In fact, the corrections promised on the title page of the 1581 second edition (Frankfurt am Main, Wechel) – *omnia nunc primum recognita et aucta per Joannem Sambucum* – and echoed in Sambucus's autobibliography, must refer to the emendations that he carried out on the faulty first edition[220].

Despite the difficulties of communication between Basel and Vienna, and the negligence of Oporinus's subcontractors, Sambucus's edition garnered positive criticism from modern editors, who refer to his careful collation of two manuscript sources for the publication of the previously unedited fourth and the fragment of the fifth *Decades*. Moreover, he compared the text of the already published first three *Decades* with a new manuscript source (now Cracow, Czart. 1415) carefully and without unnecessary emendations[221].

---

[218] John Listhius wrote notes on his copy, which are edited in Martinus Georgius Kovachich, Scriptores rerum Hungaricarum minores. Buda 1798, vol. 1, 332–338.

[219] Basel, 20 May 1568: *utinam tibi impressio melius placeat quam mihi. Sed ferendum est quod mutare iam nequeas.* ÖNB, cod. 9737^z caps. I, fol. 16.

[220] The 1581 edition contains some structural changes as well: the biography of *Attila* by Nicolaus Olahus, archbishop of Esztergom, which was inserted in the sixth book of the first *Decas* in the 1568 edition, was – rightly – moved to the appendix of the volume.

[221] De Bonfinis (n. 215), xxxii. We do not know how much of this work should be attributed to other Polish and Hungarian humanists (Krzysztof Trecy and Zsigmond Gyalui Torda), who were also earlier involved in the process of publication.

Dedication to Emperor Rudolph II
Tripartitum opus iuris consuetudinarii [...] regni Hungariae [...] studio Ioannis Sambuci. Viennae Austriae: typis Nassingerianis, sumptibus Erhardi Hilleri 1581
(Vienna, University library II 57.452)

In his bibliography, Sambucus claims to have corrected the text of the *Customary Law of Hungary* (*Tripartitum opus iuris consuetudinarii* [...] *regni Hungariae*), which was compiled by István Werbőczy (1458–1541), jurist and royal judge (*iudex regius*), and presented before the Diet of 1514 – although never sanctioned. Despite the lack of ratification, Werbőczy had the text published in Vienna in 1517, and it was often reprinted during the subsequent centuries, both in Latin and translated into Hungarian (1565), Croatian (1574) and German (1599). It also appeared in bilingual editions (1611)[222]. The *Tripartitum* (as it was often called) comprised the legal heritage of the Hungarian medieval kingdom, and its publication was important both in the Habsburg parts of Hungary and in Transylvania. After the first three editions (1517, 1545, 1561) published by the Viennese printer Johannes Singrenius the Elder and his son, Sambucus found the occasion to bring out a corrected edition in 1572, when the future emperor Rudolph II was crowned as the Hungarian king[223]. Sambucus published another edition nine years later in 1581, to which he appended a useful index prepared by Miklós Telegdi, bishop of Pécs, and Zacharias Mossóczy, bishop of Vác[224], which was often reprinted in later editions.

---

[222] István CSEKEY, A Tripartitum bibliográfiája [The bibliography of the Opus tripartitum]. In: Elemér BALÁS (ed.), *Werbőczy István*. Kolozsvár/Cluj 1942 (*Acta Iuridico-Politica* 2), 141–194.

[223] István Werbőczy, Tripartitum opus iuris consuetudinarii [...] regni Hungariae. Johannes Sambucus, [Reges Ungariae ab anno 401. ad 1072. [read: 1572] versibus descripti.] Vienna: Typis Blasii Eberi 1572.

[224] István Werbőczy, Tripartitum opus iuris consuetudinarii [...] regni Hungariae. De diversis regulis iuris antiqui. Ed. Johannes Sambucus. Nicolaus Telegdi, Zacharias Mossoczy, Index seu enchiridion omnium decretorum et constitutionum regni Ungariae ad annum 1579. usque, per causarum locos distinctum, memoriae usibusque fori maxime utile. Vienna: typis Nassingerianis, sumptibus Erhardi Hilleri 1581. Telegdi and Mossóczy recompiled the customary law of Hungary in 1584 (Decreta, Constitutiones et Articuli Regum inclyti Regni Ungariae. Tyrnavia: Telegdi 1584), where Mossóczy was responsible for the text, and Telegdi prepared the index (see Béla IVÁNYI, *Mossóczy Zakariás és a magyar Corpus Juris keletkezése* [Zacharias Mossóczy and the creation of the Hungarian Corpus Iuris]. Budapest 1926). Sambucus printed some of the medieval and yet unpublished laws of Hungary as an attachment to his second, 1581 edition of Bonfini's Decades (Frankfurt am Main: Wechel 1581): Decretorum seu articulorum aliquot priscorum Ungariae regum ad contextum Bonfinii illustrandum [...] necessariorum liber nunc primum typis proditus. See ALMÁSI (n. 2), 179, n. 107.

THE EDITIONS *EX BIBLIOTHECA SAMBUCI* AND THEIR EDITORS

Delimiting the publications coming from Sambucus's library (*ex bibliotheca Sambuci*) is more difficult than it appears at first sight. Sambucus contributed to the edition of many works but it was not always him who initiated their publication and his manuscripts did not necessarily play a central role. On the one hand, the books we label as belonging to this group are less numerous than Sambucus's *editiones* – that is, works offered to the public for the first time (see above) – since it does not include his original works or the editions of post-1500 texts in general. On the other hand, this group is broader than the series of books actually bearing the inscription *ex bibliotheca Sambuci* on their title pages[225]. What makes definition more difficult is the fact that, in the majority of cases, the works in question were not based exclusively on Sambucus's manuscript(s).

The publications reviewed in the following pages were initiated by Sambucus but philologically elaborated by others. They are the works that Jacques Auguste de Thou categorised as being published with Sambucus's support but through the efforts of others. Lacking necessary documentary sources, we are not always able to define the ways in which these editions were initiated and organised. Thus our survey of the works will be organised through a presentation of the philologist assistants and their relationship to Sambucus.

Most humanists working for Sambucus as editors of his manuscripts were Dutch contacts of Christophe Plantin, which is a sign of both Plantin's significance in Sambucus's publishing agenda and the growing importance of Dutch philology at the time. Most famously, it was Justus Lipsius (1547–1606) who consulted also one of Sambucus's Tacitus manuscripts for his edition of Tacitus's *Opera omnia*[226]. At the time when Lipsius met Sambucus in 1572 he was only one talented philologist among many others looking for a position at the

---

[225] The authors of these works were Gaius Petronius Arbiter (1565), Aristaenetus (1566), Theophylactus of Ochrid (1567), Nonnus Panopolitanus (1569), Theodorus Ducas Lascaris (1571), [Pseudo-]Hesychius Milesius (1572), Antonio Bonfini (1572), Michael Glycas (1572), Constantinus Manasses (1573), Basileus (1575), Johannes Stobaeus and Georgius Gemistus Plethon (1575), Apomasar (1577), Manuel Comnenus (1578), Manuel Palaeologus (1578).

[226] C. Cornelii Taciti historiarum et annalium libri qui exstant. Antverpiae: ex officina Christophori Plantini 1574.

imperial court[227]. In the dedication addressed to Emperor Maximilian II, Lipsius claimed that there were more erudite men in Vienna than elsewhere in an entire kingdom, which was proof of the emperor's love of science[228]. However, this was no more than a timeworn way of praising a sovereign, and Lipsius's failure to join the court clearly suggests that this flattery was in some measure wishful thinking. If Lipsius later formed a low opinion of Sambucus, it may also have been influenced by the failure of the latter to successfully intervene to obtain Lipsius a position at court[229].

Some years earlier – as suggested by their largely unstudied correspondence – Sambucus played the role of (rather unsuccessful) agent for another famous Dutch humanist, Hadrianus Junius (1511–1575)[230], who was 20 years his elder and who already enjoyed some reputation as a philologist[231]. Curiously, Sambucus appears to have promised Junius that he

---

[227] Lipsius (1547–1606) left Vienna for Jena via Leipzig (visiting Joachim Camerarius) without actually greeting Sambucus. See Stephanus Pighius's letter to Lipsius in: *Iusti Lipsi Epistolae*. Vol. I, 1564–1583. Eds. Aloïs GERLO et al. Brussels 1978, 75–78. For more on Lipsius's Viennese stay see *ibid.* 73–74; Justus Lipsius, *Iusti Lipsi Epistolae*. Vol. 13. 1600. Ed. J. PAPY. Brussels 2000, 106–111; Hendrik Désiré Louis VERVLIET, Lipsius' jeugd, 1547–1578: Analecta voor een kritische bibliografie. *Mededelingen van de Koninklijke Vlaamse Akademie voor Wetenschappen, Letteren en Schone Kunsten van België, Klasse der Letteren* 31, 7 (1969), 38–40. On the figure of Justus Lipsius, see recently Jeanine DE LANDTSHEER, Dirk SACRÉ, Chris COPPENS (eds.), *Een geleerde en zijn Europese netwerk. Catalogus van de tentoonstelling in de Centrale Bibliotheek te Leuven, 18 oktober – 20 december 2006*. Leuven 2006 (*Supplementa Humanistica Lovaniensia* 21). On Sambucus and Lipsius see Tom DENEIRE, Jeanine DE LANDTSHEER, Lipsiana in the Waller Manuscript Collection: in particular an unknown letter from Johannes Sambucus (1582) and a letter to Janus Dousa (1583) reconsidered. *Humanistica Lovaniensia* 57 (2008), 209–226.

[228] *Atque hae [...] quanti aestimes [studium doctrinae] hinc discimus, quod una Viennensis aula tua plures eruditos habeat, quam aliorum tota regna*. Reprinted in Lipsius (n. 227), vol. I, 138. Published originally in Tacitus, Antwerp: Plantin, 1574 (n. 226).

[229] Cf. ALMÁSI (n. 2), 207.

[230] On Junius, see Dirk VAN MIERT, Adrianus Junius (1511–1575). In: Henk Nellen, Steven Surdèl (eds.), *Les Humanistes des Pays-Bas*. Vol. I. Turnhout (*Collection Europa Humanistica*) [forthcoming]; Dirk VAN MIERT (ed.), *The Kaleidoscopic Scholarship of Hadrianus Junius (1511–1575)*. Leiden 2011.

[231] We have tried to order and date Junius's undated letters approximately (only letter no. 5 is written by Sambucus):
(1) late 1563?, Haarlem, in: Hadrianus Junius, Epistolae, quibus accedit eiusdem vita et oratio de artium liberalium dignitate. Ed. Petrus Junius. Dordrecht: Vincentius Caimax 1652, 403–408;

would play the role of middleman towards the emperor already in the Netherlands in 1563, when he was not even much known at court[232]. It appears that not only did the idea of an annual stipend emerge at this early point, but also the possibility of obtaining for Junius the honorary title of *comes palatinus*, which Sambucus did not even consider himself worthy of requesting in his own name, at least not until three years later when he spontaneously included it in his marriage contract[233].

---

(2) December 1563 [?], [Haarlem], in: Hadriani Junii epistolae selectae nunc primum editae. Ed. Petrus Scheltema. Amsterdam 1839, 67;
(3) January 1564, [Haarlem]. In: Junius, Epistolae selectae 1839, 65–66;
(4) 20 January 1564, [Haarlem]. In: Junius, Epistolae 1652 , 267–268;
(5) 10 February 1564, Antwerp, in: Hadrianus Junius, Emblemata. Antwerp: Plantin 1565, A3ᵛ;
(6) 1 March 1564, Haarlem, in: Hadrianus Junius, Phalli, ex Fungorum genere in Hollandiae sabuletis passim crescentis, descriptio. Delft: Schinckel 1564, Aiiʳ–Aiiiʳ and in: Junius, Epistolae 1652, 413–417;
(7) March? 1564, [Haarlem], in: Junius, Epistolae 1839, 57–58;
(8) 24 May 1564, Antwerp, in: Junius, Epistolae 1652, 385–386;
(9) 23 August 1564, [n.d.], in: Junius, Epistola 1652, 273–279;
(10) November-December 1564, [Haarlem?], in: Junius, Epistolae 1652, 408–410;
(11) January-February 1565, Antwerp, in: Junius, Epistolae 1652, 262–263;
(12) 10 March 1565, Haarlem, in: Nonius Marcellus, De proprietate sermonum. Antwerp: Plantin 1565, A6ᵛ–A7ʳ, and in: Junius, Epistolae 1652, 410–413;
(13) 2 September 1565, Amsterdam, in: Junius, Epistolae 1652, 399–403;
(14) autumn[?] 1565, Antwerp, in: Junius, Epistolae 1652, 272–273;
(15) beginning of 1568 [?] [n.d], in: Junius, Epistolae selectae 1839, 31–32.
Also see Gábor TÜSKÉS, Imitation and Adaptation in Late Humanist Emblematic Poetry: Zsámboky (Sambucus) and Whitney. *Emblematica* 11 (2001), 261–292.

[232] However, Junius was not the only one who expected Sambucus's intervention: Plantin wanted copyright privileges, Georg Cassander patronage, Hubert Goltzius a position, and Jean Matal something undefined. See ALMÁSI (n. 2), 156–157. Apparently, Johannes van den Kerckhove Polyander (1535–1598) was also in touch with Sambucus. See Bodleain Library, University of Oxford, Ms. Rawl letters 76a, 9–10.

[233] *Nihil unquam gratius feceris. Quid aio? An vero quicquam mihi esse possit gratius,* καὶ προφερέστερον ἡδὲ καὶ εὐκμερέστερον [read: εὐημερέστερον!], *quam quod tute mihi modo offers de conditionis ratione, ut alendis studiis, sublevandis (ut tuo utar verbo) lucubrationibus honorificum ac luculentum industriae subsidium deposcatur a maximis laudatissimisque Principibus. [...] Quod tunc animo incrementum, quam studiis industriaeque accessionem futuram anguraris* [read: *auguraris*] *si honoraria stipe eaque annua cohonestari me talium Principium beneficentia dignaretur? Quod si fiat, (potes autem in ea re plurimum) nae tu mihi Deus fueris in universum,* οὐ μόνον ὁ ἐκ μηχανῆς [not only from the machinery/ex machina]. *Ad id, si Comitis Palatini iustus, haud trivialis iste, titulus accederet, ut nunc sunt mores et vita (quod tu prudenter edisseris) quid me beatius.* (Undated.) Junius, Epistolae 1652 (n. 231), 407–408.

What is more important is the reason why Sambucus fashioned himself as an agent for Junius. It was precisely because Junius appeared the most suitable for involvement in his publishing programme, since his intellectual interests and abilities were so similar to Sambucus's. Apparently, Sambucus understood early on that he would need assistants for his projects. Luckily, Junius was still without a stable position (he did private teaching in Haarlem) but had a similar ambition to get into circulation and publish. Sambucus and his manuscripts were attractive to him as much for this reason as the grand idea of putting together a collection of emblems in the footsteps of Alciato, Bocchi and Sambucus himself, to be called *Emblemata*. Inspired by the idea, Junius started preparing his own emblem book, sending the poems to Sambucus in Ghent and claiming that it was dependent on his opinion whether they should be preserved or discarded[234]. Sambucus's gracious response was then printed in the front of Junius's *Emblemata* (1565) by Plantin, who became Junius's printer apparently through Sambucus's mediation[235]. Nonetheless, the hopes generated by Sambucus remained unfulfilled (and perhaps even the money promised to him remained unpaid[236]), despite the fact that Sambucus was well received in Vienna, and Maximilian's coronation was advantageous for him. By late 1565, Junius's disillusion was complete[237], but fortunately he was soon (at the beginning of 1566) appointed historian of the States of Holland and West-Friesland and given the task of writing a history of Holland. However, Junius carried on with his philological projects, such as the edition of Nonius Marcellus (which came out in 1565), Martial and the multilingual dictionary *Nomencla-*

---

[234] *Nunc reliqua ad te Emblemata in universum numero quinquagena mitto, de quibus statue quod lubet, sive ea publicum tentare velis, sive mari flammisque aboleri iubeas, susque deque ferendum putabo: tametsi non prorsus reiicula* καὶ κοπρίων ἐκβλητότερα, *ut Democriti verbis utar, ea iudicent esse nonnulli, sed tui iudicii* ἀκριβεία *momentum omne hac in re trahet.* Junius, Epistolae selectae (n. 231), 65–66 (January 1564).

[235] Cf. Junius's letter: *Plantini fidem, diligentiam et in deferendo mihi omni officio studium magnopere praedicas et id obviis ulnis ut defertur, amplector: certo typi placuerunt olim impense et quod ad Emblematum editionem attinet, moram praecipitari velim.* Junius, Epistolae selectae (n. 231), 65 (January 1564).

[236] Junius, Epistolae selectae (n. 231), 57–58 (March? 1564).

[237] On his disillusionment, see Junius, Epistolae 1652 (n. 231), 399–403 (2 September 1565), and his undated letter to Plantin (probably of 1565): *Sed promissorum qui modus erit aut finis? Interim elanguescit promissorum vanitate fervor et hebetatur animi acies.* Junius, Epistolae selectae (n. 231), 63.

tor, as well as two other projects that originated from Sambucus: the translation and edition of Eunapius and Ps.-Hesychius Milesius[238]. As reconstructed from their first exchange, Sambucus had sent Junius over a catalogue of his Greek manuscripts from Ghent[239], offering them for editing. Having scrutinised the list, Junius selected Eunapius and expressed his gratitude for the promise of support at the imperial court, which was probably intended to compensate him for his *molesta opera* – as Junius put it[240]. When Sambucus understood that he would fail to obtain what he had hoped for Junius in Vienna, the project needed to be reoriented and Sambucus stopped dealing with Junius as an editor directly. He turned to Plantin, and it was through Plantin that Junius was officially asked for the edition and translation of Eunapius. Junius found this method rather strange, although he may have understood Sambucus's motives: hopes for financial compensation now needed to be placed in Plantin[241]. However, it was only much later, when not even his hopes of the title *comes palatinus* had been realised, that Junius dropped the idea of dedicating the work to Sambucus, although he did not omit entirely his laudation, which he included in a letter to the reader[242].

The way in which the edition of Eunapius was printed is a further indication of the curious working relationship between Sambucus, Junius and Plantin. First of all, the edition of the Greek text and the Latin translation had separate title pages, paratexts, page numbers and colophons. Although in the copies known to us the two books are always bound together, their separate distribution cannot be excluded. More importantly, Plantin print-

---

[238] See n. 72.
[239] *Catalogus autorum Graecorum, quem nuper ad me dederas* θαῦμα μ' ἢ ὡς [!] σαφέστερον λέγειν ἐκπλήξιν τίνα *mihi peperit, vertat Deus* βασκανίας *omen, quam tu amuleto praesenti facillime averteris, certe si tantii operae mihi (id quod non dubito, obtestari dum fas sit, quin impetrem) praestare lubeat, meo ut aere descriptis frui detur Eunapii vicenis illis Sophistarum vitis (quas ego prorsus deperео) ne te amoris nostri ardorem clam esse pariar.* Junius, Epistolae 1652 (n. 231), 407.
[240] The term is used in another letter, in which Junius expresses his hopes that Plantin will pay for the edition of Nonius Marcellus. Junius, Epistolae selectae (n. 231), 65–66 (January 1564).
[241] Junius, *Epistolae* 1652 (n. 231), 408–410 (November–December 1564). Cf. VOET (n. 105), vol. 2, 884–885.
[242] See Junius, Epistolae selectae (n. 231), 31–32 (beginning of 1568?). For a modern edition, see Nellen, Surdèl (n. 230).

ed two variants of the volume. The special copy of the book held in the ÖNB (74.K.128) was obviously printed for Sambucus and his Vienna circle. Its dedication, written by Sambucus, is addressed to Emperor Maximilian and in it the Hungarian humanist confirms that he is bringing to light a long-awaited work (*in lucem profero*), which – together with the translation by a friend – will have a greater circulation if supported by the emperor's authority. Although the translator friend is not named, and although Sambucus is silent about the process of transcription and edition, at the end of Part 1 Junius makes clear in a letter to the reader (while eulogising Sambucus's contribution as a collector) that his job was not only the translation but also the transcription of the text. Transcribing, Junius claimed, turned out to be a great deal more difficult than had at first appeared since the manuscript, copied from the Farnese library, was full of errors. This address to the reader is followed by Junius's list of emendations, but all the other paratexts he wrote were left out of the Viennese copy: the second part starts at page 17 without Junius's dedication to Queen Elisabeth and the poem and comments he made as a translator. Curiously, in the copies that included these paratexts (which appear to be the majority)[243] it is Sambucus's dedication and the subsequent poem by his brother-in-law Colomann Eggerer that were left out. One wonders if Junius and Sambucus knew of each other's variants, or if the curious Viennese copy was the consequence of a broken friendship. In any case, it indicates that Plantin wanted to keep both parties happy – being obviously obliged to both of them. However, it also reflects the tacit way in which Sambucus was ready to appropriate the image of editor without actually lying about his role.

As regards the text by Ps.-Hesychius, the terms of collaboration appear to be slightly different. The volumes we know are similar to Eunapius, in the sense that the Greek and Latin texts are printed in two separate books, which are bound together. The first book with the Greek original is dedicated by Sambucus to the most powerful Flemish man at the imperial court, Ogier de Busbecq, while the translation is dedicated by Junius to the son of an Amsterdam patrician. Junius's postscript to the reader (following the

---

[243] Utrecht, University Library W oct 1493; BL 1067.c.14*. The copies of the Bayerische Staatsbibliothek (A.gr.b. 1484 and Biogr.c. 97) are bound in a more logical order, starting with the Latin translation and thus with Junius's dedication to Queen Elisabeth.

translation) stresses again the carelessness of Italian copiers and the need for emendations, which were noted separately except for minor cases[244].

Less awkward, but similarly unbalanced, was the relationship between Sambucus and another Dutchman, Obertus Gifanius (Hubert van Giffen) (1534–1604), who published a new edition of Lucretius's *De rerum natura*[245]. Three years younger than Sambucus, Gifanius had still not finished his studies; he would become a doctor of law in Orléans only in 1567. The edition of Lucretius was his first publication, serving to establish his credentials as an intellectual. Later on, around 1569–1570, Gifanius also maintained good contacts with Márton Berzeviczy, one of Sambucus's Hungari-

---

[244] Curiously, Junius claimed that he was almost ready with Ps.-Hesychius already in 1565, but the book came out only in 1572. Junius, *Epistolae* 1652 (n. 231), 272.

[245] Hubert Gifanius or Hubert Van Giffen (1534–1604) was a Dutch humanist and jurist. His edition of Lucretius, with various scholarly attachments, was his first publication. Having attended the Collegium Trilingue in Leuven, in 1566 Gifanius studied in Orléans as the procurator of the Natio Germanica, and became a doctor of law in 1567. Following tours in Italy, where he became acquainted with Wrocław humanists such as Johannes Crato and Thomas Rhediger, he was eventually offered a teaching position in ethics in Strasbourg. In 1583 he managed to move to Altdorf, escaping from the confessional dispute in Strasbourg. There he dedicated himself to the study of law, gaining a great reputation as a legal writer, countering the *mos Italicus*, but again running into religious controversies. In 1590 he moved to Ingolstadt, and in the last five years of his life was imperial councillor in Prague. Among his best friends was Hugo Blotius, to whom he addressed more than 100 letters. On Gifanius see *Allgemeine Deutsche Biographie* 9 (1879), 182–185; Roderich VON STINTZING, *Geschichte der deutschen Rechtswissenschaft*. Vol. 1. München 1884, 405–414; Chris L. HEESACKERS, Le Procurateur Obertus Giphanius (5 november 1566 – 4 januari 1567). In: Robert Feenstra, Cornelia M. Ridderikhoff (eds.), *L'université d'Orléans. Études néerlandaises de droit et d'histoire présentées à l'Université d'Orléans*. Orléans 1985, 133–153; Gerhard MUMMENHOFF, *Die Juristenfakultät Altdorf in den ersten fünf Jahrzehnten ihres Bestehens 1576–1626*. Diss. Erlangen 1958; Martin MULSOW, Mehrfachkonversion, politische Religion und Opportunismus im 17. Jahrhundert. Plädoyer für eine Indifferentismusforschung. In: Kaspar Greyerz et al. (eds.), *Interkonfessionalität – Transkonfessionalität – binnenkonfessionelle Pluralität. Neue Forschungen zur Konfessionalisierungsthese*. Gütersloh 2003, 132–150. On the importance of Gifanius's edition, see Ada PALMER, *Reading Lucretius in the Renaissance*. Cambridge, Mass. 2014, 165–175; for a reexamination of his Homeric scholarship and its relationship to Falkenburg's innovations, see Tania DEMETRIOU, The Homeric Question in the Sixteenth Century: Early Modern Scholarship and the Text of Homer. *Renaissance Quarterly* 68 (2015), 496–557.

an friends[246], and he discussed his emendations with Sambucus in his letters, which are unfortunately lost[247].

As Gifanius explained in the dedication and address to the reader, the copy given to him by Sambucus was an old print (a Venice edition of 1495[248]) of Lucretius annotated by Michael Marullus, which might have come to him from Piero Vettori's library[249]. Since Marullus spent a long time working on Lucretius and was very skilled in conjectures, as Hugh A. J. Munro claims, he must have "carefully collated manuscripts and editions and gathered materials from all accessible sources", among them probably also from one codex previously owned by Poliziano, thus his annotations were of great value. Nevertheless, as Munro has also shown, they were circulating in several copies and were used for Lucretius's edition already before Marullus's death in 1500. There was therefore no great novelty in Gifanius's edition; he claimed to have used Marullus's notes to see how the text had been corrupted by the first publishers. What gave value to his edition was apparently taken from the 1563–1564 edition of Denis Lambin, who was a philologist on a par with Marullus and who used five manuscripts and original conjectures

---

[246] Gifanius was well acquainted with Márton Berzeviczy (1538–1596), who studied in Paris in 1565 with Jean Dorat, but whom he met only in 1569 in Venice. See M. Antonii Mureti Epistolae. Leipzig 1866, 110 (lib. I, ep. 73). The mistaken date of this letter (1 December 1564) was corrected by Endre Veress to 1 December 1569. See Endre VERESS, Berzeviczy Márton, 1538–1596. Budapest 1911, 62.

[247] Gifanius cites a sentence from an otherwise unknown letter of Sambucus, in which the Hungarian humanist agreed to a Gellian conjecture (Noct. att. 2, 7: Tubulo for Bibulo) on a paleographical basis: de Tubulo coniectura non displicet: cum facilis sit lapsus de Tu in Bi. See Marcus Antonius Muretus, Opera omnia. Ed. David Ruhnken. Leiden 1789, I, 506.

[248] See Hugh A. J. MUNRO, Introduction. In: idem (ed.), T. Lucreti Cari De rerum natura: libri sex. Cambridge ⁴1908, 9.

[249] This may be supported by Munro's own observations on Vettori's surviving books in the Munich Staatsbibliothek. Vettori indeed had three manuscripts, suggesting his deep interest in Lucretius and the possible idea of a planned publication. Among them was a copy of the 1495 edition of Lucretius "corrected throughout by the hand of Victorius who says at the end 'contuli cum duobus codicibus, altero Ioviani Pontani, altero vero Marulli poetae Bizantii, impressis quidem, sed ab ipsis non incuriose, ut patet, emendatis, quos commodum accepi ab Andrea Cambano patritio Florentino M.D.XX. Idibus Martiis. Petrus Victorius'". MUNRO (n. 248), 11. In other words, we might suppose that Vettori, having copied Marullus's notes (taken from a printed edition) into a copy of the 1495 Venetian edition, no longer needed the original book, which he sold to Sambucus.

for his edition[250]. Gifanius also followed Lambin in his preface by putting similarly great emphasis on Lucretius's defence, even adopting some of the arguments of the Frenchman. However, his apology for Lucretius appears to be more elegantly and bravely written: he does not blame Lucretius's 'errors' on his evil Epicureanism (like Lambin), but rather tries to situate him in a philosophical context, claiming that Epicureanism – so important for a proper understanding of Latin authors – is in many respects misunderstood. Gifanius was also more elegant (shorter) in the use of his notes, which partly explains the popularity of his work, the value of which was further raised by erudite attachments.

The promises of other philological works made in the edition of Lucretius by Gifanius remained unfulfilled. Gifanius became an expert legal humanist, working first in Strasbourg, then in Ingolstadt, and finally (in 1599) joining the court of Rudolf II as imperial councillor, realising an old dream.

---

[250] See Munro's high opinion of Lambin in MUNRO (n. 248), 14–15. Cf. Edward J. KENNEY, *The Classical Text: Aspects of Editing in the Age of the Printed Book*. Berkeley, Ca. 1974, 65–67; and Jean JEHASSE, *La Renaissance de la critique. L'essor de l'humanisme érudit de 1564 à 1614*. Paris ²2002, 71–141. Gifanius's edition enraged Lambin, who criticised Gifanius for plagiarism in his lectures (see Pierre Bayle, Dictionnaire historique et critique. Rotterdam: Leers 1702, vol. 2, 1330–1331). Lambin used the harshest words against him in the third edition of his own Lucretius (which was partly motivated by desire for revenge). It is worth citing its full title: "T. Lvcretii Cari De rervm natvra, libri VI. a Dion. Lambino Monstroliensi, litterarum Graecarum in vrbe Lutetia doctore regio, olim locis innumerabilibus ex auctoritate quinque codicum manuscriptorum emendati, ac fere redintegrati, & praeterea breuibus, ac perquam vtilibus commentariis illustrati: nunc ab eodem recogniti, & longe meliores facti, planeque iam in suam pristinam integritatem restituti: cum iisdem commentariis, plus quarta parte auctis. Accesserunt hæc præterea, Vita Lucretij, eodem Lambino auctore. Præter eu[m] indice[m] qui in omnibus aliis libris ante impressis poni solitus est, omnium rerum, quæ a Lucretio singulis libris tractantur ac disputantur, capita continens, indices alij duo, vnvs, rerum, quae sunt in contextu Lucretij, & vocu[m], elocutionumque fere omnium Lucretianarum, alter, earu[m] rerum, quae sunt in commentariis Lambini. Lutetiae: Apud Ioannem Benenatum, Anno 1570." Nevertheless, Gifanius tried to respond to these charges in his private letters to Muretus, who himself claimed in turn to have been the victim of false accusations by Lambin. Although Lambin declared that he had not read the edition of his young follower, Gifanius discovered with indignation that his corrections had been tacitly taken over in the third edition of Lambinus. See John O'BRIEN, Le Lucrèce de Denys Lambin: entre revendication et prudence. In: Frank Lestringant (ed.), *La renaissance de Lucrèce*. Paris 2010, 35–46, especially 38–40. For the letter exchange of Gifanius and Muretus, and Gifanius's conflicts in Paris with Lambinus, see Muretus (n. 247), vol. 1, 500–512, 541–551.

We know considerably less about another Hellenist in Sambucus's philologist team, the Dutch Gerhard Falkenburg (Gerard Falckenburg, 1535–1578), who had studied with the same French legal humanist as Gifanius, Jacques Cujas[251]. For Plantin he prepared a bilingual first edition of Nonnus's *Dionysiaca*, which was his only text edition[252]. As he tells the reader in the dedication to Sambucus, his love for Nonnus began when reading his *Paraphrase on John's Gospel*. He discovered the *Dionysiaca* during his Italian studies but searched in vain for the manuscript. It was most probably through Plantin that his attention was called to Sambucus's codex[253]. The publication of this significant ancient epic poem was clearly remarkable, particularly in view of near contemporary plans by Johannes Oporinus and Carolus Utenhovius, both of them friends of Sambucus[254]. Falkenburg now won the day and worthily became the first editor of a text he sincerely adored. He claimed to be happy that Nonnus had led him back to fables that he had left behind in his school years and had introduced him (as a father) to the stories of Dionysus, which were truly pleasing to his soul. As for his methods

---

[251] Little is known of Gerhard Falkenburg of Nijmegen: See Conrad BURSIAN, *Allgemeine Deutsche Biographie* 6, 555. He studied law in Bourges, then continued his studies in Italy. His only publication is Nonnus's *Dionysiaca*, but recently Tania Demetriou reestablished him as a thorough 16th-century interpreter of Homer, whose notes seem to have been plagiarized by Giphanius in his edition of Homer. Cf. DEMETRIOU (n. 245), 515–520. In 1571 he was living in Cologne as a secretary (or paid companion) of the Breslau patrician Thomas Rehdiger. He corresponded with, among others, Carolus Clusius, Justus Lipsius and Bonaventura Vulcanius, and also with Janus Dousa Sr., who published some of his epigrams in 1582.

[252] Νόννου Πανοπολίτου Διονυσιακά. Nonni Panopolitae Dionysiaca, nunc primum in lucem edita, ex Bibliotheca Ioannis Sambuci Pannonii. Cum lectionibus et coniecturis Gerarti Falkenburgii Noviomagi et indice copioso. Antwerpiae: ex officina Christophori Plantini 1569.

[253] VOET (n. 105), vol. 4, 1628–1629.

[254] Cf. note 42. On Utenhovius see Willem JANSSEN, *Charles Utenhove, sa vie et son œuvre (1536-1600)*. Maastricht 1939; Leonard FORSTER, Charles Utenhove and Germany. *Daphnis* 6/4 (1977), 81–100; Philip FORD, Carolus Utenhovius: A Tale of Two Cities. In: Jeanine De Landtsheer, Henk Nellen (eds.), *Between Scylla and Charybdis. Learned Letter Writers Navigating the Reefs of Religious and Political Controversy in Early Modern Europe (1500–1700)*. Leiden 2011, 149–160. The best source on Utenhovius's attempts is Falkenburg himself in his dedication and postscript. Nonnus (n. 252), fol. *8[r] and 862. See also Jan A. VAN DORSTEN, *The Radical Arts: First Decade of an Elizabethan Renaissance*. Leyde 1970, 123–124.

of editing, he claimed to have retained the greatest respect for Sambucus's manuscript[255]:

> Ne vero fidem quis in nobis et candorem requireret, nihil mutavi; et operam dedi, ut tuum exemplar, quo solo usi fuimus, diligentissime exprimeretur. Idem in Aristaeneto et Eunapio fuit observatum; idem in Ioannis Stobaei *Physicis* tuis curabitur propediem; neque negligetur in Illustrio itidem tuo, quem cum Hadriani Junii vetere codice conversione Latina quotidie exspectamus.
>
> So that no one would resent the lack of fidelity and truthfulness in us, I have not changed anything, and I took meticulous care that your manuscript, which was the only one that we used, be printed in the most precise manner. The same was observed in [the printing of] Aristaenetus and Eunapius, and will be soon observed with your Physics of John Stobaeus, just as with your Hesychius, which we are expecting – together with the old manuscript of Hadrianus Junius and its translation – almost daily.

As we have seen, this way of proceeding coincided with Sambucus's ideas about philology. In fact, Falkenburg was as deeply against arbitrary conjectures as Sambucus, and accepted only the practice of the scrupulous collation of old codices. However, in the case of the *Dionysiaca*, Utenhovius informed him that all the manuscripts he had seen were full of errors. Thus Falkenburg adhered to Sambucus's unique copy, which had once belonged to the learned archbishop of Monemvasia, Arsenios (1465–1535). The manuscript was bought by the Hungarian humanist in Taranto for as many as 45 ducats from Andreas Darmarius, a Greek manuscript merchant and scribe from Venice[256], and was allegedly also read and emended by Sambu-

---

[255] See Nonnus (n. 252), *7ᵛ.
[256] Andreas Darmarius (Andrea Dal Mar/Dal Mare (1540– end of the 16ᵗʰ century) prepared hundreds of transcriptions of rare texts to which he had access in Venice. Cf. Otto KRESTEN, Die Handschriftenproduktion des Andreas Darmarios im Jahre 1564. *Jahrbuch der Österreichischen Byzantinistik* 24 (1975), 147–193; IDEM, Der Schreiber und Handschriftenhändler Andreas Darmarios. Eine biographische Skizze. In: Dieter Harlfinger (ed.), *Griechische Kodikologie und Textüberlieferung*. Darmstadt 1980, 406–419; Mark SOSOWER, A Forger revisited: Andreas Darmarios and Beinecke 269. *Jahrbuch der Österreichischen Byzantinistik* 43 (1993), 289–306; Kersten HAJDÚ, Andreas Darmarios in München? Über einen Handschriftenverkauf an die Herzogliche Bibliothek. *Bibliotheksforum Bayern* 22 (1994), 118–128; Pedro Pablo FUENTES GONZÁLEZ, Andrés Darmario, copista en Granada de Alejandro de Afrodisiade. *Bibliothèque d'Humanisme et Renaissance* 61 (1999), 719–728; Teresa Martínez MANZANO, Die Aufenthalte des Andreas Darmarios in Madrid und Salamanca und ihre Bedeutung für die recensio der Philostrat- und Oppian-Scholien.

cus[257]. Nevertheless, Falkenburg could not entirely do without conjectures, although he kept them separate and differentiated the more secure from the less secure. Finally, among his notes he called attention to Nonnus's borrowings from Homer and Apollonius Rhodius.

Two years after the edition of the *Dionysiaca*, Falkenburg entered the service of the above-mentioned rich Breslau patrician Thomas Rehdiger as a literary secretary[258]. In Rehdiger he chose not only a wealthy and learned bibliophile but also someone who knew the better part of the Republic of Letters, men of letters who were also members of the scholarly family of Sambucus and Plantin, including Henri II Estienne, Obertus Gifanius, Justus Lipsius, Johann Löwenklau, Theodor Pullmann, Carolus Utenhovius and Piero Vettori, participants in Sambucus's publishing projects[259].

Rheinisches Museum für Philologie 151 (2008), 400–424; Erika ELIA, *Libri greci nella biblioteca Nazionale Universitaria di Torino: I manoscritti di Andreas Darmarios*. Alessandria 2014. According to Falkenburg, it was Darmarius who sold these two volumes of the *Dionysiaca* (not his own copies) to Sambucus, as was also the case with cod. Vind. theol. gr. 70 and hist. gr. 75. Otto Kresten estimates that around 100 manuscripts can be connected to Darmarius in the collections of the ÖNB, most of which must have arrived there via Sambucus. The two men thus clearly remained in close touch in 1565–67 (cf. Otto KRESTEN, Nugae Syropulianae. Betrachtungen zur Überlieferungsgeschichte der Memoiren des Silvester Syropoulos. *Revue d'histoire des textes* 4, 1975, 75–138, here 86). Nevertheless, according to a letter of Sambucus to Hugo Blotius (27 April, 1571, Vienna), Darmarius tricked him out of his money and left for Spain without ever delivering the promised manuscripts: *Cumque tam facile tuam operam mihi deferas, te valde etiam atque etiam rogo, ipse aut per alios ad S. Georgii aediculas Graeculorum subeas atque exsciscere, num adsit Andreas dal mar* [= Dal Mare/Darmarius]. *Is enim impostor a me ante 4 annos 150 scutatos accepit certis promissis et syngrapha data, missurum se mihi quamprimum libros a me requisitos, sed nihil dum vidi, profectus erat Ilerdam cum libris manuscriptis ad Antonium Augustinum in Hispaniam. Si reversus esset, cogerem illum per amicos ad liberandam fidem; sed dissimula nomen meum, nam frater Joan*(nes) *dal mar* [Darmarius] *subolfecit, me quiddam in eos iure moliri. Poteris praetextu librorum emendorum talia cognoscere.* GERSTINGER (n. 5), 119. On the dubious practices of Darmarios in Spain, see Charles GRAUX, *Essai sur les origines du fonds grec de l'Escurial*. Paris 1880, 287–298.

[257] Cf. Sambucus's letter to Joachim Camerarius Jr. of 6 March 1569: *Nonnus est absolutus, Stobaei* φυσικὰς ἐκλογὰς *utrumque a me perlectas et multis locis emendatas praeloque subiici.* (Cambridge, Mass., The Houghton Library, Ms. Lat. 307).

[258] See n. 54 above.

[259] Most important among Rehdiger's contacts was Johannes Crato, but he also knew or corresponded with figures like Carolus Clusius, Jean Matal, Hubertus Languet, Paulus Melissus Schede, Márton Berzeviczy and Sambucus. See WACHLER (n. 54), 18–19; and the

The last figure belonging to Plantin's network among Sambucus's philologist assistants was Wilhelm Canter (Gulielmus Canterus, 1542–1575), a little-studied but generally applauded textual critic, who, after a short but assiduous life, died as a 'private philologist' at the age of 33 with an exceptional number of Greek editions behind him[260]. Canter, best known for his work on Greek tragedians, not only published several first-rate Greek poets and prose writers, relying on as many manuscripts as the Republic of Letters could provide him, but was also the author of a practical handbook on the *ars corrigendi* of Greek texts, which was a great deal more useful than either of the other two that appeared in the 16th century[261]. In fact, it was a practical guide, using a wealth of examples, on the ways in which Greek texts, from single letters to whole words, were usually corrupted by scribes. His attitude to text edition and the use of critical apparatus was as self-restrained as that of Falkenburg (who was a friend)[262], indicating the sources of his corrections and comments in the margins[263].

Canter's life was modelled on that of the scholar-monk, shunning parties and women, a lifestyle that was still highly esteemed despite the common mood against celibacy. Having received a thorough education in Leuven and Paris, and having visited a number of other French and Italian universities, also in search of manuscripts, he apparently lived on his family inheritance, keeping to a strict daily schedule and diet and dedicating his time solely to philology. His daily routine was divided between work, modest meals, daily walks and siestas and is particularly vividly described by Melchior Adam.

---

manuscript catalogue of Rehdigerische Briefsammlung in Wrocław (Wrocław: University Library, Akc. 1967/8 = Mf. 7796).

[260] Still the best on Canter is Melchior Adam, Vitae Germanorum philosophorum. Frankfurt: Impensis Jonae Rosae 1615, 272–288. Unfortunately, Adam does not indicate his sources but one may imagine that he used either an account of Wilhelm himself or of his learned brother Theodore, who also published some *Varia lectiones*. For Canter's short collaboration and potential influence on Scaliger, see GRAFTON (n. 133), vol. 1, 106 and 114.

[261] *De ratione emendandi Graecos auctores syntagma*, attached as an appendix to the third edition of his *Novae lectiones*: Gulielmi Canteri Ultraiectini Novarum lectionum libri quatuor. Antwerp: Plantin 1566. See Kenney (n. 250), 36–37.

[262] See Canter's poem in the edition of Nonnus (n. 244), fol. ‡‡2^v.

[263] See the paratexts in his Aelii Aristidis Adrianensis Oratoris clarissimi Orationum Tomi tres. Basel: Perna, 1566. In: Frank HIERONYMUS (ed.), *Griechischer Geist aus Basler Pressen*. Basel 1992. Its enlarged Internet edition was edited by Christoph SCHNEIDER and Benedikt VÖGELI at <http://www.ub.unibas.ch/kadmos/gg> (5. 2. 2015).

The texts he edited and translated for Plantin and Sambucus were the first two unpublished books of the 5th-century Joannes Stobaeus's anthology, bound together with an oration by the prolific 14th/15th-century Byzantine Neoplatonist Gemistus Pletho (Plethon). As Plantin tells readers in his dedication to Cardinal Guglielmo Sirleto (another contact that made Sambucus important for him), the mutilations and corruptions of Stobaeus's text were obvious to many, but it was Sambucus, obtaining a fuller manuscript, who first took the problem seriously[264]. However, since his manuscript was also full of errors, he obtained another from Sirleto, which he had learned about from Plantin, who in turn had been informed about the book by Fulvio Orsini[265]. To these manuscripts Plantin added a third and managed to convince Canter to make a Latin translation. The edition was late only because Plantin wanted to bring it to perfection. On Sambucus's advice he dedicated "their common efforts" to Sirleto. Plantin's approach to the edition did not exactly coincide with the views of Canter 'the translator', who, however, also stressed Sambucus's merit in finally making the full text of Stobaeus available. However, he would not reduce his role to that of mere translation, since Sambucus's codex was full of errors, even lacking punctuation. Since in some parts Stobaeus followed Plutarch closely (even in the titles of chapters), it was easier to reconstruct and emend the text. Nevertheless, Canter makes clear that in the majority of cases he relied on the great experience he had accumulated in emending Greek texts – that is, using conjectures (in fact, his marginal notes do not refer to codices). As a result, he added more than 230 emendations in the margins, where he also pointed out Stobaeus's borrowings. (It may be no accident that Canter remained silent about Sambucus's emendations, to which Sambucus referred in a letter to Camerarius Jr.: their number and quality were probably not comparable to his work[266].) However, this was not to claim that the work devoted to translation was not immense. Using only his spare time he was very efficient and quick: in a few months he spent no

---

[264] See Johannes Stobaeus, Eclogarum libri duo […]. Antwerp: Plantin 1575, 3ʳ.
[265] See Plantin's letter to Orsini of 13 June 1568: "Quant à la phisique de Stobeo, je suis joyeux que Vostre Seigneuri m'ait adverti d'où elle procède, car Sambucus m'en a rescrit, et, s'il la m'envoye pour imprimer, j'en feray le devoir, comme aussi de parler à Canterus, la première fois que je le verray ou luy rescriroy". Cited by VOET (n. 105), vol. 5, 2136–2137.
[266] See again the quotation from the letter to Joachim Camerarius Jr. in note 257.

more than 136 hours on it, *si res ad calculum vocetur*[267]. His speed may be explained by the fact that he did not refrain from using the work of earlier translators where they existed (indicating, of course, their names in the margin), newly translating only the poems that had been too freely translated. In his preface to Pletho, Canter already sounded less assured about the quality of his work, asserting that he would not have dared to join the team of translators (around Sambucus) like Hadrianus Junius, Johann Löwenklau or Laurentius Sifanus unless friends, whom he thought to be better than himself, had turned to him for advice.

Leaving aside the Low Countries, the editors still missing from our review are Johann Löwenklau, Laurentius Sifanus and Claude Aubery. Among all the editors in Sambucus's group the most significant was certainly Johann Löwenklau (Leunclavius/Leonclavius, 1541–1594), who edited seven volumes from Sambucus's library and dedicated an eighth to him – the histories of Zosimus[268].

Löwenklau was a first-class humanist and later a dedicated Orientalist, who became famous for his works on the history of the Ottoman Empire[269]. Originally from the area of Münster, he was educated in Witten-

---

[267] This last comment suggests to the modern reader that Canter wanted to let know how much he had worked for the money Plantin might have given to him.

[268] Bonfini, Symposion trimeron (n. 103); Michael Siculus Glycas, Annales, qui lectori praeter alia cognitu iucunda et utilia, Byzantinam historiam universam exhibent: nunc primum latinam in linguam transscripti et editi per Io. Lewenclaium. Ex Io. Sambuci V. C. Bibliotheca. Basel: Episcopius 1572; Constantinus Manasses, Annales Constantini Manassis: Nunc primum in lucem prolati, & de Graecis Latini facti. Basel: Episcopius 1573; LX Librorum Basilikon, id est, Universi iuris Romani, auctoritate principum Romanorum Graecam in linguam traducti. Basel: Episcopius 1575; Zosimus, Historiae novae libri VI. Basel: Perna 1576; Apomasar (Abu Ma'schar), Apomasaris Apotelesmata, sive de significatis et eventis insomniorum, ex Indorum, Persarum, Aegyptiorumque disciplinis. Depromptus ex Jo. Sambuci V. C. bibliotheca liber, Jo. Leunclaio interprete. Frankfurt: A. Wechel 1577; Commenus, Legatio [...] Commeni [...], sive Theoriani cum Catholico disputatio [...]. Basel: Perna 1578; Manuel Palaeologus, Imp. Caes. Manuelis Paleologi [...] educationis Regiae. Basel: Perna 1578.

[269] See Franz BABINGER, Herkunft und Jugend Hans Löwenklaw's. *Westfälische Zeitschrift* 98/99 (1949), 112–127; IDEM, Johannes Lewenklaws Lebensende. *Basler Zeitschrift für Geschichte und Altertumskunde* 50 (1951), 5–26; Dieter METZLER, Johannes Löwenklau. In: Robert Stupperich (ed.), *Westfalische Lebensbilder*. Vol. 13. Münster 1985, 9–44; Marie-Pierre BURTIN, Un Apôtre de la Tolérance: l'Humanist Allemand Johannes Löwenklau, dit Leunclavius (1541–1593?). *Bibliothèque d'Humanisme et Renaissance* 52 (1990), 561–570;

berg and later in Heidelberg. He made a living from occasional jobs, relying on patrons and changing locations rather frequently. His career as a philologist and Greek expert began in Basel in 1566, in the publishing house of Oporinus. Sambucus, whose very first publisher was also Oporinus (in 1552), contacted him through Oporinus and Zwinger (who was the true centre of Basel's intellectual life)[270]. When Oporinus died in 1568 and his former assistant Eusebius Episcopius (who then became a typographer himself) would not prepare Sambucus's texts for publication, the Hungarian humanist needed men who would carry on with already initiated projects (such as Bonfini's dialogues[271]) and were ready to edit his Byzantine and ancient Greek manuscripts. Löwenklau, who edited seven works *ex bibliotheca Sambuci*, turned out to be the best choice, also because his interest in the Orient corresponded to Sambucus's treasures. What Sambucus offered in return (apart from the two cases when the edition was dedicated to him) was chiefly brokerage to wealthy patrons in Vienna and Central Europe, men who shared much of his and Löwenklau's intellectual interests and religious orientation. Among them we find a man trusted by three emperors, Lazarus von Schwendi, who was brilliant both as a soldier and as a politician and the key representative of the *via media* at Maximilian's court; the diplomat and councillor Hieronymus Beck von Leopoldsdorf, who collected Oriental sources in Constantinople; the imperial councillor Count Julius von Salm, who married into a wealthy Hungarian family; Karel Žerotín, the famous erudite Moravian aristocrat; and later the Breslau patrician Jacob Monau, to mention only a few of Löwenklau's patrons[272]. Having edited the dialogues of Bonfini (1572), he translated the annals of two 12th-century Byzantine chroniclers Michael Glycas (1572) and Constantine Manasses (1573), and the *Basilika* of Leo the Wise, a Greek trans-

---

Pál ÁCS, Pro Turcis and contra Turcos: Curiosity, Scholarship and Spiritualism in Turkish Histories by Johannes Löwenklau (1541–1594). *Acta Comeniana* 25 (2011), 1–21.

[270] See Sambucus's letter to Zwinger of 21 September 1568 (*Hieronymus Volfius ad me Augusta scribens significat se de Oporini bibliotheca nihil certi adhuc cognovisse minus an Leonclabius istic sit, ad quem missurus quaedam eram*) and of 31 May 1569, in GERSTINGER (n. 5), 92 and 161–162.

[271] See n. 103.

[272] See BABINGER, *Johannes Lewenklaws Lebensende* (n. 269), esp. 10–11; BURTIN (n. 269); ALMÁSI (n. 2), 224.

lation of the *Code of Justinian*, which could function as a commentary on the original when translated back into Latin. He dedicated the histories of Zosimus to Sambucus, claiming this to be the most earnest sign of his gratitude, since it was an edition that did not originate from Sambucus. In fact, the publication of the late antique anti-Christian Zosimus was a project of Thomas Rehdiger (who died before it could come out), although apparently it was Löwenklau who managed to get hold of a copy of the single original manuscript preserved in Rome[273]. He had good reason not to give the names of the middlemen, since the manuscript was soon placed under closed access in the Vatican Library by Sambucus's erudite 'friend' the Roman censor Cardinal Guglielmo Sirleto, while its publication was probably the main reason why all of Löwenklau's publications were put on the Index in 1596[274].

Löwenklau's decision to dedicate Zosimus to Sambucus was surely not made out of disinterested gratitude, as he suggested. Sambucus, who once even promised to help open up a position for him, appeared to Löwenklau as an important potential patron[275]. Although Sambucus may have played some role in obtaining the copy of Zosimus, it was not mentioned in the dedication. Nor did Löwenklau mention that he was again lacking patrons and would be happy to pass some time in Vienna, and in particular in Sambucus's library. When Sambucus heard about the dedication he promised to send Löwenklau some *munusculum* as soon as he had read it. Probably better than a small gift, Löwenklau was soon hosted by Sambucus in Vienna for more than half a year, which apparently made both of them happy, even if Sambucus was unable to remedy Löwenklau's frustration regarding the lack of a prospective patron or position[276]. In a first account of Löwenklau's

---

[273] See Löwenklau's dedication in Zosimus (as in note 268), $a2^r$–5^r.

[274] Jésus M. DE BUJANDA (éd.), *Index des livres interdits*. Vol. IX: *Index de Rome 1590, 1593, 1596*. Sherbrooke 1994, 462 and 600. See more on the Zosimus publication in ALMÁSI, KISS (n. 1), 204, n. 851.

[275] *Saluta Leonklavium a me, et promissorum mone, cuius ingenium magni facio, industria si constans fuerit, dabo operam, ut aliquando altiore loco conspiciatur si volueriṭ* Not published by Gerstinger. See Basel, Universitätsbibliothek, Handschriften, Fr.-Gr. I 12, no. 329. Copy: *ibid.*, Mscr G2 II 8, no. 161 (8 December 1571). Cf. the letter of 9 July 1576: *Leonclavium, Virum doctissimum, suis meritis complexurus sum omni genere officiorum* [...]. GERSTINGER (n. 5), 196.

[276] According to Sambucus's correspondence, Löwenklau stayed in Vienna between 13 October 1576 and 14 April 1577. See GERSTINGER (n. 5), 198 and 214. Around April he

sojourn he informed Zwinger that they "were always together" (*quotidie una sumus*), and that his friend was using everything he had, collecting material for a future publication[277]. Several months later he gave Crato a glimpse into the intimate relationship he had with Löwenklau, affirming that Crato's letter was read to him when he and Löwenklau were preparing to consume a very modest dinner[278]. Löwenklau collected manuscripts in Sambucus's library for more than one publication[279]. In the dedication of the Latin translation of the Greek version of the 9th-century Apomasar's (Abu Ma'schar) dream-book (1577), Löwenklau claimed that the dedicatee, Hieronymus Beck, had already been able to experience during his travels in the Orient how different beliefs coexisted, as Apomasar also proved. The next translation was a multi-author volume of Byzantine historical and religious texts (*Legatio Imp. Caesaris Manuelis* [...] 1578) all collected and first published from Sambucus's library, followed by a mirror for prince written by the erudite emperor Manuel II Palaeologus (one of the last Byzantine emperors) for his son, together with other similar material (*Imp. Caes. Manuelis Palaeologi Aug. praecepta educationis regiae* [...] 1578).

Although Löwenklau's editions were all *editiones principes* they were not text editions but translations. As for his philological competence, they give little basis for judgement, although apparently it was not philological subtle-

---

may have left Vienna (perhaps also for Basel, since Sambucus asked Zwinger to take care of his case), but apparently with no success. On 12 November 1577 Sambucus informed Zwinger that Löwenklau was in Vienna together with Falkenburg (who was apparently on his way to Breslau) and asked him to obtain at least the 50 crowns that Perna had promised to him, apparently for Plotinus: *Leonclaius Vienne est, est quoque Falkenburgius nobiscum aliquamdiu mansurus, a suo comite feudorum recipiendorum caussa legatus. Te valde oro, quando Leonclaius omni patrocinio et favore dignus ita frustratus est spe allobrogica, apud Pernam 50 coronatos ei procures toties promissos.* GERSTINGER (n. 5), 229.

[277] Letter of 13 October 1576, in GERSTINGER (n. 5), 199. We do not know how long Löwenklau actually lived in Sambucus's home (if he did at all).

[278] *Tuae mihi redditae sunt, cum Leonclaius accepta salute mecum tenuiculum coenulae apparatus sumebat* [...]. Letter of 13 April 1577. GERSTINGER (n. 5), 212.

[279] Concerning Löwenklau's work Sambucus put the following notes in one of his codices: *Has prudentes, sanas, non barbare scriptas disputationes, modis conscribendi rationis artificio has descripsit latine Joh. Leonclaius una cum Damasceni libello contra Manichaeos. Josephi contra Eplasimum. Bessar. Contra Plethonem non dissimili argumento libellis. Itemque Apomasari de insomniis, Palaeologi paraeneseon libro ad Filium et aliis a me suppeditatis, per aliquot Menses 1576 Mense Xbris, quae omnia se bona gratia publicaturum est pollicitus. J. Sambucus.* Cited by GERSTINGER (n. 5), 199.

ties that interested Löwenklau but the goal of making unknown works public (similar to Sambucus), and enlarging the scientific knowledge of Byzantium, the Ottomans and the Orient in general[280]. The centre of this specific interest was Vienna (all the more so after Hugo Blotius's appointment as imperial librarian) and Löwenklau's orientation towards Vienna was through Sambucus. In 1584–1585, he took part in a diplomatic mission to Constantinople that started from Vienna, creating the foundations for publications during the next decade that concerned Ottoman history.

Besides Löwenklau, only one other German worked on Sambucus's projects: Laurentius Hubert Sifanus (1520–1579) of Bronsfeld (at Schleiden), who did excellent work on a difficult Byzantine manuscript by the 11th-century archbishop Theophylact of Ochrid (*Explanations of the Book of Acts*)[281]. Sifanus, who appears a marginal figure in the Republic of Letters, had a typical humanist career. As a highly qualified tutor to the Fugger sons Markus and Hans, for whom he worked for almost 10 years (c. 1539–1549), he even prepared a manuscript Greek grammar book for them. As a student and tutor he travelled across Europe, studying in Paris and at Italian universities. In 1556 he settled in Cologne, where he worked as professor of Greek at the Cologne Gymnasium Tricoronatum, later working at the Strasbourg Academy and finally at the University of Ingolstadt. His main opus was his publication of Gregorius of Nyssa's *Opera omnia* (Basel: Episcopius 1562), which came out with so many errors that nine years later, together with Löwenklau, Sifanus republished it. Although Sambucus was in touch with the Fuggers (having served as a tutor to Jakob Fugger in around 1559) he contacted Sifanus through the Cologne publisher Arnold Birckemann, who knew about Sifanus's special expertise in Greek manuscripts. As Sifanus tells the reader in his dedication, the text by Theophylact was sent to Birckemann, who tried to persuade him to transcribe it[282]. The copy was

---

[280] We cannot go into his philological conflict over Xenophon's edition with Henri II Estienne here, which has not yet been fully explored. See BURTIN (n. 269), 565.

[281] Theophylactus (as in note 66). On Sifanus, the best source is the article by Heinz SCHMITT. *Biographisch-Bibliographisches Kirchenlexikon*. 24 (2005), 1366–1376.

[282] As suggested in a letter to Jean Matal, when sending the copy to Birckemann Sambucus already meant it for Sifanus: *Saluta D. Sifanium: et me, intra X. dies, Theophylactum misurum significato, quemadmodum ad Bircmannos quoque scripsi*. The fragment is taken from Jean

almost illegible (scarcely anyone could read it in Cologne) and Sifanus was worried about the small letters being harmful to the eyes, and about the lack of another autograph version. He finally took on the task and, escaping from the plague, he transcribed the work in the safety of the Convent Steinfeld. Once he had finished, Birckemann also convinced him to get the mutilated copy translated, offering him tolerable conditions, but he had great difficulty completing the translation. He abandoned the work again and again when faced with problems of emendation, since each morning he was dissatisfied when reviewing the conjectures he had made the previous day (the method he typically followed). Sifanus also explained that Sambucus had sent him another manuscript to help him with dating Theophylact correctly.

Finally, mention should be made of the work of an even more marginal but intriguing figure, Claude Aubery (Aubry) (c. 1540–1596), who prepared a bilingual edition of another difficult text by the erudite emperor of Nicaea, Theodore II Ducas Lascaris (1221–1258). Aubery came from the small French village of Triaucourt (Meuse), hence his Latin name, Triuncurianus[283]. He later moved to Lausanne, where he worked as a physician, and from 1576 he taught philosophy. He was scarcely 20 years old when he brought out a new Latin translation of Theophrastus's *Characters* with erudite comments. He remained interested in medicine and philosophy throughout his life, writing textbooks and commentaries on both subjects, including a commentary on Aristotle's *Organon* (arguing for the uses of scholastic argumentation) and a physico-theological treatise on the causes of earthquakes. From the 1580s, his attention turned to religious issues and he published orations on the immortality of the soul and Christian love, although he eventually got into trouble with the Calvinist authorities on the question of justification. Under pressure from Beza (who was justly

---

Matal's letter to Georg Cassander of 6 June 1564, published in: Pieter Burman, Sylloges epistolarum a viris illustribus scriptarum. Leiden: S. Luchtmans 1727, vol. 2, 289.

[283] See *Biografia universale antica e moderna*. Vol. 3. Venice 1822, 406; Thomas FROGNALL DIBDIN, *An Introduction to the Knowledge of Rare and Valuable Editions of the Greek and Latin Classics Including an Account of Polyglot Bibles*. London ³1808, 500; Jean-François MAILLARD et al. (eds.), *L'Europe des humanistes. XIVᵉ–XVIIIᵉ siècles*. Turnhout ²1998, 44; *Dictionnaire des lettres françaises. Le XVIᵉ siècle*. Paris 2001, 81; Peter G. BIETENHOLZ, *Basle and France in the sixteenth century: the Basle humanists and printers in their contacts with Francophone culture*. Geneva 1971, 65–66.

worried that the old Aubery might influence the environment of Henry III), his views were condemned by the council of Bern (c. 1586). As a result, he converted to Catholicism and returned to Dijon[284].

As he explains in the dedication addressed to Sambucus concerning his edition of Theodore Ducas Lascaris's *De communicatione naturali libri VI*, in the summer of 1570, heading towards Tübingen, he met Löwenklau in Basel and immediately became his friend[285]. When he returned a few months later, Löwenklau mentioned Sambucus as one of the primary patrons of literary studies and, as a testimony of this, he gave him Lascaris's book to read and translate into Latin. Aubery apparently did not mind undertaking the task as he took delight in the author's philosophical system. When Sambucus received a copy of the book he promised to express his gratitude to Aubery publicly and to send him something greater at a later date[286].

This survey of Sambucus's philologist assistants raises various points for consideration. Although it is not easy to fit Sambucus into this group, it is true that these men of letters did have much in common with him. Starting with the differences, we should point out that most of the 'assistants' (with the exception of Junius and Sifanus) were younger than Sambucus. More importantly, they were socially inferior to the noble Viennese courtier, whose rank as an *imperial* historian and councillor was far above their status, not to mention the stability apparently offered by a yearly stipend of more than 400 guldens (in reality, Sambucus's pension was very irregularly paid[287]). However, even disregarding the question of rank, the relationship

---

[284] On the conflict between Beza and Aubery, see Scott M. MANETSCH, *Theodore Beza and the Quest for Peace in France, 1572–1598*. Leiden 2000, 237–239. Influenced by Beza, the Synod of Bern (1588) condemned Aubery's formulation of justification, see Henri MEYLAN, *Claude Aubery: l'affaire des 'Orationes'*. Lausanne 1937; Paul GEISENDORF, *Théodore de Bèze*. Geneva 1967, 357–359. Concerning his abjuration cf. Claudius Alberius Triuncurianus, De fide catholica apostolica romana, contra apostatas omnes, qui ab illa ipsa fide defecerunt, orationes apodicticae VI. Quibus Epistola Pauli apostoli ad Romanos scripta catholice exponitur. Bern: Jean Chiquelle 1587.

[285] Theodorus Ducas Lascaris, De communicatione naturali libri VI. Basileae: [Eusebius Episcopius] 1571, 5.

[286] *Aubero salutem: de cuius Epistola ad me publica me gratum declarabo, si ubi sit rescivero: et alia maiora ad ipsum brevi mittam.* Letter to Zwinger of 8 December 1571 (as in n. 275).

[287] See ALMÁSI (n. 2), 183–184 and 192–195.

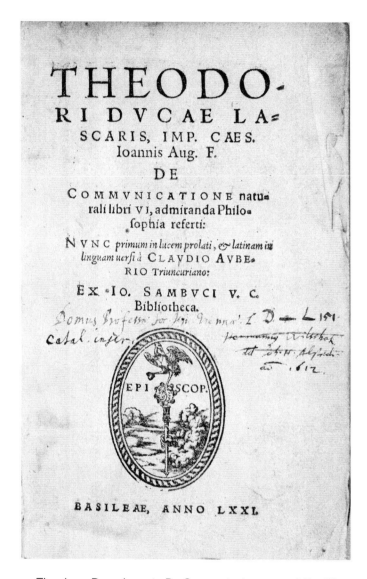

Theodorus Ducas Lascaris, De Communicatione naturali libri VI
Basileae: Episcopius 1571
(Vienna, University library I 240.480)

Sambucus maintained with his editors-translators was analogous to a patron-client relationship, despite the fact that Sambucus apparently only very rarely paid for their work. This fact alone is sufficient to explain the unbalanced nature of these relationships, which could scarcely be disguised however forceful the rhetoric of friendship sounded in their communications. If the relationship with Löwenklau was apparently smoother than with the elderly Junius, it may also be because Löwenklau better adopted the rhetoric of friendship to a patron-client model. Nor, being better informed, did he have exaggerated hopes concerning Sambucus's actual power. For Sambucus's philologist assistants, he was primarily a talented book collector dedicated to publishing, and only secondly an authority on philology. For Sambucus, his 'assistants' were little more than hardworking professionals carrying out the toilsome task of translating and transcribing. While Sambucus had some practice in the first, he clearly loathed transcribing, which was actually also described by Junius as a "nuisance" (*molesta opera*). As his career progressed, even collating could be too tiring for him. In 1573, when Sambucus offered to send Zwinger his *varias lectiones* in Aristotle, he suggested also sending him his manuscripts so that Zwinger could collect more of the problematic places, since "doing it on my own, this job of precise collating would be most annoying" (*Nam mihi soli is labor conferendi minute molestissimus esset*)[288]. Apparently, Sambucus did not regard the transcribing and translating of texts as the height of intellectual activity. Certainly he lacked the humility that these practices required.

If we look now at those aspects that linked Sambucus to this group of philologists we will see that the ties were strong enough to overcome the differences mentioned above. These people were bound together by a common love for Greek heritage. Most of them apparently also shared Sambucus's philological views – his anti-conjectural, 'non-interventionalist' attitude to philology and his insistence on the use of separate critical notes – even if they differed in the rigorousness of their actual application or the attention given to signalling the sources of their emendations. All in all, this mid-century 'anti-conjectural' generation of philologists was keen to appear decidedly more correct than earlier generations and than some of their

---

[288] GERSTINGER (n. 5), 141 (letter of 6 February 1573).

less restrained contemporaries such as Jean Dorat or Adrien Turnèbe[289]. They were not against Latin translations, although not all of them put as much stress on the publicity they could give as did Löwenklau or Sambucus. More importantly, in the same way that Sambucus was 'omnivorous' as a collector and publisher, these people were open to the transmission of any kind of texts, whether poetry or prose, Byzantine, Arabic or anti-Christian (or contrary to Christian thought), anti-Habsburg or obscene. They were fortunate to live in a period when this openness could be afforded, although in some cases there was obviously a risk of being placed on the Index – a risk that Sambucus could safely avoid by taking no actual (or only a minimal) part in the process of edition. This openness to textual tradition is parallel to the general religious attitude of this group of people. To say that they were not greatly interested in formal religious doctrine and rituals (one may wonder whether they were all regular church goers) is an understatement. What is certain is that they adopted a practical stance towards Christianity. We may form a better picture of the general religious attitude among this more or less random group of philologists if we consider the conversions of Lipsius, Gifanius and Aubery. Also typical was the Nicodemism of Junius, Sambucus and Sifanus[290]. Sifanus, who remained loyal to Catholicism, had to leave Strasbourg as soon as he was denounced for having taken part in a Carthusian mass. Even Sturm was shocked to find out he was a Papist. Later, however, in Ingolstadt, it was his Catholicism that began to be doubted when he was reported to have cited Calvin and Beza and argued against the Tridentine reforms.

---

[289] On Vettori's opinion of Turnèbe, n. 147. Cf. GRAFTON (n. 133), vol. 1, 83–87.

[290] On Junius's religious thinking see Dirk VAN MIERT, The religious beliefs of Hadrianus Junius (1511–1575). In: Rhoda Schnur (ed.), *Acta conventus Neo-Latini Cantabrigiensis: Proceedings of the Eleventh International Congress of Neo-Latin Studies (Cambridge 2000)*. Tempe, Ar. 2003, 583–594; on Sambucus, see ALMÁSI (n. 2), 329–355; ALMÁSI, MOLINO, Nikodemismus (n. 27); on Sifanus, see SCHMITT (n. 281).

CONCLUSION

How can Johannes Sambucus's philological achievements best be described? Was he a "scholar-collector, who desired to turn his acquisitions to account on his own behalf"[291], as depicted by E. J. Kenney? Or was he a philologist in the mould of Piero Vettori, who placed all his trust in manuscript evidence and preferred hunting for unedited texts to emending corrupted texts? It is hard to find a definitive answer. Very probably, his commitment to conservative textual criticism owed as much to his allegiance to Vettori as to the fact that publishing faithful copies of his own manuscripts could underscore the importance of his own collection, filled with ancient codices. Nevertheless, philology itself was still very much in a period of formation, both as a discipline and as a way of life. While the methodological foundations of philological work had been laid down since Poliziano with a distinction between manuscript witnesses and conjectures, and with the conscious appreciation of the readings of one manuscript over the other[292], there was very little space to progress without the in-depth cataloguing of the collections, paleographical systematisation or graphic reproduction of writing forms. Despite the many similar stories conveyed in the letters and prefaces of 16th-century humanists about the miraculous textual corrections they performed, there is little sign of any willingness to go further methodologically than transmitting the readings of a manuscript that might later go missing. In these circumstances, Sambucus's choice to become first and foremost a publisher of previously unedited manuscripts or manuscript readings was certainly a reasonable decision.

The place of philology in education and in 'real life' was also very much in the making. The career that Sambucus chose to pursue was certainly unique: he was adamant in his decision to stay close to the Habsburg court and to lead the life of a courtier, but at the same time he maintained an international – scholarly (rather than diplomatic) – network. Although he was not alone among his philologist contemporaries in pursuing an atypical life, he belonged to a small minority, and apparently he was the only one who remained essentially a philologist while having a prestigious position at court. It is safe to

---

[291] KENNEY (n. 250), 79.
[292] GRAFTON (n. 133), vol. 1, 9–100.

say that in the 16th century well over half of the men who produced significant philological works taught in some type of higher education institute, as philological studies had long been integrated into university curricula[293]. Another important group of philologists might be called 'independent' scholars, not in the sense of economic independence but in terms of their relative institutional independence, as they made a living by various means such as private patronage, medical and teaching practice, or employment in a publishing house. The fluctuation between these two major groups was relatively great, and not many independent scholars would insist on their real institutional independence. Only a very few enjoyed the luxury of dealing merely with philology without any, or with only very few, institutional obligations. Distinguished members of this small group were Gian Vincenzo Pinelli of Padua, considered to be one of the best philologists of the time – although publishing nothing at all[294]; Fulvio Orsini of Rome, the librarian of the Farnese; and Piero Vettori of Florence, who continued to teach at the Studio Fiorentino, even if he could probably have afforded not to. In theory, serving the emperor as imperial historian did not mean that Sambucus was left without obligations. In fact, in 1568 Maximilian ordered the *Hofzahlmaister* to pay his historian a yearly pension of 100 talers so that "he can accomplish the [writing of] histories and other subjects – with which he is charged – all the better."[295] Nevertheless, Sambucus's contribution as a historian remained

---

[293] Even if a few university teachers were more highly paid than courtiers in general, the difference in status between the two groups needs a little illumination. It is probably no accident that we have so little information on Sambucus's teaching activity at the University of Vienna.

[294] On Pinelli, see Marcella GRENDLER, A Greek Collection in Padua: The Library of Gian Vincenzo Pinelli (1535–1601). *Renaissance Quarterly* 33 (1980), 386–415; Adolfo RIVOLTA, *Catalogo dei Codici Pinelliani dell'Ambrosiana*. Milan 1933, i–xxiv; Aldo STELLA, Galileo, il circolo culturale di Gian Vincenzo Pinelli e la 'Patavina libertas'. In: Giovanni Santiello (ed.), *Galileo e la cultura padovana*. Convegno di studio promosso dall'Accademia patavina di scienze, lettere ed arti nell'ambito delle celebrazioni galileiane dell'università di Padova (13–15 febbraio 1992). Padova 1992, 307–325; Anna Maria RAUGEI, Les Correspondents. In eadem (ed.), *Une correspondance entre deux humanistes. Gian Vincenzo Pinelli et Claude Dupuy*. Florence 2001, vol. 1., xiii–xxxi; William MCCUAIG, On Claude Dupuy (1545–1594). *Studies in Medieval and Renaissance History* 12 (1991), 72–91.

[295] "Und, damit Er die Ime anbevolhne Lucubrationes et historias desto statlicher absolvieren müge [...]" Vienna, Österreichisches Staatsarchiv, FHKA, GÖ 104 (1567–68), fol. 398; and Prot. 1568 Exp (No. 277), fol. 163. The imperial order meant that Sambucus started

that of a publisher and antiquarian, which does not mean that the role (and responsibility) of being a historian did not influence his public performance as a philologist. From 1567–1568 onwards, offering the results of his philological investigations as an editor of classical or Byzantine texts was something that he could not so easily reconcile with the expectations of his office and rank as a noble courtier. Despite all these considerations, Sambucus was obviously in a privileged position, having every freedom to pursue his personal research goals and to develop a deeper interest in the little-known Greek and Byzantine authors whom he cherished the most in his collection. Being at a remove from the centres of philological debate (Rome, Florence, Paris and the Netherlands) also meant remaining more detached from the world of the lengthy commentaries and multi-volume *adversaria* that his contemporaries produced. Instead, he built up an immense collection of mostly Greek, and some Latin, manuscripts, which – in Blotius's words – could outdo the library of the French king and rival the treasures of the Vatican. Although we still do not know enough about the genesis of his manuscript collection, various data suggest that it was the result of lifelong efforts and that he invested huge energy in finding and obtaining unknown texts. Fortunately for Sambucus, his passion for collecting manuscripts corresponded with the contemporary trend in philology, the praise of 'old manuscripts', and the appreciation of great manuscript collections.

In conclusion, we suggest that Sambucus's ambiguous attitude to philology and his inconsistent performance as a philologist should be interpreted both in the framework of 16th-century philology – being part of the valuable tradition of Poliziano and Vettori – and in the social context of the Viennese court as a place with marked status expectations, while at the same time far from the philological centres of Europe. Sambucus's case demonstrates that the development of Renaissance philology should be placed in its social and infrastructural context, in which the privileged access to rare and old manuscripts had such prestige that it obtained paramount importance in philological thinking.

---

to receive his salary from two sources: 200 florins from the Hungarian Chamber and 100 talers from the Imperial Chamber (apparently for his position as a historian). His salary as a historian was later raised to 300 talers. See ALMÁSI (n. 2), 171.

Ein Bücherfund aus der Bibliothek des Johannes Sambucus

SONJA REISNER (Wien)

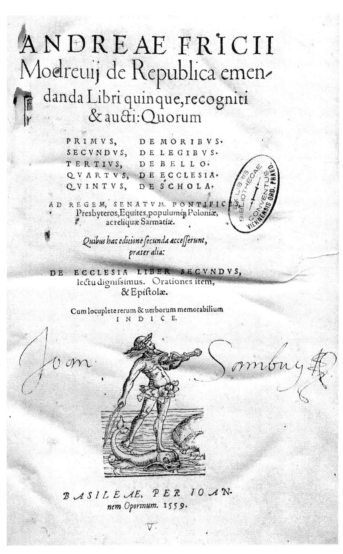

Abb. 1: Besitzvermerk des Johannes Sambucus auf dem Titelblatt von:
Andreas Fricius Modrevius, De Republica emendanda Libri quinque, recogniti &
aucti. [...] Basileae: Per Ioannem Oporinum 1559.
(Wien, Bibliothek des Dominikanerkonvents, Sign. 8884)

Der ungarische Humanist Johannes Sambucus war Zeit seines Lebens nicht nur ein vielseitig interessierter Wissenschafter, sondern auch ein großer Sammler von Handschriften[1] und Drucken. Bücher zu unterschiedlichsten Wissensgebieten wie Medizin, Geographie, Mathematik, Astronomie, Theologie, Philosophie, Musikwissenschaft sowie aus dem Bereich der lateinischen und griechischen Klassiker erwarb er nicht nur im Zuge seiner zahlreichen Reisen, die ihn unter anderem nach Frankreich, Italien, England, in die Niederlande, nach Deutschland und Ungarn führten, sowie auf der Frankfurter Buchmesse, sondern viele Werke erhielt er auch von anderen humanistischen Gelehrten und bedeutenden Druckern seiner Zeit, mit denen er in regem Austausch stand, so zum Beispiel von Crato von Kraftheim[2] oder von Christophorus Plantinus[3]. Seine Handschriftensammlung ging in mehreren Etappen an die habsburgische Hofbibliothek in Wien über, seine sehr umfangreiche Sammlung von Drucken, die in Summe über 3000 Druckwerke umfasst hatte[4], gelangte zum Teil noch zu seinen Lebzeiten an Kaiser Rudolph II., zum Teil im Jahre 1587 aus seinem Nachlass durch Sebastian Tengnagel an die Wiener Hofbibliothek. Im Jahre 1585 kamen einige Druckwerke an das Grazer Jesuitenkolleg (vermutlich im Zuge eines Notverkaufs durch die Witwe des Johannes Sambucus) und von dort schließlich an die Universitätsbibliothek Graz[5].

Doch darüber hinaus gelangten einzelne Werke aus der Bibliothek des Sambucus auch in die Bibliotheken anderer Institutionen. So stieß ich bei der systematischen Durchsicht der Frühdrucke, die sich im Besitz der Bibliothek

---

[1] Zur Handschriftensammlung des Johannes Sambucus vgl. Hans GERSTINGER, Johannes Sambucus als Handschriftensammler. In: *Festschrift der Nationalbibliothek in Wien*, hg. zur Feier des 200jährigen Bestehens des Gebäudes. Wien 1926, 251–400.
[2] Vgl. dazu beispielsweise Hans GERSTINGER, *Die Briefe des Johannes Sambucus (Zsámboky) 1554–1584*. Mit einem Anhang. Die Sambucusbriefe im Kreisarchiv von Trnava von Anton VANTUCH. Wien 1968 (*Sitzungsberichte der Österreichischen Akademie der Wissenschaften, Philosophisch-historische Klasse 255*), Brief Nr. CIX, 209 f.
[3] Vgl. dazu beispielsweise GERSTINGER, Briefe (s. Anm. 2), Brief Nr. CLII, 261f.
[4] Zum Schicksal der Bibliothek des Sambucus siehe Eleonore NOVOTNY, *Johannes Sambucus (1531–1584). Leben und Werk*. Wien: Diss. 1975, 169–174.
[5] NOVOTNY, *Sambucus* (s. Anm. 4), 173.

des Wiener Dominikanerkonvents befinden[6], auf zehn Bücher, die ursprünglich ebenfalls Teil der Bibliothek des Johannes Sambucus waren. Da in einem der Bücher (Signatur 12602) fünf verschiedene Drucke und in einem weiteren (Signatur 15101) zwei enthalten sind, beläuft sich die Gesamtzahl der Druckwerke auf fünfzehn. Neun der zehn Bände sind durch den eigenhändigen Besitzvermerk bzw. eigenhändige Notizen des Sambucus eindeutig seiner Bibliothek zuzuweisen, ein weiterer durch eine an ihn gerichtete Widmung. Ihre Erscheinungsjahre reichen von 1545 bis 1581, die Erscheinungsorte liegen vor allem im deutschen Sprachraum, lediglich drei Druckwerke stammen aus Genf (es sind dies die Signaturen 8999, 14731 und 15101/1) und eines aus Lyon (die Signatur 11765). Erwerbungsvermerke, wie sie sich in zahlreichen Handschriften aus dem Besitz des Johannes Sambucus finden[7], weisen die hier behandelten zehn Druckwerke nicht auf.

Wie diese zehn Bücher in den Besitz der Wiener Dominikaner gelangt sind, ist bisher nicht bekannt. Theoretisch wäre es denkbar, dass sie durch Kauf, Tausch oder Schenkung in die Konventsbibliothek gekommen sind. Aber in Anbetracht der Tatsache, dass Johannes Sambucus mitunter durch Geldnot dazu gezwungen war, Teile seiner wertvollen Bibliothek zu verkaufen[8], ist es nicht abwegig anzunehmen, dass die besagten Bände von den Dominikanern käuflich erworben wurden – entweder noch zu Lebzeiten des Sambucus von ihm selbst oder nach seinem Tod von seiner Witwe. Ebenso wäre aber auch denkbar, dass die Bücher über die Hofbibliothek im Wege des Tauschs oder durch Kauf an die Dominikaner gekommen sind. Denn es ist bekannt, dass die Hofbibliothek Dupla aus dem Besitz des Sambucus weitergab[9]. Da sich bis auf zwei Bücher, nämlich das mit der Signatur 11765 sowie das mit der Signatur 11933, alle Titel im Bibliothekskatalog von 1587, der von Gulyás ediert wurde, nachweisen lassen, ist es wohl am wahrscheinlichsten, dass diese Bücher zunächst im Zuge des Nachlasses an die habsburgische Hofbibliothek gelangten und erst von dort dann – sei es durch Tausch

---

[6] Dies geschah im Zuge der Beantwortung einer Anfrage, die ich im Rahmen meiner Tätigkeit als Bibliothekarin des Wiener Dominikanerkonvents zu beantworten hatte.
[7] Siehe GERSTINGER, *Sambucus als Handschriftensammler* (s. Anm. 1), 257f.
[8] Siehe GERSTINGER, *Briefe* (s. Anm. 2), 18.
[9] Siehe Pál GULYÁS, *A Zsámboky-könyvtár katalógusa (1587)*. Szeged 1992 (Adattár XVI–XVIII. századi szellemi mozgalmaink történetéhez [Materialien zur Geschichte der Geistesströmungen in Ungarn im 16.–18. Jahrhundert]12/2), 8.

oder Kauf – an den Wiener Dominikanerkonvent. Ein weiteres Argument, das für den Erwerb der Bücher über den ‚Umweg' der habsburgischen Hofbibliothek spricht, ist der Umstand, dass sich bis auf sechs Werke (8999, 11933, 12602/3, 12602/5, 12967 und 15101) alle Titel auch an der Österreichischen Nationalbibliothek nachweisen lassen, diese also als Dubletten dort möglicherweise keine Verwendung fanden.

Nun zu den Druckwerken im Einzelnen: Der Einfachheit halber führe ich die Bücher in der Reihenfolge ihrer Signaturen an.

Unter der Signatur 8884 findet sich folgender Titel (Abb. 1):

> Andreas Fricius Modrevius, De Republica emendanda Libri quinque, recogniti & aucti. [...] Quibus hac editione secunda accesserunt, praeter alia: De ecclesia liber secundus [...]. Orationes item, & Epistolae [...]. Basileae: Per Ioannem Oporinum 1559.

Es handelt sich dabei um das berühmte staatstheoretische Werk des polnischen Gelehrten Andrzej Frycz Modrzewski (1503–1572), das unter der Normnummer VD16 F 3195 (vgl. ferner VD16 F 3197, VD16 F 3198, VD16 F 3200, VD16 F 3207) im VD 16 verzeichnet ist. Das Exemplar der Wiener Dominikaner besitzt einen gut erhaltenen hellen Schweinsledereinband, der mit zahlreichen Blindstempeln verziert ist. Auf dem Titelblatt befindet sich der Besitzvermerk *Joan. Sambuci*, der, wie ich im Vergleich mit den bei Gerstinger abgedruckten Briefen[10], den bei Gerstinger wiedergegebenen Seiten aus seinem Tagebuch[11] sowie einer eigenhändigen Widmung des Sambucus an Kaiser Maximilian II.[12] feststellen konnte, von der Hand des Johannes Sambucus selbst stammt[13]. Auf dem Spiegelblatt des Hinterdeckels finden sich Notizen von einer Hand des 16. Jahrhunderts, die meines Erachtens jedoch nicht die des Johannes Sambucus ist. Im von Pál Gulyás edierten Katalog der Bibliothek des Sambucus ist dieses Werk unter

---

[10] Siehe GERSTINGER (s. Anm. 2), Briefe, Tafel XXII und XXIV.
[11] Siehe Hans GERSTINGER, Aus dem Tagebuch des kaiserlichen Hofhistoriographen Johannes Sambucus (1531–1584), Wien 1965 (Sitzungsberichte der Österreichischen Akademie der Wissenschaften, Philosophisch-historische Klasse 248, 2. Abhandlung), Tafel I–IV.
[12] Νόννου Πανοπολίτου Διονυσιακά. [...] Nunc primum in lucem edita, ex Bibliotheca Joannis Sambuci Pannonii [...]. Antverpiae: Ex officina Christophori Plantini 1569 (ÖNB *35.D.21).
[13] Zur Form des Exlibris des Johannes Sambucus siehe GERSTINGER, Sambucus als Handschriftensammler (s. Anm. 1), 256f.

der Nummer 1811 verzeichnet[14]. Die Österreichische Nationalbibliothek besitzt ebenfalls ein Exemplar dieses Werks (37.C.14).

Das nächste Druckwerk aus der Bibliothek des Wiener Dominikanerkonvents, das sich ursprünglich im Besitz des Johannes Sambucus befunden hatte, trägt die Signatur 8999. Es handelt sich dabei um folgenden Titel:

> Nicolaus Hemmingius, Syntagma institutionum Christianarum, perspicuis assertionibus ex doctrina Prophetica & Apostolica congestis, (plerisque propositis & disputatis in Academia Aifniensi) comprehensum. Genevae: Apud Eustathium Vignon 1578.

Auch dieser Druck, der im VD 16 nicht verzeichnet ist, hat einen gut erhaltenen hellen Schweinsledereinband, der mit Blindstempeln verziert ist. Dieses Werk trägt auf dem Titelblatt ebenfalls einen Besitzvermerk von der Hand des Johannes Sambucus, allerdings in stärker gekürzter Form als das vorige, nämlich *J. Samb.*. Auf dem Vorsatzblatt des Vorderdeckels befindet sich eine handschriftliche Notiz, die sich mit der Frage befasst, ob der Autor Niels Hemmingsen (Nicolaus Hemmingius; 1513–1600) Kryptocalvinist war. Meines Erachtens stammen diese Zeilen ebenfalls von der Hand des Sambucus. Dasselbe gilt auch für die Notizen zum Inhalt des Werks, die sich auf dem Spiegelblatt des Hinterdeckels befinden. Dieser Titel ist unter der Nr. 877 im von Gulyás edierten Katalog der Bibliothek des Johannes Sambucus angeführt[15]. Die Österreichische Nationalbibliothek besitzt kein Exemplar dieses Werks.

Weiters ist folgendes Werk zu nennen, das die Signatur 10422 trägt:

> Philipp Melanchthon, Corpus Doctrinae Christianae. Quae est summa orthodoxi et catholici dogmatis, complectens doctrinam puram & veram Evangelii Iesu Christi, secundum divina Prophetarum & Apostolorum scripta, aliquot libris fideli ac pio studio explicata [...] Nunc edita ad usum Ecclesiae Sanctae publicum et privatum et ad testimonium constantiae atque consensus [...] in Ecclesiis et Scholis Saxonicarum et Misnicarum [...]. Lipsiae: [In officina Ernesti Voegelini Constantiensis] 1561.

Dieses Buch trägt den gleichen Besitzvermerk *Joan. Sambuci* wie das Buch mit der Signatur 8884, und ebenso wie die beiden vorangegangenen

---

[14] Siehe GULYÁS, *A Zsámboky-könyvtár katalógusa* (s. Anm. 9), 319, Nr. 1811.
[15] Siehe GULYÁS, *A Zsámboky-könyvtár katalógusa* (s. Anm. 9), 225, Nr. 877.

Bücher ist auch dieses in einen hellen Schweinsledereinband mit Blindstempeln gebunden, wobei jedoch am Rücken sowie am Hinterdeckel das Leder nicht mehr erhalten ist. Notizen von der Hand des Sambucus sind abgesehen von seinem Besitzvermerk in diesem Band nicht zu finden. Im VD 16 trägt dieser Druck die Normnummer VD16 M 2885. Im von Gulyás edierten Bibliothekskatalog ist dieser Titel unter der Nummer 1367 zu finden[16]. Die Österreichische Nationalbibliothek besitzt zwar nicht exakt dieselbe Ausgabe dieses Werks, aber die Ausgaben Leipzig 1560 (21.E.31), Leipzig 1565 (79.E.74) sowie Straßburg 1580 (80.K.24).

Der nächste Band aus der Bibliothek des Johannes Sambucus hat die Signatur 11765 und enthält folgenden Titel:

[Guillaume d'Auvergne], Postillae maiores totius anni cum glossis, Quaestionibus & figuris. Praestantissimum Evangeliorum ac Epistolarum per anni curriculum opus, summo studio, parique fide, in studiosorum gratiam nuperrime prodit. [...] Epistolae quoque Pauli ad Senecam habentur. Index item geminus operi praefixus est, ad Evangelia, Epistolas, ac praecipuas sententias citra longae inquisitionis molestiam reperiendus. Lugduni: [Dominicus Veraarduus] 1549.

In diesem Buch findet sich auf dem Titelblatt der Besitzvermerk des Sambucus in der Form *J. Sambuci*. Auf dem vorderen Schnitt des Buchblocks ist mit Tinte in Majuskeln der Titel *Postillae maiores* notiert. Auf dem Spiegelblatt des Vorderdeckels, dem Vorsatzblatt, dem Spiegelblatt des Hinterdeckels sowie an mehreren Stellen innerhalb des Buchs finden sich Notizen von verschiedenen Händen des 16. Jahrhunderts sowie Unterstreichungen. Die handschriftlichen Marginalien stammen meines Erachtens jedoch nicht von der Hand des Sambucus. Das Buch ist in dunkles Leder gebunden und mit Streicheisenlinien sowie Blindstempeln verziert. Der Erhaltungszustand des Einbands ist nicht sehr gut. Im von Gulyás edierten Bibliothekskatalog des Johannes Sambucus ist dieser Titel nicht nachweisbar. Die Österreichische Nationalbibliothek besitzt zwar kein Exemplar derselben Ausgabe, aber eines des 1523 in Venedig erschienenen Drucks (19.W.72).

Nun zum fünften Buch aus dem Besitz des Johannes Sambucus, das sich jetzt unter der Signatur 11933 in der Bibliothek der Wiener Dominikaner

---

[16] Siehe GULYÁS, *A Zsámboky-könyvtár katalógusa* (s. Anm. 9), 270, Nr. 1367.

befindet und das das älteste der zehn Bücher darstellt. Es handelt sich dabei um folgenden Titel:

> [Philipp Melanchthon], ΤΗΣ ΘΕΙΑΣ ΓΡΑΦΗΣ ΠΑΛΑΙΑΣ ΔΗΛΑΔΗ ΚΑΙ ΝΕΑΣ ΔΙΑΘΗΚΗΣ, ΑΠΑΝΤΑ. Divinae Scripturae, Veteris ac Novi Testamenti, omnia, innumeris locis nunc demum, et optimorum librorum collatione, et doctorum virorum opera, multo quam unquam antea emendatiora, in lucem edita. Basileae: Per Ioan. Heruagium 1545 Mense Martio.

Dieser Druck, der im VD 16 die Normnummer VD16 B 2576 trägt, ist ebenfalls durch den Vermerk *J. Sambuci* auf dem Titelblatt als Besitz des Johannes Sambucus gekennzeichnet. Es trägt wie die ersten drei der vorgenannten Bücher einen mit Blindstempeln verzierten hellen Schweinsledereinband, der sich in einem recht guten Zustand befindet. Außer auf dem Spiegelblatt des Hinterdeckels finden sich keine handschriftlichen Notizen in dem Buch. Diese kurze Notiz stammt nach meinem Dafürhalten zwar aus dem 16. Jahrhundert, nicht jedoch von Sambucus selbst. Im Bibliothekskatalog, den Gulyás edierte, ist dieser Titel nicht nachweisbar. Auch die Österreichische Nationalbibliothek besitzt kein Exemplar dieses Werks.

Das nächste Buch, das sich ursprünglich in der Bibliothek des Johannes Sambucus befunden hatte, trägt die Signatur 12602 und enthält fünf verschiedene Titel. Es hat einen hellen Schweinsledereinband, der mit Blindstempeln verziert und sehr gut erhalten ist[17]. Da sich alle fünf Werke auch in dem von Gulyás edierten Katalog der Bibliothek des Sambucus in einem Band finden, ist davon auszugehen, dass wir es hier mit genau diesem Exemplar zu tun haben. Der erste darin enthaltene Titel ist folgender:

> [Hermann Hamelmann], Responsio ad dicta patrum veterum in ecclesia ut Augustini, Cyrilli, Leonis, Fulgentii, Vigilii et Theodoreti &c. Quae pro sua assertione quod Christus homo sit in loco, Cingliani adferunt, ex eorundem Patrum scriptis deprompta. Item quomodo Calvinistarum Liturgia non sit conformis Liturgiis, Quae fuerunt semper usitatae in primitiva Ecclesia. Brevis demonstratio ex Sanctorum in Ecclesia Christi Patrum scriptis petita. Adiunctis D. Chrysostomi integris sententiis de controversia & actione coenae Dominicae. [Islebiae: Excudebatur per Andream Petri 1558].

---

[17] So findet sich beispielsweise am Hinterdeckel ein Bild des Philipp Melanchthon.

Auf dem Deckblatt dieses Drucks findet sich der Besitzvermerk *Ex libris J. Sambuci*. Dieses Werk hat im VD 16 die Normnummer VD16 H 426. Innerhalb des Buches gibt es vereinzelt Notizen von der Hand des Sambucus. Bei Gulyás ist dieser Titel unter der Nummer 887 verzeichnet[18]. Die Österreichische Nationalbibliothek besitzt ein Exemplar derselben Ausgabe, es trägt die Signatur 80.M.35.

Der zweite Titel, der in diesem Band enthalten ist, ist folgender:

> Tilemanus Heshusius, De praesentia corporis Christi in coena domini. Ihenae: [Excudebat Donatus Ritzenhaim] 1560.

Er trägt keinen Besitzvermerk und weist auch ansonsten keinerlei Gebrauchsspuren wie Notizen oder Unterstreichungen auf. Im VD 16 findet sich dieses Werk unter der Normnummer VD16 H 3102. Bei Gulyás ist es unter der Nummer 887/2 verzeichnet[19]. Die Österreichische Nationalbibliothek besitzt ein Exemplar dieser Ausgabe unter der Signatur 80.L.37.

Der dritte enthaltene Titel ist:

> Matthias Flacius, Demonstrationes evidentissimae XXX. Praesentiae distributionisque corporis ac sanguinis Christi in sacra Coena, hactenus multis minus cognitae. His praemissae sunt breves summae demonstrationum, in gratiam pii Lectoris. Ursellis: Ex officina typographica Nicolai Henrici 1565.

Auch dieses Werk trägt keinen eigenen Besitzvermerk und weist keinerlei Gebrauchsspuren auf. Im VD 16 ist dieser Titel unter der Normnummer VD16 F 1340 verzeichnet. Bei Gulyás ist er unter der Nummer 887/3 angeführt[20]. Im Katalog der Österreichischen Nationalbibliothek lässt sich dieses Werk nicht nachweisen.

Das vierte enthaltene Werk ist:

> Martinus Kemnicius, Repetitio sanae doctrinae de vera praesentia corporis et sanguinis Domini in coena. Additus est tractatus complectens doctrinam de communicatione Idiomatum eodem autore. Cum indice capitum praecipuorum, quae in hoc libello explicantur. Lipsiae: [In officina Ernesti Voegelini Constantiensis] 1561.

---

[18] Siehe GULYÁS, *A Zsámboky-könyvtár katalógusa* (s. Anm. 9), 225, Nr. 887.
[19] Siehe GULYÁS, *A Zsámboky-könyvtár katalógusa* (s. Anm. 9), 225, Nr. 887/2.
[20] Siehe GULYÁS, *A Zsámboky-könyvtár katalógusa* (s. Anm. 9), 226, Nr. 887/3.

Wie die beiden vorangegangenen Werke trägt auch dieses keinen eigenen Besitzvermerk und ist ansonsten ebenfalls ohne Gebrauchsspuren. Im VD 16 findet sich dieser Titel unter der Normnummer VD16 C 2207 (außerdem VD16 C 2221). Bei Gulyás ist er unter der Nummer 887/4 angeführt[21]. Die Österreichische Nationalbibliothek besitzt das Werk des lutherischen Theologen Martin Chemnitz (1522–1586) in derselben Ausgabe (80.L.38).

Das fünfte und letzte Werk in diesem Band ist folgendes:

> Matthias Flacius, Apologia pro suis Demonstrationibus, anno superiore editis, in controversia Sacramentaria, contra Bezae cavillationes. *Sine loco*, 1566 mense Martio.

Auch in diesem Werk finden sich weder Besitzvermerk noch Gebrauchsspuren. Die Normnummer dieses Titels im VD 16 lautet VD16 F 1267. Wie die anderen vier in diesem Band enthaltenen Titel ist auch dieser bei Gulyás nachzuweisen; er trägt die Nummer 887/5[22]. Im Katalog der Österreichischen Nationalbibliothek ist dieses Werk nicht zu finden.

Der nächste Band aus der Bibliothek des Johannes Sambucus trägt die Signatur 12630 und enthält folgenden Titel:

> Pietro Vermigli, Loci communes Sacrarum literarum in Schola Tigurina Professoris ex variis ipsius authoris scriptis, in unum librum collecti, & in quatuor Classes distributi. Accesserunt huic aeditioni ab ipso authore P. Martyre scripti, nec antea publicati, Loci de Libero arbitrio, Providentia Dei, Praedestinatione, et Causa peccati. Ad haec Orationes sive Conciones, nec non Quaestiones aliquot et Responsa. Epistolae item partim Theologicae, quibus varii Loci explicantur, partim familiares. Cum Praefatione D. Rodolphi Gualtheri Tigurini de usu et utilitate Locorum Communium, et de formandis sacris Concionibus. Indice praeterea Rerum et Verborum copiosissimo. Tiguri: Excudebat Christophorus Froschoverus 1580.

Dieses Buch ist nicht durch einen Besitzvermerk auf der Titelseite als ehemaliger Besitz des Johannes Sambucus zu erkennen, sondern aufgrund einer an den Leser des Buches gerichteten Notiz von seiner Hand, die sich auf dem Vorsatzblatt befindet und die vor dem calvinistischen Inhalt des Werks warnt. Unter diese Notiz hat er seine Unterschrift gesetzt. Auch

---

[21] Siehe GULYÁS, *A Zsámboky-könyvtár katalógusa* (s. Anm. 9), 226, Nr. 887/4.
[22] Siehe GULYÁS, *A Zsámboky-könyvtár katalógusa* (s. Anm. 9), 226, Nr. 887/5.

innerhalb des Buchs finden sich vereinzelt Randnotizen von der Hand des Sambucus mit Warnungen an den Leser, so z. B. auf S. 542, wo neben der Abhandlung des Pietro Vermigli (1499–1562) zur Abendmahlslehre zu lesen ist (Abb. 2): *Caute lector istos legito laq(u)eos. latet anguis in herba* („Leser, lies diese Schlingen mit Vorsicht. Die Schlange versteckt sich im Gras"; nach Vergil, *ecl.* 3, 93). Darüber hat Sambucus sein Namenskürzel *Samb.* gesetzt.

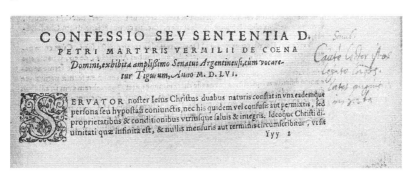

Abb. 2: Sambucus' Warnung an den Leser aus: Pietro Vermigli, Loci communes Sacrarum literarum [...]. Tiguri: Excudebat Christophorus Froschoverus 1580, 542. (Wien, Bibliothek des Dominikanerkonvents, Sign. 12630)

Auf dem Spiegelblatt des Hinterdeckels finden sich Notizen von anderen Händen des 16. Jahrhunderts. Wie die meisten der zehn Bücher ist auch dieses in einen hellen Schweinsledereinband gebunden, der mit Blindstempeln[23] verziert und dessen Erhaltungszustand recht gut ist. Im VD 16 trägt dieses Werk die Normnummer VD16 V 825. Bei Gulyás ist dieser Titel unter der Nummer 1558 verzeichnet[24]. Die Österreichische Nationalbibliothek besitzt dieses Werk in der Ausgabe Heidelberg 1603 (BE.1.K.3).

Der jüngste der zehn Bände stammt aus dem Jahre 1581 trägt die Signatur 12967 und enthält folgenden Titel:

---

[23] Auf dem Vorderdeckel ist die Kreuzigung Christi abgebildet, auf dem Hinterdeckel die Auferstehung. Da die Stempel identisch mit denen von 14731 sind, stammt der Einband wohl aus derselben Werkstätte.

[24] Siehe GULYÁS, *A Zsámboky-könyvtár katalógusa* (s. Anm. 9), 291, Nr. 1558.

Aemilius Portus, Omnes Davidis Psalmi, In Graecum carmine Heroico conversi. Basileae: Per Leonardum Ostenium, sumptibus Bern. Iobini 1581.

Das Buch ist in einen schlichten Pergamenteinband ohne jegliche Verzierungen gebunden und weist außer dem eigenhändigen Besitzvermerk des Johannes Sambucus in der Form *J. Sambuci* auf dem Titelblatt keine weiteren Gebrauchsspuren auf. Im VD 16 ist dieses Werk unter der Normnummer VD16 B 3127 verzeichnet. Bei Gulyás findet es sich unter der Nummer 858[25]. Die Österreichische Nationalbibliothek besitzt dieses Werk nicht, aber beispielsweise die lateinische Nachdichtung der Psalmen von Jacobus Latomus II., die 1587 in Antwerpen erschien (3.J.57).

Von besonderem Interesse ist meines Erachtens das folgende Buch mit der Signatur 14731, das diesen Titel enthält:

> Théodore de Bèze, Jesu Christi, D. N. Novum testamentum, Gr. & Lat. Theodoro Beza interprete. Additę sunt ab eodem summae breves doctrinę unoquoque Evangeliorum & Actorum loco comprehensae. Item, Methodi Apostolicarum epistolarum brevis explicatio. Huic autem tertiae editioni, praeter quorundam locorum recognitione, accesserunt breves difficiliorum phraseωn expositiones, et aliae quaedam annotationculae, cum ex maioribus ipsius Bezae annotationibus, tum aliunde excerptae [...]. [Genevae: Henricus Stephanus] 1580.

Die Besonderheit dieses Buches besteht darin, dass es keinen Besitzvermerk des Johannes Sambucus trägt, sondern dass sich eine Widmung von der Hand des Henricus Stephanus an Sambucus auf dem Titelblatt findet (Abb. 3): *Henr(icus) Steph(anus) D(omino) Jo(anni) Sambuco D(ono) D(edit)*.

Weitere handschriftliche Notizen und Gebrauchsspuren finden sich in dem Buch nicht. Es trägt einen hellen Schweinsledereinband, der mit Blindstempeln verziert ist und sich in einem guten Erhaltungszustand befindet[26]. Bei Gulyás ist dieses Werk unter der Nummer 795 verzeichnet[27]. Die Österreichische Nationalbibliothek besitzt zwei Exemplare dieser Ausgabe, sie tragen die Signaturen 1.L.52 und 1.L.53.

---

[25] Siehe GULYÁS, *A Zsámboky-könyvtár katalógusa* (s. Anm. 9), 222, Nr. 858.
[26] Wie auch bei 12630 ist auf dem Vorderdeckel die Kreuzigung Christi abgebildet, auf dem Hinterdeckel die Auferstehung. Die Stempel stimmen überein, der Bucheinband stammt also wohl aus derselben Werkstätte.
[27] Siehe GULYÁS, *A Zsámboky-könyvtár katalógusa* (s. Anm. 9), 215, Nr. 795.

IESV CHRISTI, D. N.
Nouũ teſtamentũ, Gr. & Lat.

Theodoro Beza interprete.

Additę ſunt ab eodē ſummæ breues doctrinę vnoquoque Euangeliorũ & Actorum loco cóptehenſæ. Item, Methodi Apoſtolicarũ epiſtolarum breuis explicatio.

Huic autem tertiæ editioni, præter quorundam locorum recognitionem, acceſſerunt breues difficilorum phraſeωn expoſitiones, & aliæ quædam annotatiuncul,æ cum ex maioribus ipſius Bezæ annotationibus, tum aliunde excerptæ: opera eorum qui in typographi epiſtola nominantur.

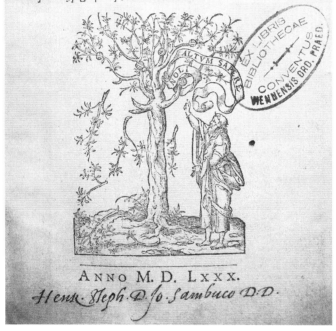

ANNO M. D. LXXX.

Henr. Steph. D. Jo. Sambuco D.D.

Abb. 3: Widmung des Henri Estienne auf dem Titelblatt von:
Jesu Christi, D. N. Novum testamentum, Gr. & Lat. Theodoro Beza interprete.
[Genevae: Henricus Stephanus] 1580.
(Wien, Bibliothek des Dominikanerkonvents, Sign. 14731)

Johannes Sambucus hatte sich bei seinem dritten Aufenthalt in Paris, der vom März 1560 bis zum Spätsommer 1561 dauerte[28], unter anderem mit dem aus der bekannten französischen Buchdruckerfamilie stammenden und bereits ab 1554 selbständig als Editor tätigen Henricus (II.) Stephanus angefreundet[29], der etwa gleich alt war wie Sambucus. Der Kontakt zwischen den beiden blieb auch nach der Rückkehr des Johannes Sambucus nach Wien weiterhin aufrecht. So standen die beiden nicht nur in Briefverkehr, sondern Henri Estienne hat Sambucus im Jahre 1575 im Zuge einer Reise nach Ungarn auch in Wien besucht[30]. Ein Brief, den Sambucus am 28. April 1581 aus Wien an Henricus Stephanus in Genf schrieb, bezeugt, dass Stephanus bisweilen Bücher an Sambucus sandte. Denn gleich zu Beginn dieses Briefs bedankt sich Sambucus für die Übersendung eines Bücherpakets[31]. Vom Erscheinungsdatum des Buchs her würde es sich ausgehen, dass auch dieses Werk, das aus der Druckerei des Henricus Stephanus selbst stammte, Teil dieser Büchersendung war.

Nun zum zehnten und letzten Band, der sich ursprünglich im Besitz des Johannes Sambucus befand. Er trägt die Signatur 15101 und enthält zwei Druckwerke. Der Titel des ersten lautet:

> Bibliotheca Studii Theologici, ex plerisque Doctorum prisci seculi monumentis collecta. Ex D. Aurelii Augustini libris in epitomen, ac locorum communium ordinem distributis. II. D. Eusebii Hieronymi Operibus ex serie tomorum in compendium redactis. III. Sententiis & dictis Orthodoxorum aliorum patrum per locos communes digestis eorundemque Similitudinibus quibus passim Scripturae loca illustrant, ad finem cuiusque Tomi additis. [Genevae]: Apud Io. Crispinum 1565.

Auch dieses Werk trägt wieder auf der Titelseite den eigenhändigen Besitzvermerk *J. Sambuci*, weist aber auch im Text vereinzelt Randnotizen von seiner Hand auf. Es findet sich bei Gulyás unter der Nummer 1544[32].

---

[28] Zum Itinerar des Johannes Sambucus siehe GERSTINGER, *Sambucus als Handschriftensammler* (s. Anm. 1), 288–290.
[29] Siehe GERSTINGER, *Briefe* (s. Anm. 2), 16. Zur Freundschaft mit Henricus Stephanus vgl. auch Endre BACH, *Un humaniste hongrois en France. Jean Sambucus et ses relations littéraires (1551–1584)*. Szeged 1932 (Études françaises 5), 20–24 sowie 51f.
[30] Siehe BACH, *Humaniste hongrois*, 23.
[31] Siehe GERSTINGER, *Briefe* (s. Anm. 2), Brief Nr. CXLIX, 258 f.
[32] Siehe GULYÁS, *A Zsámboky-könyvtár katalógusa* (s. Anm. 9), 288, Nr. 1544 und 1544/2.

Im Katalog der Österreichischen Nationalbibliothek ist dieses Werk nicht zu finden.

Der Titel des zweiten enthaltenen Werks ist:

> Procopius, Commentarii in Octateuchum, hoc est, in priores octo Veteris Testamenti libros, ex vetustissimis orthodoxorum patrum, aliorumque scriptorum enarrationibus in unum corpus & perpetuum interpretationis contextum accuratissime concinnati. Nunc primum ex antiquissimo Graeco codice manuscripto, quem amplissimae Reip. Augustanae Bibliotheca suppeditavit, in Latinum sermonem translati Conrado Clausero Tigurino interprete. Cum duplici indice [...]. Tiguri: Per Andream Gessnerum F. et Iacobum Gessnerum fratres 1555.

Dieses Werk, das im VD 16 die Normnummer VD16 P 4985 trägt, hat keinen Besitzvermerk und weist auch ansonsten keine nennenswerten Gebrauchsspuren auf. Es findet sich bei Gulyás unter der Nummer 1544/3[33]. Der Einband ist wieder ein heller Schweinsledereinband, der mit Blindstempeln verziert ist und sich in einem guten Erhaltungszustand befindet[34]. Die Österreichische Nationalbibliothek besitzt ein Exemplar dieser Ausgabe, es trägt die Signatur 7.A.20.

Zusammenfassend sind diese zehn Bände einerseits von ihrem Inhalt her vor allem ein Zeugnis für die theologischen Interessen des Johannes Sambucus, von denen auch die zahlreichen griechischen Handschriften theologischen Inhalts zeugen, die ursprünglich in seinem Besitz waren[35]. Der Umstand, dass vor allem Autoren der Reformation stark vertreten sind, zeigt, dass Sambucus dem Luthertum mit großer Sympathie zugetan war, was ihm vor allem in der beginnenden Gegenreformation unter Kaiser Rudolph II. durchaus Schwierigkeiten bereitete.

Da die Exlibris-Vermerke allesamt nur den Namen „Johannes Sambucus" in mehr oder weniger gekürzter Form enthalten, nicht aber die Angabe „Pannonius Tirnaviensis", ist davon auszugehen, dass auch die vor 1564 er-

---

[33] Siehe GULYÁS, A Zsámboky-könyvtár katalógusa (s. Anm. 9), 288, Nr. 1543[ter.].

[34] So zeigt beispielsweise ein Rollenstempel, der für den Hinterdeckel Verwendung fand, ein Bild der Lucretia.

[35] Eine genaue Auflistung der 142 heute im Besitz der Österreichischen Nationalbibliothek befindlichen griechischen theologischen Handschriften findet sich bei GERSTINGER, Sambucus als Handschriftensammler (s. Anm. 1), 349–362. Auch unter den lateinischen Handschriften, die er gesammelt hatte, sind einige theologischen Inhalts. Siehe GERSTINGER, Sambucus als Handschriftensammler (s. Anm. 1), 384–395.

schienenen Bände von ihm erst nach seiner endgültigen Niederlassung in Wien 1564 angeschafft wurden[36].

Andererseits werfen einzelne Notizen des Humanisten wie beispielsweise die über Niels Hemmingsen als Kryptocalvinist auf dem Vorsatzblatt zu dessen *Syntagma institutionum Christianarum* (Sign. 8999) oder der Vermerk mit der Warnung vor dem calvinistischen Inhalt von Pietro Vermiglis *Loci communes sacrarum literarum* (Sign. 12630) auch ein Schlaglicht auf seine Haltung in konfessionellen Fragen.

---

[36] Zur Form des Exlibris des Johannes Sambucus siehe GERSTINGER, *Sambucus als Handschriftensammler* (s. Anm. 1), 257.

Unbewusste Vermittlung griechischen Kulturerbes

Palimpseste aus dem Besitz des Johannes Sambucus

JANA GRUSKOVÁ (Wien – Bratislava)

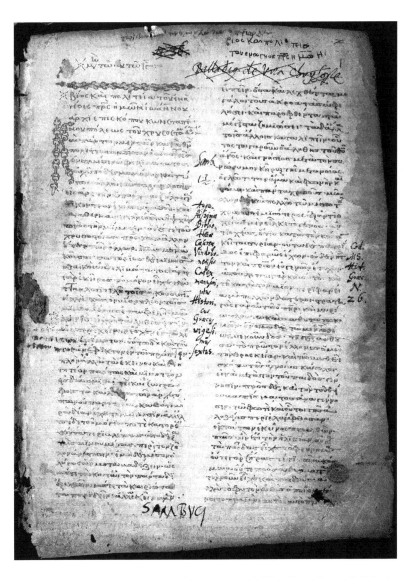

Palimpsestcodex (*Vita* des Ioannes Chrysostomos / Ailios Herodianos, Καθολική προσῳδία) mit Besitzvermerk des Johannes Sambucus
(Wien, Österreichische Nationalbibliothek, Cod. Vind. hist. gr. 10, fol. 1r)

Die umfangreiche Handschriftensammlung des Humanisten Johannes Sambucus (1531–1584) gehörte bereits zu seinen Lebzeiten zu den wichtigsten und berühmtesten Privatsammlungen Europas[*1]. Mit der Erwerbung im Jahre 1578 ging sie, noch zu Sambucus' Lebzeiten, an die habsburgische Hofbibliothek in Wien über[2], und zählt heute zu den wertvollsten Beständen der Österreichischen Nationalbibliothek. Aus dem 1035 Bücher umfassenden Bestand der griechischen Handschriften der ÖNB können heute – laut dem modernen Gesamtkatalog von Herbert Hunger, Otto Kresten, Christian Hannick und Wolfgang Lackner – 388 sicher (und 21 mit Fragezeichen) als Codices des Johannes Sambucus identifiziert werden[3]. Ihre kulturgeschichtliche Bedeutung ist eminent. Besonders während seines Stu-

---

[*] Der vorliegende Beitrag wurde im Rahmen des vom Fonds zur Förderung der wissenschaftlichen Forschung / Austrian Science Fund (FWF) geförderten Projekts P 24523-G19 *Important textual witnesses in Vienna Greek Palimpsests* verfasst, das an der Österreichischen Akademie der Wissenschaften unter der Leitung von Prof. Otto Kresten durchgeführt wird. Für weitere Details: <https://www.oeaw.ac.at/byzanz/sprache-text-und-schrift/buchkultur-palaeographie-und-palimpseste/griechische-palimpseste/project-fwf-p-24523/> sowie Jana GRUSKOVÁ, Further Steps in Revealing, Editing and Analysing Important Ancient Greek and Byzantine Texts Hidden in Palimpsests. *Graecolatina et Orientalia* 33/34 (2012), 69–82. In slowakischer Sprache ist erschienen: DIES., Sambucove rukopisy odkrývajú svoje tajomstvá [Die Handschriften des Sambucus enthüllen ihre Geheimnisse]. In: Ľudmila Buzássyová, Erika Juríková, Nicol Sipeiková (edd.), *Decus sapientiae*. Kraków 2011 (*Sambucus* Suppl. 3), 113–119.

[1] Vgl. dazu u. a. Hans GERSTINGER, Johannes Sambucus als Handschriftensammler. In: *Festschrift der Nationalbibliothek in Wien zur Feier des 200jährigen Bestehens des Gebäudes*. Wien 1926, 251–400; hier bes. 254–257; Franz UNTERKIRCHER, Hugo Blotius und seine ersten Nachfolger (1575–1663). In: Josef Stummvoll (Hg.), *Geschichte der Österreichischen Nationalbibliothek I*. Wien 1968 (*Museion* N. F. II/3, 1), 82–127; hier 116–119. Vgl. weiter die Beiträge in diesem Band und die dort zitierte Literatur.

[2] Als Sambucus um 1570 in arge finanzielle Schwierigkeiten geraten war, entschloss er sich, seine Handschriftensammlung zu verkaufen und bot sie seinem kaiserlichen Herrn für die Hofbibliothek an: GERSTINGER, Handschriftensammler (s. Anm. 1), 254, 274–284.

[3] Fast in allen seinen Handschriften befindet sich sein Exlibris, zumeist in der Form: *Joannes Sambucus Pannonius Tirnaviensis* (üblicherweise gekürzt); *Joannes Sambucus D(octor)*; *Sambucus*; *Sambuci*; *Samb.*; seltener: *Joannis Sambuci liber*; *E Sambuci libris*; *E bibliotheca* (*Ex libris*) *Joannis Sambuci*. Nach seiner Niederlassung in Wien fällt *Pannonius Tyrnaviensis* fort, dafür erscheint neben der einfachen Namensform gelegentlich *Historicus Caesar*. oder *Consiliarius et Historicus Caesar.*; vgl. GERSTINGER 1926 (s. Anm. 1), 254–257.

diums in Paris (ab 1551) mögen Sambucus' schon früher unter Camerarius in Leipzig und Melanchthon in Wittenberg begonnene und danach unter Amerbachs Leitung in Ingolstadt fortgesetzte Griechischstudien weitere Förderung gefunden haben[4]; das Griechische blieb von da an sein eigentliches Lehr- und Forschungsgebiet und griechische Handschriften die vornehmsten Objekte seiner Sammlertätigkeit, die ihren Anfang in Paris genommen haben dürfte[5]. In erster Linie ließ sich Sambucus bei der Erwerbung seiner Handschriftenschätze von philologisch-antiquarischen Prinzipien leiten, und innerhalb des Griechischen waren es speziell die philologischen, historischen und theologischen Texte, denen er mit besonderem Eifer nachspürte[6]. So erklärt Hans Gerstinger in seiner wichtigen Johannes Sambucus als Handschriftensammler gewidmeten Studie[7]:

> Die Reste der klassischen Literatur in möglichst alten, vollständigen und textlich fehlerfreien Exemplaren in tunlichster Vollzähligkeit in seiner Bibliothek zu vereinigen und sie durch Ausgaben der Welt wieder zugänglich zu machen, war sein Programm; Bemerkungen wie *vetus codex, rarus codex, codex non editus, codex correctus* (*correctior*), *codex edi deberet, edatur* u. a., die sich gelegentlich in einzelnen Handschriften vorfinden, bekunden dies, auch in seinen Praefationes und Briefen finden sich viele hiefür recht bezeichnende Stellen.

Der große Humanist wäre gewiss begeistert gewesen, hätte er gewusst, dass sich in einigen seiner Bücher unter den ihm gut bekannten Texten Fragmente anderer, noch älterer, oft einzigartiger griechischer Handschriften und wertvoller Texte verbergen. Pergament, der aus Tierhaut gewonnene Beschreibstoff, wurde nämlich im Mittelalter nicht selten wiederverwendet. Der ursprüngliche Text, der aus irgendeinem Grund verzichtbar geworden war, wurde dabei getilgt, um das kostbare Material erneut beschriften zu

---

[4] GERSTINGER, Handschriftensammler (s. Anm. 1), 262–265.
[5] GERSTINGER, Handschriftensammler (s. Anm. 1), 266f. Für das Griechische in Paris hatte speziell Stephanus' Druckerei und seine eigene wissenschaftliche Tätigkeit sowie die des Turnebus und seiner Amtskollegen und -nachfolger eine große Bedeutung. Ein wertvoller Faktor war die Gründung humanistischer Bibliotheken, vor allem der Königlichen Bibliothek, bei der ein besonderes Augenmerk auf die Zustandebringung einer möglichst umfangreichen Sammlung griechischer Handschriften gelegt wurde. Der Pariser Büchermarkt war von da an neben den italienischen Städten das Hauptziel der Sammler griechischer Handschriften; GERSTINGER, ebd.
[6] Vgl. GERSTINGER, Handschriftensammler (s. Anm. 1), 291.
[7] Ebenda.

können⁸. Einige der Codices wurden vollständig aus palimpsestierten Blättern aus (oft mehreren) älteren Handschriften hergestellt. In anderen wurde hingegen nur in bestimmten Teilen – sei es aus Mangel an weiterem Schreibmaterial, sei es zur späteren Ergänzung verlorenen Textes – palimpsestiertes Pergament verwendet⁹. Zusätzlich fanden im Laufe der Zeit gerade zweimal als Beschreibstoff verwendete Pergamentfolien mit Vorliebe eine Drittverwendung als Schutzblätter oder Stützfalze bei der Herstellung späterer Einbände[10].

Unter den griechischen Sambucus-Handschriften der Österreichischen Nationalbibliothek in Wien befinden sich folgende *codices rescripti*, wobei das Ausmaß der jeweiligen Palimpsestierung nach den oben genannten Kategorien variiert: Vind. hist. gr. 10; Vind. phil. gr. 158; Vind. phil. gr. 286; Vind. iur. gr. 18; Vind. theol. gr. 27; Vind. theol. gr. 127; Vind. theol. gr. 158; Vind. theol. gr. 164; Vind. theol. gr. 177; Vind. theol. gr. 268.

Sambucus hat gewiss in seinen Palimpsesten die bei normalem Licht erkennbaren Spuren der getilgten Schrift sehen, vielleicht sogar einige kleine Stellen entziffern können. Für eine entsprechende Lesbarmachung getilgter Schriften hatte man zu seiner Zeit jedoch noch keine technischen Mittel zur Verfügung, sodass diese Texte weiter unentdeckt bleiben mussten.

---

[8] Für die Tilgung eines Textes können generell verschiedene Gründe ausschlaggebend gewesen sein. Ein Text wurde etwa dann unbrauchbar, wenn er in seinem Kulturbereich nach inhaltlich an Aktualität verloren hatte. Auch formale Gründe konnten zur Palimpsestierung führen; so wurden etwa seit dem 9. Jahrhundert oft griechische Majuskelcodices palimpsestiert. Ebenfalls konnte eine mechanische Beschädigung der ursprünglichen Handschrift als Grund für das Palimpsestieren der Blätter dienen. Es ist aber auch damit zu rechnen, dass man bei einem Bedarf an Pergament nach Büchern, die in mehreren Exemplaren vorhanden waren, gegriffen hat. Vgl. Jana GRUSKOVÁ, *Untersuchungen zu den griechischen Palimpsesten der Österreichischen Nationalbibliothek. Codices Historici, Codices Philosophici et Philologici, Codices Iuridici*. Wien 2010 (Veröffentlichungen zur Byzanzforschung XX, Denkschriften der philosophisch-historischen Klasse der ÖAW 401), 17–21 (Einleitung).

[9] Dabei in einer bunt gemischten Abfolge und manchmal sogar kopfständig.

[10] Vgl. GRUSKOVÁ, *Untersuchungen* (s. Anm. 8), 17f. Bei einer Wiederverwendung des Pergaments wurden zumeist Doppelblätter bzw. Einzelblätter in ihrem ursprünglichen Format, d. h. wieder als Doppel- und Einzelblätter, gebraucht. Nicht selten hat man jedoch ältere Blätter im neuen Codex zu Doppelblättern gefaltet. Manchmal wurden sogar ursprüngliche Blatthälften zu (kleineren) Doppelblättern oder originale Doppelblätter zu (größeren) Einzelblättern umfunktioniert. Bei allen soeben genannten Varianten konnte das Pergament zusätzlich mehr oder weniger beschnitten worden sein; vgl. a. a. O., 18f.

Dass die getilgte Schrift eines palimpsestierten Pergamentblattes überhaupt wiederzugewinnen ist, d. h. lesbar gemacht werden kann, bzw. noch teilweise mit bloßem Auge zu erkennen ist, liegt an den Eigenschaften des Pergaments und an der Zusammensetzung der von den Schreibern verwendeten Tinte. Im 18. und 19. Jahrhundert wurden chemische Verfahren auf der Basis von Tinkturen (sogenannte Reagenzien) zur Lesbarmachung der getilgten Schriften angewandt. Diese Experimente lieferten zwar in einigen Fällen sensationelle Textfunde[11], haben jedoch zur weitgehenden Zerstörung der Pergamentoberfläche durch chemische Beschädigung und Dunkelfärbung geführt. Von derartigen Methoden hat man daher seit dem Beginn des 20. Jahrhunderts Abstand genommen. Im 20. Jahrhundert kamen photographische Verfahren und vor allem die Anwendung des UV-Lichtes zum Einsatz, die dann bei der Lesbarmachung getilgter Texte einen wesentlichen Fortschritt bedeuteten[12]. Dank dieser technischen Möglichkeiten konnten viele der Sambucus-Palimpseste bereits bei der in den 60er bis 90er Jahren des 20. Jahrhunderts durchgeführten Gesamtkatalogisierung der griechischen Handschriftenbestände der Österreichischen Nationalbibliothek weitgehend entziffert und bearbeitet werden. Einige der in den Sambucus-Palimpsesten verborgenen Texte ließen sich jedoch erst in den letzten 15 Jahren näher erforschen, nicht zuletzt dank der modernen Digitalisierungstechnik zur Lesbarmachung getilgter Texte[13]. Eine neue, systematische, durch die genannten technischen Fortschritte ermöglichte Bearbeitung der griechischen Palimpseste der ÖNB, und darunter auch der Sambucus-Palimpseste, hat mit dem europäischen Pilotprojekt „*Rinascimento virtuale – Digitale Palimpsestforschung*" in den Jahren 2003–2004[14] begon-

---

[11] Man denke etwa an das Strabon-Palimpsest oder an Ciceros Schrift *De re publica*, die zu Anfang des 19. Jahrhunderts von Kardinal Angelo Mai in einem Palimpsestcodex der Biblioteca Apostolica Vaticana (Cod. Vat. lat. 5757) entdeckt wurde.

[12] Vgl. GRUSKOVÁ, *Untersuchungen* (s. Anm. 8), 19f. (mit Literatur).

[13] Vgl. GRUSKOVÁ, *Untersuchungen* (s. Anm. 8), 20–26 (mit Literatur). Für die Arbeit an Originalen stehen inzwischen qualitativ hochwertigere und sehr viel bequemer zu benutzende UV-Lampen (bzw. UV-Handlupen) als noch vor einigen Jahrzehnten zur Verfügung.

[14] Vgl. Dieter HARLFINGER in Zusammenarbeit mit Jana GRUSKOVÁ, Daniel DECKERS, Koen VANHAEGENDOREN (Hg.), *Rinascimento virtuale – Digitale Palimpsestforschung. Perspektiven des Netzwerks in den Beitrittsländern Mittel- und Osteuropas und in angrenzenden Staaten*. Berichtband der RV-Tagung in Bratislava, 28.–29. Juni 2002. Bratislava 2002, sowie die Inter-

nen und wurde danach in zwei an der Österreichischen Akademie der Wissenschaften (Byzanzforschung) unter der Leitung von Otto Kresten von der Autorin dieser Zeilen in Zusammenarbeit mit ausländischen Kooperationspartnern und mit Unterstützung von Ernst Gamillscheg durchgeführten und zum großen Teil vom österreichischen Fonds zur Förderung der wissenschaftlichen Forschung (FWF) geförderten Projekten fortgesetzt[15].

Welche Textschätze der klassischen und der byzantinischen Literatur verbergen sich aber in den unteren Schichten von Sambucus' Palimpsesten? Wieweit konnten sie bisher lesbar gemacht, entziffert und erforscht werden? Um den Antworten auf diese Fragen näher zu kommen und dieses bisher nur wenig bekannte Verdienst von Sambucus' Sammeltätigkeit zu illustrieren, seien im Folgenden einige Beispiele kurz präsentiert.

Unter den zum Bestand der *Codices theologici* der ÖNB gehörenden Sambucus-Handschriften befinden sich, wie bereits gesagt, sechs Palimpseste[16]. Im Codex Vind. theol. gr. 27 wurden etwa sieben Doppelblätter einer ins 11. Jahrhundert datierbaren Handschrift im 14. Jahrhundert zu Einzelblättern umfunktioniert, um die Textlücken in einer im 11. Jahrhundert entstandenen

---

netpräsentation *Rinascimento virtuale / Digitale Palimpsestforschung. Rediscovering written records of a hidden European cultural heritage* <http://www.rinascimentovirtuale.eu/>.

[15] In den Projekten: *Griechische Palimpseste* (2005–2008; vgl. GRUSKOVÁ, *Untersuchungen*, s. Anm. 8, 19f.); FWF-Projekt P 24523-G19 *Important textual witnesses in Vienna Greek Palimpsests* (s. Anm. *) und FWF-Projekt P 28112-G25 *Scythica Vindobonensia* (2015–2018) <https://www.oeaw.ac.at/byzanz/sprache-text-und-schrift/buchkultur-palaeographie-und-palimpseste/scythica-vindobonensia/>).

[16] Zum Cod. Vind. theol. gr. 127 vgl. Herbert HUNGER, Otto KRESTEN, Christian HANNICK, *Katalog der griechischen Handschriften der Österreichischen Nationalbibliothek III/2. Codices theologici 101–200*. Wien 1984 (*Museion* N. F. IV/1, 3, 2), 96–97. Im Cod. Vind. theol. gr. 158 wurde zur Stützung einer Lage in dem neuen Buchblock ein Pergamentfalz (fol. 204/1, 210/1) aus einem palimpsestierten Majuskelcodex des 10. Jahrhunderts (Evangelienlektionar) verwendet; vgl. HUNGER, KRESTEN, HANNICK, *Katalog*, 231–238; Jana GRUSKOVÁ, Christian GASTGEBER, Zur Wiederverwertung von Handschriften mit Bibeltexten am Beispiel griechischer Codices der Österreichischen Nationalbibliothek. *Biblos* 52/1–2 (2003), 59–74 (bes. 71 mit Abbildung). Zum Cod. Vind. theol. gr. 164 vgl. HUNGER, KRESTEN, HANNICK, *Katalog*, 253–257. Der im 15./16. Jahrhundert hergestellte Cod. Vind. theol. gr. 268 enthält in den Schutzblättern getilgte Majuskelfragmente (10. Jahrhundert) eines Lektionars (ohne obere Schrift): Vgl. Herbert HUNGER, Wolfgang LACKNER, Christian HANNICK, *Katalog der griechischen Handschriften der Österreichischen Nationalbibliothek III/3. Codices theologici 201–337*. Wien 1992 (*Museion* N. F. IV/1, 3, 3), 230–234.

griechischen Handschrift mit *Orationes* des Gregor von Nazianz zu ergänzen (fol. 4, 48, 74, 87, 100, 168)[17]. Diese Blätter, die von Herbert Hunger und Otto Kresten weitgehend entziffert und gründlich analysiert wurden, enthalten Fragmente eines Heirmologions (teilweise mit paläobyzantinischer Notation), eines der wichtigsten Gesangsbücher der byzantinischen liturgischen Musik. Zu dem um die Mitte des 12. Jahrhunderts geschriebenen Codex Vind. theol. gr. 177 mit Psalmen und Oden wurden im 15. Jahrhundert vier palimpsestierte Blätter zugebunden, um einerseits einen Textverlust zu reparieren (fol. 6), andererseits um den Buchblock zu schützen (fol. 207–209); diese vier Blätter stammen aus einem im 10. Jahrhundert hergestellten Codex und enthalten Fragmente aus dem Psalmenkommentar des Diodoros von Tarsos, eines Theologen des 4. Jahrhunderts n. Chr.[18].

Der 33 Folien umfassende, vollständig aus palimpsestiertem Pergament hergestellte Codex Vind. hist. gr. 10[19] enthält in der heute lesbaren oberen Textschicht ein Fragment der metaphrastischen *Vita* des Ioannes Chrysostomos. Die griechische Minuskelschrift lässt sich ins ausgehende 12. Jahrhundert datieren. Johannes Sambucus hat den Codex in dem heutigen fragmentarischen Zustand und ohne Autorenangabe um 1,5 Dukaten erworben (siehe sein Exlibris auf fol. 1ʳ, Abb.1)[20]; er hat dabei aber nicht gewusst, dass sich unter der chrysostomischen Lebensgeschichte ein Text verbirgt, der von zentraler Bedeutung nicht nur für die griechische Sprache und Grammatik ist, sondern auch wertvolle Reste der griechischen Literatur enthält. Kurz vor dem Jahre 1960 gelang es nämlich Herbert Hunger, in

---

[17] Das aus derselben originalen Handschrift stammende fol. III wurde dabei als Schutzblatt verwendet: Vgl. Herbert HUNGER, Otto KRESTEN, *Katalog der griechischen Handschriften der Österreichischen Nationalbibliothek III/1. Codices theologici 1–100.* Wien 1976 (Museion N.F. IV/1, 3, 1), 44–47.

[18] Vgl. dazu HUNGER, KRESTEN, HANNICK, *Katalog* 1984 (s. Anm. 16), 316–327. Seit dem Frühjahr 2016 stehen uns für diese Blätter multispektrale von Mitarbeitern des Centre of Image and Material Analysis in Cultural Heritage, Wien (<http://hrsm.caa.tuwien.ac.at/>), im Rahmen des Projekts „*Analysis and Conservation of Cultural Heritage – Modern Imaging and Material Analysis Methods for the Visualization, Documentation and Classification of Historical Written Material (Manuscripts)*" hergestellte Aufnahmen zur Verfügung.

[19] Zum Codex vgl. Herbert HUNGER, *Katalog der griechischen Handschriften der Österreichischen Nationalbibliothek I. Codices historici, Codices philosophici et philologici.* Wien 1961 (Museion N. F. IV/1, 1), 15; GRUSKOVÁ, *Untersuchungen* (s. Anm. 8), 31–41, 173–178 (mit Literatur und Abbildungen).

[20] Vgl. GERSTINGER, Handschriftensammler (s. Anm. 1), 378.

zehn Blättern dieses Codex Fragmente einer Minuskelhandschrift des beginnenden 10. Jahrhunderts mit der *Allgemeinen Akzentlehre* des Griechischen (*De prosodia catholica*, Καθολικὴ προσῳδία) des Ailios Herodianos, eines der berühmtesten antiken griechischen Grammatiker, zu entdecken. Auf fol. 1ʳ–8ᵛ und 24ʳ–25ᵛ konnte Hunger mit Hilfe des UV-Lichts gründlich getilgte Reste von Buch 5, 6 und 7 dieses bedeutenden, dem Kaiser Marcus Aurelius (reg. 161–180 n. Chr.) gewidmeten Werkes entziffern. Eine erste kurze Beschreibung wurde von Hunger in dem im Jahr 1961 erschienenen Katalog veröffentlicht[21]. Im Jahre 1967, nach wiederholten Ansätzen zu verbesserten Lesungen im Laufe von etwa zehn Jahren, folgte dann eine eingehende Studie aus der Feder Hungers, auch wenn noch der größere Teil des Textes unentziffert war und viele Einzelheiten weiterhin ungeklärt bleiben mussten[22]. Dementsprechend umfasste das Ergebnis etwa 25% des Textes, bot aber dennoch wertvolles Material, darunter auch eine Rekonstruktion der originalen Blattabfolge. Erschlossen werden konnten neben mehreren Regeln der *Prosodia* und (teilweise unbekannten) Glossen zahlreiche Zitate aus schon bekannten antiken Texten, aber auch nicht wenige neue Klassikerzitate, die zur Exemplifizierung der Regel dienten[23]. Von den berühmten Namen sind hier vor allem Homer, Hesiod, Aischylos, Sophokles, Euripides, Aristophanes, Pindar, Thukydides, Aristoteles und Kallimachos zu nennen[24]. Eine hohe Resonanz unter den klassischen Philologen ließ nicht

---

[21] Vgl. HUNGER, *Katalog* (s. Anm. 19), 15. Zu Ailios Herodianos und seinem Werk vgl. bes. August LENTZ, *Herodiani Technici reliquiae. Tomus I praefationem et Herodiani prosodiam catholicam continens*. Leipzig 1867 (repr. Hildesheim 1965; *Grammatici Graeci* 3.1); Hermann SCHULTZ, Herodianos Nr. 4. RE VIII 1 (1912), 959–973; Andrew R. DYCK, Aelius Herodian: Recent Studies and Prospects for Future Research. In: *Aufstieg und Niedergang der Römischen Welt*. II: *Principat*. Bd. 34/1 (Berlin, New York 1993), 772–794.

[22] Herbert HUNGER, Palimpsest-Fragmente aus Herodians Καθολικὴ προσῳδία, Buch 5–7, Cod. Vindob. hist. gr. 10. *Jahrbuch der Österreichischen Byzantinischen Gesellschaft* 16 (1967), 1–33.

[23] Hungers Untersuchungen ermöglichten unter anderem den Nachweis, dass Herodians Καθολικὴ προσῳδία im 10. Jahrhundert in Byzanz, wenn nicht in der Originalfassung, so jedenfalls in einer ausführlicheren, an guten Zitaten reicheren Redaktion abgeschrieben worden war, als sie sich bis dahin aus den spätantiken und byzantinischen Grammatikern rekonstruieren ließ; vgl. HUNGER, Palimpsest-Fragmente (s. Anm. 22), 1 und 30.

[24] Vgl. z. B. Martin WEST, Notes on newly-discovered fragments of Greek authors. *Maia* 20 (1968), 195–205 (bes. 197–205); Johannes Th. KAKRIDIS, Ποικίλα ἑλληνικά. *Hellenica* 21 (1968), 149–159 (bes. 149–154); François LASSERRE, Trois nouvelles citations poétiques. *Museum Helveticum* 26 (1969), 80–87; Carlo GALLAVOTTI, *Empedocle: Poema fisico e lustrale*.

lange auf sich warten. Es ist daher gut zu verstehen, dass der Codex Vind. hist. gr. 10 einer der ersten Kandidaten war, als man am Beginn des 21. Jahrhundert im Rahmen des oben erwähnten EU-Projekts „Rinascimento virtuale" nach wertvollen Palimpsesten suchte, die mit Hilfe der modernsten (dementsprechend kostspieligen) multispektralen Aufnahmetechnik und Bildverarbeitung lesbar gemacht werden sollten. Zum Einsatz kam hier das spezielle, von Daniele Broia erstellte Kamerasystem RE.CO.RD der italienischen Firma Fotoscientifica aus Parma. Den Klassischen Philologen Klaus Alpers aus Hamburg, Oliver Primavesi aus München und der Autorin dieser Zeilen wurde die weitere Bearbeitung der Herodian-Fragmente anvertraut. An der Entzifferung und Analyse des Textes wird zur Zeit intensiv gearbeitet; erste Ergebnisse liegen bereits vor[25].

Schon Herbert Hunger erkannte, dass die untere Schrift der übrigen Blätter des Codex Hist. gr. 10 (d. h. fol. 9^r–23^v und 26^r–33^v) mit Herodian nichts zu tun hat[26]. Bei der oben genannten Untersuchung konnte dann festgestellt werden, dass eben diese Blätter aus einem um das Jahr 1000 (bzw. ein wenig später) geschriebenen Minuskelcodex stammen und Fragmente eines bisher unbekannten „Florilegiums" der Basiliken, des ausführlichsten gesetzgeberischen Textes des byzantinischen Rechts, enthalten. Bernard H. Stolte, ein Spezialist für die Rechtsgeschichte in Byzanz, wurde zur Kooperation eingeladen. Die entdeckte juristische Handschrift wurde nach dem heutigen Aufbewahrungsort *Florilegium Basilicorum Vindobonense*

Milano 1975, 58, 243–244; Nicolaus VAN DER BEN, *The Proem of Empedocles' Peri Physios. Towards a New Edition of All the Fragments*. Amsterdam 1975, 15, 68–69; Günther ZUNTZ, Textkritische Anmerkungen zu Aischylos' 'Hepta'. *Hermes* 111 (1983), 259–281; hier 264ff.

[25] Vgl. dazu Oliver PRIMAVESI, Klaus ALPERS, Jana GRUSKOVÁ, Aus den Untersuchungen zum Wiener Herodian-Palimpsest (in Vorbereitung); Oliver PRIMAVESI, Klaus ALPERS, Empedokles im Wiener Herodian-Palimpsest. *Zeitschrift für Papyrologie und Epigraphik* 156 (2006), 27–37; GRUSKOVÁ, *Untersuchungen* (s. Anm. 8), 35–37, 173–174 (Abbildungen). Vgl. auch Ernst GAMILLSCHEG, Der Codex des Herodian in der Österreichischen Nationalbibliothek. Zur Anwendung neuer Technologien in der Handschriftenforschung. In: Véronique Somers (Hg.), *Palimpsestes et éditions de textes: les textes littéraires. Actes du colloque tenu à Louvain-la-Neuve (septembre 2003).* Louvain-la-Neuve 2009 (*Publications de l'Institut orientaliste de Louvain* 56), 101–110 (mit Abbildungen). Seit Ende 2015 stehen multispektrale von Mitarbeitern (vor allem von Fabian Hollaus) des Wiener Centre of Image and Material Analysis in Cultural Heritage im Rahmen des in Anm. 18 genannten Projekts hergestellte Aufnahmen zur Verfügung.

[26] Vgl. HUNGER, Palimpsest-Fragmente (s. Anm. 22), 2.

genannt. Ergebnisse einer ersten Analyse liegen vor[27]: Erhalten geblieben sind hier mit Randscholien ausgestattete Fragmente (Teile bzw. Auszüge) aus den Büchern II, III, V–X, XVI und XIX der Basiliken. Besonders zu betonen ist die Tatsache, dass auf den Blättern 14 und 33 Textpassagen des bisher nur ganz fragmentarisch durch Testimonien rekonstruierten Buches XIX (teilweise mit umfangreichen Randscholien) entziffert werden konnten. Eine Edition und eine eingehende Analyse des Florilegiums sind in Vorbereitung[28].

Den philologischen Interessen des Sambucus ist es gewiss zuzuschreiben, dass er auf einer seiner Reisen einen 239 Blätter umfassenden Codex mit dem sogenannten *Etymologicum Gudianum*, einem für die byzantinische Kulturgeschichte signifikanten, im 11. Jahrhundert entstandenen und später mit Vorliebe verwendeten Lexikon, gekauft hat. Die Handschrift, die heute unter der Signatur Cod. Vind. phil. gr. 158[29] in der ÖNB aufbewahrt wird, wurde im 13. Jahrhundert in Süditalien (Salento, Terra d'Otranto) hergestellt. Die Identifizierung eines der zwei zusammenarbeitenden Kopisten als „Copista del Dioscoride" von Daniele Arnesano erlaubte eine Präzisierung des Entstehungszeitraumes und des Entstehungsortes der Handschrift[30], bei deren Herstellung durchwegs Pergamentblätter aus älteren, palimpsestier-

---

[27] Vgl. Jana GRUSKOVÁ, Zwei neue Basiliken-Handschriften in der Österreichischen Nationalbibliothek I: Paläographisch-kodikologische Analyse (mit vier Tabellen und 30 Tafeln). In: Christian Gastgeber (Hg.), *Quellen zur byzantinischen Rechtspraxis. Aspekte der Textüberlieferung, Paläographie und Diplomatik. Akten des internationalen Kongresses (Wien, 5.–7. November 2007).* Wien 2010 (Veröffentlichungen zur Byzanzforschung XXV, Denkschriften der philosophisch-historischen Klasse der ÖAW 413), 107–138, 153–182 (bes. 107–122, 154–166, mit Literatur und Abbildungen); Bernhard H. STOLTE, Zwei neue Basiliken-Handschriften in der Österreichischen Nationalbibliothek II: Rechtshistorische Analyse (mit 30 Tafeln), ebenda, 139–182 (bes. 139–146); GRUSKOVÁ, *Untersuchungen* (s. Anm. 8), 37–41, 176, 178 (mit Abbildungen). – Zum Text der Basiliken: Herman J. SCHELTEMA, (Douwe HOLWERDA), Nicolaas VAN DER WAL, *Basilicorum libri LX.* Series A: *Text.* Series B: *Scholia.* Groningen 1953–1988 (*Scripta Universitatis Groninganae*).

[28] Von Bernard H. Stolte und Jana Grusková mit Unterstützung von Otto Kresten.

[29] Zum Codex vgl. HUNGER, *Katalog* (s. Anm. 19), 261; GRUSKOVÁ, *Untersuchungen* (s. Anm. 8), 54–102; 182–211 (mit Literatur und Abbildung); Rezension: Paul CANART, *Scriptorium* 66, 1 (2012), 46*–47*. Sambucus' Exlibris befindet sich auf fol. II^v; vgl. GERSTINGER, Handschriftensammler (s. Anm. 1), 371.

[30] Vgl. Daniele ARNESANO, Il «Copista del Dioscoride». Un anonimo salentino del secolo XIII. *Bollettino dei Classici* III/24 (2003), 29–55 (Tav. I–V) (30, 41–42, 48, 49, Tav. IV); GRUSKOVÁ, *Untersuchungen* (s. Anm. 8), 59 (mit Literatur).

ten Codices verwendet wurden: aus einer Majuskelhandschrift des 9. Jahrhunderts und aus (ca.) elf verschiedenen Minuskelhandschriften des 10. bis 12. Jahrhunderts. Unter den getilgten Texten befinden sich Fragmente des Alten Testaments, eines Evangelienlektionars und hymnographischer, hagiographischer und homiletischer Texte. Besondere Bedeutung besitzen darunter die Blätter mit der griechischen Vita Τοῖς τετηρηκόσιν des Ioannes von Damaskos (*Bibliotheca hagiographica Graeca* 884; *Patrologia Graeca* 94, 429–489); es handelt sich dabei um den ältesten erhaltenen Textzeugen dieser Vita, dessen Entstehung sich paläographisch in die zweite Hälfte des 11. Jahrhunderts (bzw. um 1100) datieren lassen könnte[31]. Eine neue, eingehende Auswertung des Palimpsests liegt nun in den Händen von Robert Volk (Edition der Vita) und Erich Lamberz (vertiefte paläographische Analyse) von der Bayerischen Akademie der Wissenschaften.

Von großem Interesse sind die Entstehungsumstände jener Schulbücher und Grammatiken, mit deren Hilfe die Kontinuität des Wissens um die klassische Gräzität angestrebt wurde. Der Sambucus-Codex Vind. phil. gr. 286[32], für dessen Herstellung der im ersten Drittel des 15. Jahrhunderts in Konstantinopel tätige Kopist und Lehrer Georgios Baiophoros verantwortlich ist (fol. 13–83, +43/1)[33], enthält in seiner oberen Textschicht eine dieser Grammatiken, die *Erotemata* des Manuel Moschopulos (Ende 13./ Anfang 14. Jahrhundert)[34], eines der bedeutendsten Philologen der Palaiologenzeit. Georgios Baiophoros hat dabei Pergament aus ca. 13 älteren Minuskelhandschriften des 10.–12. Jahrhunderts herangezogen[35]. Alle diese

---

[31] Mehr dazu bei GRUSKOVÁ, *Untersuchungen* (s. Anm. 8), 55, 88–90, 203–205 (mit Literatur und Abbildungen). In der erhaltenen Überschrift auf fol. 109ʳ wird als Verfasser ein Ioannes, Patriarch von Jerusalem, genannt. Für das Palimpsest stehen seit dem Frühjahr 2016 multispektrale von Mitarbeitern des Centre of Image and Material Analysis in Cultural Heritage im Rahmen des in Anm. 18 genannten Projekts hergestellte Aufnahmen zur Verfügung.

[32] Zum Codex HUNGER, *Katalog* (s. Anm. 19), 385f.; GRUSKOVÁ, *Untersuchungen* (s. Anm. 8), 103–129, 212–218 (mit Literatur und Abbildungen); CANART, Rez. (s. Anm. 29), 46*–47*. Das Sambucus-Exlibris befindet sich auf fol. 1ʳ; vgl. GERSTINGER, Handschriftensammler (s. Anm. 1), 375.

[33] Vgl. Ernst GAMILLSCHEG, Zur handschriftlichen Überlieferung byzantinischer Schulbücher. *Jahrbuch der Österreichischen Byzantinistik* 26 (1977), 211–230 mit vier Tafeln; bes. 226f.

[34] Zu Manuel Moschopulos vgl. *Prosopographisches Lexikon der Palaiologenzeit* (*PLP*) 19373 (VIII 37).

[35] Mehr dazu bei GRUSKOVÁ, *Untersuchungen* (s. Anm. 8), 106–129, 212–218 (mit Literatur und Abbildungen).

Codices homiletischen, hagiographischen und liturgischen Inhalts stammten aller Wahrscheinlichkeit nach aus der Bibliothek seines Klosters, d. h. des Prodromu-Petra-Klosters zu Konstantinopel[36]. Erhalten geblieben sind hier z. B. Minuskelfragmente des 11. Jahrhunderts aus *Scripta anonyma adversus Iudaeos* (fol. 15^{rv}, 18^{rv}, 30^{rv}, 33^{rv}, 44^{rv}, 47^{rv}, 60^{rv}, 63^{rv})[37].

Im Jahre 1562 hat Johannes Sambucus um fünf Dukaten eine kleinformatige Handschrift des 11. Jahrhunderts von 81 Blättern juristischen Inhalts erworben, den heutigen Codex Vind. iur. gr. 18[38]. Die unterschiedliche Hand und die divergierende *mise en page* der (oberen) Schrift der ersten acht Blätter (fol. 1–8) wie auch die inhaltliche Trennung des Textes von dem danach folgenden Teil (fol. 9–81) weisen darauf hin, dass die erste Lage ursprünglich nicht zu dem restlichen Codex gehörte[39]. Für den zweiten Teil, der einen Prochironderivat und einige andere juristische Texte enthält, lässt

---

[36] Baiophoros' fruchtbare Kopistentätigkeit und seine Vorliebe für die Verwendung palimpsestierten Pergaments bei der Herstellung von Schulbüchern, von denen mehr als 20 auf uns gekommen sind, erlaubt es, einzelne Aspekte dieser historischen Wiederverwertung des kostbaren Schreibmaterials in einem Kloster der byzantinischen Hauptstadt in den ersten Jahrzehnten des 15. Jahrhunderts näher zu untersuchen. Vgl. dazu GAMILLSCHEG, Schulbücher (s. Anm. 33); Ernst GAMILLSCHEG, Zur Rekonstruktion einer konstantinopolitaner Bibliothek. *Rivista di Studi Bizantini e Slavi* I (= *Miscellanea Agostino Pertusi* I) (1981), 283–293 (284) (mit Literatur und Datierungsvorschlägen); Jana GRUSKOVÁ, Neue Ergebnisse aus der Palimpsestforschung an der Österreichischen Nationalbibliothek: Aus der Werkstatt des Schulmeisters. In: Santo Lucà (Hg.), *Libri palinsesti greci: conservazione, restauro digitale, studio*. Atti del Convegno internazionale (Roma – Grottaferrata, 21–24 aprile 2004). Roma 2008, 295–311; Annaclara CATALDI PALAU, Un nuovo manoscritto palinsesto di Giorgio Baiophoros. In: *Libri palinsesti greci* (a. a. O.), 263–277 (271, 275); DIES., *Studies in Greek manuscripts I–II*. Spoleto 2008, 197–234, 303–344 (mit Tafeln); GRUSKOVÁ, *Untersuchungen* (s. Anm. 8), 102–129, 212–218 (mit Literatur und Abbildungen).

[37] Mehr dazu bei GRUSKOVÁ, *Untersuchungen* (s. Anm. 8), 114–116.

[38] Vgl. Herbert HUNGER, unter Mitarbeit von Otto KRESTEN, *Katalog der griechischen Handschriften der ÖNB II. Codices juridici, Codices medici*. Wien 1969 (Museion N. F. IV/1, 2), 33–34; GRUSKOVÁ, *Untersuchungen* (s. Anm. 8), 130–169, 219–245 (mit Literatur und Abbildungen); CANART, Rez. (s. Anm. 29), 46*-47*. Das Exlibris *J. Sambuci P. T.* befindet sich auf fol. 1^{r}, eine eigenhändige Eintragung des Humanisten auf fol. III^{v}; vgl. GERSTINGER, Handschriftensammler (s. Anm. 1), 326 und 362 (mit berechtigten Zweifeln, dass Sambucus den Codex in Neapel angekauft haben könnte).

[39] Zum juristischen Inhalt beider Teile: Ludwig BURGMANN, Marie Theres FÖGEN, Andreas SCHMINCK, Dieter SIMON, *Repertorium der Handschriften des byzantinischen Rechts* I. Frankfurt am Main 1995 (Forschungen zur byzantinischen Rechtsgeschichte 20), 367 (Nr. 321); GRUSKOVÁ, *Untersuchungen* (s. Anm. 8), 140–142 (mit Literatur).

sich paläographisch süditalienische Herkunft postulieren[40]; die erhaltenen Kustoden weisen jedoch darauf hin, dass der Codex, dem fol. 9–81 entstammen, im Originalzustand ca. 185 Blätter umfasst haben dürfte[41]. Auf fol. III[v] gibt Sambucus folgende Wertschätzung des Buches: *Si integer esset, magni pretii esset*. Die (oberen) juristischen Texte beider Teile wurden zur Gänze auf palimpsestierten Blättern mehrerer (insgesamt ca. 14) älterer Majuskel- und Minuskelhandschriften des 6. bis 11. Jahrhunderts ursprünglich liturgischen, homiletischen, historischen, juristischen bzw. medizinischen Inhalts geschrieben[42]. Viele dieser Texte wurden bereits von Herbert Hunger und Otto Kresten bei der Katalogisierung des Codex identifiziert, einige konnten erst in den letzten Jahren entziffert und untersucht werden. Zu den erstgenannten gehören etwa die medizinischen Texte aus dem 10. Jahrhundert mit Rezepten gegen Kopfschmerzen und für Schlafmittel auf fol. 48 und 53[43] – der Arzt Johannes Sambucus hätte sie bestimmt mit Interesse gelesen. Unter den letztgenannten ist vor allem das neuentdeckte, möglicherweise aus dem ansonsten verlorenen griechischen Original der Chronik des Eusebios von Kaisareia stammende Textfragment (fol. 32+39), das sogenannte *Eusebii Chronici fragmentum Vindobonense*, zu nennen[44].

In seiner am Beginn des 4. Jahrhunderts n. Chr. verfassten *Chronik* hat Eusebios versucht, die gesamte Weltgeschichte bis in seine Zeit chronologisch

---

[40] Vgl. Guglielmo CAVALLO, La circolazione di testi giuridici in lingua greca nel Mezzogiorno medievale. In: Manlio Bellomo (Hg.), *Scuole, diritto e società nel Mezzogiorno medievale d'Italia II*. Catania 1987 (*Studi e ricerche dei „Quaderni Catanesi"* 8), 87–136 (bes. 94f., 108, 118 mit einer Abbildung); GRUSKOVÁ, *Untersuchungen* (s. Anm. 8), 131f., 138–142, 219–245 (mit Literatur und Abbildungen).

[41] Zu weiteren Details GRUSKOVÁ, *Untersuchungen* (s. Anm. 8), 138–140.

[42] Vgl. GRUSKOVÁ, *Untersuchungen* (s. Anm. 8), 132–138, 142–169.

[43] Vgl. HUNGER, KRESTEN, Katalog (s. Anm. 38), 33f.; vgl. auch Dieter HARLFINGER, Carl Wolfram BRUNSCHÖN, Maria VASILOUDI, Die griechischen medizinischen Palimpseste (mit Beispielen ihrer digitalen Lektüre), in: *Ärzte und ihre Interpreten: Medizinische Fachtexte der Antike als Forschungsgegenstand der Klassischen Philologie. Fachkonferenz zu Ehren von Diethard Nickel*. München, Leipzig 2006 (*Beiträge zur Altertumskunde* 238), 143–164 (bes. 161 mit Abbildung); GRUSKOVÁ, *Untersuchungen* (s. Anm. 8), 158–159, 239 (mit Abbildung). Die Fragmente zählen auch Ingredienzien für sogenannten Dreckapotheke auf.

[44] Mehr dazu bei GRUSKOVÁ, *Untersuchungen* (s. Anm. 8), 151–153, 234f. (mit Literatur und Abbildungen) und bei Jana GRUSKOVÁ, Zur Textgeschichte der Weltchronik des Eusebios zwischen Okzident und Orient („Eusebii Chronici fragmentum Vindobonense" – ein neues griechisches Handschriftenfragment). In: Erika Juhász (Hg.), *Byzanz und das Abendland. Begegnungen zwischen Ost und West*. Budapest 2013, 43–51 (mit Abbildung eines Details).

zu erfassen[45]. Im einleitenden Teil, in der sogenannten Χρονογραφία, bot er eine nach Völkern geordnete, quellenkritische, auf Exzerpten aus früheren, heute zumeist verlorenen, Autoren fußende Studie, in der er die chronologischen Systeme verschiedener Völker des Altertums erörterte. Den Hauptteil der *Chronik*, die sogenannten Χρονικοὶ κανόνες, bildete dann eine synchronistische Darstellung der Weltgeschichte in parallelen chronologischen Tabellen von Daten und Ereignissen. Die *Chronik* des Eusebios gehörte zu den einflussreichsten Werken der Spätantike und des Mittelalters in vielen Kulturen des Ostens und des Westens. Wesentlich trugen dazu die bald nach der Abfassung des Werkes entstandenen Übersetzungen bei, die dann eine selbständige Überlieferung und ein eigenes Nachleben in ihren Kulturbereichen entwickelten, wie etwa die von Hieronymus angefertigte, leicht erweiterte lateinische Übersetzung des zweiten Buches, d. h. der chronologischen Tabellen (*Canones*)[46], oder die im 6. bzw. (nach den jüngsten Untersuchungen eher) im 5. Jahrhundert entstandene armenische Übersetzung der gesamten *Chronik*[47]. Es waren gerade diese Übersetzungen und daneben zahlreiche spätere, auf die *Chronik* des Eusebios zurückgreifende Autoren, besonders der am Ende des 8. bzw. zu Beginn des 9. Jahrhunderts tätige byzantinische Gelehrte Georgios Synkellos in seinem Werk Ἐκλογὴ χρονογραφίας[48], die das

---

[45] Vgl. u. a. *Clavis patrum Graecorum* (CPG) 3494; Alden A. MOSSHAMMER, *The Chronicle of Eusebius and Greek Chronographic Tradition*. Lewisburg, London 1979, bes. 15–83 (mit Literatur); Richard W. BURGESS, *Studies in Eusebian and Post-Eusebian Chronography*. Stuttgart 1999, bes. 21–110.

[46] Vgl. *Clavis patrum Latinorum* (CPL) 615c; *Clavis patrum Graecorum* (CPG) 3494; Rudolf HELM, *Eusebius Werke VII: Die Chronik des Hieronymus. Hieronymi Chronicon.* 1. Teil: *Text*. Berlin 1913 (*Die griechischen christlichen Schriftsteller* 24); 2. Teil: *Lesarten der Handschriften und Quellenkritischer Apparat zur Chronik*. Berlin 1926 (*Die griechischen christlichen Schriftsteller* 34); verbesserte Auflage in einem Band: Berlin ²1956 (*Die griechischen christlichen Schriftsteller* 47); Berlin ³1984 (Nachdruck mit einer Vorbemerkung von Ursula Treu).

[47] Vgl. u. a. Armenuhi DROST-ABGARJAN, Ein neuer Fund zur armenischen Version der Eusebios-Chronik. In: Martin Wallraff (Hg.), *Julius Africanus und die christliche Weltchronistik*. Berlin, New York 2006, 255–262 (hier 255; zur Datierung 256); Alfred SCHOENE, Heinrich PETERMANN, *Eusebi Chronicorum libri duo*. Vol. I: *Eusebi Chronicorum liber prior*. Berlin 1875; Alfred SCHOENE, Heinrich PETERMANN, Emil ROEDIGER, *Eusebi Chronicorum libri duo*. Vol. II: *Eusebi Chronicorum canonum quae supersunt*. Berlin 1866; Josef KARST, *Eusebius Werke V: Die Chronik. Aus dem Armenischen übersetzt mit textkritischem Commentar*. Leipzig 1911 (*Die griechischen christlichen Schriftsteller* 20).

[48] Vgl. Alden A. MOSSHAMMER, *Georgii Syncelli Ecloga chronographica*. Leipzig 1984. Vgl. auch MOSSHAMMER, *Chronicle* 1979 (s. Anm. 45), 29–30, 38–41.

Werk der modernen Welt übermittelt haben, da das griechische Original des Eusebios die Neuzeit nicht erreicht hat. Es lässt sich daher gut verstehen, dass die Überraschung groß war, als vor ein paar Jahren in der unteren Textschicht von fol. 32^{rv}+39^{rv} der Sambucushandschrift Codex Vind. iur. gr. 18 ein vier Codexseiten umfassendes griechisches Fragment aus dem ersten Buch der *Chronik* des Eusebios, aus dem Kapitel „Wie die Chaldäer die Chronik schreiben", identifiziert werden konnte. Den unteren, einspaltig zu 20 Zeilen pro Seite angeordneten, parallel zur oberen Schrift verlaufenden griechischen Minuskeltext hat eine ins 10. Jahrhundert (vielleicht sogar ein wenig früher) datierbare Hand geschrieben. Die weitgehende Übereinstimmung mit der armenischen Übersetzung erlaubt den Schluss, dass das Wiener Doppelblatt aus einer direkten Abschrift des griechischen Originals bzw. aus einer Abschrift der von Mosshammer vermuteten gemeinsamen Vorlage der armenischen Übersetzung und der bei Synkellos erhaltenen Exzerpte[49] gestammt haben könnte[50].

Der Historiker und Philologe Johannes Sambucus, der halb Europa nach neuen Texten und verborgenen Handschriften durchforstet hatte, wäre gewiss begeistert gewesen, dass sich in seinen Handschriften ein solcher Schatz an Resten wichtiger Textzeugen der griechischen und der byzantinischen Literatur erhalten hat.

---

[49] Vgl. MOSSHAMMER 1984 (s. Anm. 48), XXVI.
[50] Mehr dazu in den in Anm. 45 genannten Beiträgen. Für eine genauere Erfassung des Wiener Fragments wurden die beiden Blätter im Rahmen des in Anm. * genannten FWF-Projekts in Kooperation mit dem technischen Team der *Early Manuscripts Electronic Library* (EMEL) aus California (<http://emel-library.org/>) im Jahre 2013 multispektral aufgenommen; die Bilder wurden danach durch ein Team von imaging scientists speziell verarbeitet, um die getilgte Schrift lesbar zu machen. An der weiteren Entzifferung und Analyse des Fragments wird zur Zeit intensiv gearbeitet; vgl. Jana GRUSKOVÁ, Olivier GENGLER, The Vienna Greek Palimpsest of the Chronicle of Eusebius (Codex Vind. iur. gr. 18, fols. 32 and 39) (in Vorbereitung).

Die *editio princeps* der *Dionysiaka* des Nonnos von Panopolis (1569)

Ex bibliotheca Ioannis Sambuci

HERBERT BANNERT (Wien)

ΝΟΝΝΟΥ
ΠΑΝΟΠΟΛΙΤΟΥ
ΔΙΟΝΥΣΙΑΚΑ.

NONNI PANOPOLITAE
DIONYSIACA,
NVNC PRIMVM IN LVCEM EDITA,
EX
Bibliotheca Ioannis Sambuci Pannonij.

CVM *lectionibus*, *& coniecturis Gerarti Falkenburgij Nouiomagi*, *& Indice copioso.*

ANTVERPIÆ,
Ex officina Chriſtophori Plantini.
cIɔ Iɔ LXIX.

Abb. 1: Titelblatt der *editio princeps* der *Dionysiaka*.
Νόννου Πανοπολίτου Διονυσιακά. [...] Nunc primum in lucem edita, ex Bibliotheca Ioannis Sambuci Pannonii [...]. Antverpiae: Ex officina Christophori Plantini 1569 (Wien, Universitätsbibliothek I 249.157)

Im Jahre 1583 ließ Johannes Sambucus auf einem mit 25. März datierten, einseitig beschriebenen und in drei Spalten gegliederten, bei Leonhard Nassinger in Wien[1] gedruckten Folioblatt eine Zusammenstellung seiner gedruckten, noch nicht gedruckten und in Planung befindlichen Ausgaben und sonstigen Arbeiten erscheinen, zu einem Zeitpunkt, als er innerhalb eines Jahres keine neuen Publikationen vorweisen konnte: Die lange geplante Ausgabe des Dioskurides (*De materia medica*), in die Sambucus zu Recht große Hoffnungen gesetzt hatte, war gescheitert, und auch manch andere Pläne – Ausgaben von Aristoteles' *De generatione et corruptione* und der *Historia animalium* – ließen sich nicht verwirklichen, verhindert zum Teil durch rivalisierende Bearbeiter, zum Teil durch das Faktum, dass in Wien ein versierter und geschäftsfreudiger Drucker fehlte und Sambucus somit von den Zentren des Buchdrucks abgeschnitten war[2]. Den *Catalogus librorum quos Ioan. Sambucus vel suos typis edidit, vel bibliothecae aliena pignora prodidit, vel praecipue adhuc divulganda prae manibus habet*[3] hat er wohl aus Enttäuschung darüber publik gemacht, dass viele wertvolle Handschriften, deren Herausgabe er selbst in Angriff genommen oder Anderen überlassen hatte, teils aus Unfähigkeit, teils durch Neid verhindert, nicht mit der gebotenen Schnelligkeit der Publikation zugeführt werden konnten. Die Selbstbibliographie sollte eine Rechtfertigung sein, und die Enttäuschung manifestiert sich in den vielen Fehlern und Ungenauigkeiten, die darauf hindeuten,

---

[1] Nassinger druckte 1579/80 bis 1591 in Wien, zunächst unter der Adresse „in der Weyhenburgk bey den Blawen Lilgen" (heute Weihburggasse, Ecke Liliengasse, Wien, 1. Bezirk; in der nächsten Parallelstraße, in Richtung Stephansplatz, befand sich das Stadtwohnhaus von Johannes Sambucus, Singerstraße 3). Vgl. Anton MAYER, *Wiens Buchdrucker-Geschichte 1482–1882*. Wien 1883–1887, Bd. 1, 128–135; Christoph RESKE, *Die Buchdrucker des 16. und 17. Jahrhunderts im deutschen Sprachraum*. 2., überarbeitete und erweiterte Auflage, Wiesbaden 2015 (Beiträge zum Buch- und Bibliothekswesen 51), 972.

[2] Hans GERSTINGER, *Die Briefe des Johannes Sambucus (Zsamboky), 1554–1584*. Mit einem Anhang: Die Sambucusbriefe im Kreisarchiv von Trnava, von Anton VANTUCH. Wien, Graz 1968 (Sitzungsberichte der Österreichischen Akademie der Wissenschaften, philosophisch-historische Klasse 255), 286–289 (zu Aristoteles) und 297–302 (zu Dioskurides).

[3] Der *Catalogus* wurde bekannt gemacht von Gedeon BORSA, James E. WALSH, *Eine gedruckte Selbstbibliographie von Johannes Sambucus*. Magyar Könyvszemle 85 (1965), 127–133 <http://mek.oszk.hu/03300/03301/html/bgkvti_2/bgki0262de.htm> (3. 10. 2016).

dass Sambucus das Blatt rasch und aus dem Gedächtnis zusammengestellt hat. Denn bei der Jagd nach Publikationen, nach Erstausgaben, hatten Andere wohl die besseren Verbindungen, zu Buchdruckern und auch zu Geldgebern[4].

JOHANNES SAMBUCUS UND SEINE HANDSCHRIFT DER *DIONYSIAKA*:

COD. VIND. PHIL. GR. 45 UND 51

Johannes Sambucus wurde im Juli 1531 in Tyrnau (Nagyszombat, heute Trnava in der Slowakischen Republik) geboren und starb am 13. Juni 1584 als Kaiserlicher Hofrat, Hofmedicus und Hofhistoriographus in Wien[5]. Seine Bibliothek von ca. 3000 Drucken und Handschriften war zu seiner Zeit vermutlich die größte Privatbibliothek der Welt[6]. Auf seinen Reisen durch Deutschland, Belgien, Holland, Frankreich und vor allem Italien hat er 22 Jahre lang auch Handschriften griechischer und lateinischer Autoren gesammelt und viele davon für Erstausgaben selbst herangezogen oder an Andere weitergegeben[7].

---

[4] Vgl. Hans GERSTINGER, *Johannes Sambucus als Philologe*. Wiener Studien 79 (1966), 551–556 (552 Anm. 1 aus 551); Gábor ALMÁSI, *The Uses of Humanism. Andreas Dudith (1533–1589), Johannes Sambucus (1531–1584), and the East Central European Republic of Letters*. Leiden 2009 (Brill's Studies in Intellectual History 185), 225f.

[5] Zur Biographie des Sambucus: GERSTINGER, Briefe (s. Anm. 2), 11–20; ALMÁSI (s. Anm. 4), 145–197; Richard HOCHE, Allgemeine Deutsche Biographie 30 (1890), 307f.; Gábor BARTA, Neue Deutsche Biographie 22 (2005), 405f.; Endre BACH, *Un humaniste hongrois en France. Jean Sambucus et ses relations littéraires (1551–1584)*. Szeged 1932; Eleonore NOVOTNY, *Johannes Sambucus (1531–1584). Leben und Werk*. Wien: phil. Diss. (masch.) 1975.

[6] Vgl. Hans GERSTINGER, *Johannes Sambucus als Handschriftensammler*. In: Festschrift der Nationalbibliothek in Wien. Hg. zur Feier des 200jährigen Bestehens des Gebäudes. Wien 1926, 251–400 (zu den Handschriften); einen Katalog der Bibliothek hat Pál Gulyás 1941 zusammengestellt: Pál GULYÁS, *A Zsámboky-könyvtár katalógusa (1587)*. Szeged 1992 (Adattár XVI–XVIII. századi szellemi mozgalmaink történetéhez 12/2), Neudruck von: Pál GULYÁS, *Sámboki János könyvtára* [Die Bibliothek des Johannes Sambucus]. Budapest 1941. Die Handschriften bilden einen erheblichen Teil des Handschriftenbestands der Österreichischen Nationalbibliothek in Wien.

[7] Die Paratexte von Sambucus' Editionen bzw. Editionen *ex bibliotheca Sambuci* liegen in einer modernen Edition vor; eine umfangreiche (im vorliegenden Band in englischer Fassung aktualisierte) Einleitung ist Sambucus' gelehrten Netzwerken und philologischen Prinzipien gewidmet: Gábor ALMÁSI, Gábor Farkas KISS, *Humanistes du bassin des Carpates II. Johannes Sambucus*. Turnhout 2014 (Europa humanistica 14).

Der vielleicht bedeutendste Kauf gelang Sambucus im Winter 1563, als er auf einer ausgedehnten Italienreise nach Tarent gekommen war und dort die um 1550 geschriebene Handschrift der *Dionysiaka* des Nonnos von Panopolis aus dem Besitz des Arsenios Apostolios[8], Erzbischofs von Monemvasia, um 38 + 7 = 45 Gold-Florin erwerben konnte: Er vermerkt auf Folio 1a des Codex, der sich heute als Cod. phil. gr. 45 in der Österreichischen Nationalbibliothek befindet[9]: *Tarenti emit Sambucus 38* (korrigiert aus 28) Δ *et Saphiro valoris 7* Δ *1563*. Der Preis ist für eine so junge Handschrift ungewöhnlich hoch, der Grund ist wohl, dass der Text noch unediert war und daher der Preis gesteigert werden konnte[10]. Die Handschrift wurde 1754 neu gebunden, der Besitzvermerk des Arsenios fehlt heute. Im letzten Satz des an den Leser gerichteten Nachworts der *editio princeps* schreibt Falkenburg:

> Vale, et Joanni Sambuco, qui Nonni exemplar, quo olim Arsenius Monembasiae Episcopus usus fuit, Tarenti a se XLV aureis emtum, benignissime nobiscum communicavit, bene precare.
> Νόννου Πανοπολίτου Διονυσιακά 1569, 862

Es ist dies heute der einzige Hinweis auf den Vorbesitzer, und der Preis ist aus der Notiz in der Handschrift errechnet – wohl auch, um den besonderen Wert und die hohen Kosten noch einmal zu betonen: Unmittelbar zuvor hat Falkenburg die Hoffnung ausgesprochen, dass die mühevolle Arbeit an der Edition auch dazu führen möge, in italienischen Bibliotheken verborgene Nonnos-Handschriften zu suchen – bis heute leider ohne Erfolg[11].

---

[8] Arsenios Apostolios (1468/69–1535), aus Kandia in Kreta, arbeitete als Kopist griechischer Werke in Kreta, Florenz und Venedig, besorgte Ausgaben u. a. der Euripidesscholien und war als Sprachlehrer tätig (und Griechischlehrer des Franciscus Portus). Vgl. Deno John GEANOKOPLOS, *Bisanzio e il Rinascimento. Umanisti Greci a Venezia e diffusione del Greco (1400–1535)*. Roma 1967, 195–237; Pieter G. BIETENHOLZ, *Contemporaries of Erasmus* I (1985), 68f. Vgl. auch ALMÁSI, KISS (s. Anm. 7), 124f. Anm. 623.

[9] Die Handschrift ist, wie die anderen *Dionysiaka*-Handschriften auch, über Zwischenstufen eine Abschrift nach L (Cod. Laurentianus Mediceus 32.16); vgl. *Nonni Panopolitani Dionysiaca recensuit Arthurus* LUDWICH, 2 Bde. Leipzig 1909–1911, Bd. I, X–XVI, und *Nonni Panopolitani Dionysiaca recognovit Rudolfus* KEYDELL, 2 Bde. Berlin 1959, Bd. I, *24–*35; siehe auch unten Anm. 38. Zur Geschichte der Handschrift und zu den Umständen des Erwerbs durch Sambucus vgl. GERSTINGER (s. Anm. 6), 290 und 299.

[10] Dass beim Kauf von Handschriften Schmuckstücke, Ringe oder Edelsteine zusätzlich gegeben wurden, ist auch sonst bezeugt; vgl. GERSTINGER (s. Anm. 6), 299.

[11] Vgl. GERSTINGER (s. Anm. 6), 299 mit Anm. 1.

Die *Dionysiaka* des Nonnos waren zu dieser Zeit in literarischen Kreisen bekannt, denn schon Angelo Poliziano (1454–1494) hatte auf sie hingewiesen, von der Existenz der Handschrift in Florenz aber scheint man nichts gewusst zu haben[12]. Da die Paraphrase auf das Johannes-Evangelium um die Jahrhundertwende bei Aldus Manutius in Venedig zum ersten Mal gedruckt worden war (1504[13]), wusste man wohl um den Dichter, und auch im Widmungsschreiben des Gerart Falkenburg an Johannes Sambucus in der *editio princeps* der *Dionysiaka* ist deutlich ausgesprochen, dass die Paraphrase gelesen und studiert und gerade dadurch die Sehnsucht nach dem anderen Werk gesteigert wurde[14]:

> sed multo maximum est tuum in nos promeritum, quod hunc nobis uberrimum laetissimumque universae eloquentiae, et poëseos fontem, tot annis frustra, desideratum aperueris.

DIE *EDITIO PRINCEPS* DER *DIONYSIAKA* DES NONNOS VON PANOPOLIS
BETREUT VON GERART FALKENBURG, GEDRUCKT IN DER OFFICINA PLANTINIANA, ANTWERPEN 1569

Gerart Falkenburg[15], um 1538 in Nimwegen (Nijmegen, Neumagen, Grafschaft Geldern, Hansestadt seit 1402) geboren, studierte in Bourges bei Jacobus Cuiacius (Jacques Cujas, 1520–1590), dem berühmten antiken Rechtshistoriker, und später in Italien die Rechte, war dann in Paris bei Auratus (Jean Dorat, 1508–1588) und im Jahre 1563 in England[16]; mit Janus

---

[12] S. unten Anm. 38.
[13] Zur editio Aldina und zu ihrer Datierung vgl. Gianfranco AGOSTI, *Prima fortuna umanistica di Nonno*. In: Vincenzo Fera, Augusto Guida (Hgg.), *Vetustatis indagator. Scritti offerti a Filippo Di Benedetto*. Messina 1999 (*Percorsi dei Classici* 1), 89–114; hier 90–105.
[14] Sambucus besaß die Paraphrase in der mit einer lateinischen Übersetzung versehenen Ausgabe des Ioannes Bordatus (Paris 1561): GULYÁS (s. Anm. 6), 312 Nr. 1742/1.
[15] Zu Gerart (Geraart, Gerhard, Gerhardus) Falkenburg ist nicht allzuviel bekannt; vgl. Friedrich August ECKSTEIN, *Nomenclator philologorum*. Leipzig 1871, 152; Conrad BURSIAN, *Allgemeine Deutsche Biographie* 6 (1877), 555. Vgl. ALMÁSI, KISS (s. Anm. 7), LIX–LXI.
[16] Einen Brief von Jean Dorat an Falkenburg, der auf Juni 1570 zu datieren ist und in dem Dorat von einigen von ihm übersetzten Partien aus den *Dionysiaka* (nicht aber von der bereits erschienenen Ausgabe) spricht, hat Marie-Jeanne DURRY, *Une lettre inedite de Dorat*. In: *Mélanges d'Histoire Littéraire de la Renaissance offerts à Henri Chamard*. Paris 1951, 63–69, be-

Dousa d. Ä., Justus Lipsius, Hadrianus Junius und anderen stand er in Briefkontakt[17]. Ende der 1560er Jahre war er in Antwerpen und wurde von Plantin oder von Sambucus selbst oder über Vermittlung eines der beiden mit der editio princeps der Dionysiaka betraut, doch dann verliert sich seine Spur, und auch Hadrianus Junius konnte in einem Ende des Jahres 1574 zu datierenden Brief an Falkenburg nur Vermutungen über seinen Aufenthalt anstellen und bedauert, außer dem Widmungsschreiben in der Ausgabe der Dionysiaka von 1569 nichts mehr von ihm gelesen zu haben[18]: *Nihil tui apud me est praeter epistulam illam, eruditionis plenam, quae Nonno praefixa legitur.* Später war Falkenburg im Dienste des Breslauer Patriziers und Bankiers Nicolaus Rehdiger d. J. (1525–1587) und im Gefolge des Grafen Hermann von Neuenahr d. J. (1520–1578) in Köln, als dessen Gesandter er schließlich im Jahre 1577 bei Sambucus in Wien auch zu Gast war[19]. Am 8. September 1578 ist er an den Folgen eines Reitunfalls gestorben.

Die editio princeps der Dionysiaka ist in einem schön gedruckten, mit kunstvoller (stark ligierter und nicht leicht lesbarer) griechischer Typographie versehenen Band, dem – unter Einarbeitung der in den *Miscellanea* von Angelo Poliziano (1454–1494) schon 80 Jahre zuvor veröffentlichten Notizen und Verbesserungen – reichlich Varianten von Falkenburg selbst, von Karl von Utenhove (1536–1600), von Wilhelm Canter (1542–1575), gelegentlich auch von seinem Bruder Theodor Canter (1545–1617), und von Johannes Goropius Becanus (1519–1572), nicht aber solche des Sambucus beigegeben sind (auf insgesamt 40 Seiten[20]), Mitte bis Ende März 1569 in

---

kannt gemacht. Der Aufenthalt in England lässt sich aus einem der letzten Sätze des Widmungsschreibens belegen (datiert mit 22. Februar 1569), wo es über Karl von Utenhove heißt: *cuius acerrimum ingenium multorum mihi sermone Lutetiae cognitum, in Anglia annis abhinc amplius quinque, non sine maxima voluptate me perspexisse memini.*

[17] Einige Briefe Falkenburgs an Ianus Dousa sind von diesem publiziert, darunter ein die Ausgabe der Dionysiaka betreffendes Schreiben: Iani Dousae Nordovicis schediasma succidaneum nuperis ad Tibullum praecidaneis addendum. Eiusdem ad familiarem quandam Gerardi Falkenburgii Epistolam responsio, ab adulescentulo iam olim commentata et scripta [...] Gerardi Falkenburgii Epigrammata quaedam Graeca. Antverpiae: Ex officina Christophori Plantini 1582, 43–45.

[18] Hadr. Junii Epistolae (s. unten Anm. 21), 477f.

[19] Sambucus an Theodor Zwinger (12. November 1577); GERSTINGER (s. Anm. 2), 229f.

[20] *Editio princeps*, 863–899: *Gerarti Falkenburgii Nouiomagi in Nonni Dionysiaca lectiones, et coniecturae*; 901–902 folgt eine von Plantinus beigefügte, nachträglich eingesandte Liste mit Lesarten von Wilhelm Canter, die nur den ersten Band der Handschrift betrifft (*Gulielmi*

Antwerpen bei Christophorus Plantinus erschienen (das Widmungsschreiben an Sambucus ist mit 22. Februar 1569 datiert).

> Νόννου Πανοπολίτου Διονυσιακά. Nonni Panopolitae Dionysiaca, Nunc primum in lucem edita, ex Bibliotheca Ioannis Sambuci Pannonii. Cum lectionibus, et coniecturis Gerarti Falkenburgii Nouiomagi, et Indice copioso. Antverpiae: Ex officina Christophori Plantini MDLXIX.

Über die Vorbereitungen zur Edition und über Verbindungen zwischen Sambucus und Falkenburg ist nur wenig bekannt. Hadrianus Junius, der sich jedenfalls mit dem Text beschäftigt und dessen Textvorschläge Falkenburg in sein Verzeichnis der *lectiones et coniecturae* aufgenommen hat, schreibt in einem auf den 24. Mai 1564 datierten Brief aus Antwerpen an Sambucus[21]:

> Eunapium ut describendum cures, et si fieri potest etiam Nonnii Dionysiaca, quod ad Epithetorum meorum editionem maxime necessaria videantur, obsecratum te velim.

Daraus ergibt sich, dass zu dieser Zeit die Handschrift offenbar nicht in Antwerpen zur Verfügung stand.

Der Druckvorgang selbst, mit dem Sambucus, wie es scheint, nicht befasst war, und die Zeit der Bearbeitung und bis zur Auslieferung der Ausgabe in Antwerpen ist hingegen gut belegt und kann nachvollzogen werden: In einem in großer Eile (*raptim*) geschriebenen Brief vom 8. Jänner 1568 an Theodor Zwinger in Basel, der als Korrektor für die Offizin Oporinus tätig

---

Canteri Emendationes Nonni partis prioris). Lesarten des Sambucus sind nicht ausgewiesen. – Von Johannes Goropius Becanus ist, nach dem Widmungsschreiben Falkenburgs an Sambucus, ein in der alkäischen Strophe verfasstes Gedicht an Sambucus dem Text der *editio princeps* des Nonnos vorangestellt.

[21] Hadr. Junii Epistolae, Quibus accedit Eiusdem Vita et Oratio De Artium liberalium dignitate. Dordrechti: Apud Vincentium Caimax, Bibliopolam, Anno 1552 (recte 1652), 386; der Brief ist überschrieben: 385 *Hadr. Iun. Ioanni Sambuco, Pannonio ni fallor*. Das angesprochene Werk ist: Nomenclator, omnium rerum propria nomina variis linguis explicata indicans, Hadriano Iunio medico auctore. Antverpiae: ex officina Christophori Plantini 1567. Eine Komplikation ergibt sich daraus, dass Hadrianus Junius im selben Brief (und in anderen Briefen) auch über seine Arbeit an der Edition des „Nonnius" (Nonius Marcellus, *De compendiosa doctrina*) spricht, die mit dem Titel (des ersten Buches) *De proprietate sermonum* 1565 bei Plantin gedruckt wurde. Eine Handschrift des Nonius Marcellus befand sich offenbar nicht im Besitze des Sambucus, denn aus dem Widmungsschreiben des Hadrianus Iunius an Kaiser Maximilian II. geht hervor, dass Sambucus ihn auf eine Handschrift im Besitz des Hofes aufmerksam gemacht hat.

war, kündigt Sambucus die Ausgabe des Nonnos als im Druck befindlich an[22]: *Scis Nonni Διονυσιακά et ἐκλογὰς φυσικάς Stobaei nunc a Plantino imprimi et alia brevi.* Am 25. März 1568 schreibt Plantinus an den Kardinal Antoine Perrenot de Granvelle (1517–1586)[23]: „J'ay reçu Dionysiaca Nonni, que m'a envoyé Mr. Sambucus pour l'imprimer et quelques autres livres grecques aussi." Am 24. August 1568 schreibt Sambucus an Crato von Kraftheim in Wien, dass die *Dionysiaka* bis zur Frankfurter Messe im Herbst verfügbar sein werden[24]: *Nonni Διονυσιακὰ hoc Francfurtensi mercatu habebimus.* Am 1. September 1568 heißt es auch in einem Brief an Petrus Victorius in Florenz, dass dieser die Ausgabe in zwei Monaten mit vielen Verbesserungen des Texts erhalten werde[25]: *Nonni quoque Διονυσι(α)κὰ intra duos menses elegantissime impressa typis non paucis locis correctis habebis.* In einem Brief an Fulvio Orsini (1529–1600), der nicht datiert, aber zwischen 26. März und 3. April 1569 verfasst ist, schreibt inzwischen Christoph Plantin[26]: *Dionysiaca Nonnii Graeca, alienis sumptibus adjuta, (mirum etenim quantum his temporibus nostrae frigeant tabernae) impressi.*

Am 29. März 1569 schickt Falkenburg ein Exemplar aus Antwerpen an Ianus Dousa nach Noordwijk und teilt mit, dass Hadrianus Junius schon eines erhalten hat[27]. Am 6. April 1569 berichtet dann Sambucus Petrus Victorius in Florenz, dass er neue Handschriften des Aischylos entdeckt habe, bei denen freilich auch, wie im Laurentianus 32.9, der Anfang der *Choephoren* fehlt, dafür aber ein Rollenverzeichnis beigegeben ist, und erwähnt dabei, dass die *Dionysiaka* schon erschienen seien, er aber noch kein Exemplar erhalten habe[28]: *Διονυσιακὰ iam excurrunt, sed impressum integrum exemplum ad me adhuc non pervenit.* Ein in weißes Pergament gebundenes

---

[22] GERSTINGER (s. Anm. 2), 83f. mit Kommentar.
[23] *Correspondance de Christophe Plantin*. Publiée par Max ROOSES. Bd. 3. Antwerpen 1911, 41 (online zugänglich: <http://archive.org/stream/correspondancede03>). Vgl. auch die Angaben bei GERSTINGER (s. Anm. 2), 84, mit weiteren Hinweisen.
[24] GERSTINGER (s. Anm. 2), 88.
[25] Es bleibt unklar, ob Sambucus damit auch eigene Korrekturen meint, die aber – soweit ich sehe – nicht ausgewiesen sind. GERSTINGER (s. Anm. 2), 89f.
[26] *Correspondance de Christophe Plantin* (s. Anm. 23), Bd. 2. Antwerpen 1885, 45 <http://archive.org/details/correspondancede02plan>. Am Ende des Briefes heißt es: *Aveo scire, num in Bibliotheca Farnesiana sint Nonnii Dionysiaca. D. Falkenbergus te plurimum salutat.* (2, 46).
[27] Iani Dousae schediasma (s. Anm. 17), 43–45.
[28] GERSTINGER (s. Anm. 2), 99f.

Exemplar hat er schließlich unter dem Datum 8. Juni 1569 Kaiser Maximilian überreicht und auf das Verso der Vorsatzseite eine eigenhändige Widmung geschrieben:

> Maximiliano II Invictissimo / clementissimoque Caesari D(omi)n(o) / D(omi)n(o) suo gratissimo etc. / Infimus Clientulus et subditissimus / D. Joan Sambucus. V(estrae) M(aiestatis) / Cons(iliarius) et histor(icus) / MDLXIX. 8. Junii.

Allerdings erscheint die Widmung nicht sehr sorgfältig ausgeführt, in gewöhnlicher Schrift geschrieben, mit in den Briefen vielfach bezeugten Floskeln. Dies könnte eine von Gábor Almási beobachtete zeitliche Koinzidenz erklären: Die Widmung ist mit 8. Juni datiert, drei Tage vor einer Verhandlung in einem langwierigen Erbschaftsstreit im Zusammenhang mit Liegenschaften in Trnava, für die Sambucus Kaiser Maximilian um Intervention gebeten hat, die dann auch zur Inbesitznahme der Liegenschaften durch den Kaiser und damit dem Entzug des Verfügungsrechts für die Gegner des Sambucus geführt hat[29].

DAS WIDMUNGSSCHREIBEN VON GERART FALKENBURG AN JOHANNES SAMBUCUS

Das von Falkenburg der Ausgabe vorangestellte Widmungsschreiben an Johannes Sambucus ist nach einer Vorlage gesetzt, die vorne in den ersten Band der Handschrift (cod. Vind. Phil. gr. 45) eingeklebt wurde und erhalten ist (s. Abb. 5)[30]. Die Vorlage, in gut lesbarer Schrift, wurde von einem Schreiber geschrieben, ist aber an manchen Stellen von einer anderen Hand, wohl von Falkenburg selbst, korrigiert. Außer dem wiederholten Dank an Sambucus für die Möglichkeit, den Text zu edieren, finden sich auch Angaben zu Autor und Werk, die das Wissen um Nonnos zu dieser Zeit dokumentieren – und auch dokumentieren, dass lange Zeit nichts wesentlich darüber hinaus mitgeteilt werden konnte.

---

[29] ÖNB *35.D.21; ALMÁSI (s. Anm. 4), 171 mit Anm. 104. Wann Sambucus seine Belegexemplare erhalten hat, ist unbekannt, doch erscheint der Zeitraum von Ende März bis Anfang Juni für einen dem Kaiser gewidmeten Band etwas lange. Ein Exemplar hatte er jedenfalls auch in seiner eigenen Bibliothek: GULYÁS (s. Anm. 6), 313 Nr. 1748. – Die Universitätsbibliothek Wien besitzt ein in geprägtes braunes Leder gebundenes Exemplar aus dem Besitz des Wiener Jesuitenkollegs (Vermerk auf dem Titelblatt: *Collegii Socie: Jesu Cata: inscriptus Anno 1609*; s. Abb. 1 auf S. 162).

[30] Vgl. die kritische Edition des Widmungsbriefs im Anhang, unten S. 184–205.

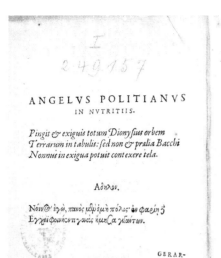

Abb. 2: Widmungsschreiben Falkenburgs an Sambucus.
Νόννου Πανοπολίτου Διονυσιακά. [...] Nunc primum in lucem edita, ex Bibliotheca Ioannis Sambuci Pannonii [...]. Antverpiae: Ex officina Christophori Plantini 1569 (Wien, Universitätsbibliothek I 249.157)

Falkenburg stellt fest, dass über die Lebenszeit und die Lebensumstände des Nonnos nichts bekannt ist außer seiner Heimatstadt Panopolis in Unterägypten, einem Zentrum der Bildung und der Rhetorik. Die Identität mit dem gleichnamigen Bischof von Edessa lehnt er ab[31], bezeichnet Nonnos als einen Zeitgenossen des Heliodor und des Synesios, und hält fest, dass die Kenntnis des Namens des Autors Angelo Poliziano verdankt wird. Den Namen erklärt er sich damit, dass in Ägypten fromme Männer und Frauen

---

[31] Einen Überblick über die Diskussion der Identität mit Nonnos von Edessa gibt ACCORINTI (s. Anm. 38), 1110–1111.

Nonni und *Nonnae* genannt worden wären[32]; dies ergibt sich wohl aus dem Verdienst, das sich Nonnos durch die Paraphrase des Johannesevangeliums erworben hat, die von Falkenburg anerkannt und gelobt und, infolge der vergleichbaren Art der Darstellung und auch ähnlicher Ausdrücke und auch Versteile, die er in den Anmerkungen verzeichnet hat, als Beweis für die Identität des Autors herangezogen wird. Zum Thema der Dionysostaten erwähnt Falkenburg die verlorenen *Bassarika* des Dionysios[33]; zur Frage nach einem weiteren Epos des Nonnos, einer Gigantomachie, deren Existenz man aus dem Zweizeiler in der *Anthologia Graeca* 9, 198 erschlossen hat, verweist Falkenburg nachdrücklich darauf, dass Nonnos die Inder als *Gigantes* bezeichnet und infolgedessen die Bemerkung „ich habe scharenweise Giganten niedergemäht" durch den Inhalt der *Dionysiaka* ausreichend gerechtfertigt ist[34]. Falkenburg lobt den reichen Inhalt, die originellen Wortbildungen, die klingenden und eingängigen Epitheta, die man nirgends sonst finden kann, er lobt die Nähe des Gedichts zu Homer und erklärt es geradezu zu einem vollständigen Ersatz des homerischen Epos. Einen weiteren Nutzen sieht er darin, dass durch die *Dionysiaka* die Geschichten bei Ovid ebenso erschlossen und ergänzt werden, wie dereinst Vergil durch die Kenntnis Homers bereichert wurde (et vice versa)[35]. Umso weniger verständlich sei es, dass Kritiker das Gedicht, und zwar zumeist, ohne es wirk-

---

[32] Der locus classicus für das Wort *nonna* ist Hieronymus, Ad Eustochium de custodia virginitatis (epist. 22, 16): *illae* (sc. viduae) [...] *castae vocantur et nonnae*; vgl. auch epist. 117, 6, und Regula Benedicti cap. 63, 12 (*nonnus* als ehrenvolle Bezeichnung für einen älteren Mönch: *sed priores iuniores suos fratrum nomine, iuniores autem priores suos nonnos vocent, quod intellegitur paterna reverentia*). Vgl. ACCORINTI (s. Anm. 38), 1108.

[33] Dionysios, Epiker aus (vermutlich) hellenistischer Zeit, Verfasser der *Bassarika* (über den Indienzug des Dionysos); erwähnt bei Stephanos von Byzanz (5./6. Jh. n. Chr.). Dionysii Bassaricon et Gigantiadis fragmenta cum prolegomenis, Italica versione et indicibus edidit Henricus LIVREA. Romae 1973 (*Bibliotheca Athena* 12).

[34] Das Epigramm hat Falkenburg, zusammen mit drei Versen des Angelo Poliziano (s. u. Anm. 47), als Motto auf die Rückseite des Titels gesetzt (s. Abb. 2): Νόννος ἐγώ· Πανὸς μὲν ἐμὴ πόλις, ἐν Φαρίῃ δὲ / ἔγχεϊ φωνήεντι γονὰς ἤμησα Γιγάντων. („Nonnos heiße ich, stamme aus Panstadt. In Pharia [Alexandrien] mähte / ich mit dem klingenden Schwert meiner Rede die Giganten scharenweise nieder.")

[35] Aus Falkenburgs Anregung wurde in der modernen Nonnosforschung (ausgehend von Julius BRAUNE, Nonnos und Ovid. Greifswald 1935) eine Diskussion über die mögliche Rezeption der *Metamorphosen* durch Nonnos. Eine (reservierte) Kurzdarstellung bietet: Elizabeth FISHER, Ovid's Metempsychosis. The Greek East. In: James G. Clark, Frank T. Coulson, Kathlen L. McKinley (eds.), Ovid in the Middle Ages. Cambridge 2011, 26–47; hier 29.

lich zu kennen, verwerfen und sich abfällig über den Dichter äußern. Die Freude und der Genuss, den ihm der bislang unbekannte Text bereitet, haben aber, wie Falkenburg nachdrücklich betont, nicht dazu geführt, dass er willkürlich und, wie sonst bei Erstausgaben seiner Zeit üblich, nach eigenem Ermessen in den Text eingegriffen hätte[36]: Aus Ehrfurcht vor der wertvollen Handschrift hat er den Text exakt nach der Vorlage wiedergegeben, dafür aber in den beigefügten *Lectiones et coniecturae* (Abb. 3) Lesarten und Verbesserungen zusammengestellt, zum überwiegenden Teil eigene, aber auch solche von anderen (Angelo Poliziano), die sich mit dem Text beschäftigt haben, oft sehr lange beschäftigt haben, wie er mit einem Seitenblick auf Carolus Utenhove bemerkt: dieser sollte eine lateinische Übersetzung anfertigen, hatte den Text, und zwar in mehreren Abschriften, lange Zeit zur Verfügung und hat dennoch seine Arbeit offenbar nicht zu Ende bringen können[37]. Falkenburg schließt mit einem weiteren Dank an Sambucus und der Hoffnung, mit der Edition und den Verbesserungen sowie der Erschließung des Textes durch reichliche Indizes gewissermaßen die Leihgebühr für die lange Zeit der Abwesenheit der Handschrift entrichtet zu haben.

---

[36] Im Nachwort an den Leser schreibt Falkenburg: *coniectores, ut araneae ex se telas texunt, ita pleraque ex ingenio suo, cui nimium solent fidere, proferunt, quae auctoribus ipsis οὐδ' ὄναρ οὐδ' ὕπαρ in mentem venissent. Qua corrigendi ratione factum fuit, ut si nunc veteres illi reviviscant, sua agnoscere scripta vix ipsi possint.* („Die Konjekturenmacher, wie Spinnen die Netze aus sich heraus weben, so veröffentlichen sie zumeist aus ihrer genialen Phantasie, der sie allzusehr zu vertrauen pflegen, was den Autoren selbst nicht im Schlaf und nicht im Traum eingefallen wäre. Durch diese Methode des Korrigierens ist es soweit gekommen, dass jene alten Schriftsteller, wenn sie jetzt zum Leben erwachen würden, ihre eigenen Texte selbst kaum wiedererkennen könnten.")

[37] Die Übersetzung von Utenhove kann nicht nachgewiesen werden; unklar bleibt auch, was die Mitteilung *et plura huius libri habuit exemplaria* bedeutet. Die Mehrzahl wird übrigens auch vom Comte de Marcellus angezweifelt (s. Anm. 38, XVI). Schon in einem Brief aus Paris an Hieronymus Wolf in Augsburg vom 12. Dezember 1560, in dem Sambucus den jungen, gerade bei Jean Dorat in Paris studierenden Karl Utenhove empfiehlt, wird auf die in Arbeit befindliche lateinische Übersetzung der *Dionysiaka* hingewiesen; vgl. GERSTINGER (s. Anm. 2), 51; AGOSTI (s. Anm. 13), 112. Zu Utenhove vgl. ALMÁSI, KISS (s. Anm. 7), 119 Anm. 602 und 135 Anm. 650.

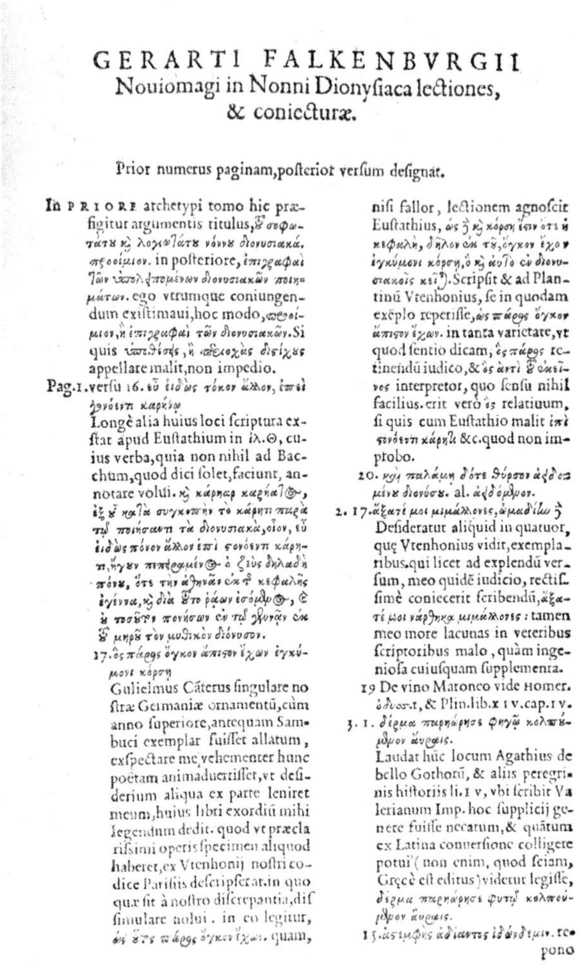

GERARTI FALKENBVRGII
Nouiomagi in Nonni Dionysiaca lectiones, & coniecturæ.

Prior numerus paginam, posteriot versum designat.

IN PRIORE archetypi tomo hic præfigitur argumentis titulus, τοῦ σοφωτάτου καὶ λογιωτάτου νόννου διονυσιακά. προοίμιον. in posteriore, ἐπιγραφαὶ τῶν ὑποτ[illegible]μένων διονυσιακῶν ποιημάτων. ego vtrumque coniungendum existimaui, hoc modo, προοίμιον, ἢ ἐπιγραφαὶ τῶν διονυσιακῶν. Si quis ὑποθέσεις, ἢ περιοχὰς διστίχους appellare malit, non impedio.

Pag. 1. versu 16. εὖ εἰδὼς τόκον ἄλλον, ἐπεὶ ἠνόεντι καρήνῳ

Longè alia huius loci scriptura exstat apud Eustathium in ἰλ. Θ, cuius verba, quia non nihil ad Bacchum, quod dici solet, faciunt, annotare volui. καὶ κάρηαρ καρηνάτου, ἐξ οὗ κατὰ συγκοπὴν τὸ κάρητι παρὰ τῷ ποιήσαντι τὰ διονυσιακά, οἷον, εὖ εἰδὼς πόνον ἄλλον ἐπὶ στονόεντι κάρητι, ἤγουν πεπειραμένος ὁ ζεὺς δηλαδὴ πόνου, ὅτε τὴν ἀθηνᾶν ἐκ τῆς κεφαλῆς ἐγέννα, καὶ διὰ τοῦτο ῥᾷον ἐσόμενος, ἐπεὶ [illegible] τοσοῦτον πονήσων ἐν τῷ γεννᾶν ἐκ τοῦ μηροῦ τὸν μυθικὸν διόνυσον.

17. ὃς πάρος ὄγκον ἄπιστον ἔχων ἐγκύμονι κόρσῃ

Gulielmus Canterus singulare nostræ Germaniæ ornamentum, cùm anno superiore, antequam Sambuci exemplar fuisset allatum, exspectare me vehementer hunc poëtam animaduertisset, vt desiderium aliqua ex parte leniret meum, huius libri exordium mihi legendum dedit. quod vt præclarissimi operis specimen aliquod haberet, ex Vtenhonij nostri codice Parisiis descripserat. in quo quæ sit à nostro discrepantia, dissimulare nolui. in eo legitur, ὡς ὅτε πάρος ὄγκον ἔχων. quam, nisi fallor, lectionem agnoscit Eustathius, ὡς ἡ καὶ κόρση ἐστιν ὅτι ἡ κεφαλή, δῆλον ἐκ τοῦ, ὄγκον ἔχων ἐγκύμονι κόρσῃ, ὃ καὶ αὐτὸ ἐν διονυσιακοῖς κεῖται. Scripsit & ad Plantinum Vtenhonius, se in quodam exemplo reperisse, ὡς πάρος ὄγκον ἄπιστον ἔχων. in tanta varietate, vt quod sentio dicam, ὃς πάρος retinendum iudico, & ὃς ἀντὶ τοῦ ἐκεῖνος interpretor, quo sensu nihil facilius. erit verò ὃς relatiuum, si quis cum Eustathio malit ἐπὶ στονόεντι κάρητι &c. quod non improbo.

20. καὶ παλάμῃ δότε θύρσον ἀεξομένου διονύσου. al. ἀεξόμενον.

2. 17. ἄξατέ μοι μιμάλλονες, ἀμαδίων [illegible]

Desideratur aliquid in quatuor, quæ Vtenhonius vidit, exemplaribus. qui licet ad explendum versum, meo quidem iudicio, rectissimè coniecerit scribendum, ἄξατέ μοι νάρθηκα μιμάλλονες: tamen meo more lacunas in veteribus scriptoribus malo, quàm ingeniosa cuiusquam supplementa.

19 De vino Maroneo vide Homer. ὀδυσσ. ι, & Plin. lib. XIV. cap. IV.

3. 1. δέρμα πυρηνάρησι φυγῷ κολπούμενον αὔραις.

Laudat hunc locum Agathius de bello Gothorum, & aliis peregrinis historiis li. IV, vbi scribit Valerianum Imp. hoc supplicij genere fuisse necatum, & quantum ex Latina conuersione colligere potui (non enim, quod sciam, Græcè est editus) videtur legisse, δέρμα πυρηνάρησι φυτῷ κολπούμενον αὔραις.

15. ἀστεμφὴς ἀδίαντος ἰδάνδειμιν. repono

Abb. 3: *Lectiones et coniecturae* aus der *editio princeps* der *Dionysiaka*. Νόννου Πανοπολίτου Διονυσιακά. [...] Nunc primum in lucem edita, ex Bibliotheca Ioannis Sambuci Pannonii [...]. Antverpiae: Ex officina Christophori Plantini 1569 (Wien, Universitätsbibliothek I 249.157)

TEXTGESCHICHTE DER *DIONYSIAKA*[38]

Der Text der *Dionysiaka* ist, wie die Durcharbeitung der Überlieferung durch Arthur Ludwich ergeben hat, in nur einer Handschrift überliefert, dem *Codex Laurentianus Mediceus 32.16* (L). Das Manuskript entstand in der Werkstatt des Maximos Planudes in Konstantinopel und ist datiert auf den 1. September 1280 (fol. 8ᵛ). Der Codex wurde 1423 von Francesco Filelfo von seiner Schwiegermutter Manfredina Doria, der Witwe des Johannes Chrysolaras, gekauft und 1427 nach Italien gebracht. Nach dem Tod des Filelfo (1481) kam die Handschrift in die Bibliotheca Laurenziana[39]. Die *Dionysiaka* stehen am Anfang der Sammelhandschrift (fol. 9ʳ–173ʳ)[40]. Der Name des Autors ist nicht genannt und blieb zunächst unbekannt. Erst Angelo Poliziano (1454–1494), der sich ab 1472 mit dem Text beschäftigte, nennt im Jahre 1482 den Namen des Nonnos von Panopolis als des Autors. Diese

---

[38] Zur Textgeschichte: Marie-Louis Jean André Charles Lodoïs de Martin du Tyrac, Comte de Marcellus (ancien ministre plénipotentiaire), *Nonnos, Les Dionysiaques ou Bacchus. Poëme en XLVIII chants*. Grec et Français. Paris: Librairie de Firmin Didot Frères 1856, XII–XIX; Arthur LUDWICH, Über die handschriftliche Überlieferung der Dionysiaka des Nonnos. Hermes 12 (1877), 273–299; Arthur LUDWICH in der Praefatio der Teubner-Ausgabe von 1909, X–XVI (s. Anm. 9); Rudolf KEYDELL in der Praefatio der Ausgabe von 1957, *25–*35 (s. Anm. 9); ferner: Francis VIAN, im ersten Band der Les Belles Lettres Edition (1976; ²2003), LXI–LXXIV, und Fabrizio GONNELLI, *Introduzione: Per una storia della fortuna di Nonno*. In: Nonno di Panopoli, Le Dionisiache. Vol. II: canti XIII–XXIV. Milano 2003 (²2008), 7–50. Vgl. die zusammenfassende Darstellung von Domenico ACCORINTI, Nonnos von Panopolis. *Reallexikon für Antike und Christentum* 25 (2013), 1107–1129; hier 1113f. Dazu jetzt: Claudio DE STEFANI, Brief Notes on the Manuscript Tradition of Nonnus' Works. In: Domenico Accorinti (ed.), *Brill's Companion to Nonnus of Panopolis*. Leiden, Boston 2016, 671–690; hier 672–679.

[39] Cod. Laurentianus Mediceus pl. 32.16, fol. 8ᵛ ποιηταὶ πλείους πρῶτον διονυσιακά, darunter in der nächsten Zeile: *poetae plures primum dionysiaca* (sic!); darunter: φραγκίσκου φιλέλφου *francisci philelfi*; darunter wiederholt: φραγκίσκου φιλέλφου *francisci philelfi / emptus Constantinopoli* ἀπὸ τῆς (über der Zeile: μεθίσου) γυναικός; *viri clarissimi Iohannis Chrysolarae sub / anno Mº CCCCº XXIIIº pridie nonas Ianuarias*. Am Fuß der Seite stehen drei Zwölfsilber: εἴληφε καλῶς ἡ βίβλος αὕτη πέρας / τοῦ πρὶν Μανουήλ, ἀρτίως δὲ Μαξίμου / θεὸν βοηθὸν τῇδε συγκεκτημένου. Vgl. Paul MAAS, *Byzantinisch-neugriechisches Jahrbuch* 4 (1923), 267f. und Alexander TURYN, *Dated Greek Manuscripts of the Thirteenth and Fourteenth Centuries in the Libraries of Italy*. Urbana, Chicago, London 1972, 28–39 mit pl. 16–23. – Die *Dionysiaka* enden auf fol. 173ʳ der Handschrift, und am Fuß von fol. 173ʳ steht von der Hand des Kopisten: Δόξα σοι ὁ Θεός, ὅτι μὲ τὸ ἀπεξέβαλες.

[40] Der Cod. Laurentianus 32.16 enthält außerdem folgende Texte: Theokrit, Apollonios von Rhodos, Hesiod, Oppian, Moschos, Nikander, Triphiodor, Phokylides, Gregor von Nazianz, Delphische Orakel, Versrätsel, und Epigramme auf das Hippodrom von Konstantinopel.

Zuordnung wurde 1907 durch den *Berliner Papyrus 10567* (aus dem 6./7. Jahrhundert n. Chr.) bestätigt.

Eine weitere Handschrift hat Cyriacus von Ancona (ca. 1391–1455) am 26. 11. 1444 im Kloster Lavra auf dem Berg Athos gelesen (und 33 Verse vom Anfang des Gedichts abgeschrieben). Es scheint sich um eine von dem im Laurentianus überlieferten Text unabhängige Fassung gehandelt zu haben, die mit der Textfassung des Berliner Papyrus zusammengeht. Die Handschrift ist heute verloren[41].

> q Vo pacto inuenta sit purpura, non alienum fuerit hic refer
> re, uel ut graeci poetae Nóni locus intelligatur, uel ut fabella
> praequam lepida, latinis intacta, noscatur. Est autem apud
> Polluce libro de uerbis idoneis ad Commodum primo, in hanc sen‑
> tentiam. Tyrii ferunt, inquit, captum amore Herculem Nymphæ cu
> iusdam indigenæ, cui nomen Tyro, sequebaturq; eum, inquiunt, ca‑
> nis antiquo more, quo dominum canes usq; etiam ad contionem eo
> mitabantur. Quare canis hic Herculeus, irreptantem scopulis purpu
> ram conspicatus, peresa caruncula, sua sibi labra, cruore puniceo infe‑
> cit. Cum igitur ad puellam Hercules adiisset, delectata illa insueta tin‑
> ctura, quam ceu florentem in eius canis labris aspexisset, affirmauit, si‑
> bi cum illo posthac nihil fore, nisi ad se uestem afferret, etiam canis il‑
> lius labris splendidiorem. Quo circa inuenta Hercules animante, col
> lectoq; sanguine, munus puellae detulit, primus (ut Tyrii dictitant) au
> ctor puniceæ infecturae. Nos igitur í Rustico nostra, propter hoc ipsú
> deniq; concham diximus Herculeam, cú purpuram significaremus.
> Porro autem Nóni poetae uersiculi super hac ipsa fabula, sic in libro
> quadragesimo Dionysiacon, inueniuntur.
>
> Καὶ τυείης σκοπιαζι δεδυμέρα φαρτανόχλω
> Γ'ορφυρίους ασπιδῆρας ἀκοντίζουτα Θηλασυκς.
> Ἡ χηνώαλιεργὸς ἐπαπαλοῖσιν ἐρίπτων
> Ἐνδόμυχεν χρονηῖσι γραάσι θεσκέλοις ἰχνύη,
> Χιονίας πορφυρι παιδικῷ, ἐνδόοι κόχλου
> Χέλια φωνίζας διερῷ πυρί, τοῖ ποτε μοῦνω
> Φαισρὸρ ἀλιχεαίνων ἐρυθαίνετο φᾶρος ἀνάκτων.

Abb. 4: *Misc.* I, 12: *Quomodo inventa purpura, simul explicatus Nonni locus, graeci poetae*. Angelo Poliziano, Opera, Venedig: Aldus (Juli) 1498, Ciiii^v
(Wien, Universitätsbibliothek II 138.230)

---

[41] Exzerpt in MS Vat. lat. 5250² fol. 19ᵛ. Siehe auch Aubrey DILLER, A Lost Manuscript of Nonnus' Dionysiaca. *Classical Philology* 48/3 (Juli 1953), 177; vgl. Barry BALDWIN, A ‚lost manuscript' of Nonnus' Dionysiaca. *Scriptorium* 37 (1983), 110–112. Zu Cyriacus von Ancona: Edward W. BODNAR, Clive FOSS (eds.), *Cyriac of Ancona*. Cambridge, Mass. 2003.

Nach der *editio princeps* der Paraphrase des Johannes-Evangeliums im Jahre 1504 hatte Aldus Manutius ab 1508 auch die Absicht, die *Dionysiaka* zu edieren, und es wurde Pietro Candido (ca. 1460–1513), der Camaldulenser aus Casentino, mit der Vorbereitung der Ausgabe betraut, und vielleicht sollte für diese Ausgabe die Handschrift vom Athos oder auch eine der bekannten Abschriften des Codex Laurentianus Mediceus 32.16 verwendet werden[42]. Falkenburg teilt dazu im Widmungsbrief ohne nähere Angaben mit, dass Aldus Manutius eine Handschrift von Johannes Laskaris (1445–1534) erhalten habe, und später, im Jahre 1556, Johannes Oporinus (1507–1568) in Basel eine Handschrift aus Italien zur Verfügung hatte, und mit gewissem Stolz lässt Falkenburg durchblicken, dass sich bei beiden Druckern wohl niemand gefunden hat, der imstande gewesen wäre, den Text zu edieren. 1553 bemühte sich auch Paulus Manutius, Franciscus Portus für eine Edition der *Dionysiaka* zu gewinnen, vielleicht auch, weil er von der Handschrift des Arsenios wusste, die dann im Winter 1563 von Sambucus in Tarent gekauft wurde[43].

WEITERE AUSGABEN, AUCH MIT LATEINISCHER ÜBERSETZUNG

Der erste lateinische Übersetzer war eigentlich Angelo Poliziano, der anlässlich seiner Beschäftigung mit dem Text in Florenz (Laurentianus 32.16) in den Jahren ab 1472 nicht nur den Namen des Autors erkannte, sondern den Text exzerpiert und in den *Miscellanea* auch einige Passagen übersetzt hat (cap. 11, 12, 80; Abb. 4)[44]. Wie aus Polizianos Bemerkungen hervorgeht, hat er 1481 die *Dionysiaka* gelesen (ohne Autornamen), im selben Jahr finden sich erste Bemerkungen zum Text im Kommentar zu den *Silvae* des Statius, ebenso 1482 im Kommentar zu den *Fasti* Ovids[45]. Im Kommentar zu den *Satiren*

---

[42] Vgl. AGOSTI (s. Anm. 13), 109–111.
[43] Vgl. AGOSTI (s. Anm. 13), 112f.
[44] Vgl. cap. 36, 46 und 57 der (1972 erstmals gedruckten) zweiten Centurie: Angelo Poliziano, *Miscellanorum Centura secunda*, per cura di Vittorio BRANCA e Manlio PASTORE STOCCHI, editio minor. Firenze 1978.
[45] Angelo Poliziano, *Commento inedito alle Selve di Stazio*. A cura di Lucia CESARINI-MARTINELLI. Firenze 1978, 447. Angelo Poliziano, *Commento inedito ai Fasti di Ovidio*. A cura di Francesco LO MONACO. Firenze 1991, 102f., 257–261; 177f., 295f., 338.

des Persius 1482/83[46] und in den *Nutricia* von 1491 nennt er den Namen Nonnos, den er vielleicht den *Historien* des Agathias (4, 23, 5) entnommen hat[47]. Allerdings ist nicht zu belegen, dass und woher er die *Historien* kannte: Die lateinische Übersetzung des Christophorus Persona (1416–1486) erschien 1516 im Druck, kursierte aber in mehreren Abschriften bereits zu Lebzeiten Polizianos[48], die *editio princeps* wurde erst 1594 bei Plantinus in Leiden gedruckt (nach dem Text des Cod. Vat. gr. 151 – möglicherweise hat Poliziano diese Handschrift gekannt)[49].

Die erste vollständige lateinische Übersetzung der *Dionysiaka*[50] in Hexametern wurde dann schließlich vom Rostocker Philologen, Theologen und Astronomen Eilhard Lubin (1565–1621) auf der Basis der Erstedition, deren Text mit abgedruckt wurde, erstellt:

> Νοννου Πανοπολιτου Διονυσιακα. Nonni Panopolitae Dionysiaca. Nunc denuo in lucem edita, et Latine reddita per Eilhardvm Lvbinvm Poëseos in Academia Rostochina professorem. Ex Bibliotheca Ioannis Sambvci Pannonij. Cum lectionibus, et coniecturis Gerarti Falkenbvrgii Nouiomagi, et Indice copioso. Hanoviae: typis Wechelianis apud Claudium Marnium et heredes Iohannis Aubrii 1605.

Fünf Jahre später wurde diese zweisprachige Ausgabe mit dem Text von Falkenburg und mit der Übersetzung von Lubin in Hanau in einer unveränderten Fassung noch einmal gedruckt, erweitert um eine zur selben Zeit in Leiden auch als Monographie erschienene, zusammenfassende Publikation mehrerer Abhandlungen und Kommentare zu der noch immer unbefriedi-

---

[46] Angelo Poliziano, *Commento inedito alle Satire di Persio*. A cura di Lucia CESARINI-MARTINELLI e Roberto RICCIARDI. Firenze 1985, 47–49.

[47] Falkenburg hat die Verse als Dreizeiler (unter der Überschrift: *Angelus Politianus in Nutritiis*) auf die Versoseite des Titelblatts, dem Widmungsschreiben gegenüber, gesetzt (s. Abb. 2): *Nutricia* 424–426 *Pingit et exiguus totum Dionysius orbem / Terrarum in tabulis: sed non et proelia Bacchi / Nonnus in exigua potuit contexere tela* („In kleinen Bildtafeln hat Dionysios, sc. von Alexandrien, der Periheget, den ganzen Erdkreis aufgezeichnet: Aber die Kämpfe des Bacchus konnte Nonnos nicht in kleine Stoffe einweben"). Im Nachwort an den Leser nimmt er darauf Bezug: *coniectores, ut araneae ex se telas texunt* [...].

[48] Agathiae Myrinaei Historiarum libri quinque. Rec. Rudolfus KEYDELL. Berlin 1967, XVf.; vgl. AGOSTI (s. Anm. 13), 106f.

[49] Francis VIAN, Ange Politien lecteur des poètes grecs (1997). In: Domenico Accorinti (Hg.), *L'épopée posthomérique. Recueil d'études*. Alessandria 2005, 609–620; hier 617ff.; und AGOSTI (s. Anm. 13), 105–108. Vgl. auch Alessandro DANELONI, Le note del Poliziano al testo delle Dionisiache nel Laur. 32, 16. *Studi medievali e umanistici*, Messina 2 (2004), 341–347.

[50] Zur Übersetzungsarbeit von Karl Utenhove s. Anm. 37.

genden Textsituation des Gedichts[51], mit vielen zusätzlichen Korrekturen und Lesarten von Petrus Cunaeus (1586–1638), Daniel Heinsius (1580–1655) und Joseph Scaliger (1540–1609), nunmehr ein Band von insgesamt über 1800 Seiten und damit ein Kompendium der Nonnosforschung und -interpretation der Zeit:

> ΝΟΝΝΟΥ ΠΑΝΟΠΟΛΙΤΟΥ ΔΙΟΝΥΣΙΑΚΑ. Nonni Panopolitae Dionysiaca. Petri Cunaei Animadversionum liber. Danielis Heinsii Dissertatio de Nonni Dionysiacis et ejusdem Paraphrasi. Josephi Scaligeri Coniectanea. Cum vulgata versione, et Gerarti Falkenburgii lectionibus. Hanoviae: Typis Wechelianis, apud Claudium Marnium & haeredes Ioannis Aubrii 1610.

In der Zwischenzeit war in Genf 1606 im Rahmen einer groß angelegten Sammlung griechischer Dichtung – ohne Nennung von Falkenburg und Lubin – deren Text und Übersetzung, zusammen mit vielen anderen griechischen Autoren, in einem zweisprachigen Band von Jakob Lectius herausgebracht worden[52]:

> ΟΙ ΤΗΣ ΗΡΩΙΚΗΣ ΠΟΙΗΣΕΩΣ ΠΑΛΑΙΟΙ ΠΟΙΗΤΑΙ ΠΑΝΤΕΣ. Poetae Graeci veteres carminis heroici scriptores, qui extant, omnes. Apposita est e regione Latina interpretatio. Notae item et variae lectiones in margine adscriptae. Cura et recensione Iac. Lectii. Accessit et Index rerum et verborum locupletissimus. Aureliae Allobrogum [Genf]: Excudebat Petrus de la Rouiere, sumptibus Caldorianae Societatis Anno MDCVI [1606].

Und schließlich seien noch weitere verdienstvolle Textausgaben oder Teilausgaben mit Übersetzung erwähnt, die bewirkt haben, dass die *Dionysiaka* einem kleinen, aber interessierten und kompetenten Rezipientenkreis bekannt und zugänglich waren:

> Nonni Dionysiacorum libri sex, ab octavo ad decimum tertium, res Bacchicas ante expeditionem Indicam complectentes. Emendavit, omnium Nonni librorum argumenta et notas mythologicas adjecit Georgius Henricus Moser, Ulma-Bavarus, seminarii philologici Heidelbergensis sodalis. Praefatus est Fridericus Creuzer. Heidelbergae: ex libraria Mohrii et Zimmeri academica 1809.

---

[51] Petri Cunaei Animadversionum Liber in Nonni Dionysiaca. In quo quid sit de hujus autoris virtutibus et vitiis habendum, ostenditur. Danielis Heinsii Dissertatio De Nonni Dionysiacis, et ejusdem Paraphrasi. Iosephi Scaligeri Coniectanea. Ad editionem Plantini et Wecheli. Lugduni Batavorum: Ex officina Lodivici Elzeviri 1610.

[52] Die Ausgabe erwähnt GONNELLI (s. Anm. 38), 26 Anm. 43.

Friedrich Graefe, Νοννου του Πανοπολιτου τα κατα Ὑμνον και Νικαιαν. Des Nonnos Hymnos und Nikaea. St. Petersburg: Gedruckt bey Pluchart und Comp. 1813 (Versübersetzung, Text griechisch und deutsch).
Christian Friedrich Graefe (ed.), Nonni Panopolitae Dionysiacorum libri XLVIII. Suis et aliorum conjecturis emendavit et illustravit Fridericus Graefe. Lipsiae: sumptibus Fr. Chr. Guil. Vogelii 1819 et 1826.

Die beiden zuletzt genannten Arbeiten von Graefe führen in das erste Zentrum der Nonnos-Rezeption, nach St. Petersburg. Zu Beginn des 19. Jahrhunderts. beschäftigten sich dort zwei Gelehrte mit dem Text des Nonnos von Panopolis und publizierten erste philologische Arbeiten: Christian Friedrich Graefe (1780–1851), ein deutscher Archäologe und Philologe im Dienste des Zaren, und Graf Sergej Semjonowitsch Uwarow (1785–1855), Präsident der Akademie der Wissenschaften in St. Petersburg und Minister unter Zar Alexander I. (1801–1825). Für das Buch von Graefe (1813), in dem zum ersten Mal ein Teil der *Dionysiaka*, die Geschichte von der Nymphe Nikaia und von Liebe und Tod des Hirten Hymnos in den Büchern 15 und 16, auf der Textbasis der *editio princeps* von Falkenburg und der auf diese folgenden Verbesserungen des Textes, ins Deutsche übersetzt und kommentiert wurde, verfasste Uwarow ein Vorwort, und im Jahr 1817 schrieb er die erste Würdigung des Dichters, die erste Monographie über Nonnos, aus Verehrung für die deutsche Altertumswissenschaft – er hatte in Göttingen studiert – in deutscher Sprache[53].

Und so erreichte die Kenntnis des Dichters auch Weimar, denn Uwarow hatte das Buch Graefes an Johann Wolfgang von Goethe gesandt, der als Dank am 9. Mai 1814 an Uwarow schrieb[54]:

---

[53] Sergej Semjonowitsch Uwaroff, *Nonnos von Panopolis, der Dichter. Ein Beytrag zur Geschichte der griechischen Poesie.* St. Petersburg 1817.

[54] Georg SCHMID, Goethe und Uwarow und ihr Briefwechsel. Sonderdruck aus: *Russische Revue* 28/2, St. Petersburg 1888, 20f. Vgl. Ernst GRUMACH, *Goethe und die Antike.* Potsdam 1949, 321; *Goethes Leben von Tag zu Tag. Eine dokumentarische Chronik* von Robert STEIGER und Angelika REIMANN. Bd. VI: *1814–1820.* Zürich, München 1993, 66. Hans RUPPERT (Hg.), *Goethes Bibliothek. Katalog.* Weimar 1958, 183 Nr. 1314 und 1315: Sowohl das Buch von Graefe als auch Uwarows Monographie befinden sich in Goethes Bibliothek, nicht aber eine Textausgabe des Nonnos. (Übrigens besaß Goethe auch die *Emblemata* von Sambucus in der ersten Auflage von 1564: RUPPERT 211 Nr. 1478.) Weitere Angaben finden sich in Nina ARINGER, Herbert BANNERT, Nicole KRÖLL, *Der Forschungsbericht: Nonnos von Panopolis. 1. Bericht: Dionysiaka, umfassend im Wesentlichen die Jahre 1980–2010.* Anzei-

Mit dem Herausgeber des griechischen und übersetzten Gedichtes bin ich völlig einverstanden: denn obgleich das Leben kurz genug ist und wir schon zufrieden seyn dürfen, wenn wir uns mit den besten Werken der Alten bekannt machen und befreunden können, so ist doch für alle Diejenigen, welche sich den Kunstbetrachtungen ernsthaft widmen, höchst erwünscht, wenn man ihnen Gelegenheit giebt, auch in diejenigen Zeiten zu schauen, wo zwar noch immer Geist, Leben, Leidenschaft und Talent in dem Menschen wohnen, aber nicht mehr zu einer freyen, reinen Ausbildung gelangen können, weil gerade die trefflichsten Vorgänger den Nachfolger in Überbildung, ja Verbildung hintreiben. Auf alle Fälle stellt das hier übersetzte Werk einen kräftigen und gefühlvollen und zugleich wundersam-sprachgebildeten und rhythmisch geübten Poeten dar. Mir und meinen Freunden hat das ganze Heft sehr angenehme Stunden gebracht.

Es war also, wie es scheint, die Hoffnung, die Gerart Falkenburg im Widmungsschreiben an Sambucus ausgesprochen hatte, dass nämlich die Zweifel über den Wert einer späten Dichtung weichen mögen der Freude über den Reichtum an Phantasie und dass die erfindungsreiche Sprache und die Buntheit der Geschichten des Nonnos diejenigen erfreuen mögen, die sich ernsthaft und eingehend mit dem Dichter und seinem kulturellen Umfeld beschäftigen wollen, fürs Erste aufgegangen[*].

---

ger für die Altertumswissenschaft 64 (2011), 1–44; hier 1–6; Herbert BANNERT, Nicole KRÖLL, Der Forschungsbericht: Nonnos von Panopolis. 2. Bericht: Dionysiaka, umfassend die Jahre 2010–2016. Anzeiger für die Altertumswissenschaft 69 (2016), 129–174; hier 129.

[*] Die Arbeit entstand im Rahmen des Projekts P 21088-G20 Religion und Poesie in der Dichtung des Nonnos von Panopolis, gefördert vom österreichischen Fonds zur Förderung der wissenschaftlichen Forschung (FWF). – The research was funded by the Austrian Science Fund (FWF): P 21088-G20 Religion and Poetry in the Epic of Nonnus of Panopolis. Für vielfache Unterstützung, besonders für die Hilfe zur Kenntnis der Handschrift und der Entstehungsgeschichte der editio princeps danke ich Christian Gastgeber (Wien).

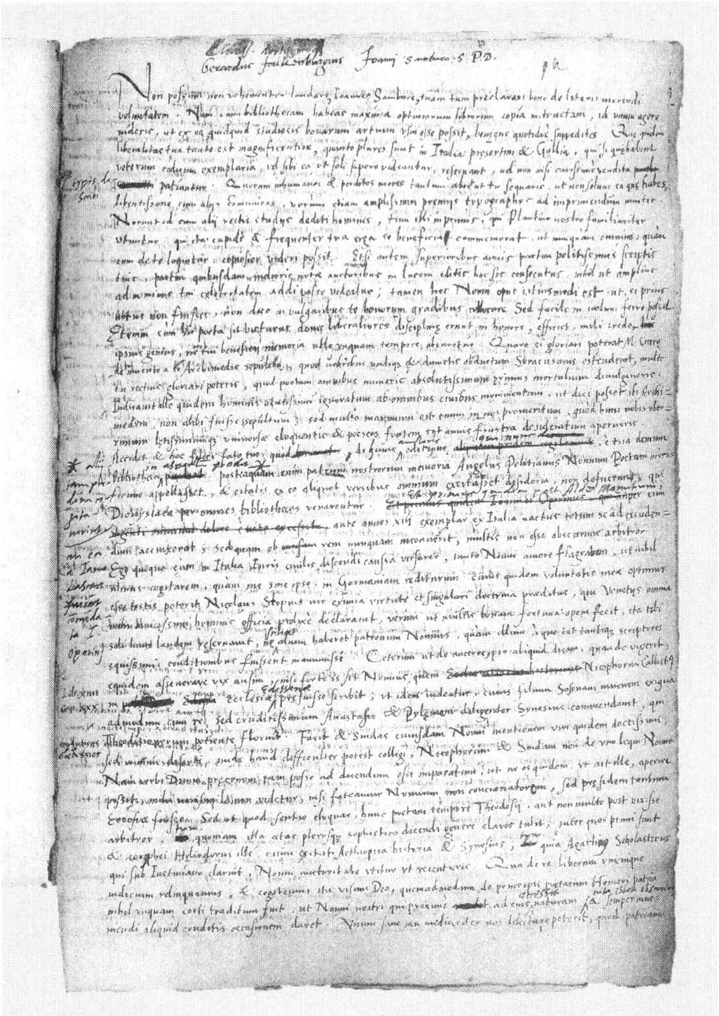

Abb. 5: Druckvorlage für das Widmungsschreiben Falkenburgs an Sambucus
(Wien, Österreichische Nationalbibliothek, Cod. phil. gr. 45)

ANHANG

Für den Widmungsbrief an Johannes Sambucus, den Gerart Falkenburg der *editio princeps* vorangestellt hat (ohne Paginierung), existiert ein handschriftlicher Entwurf, der dem ersten Band des Nonnos-Codex aus dem Besitz des Sambucus vorgebunden ist (Wien, Österreichische Nationalbibliothek, Cod. phil. gr. 45). Er ist kalligraphisch von einem Schreiber für den Setzer geschrieben; handschriftliche Verbesserungen und Ergänzungen stammen vermutlich von der Hand Falkenburgs.

Im Folgenden ist der Text nach dem Druck der *editio princeps* wiedergegeben, übersetzt und mit Sacherklärungen (in Fußnoten zur Übersetzung) versehen[55]; die Marginalien des Drucks sind in eckigen Klammern in den Text integriert. Der Apparat verzeichnet die (wenigen) Druckfehler der *editio princeps*; weiters die Abweichungen des handschriftlichen Entwurfs bzw. dessen Erstfassung mit den Korrekturen und Ergänzungen:

S = 1. Hand: der Schreiber
F = 2. Hand: Falkenburg

---

[55] Die Paratexte der *editio princeps* publizierte bereits Beriah BOTFIELD, *Praefationes et epistolae editionibus principibus auctorum veterum praepositae / Prefaces to the First Editions of the Greek and Roman Classics and of the Sacred Scriptures*. London, Cambridge 1861, 572–584. Sämtliche Paratexte mit kurzen Inhaltsangaben und Übersetzungen der Graeca bieten auch ALMÁSI, KISS, *Humanistes du bassin des Carpates* (s. Anm. 7), 124–142. Der handschriftliche Entwurf aus Cod. phil. gr. 45 ist nicht herangezogen.

GERARTVS FALKENBVRGIVS NOVIOMAGVS IOANNI SAMBVCO S. D.

Non possum non vehementer laudare, Ioannes Sambuce, tuam tam praeclaram bene de litteris merendi voluntatem. nam cum bibliothecam habeas maxima optimorum librorum copia instructam, id unum agere videris, ut ex ea, quidquid studiosis bonarum atrium usui esse possit, benigne quotidie suppedites. Quae quidem liberalitas tua tanto est magnificentior, quanto plures sunt in Italia praesertim et Gallia, qui, si quae habent veterum codicum exemplaria, vel sibi ea, ut soli sapere videantur, reservant, vel non nisi carissime vendita typis describi patiuntur. Quorum inhumanos et perditos mores tantum abest ut tu sequaris, ut non solum ea quae habes, libentissime cum aliis communices, verum etiam amplissimis praemiis typographos ad imprimendum invites. Norunt id cum alii rectis studiis dediti homines, tum illi in primis, qui Plantino nostro familiariter utuntur. qui ita cupide, et frequen|ter tua erga se beneficia comemorat, ut numquam omnino, quam cum de te loquitur, copiosior videri possit. Etsi autem superioribus annis partim politissimis scriptis tuis, partim quibusdam melioris notae auctoribus, in lucem editis, hoc sis consecutus, nihil ut amplius ad nominis tui celebritatem addi posse videatur; tamen hoc Nonni opus istiusmodi est, ut, si prius notus non fuisses, non dico in vulgaribus te honorum gradibus collocare, sed facile in caelum ferre possit. Etenim cum hic poeta sit victurus, donec liberaliores disciplinae erunt in honore, efficiet, mihi crede, ipsius Genius, ne tui beneficii memoria ullo unquam tempore obscuretur. Quare si gloriari poterat M. Cicero de invento a se Archimedis sepulcro, quod ipse vepribus undique et dumetis obductum Syracusanis ostenderat, multo tu rectius gloriari poteris, quod poetam omnibus numeris absolutissimum primus mortalium divulgaveris. Indicavit ille quidem hominis acutissimi ignoratum ab omnibus civibus monumentum, ut dici posset, ibi Archimedem, non alibi fuisse sepultum; sed multo maximum est tuum in nos promeritum, quod hunc nobis uberrimum laetissimumque universae eloquentiae, et poëseos fontem, tot annis frustra, desidera|tum aperueris.

---

23 Cicero, *Tusc.* 5, 64 *Cuius ego quaestor ignoratum ab Syracusanis, cum esse omnino negarent, saeptum undique et vestitum vepribus et dumetis indagavi sepulcrum.*

I Gerardus Falkenburgius Ioanni Sambuco S. P. D.; Clariss. doctissimoque s. l. || **9** praelo committi; typis describi **F** *marg.* || **I I** communicas || **I3** imprimis || **22** hoc ipsius genius || **24** vebribus || **28** monimentum

GERART FALKENBURG AUS NIMWEGEN GRÜSST JOHANNES SAMBUCUS PANNONIUS

Ich kann, Johannes Sambucus, Deine allseits bekannte und äußerst verdienstvolle Hingabe an die Wissenschaften nur in höchsten Tönen loben. Denn obwohl Du im Besitz einer Bibliothek bist, die mit einer ungeheuren Anzahl erstklassiger Bücher ausgestattet ist, bist Du offenbar einzig und allein darum bestrebt, aus ihren Beständen für die an den Schönen Künsten Interessierten von Tag zu Tag freundlicher Weise zur Verfügung zu stellen, was immer ihnen von Nutzen sein könnte. Diese Deine Freigiebigkeit ist umso großzügiger, weil es ja in Italien und besonders in Frankreich einige Leute gibt, die, wenn sie Exemplare alter Handschriften besitzen, diese entweder für sich selbst aufbewahren – offenbar, damit nur sie alleine Kenner zu sein scheinen –, oder nur gegen eine äußerst hohe Summe erlauben, dass sie gedruckt werden. Dass Du Dich deren jedem Humanismus widersprechendem und abstoßendem Verhalten anschließt, liegt Dir so fern, dass Du nicht nur das, was Du besitzt, mit großer Freude an Andere weitergibst, sondern auch mit reichen Gaben die Drucker dazu einlädst, es zu drucken. Das haben schon manch andere Leute erfahren, die sich mit den richtigen Studien beschäftigen, vor allem aber die, welche mit unserem Freund Plantinus immer wieder gerne zusammenarbeiten. Der spricht so gerne und oft von Deinem Entgegenkommen ihm gegenüber, dass er überhaupt niemals als wenn er von Dir spricht ausführlicher erscheinen könnte. Wenn Du aber auch mit den in den letzten Jahren von Dir publizierten, teils ausgezeichneten Texten, teils manchen besser beachteten Autoren dieses Ziel verfolgt hast, könnte wohl nichts mehr der Berühmtheit Deines Namens hinzugefügt werden; doch dieses Werk des Nonnos ist von der Art, dass es Dich, wenn Du nicht schon vorher bekannt gewesen wärst, ich sage nicht, in einfache Arten von Ehrenbezeugungen versetzt, sondern Dich leicht in den Himmel hätte tragen können. Denn wenn dieser Dichter solange leben sollte, bis freiere Künste in Ansehen stehen werden, würde, glaube mir, sein Genius bewirken, dass die Erinnerung an Deine Wohltat niemals durch die Zeit verblassen wird. Wenn daher M. Cicero voll Stolz sein konnte über das von ihm gefundene Grab des Archimedes, das er persönlich, überall von Dornen und Gebüsch versteckt, den Syrakusanern gezeigt hat, könntest Du mit viel größerer Berechtigung darauf stolz sein, dass Du den in jeder Hinsicht vollkommensten Dichter als Erster unter den Menschen bekannt gemacht hast. Jener hat zwar auf das von allen Einheimischen unbeachtete Grabmal eines Menschen mit herausragendem Verstand hingewiesen, so dass man sagen konnte, dass Archimedes dort und nicht irgendwo anders begraben sei; aber noch viel mehr hast Du Dich uns gegenüber verdient gemacht, weil Du uns diesen überreichen und große Freude bringenden Quell der gesamten Beredsamkeit und Dichtung geöffnet hast, auf den wir sehnsüchtig so viele Jahre vergeblich gewartet haben.

Accidit et hoc felici fato tuo, quod de huius auctoris editione, qui e tua demum bibliotheca in aspectum prodit, alii iam pridem cogitaverint. Posteaquam enim patrum nostrorum memoria Angelus* *[In Miscellaneis]* Politianus Nonnum poëtam mirificum appellasset, et citatis ex eo aliquot versibus omnium excitasset desideria, non defuerunt, qui Dionysiaca per omnes bibliothecas venarentur. Et primus quidem, post Aldum Manutium, cui ea a Iano Lascare fuerant commendata, I. Oporinus ante annos XIII exemplar ex Italia nactus, totum se ad excudendum accinxerat; sed quam ob rem nunquam incoaverit, multis non esse obscurum arbitror.

    Ego quoque cum in Italia Iuris civilis discendi caussa versarer, tanto Nonni amore flagrabam, ut nihil minus cogitarem, quam me sine ipso in patriam rediturum. cuius quidem voluntatis meae optimus esse testis poterit Nicolaus Stopius, vir eximia virtute, et singulari doctrina praeditus, qui Venetiis omnia mihi amicissimi hominis officia prolixe declaravit. Verum ut multis bonam fortuna spem fecit, ita tibi soli hanc laudem reservavit, ne scilicet alium haberet patronum Nonnus, quam illum, a quo tot tantique scriptores aequissimis conditionibus fuissent manumissi.

    Ceterum | ut de auctore ipso aliquid dicam, quando vixerit, equidem asseverare vix ausim, nisi forte is sit Nonnus, quem Nicephorus Callistus *[libro xiiii. cap. xxx.]* Ecclesiae Edessenae praefuisse scribit; ut idem videatur, cuius filium Sosenam iuvenem exigua admodum cum re, sed eruditissimum, Anastasio et Pylaemeni diligenter *[in epist.]* * Synesius commendavit, qui Theodosio rerum potiente floruit. Facit et *[in dictione Σαλούστιος]* * Suidas cuiusdam Nonni mentionem viri quidem doctissimi, sed minime diserti. unde haud difficulter potest colligi, Nicephorum et Suidam non de

---

34 Poliziano, *Miscellaneorum centuria prima* 11 (ed. Ald. 1498, Ciii^v) ǁ **50** Nicephorus, *Eccles. hist.* 14, 30 (PG 146, 1156D) ǁ **53** Synesius, *epist.* 43; 102 (Synésios de Cyrène, Correspondance. Texte établi par Antonio GARZYA, traduit par Denis ROQUES. Vol. 2: Lettres I–LXIII. Vol. 3: Lettres LXIV–CLVI. Paris 2003) ǁ **55** Suda Σ 62

32 quod ~~hic auctor~~; de huius editione; auctoris s. l. ǁ **33** ~~alii iam pride.m cogitarunt~~; qui nunc ~~demum~~ **F** s. l.; e tua demum bibliotheca ~~prodeat~~; in aspectum prodit * **F** s. l.; * alii iam pridem cogitaverint **F** mg. ǁ **37** ~~Et primus quidem Ioannes Oporinus, qui nuper cum ingenti omnium dolore e vita excessit~~; Et primus quidem, post Aldum Manutium **F** s. l.; cui ea a Iano Lascare fuerant commendata, I. Oporinus **F** mg. ǁ **40** ~~causam~~ rem **S** ǁ **43** patriam] Germaniam ǁ **47** scilicet **S** s. l. ǁ **50** quem ~~Ecclesiasticus historicus~~; libro xiiii. cap. xxx. **S** mg. ǁ **51** in ~~urbe quae~~ (?) ~~Edessa~~; Edessenae **F** s. l. ǁ **54** * in dictione σαλουστιος **S** mg.

Es kommt zu Deinem glücklichen Geschick noch dazu, dass an eine Ausgabe dieses Autors, der jetzt gerade aus Deiner Bibliothek in die Öffentlichkeit tritt, Andere schon früher gedacht haben. Denn nachdem zur Zeit unserer Väter Angelus Politianus *[am Rand: In den Miscellanea]* den wundersamen Dichter Nonnos genannt und mit einigen aus ihm zitierten Versen die Sehnsucht von allen geweckt hatte[56], fehlte es nicht an Leuten, die in allen Bibliotheken nach den *Dionysiaka* auf der Jagd waren. Denn als Erster, nach Aldus Manutius, dem sie von Johannes Laskaris anvertraut worden waren, gelangte Johannes Oporinus vor dreizehn Jahren in den Besitz eines Exemplars aus Italien und bereitete den Druck des Ganzen vor. Warum er aber niemals damit begonnen hat, ist Vielen, glaube ich, nicht ganz unverständlich.

Und als ich selbst mich zum Studium des Bürgerlichen Rechts in Italien aufhielt, beherrschte mich eine so heiße Liebe zu Nonnos, dass ich an nichts weniger dachte als daran, ohne ihn in die Heimat zurückzukehren. Der beste Zeuge für diese meine feste Entschlossenheit könnte Nicolaus Stopius sein, ein Mann von herausragender Fähigkeit und ausgestattet mit einzigartiger Gelehrsamkeit, der mir in Venedig alle Gefälligkeiten eines eng befreundeten Mannes freigiebig erwiesen hat[57]. Wie aber das Glück vielen gute Hoffnung gemacht hat, so hat es für Dich allein die Ruhmestat vorgesehen, dass nämlich Nonnus keinen anderen Schutzherrn haben sollte, als jenen, von dem so viele und so bedeutende Schriftsteller zu genau denselben Bedingungen in die Freiheit entlassen worden sind.

Und außerdem, damit ich auch etwas über den Autor selbst sage, wann er gelebt haben könnte, würde ich kaum ernsthaft zu behaupten wagen, wenn es sich nicht um eben jenen Nonnos handelte, von dem Nikephorus Kallistus *[am Rand: Buch 14, cap. 30]* schreibt, dass er der Kirche in Edessa vorgestanden wäre; und dass es derselbe zu sein scheint, dessen Sohn Sosena, einen jungen Mann von bescheidenem Vermögen, aber außerordentlicher Bildung, Synesius[58] *[am Rand: in den Briefen]* nachdrücklich dem Anastasius und dem Pylaemenes anvertraut hat, der zur Zeit lebte, als Theodosius sich der Herrschaft bemächtigte. Auch die Suda *[am Rand: im Lemma Σαλούστιος]* erwähnt einen gewissen Nonnos, einen zwar außerordentlich gelehrten, aber im Stil ganz unbedeutenden Mann. Daraus kann unschwer geschlossen werden, dass Nikephorus und die Suda nicht ein und denselben Nonnos mei-

---

[56] Zu Polizianos Beschäftigung mit Nonnos in den *Miscellanea* vgl. Anm. 45.
[57] Nikolaus de Stoop aus Aalst in Flandern (? –1568, Venedig), Dichter und Gelehrter, beteiligte sich an Texteditionen und war zeitweise Begleiter von Andreas Vesalius (1514–1564) in Italien.
[58] Synesios von Kyrene (ca. 370–412 n. Chr.), neuplatonischer Philosoph, ab 411 Bischof von Ptolemais. Erhalten sind u. a. eine Briefsammlung, Hymnen (im dorischen Dialekt) und eine in Konstantinopel gehaltene Rede über das Königtum. Vgl. zuletzt: Helmut SENG, Lars HOFFMANN (Hgg.), *Synesios von Kyrene. Politik – Literatur – Philosophie*. Turnhout 2012 (*Byzantios. Studies in Byzantine History and Civilization* 6).

uno loqui Nonno. nam verbi divini praeconem tam esse infantem posse, ὥστε μὴ διᾶραι τὸ στόμα δύνασθαι πρός γε λόγων ἐπιεικῶν σύνθεσιν, mihi verisimile non videtur, nisi fateamur Nonnum non concionatorem, sed praesidem tantum Ecclesiae fuisse. Sed, ut quod sentio eloquar, hunc 60 poetam tempore Theodosii, aut non multo post vixisse arbitror: tum quoniam illa aetas plerosque sophistico dicendi genere claros tulit, inter quos primi sunt, et coryphaei, Heliodorus ille, cuius exstat Aethiopica historia, et Synesius; tum quia *[lib. IV. de bello Gothorum]* * Agathius, qui sub Iustiniano claruit, Nonni auctoritate utitur ut recentioris. Qua de re 65 liberum unicuique iudicium relinquamus, et cogitemus ita visum Deo, quemadmodum de principis poetarum Homeri patria nihil unquam certi traditum fuit, ut Nonni nostri, qui proxime ad | eius accessit naturam, vita esset obscurior, et semper inveniendi aliquid eruditis occasionem daret. Unum sane illud non mediocriter nos delectare poterit, quod patria 70 Nonno fuerit Panos Aegypti oppidum, quam regionem Graecia ad percolenda omnibus bonis artibus ingenia magistram habuit. quod verum esse, si nihil aliud, vel hoc satis superque probat, quod prisci illi Graeci, Plato, Pythagoras, Thales, Solon, Lycurgus et ceteri, qui familiam in philosophia ducebant, tanquam ad mercaturam sapientiae, et doctrinae in 75 Aegyptum fuerint profecti. Neque silentio praetereundum existimavi, quod olim Aegyptii viros, et virgines pietate, et vitae sanctimonia insignes, Nonnos, et Nonnas appellaverint. Non enim obscure quis inde divinaverit nostro poetae propter sanctissimos, et innocentissimos mores, illud nomen a suis popularibus fuisse inditum. Argumentum operis lepidissi- 80 mum est de Bacchi progenie, miraculis, peregrinationibus, bello cum Deriade Indorum rege, et aliis, trophaeis, et triumphis: in quo et Dionysius se exercuit, cuius Bassarica a Stephano citantur.

---

58 Suda Σ 62 || **64** Agathias 4, 23, 5 Agathiae Myrinaei Historiarum libri quinque. Rec. Rudolfus KEYDELL. Berlin 1967, 152 || **83** Stephanus, *Ethnica* s. v. Γάζος

57 tam – σύνθεσιν] tam posse ad dicendum imparatus, ut ne os quidem, ut ait ille, aperire posset || **61** et tum **F** *s. l.* || **64** hic (?) tum **F** *s. l.*; Agathius Scholasticus || **68** proxime accedat ad eius naturam; accessit **F** *s. l.* || **68** vita esset obscurior **F** *s. l.* || **70** patriam habuerat || **71** panon || **73** Plato **F** *mg.* || **74** Thales, Solon, Pythagoras, Lycurgus || peregrinationibus] *deest* || et aliis] *desunt* || **83** Bacchica; Bassarica **F** *mg.*; a Stephano de urbibus nen. Denn dass der Verkünder des göttlichen Wortes so unbedarft sein kann, dass er den Mund nicht aufmachen sollte zur Komposition der passenden Worte, scheint mir unwahrscheinlich, wenn wir nicht zugestehen, dass Nonnos nicht ein Prediger, sondern nur der Vorstand der Kirchengemeinde war. Aber damit ich ausspreche, was ich meine: Ich glaube, dass dieser Dichter zur Zeit des Theodosius oder nicht viel später gelebt hat[59]: weil nämlich diese Zeit besonders viele im sophistischen Redestil berühmte Männer hervorgebracht hat, unter denen die ersten und hervorragenden jener Heliodor[60], von dem die *Äthiopische Geschichte* überliefert ist, und Synesius sind; und dann weil Agathias[61] *[am Rand: Buch 4 Über den Gotenkrieg]*, der zur Zeit des Justinian bekannt war, das Werk des Nonnos als jüngst erschienen bezeichnet. Daher wollen wir jedem sein freies Urteil überlassen und auch glauben, dass es Gott auch so erschienen ist, insoferne ja über die Heimat Homers, des Ersten unter den Dichtern, nichts Sicheres überliefert war, so dass das Leben von unserem Nonnos, der dessen Natur am Nächsten kommt, im Dunkeln bleibt und für alle Zeit den Gebildeten die Möglichkeit bietet, irgendetwas herauszufinden. Das Eine aber kann uns gewiss eine nicht geringe Freude bereiten, nämlich dass die Heimat des Nonnos die Stadt des Pan in Ägypten war, eine Gegend, die Griechenland Lehrmeisterin war zur Ausbildung der Geistesgaben in allen schönen Künsten. Dass dies richtig ist, kann – wenn schon nichts Anderes – die Tatsache hinlänglich beweisen, dass jene alten Griechen, Platon, Pythagoras, Thales, Solon, Lykurg und andere, die ihre Anhängerschaft in der Philosophie leiteten, ebenso zum vorteilhaften Handel mit Weisheit und Wissen nach Ägypten gereist sind. Und ich bin auch der Meinung, dass man nicht mit Schweigen übergehen darf, dass in früheren Zeiten die Ägypter Männer und Frauen, die sich durch Frömmigkeit und Keuschheit auszeichneten, Nonni und Nonnae genannt haben[62]. Denn ganz klar könnte man daraus ableiten, dass unserem Dichter wegen seiner überaus heiligsamen und unbescholtenen Charaktereigenschaften dieser Namen von seinen Landsleuten beigegeben worden war.

Das überaus originelle Thema seines Werkes ist die Familie des Bacchus, seine Wundertaten, seine Reisen, der Krieg mit Deriades[63], dem König der Inder, und mit Anderen, seine Siege und Triumphe: Mit diesem Thema hat sich auch Dionysios[64] beschäftigt, dessen *Bassarika* von Stephanos erwähnt werden.

---

[59] Ca. 400–470 n. Chr.: ACCORINTI (s. Anm. 38), 1108–1110.
[60] Heliodor von Emesa (3. Jh. n. Chr.), Verfasser der Geschichten von Theagenes und Charikleia (*Aithiopika*, 10 Bücher).
[61] Vgl. Anm. 48.
[62] Vgl. Anm. 32.
[63] König Deriades, Sohn des Flusses Hydaspes und der Nymphe Astris, Nonnos, *Dion.* 26–40.
[64] Vgl. Anm. 33.

Tanta vero est in hoc libro orationis copia, et dulcedo, tanta rerum varietas, tam bene decorum ubique servatum, vix ut quicquam desiderari possit. Aeschylum accepimus dicere solitum | suas tragoedias esse τεμάχη τῶν μεγάλου ὁμήρου δείπνων: sic huius poetae ornamenta nihil esse aliud possumus dicere, quam luculentam Homerici carminis paraphrasin. ita in universo Homeri corpore nihil pulcri est, nihil magnopere utile, quod hic noster non ingeniose fuerit aemulatus. Atque ego crediderim, si Homerus amissus esset, nec ulla exstarent de imitatione praecepta, ea omnia, quae in illo admirari solemus, ex hoc fonte hauriri posse, et restitui. Si autem verum est id, quod vulgo dici solet, nos illorum mores, atque adeo animos induere, quibuscum familiariter versamur, quis hic non constituat quasi quandam μετεμψύχωσιν, et credat Nonnum Homeri animum, cuius poema nunquam de manibus deposuit, assiduo lectionis usu lucri fecisse? quis hoc non libenter fateatur, cum ita divinum illum poetam ad imitandum sibi proposuerit, ut non, quod ceteri facere solent, Pierides, sed Homericas plerunque Musas invocet? Neque sane praesentiores alibi Deas reperire potuisset. Siquidem non tantum opes, et animum, sed et verba non nihil Homericis grandiora cumulate illi subministrarunt, et suggesserunt. Sunt hic, fateor, permulta, quae Critici in dubium vocabunt, et contendent in Tragico esse, quam Epico tolerabiliora: quae ut So-phi|stico saeculo ab illis condonari possunt, ita mihi orationis aequabilitas, et similitudo admirabilis sonantium verborum, et epithetorum sesquipedalium elegantia, et iuconditate perfusa mirum in modum placet. adeo ut quod illi forsan vitio vertent, ego in minime vulgari laude ponam. Nam haec grandis, et elata Nonni compositio tam ubique sibi constat, tam dilucida, tamque suavis est, ut nullo labore conquisita, et sua sponte fusa videatur. quod cum alii olim, qui illa ingenii dexteritate, quae ad hanc rem requiritur, carebant, labore, diligentia, et vigiliis assequi conarentur, accidit ut illorum in sublimi eloquendi genere scripta industriam magis, et curam, quam naturam redolerent, ideoque in varias reprehensiones incurrerent.

---

86 Athenaeus, *Deipnosoph.* 8, 347e || **99** Nonnus, *Dion.* 25, 1–10; 25, 253–270; 32, 184

86 τεμά || **103** contendant e **F** *s. l.*; Ethico Epico **F** *s. l.* || **104** ab illis condonari possunt, ita mihi orationis aequabilitas, et similitudo **F** *mg.* || **108** ubi

Es ist solch eine Fülle an Redekunst in diesem Werk, und Wonne, eine solche Buntheit der Darstellung, es ist überall fein die Anmut gewahrt, dass kaum ein Wunsch offen bleiben könnte. Wir wissen, dass Aischylos zu sagen pflegte, seine Tragödien seien „Schnittstücke vom Mahle des großen Homer": So können wir auch sagen, dass die Zierstücke dieses Dichters nichts Anderes sind, als eine treffliche Paraphrase des homerischen Epos. So gibt es in der gesamten Homerischen Dichtung nichts Schönes, nichts von bedeutendem Nutzen, das dieser unser Dichter nicht in genialer Weise nachgeahmt hätte[65]. Ich würde sogar behaupten, wenn Homer verloren wäre, und es keinerlei Angaben gäbe über die Nachahmung, dann könnten wir all das, was wir bei jenem zu bewundern pflegen, aus dieser Quelle schöpfen und ersetzen!

Wenn das wirklich wahr ist, was man allgemein zu sagen pflegt, dass uns deren Lebensart und auch sehr deren Denkweise anziehen, mit denen wir uns gerne und ausführlich beschäftigen, wer könnte dann da nicht gewissermaßen eine Metempsychose (Seelenwanderung) feststellen und glauben, dass Nonnos die Seele Homers, dessen Dichtung er niemals aus den Händen legte, durch beständige Lektüre mit Gewinn zu seinem Eigentum gemacht habe? Wer würde denn nicht freimütig zugeben, dass er, weil er sich den göttlichen Dichter zum Vorbild genommen hat, nicht, was die Anderen zu tun pflegen, die Pieridischen, sondern zumeist die homerischen Musen anruft? Und gewiss hätte er anderswo keine wirksameren Göttinnen finden können! Und so haben sie ihm nicht nur die Mittel und auch die geistige Fähigkeit, sondern auch noch Wörter in großer Menge zur Verfügung gestellt und herbeigeschafft, die nichts weniger sind als viel prächtiger als die Homerischen. Darunter, das gebe ich zu, sind sehr viele, die Kritiker in Zweifel ziehen werden, und von denen sie sagen werden, dass man sie bei einem tragischen Dichter leichter ertragen kann als bei einem Epiker: Aber so, wie diese von ihnen einer sophistischen Epoche zugerechnet werden können, so gefällt mir in ganz wunderbarer Weise die Gleichmäßigkeit der Rede und die bewundernswerte Ähnlichkeit der Wortklänge und die Eleganz der endlos langen Epitheta, durchdrungen von Anmut, so sehr, dass ich genau das, was diese vielleicht als Fehler betrachten, mit keineswegs gewöhnlichem Lob versehen möchte. Denn diese großartige und erhabene Dichtung des Nonnos ruht überall so sehr in sich selbst, ist so rein und klar, so anmutig, dass sie durch keinerlei Kraftanstrengung zusammengestellt, sondern wie von selbst entströmt zu sein scheint. Obwohl in alter Zeit manch Andere, die eine solche Gewandtheit des Geistes nicht hatten, dies durch Arbeit, Fleiß und durchwachte Nächte zu erreichen versuchten, ist das Ergebnis dennoch, dass ihre im hohen Stil der Beredsamkeit abgefassten Schriften mehr nach Fleiß und Bemühung als nach der Natur riechen und sich infolgedessen vielfältiger Kritik aussetzen.

---

[65] Vgl. Herbert BANNERT, Nicole KRÖLL, Nonnus and the Homeric Poems. In: Domenico Accorinti (ed.), *Brill's Companion to Nonnus of Panopolis*. Leiden, Boston 2016, 481–506.

Neque vero hoc solum natura duce, comite doctrina Nonnus fuit consecutus, ut in hoc haudquaquam fucato eloquentiae splendore excelluerit: sed etiam non mediocri significantissimorum verborum, et epithetorum numero linguam Graecam auxit; ne quid interim de illis versibus dicam, qui iure optimo proverbiorum vice usurpari poterunt.

Quae cum ita se habeant, optarim severiores illos aestimatores, antequam iudicium de hoc auctore faciant, bis terve universum opus legere, et relegere. Multa vi|debuntur prima fronte absurda, plura perperam detorta, plurima tanquam indigna poësi reiicienda. quae, diligenti habita inquisitione, Nonno praecipuum a nobis amorem conciliant, cumque excelso atque eminenti loco statuunt. hoc mihi evenisse negare non possum: neque dubito quin idem accidere possit aliis studio, et voluntate a Musis non abhorrentibus. Hortor igitur Graecae linguae studiosos, ne ita se affectibus rapi patiantur, ut hunc auctorem visum quidem, sed incognitum damnent, qua peste in re litteraria nulla perniciosior excogitari potest. Hinc fit, ut et recte dicta calumniemur, et callida, et inepta aliorum argumenta, opinione, et favore ducti, pro veris etiam inviti saepe defendamus. Unde non sine magno animi mei dolore recordari possum, complures non tinctos, sed probe litteris imbutos eo dementiae progredi, ut et a libris, quos nunquam inspexerunt, abhorreant, nonnullorum saltem auctoritate impulsi, qui apud vulgus videri, quam esse docti malunt. Quibus equidem non invideo, modo ne moleste ferant nos liberalissimam animi remissionem e Dionysiacis petere. Coepi autem ego Nonnum mirabiliter diligere, et suspicere, cum primum Euangelicae historiae sancti Ioannis conversionem ipsius accurate | perlegissem. quam propter religiosam, et ad rem accommodatam dictionis maiestatem plurimi semper feci. nam quod antea vix fieri posse putabam, ut tam sublimem materiam numerosa caperet oratio, id ita omnibus suis partibus perfectum expletumque in illo carmine animadverti, ut saepe unum Nonni malim epitheton, quam prolixa aliorum commentaria.

---

141 fieri **F** s. l.

Denn nicht nur das hat Nonnos unter der Führung der Natur, begleitet von seiner Gelehrsamkeit, vollbracht, so dass er sich in einem in keiner Weise verfälschten Glanz der Beredsamkeit hervortun konnte, sondern er hat die griechische Sprache mit einer nicht unbedeutenden Anzahl besonders bezeichnender Wörter und Beiwörter bereichert – und dabei möchte ich noch gar nicht über die Verse sprechen, die mit vollem Recht den Status von Sprichwörtern für sich beanspruchen können.

Unter diesen Voraussetzungen möchte ich doch hoffen, dass diese Kritiker, bevor sie ein Urteil über den Autor abgeben, sein ganzes Werk zweimal und dreimal lesen und wieder lesen! Vieles wird auf den ersten Blick abgeschmackt, mehr noch völlig verkehrt, sehr vieles echter Dichtung unwürdig und daher abzulehnen erscheinen; doch genau dies gewinnt Nonnos nach sorgfältiger Untersuchung unsere besondere Zuneigung und setzt ihn auf einen erhabenen und weithin sichtbaren Rang. Dass mir dies so geschehen ist, kann ich nicht leugnen, und ich zweifle nicht, dass es auch Anderen so ergehen könnte, wenn sie in ihrem Eifer und ihrer Haltung den Musen verbunden sind. Daher fordere ich die Liebhaber der griechischen Sprache auf, dass sie sich von ihren Empfindungen nicht dazu hinreißen lassen, diesen Dichter zwar angesehen, aber nicht näher kennengelernt zu haben und ihn dennoch verdammen, ein Unheil, das in der Literaturwissenschaft schlimmer nicht erdacht werden könnte. Denn aus diesem Grunde geschieht es, dass uns auch richtig Verfasstes dunkel bleibt, und wir hinterlistig erfundene und geistlose Urteile von Anderen, durch vorgefasste Meinung und Zuneigung verleitet, sehr oft auch gegen unseren Willen an Stelle der Wahrheit verfechten. In diesem Zusammenhang kann ich mich nicht ohne großen Schmerz aus meinem Gedächtnis erinnern, dass sehr viele Leute, die nicht nur einen äußeren Anstrich von Literaturkenntnis haben, sondern von ihr regelrecht durchdrungen sind, in ihrer Unzurechnungsfähigkeit so weit fortgeschritten sind, dass sie vor Büchern zurückschrecken, die sie nie in der Hand gehabt haben, und sie lassen sich dabei von der Autorität einiger Weniger leiten, die bei der breiten Masse lieber gebildet erscheinen wollen, als es auch tatsächlich zu sein. Ich neide es ihnen nicht, solange sie es nicht als eine Art Belästigung empfinden, dass wir außerordentlich reiche Erholung des Denkens aus den Dionysiaka beziehen. Ich selbst habe in dem Augenblick begonnen, Nonnos ganz wunderbar zu schätzen und zu bewundern, als ich seine Übertragung der Evangeliendarstellung des heiligen Johannes genau durchgelesen hatte[66]. Wegen ihrer frommen und der Erhabenheit der Sache angepassten Diktion habe ich sie stets überaus geschätzt. Denn ich hätte früher kaum je glauben können, dass eine in Versen gebundene Erzählung einen derart erhabenen Stoff bewältigen könnte, und gerade das habe ich in diesem Gedicht in allen Teilen vollkommen und erfüllt gefunden, dass ich oft lieber ein einziges Epitheton des Nonnos lieber hätte als die weitschweifigen Kommentare von Anderen.

---

[66] Vgl. Anm. 13 und 14.

Sed mirari satis nequeo reperiri quosdam, qui negent Dionysiaca, et Eu- 145
angelicam illam paraphrasin eiusdem esse Nonni. quos quid moveat, equidem ignoro, nisi existiment unum hominem in tam dissimilibus argumentis
elaborare non potuisse. quod quam probabiliter dici possit, ipsi viderint.
Carminis sane eadem est in Paraphrasi ratio, quae in Dionysiacis, epitheta
eadem, filum orationis idem, usqueadeo ut hemistichi et integri versus hinc 150
in illam deriventur, quos suis locis indicavimus. Si vero hoc satis non est,
sufficiat Suidae [in voce νόννος] auctoritas, qui disertis verbis tradit paraphrasin a Nonno Panopolite fuisse confectam; quem Dionysiaca scripsisse
Agathius testatur, et vetus illud distichon, quod vel ab ipso Nonno, vel alio
ipsius perquam studioso Dionysiacis olim praefixum fuit. Neque enim am- 155
plius sunt audiendi, qui aliam ex eo Nonni Gigantomachiam commenti
fuerunt, cum ipse in Diony|siacis Indos Gigantes appellet.

Dicat nunc aliquis a Musis aversus, Quid proderunt mihi Dionysiaca,
non absimilia veris Luciani narrationibus, in quibus nihil veri, sed fabulosa
sunt omnia? malo historiae guttam, quam fabularum Oceanum. Cui, cum 160
iam a doctissimis quibusque, abunde sit demonstratum, quid sub fabularum involucris lateat, cantilenam eandem canere nolo. veruntamen si
quisquam est inter Graecis litteris eruditos tam animo agresti ac duro, cui
haec leviora studia ἀπροσδιόνυσα videantur, illum certe non solum pi-
geat, verum etiam pudeat stultitiae, et inscientiae suae. 165

---

154 *Anthologia Graeca* 9, 198 || 157 Nonnus, *Dion.* 31, 173; 48, 13 et passim

152 in voce νόννος || 153 Panopolita || 154 Agathias || 156 Neque – appellet *desunt* || 160 ~~guttulam~~ (?) guttam **F** *s. l.* || 163 ~~duro ac~~ agresti; ac duro **F** *s. l.* | 165 inscitiae ē *s. l.*

Doch kann ich mich nicht genug wundern, dass sich immer wieder welche finden, die leugnen, dass die Dionysiaka und jene Paraphrase des Evangeliums von demselben Nonnos stammen. Was diese Leute dazu bewegt, das weiß ich nicht, außer vielleicht dass sie der Meinung sind, dass ein einzelner Mensch in so verschiedenen Themenbereichen nicht arbeiten kann; dass dies etwas glaubhafter behauptet werden kann, mögen sie selbst sehen! Es ist die Art und Weise der Dichtung in der Paraphrase mit Sicherheit dieselbe wie in den Dionysiaka, die Epitheta sind dieselben, die Linie der Darstellung ist dieselbe, und das geht so weit, dass halbe und ganze Verse von diesen in jene übernommen werden, was wir an den entsprechenden Stellen verzeichnet haben. Wenn das aber noch nicht genug ist, möge die Autorität der Suda dafür ausreichend sein, die in klaren Angaben überliefert, dass die Paraphrase von Nonnos aus Panopolis angefertigt wurde, von dem Agathias bezeugt, dass er die Dionysiaka geschrieben hat, und auch das alte Distichon, das entweder von Nonnos selbst oder von einem anderen respektablen Gelehrten einst den Dionysiaka vorangestellt worden war[67]. Und man darf auch nicht weiter auf diejenigen hören, die sich aufgrund dieses Distichons ausgedacht haben, dass es noch eine andere Gigantomachie des Nonnos gäbe, obwohl er in den Dionysiaka die Inder als Giganten bezeichnet.

Es könnte nun einer, der den Musen ganz ferne steht, sagen: „Was bringen mir die Dionysiaka, die den wahren Geschichten des Lukian nicht unähnlich sind, in denen nichts wahr, sondern alles fabelhaft ist? Ich will lieber einen Tropfen Geschichte als einen Ozean von Geschichten!" Da ja schon, und gerade auch von den besten Gelehrten, mehr als genug nachgewiesen wurde, was unter dem Deckmantel der Geschichten verborgen ist, will ich dieselbe alte Leier nicht noch einmal singen. Wenn aber nun doch unter den in griechischer Literatur Gebildeten einer mit einer ebenso einfältigen wie hartnäckigen Meinung ist, dem diese weniger ernsthafte Beschäftigung „undionysisch"[68] erscheint, dem sollen seine Dummheit und sein Unwissen nicht nur unangenehm sein, sondern er soll sich dafür schämen.

---

[67] Vgl. Anm. 34.
[68] Das Wort ist in der griechischen Literatur belegt bei Lukian, *Bacchus* 6, 5; Plutarch, *Quaestiones Convivales* 2, 612e9 und 671e11; Athenaios, *Deipnosophistai* 11, 85, 41; 15, 12, 6; Heliodor, *Aithiopika* 3, 10, 2; Eunapios, *Historiae* (1, 211, 3 DINDORF = fr. 1, 86 BLOCKLEY); die *editio princeps* der *Vitae philosophorum et sophistarum* des Eunapios, nach einer unbekannten, sehr fehlerhaften Handschrift, war gerade im Jahr zuvor, 1568, bei Plantin erschienen (besorgt von Hadrianus Junius, mit lateinischer Übersetzung); Falkenburg steuerte ein griechisches Epigramm auf Eunapios bei (*editio princeps*, p. 16); ob auch Kenntnis der Historienfragmente angenommen werden kann, ist fraglich. Sicher war Falkenburg jedoch mit dem Beleg bei Cicero, *Att.* 16, 13 vertraut. Er verwendet das Wort noch einmal in seinem an den Leser gerichteten Nachwort, als er über seine im Folgenden angeführten Konjekturen und Verbesserungen spricht: 862 *Si vero, quod mirum non est, multi occurrant iactus* ἀπροσδιόνυσοι, *tuae humanitatis erit non tam quid Nonno conveniat, quam quae mea fuerit voluntas, expendere.*

Ad me quod attinet, equidem solide gaudeo, huius praesertim infelicis belli tempore, quo nulla mihi iura sapiunt, hunc auctorem oblatum ad recolenda illa studia, quorum ab adolescentia cupidissimus fui. in quo ut libentissime acquievi, ita uberrimos mei laboris fructus cepi. primum enim per amoenissimos omnium fabularum labyrinthos me ad Liberum patrem deduxit, eiusque res gestas, tanquam in tabula depictas, ita oculis meis subiecit, ut animum contemplando ne nunc quidem explere possim. Deum immortalem, quanta hic consiliorum, occasionum, et eventuum varietas! quam elegantes locorum descriptiones! quot ritus, et consuetudines! Animi vero | motus, omniaque communis vitae officia ita decore hic exprimuntur, ut humanos, et amabiles scriptoris mores liceat agnoscere. Quid hic reliquas digressiones, quas ἐπεισόδια vocant Graeci, enumerem, ex quibus non exigua utilitas ad Philosophos, Oratores, et Historicos dimanabit? Est hic, in quo se Astrologi exercere possint, neque deest quod oblectet Medicos, habent et quod venerentur Iurisconsulti nostri.

    Adde quod hic multa videre liceat, quae apud alios non tantum non sunt obvia, sed nusquam in libris impressis reperiuntur. Ad Ovidii quoque Metamorphosin illustrandam, ceterorumque Graecorum et Latinorum poetarum explicationem non parum Nonnus adiumenti attulerit. Iuvabit interdum floridiora quaedam loca conferre, et, quod uni deest, ex altero supplere. Quae collatio quantum conducat ad utriusque linguae cognitionem parandam, illi intelligunt, qui Virgilio interprete Homerum familiarem sibi fecerunt.

---

170 Bacchum || **179** neque deest quod oblectet Medicos, habent et quod venerentur Iurisconsulti nostri **F** *mg.* || **180** quorum perhonorifica hic fit mentio

Was mich betrifft, ich freue mich mit gutem Grunde sehr, besonders in der Zeit dieses unseligen Krieges,[69] in dem mir Rechtsangelegenheiten gar nicht zusagen, dass mir dieser Autor anvertraut wurde, um jene Studien wieder aufzunehmen, nach denen ich mich seit meiner Jugendzeit ganz besonders gesehnt habe. Und ebenso, wie ich mich in diese mit großem Vergnügen eingefunden habe, habe ich aus meiner Arbeit auch überaus reichen Ertrag erhalten. Denn zuerst hat sie mich durch die reizvollsten Irrwege aller möglichen Mythen zu Vater Bacchus geführt und mir seine Taten, wie auf einem Bilde gemalt[70], so lebendig vor meine Augen gestellt, dass ich meine Phantasie bei der Betrachtung auch jetzt noch nicht zur Gänze ausfüllen könnte. Großer Gott, welche Abwechslung an Versammlungen, Vorfällen und Ereignissen gibt es hier! Welch elegante Beschreibungen von Orten! Wie viele Riten und Gebräuche! Gemütsbewegungen und alle anderen Begebnisse eines normalen Lebens werden hier mit solcher Zierlichkeit dargestellt, dass man die humane und liebenswerte Gesinnung des Verfassers gut erkennen kann. Warum soll ich hier noch die übrigen Exkurse, die die Griechen Episoden nennen, aufzählen, aus denen ein nicht geringer Nutzen auf Philosophen, Redner und Historiker ausstrahlen wird? Hier ist der Ort, an dem sich Astrologen bilden können, und es fehlt auch nichts, was Ärzte erfreuen könnte, und auch unsere Rechtsgelehrten haben etwas, womit sie sich ehrfurchtsvoll beschäftigen können.

Denk dir noch dazu, dass man hier Vieles sehen kann, was bei Anderen nicht nur nicht vorkommt, sondern nirgendwo in gedruckten Büchern aufgefunden werden kann. Und auch zur Illustration der Metamorphosen des Ovid[71] sowie zur Erklärung der übrigen griechischen und lateinischen Dichter sollte Nonnos nicht wenig Hilfestellung bieten. Es wird hilfreich sein, manch blumig-bunte Stellen zu vergleichen und, was der einen fehlt, aus der anderen zu ergänzen. Wieviel eine solche Zusammenschau dazu beitragen könnte, die Kenntnis jeder der beiden Sprachen zu verbessern, wissen diejenigen, die sich durch die Vermittlung Vergils mit Homer vertraut gemacht haben.

---

[69] Es handelt sich wohl um den Dritten Hugenottenkrieg: In der Schlacht von Jarnac (Dép. Charente) am 13. März 1569 siegten die Katholiken, geführt vom späteren Marschall de Tavannes und dem Herzog von Anjou, dem späteren König Heinrich III. Oder Falkenburg meint den Beginn der Auseinandersetzungen zwischen der spanischen Krone und den Niederlanden, die am 23. Mai 1568 zur Schlacht von Heiligerlee (Provinz Groningen) und zum ersten Sieg der Aufständischen unter der Führung von Ludwig und Adolf von Nassau führte (Beginn des Achtzigjährigen Krieges, Abfall der Niederlande, Westfälischer Frieden 1648).

[70] Vgl. den Dreizeiler des Angelus Politianus, der von Falkenburg als Motto gewählt wurde – s. oben Anm. 34.

[71] Vgl. Anm. 35.

Postremo id est in hoc inexhausto omnium bonorum thesauro singulare, ut si vel centies studiose diligenterque illum evolveris, et excusseris, semper aliquid apportet novi, semper aliquid moneat quod nesciveris, semper incredibili animum voluptate pascat. Quare summopere est deplorandum, esse in hoc libro quae|dam et temporum vitio, et librarii incuria, qui saepius alio dictante scripsisse videtur, minus integra et depravata; quorum tamen maxima pars eiusmodi est, ut coniecturae aleam non gravate admittere videatur. Ne vero fidem quis in nobis, et candorem requireret, nihil mutavi; et operam dedi, ut tuum exemplar, quo solo usi fuimus, diligentissime exprimeretur. idem in Aristaeneto, et Eunapio fuit observatum: idem in Ioannis Stobaei Physicis tuis curabitur propediem; neque negligetur in Illustrio itidem tuo, quem cum Hadriani Iunii V. C. conversione Latina quotidie exspectamus.

190

195

200

198 ΑΡΙΣΤΑΙΝΕΤΟΥ ΕΠΙΣΤΟΛΑΙ ΕΡΩΤΙΚΑΙ [...] E Bibliotheca V. C. Ioan. Sambuci. Antverpiae: ex officina Christophori Plantini 1566. || **198** ΕΥΝΑΠΙΟΥ ΤΟΥ ΣΑΡΔΙΑΝΟΥ ΒΙΟΙ ΦΙΛΟΣΟφων καὶ σοφιστῶν. E bibliotheca Ioan. Sambuci Pannonii Tirnauiensis. Antverpiae: ex officina Christophori Plantini 1568. EVNAPIVS SARDIANVS De vitis philosophorum et sophistarum, nunc primum Graece et Latine editus, interprete Hadriano Junio Hornano. Antverpiae: ex officina Christophori Plantini 1568. || **199** IOANNIS STOBAEI ECLOGARVM LIBRI DVO quorum prior Physicas, posterior Ethicas complectitur, nunc primum Graece editi; interprete Gulielmo Cantero. Una et GEORGII GEMISTI PLETHONIS DE REBVS PELOPONNESIACIS ORATIONES DVAE, Eodem Gulielmo Cantero interprete. Accessit et alter eiusdem Plethonis libellus Graecus De virtutibus. Ex bibliotheca C. V. I. Sambuci. Antverpiae: ex officina Christophori Plantini 1575. || **200** ΗΣΥΧΙΟΥ ΜΙΛΗΣΙΟΥ ΙΛΛΟΥΣΤΡΙΟΥ ΠΕΡΙ τῶν ἐν παιδείᾳ διαλαμψάντων σοφῶν. Ex bibliotheca Ioannis Sambuci Pannonii Tirnauiensis. Antverpiae: ex officina Christophori Plantini 1572.

190 studiose; studioso *ed. pr., corr.* || et excusseris **S** *s. l.* || **196** admitti || **199** in Ioannis Stobaei Physicis tuis curabitur propediem; neque negligetur *desunt*; idem in Illustrio tuo curabitur

Und schließlich ist einzigartig an diesem unerschöpflichen Schatz von allem Schönen, dass du, auch wenn du ihn hundertmal eifrig und aufmerksam ausgebreitet und durchgearbeitet hast, er dir doch stets irgendetwas Neues bringt, stets etwas auffällt, das du nicht gewusst hast, stets den Geist mit unglaublichem Vergnügen versorgt. Aus diesem Grunde ist es außerordentlich beklagenswert, dass es in diesem Buch infolge von Altersschäden und auch durch die Nachlässigkeit des Schreibers, der recht oft nach dem Diktat eines Anderen geschrieben zu haben scheint, manche unvollständige und verdorbene Stellen gibt, die aber größten Teils von der Art sind, dass sie den Glückstreffer einer Konjektur nicht ungern zulassen dürften. Damit aber niemand bei mir Zuverlässigkeit und Redlichkeit einmahnen könnte, habe ich grundsätzlich nichts geändert, und ich habe mich bemüht, dass dein Exemplar, das ich als einziges benützt habe, in allen Details ganz genau gedruckt würde. Auf dieselbe Vorgehensweise wurde bei Aristainetos[72] und auch bei Eunapios[73] geachtet, und ebenso wird sie demnächst bei deiner Physik des Stobaios[74] angewendet werden, und sie wird genauso wenig vernachlässigt werden in deinem [Hesychius] Illustrius, den wir, zusammen mit der Übersetzung von Hadrianus Junius, täglich erwarten[75].

---

[72] Die *editio princeps* des Aristainetos wurde 1566 von Sambucus bei Plantin in Antwerpen herausgegeben, die einzige Handschrift (geschrieben um 1200; Wien, ÖNB, Cod. phil. gr. 310) stammt aus seinem Besitz. ALMÁSI, KISS (s. Anm. 7), 71–73.

[73] Die *editio princeps* der Sophistenviten des Eunapios als Einzelausgabe ist 1568 bei Plantin erschienen, mit dem griechischen Text bearbeitet von Sambucus und einer lateinischen Übersetzung von Hadrianus Junius, nach einer sehr fehlerhaften, heute verlorenen Handschrift, einer Abschrift des Cod. Laurentianus Mediceus 86, 7 (was weder Sambucus noch Hadrianus Junius noch Falkenburg wussten); vgl. *Eunapii Vitae Sophistarum*, rec. Ioseph GIANGRANDE. Rom 1956, VII–VIII). Falkenburg hat zu dieser Ausgabe vier griechische Disticha beigesteuert. Eine genaue Beschreibung der Entstehungsstadien von Text und Übersetzung gibt GERSTINGER (s. Anm. 2), 303–305, vgl. GERSTINGER (s. Anm. 6), 348 und ALMÁSI, KISS (s. Anm. 7), LVIf.

[74] Die Ausgabe der ersten beiden Bücher des Stobaios, zusammen mit Schriften des Georgios Gemistos Plethon von Johannes Sambucus herausgegeben und von Wilhelm Canter mit einer lateinischen Übersetzung versehen, wurde 1575 bei Plantin in Antwerpen gedruckt; über die zugrunde liegenden Handschriften und deren Verbleib vgl. GERSTINGER (s. Anm. 2), 315–317 und GERSTINGER (s. Anm. 6), 348. ALMÁSI, KISS (s. Anm. 7), 192–204.

[75] Hesychios Milesios (Hesychius Illustrius), Περὶ τῶν ἐν παιδείᾳ διαλαμψάντων σοφῶν, wurde 1572 mit dem griechischen Text und der lateinischen Übersetzung von Hadrianus Junius (mit Anmerkungen und Lesarten im Anhang) bei Plantin in Antwerpen gedruckt; griechische und lateinische Version haben jeweils ein eigenes Titelblatt, ALMÁSI, KISS (s. Anm. 7), LVII und 155–161. Die Handschrift des Hesych ist in der ÖNB nicht vorhanden, scheint also nicht mehr an Sambucus zurückgekommen zu sein. Vgl. GERSTINGER (s. Anm. 2), 305.

Hanc rationem si omnes typographi sequerentur, neque quorumvis emendationes infarcirent, multo facilius cum veteribus auctoribus in gratiam rediremus. Dici enim vix potest, quoties nostrum nos fallat iudicium, cum saepe illa, quae heri pro oraculis habuerimus, repudiemus, et nihili faciamus hodie. Quocirca non male illum olim iudicasse arbitror, qui interrogatus quodnam Homeri exemplar omnium esset optimum, respondit, Id quod minime correctum. Quod, si unquam verum fuit, nos in dies verissimum experimur, quando plerique tantum sibi sumunt, ut in veterum scriptis non aliter ac suis quidvis sibi licere putent. Hanc ob caussam, etsi viderem | in tuo archetypo plura vulnera, quae vel mediocriter Graece doctus sanare posset; malui tamen seorsum meas quasdam de locis suspectis annotare coniecturas, et lectiones, quam quae mihi temere fortasse in mente venerunt, passim in contextum, ut vocant, inserere.

    Volui autem hoc labore illis tantum prodesse, qui a libris mendosis plane abstinere solent, ut habeant a me saltem aliquid, quod ad Nonnum intelligendum faciat. quam voluntatem meam spero lectores in optimam partem accepturos, quoad prodeant alii, qui ex vetustorum codicum fide loca vacua suppleant, et mutila laceraque restituant. quam palmam nemo, ut opinor, praeripiet Carolo Utenhovio Caroli praestantissimi viri filio; cuius acerrimum ingenium multorum mihi sermone Lutetiae cognitum, in Anglia annis abhinc amplius quinque, non sine maxima voluptate me perspexisse memini. Ille enim ante tot annos vertere Nonnum coepit, ut credibile sit interea multas illum paginas pervolutando manibus contrivisse. neque video quis melius Latine Nonnum reddere possit, quam ille, qui et in poëtarum omnium scriptis assiduissime fuit versatus, et plura huius libri habuit exemplaria. Exspectabunt idcirco docti non tantum Latinam ab illo interpretationem, sed etiam au|ctorem ipsum ab omnibus mendis vindicatum. Atque utinam sua tam cito proferat, quam avide hactenus a quam plurimis fuerunt expetita, memor veteris proverbii: Bis dat, qui cito dat.

---

230 Publilius Syrus, *sent.* 64 (Erasmus, *Adag.* 791/1.8.91)

205 oraculis **S**; oculis *ed. pr., corr.* || **228** perpolitam ab illo Latinam interpretationem

Wenn alle Buchdrucker diese Vorgangsweise befolgten, und nicht Verbesserungen von irgendwelchen Leuten hineinstopfen würden, könnten wir viel leichter mit den alten Autoren in Freundschaft verkehren. Denn es ist kaum zu sagen, wie oft unser Urteil uns täuschen kann, wenn wir oft das, was wir gestern klar vor Augen gehabt haben, zurückweisen und heute für Unsinn halten müssen. Deshalb glaube ich auch, dass jener dereinst nicht schlecht geurteilt hat, der auf die Frage, welche Ausgabe des Homer denn die beste von allen sei, geantwortet hat: „die mit den wenigsten Korrekturen." Wenn das jemals wahr gewesen ist, erfahren wir es heutzutage als absolute Wahrheit, wenn die Meisten für sich in Anspruch nehmen, dass sie glauben, in den Schriften der Alten steht ihnen nichts Anderes frei als in ihren eigenen[76]. Aus diesem Grund, und obwohl ich in deinem Archetypus viele Schäden erkennen konnte, die auch ein in der griechischen Sprache nur mittelmäßig Bewanderter hätte heilen können, wollte ich doch lieber getrennt meine Konjekturen zu verdächtigen Stellen verzeichnen, und ebenso die Lesarten, als das, was mir vielleicht zufällig gerade in den Sinn kam, jeweils in den Kontext, wie man so sagt, einfügen.

Ich wollte auch mit dieser Arbeit nur jenen einen Nutzen erweisen, die sich von fehlerhaften Büchern völlig fernzuhalten pflegen, damit sie wenigstens Etwas von mir haben, was zum Verständnis des Nonnos beitragen kann. Diesen meinen Wunsch, hoffe ich, werden die Leser positiv aufnehmen, insofern ja andere vortreten können, die nach dem Zeugnis alter Handschriften Leerstellen ausfüllen und Zerstörtes und Zerrissenes wiederherstellen. Diese Auszeichnung, glaube ich, wird niemand dem Carolus Utenhove, dem Sohn des hervorragenden Carolus, wegnehmen; von seinem überaus scharfen Verstand, erinnere ich mich, wurde mir im Gespräch mit Vielen in Paris berichtet, und in England, vor mehr als fünf Jahren, konnte ich mich dann nicht ohne große Bewunderung selbst davon überzeugen. Denn er hat vor so vielen Jahren begonnen, Nonnos zu übersetzen, dass es durchaus glaubhaft ist, dass er inzwischen viele Seiten bei der genauen Lektüre mit seinen Händen abgewetzt hat. Und ich sehe auch niemanden, der Nonnos besser ins Lateinische übersetzen könnte, als er, der mit den Texten aller Dichter unablässig beschäftigt gewesen ist und außerdem mehrere Exemplare dieses Buches bei sich hatte. Es werden infolgedessen die Gebildeten von ihm nicht nur eine (geschliffene) lateinische Übersetzung erwarten, sondern auch einen Autor, der von allen Mängeln befreit ist. Und möge er seine Arbeit so schnell herausgeben, wie sie bis jetzt ungeduldig von den Meisten verlangt worden ist, eingedenk des alten Sprichwortes: Doppelt gibt, wer schnell gibt.

---

[76] Vgl. Anm. 36.

Lectiones vero et coniecturas meas, Ioannes Sambuce, visum fuit tibi potissimum quasi tacito fenoris nomine, quam diu Nonno caruisti, debitas, dedicare; tum ut aditum ad tuam mihi amicitiam aperiant, tum ut animi erga te mei gratitudinem publice testatam relinquant. Quem laborem meum si tibi non displicuisse intellexero, fructum amplissimum videbor consecutus, et ad maiora posthac alacrius accedam. 235

Vale. Antverpia, VIII. kal. Martias, anno a Christo Servatore nato M. D. lxix.

---

235 reliquant etc. *desunt cetera*

Meine Lesarten aber und meine Konjekturen, Johannes Sambucus, so schien es mir, sollen dir, der du so lange deinen Nonnos entbehren musstest, am ehesten quasi unter der stillschweigenden Bezeichnung eines Zinsgewinnes, als Schuldentilgung gewidmet werden; dann mögen sie mir einen Zugang zu deiner Freundschaft eröffnen, dann mögen sie als Zeugnis meiner Dankbarkeit dir gegenüber öffentlich sichtbar bleiben. Wenn ich erkannt haben werde, dass meine Arbeit dir nicht missfallen hat, werde ich für mich offensichtlich reichlichen Lohn erhalten haben, und umso eifriger werde ich dann etwas noch Größeres anfangen.

Herzlichen Gruß!

Antwerpen, am 22. Februar im Jahre nach der Geburt Christi des Erlösers 1569.

Johannes Sambucus und seine Hunde Bombo und Madel

HERBERT BANNERT (Wien)

Abb. 1: Porträt des Sambucus. Emblemata et aliquot nummi antiqui operis. Antverpiae: ex officina Christophori Plantini 1566
(Wien, Universitätsbibliothek I 125.521)

> „Dem Hunde, wenn er gut gezogen, / Wird selbst ein weiser Mann gewogen."
> Johann Wolfgang von Goethe, *Faust I*, v. 1174f. (Wagner)

Auf seinen Reisen begleiteten Sambucus seine beiden Hunde Bombo und Madel, und auf Holzschnitten ab der ersten Auflage (1564) der *Emblemata* hat Sambucus die Hunde mit in das Bild genommen: im Emblem FIDEI CANUM EXEMPLUM, einer Dokumentation seiner vielen Reisen durch Europa, zu Pferde und mit beiden Hunden als Begleitung, und auf demselben Bild, weiter im Hintergrund, noch einmal zu Schiff, und wieder sind die Hunde mit im Boot (Abb. 2)[1]. Auf dem Autorenporträt der zweiten Auflage von 1566 (Abb. 1) posiert Sambucus selbst mit dem Hund Bombo (der ein Stachelhalsband trägt[2]). Am unteren Bildrand ist, wie auf dem Bild des Emblems, auch hier der Name Bombo dazugesetzt.

Warum ist in der zweiten Auflage von 1566 das Titelbild geändert, während in allen anderen Ausgaben (erste Auflage 1564, dritte Auflage 1569, unveränderte Auflagen 1576 und 1584) und auch in den Übersetzungen

---

[1] Das Emblem ist schon in der ersten Ausgabe von 1564 enthalten (p. 164f.; vgl. p. 143 der Ausgabe von 1566; p. 163 in allen folgenden Auflagen). Eine kurze Zusammenstellung der Dokumente zu Sambucus und seinen Hunden bietet die Internetpublikation Antonio Bernat VISTARINI, Emilio BLANCO, John T. CULL and Tamás SAJÓ, His Master's Voice. Johannes Sambucus and his dog Bombo. *Silva de varia lección* 3, 15-12-2004 <www.studiolum.com/en/silva3.htm> bzw. <http://www.emblematica.com/en/silva3.htm> (19. 12. 2016).

[2] Das Stachelhalsband, mit nach außen gekehrten Stacheln, schützt den Hund vor Bissen und anderen Angriffen und wird auch heute noch bei Hirten- und Jagdhunden verwendet. Pollux aus Naukratis in Ägypten (2./3. Jh. n. Chr.), Verfasser eines Sachwörterbuchs (*Onomasticon*), vermerkt dazu im Kapitel über Jagdhunde 5, 55 κόσμος δὲ κυνῶν δέραια μέν, ἱμὰς πλατὺς περὶ τῷ τραχήλῳ, στερεός, ὃς καὶ περιδέραιον καὶ περιδερὶς ὀνομάζεται· ἔνδοθεν δ'αὐτῷ ὑπερράφθω ἀρνακίς, ὡς μὴ τρίβοιτο ὑπὸ τοῦ λώρου ἡ δειρὴ τοῦ κυνός. [...] ἧλοι δ'ἢ ἐγκεντρίδες ἔπεισι ταῖς τελμονίαις („Denn die Zierde der Hunde sind die Halsbänder, ein Lederriemen, breit und fest um den Nacken, der auch Rundhalsband und Halskette genannt wird: auf dessen Innenseite ist ein Schaffell eingenäht, damit der Hals des Hundes nicht durch den Riemen gerieben wird. [...] Und Nägel oder Stacheln sind befestigt in den Riemenstreifen."). – Halsband und Leine werden schon in den Solonischen Gesetzen für die Hundehaltung vorgeschrieben: Plutarch, Solon 24, 4 Ἔγραψε δὲ καὶ βλάβης τετραπόδων νόμον, ἐν ᾧ καὶ κύνα δάκνοντα παραδοῦναι κελεύει κλοιῷ τριπήχει δεδεμένον· τὸ μὲν ἐνθύμημα χάριεν πρὸς ἀσφάλειαν. („Er, sc. Solon, verfasste auch eine Gesetzesbestimmung betreffend Schadensfälle mit Vierbeinern, in der er verbindlich vorschrieb, dass ein bissiger Hund mit einem Halsband zu versehen und an einer drei Ellen langen Leine festzubinden sei; das ist doch eine gute Erfindung in Richtung mehr Sicherheit!")

(französische Übersetzung 1566, niederländische 1567) das Porträt der ersten Auflage oder ein Porträt ohne den Hund verwendet wurde? Sambucus hatte 1566 die Zeit seiner Reisen, auf denen ihn die Hunde stets begleitet hatten, beendet und sich in Wien niedergelassen. Vielleicht wollte er das dokumentieren und damit auch ein privates Detail mitteilen[3].

Wenn man den Angaben über die Benennung von Hunden in der Antike folgt, dann geht der Name Bombo wohl auf βόμβος, „dumpfer, tiefer Laut" und somit auf das Bellen des Hundes mit tiefer Stimme zurück, nicht ungewöhnlich für einen Rüden[4]. Der Name Bombo ist übrigens auch heute als Hundename gebräuchlich, wie ein Blick in einschlägige Tier- und Haustiertauschbörsen zeigt[5]. Der Name von Bombos Mutter, der Hündin Madel[6], ist dagegen nicht dazugesetzt, findet sich aber im Text der jambischen Dimeter des Emblems *FIDEI CANUM EXEMPLUM*:

> Sit quanta odori vis canis,
> Et quae fides erga suos
> Heros, monere quos vides
> Possunt mei canes duo
> Bombo cui nomen dedi,   5
> Matri et Madel simillimae.
> Hi me sequuntur per mare,
> Terras per, et cunctos locos.
> Lutetia hoc frequens tulit,

---

[3] Vgl. Gábor ALMÁSI, *The Uses of Humanism. Andreas Dudith (1533–1589), Johannes Sambucus (1531–1584), and the East Central European Republic of Letters*. Leiden 2009 (Brill's Studies in Intellectual History 185), 145–197; hier 229.

[4] „Bombo" ist die (argentinische) Bezeichnung für eine mit zwei Fellen bespannte große Trommel, die zur Begleitung des Tango verwendet wird. – Ein Beispiel für die Benennung einer Hündin nach ihrer Eigenschaft, ein flinker und guter Jagdhund zu sein, findet sich bei Arrian (der sich, in Anlehnung an sein Vorbild, Xenophon nennt), *Cynegeticus* 5, 6 ὥστε οὐκ ἂν ὀκνήσαί μοι δοκῶ καὶ τὸ ὄνομα ἀναγράψαι τῆς κυνός, ὡς καὶ ἐς ὕστερον ἀπολελεῖφθαι αὐτῇ, ὅτι ἦν ἄρα Ξενοφῶντι τῷ Ἀθηναίῳ κύων, Ὁρμὴ ὄνομα, ὠκυτάτη τε καὶ σοφωτάτη καὶ ἱερωτάτη („Also, glaube ich, sollte ich nicht zögern, auch den Namen der Hündin aufzuschreiben, damit sie auch in Zukunft in Erinnerung bleibt: Xenophon aus Athen hatte eine Hündin mit Namen Hormé [,Schnelligkeit'], sehr schnell, sehr klug, und herrlich stark.")

[5] Ein Beispiel: „ein neues Zuhause für einen Labrador-Mischling, Name: Bombo [...], ein Rüde [...]"; <http://www.windhundtreff.eu/index.php?page=Thread&threadID=20609> (3. 4. 2014).

[6] ,Madel' oder ,Madl', österr. ugs. für ,Mädchen'. Duden-Wörterbuch s. v.: Madel, das; Wortart: Substantiv, Neutrum; Gebrauch: süddeutsch, österreichisch. <http://www.duden.de/rechtschreibung/Madl> (1. 6. 2017).

Videre Romam nescii, 10
Νεάν τε καὶ καλὴν πόλιν,
Et Teutonae terrae procul
Partem quae habetur optima.
Belgas peragrarunt simul,
Ducentur et spero breui 15
Dulcem in vocantem et patriam.
Merentur hi famam canes.
Sensus inesse cur neges
His bestiis sequacibus?

Sambucus, Emblemata 1566, 143

Abb. 2: *FIDEI CANUM EXEMPLUM*. Emblemata et aliquot nummi antiqui operis. Antverpiae: ex officina Christophori Plantini 1566, 143
(Wien, Universitätsbibliothek I 125.521)

Welch ausgeprägten Geruchssinn ein Hund hat,
und welch treue Ergebenheit gegenüber seinen
Herrn, das können meine beiden Hunde bezeugen,
die du hier siehst.
Den einen habe ich Bombo genannt, 5
und seine ihm sehr ähnliche Mutter Madel.
Sie begleiten mich zur See
und zu Lande und an allen Orten.
So hat Paris sie oft aufgenommen,
sie haben Rom gesehen, ohne es zu wissen, 10
und auch das schöne Neapel,
und von deutschen Landen den fernen
Teil, der als der schönste gilt.
Belgien haben sie gemeinsam bereist,
und bald werden sie, das hoffe ich, 15
auch dem süßen Ruf des Vaterlandes folgen.
Es verdienen diese Hunde ihren Ruf!
Warum sollte man leugnen, dass
diese treu folgenden Tiere Gefühle haben?

Eine Folge der Beigabe des Namens des Hundes war übrigens, dass Joseph Heller 1823 in seiner *Geschichte der Holzschneidekunst*[7] Bombo als den Namen eines Holzschneiders angibt, der u. a. für Sambucus gearbeitet habe. Dies führt wiederum zu berechtigter Entrüstung derer, die die Hintergründe und die Verbundenheit des Sambucus mit seinen Hunden offenbar genauer kannten. Im *Künstlerlexikon* von Georg Kaspar Nagler (1835) heißt es[8]:

> Bombo, nach Heller (Gesch. der Holzschneidekunst S. 171) ein Formschneider, der an den Sinnbildern des Johann Sambucus (Emblemata J. Sambuci) arbeitete. Heller sagt, dass er von diesem Künstler keine weitere Nachricht kenne, was wohl zu glauben ist, denn dieser Bombo ist kein Künstler, sondern ein Hund. Der Name steht unter dem einen der beiden Hunde, welche den Reiter begleiten, und dieser heisst Bombo, wie die unter dem Bilde stehenden Verse:

---

[7] Geschichte der Holzschneidekunst von den ältesten bis auf die neuesten Zeiten, nebst zwei Beilagen, enthaltend den Ursprung der Spielkarten und ein Verzeichniß der sämmtlichen xylographischen Werke. Bamberg: im Verlage bei Carl Friedrich Kunz 1823, 171.

[8] Neues allgemeines Künstler-Lexicon oder Nachrichten von dem Leben und den Werken der Maler, Bildhauer, Baumeister, Kupferstecher, Formschneider, Lithographen, Zeichner, Medailleure, Elfenbeinarbeiter, etc. bearbeitet von Dr. G(eorg) K(aspar) Nagler. Zweiter Band: Börner – Cleoetas. München: Verlag von E. A. Fleischmann 1835, 27.

Bombo cui nomen dedi
Matri et Madel simillimae

beweisen. Heller schrieb indessen hier nur dem unsicheren Papillon[9] nach, welcher sagt, dass der Name eines Formschneiders Bombo auf einigen Blättern von Johann Sambucus Sinnbildern stehe.

Auch Füssly[10] zählt nach Papillon in seinem Lexicon den Hund Bombo unter die Formschneider.

Porträts von Gelehrten mit Hunden sind in der tierverliebten Renaissance auch sonst nicht selten[11]: Conrad Celtis (1459–1508) ist auf dem Frontispiz der *Amores* mit seinem Hund Lachne (benannt nach Ovid, met. 3, 222) abgebildet, Sambucus' Zeitgenosse Justus Lipsius (1547–1606) ließ sich gerne mit einem seiner drei Hunde (namens Saphyrus) porträtieren, und schon von Petrarca (1304–1374) gibt es Darstellungen, die ihn mit einem Hund zeigen – er hat zwei Hunden, die sein Landleben in Vaucluse teilten, literarische Denkmäler gesetzt[12].

Die Verbundenheit des Sambucus mit seinen beiden Reisebegleitern hat aber über die persönliche Note hinaus wohl noch einen weiteren, literarischen Bezug, der bis zu den homerischen Epen zurückreicht, denn dass zwei Hunde einen des Öfteren auch allein Reisenden begleiten, ist weiter nicht

---

[9] Jean-Michel Papillon (1698–1776), Holzschneider, Verfasser von Artikeln in der Encylopédie und eines Traité historique et pratique de la gravure en bois. Paris: Pierre-Guillaume Simon 1766, 525 zu Bombo.

[10] Johann Rudolf Füssli (1709–1793), Allgemeines Künstlerlexikon, oder: Kurze Nachricht von dem Leben und den Werken der Maler, Bildhauer, Baumeister, Kupferstecher, Kunstgiesser, Stahlschneider [...]. Erster Theil. Zürich: Orell, Füßli und Compagnie 1779, 86.

[11] Vgl. Jan PAPY, Lipsius and His Dogs: Humanist Tradition, Iconography and Rubens' Four Philosophers. *Journal of the Warburg and Courtauld Institutes* 62 (1999), 167–198; hier 185–190. Zur Präsenz von Hunden in Darstellungen der humanistischen Studierstube vgl. auch Gadi ALGAZI, At the Study. Notes on the Production of the Scholarly Self. In: David Warren Sabean, Malina Stefanovska (eds.), *Space and Self in Early Modern European Culture*. Toronto 2012, 17–50; hier 28–34. Zu Hunden als Motiv von Emblemen vgl. Arthur HENKEL, Albrecht SCHÖNE, *Emblemata. Handbuch zur Sinnbildlichkeit des XVI. und XVII. Jahrhunderts*. Stuttgart 1967, 556–585, und auch die Internetseite: *French Emblems at Glasgow* <http://www.emblems.arts.gla.ac.uk/french/index.php> (30. 1. 2017).

[12] Petrarca, Fam. 13, 11 (*De natura et fide canum*) und Epyst. 3, 5. Vgl. Silvia RIZZO, Il cane spagnolo di Petrarca (Epyst. 3, 5). *Rivista Letteraria Libera. La Recherche.it.* Associazone culturale <http://www.larecherche.it/testo.asp?Id=409&Tabella=Saggio> (30. 1. 2017). Zu dem bei Papy (s. Anm. 11) genannten Zabot vgl. dagegen Angelo PIACENTINI, L'epitaffio al cane Zabot attribuito a Petrarca. *Studi petrarcheschi* n.s. 23 (2010), 189–212.

verwunderlich: Schon in der *Odyssee* verlässt Telemachos das Gehöft des Schweinehirten Eumaios in Begleitung von „zwei schnellen Hunden" (*Od.* 2, 11 und öfter)[13].

Auch Arzt und Ärztin, die in der Antike ja Wanderärzte waren – Sambucus hatte 1555 an der Universität Padua ein Medizin-Lizenziat erlangt und konnte sich *medicus* nennen –, reisten in Begleitung von Dienern und Schülern und, wohl aus Sicherheitsgründen, mit Hunden. Auch dafür findet sich eine – sogar bildlich dokumentierte – Parallele auf dem berühmten Grabrelief der Ärztin Mousa aus Byzantion (ca. 100 v. Chr.), die eine Buchrolle in der Hand hält (wohl ein Hinweis auf medizinische Ausbildung auf der Basis von Lehrbüchern) und in Begleitung einer Dienerin und zweier Hunde dargestellt ist[14].

Ein Denkmal für einen treuen Hund hat auch Nonnos in die *Dionysiaka* eingefügt: Erigone, die sich aus Verzweiflung über den Tod ihres von trunkenen, sich vergiftet wähnenden Bauern erschlagenen Vaters Ikarios im Wald erhängt hat, wird von ihrem treuen Hund Maira bewacht und vor wilden Tieren geschützt; schließlich veranlasst der Hund vorbeiziehende Wanderer, die Tote zu bestatten und hilft beim Ausheben des Grabes. Die Stelle bewacht er bis zu seinem eigenen Tod.

<pre>
καὶ θάνε, καὶ μόρον εἶχεν ἑκούσιον· ἀμφὶ δὲ κούρην   225
πυκνὰ κύων δεδόνητο, καὶ ἴαχε πένθιμον ἠχὼ
ὄμμασι θηρείοισι νοήμονα δάκρυα λείβων.
οὐδὲ κύων ἀφύλακτον ἐρημάδα κάλλιπε κούρην,
ἀλλὰ φυτῷ παρέμιμνεν ἐπήλυδα θῆρα διώκων,   230
πόρδαλιν ἠὲ λέοντα· παρερχομένοισι δ' ὁδίταις
νεύμασιν ἀφθόγγοις ἐπεδείκνυεν ἄζυγα κούρην
δεσμοῖς ἀγχονίοισι περίπλοκον ὑψόθι δένδρου.
οἱ δέ μιν οἰκτείροντες ἀνήιον εἰς φυτὸν ὕλης
ἴχνεσιν ἀκροτάτοισιν, ἀπ' εὐπετάλων δὲ κορύμβων   235
</pre>

---

[13] Zur Darstellung von Hunden in der antiken Literatur und Kunst vgl. z. B. Saara LILJA, *Dogs in Ancient Greek Poetry*. Helsinki 1976 (*Societas Scientiarum Fennica. Commentationes Humanarum Litterarum* 56); A. A. PHILLIPS, M. M. WILLCOCK (eds.), *Xenophon and Arrian, On Hunting*. Warminster 1999; Joris PETERS, Ein Hundeleben in der Antike. *Antike Welt* 5 (2005), 8–16; Tanja STROBLMAYR, *Mensch und Hund in der griechisch-römischen Antike*. Uelvesbüll 2011 (ursprünglich Diss. Universität Salzburg 2011).

[14] Istanbul, Archaeological Museum, *Supplementum Epigraphicum Graecum* 24.811; vgl. Antje KRUG, *Heilkunst und Heilkult. Medizin in der Antike*. München ²1993, 196 Abb. 87.

παρθενικὴν ἀδμῆτα κατήγαγον· ἀγχιφανῆ δὲ
γαῖαν ἐκοιλαίνοντο πεδοσκαφέεσσι μακέλλαις.
τοῖς ἅμα καὶ πεπόνητο κύων πινυτόφρονι θυμῷ,
πενθαλέῳ δ' ἐβάθυνε πέδον τεχνήμονι ταρσῷ,
θηγαλέοις ὀνύχεσσι χυτῆς χθονὸς ἄκρα χαράσσων. 240
καὶ νέκυν ἀρτιδάικτον ἐπεκτερέιξαν ὁδῖται·
καὶ ξυνῆς μεθέπων ὑποκάρδιον ὄγκον ἀνίης
εἰς ἑὸν ἔργον ἕκαστος ἀνέδραμεν ὀξέι ταρσῷ·
αὐτὰρ ὁ μοῦνος ἔμιμνε κύων παρὰ γείτονι τύμβῳ
Ἠριγόνης ὑπ' ἔρωτι, θελήμονι δ' ὤλετο πότμῳ. 245

Nonnos, *Dionysiaka* 47, 225–245

Und sie starb, und hat freiwillig den Tod auf sich genommen. Doch das Mädchen
umkreiste ständig der Hund, und der winselte in seiner Trauer
und aus seinen Augen vergoss er – obwohl nur ein Tier! – Tränen des Mitgefühls.
Und der Hund ließ das Mädchen nicht unbewacht allein,
sondern blieb bei dem Baum und verscheuchte streunende wilde Tiere,
Panther oder Löwe. Und vorbeikommende Wanderer
machte er mit Zeichen, ohne Laut zu geben, auf das unschuldige Mädchen aufmerksam,
mit würgendem Strick umwunden hängend hoch oben am Baum.
Die hatten Erbarmen und kamen heran zum Baumstamm
auf Zehenspitzen, und aus dem dichten Blätterwerk der Äste
holten sie die unberührte Jungfrau herunter; und ganz in der Nähe
hoben sie in der Erde eine Grube aus mit Boden-Stechspaten.
Gemeinsam mit ihnen arbeitete auch der Hund mit verständigem Wissen,
machte traurig eine Vertiefung im Boden mit geschickten Pfoten
und mit scharfen Krallen scharrte er die Oberfläche zu aufgeschütteter Erde.
Und es bestatteten den eben erst vom Schicksal bestimmten Leichnam die Wanderer.
Es trug im Herzen ein jeder einen Teil von der Last der Trauer
und wandte sich seinen eigenen Geschäften zu mit schnellem Schritt.
Der Hund aber harrte alleine aus neben dem Grabhügel
in Liebe zu Erigone, und dort starb auch er, freiwillig, in sehnsüchtiger Treue.

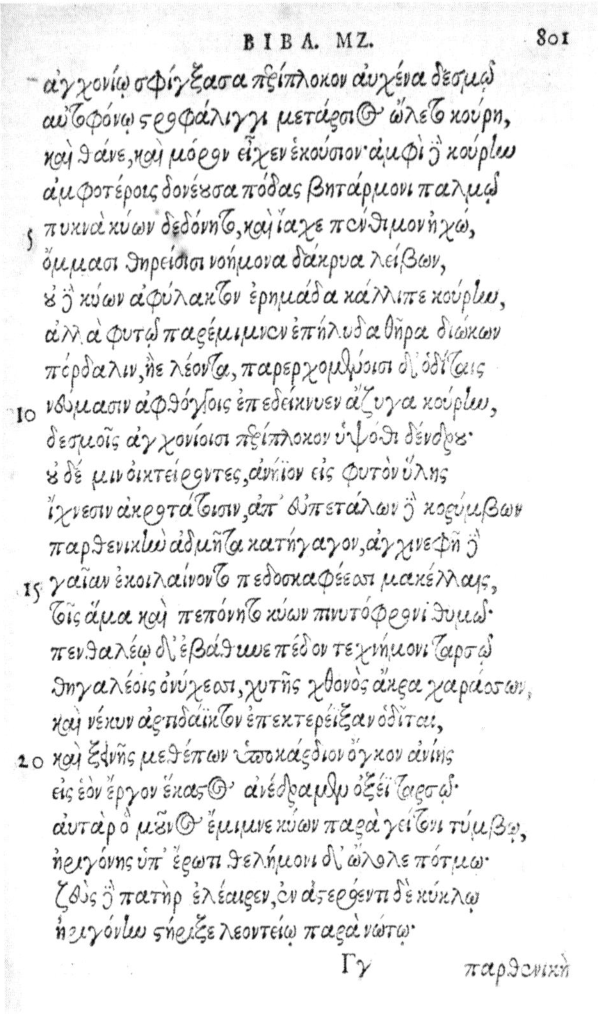

Abb. 3: Nonnos, *Dionysiaka* 47, 223–247 aus der *editio princeps*.
Νόννου Πανοπολίτου Διονυσιακά. […] Nunc primum in lucem edita, ex Bibliotheca
Joannis Sambuci Pannonii […]. Antverpiae: Ex officina Christophori Plantini 1569, 801
(Wien, Universitätsbibliothek I 249.157)

Die Janus-Pannonius-Edition und das fragmentarische Brandolini-Manuskript von János Zsámboky

GYULA MAYER (Budapest)

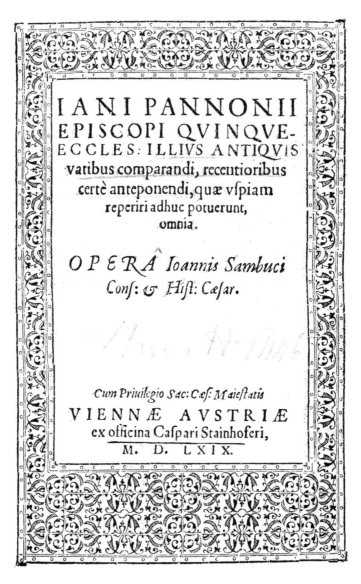

Abb. 1: Titelblatt der Janus Pannonius-Ausgabe des Johannes Sambucus. Wien 1569 (Országos Széchényi Könyvtár, App. H. 432)

Der erste eigenständige Janus Pannonius-Druck ist 1512 erschienen[1]. Die Absicht späterer Editoren war teils die Veröffentlichung neuer, bis dahin nicht publizierter Werke des Dichters, teils eine Zusammenfassung des Materials ihnen bekannter, früherer Werkausgaben. Der von János Zsámboky (Johannes Sambucus) edierte Wiener Sammelband von 1569[2] war bekanntlich über zweihundert Jahre lang die vollständigste Ausgabe der Arbeiten des Janus Pannonius. Am Anfang des Drucks befindet sich ein Vorspann von vier Folioblättern, gefolgt von 132 arabisch und 94 römisch durchnummerierten Folios. Der Vorspann mit dem Bogenzeichen (:) enthält – außer dem Titelblatt – Zsámbokys Widmung an den Wesprimer Bischof János Liszti[3] sowie seine Hendekasyllaben an Janus. Das Material der arabisch durchnummerierten Folios wurde vom Editor – mit geringfügigen Änderungen – aus der Basler Ausgabe von 1555[4] übernommen, das Gedicht vom Ende des an László Vetési adressierten Briefes zu den Epigrammen umgestellt, zwei Gedichte von Pál Istvánffy aus der Ausgabe des Adrian Wolfhard[5] (1491–1544) übernommen und schließlich ein auf

---

[1] Ioannis Pannonii [...] Panegyricus in laudem Baptistae Guarini [...] conditus. Viennae Austriae: in aedibus Hieronymi Vietoris et Ioannis Singrenii 1512 (VD16 J 192).

[2] Iani Pannonii [...] quae uspiam reperiri adhuc potuerunt; omnia. Opera Ioannis Sambuci. Viennae: Kaspar Stainhofer 1569 (VD16 ZV 24520). Zu Sambucus' Wiener Ausgabe vgl. Iani Pannonii Opera quae manserunt omnia. Volumen I: Epigrammata. Fasciculus 1: Textus. Edidit, praefatus est et apparatu critico instruxit Iulius MAYER, similia addidit Ladislaus TÖRÖK. Budapest 2006, 25f. Im Folgenden steht für Gedichte dieser kritischen Ausgabe die Sigle „M."; die Abkürzung „Tel." bezieht sich auf die Teleki–Kovásznai-Edition: Ianus Pannonius, Poemata quae uspiam reperiri potuerunt omnia. Pars I. Trajecti ad Rhenum 1784. Die Sigle „Eh" bezieht sich in der kritischen Ausgabe auf Sambucus' Wiener Ausgabe von 1569; im Editionsanhang dieses Beitrags ist zu „E" vereinfacht.

[3] Das (ein?) Privatexemplar des Mäzens wird heute in der Universitätsbibliothek der ELTE Budapest aufbewahrt: *Mátyás király – Magyarország a reneszánsz hajnalán: Katalógus* [König Matthias – Das Ungarn der Frührenaissance: Katalog]. Budapest 2008, 18 und Tafel V.

[4] Iani Pannonij [...] opera multo nunc demum quam unquam antea & auctiora & emendatiora, in lucem edita. Basileae: Oporinus (VD16 J 189). In der kritischen Ausgabe (s. Anm. 2) „Ec".

[5] Ioannis Pannonii [...] Panegyricus Iacobo Antonio Marcello patritio Veneto. Bononiae: Hieronymus de Benedictis 1522. – RMK (Károly SZABÓ, *Régi magyar könyvtár*) III, 250, fol. Pii^{r-v}. Zu Wolfhard vgl. Johanna ERNUSZT, *Adrianus Wolphardus*. Budapest 1939, deutsche Zusammenfassung *Egyetemes Philologiai Közlöny* 63 (1939), 209.

den im Februar des Editionsjahres 1569 verstorbenen Miklós Oláh gedichtetes Epitaph mitabgedruckt. Für den zweiten, römisch durchnummerierten Teil der Ausgabe hatte Zsámboky das Material seiner Paduaner Edition von 1559[6] erweitert. Auf dem Verso des Titelblattes liest man folgende Angabe:

> LECTOR. Altera libri pars, cuius foliorum numeri sunt notis Romanis insignes, tota nunc primum in lucem prodit: Olim quoque extabat altera, haec te scire volui, vt in colligando, vtramcunque partem velles, praeponeres, quod initio, antea vulgata his connectere, non constitueramus.

Zsámbokys Formulierung bezüglich der hier zum ersten Mal veröffentlichten Gedichte ist zwar nicht ganz genau; es ist aber verständlich, dass er seine früheren Ausgaben[7] sowie die ihm offensichtlich unbekannten Krakauer Hefte[8] nicht berücksichtigt hatte. Der römisch durchnummerierte zweite Teil mit den neuen Texten enthält nun Folgendes:

I^r–V^v: *Ad Ludouicum Gonzagam Carmen*
V^v–XII^r: *Eranemus hoc est Ventorum contentio*
XII^v–XVII^r: *Bartolomeo Fontio respondet*
XVII^v–XLII^r: [Elegiae]
XLII^r–XLVI^r: *Iani Pannonii De laudibus Pontific: & rerum humanarum conditione*
XLVI^v–XCII^r: *Epigrammata eiusdem Pan: et lusus iuveniles*
XCII^r–XCIII^r: *In Epiphaniam*
XCIII^r–XCIIII^r: *Tres epistolae eiusdem Pannonii, Veronae repertae.*
Pan: Andr: Iulio S.
Ian: Pan: in nupt: Land: nomine Guar:
Tibaldeo poetae Ferrarień. Pannon: suus S.

Lassen wir nun diesen Teil des Zsámboky-Bandes im Hinblick auf die Frage, auf welche Quellen der Herausgeber zurückgegriffen haben könnte, Revue passieren.

---

[6] Iani Pannonii […] Lusus quidam et epigrammata, nunc primum inventa et excusa. Patavii: („Ed").
[7] Abgesehen von der Paduaner Edition den Druck des *Eranemus* im Anschluss an die ungarische Königsserie: Reges Ungariae ab anno Christi 401 usq. ad 1567. Item Iani Pannonii […], Eranemus, nunc repertus et ed. a Joanne Sambuco. Viennae: Kaspar Stainhofer 1567. („Eg").
[8] Opusculum Francisci Uiihelini […]. Insunt praeterea Ioannis Pannonii […] Epigrammata […] hactenus non impressa. Cracoviae: Hieronymus Vietor mense Iunii 1518 bzw. Epigrammata, antea non impressa. Cracoviae: Hieronymus Vietor mense Augusto 1518. In der kritischen Ausgabe (s. Anm. 2) „Js" und „Jt".

Fol. I^r–V^v

Zwei Handschriften des *Gonzaga-carmens* sind uns erhalten: eine Vatikanische und eine Sevillaner. Zsámboky wird keine dieser beiden gekannt und muss sich folglich auf ein weiteres – uns nicht bekanntes – Manuskript gestützt haben.

Fol. V^v–XII^r

Der *Eranemos* blieb ebenfalls in zwei Manuskripten erhalten, einem Wiener sowie dem (sog. ersten) Sevillaner. Die Wiener Handschrift (Österreichische Nationalbibliothek, Cod. 9977), aus der Zsámboky dieses Werk in einem eigenständigen Druck bereits zwei Jahre früher herausgegeben hatte, gelangte aus Zsámbokys Besitz in die Kaiserliche Bibliothek[9].

Fol. XII^v–XVII^r

Die Elegie mit der Überschrift *Bartolomeo Fontio respondet Florentiae Ian: Pan:* von 254 Versen wurde von Sámuel Teleki (1739–1822) und Sándor Kovásznai (1730–1792), die Janus' Autorenschaft in ihrer Anmerkung zum Gedicht in der Utrechter Ausgabe philologisch penibel in aller Ausführlichkeit widerlegen[10], in ihrer Janus-Ausgabe unter fremden Gedichten als viertes Stück der *Appendix carminum* (I, 671–687) veröffentlicht. Ihr Verfasser – wie von Teleki und Kovásznai nachgewiesen und auch von der späteren Forschung angenommen – war Angelo Poliziano[11]. Hierzu nur ein kurzes Zitat von Teleki–Kovásznai: „*quemvis potius quam Ianum Pannonium hujus epistolae scriptorem fuisse, id vero his argumentis omni exceptione majoribus conficiemus.*"

Fol. XVII^v–XLII^r

Es folgen fünfzehn weitere Elegien (bei Teleki–Kovásznai unter II, 4–18), von denen uns laut der Tabelle in der Monographie von Csaba Csapodi (1910–2004) alles in allem jedoch nur sieben auch in Handschriften erhal-

---

[9] István BORZSÁK, Die Janus Pannonius-Ausgaben des Sambucus. *Acta Antiqua Academiae Scientiarum Hungaricae* 21 (1973), 361–374; hier 365.

[10] Vgl. Tel. I, p. IX.

[11] Vgl. István HEGEDŰS, Bartolomeo della Fonte. *Irodalomtörténeti Közlemények* 12 (1902), 1–19; hier 5f. und (mit Hinweis auf Concetto MARCHESI, *Bartolomeo Della Fonte*. Catania 1900, 42f.) József HUSZTI, Platonista törekvések Mátyás király udvarában [Platonistische Bestrebungen am Hof von Matthias]. *Minerva* 3 (1924), 153–222; hier 178–180 (italienisch: Tendenze platonizzanti alla corte di Mattia Corvino. *Giornale critico della filosofia italiana* 11, 1930, 1–287; hier 24–26); des Weiteren Ladislaus JUHÁSZ, *Commentatio critica ad edendas Iani Pannonii elegias*. Szeged 1929, 12.

ten seien¹². Dabei erweist sich einerseits eine positive Angabe von Csapodi als falsch, anderseits finden sich zwei andere Elegien, deren Manuskripte von ihm nicht angeführt werden, so dass die Manuskripte bei insgesamt sieben von den fünfzehn Gedichten (II, 4, 6, 12–14 und 18) als verschollen betrachtet werden müssen[13]. Zweifel in Hinblick auf die Authentizität ergeben sich nur beim letzten Stück – worauf weiter unten noch eingegangen werden soll.

Fol. XLVI^v–XCII^r

Die nächste größere Einheit des Bandes enthält Epigramme (etwa 300). 145 von diesen wurden von Zsámboky bereits in seiner Paduaner Ausgabe von 1559 publiziert (wobei er die Stücke 283–284 M. zusammen als ein Gedicht behandelt). Die Epigramme stammen ausnahmslos aus dem Ofener (Budaer) Corpus[14], und haben somit eine gesicherte handschriftliche Überlieferung. Die Ausgabe von Padua beruht offensichtlich auf demselben Manuskript wie auch noch die zehn Jahre jüngere Wiener Edition. Laut Vorwort der Paduaner Edition von 1559 soll Zsámboky auch von János Liszti ein Janus-Manuskript erhalten haben: Man erfährt hier ferner auch, dass Zsámboky nur eine Auswahl der darin enthaltenen Gedichte abgedruckt hat[15]. Nichts spricht also gegen die Annahme, dass auch ihm ein Manuskript gleichen Umfangs und Inhalts zur Verfügung stand wie etwa das des Beatus Rhenanus oder des Stanislaus Sauer, wobei die von Zsámboky herangezogene Handschrift nicht auffindbar ist. Im Vergleich zur Paduaner Ausgabe nahm Zsámboky gewisse Änderungen an der Reihenfolge der Gedichte vor: so trug er die nicht in Disticha abgefassten Stücke in einem besonderen Teil am Ende des Bandes zusammen (fol. LXXXIV^v–XCIII^r = *epigr.* I, 313 – II, 24 Tel.)[16]. Nach *epigr.* I, 240 Tel. (=236 M.) auf fol. LXXII^v steht der Kustos *Ad Luciam* – d. i. der Titel von *epigr.* I, 244 Tel. (=240 M.). Letzteres Gedicht bringt jedoch – zumal vom Metrum her Hendekasyllabus – erst fol. XC^r, was dafür zeugt, dass Zsámbokys Reihenfolgenänderungen kaum handschriftlich bedingt gewesen sein können.

---

[12] Csaba CSAPODI, *A Janus Pannonius-szöveghagyomány* [Die Überlieferung des Janus-Pannonius-Textes]. Budapest 1981, 55.
[13] MAYER-TÖRÖK (s. Anm. 2), *Iani Pannonii Opera quae manserunt omnia*. Vol. II: *Elegiae*. Fasc. 1: *Textus*. Budapest 2014, 33.
[14] MAYER (s. Anm. 2) I, 1, 35ff.
[15] Zitiert auch in BORZSÁK (s. Anm. 9), 364: „*selegi de multis pauca et de bonis meliora.*"
[16] Vgl. Ladislaus JUHÁSZ, *Quaestiones criticae de epigrammatibus Iani Pannonii*. Roma 1929, 7.

Fol. XCII^r–XCIII^r

Den Epigrammen aus dem Ofener Corpus folgt ein *carmen sapphicum In Epiphaniam* (XCII^r–XCIII^r), für das lange Zeit keine andere Quelle bekannt war. Teleki–Kovásznai hatten das Gedicht als Stück II, 24 der Epigramme veröffentlicht und schrieben es einer fremden Hand zu:

> Ceterum totum hoc carmen non Iani, sed barbari nescio cujus rudem foetum esse facile sentiet, qui modo naso voluerit uti. Nec MStum habet, nec ullae praeter Sambucinam editiones, quae ante illam prodierunt.

István Hegedűs (1848–1925) charakterisiert das Gedicht wie folgt:

> Es ist im sapphischen Metrum geschrieben und besteht aus acht Strophen. Es erzählt in einfacher Sprache und im andächtigen Ton der christlichen Hymnen von der Huldigung der Hirten, der Könige und der Magier. Herodes bat die Könige, ihm auf ihrem Rückweg die Geburt des Kindes zu melden. Diese aber, überaus froh, den König der Welt gesehen zu haben, kehren in der Stille der Nacht in ihre Länder zurück und singen dort das Lob des Herrn. Herodes, angst und bange, lässt alle Säuglinge ermorden. / Christus flüchtet da nach Ägypten / mit seiner Heiligen Mutter, während das Blut von Säuglingen / hier den Boden tränkt.[17]

In seinem Kurzkommentar von 1968 meint László Juhász (1905–1970), dass weder die Form (d. h. die sapphische Strophe) noch der Inhalt des Gedichts für eine Autorschaft des Janus Pannonius sprächen. Das erste Argument wird durch das aus dem ersten Sevillaner Codex bekannte Gedicht (*epigr.* 453 M.) an einen deutschen Dichter namens Heinrich (d. h. Heinrich von Gundelfingen)[18] mit seiner ebenfalls sapphischen Form aufgehoben; auf

---

[17] „Sapphói mértékben van írva, 8 versszakot alkot. Egyszerű nyelven, a keresztyén hymnusok áhítatos hangján szól. Elmondja a pásztorok, a királyok és a mágusok hódolatát. Herodes megkérte a királyokat, hogy visszatértükben jelentsék meg a gyermek születését. De ők boldogan, hogy megláttak a világ fejedelmét, az éj csöndjében visszatérnek hazájukba, és otthon zengik az Úrnak dicséretét. Herodes féltében lekonczolja a gyermekeket. / Krisztus Egyiptomba menekszik ottan / Szent anyjával, míg csecsemők vérétől / Ázik a föld itt." István HEGEDŰS, Janus vallásos költeményei [Die religiösen Gedichte von Janus]. *Akadémiai Értesítő* 24 (1913), 159–171; hier 163. Die im obigen Zitat wiedergegebene Stelle im Wortlaut des Originals: *Cautus Herodes pueros trucidat, / Christus Aegyptum fugit in propinquam / Matre cum sancta, madet innocentum / Sanguine tellus.*

[18] Ágnes RITOÓK-SZALAY, Poetischer Briefwechsel von Humanisten. *Acta classica Universitatis scientiarum Debreceniensis* 34/35 (1998/99), 103–115; hier 113ff. und L'edizione critica del-

das zweite Argument wird später noch eingegangen. Wie dem auch sei, ist es László Juhász bereits 1931 gelungen, Raffaello Zovenzoni (1431–1485) als Autor des Gedichts zu identifizieren[19].

Fol. XCIII^r–XCIIII^r

In Zsámbokys Ausgabe folgen diesem Text *Tres Epistolae Pannonii, Veronae repertae* (*Epist.* XX–XXII Tel.), an deren Authentizität Teleki und Kovásznai ebenfalls mit gutem Grund gezweifelt und die sie auf etwas später als Janus' Zeit datiert haben. Hierzu soll Janus' Monograph József Huszti (1887–1954) zitiert werden:

> Von Sámuel Telekis kritischer Scharfsicht zeugt, dass er alle drei angeblichen Janus-Briefe für verdächtig hielt. [...] In Bezug auf den ersten Brief stellte Sabbadini fest, dass dieser von Guarino an Andreas Julianus verfasst wurde. Auch über den zweiten »Brief« wies er nach, dass er eigentlich aus einer Rede von Guarino [...] stammt, wobei er zugleich dessen zahlreiche Handschriften aufzählt.[20]

Der Adressat des dritten Briefes ist Antonio Tebaldeo. Huszti schließt – da er Tebaldeos Geburt auf das Jahr 1456 datiert – Janus' Autorschaft aus und und stellt die Frage, ob der Brief nicht etwa von Péter Garázda (1450?–1507) verfasst worden sein könnte[21] – hierüber wissen wir vorläufig jedoch nichts Sicheres.

---

le opere di Janus Pannonius. In: Rhoda Schnur (Hg.), *Acta Conventus Neo-Latini Budapestinensis*. Tempe 2010, 613–620; hier 619f.

[19] László JUHÁSZ, *Adalékok az 1437–1490. évekből* [Miszellen aus den Jahren 1437–1490]. Budapest 1931, 8–10, mit Hinweis auf Carmina illustrium poetarum Italorum. Bd. XI. Florenz 1719, 480f.; vgl. László JUHÁSZ, Janus Pannonius epigrammáinak szövegkritikájához és herméneutikájához [Zur Textkritik und Hermeneutik der Epigramme des Janus Pannonius]. *Filológiai Közlöny* 14 (1968), 146–185; hier 183f. Die von László Fejérpataky gefundene Kopie von Németújvár (vgl. CSAPODI, s. Anm. 12, 12) wurde womöglich – wie aus den von Juhász veröffentlichten variae lectiones zu schließen ist – aufgrund von Zsámbokys Ausgabe verfertigt. Juhász stellte sich das zwar eher umgekehrt vor – was jedoch praktisch auszuschließen ist. Die moderne Ausgabe des Gedichts: Baccio ZILIOTTO, *Raffaele Zovenzoni: La vita, i carmi*. Trieste 1950, 134f., vgl. auch 168. Weitere Literatur in Tibor KARDOS, Janus Pannonius és a középkor [Janus Pannonius und das Mittelalter]. *Filológiai Közlöny* 19 (1973), 1–20; hier 9.

[20] József HUSZTI, *Janus Pannonius*. Pécs 1931, 337, Anm. 4.

[21] József HUSZTI, Ant. Thebaldeus költeménye Mátyás királyhoz [Gedicht des Ant. Thebaldeus an König Matthias]. In: Imre Lukinich (Hgg.), *Emlékkönyv gróf Klebelsberg Kuno negyedszázados kulturpolitikai működésének emlékére születésének ötvenedik évfordulóján*. [Festschrift zu

Fol. XLII^r–XLVI^r
Im Folgenden kommen wir zur letzten der von Zsámboky erstmals herausgegebenen Elegien (II, 18 Tel.). Zsámboky bringt diese unter dem Titel *De laudibus Pontific: & rerum humanarum conditione*, Teleki–Kovásznai als *Consultatio Dei Patris et Filii de perdendo hominum genere; quos tandem B. Virgo exorat*. Ihre Textüberlieferung beruht, wie oben gezeigt, ausschließlich auf Zsámbokys Ausgabe (im Folgenden als „E", XLII^r–XLVI^r). Im Hauptteil ihrer Ausgabe merken Teleki–Kovásznai vorerst nur an, dass ihr Text verderbte und lückenhafte Stellen aufweist (bzw. nicht vollkommen ausgearbeitet ist). Im – wie gewöhnlich – erst nachträglich abgefassten Vorwort wird sogar ihre Authentizität in Zweifel gezogen: „*carmen de rerum humanarum conditione, quod admodum est depravatum, nec Jani videtur esse*" (I, p. IX).

In seiner Rede von 1912 an der Ungarischen Akademie der Wissenschaften versuchte István Hegedűs, die von ihm selbst gestellte Frage zu beantworten:

> Können wir von einem religiösen Gedicht oder noch mehr von wahrer religiöser Stimmung sprechen bei einem Dichter, von dem – als einem Renaissance-Geist durch und durch – mit noch mehr Recht behauptet werden kann, was ein Biograph Goethes in Bezug auf dessen Genie als Motto zitiert: als Künstler Polytheist, als Naturforscher Pantheist.[22]

Hegedűs ist bestrebt, Argumente pro wie kontra gleichermaßen sachlich zu erwägen, und beruft sich mit Recht auf das Epigramm mit dem Titel *De signis quae Moldavis erepta templo Virginis Budae* (d. i. *fixa fuerant*). Im Dezember 1467 wurde Matthias' Heer vom Woiwoden Stephan in den Hinterhalt gelockt, infolge dessen es schwere Verluste erlitt und auch der König selbst verwundet wurde. Das ungarische Heer, das tüchtig stand-

---

Ehren der 25-jährigen kulturpolitischen Tätigkeit von Kuno Graf Klebelsberg zu seinem 50. Geburtstag]. Budapest 1925, 349f.

[22] „Lehet-e vallásos költeményről beszélni, vagy meg inkább igaz vallásos hangulatról, annál a költőnél, kiről, mint minden ízében renaissance szellemről, még több joggal elmondhatni, amit Goethe egyik életrajzírója jeligeképpen alkalmaz e lángészre, hogy mint művész polytheista, mint bölcsész pantheista." Hegedűs, (s. Anm. 17), 159. Hegedűs schreibt *Ep*. II, 24 und *El*. II, 18 bereits in einem früheren Hinweis – Joannes Pannonius éneke [Der Gesang des Janus Pannonius]. *Irodalomtörténeti Közlemények* 10 (1900), 243–245; hier 244 – Janus zu, wie vor ihm übrigens auch schon Rényi REZSŐ, A humanismus jelleme [Der Charakter des Humanismus]. *Irodalomtörténeti Közlemények* 2 (1892), 1–32; hier 20.

hielt, brachte die vom Feind erbeuteten Fahnen in die Kirche der Heiligen Jungfrau zu Ofen. Janus selbst – der die Ereignisse an Ort und Stelle mit erleben konnte[23] – fleht Maria in einem Gedicht an[24]. Die Texttradition des Epigramms lässt nicht den geringsten Zweifel an der Authentizität des Gedichts zu.

Etwas komplizierter sieht es bei Elegie II, 18 (Tel.) aus. Husztis Zusammenfassung des Inhalts:

> Gottvater betrachtet das irdische Leben und sieht, dass die Menschen in verschiedenartigen Sünden versunken sind. Er erzürnt sich gegen das undankbare Menschengeschlecht und beruft zum Zwecke der Beratung zu Vergeltungsmaßnahmen den Himmlischen Rat ein. Als erstes berichtet er selbst über die entartete Lage, anschließend unterbreitet er seinen Vorschlag, nach dem das Leben auf Erden mit Feuer ausgerottet werden sollte, und fordert sogleich die Versammlungsteilnehmer auf, ihre Meinung zu äußern. Als Erste meldet sich die Muttergottes zu Wort und bittet nach langwieriger Begründung um Gnade für das menschliche Geschlecht. Das Gedicht bricht [...] noch während der Rede der Heiligen Jungfrau ab. Die in den Ausgaben enthaltenen weiteren zehn Verse können [...] zum Vorausgehenden in keinerlei Beziehung gesetzt werden.[25]

Hegedűs hat zwar versucht, die *lacuna* zu überbrücken, konnte Huszti jedoch – der die fraglichen zehn Verse für ein Fragment eines anderen Gedichts hielt – von der Richtigkeit seiner Lösung nicht überzeugen.

Wie schwer es ist, die Authentizität des Gedichts an sich zu beurteilen, zeigt auch, dass László Juhász sie 1929 – in Anlehnung an Teleki–Kovásznai – zunächst zwar noch in Frage gestellt hatte[26], seine Einwände jedoch – unter dem Einfluss von Husztis später publizierter stilkritischer Argumentation[27] –

---

[23] CSAPODI (s. Anm. 12), 79, wo freilich *mense Decembri* zu lesen ist.
[24] Epigr. I, 10 Tel. = 432 M., vgl. HUSZTI, Janus Pannonius (s. Anm. 20), 268.
[25] „Az Atyaisten szemügyre veszi a földi életet, s látja, hogy az emberek a bűnök különböző formáiba merültek. Haragra lobban a hálátlan emberi nem iránt s a megtorló lépések megbeszélése céljából összehívja az égiek tanácsát. Először ő maga ismerteti az elfajult helyzetet, majd előterjeszti javaslatát, hogy a földi életet tűzzel pusztítsák el s egyúttal felszólítja a gyűlés résztvevőit véleményük nyilvánítására. Az első hozzászóló a Boldogságos Szűz, aki hosszadalmas megokolással az emberi nem számára irgalmat esdekel. A költemény [...] még a Boldogságos Szűz beszéde közben megszakad. A kiadásokban található további tíz sor [...] az előzőekkel semmiféle logikus kapcsolatba nem hozható."
[26] JUHÁSZ, Commentatio critica (s. Anm. 11), 12.
[27] HUSZTI, Janus Pannonius (s. Anm. 20), 68–70.

nach kurzer Zeit wieder aufgab und für das Gedicht als authentischen Janus-Text Stellung nahm[28]. Sándor V. Kovács (1931–1986) nimmt es in die erste bilingue Ausgabe von 1972 hingegen nicht auf, und auch Csapodi dürfte es aus demselben Grund abgelehnt haben[29]. Mit seiner von Husztis Beweisführung abweichenden, jedoch äußerst bedenklichen Argumentation – das Gedicht im Lichte des rhapsodisch-instabilen Verhältnisses zwischen Janus und dem König interpretierend – plädierte Béla Karácsonyi (1919–1995) bei der 1972-er Jubiläumskonferenz für dessen Authentizität[30]. Karácsonyis Grundgedanke wird von Tibor Kardos (1908–1973) in seiner postum erschienenen Studie akzeptiert: durch den Entwurf einer monumentalen gattungs- und philosophiegeschichtlichen Skizze gelingt es ihm nämlich, Janus' Autorschaft mit neuen Argumenten zu untermauern[31] – so wird der Text von V. Kovács als Janus' Werk in die zweite bilingue Ausgabe von 1987 ebenfalls mit aufgenommen.

Offensichtlich kann ein dezisives Argument auch in diesem Fall nur durch Erschließung der handschriftlichen Texttradition geboten werden. Das Gedicht ist in einem Codex gemischten Inhalts der Österreichischen Nationalbibliothek (Cod. 3324) mit auffindbar – zumindest sein Anfang und sein Ende[32]: Auf fol. 45^v (im Weiteren **S**) sind nämlich zwar die ersten sechs Zeilen des fraglichen Textes zu lesen, wobei die folgenden drei Folios aus dem Bogen herausgeschnitten wurden. Da eine Codexseite 32 Zeilen

---

[28] Ladislaus JUHÁSZ, De edendis Iani Pannonii operibus quae supersunt omnibus. Szeged 1929, 7. Anhand der Huszti-Stelle wird das Werk auch von István BORZSÁK (s. Anm. 9), 361 dem Janus zugeschrieben.

[29] CSAPODI (s. Anm. 12), 21. An der Stelle, auf die er sich beruft (Sándor V. KOVÁCS, Az újkori Janus Pannonius-filológia [Die Janus Pannonius-Philologie der Neuzeit]. In: Tibor Kardos, Sándor V. Kovács (Hgg.), Janus Pannonius: Tanulmányok [Janus Pannonius: Studien]. Budapest 1975, 563–585; hier 572f.; Vgl. Sándor V. KOVÁCS, Eszmetörténet és régi magyar irodalom: Tanulmányok [Geistesgeschichte und ältere ungarische Literatur: Studien]. Budapest 1987, 337–341, wird von Kovács nicht behauptet, dass das Gedicht nicht von Janus stammt.

[30] Béla KARÁCSONYI, Janus Pannonius és a centralizáció [Janus Pannonius und die Zentralisierung]. In: Janus Pannonius: Tanulmányok (s. Anm. 29), 93–118; hier 115.

[31] KARDOS, (s. Anm. 19), 6, 9–13. In Anm. 28 wird von Kardos die Entscheidung von V. Kovács aus dem Jahr 1972 subtil kritisiert. In seinem Gedankengang tauchen natürlich auch die im Volk wurzelnden Ketzerbewegungen mehrmals auf.

[32] Otto MAZAL, Handschriften mittelalterlicher Augustiner-Eremiten in der Österreichischen Nationalbibliothek. Augustinianum 4 (1964), 265–330; hier 324f., bzw. schon früher von Erzsébet MAYER (s. Anm. 35).

enthält, verwundert es auch nicht, dass wir auf dem nächsten Folio (fol. 46ʳ) den auf Zeile 198 folgenden Teil des Gedichts wiederfinden. Wird nun auch die Überschrift über den Anfangszeilen betrachtet, liest man mit einiger Enttäuschung allerdings Folgendes: *Lippi Brandolini de laudibus beatissimi patris Sisti quarti pontificis Maximi Libellus incipit.*

Der blinde Humanist Aurelio Lippo Brandolini aus Florenz (um 1454–1497) ist der ungarischen Kulturgeschichte nicht unbekannt[33], zumal er ja eine kurze Zeit auch an Matthias' Hof verbrachte und als Hauptfiguren seiner ebenda in Angriff genommenen staatstheoretischen Arbeit der ungarische König und dessen Sohn János Corvinus erscheinen[34].

Der hierdurch erwachende Verdacht bezüglich der Autorschaft wird zur Gewissheit, wenn man auch die übrigen – von Erzsébet Mayer bereits 1938 gesammelten – Manuskripte mit den Werken des Aurelio Brandolini einsieht[35]. Drei weitere Handschriften seines Papst Sixtus IV. (1471–1484) gewidmeten Gedichtkranzes sind uns bekannt: eine in Rom (Biblioteca Nazionale Centrale, Ms. S. Giovanni e Paolo 7 [1823] = **G**) und zwei im Vatikan (Vat. Lat. 5008 = **V** und Urb. Lat. 739 = **U**). In Bezug auf die letzten zehn Zeilen bei Zsámboky behielt Huszti Recht, und es ist kein Zufall, dass sich diese in der Wiener Handschrift am Anfang der Seite befinden. Das Gedicht mit dem Anfang *Sederat omnipotens* ist in der Tat bruchstückhaft und die zehn Schlusszeilen bilden das Ende eines anderen, ebenfalls von Brandolini verfassten Gedichts mit dem Titel *Epigramma de Eucharistia*.

Nun wird die nahe liegende Annahme, dass die Wiener Handschift mit dem ehemals bei Zsámboky bzw. in seinem Besitz befindlichen Manuskript identisch ist, leicht zur Gewissheit. Am Eingang des Heftes (fol. 22ʳ) findet man den eigenhändigen Eintrag des ungarischen Humanisten. Zum Ver-

---

[33] Brandolini, Aurelio Lippo. KŐSZEGHY Péter et al. (Hgg.), *Magyar művelődéstörténeti lexikon* [Lexikon zur ungarischen Kulturgeschichte]. Budapest I (2003), 440–442.

[34] Hierzu zuletzt István PUSKÁS, Monumento al Principe: Il dialogo di Aurelio Lippo Brandolini intitolato De comparatione rei publicae et regni. *Nuova Corvina* 20 (2008), 187–193. Die frühere Fachliteratur zum Autor wird zitiert von Elisabeth SCHRÖTER, Der Vatikan als Hügel Apollons und der Musen: Kunst und Panegyrik von Nikolaus V. bis Julius II. *Römische Quartalschrift* 75 (1980), 208–240; hier bes. 212 und 215–217.

[35] Erzsébet MAYER, Un umanista italiano della corte di Mattia Corvino: Aurelio Brandolini Lippi. *Annuario / Studi e documenti italo-ungheresi della R. Accademia d'Ungheria di Roma* 2 (1937) [Roma 1938], 123–167; hier 164.

gleich – wenn dies sich nach alledem überhaupt noch als notwendig erweist – sind die von Hans Gerstinger veröffentlichten Einträge zugänglich[36].

Es scheint also unwiderlegbar, dass die Gutgläubigkeit von Hegedűs und anderen Zsámboky gegenüber als nicht hinreichend begründet gelten kann: Zsámboky wird Janus' Dichtkunst nicht nur durch die Weglassung gewisser ‚unangenehmer' Epigramme leichter verdaulich gemacht, sondern sie durch einen frommen Betrug sogar noch ‚angereichert' haben – wobei er auch den Habitus der an der Finanzierung der zu druckenden Bände beteiligten Personen im Auge zu behalten trachtete. In Kenntnis der Handschriften wäre es ein Leichtes, über die – beträchtlich divergierende Ansichten vertretenden – Philologen den Stab zu brechen, die die *Consultatio* in ihr von Janus gemaltes Bild einzufügen versuchten und später auch einfügen konnten – dies wäre jedoch kaum billig. Ihre Interpretationen zeugen zwar nicht weniger vom modernen Philologen und seiner Zeit als von Janus und dessen Epoche – immerhin waren sie trotz ihres fehlerhaften Grundkonzeptes imstande, zum Gedicht (bzw. unter dem Vorwand des Gedichts) auch durchaus gültige Beobachtungen anzustellen. Ja, es mag sogar sein, dass der Zufall – oder gar die Vorsehung? – aus den beiden Brandolini-Bruchstücken ein gelungeneres und liebenswürdigeres Gedicht zustande gebracht hat, als es das Lied in seiner auf Sixtus IV. zugeschnittenen Ganzheit ursprünglich gewesen war[37]. Nach dem Gedicht soll auf Vorschlag und Bitte der Heiligen Jungfrau nämlich ein mit allen Tugenden gesegneter Hirte auf die Erde geschickt werden, der der herumirrenden Herde den richtigen Weg weist. Gott gibt der Bitte nach und der hl. Franziskus erklärt sich bereit, Erzieher und Patron des zu dieser Aufgabe Auserwählten zu werden (Francesco della Rovere wurde ab seinem neunten Lebensjahr bei den Franziskanern erzogen und später auch selbst Mönch dieses Ordens). Der Herr erschafft die Seele, die auf die Erde herabgestiegen den Namen Sixtus bekommt; im

---

[36] Hans GERSTINGER, Johannes Sambucus als Handschriftensammler. In: *Festschrift der Nationalbibliothek in Wien*, hg. zur Feier des 200jährigen Bestehens des Gebäudes. Wien 1926, 251–400; hier Tafel II.

[37] Wie es in Brandolinis Widmung zu lesen ist: *Offero igitur benignitati tuae conscriptos a me diversis temporibus libros tres, quorum primus, qui perpetuo carmine scriptus est, mores et laudes Sisti ab ipso vitae exordio summatim continet, immo etiam caelestium consilio adhibito causas explicat, quibus Sistum in terras mittere necesse fuerit.*

verbleibenden umfangreicheren Teil des Werkes werden sein Leben und hauptsächlich seine Verdienste beschrieben.

Kurzum: Wir sind ein paar Janus-Gedichte ärmer geworden[38]. Dem muss der Gerechtigkeit halber jedoch gleich hinzugefügt werden, dass wir Zsámboky für seine auf die Erhaltung der authentischen Janus-Texte gerichtete Tätigkeit trotz seiner kleinen Finte nach wie vor zu Dankbarkeit verpflichtet sind. Die mutmaßliche editorische Absicht erklärt zwar, aus welchem Grund bzw. zu welchem Zweck die Brandolini-Gedichte in den Janus-Band gekommen sind, es ist jedoch weiterhin fraglich, warum sie darin ausgerechnet in dieser Form erscheinen. Ein Vergleich der Manuskripte in Wien und Italien mag zu einer adäquaten Antwort auf diese Frage verhelfen.

Struktur und Text der drei italienischen Manuskripte sind im wesentlichen identisch. Der *Codex Urbinas* ist eine 1517-er Kopie der neuen, „wiederaufgewärmten" Ausgabe des Werkes, die 1505 von Raffaello Brandolini (1465–1517), dem jüngeren Bruder des Verfassers, angefertigt, und dem Kardinal Galeotto della Rovere, dem Neffen von Papst Julius II., gewidmet wurde. Von dem aus diesem Grund verfassten Vorwort abgesehen hat er den gleichen Inhalt wie die anderen zwei italienischen Codices. Genauer gesagt: **V** weist an seinem Anfang geringfügige Mängel auf, so dass **G** als das einzig vollständige Exemplar der Originalausgabe gelten kann. In dieser Handschrift wurden die letzten beiden Zeilen eines Epigramms im Nachhinein getilgt[39]: diese Zeilen finden sich in **V** und **U** auch nicht mehr, folglich erscheint die Abhängigkeit der Vatikanischen Manuskripte von der römischen Handschrift als beinahe sicher.

Das ominöse Wiener Manuskript enthält offensichtlich die gleiche Gedichtsammlung wie die italienischen Handschriften, und zwar ohne das

---

[38] Ein andersartiger Zusammenhang kann jedoch angenommen werden: László Török, Mitherausgeber unserer gemeinsamen kritischen Edition der Werke des Janus Pannonius, meinte nach der Lektüre vorliegender Studie, dass Brandolini sein hier besprochenes Werk in Kenntnis von Janus' Gedichten verfasst hatte. Als von ihm als Beispiele angegebene Parallelen wären etwa folgende zu nennen: zu Zeile 64: *Eleg.* II 12, 8 Tel. = 5, 8 M.; zu Zeile 132: *Eleg.* I, 10, 32 Tel. = 28, 32 M. und I, 6, 108 Tel. = 24, 108 M.; Zeile 152: *Eleg.* II, 15, 22 Tel. = 13, 22 M. und I, 2, 28 Tel. = 20, 28 M.; Zeile 201: *Epigr.* I, 4, 7 = 376, 7 M.; Zeile 208: *El.* I, 6, 90 Tel. = 24,90 M.

[39] Giuseppe DE LUCA, Un umanista fiorentino e la Roma rinnovata da Sisto IV. *Rinascita* I (1938), 74–90; hier 85. Im hier veröffentlichten Text lautet *Epigr.* X, 7 richtig: *Haec domus augustis fuerat satis omnibus una*; X, 14 richtig: *Cumque uiris Zeusis cederet ipse suis.*

Vorwort der zweiten Ausgabe, wobei die Reihenfolge der Texte von der in den italienischen Codices abweicht. In der Wiener Handschrift findet sich ein einziges Gedicht, das in den italienischen nicht zu finden war. Sollte es in diesen tatsächlich nicht enthalten sein, so zeugt das Wiener Manuskript von den Spuren einer anderen Redaktion. Die Existenz dieser Redaktion und ihr Verhältnis zur italienischen könnten durch die Kollationierung des gesamten Textes geklärt werden; hierfür vermag leider auch der unten abgedruckte Abschnitt nicht genügend Anhaltspunkte zu bieten.

Die Originalstruktur des Wiener Manuskripts lässt sich hingegen mit großer Wahrscheinlichkeit rekonstruieren. In ihm fehlen – wie oben bereits erwähnt – drei (herausgeschnittene) Folios, aufgrund deren Zsámboky in seiner 1569-er Ausgabe die Passage *Eleg.* II, 18, 7–198 Tel. publizierte. Es fällt schwer, den Gedanken loszuwerden, dass diese zwei Umstände miteinander in Verbindung gebracht werden könnten: d. h. dass Zsámboky die wenigen Anfangs- und Schlusszeilen des von ihm zur Veröffentlichung bestimmten Textes selber abschrieb bzw. abschreiben ließ – zumal diese sich auf auch andere Texte (noch dazu selbst Brandolinis Namen) enthaltenden Seiten befanden –, die mittleren drei Folios hingegen kurzerhand herausschnitt und dem Drucker übergab. Wie es sich aber in derartigen Situationen nicht selten ergibt, gelangten die fraglichen drei Folios nach Satz und Druck des Textes nicht mehr an ihre ursprüngliche Stelle zurück.

Der Umstand, dass dem Anfang von Brandolinis Kleinepos[40] (*Eleg.* II, 18, 1–198 Tel.) in Zsámbokys Manuskript unmittelbar der Schluss des *Epigramma de Eucharistia* (*Eleg.* II, 18, 201–210 Tel.) folgte, ist auf zweierlei Weisen zu erklären: Entweder zeigte die Handschrift schon bei ihrer Entstehung diese Anordnung oder ihre Folios gerieten später durcheinander.

Der Codex, dessen Teil heute 25 Folios mit den Brandolini-Gedichten (fol. 22–46) bilden, ist derart eng gebunden, dass sich seine Bogeneinteilung zwar nicht mit letzter Gewissheit feststellen lässt, aber mit großer Wahrscheinlichkeit aussieht, wie folgt: fol. 23–30 und 32–39 zwei Quaternionen, 40+46 sowie 44+45 zwei Bifolien, die übrigen Folios stehen allein[41]. Wenn

---

[40] Sein Inhalt wird von DE LUCA (s. Anm. 39), 79f. zusammengefasst, der anhand der Gattung – allerdings ohne dessen Namen zu erwähnen – Gabriele D'ANNUNZIOs Werk *Il libro ascetico della giovane Italia* als zeitgenössische Parallele zitiert.

[41] Die Angaben zur Bogeneinteilung verdanke ich der freundlichen Mitteilung von Christian Gastgeber.

man die sich aneinander anschließenden Textteile aufgrund der italienischen Handschriften zusammenfügt, ist die ursprüngliche Reihenfolge der Folios folgendermaßen zu rekonstruieren: 44–45, die herausgeschnittenen drei Folios, 22–35, 40, 46, 36–39, 41–43. Unter Berücksichtigung der zusammengehörenden Folios ergeben 22–31 und 32–39 (in ihrer Mitte mit 40+46) zwei regelrechte Quinionen.

Die Reihenfolge der Texte ist mit der der italienischen zwar auch so nicht in jeder Hinsicht identisch, so dass die oben gestellte Frage auch weiterhin offen bleiben muss. Es lässt sich allerdings eine weitere, äußerst wahrscheinliche Hypothese aufstellen: Die im Kleinepos fehlenden Zeilen nach den herausgeschnittenen drei Folios und die jenen folgenden fünf Gedichte in den italienischen Handschriften könnten mit ziemlicher Genauigkeit auf weiteren fünf Folios platziert werden – woraus folgt, dass den Anfang der Wiener Handschrift ebenfalls ein Quinio gebildet haben könnte.

Demnach wird das Wiener Manuskript ursprünglich annähernd drei Viertel des Materials der italienischen Handschriften enthalten haben (fol. 43^v ist leer, es kann also auch aus diesem Grund nicht als eine vollständige Kopie von jenen gelten). Bereits als Zsámboky es erwarb, war es fragmentarisch: einzelne seiner Bifolien waren entzwei gerissen bzw. ihre Reihenfolge vermischt worden. Das Fehlen von drei Folios wird jedoch – wie oben schon erörtert – wohl auf Zsámbokys Rechnung zu setzen sein.[*]

---

[*] Die Forschungen wurden mit Unterstützung des Forschungsprogramms OTKA NN 104.456 des Nationalen Forschungsfonds Ungarn durchgeführt und sind in ungarischer Sprache bereits publiziert: Zsámboky János Janus Pannonius-kiadása és csonka Brandolini-kézirata. *Irodalomtörténeti Közlemények* (ItK) 115 (2011), 202–216. An dieser Stelle darf ich mich bei Géza Szentmártoni Szabó für seine freundliche Hilfe und bei Balázs Sára für die deutsche Übersetzung der ungarischen Fassung recht herzlich bedanken.

ANHANG

Im Folgenden wird nun der aufgrund der Manuskripte revidierte Text von Brandolinis Gedichten vorgestellt. Dies bedeutet, dass erstmals auch die am Schluss des in der Fachliteratur als *Consultatio* bekannten Ps.-Janus-Gedichts fehlenden 30 Zeilen (199–228) sowie die ersten sechs Zeilen des Brandolini-Epigramms mit dem Titel *De Eucharistia* (gedruckt) zu lesen sind, die von Zsámboky an den voraufgehenden Text angefügt, von Teleki und Kovásznai aber – durch zwei punktierte Zeilen – von diesem wieder abgetrennt worden waren. Von dem mehr als tausend Verse umfassenden Kleinepos soll hier ausschließlich sein (für die dem Janus zugeschriebene Elegie als ausschlaggebend betrachtetes) erstes Viertel veröffentlicht werden, und zwar in einer Form wiedergegeben, die der in der Janus-Ausgabe verwendeten möglichst nahe kommt.

G Rom, Biblioteca Nazionale Centrale, Ms. S. Giovanni e Paolo 7 [1823]
S Wien, ÖNB, Cod. 3324
U Biblioteca Vaticana, Urb. Lat. 739
V Biblioteca Vaticana, Vat. Lat. 5008

E editio Viennae: Kaspar Stainhofer 1569 (VD16 ZV 24520)
M. Iani Pannonii Opera quae manserunt omnia. [...] Edidit [...] Iulius MAYER, similia addidit Ladislaus TÖRÖK. Budapest 2006
Tel. editio Trajecti ad Rhenum 1784

Quid tantum sanctos stupet vrbs Romana Catones?
Quidue stupet septem terra Pelasga viros?
Socrate quidne suo doctæ lætantur Athenæ?
E quibus huic aliquem præposuisse nefas.
Doctus Romano, doctus sermone Pelasgo,
Siue velit prosa scribere, siue metro.
Cùm dicit prosa, Ciceronem dicere iures,
Cùm cantat numeris crediture esse Maro.
Plurima conscripsit per se sermone Latino,
Plurima de Graia transtulit historia.
Inclyta semper erunt rerum monumenta, vigebunt
Cum tot magnificis scripta voluminibus.
Semper erunt libri, qui scilicet ipsius omnes
Præscriptum summo margine nomen habent.
Per quos æternùm viuet mage splendida fama,
Donec erit Phœbus, sidera donec erunt.
Nec plus à magno scripti Cicerone libelli
Stabunt, aut nomen Quintiliane tuum,
Et cum Getulo sauus Catilina lugurtha,
Et cum Romana Lucius historia.
Clarus ab Eois quà Sol iubar exerit vndis,
Quà rubro emeritos gurgite condit equos,
Zona vaporifero quà subiacet ardua Cancro,
Quà micat in gelido Mænalis vrsa polo:
Hunc omnes nouère hominem, nec laudibus vllis,
Clara potest tanti crescere fama viri.

Finem

XLII

Finem igitur præstat longis imponere verbis,
Ne reus immensæ garrulitatis agar,
Sed prius æterno qui colligat omnia nexu,
Orabo summum supplice voce patrem:
Vt det contiguis concordem ducere vitam,
Vos placido dictis ore fauete meis.

IANI PANNONII DE
laudibus Pontific: & rerum humanarum conditione.

Sederat omnipotens medio sublimis olympo,
Subdideratq́; oculis condita cuncta suis.
Lustrabat tractusq́; maris, terrasq́; patentes,
Quidquid & astriferi clauditur axe poli:
Paulatimq́; hominum defixi lumina rebus,
Vt studia humani cerneret ingenij.
Vt vitam & mores, vt vota & gaudia nosset,
Quod quisq́; effugeret, quod sequeretur opus,
Conspicit implicitum tam multis fraudibus orbem,
Tot scelerum facies, & mala tanta videt.
Insanas hominum curas, vota improba cernit,
Et nullo in terris esse in honore Deos.
Hic perit excidijs vrbes, per tela, per ignes
Tendit, vt innumeras vndiq́; cogat opes.

M ij   Ille

Quid faciant vili membrorum carcere septi?
Quid faciat vili massa subacta luto?
Tu quoq́; deposito fateamur vera timore,
Das tantis causam, materiamq́; malis.
Imbelles homini sensus, stimulosq́; dedisti,
Duxisti è fragili mollia membra luto.
Quid referan tot opes insani pabula luxus,
Quid Veneris stimulos, ingluuiemq́; gulæ?
Præterea quamuis obnoxia vita periclis
Me miseram quantis continuata malis.
Et mirum est siquid mortalia pectora peccant?
Quis valeat tantos exuperare dolos?
Sed tamen agnoscunt crimen, culpamq́; fatentur,
Et facti veniam, supplicium q́; petunt.
Nec sunt magna tamen mortalis crimina culpæ,
Si modò de miseris credere vera potes.
Quæ virtus totum, pietasq́; est magna per orbem
Totaq́; delubris terra referta tuis.
Aspice quæ plenis hinc atq́; hinc sedibus omnes
Circumstant animæ, quis nisi terra dedit?
Sed sanè sint magna hominum peccata, nec vsquam
Sit pietas esto, sit tibi nullus honos.
Supplicijs fontes (nisi mauis parcere cunctis)
Da decet: hoc omnes æquius esse putant.
Si tamen haud vllæ possunt te flectere causæ
Et certum est pœnas sumere ab orbe graues,

Aspice

XLVI

Aspice supplicijs fontes, & noxia tantum
Corpora, at immeritum perdere parce genus.
Magna fuère quidem, & quæ vllis promittere votis
Vel quamuis auidus non foret ausus homo.
At quantum est minimo totum se inmittere pani,
Et magnum exiguo claudere in orbe Deum?
Quantum est se nobis totum præbere fruendum,
Et tamen à toto comminuisse nihil?
Cùm dedit illa quidem, vicit sua munera Christus,
Cùm dat se donis vincitur ipse suis.
O amor, ô pietas, post omnia se dedit ipsum,
Qui se iam dederat plus dare quid poterat?

N ij   EPI.

Abb. 2ab: Beginn und Schluss des Gedichts des Aurelio Lippo Brandolini in der Janus Pannonius-Ausgabe des Johannes Sambucus, Wien 1569, XLIIr–XLVIr (Országos Széchényi Könyvtár, App. H. 432)

LIPPI BRANDOLINI DE LAUDIBUS BEATISSIMI PATRIS SISTI IIII PONTIFICIS MAXIMI LIBELLUS INCIPIT

Scelera humani generis a Deo dum terras intueretur conspecta

    Sederat omnipotens medio sublimis Olympo,
        subdideratque oculis condita cuncta suis.
    Lustrabat tractusque maris, terrasque patentes,
        quicquid et astriferi clauditur axe poli.
    Paulatimque hominum defixit lumina rebus,   5
        ut studia humani cerneret ingenii,
    ut vitam et mores, ut vota et gaudia nosset,
        quod quisque effugeret, quod sequeretur opus.
    Conspicit implicitum tam multis fraudibus orbem,
        tot scelerum facies et mala tanta videt.   10
    Insanas hominum curas, vota improba cernit,
        et nullo in terris esse in honore deos.
    Hic petit excidiis urbes per tela, per ignes;
        tendit, ut innumeras undique cogat opes.
    Ille armis violat leges hominesque deosque,   15
        subdat ut imperio regna aliena suo.
    Ense petunt alii fratres carosque parentes,
        cumque suis alii bella nefanda gerunt.
    Furta iuvant multos, fenus saevaeque rapinae,
        fanaque direptis, proh, spoliata deis.   20
    Decipit hic dominum, fraudem parat ille clienti,
        emtori varios iniicit ille dolos.
    Pars amat ingentes sumptus luxumque superbum,
        laetaque magnificas aedificare domos.
    Pars Venerem sequitur caecique Cupidinis ignes,   25
        pars sequitur rapidam luxuriosa gulam.
    Hi spernunt Stygiosque lacus poenasque malorum,
        quaeque manent animas praemia certa pias.
    Contemnunt illi superos superumque parentem,
        nec pudor est ullos esse negare deos.   30

I GUV S (ll. 1–6) **E** (ll. 1–198) Tit. Lippi ... incipit *hab.* **GUVS** Scelera ... conspecta *hab.* **GUV** Iani Pannonii de laudibus Pontific: & rerum humanarum conditione **E** Consultatio Dei Patris et Filii de perdendo hominum genere; quos tandem B. Virgo exorat *Tel.* || **5** Paullatimque *Tel.* | defixi **E** || **12** 'pro: nullo in terris, *legendum*: nullo terris' *Tel.* || **18** nephanda **U** || **20** Phanaque **GUVE** | proh spoliata] exspoliata *Tel.* || **21** clienti] parenti **E***Tel.* || **26** rabidam **E***Tel.*

Indignatio Dei, concilium deorum omnium et ipsius oratio de humano genere delendo

His pater attonitus studiis votisque virorum,
  hoc doluit vili posse licere luto.
Indoluit simul et magnas exarsit in iras,
  aestuat, ira gravi mista dolore fremit,
ut quondam pleno fluctus furit actus aeno,   35
  aut ubi sulfureis mons sonat intus aquis.
Tandem ubi conceptus paulum deferbuit aestus,
  concilium toto convocat inde polo.
Undique conveniunt superi, circaque residunt,
  incipit a solio sic prior ipse suo: 40
'Ecquid caelicolae vestros spectatis alumnos,
  cernitis humanum, quo ruat usque, genus,
quem tandem inveniet nostra haec patientia finem,
  aut haec ducemus quam toleranda diu?
Quis iam virtuti locus est toto orbe relictus,   45
  quis toto sceleri non patet orbe locus?
Quid non dira fames auri regnique cupido
  fas putat, immo sibi quid putat esse nefas?
In venerem ruit omne genus, gula conficit omnes,
  vitaque pro rapida perditur ingluvie.   50
Iam mores legesque omnes, iura omnia pulsa,
  religio, pietas, canaque pulsa fides.
Caedibus et bellis, et fuso sanguine flagrat
  terra, nec est nati tutus ab ense parens.
Concurrit ruptis inter se legibus orbis,   55
  in clademque ruunt omnia versa suam.
Mersa est flagitiis tellus, de culmine summo
  pendet, et in praeceps corruit omne genus.
Nos neque iam norunt, nec caelo vivere credunt,
  aut quenquam aetherei sceptra tenere poli.   60
Fulmina contemnunt, poenas et Tartara rident,
  et quisquam in terris numina nostra colat?
Heu, genus ingratum, nostra sub imagine cretum
  poenitet e facili compositumque luto.
Nonne mare et terras, quemque ipsi habitamus, Olympum,   65
  e nihilo nostrae constituere manus?

|| **31** *Tit. hab.* **GUV** generi **V** || **34** fremens *Tel.* || **35** actus aeno] actus * **E** actus in alto *reposuimus*: in alto *Tel.* || **36** *forte leg.* tonat *Tel.* || **37** paullum *Tel.* || **41** Et quid **V** || **44** tolleranda **U** || **48** imo *Tel.* || **52** Relligio *Tel.* || **64** *forte leg.* composuisset *Tel.*

Quisnam opibus terram, quis piscibus imbuit undas?
  Quis posuit nitido sidera clara polo?
Edita sunt nostro – quis nescit? – numine cuncta,
  sunt tamen ingratis edita cuncta viris.　　　　　　　　　　　70
Nos illis gravidam numeroso munere terram,
  nos dedimus latum, qua patet usque, mare.
Spem quoque praebuimus regni post omnia nostri,
  atque huius socios iussimus esse poli.
Illi autem elati imperio rebusque secundis　　　　　　　　　　　75
  vertere in cladem munera nostra suam.
Segnitie mollique animos deperdere luxu
  coepere et miris degenerare modis.
Sed neque destitimus carum praestare parentem,
  humanumque omni parte iuvare genus.　　　　　　　　　　　80
Tradidimus sacras caeli de vertice leges,
  sed sprevit leges impia turba meas.
Misimus et vates, vates sprevere sacratos,
  misimus atroces, nec timuere, viros.
Denique conceptum divini numine verbi,　　　　　　　　　　　85
  in terras natum mittere non piguit.
Immo ego descendi, pariter descendimus ambo,
  sedimus et gremio, diva pudica, tuo.
Vos mihi, caelicolae, testes, quis me impia poenis
  sustulerit leto turba redempta meo.　　　　　　　　　　　90
Sed mea praetereo pereunti debita mundo
  fata; quis e vobis non mala mille tulit?
Quot ferro, quot aqua absumpti, quotque igne cremati?
  Corpora quot rapidis dilaniata feris?
Ecquid, ut aetherea pellant nos sede, moramur,　　　　　　　　95
  et caelo admotis montibus arma ferant?
Tollamus scelerum auctores, causasque malorum,
  deleat invisum flamma inimica genus.
Iam satis humani tulimus ludibria fastus,
  sat vobis, superi, sat tibi, diva, datum.　　　　　　　　　　　100
Desine me genitrix lacrimosis flectere verbis,
  desinite ingratas vos mihi ferre preces.
Consulite in medium, et vanas deponite mentes,
  solvatur tantis terra polusque malis.'

71 illi **VE** || 89 queis **E** quîs *Tel.* || 94 rabidis *Tel.* | dilanita **V** || 103 varias **E***Tel.*

Deorum fremitus et Beatae Virginis oratio de humano genere servando
  Talibus attoniti dictis diversa fremebant,   105
    obscuroque dabant murmura caeca sono,
  ut procul in silvis cum surgere ventus opacis
    incipit, aut imis murmurat unda vadis.
  Atque ibi deiecto mater maestissima vultu
    suppliciter tales fundit ab ore sonos: 110
  'Nate, tuae (quid enim superest?) spes unica matris,
    quo solo videor nomine freta loqui.
  Nate, quid indignas, mitissime, surgis in iras,
    quae nova tam subiti causa furoris adest?
  Et quae tanta tuum laeserunt crimina numen,   115
    ut nullus veniae iam locus esse queat?
  Quid, tua non omnem superat clementia culpam?
    Anne animum minuit noxa aliena tuum?
  Ulcisci quos, nate, paras, quos perdere tentas?
    Cum quibus, o superum maxime, bella geris?   120
  Nonne hominum genus ecce tuum, tua pignora perdis,
    duxerat e molli quos tua dextra luto.
  Quid iuvat invalido Martem exercere sub hoste,
    quid iuvat in praedam saevior esse tuam?
  Quae tibi cum vili bella aut certamina caeno,   125
    aut quae deletis laus tibi parta viris?
  Cui mare, cui terras, cui cetera tradis habenda?
    Quae rerum facies, nate, quis usus erit?
  Frustra igitur magni moles erit edita mundi?
    Frustra erit ad motus inrequieta suos?   130
  Fulgebunt nitido nequicquam sidera caelo,
    et peragent notas per sua signa vias?
  Cui feret innumeros tellus uberrima fructus?
    Servabit tantas cui gravis alvus opes?
  Cui pecudes alet illa suas, volucresque ferasque,   135
    et vaga cui pisces nutriet unda suos?
  Sublatis tot, Nate, viris tua dona perire
    et squalere tuum sic patieris opus?
  Ferre potes vacuum caesis cultoribus orbem,
    heredem tantis nec superesse bonis?   140

105 *Tit. hab.* **GUV** || 115 Ec **G** || 120 Superûm *Tel.* || 125 aut] ac **E***Tel.* | caeno] gente **E***Tel.* || 135 ille **E** || 136 suas **E**

Sed tibi sic placitum; sint omnia condita frustra,
    et pereat tanti, Nate, laboris opus.
Numne etiam poteris caelo delapsus ab alto
    nequicquam in nostro procubuisse sinu?
Num poteris laceros variis cruciatibus artus   145
    nequicquam indignae, nate, dedisse neci?
Nequicquam tantos poterit tolerasse dolores,
    obsequitur iussis dum pia turba tuis?
Si te nulla movet tantorum causa laborum,
    at moveat, debet quem tibi mundus, honos.   150
Quis tibi sacra feret, quis templa arasque dicabit?
    Quis sparget nomen cuncta per ora tuum?
Nemo aderit, qui vota ferat, qui numen adoret,
    quin nullum in terris iam tibi numen erit.
Otia ages caelo, duces inglorius aevum,   155
    et tua te facient munera nulla deum.
Cui veniam dabis, admisso quem crimine plectes?
    Ostendes cui te per tua iura deum?
Iactabis vacuis nequicquam fulmina terris,
    fulminibus nemo, qui moveatur, erit.   160
Non pater exhausto, non rex, non arbiter, orbe,
    – quid multa? – exhausto non eris orbe deus.
Non faciunt simulacra deos, non templa, nec arae;
    imperium in cunctos arbitriumque facit.
Cui porro imperites, tua quem sententia damnet,   165
    si tibi subiectum deleat ira genus?
At vitiis intenti homines, iacet obruta virtus,
    nec quisquam toto iam colit orbe deum.
Labitur interdum, varioque errore tenetur
    infirmum, fateor, desipiensque genus.   170
Quid faciant vili membrorum carcere saepti?
    Quid faciat turpi massa subacta luto?
Tu quoque (deposito fateamur vera timore)
    das tantis causam materiamque malis.
Inbelles homini sensus stimulosque dedisti,   175
    duxisti e fragili mollia membra luto.
Quid referam tot opes, insani pabula luxus?
    Quid veneris stimulos ingluviemque gulae?

---

141 *forte legendum:* Si tibi sic. *vel:* Sed tibi si. *Tel.* || 143 Tune E*Tel.* || 150 honor E*Tel.* || 162 erit E || 169 vanoque GUV || 172 turpi] vili E*Tel.*

Praeterea quantis obnoxia vita periclis,
    me miseram, quantis continuata malis!   180
Et mirum est, si quid mortalia corpora peccant?
    Quis valeat tantos exsuperare dolos?
Sed tamen agnoscunt crimen, culpamque fatentur,
    et facti veniam suppliciumque petunt.
Nec sunt magna tamen mortalis crimina culpae,   185
    si modo de miseris credere vera potes.
Quin virtus totum pietasque est magna per orbem,
    totaque delubris terra referta tuis.
Aspice, quae plenis hinc atque hinc sedibus omnes
    circumstant animae; quis, nisi terra, dedit?   190
Sed sane sint magna hominum peccata, nec usquam
    sit pietas, esto, sit tibi nullus honos.
Suppliciis sontes (nisi mavis parcere cunctis: (197 T.)
    hoc decet, hoc omnes aequius esse putant),   (198 T.)
si tamen haud ullae possunt te flectere causae,   (193 T.)
    et certum est poenas sumere ab orbe graves,
affice suppliciis sontes et noxia tantum
    corpora, at immeritum perdere parce genus.   (196 T.)
Quin potius veniam tua det clementia cunctis,
    officioque omnes demereare tuo.   200
Hoc decet, hoc una cuncti te voce precamur,
    hoc polus, hoc tellus orba futura rogat.
Aspice concessum genitis mortalibus orbem,
    neve tui tantum perde laboris opus.
Aspice confossum numeroso vulnere corpus,   205
    et tua pro miseris pendula membra viris.
Aspice (si vero dicor tibi nomine mater)
    hunc uterum, haec labris ubera trita tuis.
Aspice bis senos, fidissima pectora, fratres,
    quaeque tenet meritum turba beata polum.   210
En laceros tendunt artus discerptaque membra
    et sua mortali vulnera facta manu.
Ne, rogo, tam multos perdi patiare labores,
    neve velis tantas spernere, nate, preces.

---

179 quamuis **E** || **181** corpora] pectora **UE**Tel. || **184** suppliciumque] supplice voce Tel. || **187** Quae **E** || **189** Asspice Tel. || plene hinc **UV** plenhic **G** || **190** animas Tel. || **193** Suppliciis … putant] post parce genus hab. Tel. | (nisi … putant) **U** || **194** Hoc decet] Hoc docet **U** Da decet **E**Tel. || **199** desinit **E** || **208** hubera **GU**

Serva homines, genus, alme, tuum; tua pignora serva, 215
    materiam laudi da superesse tuae.
Sola etenim aeternas tibi dat clementia laudes;
    ut semper possis parcere, parce viris.
Comprime susceptas, qui cetera comprimis, iras,
    diraque saevitiae comprime tela tuae. 220
Redde age te placidum, mundo te redde serenum,
    nostraque sollicito pectora solve metu,
et, tibi quas homines omni pro crimine poenas
    debuerant, larga, nate, remitte manu.
Hac liceat peccasse tenus; iam nulla videbis 225
    crimina, nil posthac, quod verearis, erit.
Ipsa ego praestabo, quicquid peccabitur in te,
    si digna est, nostram do tibi, nate, fidem.'

222 solicito **U** || 225 licet **U**

DE EUCHARISTIA. EPIGRAMMA XXXVII.

Virgineum in gremium caelo descendere ab alto,
    ingentemque humili cingere carne deum,
inter mortales miseram traducere vitam
    indignamque viro sponte subire necem,
reddere se nobis et morte resurgere victa, 5
    et nobis primum sponte aperire polum
magna fuere quidem, et quae ullis promittere votis (201 T.)
    vel quamvis avidus non foret ausus homo.
At quantum est minimo totum se immittere pani,
    et magnum exiguo claudere in orbe deum?
Quantum est se nobis totum praebere fruendum, (205 T.)
    et tamen e toto comminuisse nihil?
Cum dedit illa quidem, vicit sua munera Christus,
    cum dat se, donis vincitur ipse suis.
O amor, o pietas, post omnia se dedit ipsum! 15
    Qui se iam dederat, plus dare quid poterat? (210 T.)

1 **GUV S** (ll. 7–16) **E** (ll. 7–16) *Tit. hab.* **GUV** eucaristia **GU** Epi. 37 De eucaristia **G** || 12 e] a **E***Tel.* || 16 lineam *in mg. add.* **G**

Iohannes Sambucus und die *Donatio Constantini*

CHRISTIAN GASTGEBER (Wien)

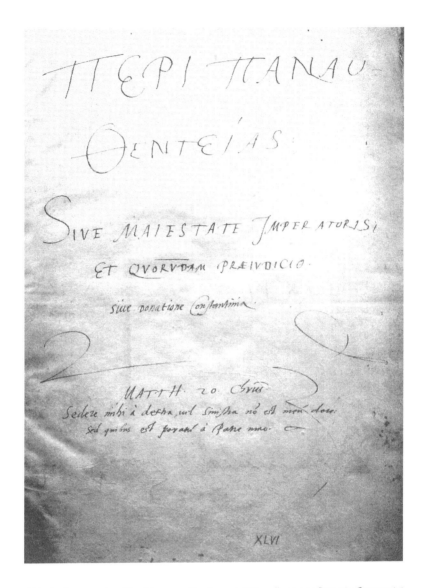

Abb. 1: Autographes Titelblatt von Sambucus' Abhandlung zur *Donatio Constantini* (Wien, Österreichische Nationalbibliothek, Cod. 9534, fol. 1r)

Meliora sunt vulnera diligentis quam oscula blanda fraudantis.
Sambucus' Leitspruch nach *Prov.* 27, 6
(ÖNB, Cod. 9534, fol. 3ᵛ)

Als sich Iohannes Sambucus 1571 an der Debatte um die Echtheit der so genannten *Donatio Constantini* beteiligte, blickte diese wissenschaftliche Debatte schon auf eine Reihe von Traktaten zurück, und immer mehr entwickelte sich die Diskussion zu einer Auseinandersetzung zwischen Kirche bzw. kirchlichen Privilegien und humanistischem bzw. in weiterer Folge protestantischem sowie kaiserlichem Einspruch auf der Basis hermeneutischer Überlegungen. Sambucus leistete dazu seinen Beitrag, und zwar nicht bloß in der Rezeption der Einwände seiner kritischen Vorgänger, sondern indem er neue Quellen aus seiner eigenen umfangreichen griechischen Bibliothek beisteuerte, darunter auch einen der ersten Papyri, der während der Renaissancezeit über die Alpen in den Norden gebracht wurde.

DIE EDITION, DIE NIE ERSCHIEN

Sein Werk „Über die Allmacht bzw. die Majestät des Kaisers und das Vorurteil einiger bzw. die Konstantinische Schenkung" (Περὶ Παναυθεντείας sive de maiestate imperatoris et quorundam praeiudicio sive donatione Constantinia) liegt bislang – mit Ausnahme der *Praefatio* und dem in Deutsch verfassten, eingelegten Begleitbrief des Autors an den Kaiser[1] – noch in keiner Edition vor[2]. Wiewohl eine kleine Einschränkung voranzuschicken ist, denn das Werk war bereits in den 70er Jahren des 17. Jahrhunderts für eine Druckausgabe geplant. Diese wollte der Präfekt der kaiserlichen Hofbibliothek Peter Lambeck (1663–1676) besorgen. Er kündigte das Werk in seinem *Catalogus librorum quos Petrus Lambecius Hamburgensis J(uris) U(triusque) D(octor), S. Caes. Maiestatis consiliarius, historiographus ac bibliothecarius, composuit et in lucem edidit ab anno aetatis decimo nono usque ad quadragesimum*

---

[1] Ediert bei Hans GERSTINGER, *Die Briefe des Johannes Sambucus (Zsamboky) 1554–1584. Mit einem Anhang: Die Sambucusbriefe im Kreisarchiv von Trnava* von Anton Vantuch. Wien 1968 (ÖAW, Phil.-hist. Kl., Sitzungsberichte 255), 120–122 (Nr. XLVI).

[2] Die Ausführungen hier verstehen sich daher gewissermaßen als Praeliminaria zu einer vom Verfasser geplanten kritischen Ausgabe mit Übersetzung und Kommentar.

quintum; nempe ab anno Christi MDCXLVII usque ad annum MDCLXXIII[3] an. Unter Nr. 18 wird genannt:

> Syntagma Rerum Germanicarum sive Germanicarum Rerum Scriptores varii, variaque Acta publica, ex Augustissimâ Bibliothecâ Caesareâ Vindobonensi in lucem edita cum Annotationibus necessariis, Chronologiâ accuratâ, & amplissimis Indicibus, Geographico inprimis & Genealogico; Vindobonae sive Wiennae, typis Matthaei Cosmerovii, S. Caes. Majestatis Typographi, A. 1673 aliquot Tomis in folio, cum multis Iconismis & Tabulis aeri incisis.
>
> Lambeck, *Catalogus* 1673, 45

Das Werk wird dann im Folgenden als in Druck befindlich angeführt, allerdings mit gewissen Verzögerungen[4]; im Voraus gibt Lambeck daher in diesem *Catalogus librorum* einen Einblick in den Inhalt; als Nr. 61 wird angeführt:

> *Joannis Sambuci Liber de Panauthentiâ sive Majestate Imperatoris, & quorundam praejudicio sive Donatione Constantinianâ, qui exstat autographus in Augustissimâ Bibliothecâ Caesareâ, & Imp. Maximiliano II ab ipso dedicatus atque oblatus est* A. 1571 d. 22 Julii.
>
> Lambeck, *Catalogus* 1673, 63

Am Ende der Aufzählung wird noch einmal auf die Drucklegung zum Zeitpunkt der Katalogabfassung (1673) hingewiesen:

> Haec igitur & alia longè plura ejus generis *Monumenta atque Acta publica* inserentur suprà memorato *Syntagmati Rerum Germanicarum*; cujus impressio uti anno hoc 1673 feliciter jam est inchoata, sic in manu DEI OPT. MAX. est, ut suo deinceps tempore aequè felix sequatur.
>
> Lambeck, *Catalogus* 1673, 65

In der Tat dürfte es allerdings nur zu einer Vorankündigung (bestenfalls noch eines Teilprobeandrucks [wohl gar nur des Titelblattes?]) gekommen sein, wie dies etwa für Lambecks ersten Teils des neunten Buches der *Commentarii de Augustissima Bibliotheca Caesarea Vindobonensi* bezeugt ist[5]. Trotz

---

[3] Wien: Matthaeus Cosmerovius 1673 (VD 17: 23:234137S).

[4] A. o., 45: *Quandoquidem autem amplum hoc & diffusum Opus iam quidem sub prelo est, ob magnitudinem tamen suam & multiplicis argumenti varietatem non adeò praepropere potest accelerari, ut quidam arduorum hujusmodi laborum ignari absurdè opinantur,* […].

[5] Es ist derjenige Teil, den er bis zu seinem Tod abschließen konnte; dazu sind das Originalmanuskript und ein (Einzel?)Druck (bislang nur in der Österreichischen Nationalbibliothek nachgewiesen) erhalten. Siehe Christian GASTGEBER, *Miscellanea Codicum Graecorum*

des Eindruckes einer unmittelbar bevorstehenden Publikation haben Lambecks Nachfolger Daniel Nessel (1680–1700) und Adam František Kollár (1772–1777 [1783]) explizit auf die nicht erfolgte Drucklegung aufmerksam gemacht.

Lambecks unmittelbarer Nachfolger, Daniel Nessel, hat in seiner *Sciagraphia*[6] auf das niemals in Druck gegangene Werk hingewiesen, tatsächlich gab es nicht einmal ein Druckvorbereitungsexemplar, nur das Titelblatt ließ Lambeck offensichtlich drucken. Es reiht sich damit dieses geplante Werk in eine Gruppe anderer gigantomanischer Corpora, die Lambeck geplant, aber nie zu Ende geführt hat wie seine Literaturgeschichte[7] oder seinen Katalog aller Handschriften und Einzeleditionen zur Bibliotheksgeschichte[8]. Nessel wurde schließlich ersucht, die Edition selbst nach Lambecks Vorarbeiten durchführen, wozu er ein Konzept vorbereitete und in Druck geben ließ; er wollte den Lambeck'schen Plan noch um zusätzliche Texte erweitern, letztlich blieb es jedoch auch bei ihm nur bei diesem Publikationskon-

---

Vindobonensium II: Die griechischen Handschriften der Bibliotheca Corviniana in der Österreichischen Nationalbibliothek. Provenienz und Rezeption im Wiener Griechichhumanismus des frühen 16. Jahrhunderts. Wien 2014 (ÖAW, Denkschriften der phil.-hist. Kl. 465; Veröffentlichungen zur Byzanzforschung 34), 119.

[6] Sciagraphia sive Prima Delineatio et Brevis Notitia Magni Corporis Historici, hactenus Inediti, brevi tamen, DEO volente, Edendi, in varia *Syntagmata*, diversosque *Tomos* ratione diversitatis materiae nempe Historiarum et Antiquitatum Sacrarum, sive, Ecclesiasticarum, Germanicarum, Austriacarum, Hispanicarum, Hungaricarum, Bohemicarum, Polonicarum, Sinensium, Mexicanarum, Monetariarum sive Numismatum veterum concinne divisi, quod ex inaestimabilis Thesauri *Augustissimae Bibliothecae Caesareae Vindobonensis* antiquissimis rarissimísque Autographis Codicibus Manuscriptis nunc primum erutum, accuratè digestum collectúmque, summâ fide & diligentiâ descriptum, se publicis usibus benevolè communicaturum, pollicetur DANIEL de NESSEL, J. C. Sac. Caes. Maj. Consiliarius et Bibliothecarius Aulicus. Vindobonae: Joannes Jacobus Mann 1692 (VD 17 12:156396X).

[7] Petri Lambecii Hamburgensis liber primus Prodromi Historiae Literariae nec non libri secundi capita quatuor priora cum appendice, quae SCIAGRAPHIAM continet, sive primam delineationem praecipuarum Personarum ac Rerum, de quibus, volente Deo, reliquis triginta duobus ejusdem Libri Capitibus plenius & accuratius agetur. Accedunt insuper Tabulae duae Chronographiae universalis quarum priori successio omnium Seculorum à creatione Mundi usque ad initium vulgaris Aerae Christianae, posteriori autem continuatio eorundem ab initio vulgaris Aerae Christianae usque ad nostram aetatem exhibetur. Hamburgi: Michael Pfeiffer 1659 (VD 17 23:231465Z).

[8] Plan dazu am Ende von Band 5 der *Commentarii*, die auf 25 Bände konzipiert wurden. Siehe GASTGEBER, *Miscellanea* (s. Anm. 5), 118f.

zept. Bemerkenswerterweise hat er dazu Sambucus' Abhandlung (aus theologisch-politischer Räson?) nicht aufgenommen[9]:

> Nondecim annorum periodus elapsa est, ex quô Cl. Dominus *Lambecius*, meus in Praefecturâ Bibliothecaria Antecessor, in *Catalogo Librorum à se editorum & deinceps edendorum*, pag. 45 orbi litterario promisit, se *Syntagma rerum Germanicarum variósque Autores & Acta Publica*, ex Augustissimâ Bibliothecâ Caesareâ Vindobonensi in lucem editurum, cum *Annotationibus* necessariis, *Chronologiâ* accuratâ, & amplissimis *indicibus* Viennae typis Cosmerovianis A. C. 1673. Qui certè utilissimus labor communi Eruditorum acclamatione & suffragio exceptus, summóque desiderio ejus usura expetita fuit. Quandoquidem autem amplum & diffusum Opus ob magnitudinem suam, & multiplicis argumenti varietatem non adeò praepoperè poterat accelerari, accessit insuper fatalis necessitas, quae post septennium mortalitati eum exemit, promissosque hosce conatûs non intervenit tantùm, verùm prorsus in ipsis primordiis suffocavit. Ego postea Muséum ejus & loculamenta anxiâ curiositate excutiens, expressi mandati CAESAREI autoritate munitus, seriò indagavi ac edoceri allaboravi, quoúsque in *Syntagmate Rerum Germanicarum* elaborando Lambeciana industria olim processisset, & quid praelo maturum nobis reliquisset; Sed post absolutam inquisitionis diligentiam magnâ spe excidi, quippe **praeter frontispicium sive nudum titulum operis impressum, duos tantùm Autores ex autographis Manuscriptis Caesareis ab Amanuense descriptos** reperi, minutissimam certè portionem tam vasti & diffusi meditati Syntagmatis. Non defuerunt nihilominùs multi Illustres & celeberrimi Viri, qui iteratis humanissimis literis me publico nomine interrogârunt, numne deinceps *Syntagmatis* illius *Rerum Germanicarum* publicè exponendi luci insuper spes aliqua superesset, quin imò me instanter rogarunt, ut Lambecianam fidem liberarem, nec tàm utilissimum *Germanicae Historiae ineditae incognitaeque Supplementum* publicis usibus inviderem. Ego proinde tot invitamentis allectus, proprióque ac innato desiderio Rempubl. Literariam, pro meo modulo, promovendi, praecipue autem ex incomparabili Augustissimae Bibliothecae Thesauro abundantissimos Historiae ac politioris literaturae rivulos in alienas segetes, derivandi, induxi animum, rem bonis avibus aggredi, & non sine maximis laboribus & exantlatis lucubrationibus, non ea tantùm quae illustris Dominus *Lambecius* edenda promiserat, sed plura alia & potiora documenta & monumenta Historica inedita collecta, uni Magno Corpori includere, & ratione diversitatis argumenti in specialia *Volumina* dispertiri, quorum *Sciagraphiam* & specialem Recensionem uno quasi intuitu hîc vides. Continebit igitur hoc Opus meros *Scriptores ineditos, Acta publica, Monumenta Literaria, Diplomata, Rescripta, Epistolas, Decreta, Antiquitates, & Res Memorabiles*, speciatim *Eccle-*

---

[9] Sciagraphia (s. Anm. 6), fol.)(2ʳ–)(3ᵛ.

siasticas, Germanicas, Austriacas, Hispanicas, Hungaricas, Bohemicas, Polonicas, Chinenses, Mexicanas, Monetarias, & totum hoc Systema, in meo Muséo sollicitâ custodia asservatum, ita concinnè jam à me dispositum, digestum, ac impressioni typographicae praeparatum est, ut non tantum primâ die, verùm etiam, si aliquid humanitùs mihi contingeret, deinceps praelo haud difficulter submitti possit; Sed sine meis Notis aut Observationibus, quas si elaborando annectere vellem, alterutrum eveniret, nempè ut inanibus promissis Lectorem lactarem, aut mihi Triseclisenis aetatem vanè pollicerer. Cum verò tot volumina non exiguam sumptuum impressoriorum Summam requirant, in id sedulò incumbam, ut Magnates & Patronos inveniam, qui suâ Munificentiâ conatûs meos promoveant. De reliquo benè vale, LECTOR, & laboribus meis fave.

Nessel, *Sciagraphia* 1692, fol.)(2ʳ–)(3ᵛ

Kollár fasste den Stand der Arbeit in dem überarbeiteten Neudruck von Lambecks *Commentarii* (im ersten Band, in seinen *Supplementa* zur Bibliotheksgeschichte Lambecks bis zu seiner Zeit) 1766 folgendermaßen zusammen und kommentierte die beabsichtigte Edition aus eigenen Aufzeichnungen (*adversaria*), da von protestantischer Seite mittlerweile der von Sambucus ins Treffen geführte Papyrus mit einem Teil der Unterschriften von Konzilsteilnehmer (darunter des Bischofs von Athen in subordinierter Position, aber als Legat des Papstes) als Nachweis des inexistenten päpstlichen Machtanspruches (fälschlich) interpretiert wurde[10]:

> Alterum Lambecii nostri Opus, de quo sententiam meam cum Lectoribus communicaturum me esse, supra sum pollicitus, est celeberrimum illud *Syntagma Rerum Germanicarum*, cujus & olim ingens fuit expectatio, & nunc in desiderio est eruditorum quorundam hominum. Quippe Lambecius noster in Catalogo librorum suorum, quos aut edidit, aut sese editurum esse speravit, [...] de hoc-

---

[10] Petri Lambecii Hamburgensis Commentariorum de Augustissima Bibliotheca Caesarea Vindobonensi liber primus [...] Editio altera opera et studio Adami Francisci Kollarii [...]. Vindobonae: Iohannes Thomas de Trattnern 1766, Sp. 541–543. Angeführt zunächst aus Lambecks Beschreibung in seinem *Catalogus* auf Sp. 522. Bereits einleitend dazu wird erwähnt (Sp. 499–500, Anm. 3): *Hoc Syntagma quod post LAMBECII mortem vix inchoatum in ejus Museo repertum est, jussus fuit perficere edereque successor ipsius DANIEL NESSELIUS: At nec ab eo quicquam in hoc genere prodiit praeter solam Sciagraphiam quam vocat Magni Corporis Historici hactenus inediti, brevi tamen, Deo volente, edendi, in varia Syntagmata diversosque tomos divisi &c. Vindobonae A. 1693. 4 vulgavit praeterea Anno 1690 Vindobonae in Fol. Prodromum Historiae Pacificatoriae, sive indicem Chronologicum Corporis Historico-Politici Publicarum Pacificationum, Confoederationum &c. ab A. Christi MCCC ad MDCLXXXV, sed & hoc opus ipsum nunquam vidit lucem. Obiit Nesselius Anno MDCC. FABR.*

ce *Rerum Germanicarum Syntagmate* ita scripsit, quasi magna fuit parte jam typis excusum, aut prelo paratum, brevi esset in lucem proditurum. Nesselius quidem in epistola sua, ad Lectorem scripta, quam *Sciagraphiae suae Magni Corporis Historici* praefixit, erronea ista opinione Historiae Germanicae studiosos liberare studuit; verum apud cultores Lambecii, a quibus ea de re per litteras frequenter egomet compellatus fui, invenisse fidem non videtur. Igitur ut horum desideriis una opera plene satisfaciam, & eos Scriptores vetustos omnes, quorum desiderio populares suos incendit noster, clara in luce collocem; agam hic de singulis, pro viribus quidem meis, diligenter [...] Promam autem, quae hic, Lector, leges, partim ex Commentariis Gentiloti nostri, partim ex adversariis meis, ad quae, o utinam, nihil unquam aliud, nisi quod huc faceret, retulissem! sed nimirum quia ingenio, diligentia, eruditione ac fortuna adeo ipsa immortali Lambecio longe sum inferior, periculis saltem & infortuniis eidem esse debui persimilis; quanquam ne hoc quidem pacto simillima est rerum fortunarumque nostrarum ratio: nam illi pro sudoribus suis, inique ac superbe habito, ingrata solum urbs natalis; at mihi cinerique meo patria mea ferme universa justissimarum querelarum causam praebuit aeternam. Attamen ne haec quidem unquam a fortis me officio viri avertet: nefas enim mihi sit serenitatem animi mei pacemque idcirco amittere, qui orbem terrae universum pro germana semper patria adhuc {tria}[11] habuerim, & iis, quibus placere studebam, concivibus meis, id est, ingenio, virtute, doctrina et veritatis studio illustribus viris, nondum etiam displicuerim. Redeo ad diverticulum, et Scriptorum rem, quos Lambecius promisit, censere aestimareque instituo.

Lambeck, *Commentarii*, ed. Kollár, 1766, I, Sp. 541–543

Zum Objekt selbst folgt eine ausführliche Auseinandersetzung mit der von Sambucus herangezogenen neuen Quelle, dem Papyrus mit den Unterschriften der Teilnehmer (der 17. Sitzung) des Sechsten Ökumenischen Konzils (*Constantinopolitanum tertium*) 680/81[12]. Der Papyrus hatte so großes Interesse des Kaisers erweckt, dass selbiger 1596 zu Kaiser Rudolf II. nach Prag transportiert wurde; zu Lambecks Zeit wusste man nichts mehr von seinem Verbleib und hatte nur eine fehlerhafte Abschrift zur Verfügung; erst

---

[11] tria sollte mit dem Reklamanten [ad-]huc der vorangehenden Seite wie auf den anderen Seiten übereinstimmen (Reklamant – erstes Wort der Folgeseite). Offensichtlich ein Lapsus des Druckers der huc in der Vorlage in sinnloses tria verlesen hat.

[12] Dazu grundlegend Giuseppe DE GREGORIO, Otto KRESTEN, Il Papiro conciliare P. Vindob. G 3: Un 'originale' sulla via da Costantinopoli a Ravenna (e a Vienna). In: Laura Pani, Cesare Scalon (edd.), *Le Alpi porta d'Europa. Scritture, Uomini, Idee da Giustiniano al Barbarossa. Atti del Convegno internazionale di studio dell'Associazione italiana dei Paleografi e Diplomatisti. Cividale del Friule (5–7 ottobre 2006)*. Spoleto 2009, 233–379.

unter dem Bibliothekspräfekten Pio Nicolò de Garelli (1675–1739) konnte das wertvolle Stück wieder aus dem Besitz mittlerweile Kaiser Karls VI. 1723 in die Wiener Hofbibliothek überführt werden; Kollár erwähnt zudem, dass der Papyrus zu einer Bibliotheksattraktion geworden ist[13]:

> *Joannis Sambuci Liber de Panauthentia, sive Majestate Imperatoris, & quorundam praejudicio, sive Donatione Constantiniana.* Non liber, sed epistola potius, *in qua*, inquit Gentilotus[14], *evertit fictitiam illam donationem Constantini iisdem rationibus & argumentis, quae ab aliis adferuntur, & passim nota sunt. Meminit in illa indicis cujusdam vetusti, in papyru arundinea scripti, qui Trullanae Synodi nomina Patrum, ipsorum, ut putat, manu rata testataque continet; ubi XXII. Joannem Episcopum Atheniensem, Roma ablegatum non principe loco sedisse colligitur. Eundem hunc indicem esse reor atque illum, quem Sambucus An. MDLXXXIII ad L. Schraderum*[15] *misit, Seldenus vulgavit*[16]*, & Labbeus*[17] *Tom. II. Concil. pag. 54.55 Nycaenae Synodo subtexuit non Trullanae, ut statuit Sambucus: & quidem recte, quemadmodum indiculum istum cum subscriptionibus Trullanae Synodi conferenti patebit; qua de re lectorem monere non inutile visum est.* Hactenus Gentilotus; cujus facilitatem ego quidem vehementer miror, qua persuaderi sibi ab Labbeo passus est, subscriptiones istas Nicaenae Synodo recte subjici: postquam a Lambecio jam pridem ei, cujus revera sunt, Concilio fuerint redditae. At vero rem lectori Catholico non ingratam facturum me esse arbitror, si de celebri hoc fragmento, quod ab hospitibus nostris toties videri expetitur, diligentius hic egerim; eo potissimum, quod tum Seldenus, tum etiam alii, in argumentum illud sumere non sunt gravati, quo Hierarchiam Ecclesiae Catholicae, ab ipsomet Divino Praeceptore institutam, supremum praeterea in spiritualibus summorum Pontificum principatum, potestatemque clavium, per summam temeritatem oppugnarent. Niliacam ergo chartam istam Ravenati in Ecclesia Parochiali a Bartholomaeo Bembo, Petri Bembi avo, Sambucus noster Patavii anno MDLIII a Torquato Bembo comparavit. Testatum hocce reliquit Sambucus in apographo earundem subscriptionum suo, quod Lambecius inter ejusdem schedas forte fortuna repertum, codici Graeco, ne deperiret, adsui curavit [*Histor.*

---

[13] Kollár, Commentarii I (s. Anm. 10), 593–598.
[14] Johann Benedikt Gentilotti von Engelsbrunn (1672–1725); Präfekt der Wiener Hofbibliothek (1705–1723).
[15] Laurentius Schraderus (Lorenz Schrader, 1538–1606), Verfasser der Monumentorum Italiae, Quae hoc nostro saeculo & à Christianis posita sunt, LIBRI QUATUOR. Helmaestadii: Iacobus Lucius Transylvanus 1592.
[16] John Selden (1584–1654) zitiert den Papyrus in seinen Eutychii Aegyptii, Patriarchae Orthodoxorum Alexandrini, Scriptoris, ut in Oriente admodum Vetusti ac Illustris, ita in Occidente tum paucissimis Visi tum perraro Auditi, Ecclesiae suae Origines. London: Richard Bishop 1642, 125–127.
[17] Philippe Labbé (1607–1667).

Ecclesiast. ex recensione LAMBECII XLIV. nunc vero LVIII][18]. Primus omnium Schraderus laudatae chartae Niliacae exemplar a Sambuco habuit, quod Seldenus postea Typis evulgavit in notis suis ad fragmentum Historiae Eutychii Patriarchae Alexandrini: unde depromptum Synodo Nicaenae Labbaeus prorsus incaute adsuit [*Tom. II. pag. 54*]. Lambecius noster apographum alterum, in Bibliotheca nostra ut modo monui, repertum, tertio edidit [*Comment. Tom. VIII. pag. 408*]: unde ellucescit, tria haec laudatae chartae exemplaria ex apographis solum typis excusa fuisse: autographum enim ne Lambecio quidem usquam est visum; en illius verba: *Hucusque,* inquit, *fragmentum illud subscriptionum Synodalium, quod Joannes Sambucus in vetustissima charta Niliaca scriptum, Patavii An. 1553 sibi comparavit; quodque post ipsius mortem, quae in annum Christi 1584 incidit, translatum quidem fuit in Augustissimam Bibliothecam Caesaream Vindobonensem, sed postea A. 1596 Imperatori Rudolpho II. Ejusdem videndi cupido, authenticum sive originale Pragam missum est. Quo autem deinde illud pervenerit, & an in rerum natura adhuc supersit; & alicubi latitet; hoc mihi prorsus est incognitum. Ne igitur apographo quoque accidat, quod authentico sive originali jam accidit, curavi illud Codici manuscripto Historico Graeco quadragesimo quarto, de quo in praesens ex professo agitur, in fine adglutinari, & quantum humanitatis fieri potest, conservationi ejus providerI.* Haec ille. Verum enimvero non recte lectorum commodis hac Lambecii cura esset consultum, nisi ipsumet autographum, Augusti Caesaris Caroli VI. illustris Pii Nicolai Garellii Bibliothecae nostrae tum Praefecti precibus inclinati, jussu, Pragae quam diligentissime investigatum repertumque ad Bibliothecam nostram an. MDCCXXIII redivisset: nihil enim unquam quidquam majori oscitantia ex autographis Graecis exscriptum vidi legique, ac sint subscriptiones istae, quas Seldenus, Labbaeus & Lambecius cum eruditis communicaverunt: nam ut alia peccata omittam, quae omnem fere versum turpiter vitiant, principio statim pro illis: ἐπαρχίας ὁρίσας ὑπέγραψα, autographum integre scriptum habet Θεόδωρος ἐλέει Θεοῦ ἐπίσκοπος τῆς μετιληνῶν μητροπόλεως τῆς α΄ τῶν Ἀρμενίων ἐπαρχίας ὁρίσας ὑπέγραψα. [Es folgen weitere Fehler aus der kopialen Überlieferung].

Atque haec speciminis gratia heic adscripta lectori, spero, sufficient. Ad autographum porro quod attinet, Seldenus, Labbeus, & Gentilotus opinione sua falsi sunt, quando ὑπογραφὰς istas Patrum Nicaenae Synodi esse arbitrati, eidem Synodo tribuerunt: sunt enim prorsus eaedem cum illis, sed principio & fine mutilae, quas Labbeus cum Concilio una Constantinopolitano tertio, Generali vero sexto, luce publica donavit [*Concil. Tom. VI. pag. 1028*], ut recte observarat Lambecius, Sambucum sequutus, qui eas, levi errore, ad Trullanam sive Quinisextam, retulerat. Evanescunt ergo ad hanc lucem tum Sambuci tenebrae, tum Seldeni conatus longe vanissimi, qui adserere ausus est, eo in Concilio, cujus subscriptiones istae essent, Legatos Romanae Sedis haudquaquam principe loco rebus ibi gestis

---

[18] ÖNB, Cod. hist. gr. 56, als Adligat am Ende; siehe dazu noch unten, Anm. 38.

praefuisse: nam in subscriptionibus integris Synodi Constantinopolitanae tertiae, Oecumenicae vero sextae, primo omnium loco leguntur tres, nimirum Theodorus & Georgius S[anctae]. R[omanae]. E[cclesiae]. Presbyteri cum Joanne ejusdem Ecclesiae Diacono, cum potestate, singulis adscripta: τὸν τόπον ἐπέχων Ἀγάθωνος τοῦ μακαριωτάτου καὶ οἰκουμενικοῦ Πάπα πόλεως ῥώμης. *Locum tenens Agathonis beatissimi & oecumenici Papae Urbis Romanae.* Unde liquet, Joannem illum Athenarum Episcopum, qui tum in charta nostra, tum etiam apud Labbeum Legatum se Apostolicae Sedis Romae veteris scribit, & non principem locum, sed suum, id est, Episcopi Athenarum, occupat; aut peculari quadam cum potestate adfuisse, aut certe Vicaria quidem, sed solum honoraria esse gavisum. De vetustate chartae nostrae sentiant, per me licet, alii arbitratu suo; nam mihi quidem & una eademque exarata manu, & longe junior, quam multi velint, esse videtur. Retinent me in hac sententia in primis librarii vitia, ex recentiori Graecum idioma pronunciandi ratione orta. Sic, verbi causa, Gregorius Mitylenes Episcopus hic scribitur: μιτυλινέων πόλεως ἐπίσκοπος pro μιτυληναίων. [sic!, es folgen weitere orthographische Fehler].

Quibus in verbis tametsi syllabae sint. Quaedam [Satztrennung sic!], quas, utrovis modo recte scribi posse, non negem; tamen sunt non nullae aliae, quae recentiorum Graecorum, ut dixi, idioma suum pronunciandi modum liquido indicant. Sed demus ultro, omnia recte, bene, probe, coaeva praeterea, & ipsorum adeo Patrum manu esse scripta, quid tum postea? Nimirum subscriptiones Oecumenicae Synodi sextae novum robur accipient, ubi οἱ τὸν τόπον ἐπέχοντες Ἀγάθωνος τοῦ μακαριωτάτου Πάπα primo omnium loco subscripti leguntur. Valeat ergo δυστυχής cum Eutyche suo Seldenus, valeant pariter alii, quos Anarchiae suae in Oriente patrocinia frustra quaerere, sequenter vidimus. Haec promissi Lambeciani gratia; nam ad Sambucum quod attinet, vehementer sane miror Virum cetera doctum & prudentem, in hoc mustaceo laureolam quaerere voluisse.

Lambeck, *Commentarii*, ed. Kollár, 1766, I, Sp. 593–598

Auch die Fachwelt wurde sehr bald über das Ausbleiben des *Syntagma*, d. h. über den nie ausgeführten Druck und über Nessels Versuch, das Werk zu Ende zu bringen (oder besser überhaupt in Angriff zu nehmen) in einschlägigen Informationsquellen informiert[19].

---

[19] Johan Peter Nicerons Nachrichten von den Begebenheiten und Schriften berühmter Gelehrten mit einigen Zusätzen, herausgegeben von Friedrich Eberhard Rambach, Neuzehnter Theil. Halle: Christoph Peter Franckens 1759, 27–28. – Vgl. ferner Friedrich Gladovs Versuch Einer vollständigen und accuraten Reichs-Historie von Teutschland, Darinnen die Geschichte der Teutschen von den Zeiten der Römer an biß auf den Badischen Frieden, Nebst deutlicher Anzeigung der vornehmsten Veränderungen im Reiche und deren wahren Ursachen pragmatisch beschrieben, Als eine richtige Einleitung in ein gründliches Teutsches

SAMBUCUS' ZUGANG ZUR KONSTANTINISCHEN SCHENKUNG

In einer noch erhaltenen autographen Abschrift, Cod. 9534 der Österreichischen Nationalbibliothek[20], widmete Sambucus seine Abhandlung am 22. Juli 1571 Kaiser Maximilian II.[21]; die Widmung[22] selbst schließt mit der Datierung *Kal. Quinctil. 1571*, was dem 1. Juli 1571 entspricht; mit selbem Datum endet auch der Traktat auf fol. 16^v (vor der Appendix mit der griechischen Version der *Donatio Constantini*, fol. 17^r–18^r, mit einer kurzen lateinischen Widerlegung deren Authentizitätsanspruches zur Zeit Kaiser Konstantins[23]). Schließlich ist zur Widmung noch ein kleiner autographer Zettel eingeklebt, der in deutscher Sprache ebenso an den Kaiser gerichtet ist und als Antidoron für das Werk um eine finanzielle Unterstützung ersucht; er war offensichtlich gesondert dem Werk bei der Übergabe an den Kaiser beigelegt. Diese Beilage datiert vom 5. August 1571.

Mit dem Jahr 1571 steht das Werk im Zusammenhang mit Sambucus' steigender Bedeutung am Hof und seinen vermehrten Hoffunktionen und -titel[24] – sowie damit verbundenen finanziellen Zuwendungen. Insbesonde-

---

Staats-Recht, vorgestellet, und durchgehends mit glaubwürdigen Zeugnissen alter und neuer Scribenten bewiesen werden. Nebst ausführlichen Registern. Leipzig und Halle: Felix du Serre 1717, 18 mit Anm. x: „Im übrigen übergehen wir mit Stillschweigen, was Lambecius, Nesselius, Tenzel und Weber versprochen haben". Léopold Delisle berichtet von Einzelseiten (feuilles tirées), die sehr selten seien; es handelt sich offensichtlich um das in Druck gegebene Titelblatt: „ils ont été en tête le titre de Codex epistolaris Carolinus". Delisle in der Besprechung der *Bibliotheca rerum germanicarum tomus quartus. Monumenta Carolina* von Philippe Jaffé in: *Bibliothèques de l'École des Chartes* 29 (1868), 190.

[20] 1. Teil (fol. 1^r–18^r): Περὶ Παναυθεντείας sive de maiestate imperatoris et quorundam praeiudicio sive donatione Constantinia; 2. Teil, Anhang (fol. 19^r–23^r): Caesares Austrii X, descripti per Iohannem Sambucum (von Rudolf bis Maximilian II.) in elegischen Distichen. Zur Handschrift siehe die aktualisierte Beschreibung unter <http://data.onb.ac.at/rec/AL00177812> (13. 8. 2015). Siehe auch Franz UNTERKIRCHER, *Die datierten Handschriften der Österreichischen Nationalbibliothek von 1501 bis 1600*. Wien 1976 (Katalog der datierten Handschriften in lateinischer Schrift in Österreich 4), 86.

[21] Wien, ÖNB, Cod. 9534, fol. 3^r: *XXII. Julii Redituí Augusti MDLXXI*. Als Abschluss einer jeweils über zwei Seiten laufenden (1^v–2^r, 2^v–3^r) Inscriptio des Kaisers.

[22] Wien, ÖNB, Cod. 9534, fol. 4^r–5^r. Ediert bei GERSTINGER, *Briefe* (s. Anm. 2), 121–122.

[23] Diese Passage ist unten, S. 263f., ediert.

[24] Sambucus' Karriereentwicklung (siehe dazu Gábor ALMÁSI, *The Use of Humanism. Johannes Sambucus [1531–1584], Andreas Dudith [1533–1589], and the Republic of Letters in East Central Europe*. Leiden 2009 [Brill's Studies in Intellectual History 185], 245–190):

re seine Position als Hofhistoriograph ab 1566 nach dem Tod des vorangehenden Amtsinhabers Wolfgang Lazius (19. Juni 1565) und der neue Titel eines *consiliarius aulae* Ende der 60er Jahre[25] forderte regelrecht dazu auf, in einem anschwellenden Streit zwischen dem Kaiser und Papst Pius V. die Macht Letzteres in die Schranken zu weisen und gegen dessen Ansprüche, die auch auf der Konstantinischen Schenkung basierten, Stellung zu beziehen[26], nicht zuletzt weil sich Sambucus mit einer gut argumentieren Widerlegung der weiterhin gewogenen Gunst des Kaisers sicher sein wollte. Zudem bereitete es dem Kryptoprotestanten[27] Sambucus gewiss eine Genugtuung, eine solche antirömische Schrift mit kaiserlichem Segen zu verfassen.

Der Streit selbst entzündete sich an der Person Cosimo I de' Medici und dem Großherzogtum der Toskana[28]. Im Machtstreit zwischen Ferrara und Florenz bemühte sich Herzog Cosimo de' Medici um eine Rangerhöhung des florentinischen reichsunabhängigen, freien Staates zum Königtum, woraus letztlich nur ein Großherzogtum wurde. Die entsprechende Bulle (mit Verleihung der Würde des Großherzogtums der Toskana mit Königskrone) besorgte man sich vom Papst am Kaiser vorbei; am 13. Dezember 1569 wurde sie in Florenz von Michele Bonelli, Neffen des Papstes Pius V., überreicht. Die Folge war nicht nur eine Enttäuschung des Hauses Este in Ferrara mit Herzog Alfonso II. an der Spitze, sondern vielmehr noch eine Entrüstung des Kaisers über die Ingerenz des Papstes in kaiserlichen Agenden. Florenz hatte zuvor durch enge Beziehungen nach Rom den Papst für diese Rangerhöhung ins Spiel gebracht, der dem Kaiser zwar eine Entschei-

---

1557	*aulae familiaris*
1566	Hofhistoriograph: *historicus*
1567	*medicus aulicus; comes palatinus*
1568 ca.	*consiliarius aulae*

[25] Siehe dazu ALMÁSI, *The Use of Humanism* (s. Anm. 24), 169–170.
[26] [...] ut Tua Maiestas videret, quanti Germanici, hoc est universi nominis Christiani imperii dignitas aestimanda, quo loco res Romanorum sint habendae [...] (Widmung: GERSTINGER, *Briefe* [s. Anm. 2], 121).
[27] Siehe dazu ALMÁSI, *The Use of Humanism* (s. Anm. 24), 329–356.
[28] Siehe dazu Viktor BIBL, Die Erhebung Herzog Cosimos von Medici zum Grossherzog von Toskana und die kaiserliche Anerkennung, 1569–1576. *Archiv für österreichische Geschichte* 103 (1913), 1–162; Imre TEGLASY, Über das Schicksal der Donatio Constantiniana im 16. Jahrhundert. Ein unbekanntes Werk des Johannes Sambucus (Zsámboky) über die kaiserliche Plenipotenz. In: August Buck, Tibor Klaniczay, Sarolta Katalin Németh (Hgg.), *Geschichtsbewusstsein und Geschichtsschreibung in der Renaissance*. Budapest, Leiden 1989, 85–96.

dung für den in Rom anhängigen Prozess zubilligte, aber unter Bedingungen, die für den Kaiser unvertretbar und seine Macht beschränkend waren, wie ein Breve Papst Pius' vom 10. Juli 1567 formulierte[29]. Kaiser Maximilian II. griff daher zu einer bekannten Habsburger-Taktik: die Zeit verstreichen lassen und weder für Ferrara noch Florenz eine Entscheidung treffen (mit beiden Häusern war Habsburg auch verwandtschaftlich verbunden), bis die Entscheidung schließlich nicht mehr bei der Kurie, deren Wanken zwischen den beiden Familien ebenso unsicherer Verhandlung entgegensah, sondern beim Papst selbst fiel. Der Kaiser wurde nur mehr rein formal um Zustimmung ersucht, was man taktisch-diplomatisch zunächst auch erreichte oder erreicht zu haben interpretierte. Die folgende Protestwelle der Ferrara-Verbündeten und die Empörung des Kaisers wusste Florenz dann jedoch durch die Unterstützung der Heiligen Liga (25. Mai 1571) mit Papst Pius V., Spanien, Neapel, Sizilien, Venedig, Genua und Florenz, Savoyen, Parma, Urbino und den Maltesern gegen die Türken etwas zu besänftigen – eine Notlösung aus der immer bedrohlicheren Angriffsgefahr gegen Florenz und Rom seitens des Kaisers, Spaniens und Frankreichs. So zog sich der Streit lange Zeit nach der päpstlichen Bulle von 1569 hin und schwoll im Jahre 1571 mit der Anklage Alfonsos II. d'Este beim kaiserlichen Gericht an (was ihm als kaiserlicher Lehensmann für das Herzogtum Modena und Reggio möglich war), bis man sich unter politisch-militärischem Druck seitens Florenz um Akkordverhandlungen mit Empfang der vom Papst verliehenen Würde aus der Hand des Kaisers einigte. Den wirklichen Abschluss fand die Auseinandersetzung erst Ende 1575.

Damit gewinnt der Trakat gleich noch eine weitere Nuance, indem durch das Werk eben nicht nur die Position des Kaisers wieder historisch fundiert untermauert werden und u. a. durch neue weitere[30] Quellen die vom Papst ins Treffen geführte Schenkung als Fälschung erwiesen werden soll – selbst schon in einer langen Tradition von Kritiken, die bis auf Nikolaus von Kues zurückgehen –, sondern indem auch sehr subtil und mit aller Vorsicht generell gegen das päpstliche Machtkonstrukt zugunsten der pro-

---

[29] BIBL, Erhebung (s. Anm. 28), 37.
[30] Auf diesen Aspekt legt Sambucus besonderen Wert: *Caeterum leget Tua Maiestas quaedam ab aliis non lecta neque fortassis observata*. Widmung: GERSTINGER, Briefe (s. Anm. 2), 121.

testantischen Seite angekämpft wird³¹. Dies macht Sambucus sehr diplomatisch durch die Einbeziehung autoritativer Quellen, wie Münzen, der griechischen Version der Konstantinischen Schenkung, wie er sie einer seiner Handschriften gefunden hat und die von der lateinischen, vom Papst vorgebrachten in wichtigen Punkten abweicht³², sowie durch ein einzigartiges Stück, das er in Italien erwerben konnte: ein ‚Original' eines Konzilspapyrus. Auf dieses einmalige Stück sei im Folgenden der Schwerpunkt gelegt.

DER KONZILSPAPYRUS ÖNB, P. VINDOB. G 3 IN SAMBUCUS' ARGUMENTATION GEGEN DIE KONSTANTINISCHE SCHENKUNG

Das Dokument, das Sambucus aus Italien erwarb, ist als Rarität bis heute erhalten und wird in der Payprussammlung der Österreichischen Nationalbibliothek unter der Signatur P. Vindob. G 3 aufbewahrt. Es handelt sich dabei um ein Fragment von 35 Unterschriften (beginnend mit der 25. nach der modernen Edition) der Konzilsteilnehmer des *Constantinopolitanum tertium* (680), und zwar zum Ende der 17. Sitzung, erhalten als Rotulus in Form einer *transversa charta* von 66–69 × 31 cm³³. Allerdings zeigte eine genaue Analyse des Schriftduktus, dass mit diesem Papyrus kein Original mit autographen Unterschriften vorliegt, sondern, wie bereits von Kollár kritisch angemerkt wurde, eine Kopie einer einzigen Hand, die jedoch während des Konzils als *copia imitativa* angelegt wurde³⁴. Für die griechische

---

[31] Man vergleiche etwa aus der Widmung an Kaiser Maximilian II. den zweideutigen Satz: *Tuum est et religionem perversam emendare et constitutam tueri. Pontifici res fidei tuo subsidio augenda, si recte sentiat, relinquatur.* GERSTINGER, *Briefe* (s. Anm. 2), 122.

[32] Dieses „graecum θέσπισμα Constantino tributum" (GERSTINGER, *Briefe*, s. Anm. 2, 122) wird dann auch in einer Appendix am Ende (fol. 17ʳ–18ʳ) ediert. Auf die Überlieferung der griechischen Version, die ab dem 11. Jahrhundert in Byzanz auftaucht und dann in juristischen Sammlungen verbreitet wurde (von wo sie Sambucus übernahm), wird im Detail im Rahmen der geplanten Edition von Sambucus' Schrift eingegangen; vgl. zu diesem Themenkomplex unten, Anm. 50.

[33] Siehe die genaue Analyse mit den Textverlusten in DE GREGORIO, KRESTEN, *Papiro conciliare* (s. Anm. 12), 242–244.

[34] DE GREGORIO, KRESTEN, *Papiro conciliare* (s. Anm. 12), 252–259. Zu den historischen Umständen dieser copia (bzw. insgesamt fünf copiae für die fünf Patriarchenstühle) siehe a. o., 282–296, 310–313; zusammenfassend (295–296): „Noi possediamo, dunque, un frammento di uno di questi cinque originali (sui sei approntati) dell'ὅρος della XVII sessione recanti le copie imitative 'ufficiali' delle firme dei vescovi: un'operazione, questa, condotta sicuramente,

Version der 17. Sitzung stellt das Papyrusfragment den einzig erhaltenen Textzeugen dar. Dass sich das Stück erhalten hat, verdankt sich wohl einzig dem Umstand, dass diese originale konstantinopolitanische Kanzleikopie Ende des 7. Jahrhunderts in den Westen nach Ravenna kam[35] und hier die Jahrhunderte überdauern konnte. Eine Analyse und besagte Wertung des Dokuments verdankt sich einer detaillierten Studie von Giuseppe De Gregorio und Otto Kresten[36].

1553 erwarb Sambucus in Padua[37] von Torquato Bembo den Papyrus, der, wie auf dem Papyrus selbst vermerkt, einst im Besitz des Bartolomeo Bembo in Ravenna war[38]. Der Erwerb in Padua ist durch eine vermutlich

---

stando almeno a quanto abbiamo già mostrato sotto il profilo paleografico per il P. Vindob. G 3, da un membro di una delle due cancellerie centrali della capitale."

[35] DE GREGORIO, KRESTEN, Papiro conciliare (s. Anm. 12), 350–358: zur Verbindung mit dem *notarius Iohannicius* des Exarchen von Ravenna und zu dessen vermutetem Erwerb des Papyrus als Schriftmuster.

[36] Siehe Anm. 12.

[37] Siehe Hans GERSTINGER, Johannes Sambucus als Handschriftensammler. In: *Festschrift der Nationalbibliothek in Wien*, hg. zur Feier des 200jährigen Bestehens des Gebäudes. Wien 1926, 294–295; DERS., *Briefe* (s. Anm. 2), 19–20; DE GREGORIO, KRESTEN, Papiro conciliare (s. Anm. 12), 234–239, 358–361.

[38] „Ebi in Ravena cita antica nel d°mo in la libreria B(ar)tolamio Bembo I(uris). V(triusque). D(octor)."; ediert bei DE GREGORIO, KRESTEN, Papiro conciliare (s. Anm. 12), 345 mit Abb. auf Taf. I. – Die vier Abschriften stammen nicht von Sambucus; Peter Lambeck hatte bei seiner Katalogbeschreibung des Codex hist. gr. 56 (Commentarii, vol. 8 [s. Anm. 47], 408–410) das Original noch nicht zur Verfügung (es lag noch in Prag, siehe oben das Zitat zu Anm. 18) und bei seiner Edition der Abschrift schon diesbezüglich bemerkt: „Quod superest, obiter hâc occasione moneo, me nuper in *Augustissimâ Bibliothecâ Caesareâ* inter *Ioannis Sambuci* schedas fortuito invenisse notabile aliquod *Fragmentum Subscriptionum quarundam Synodalium*, vel ab ipsius amanuensi, vel ab aliquo alio ita descriptum, ut optimâ fide hic à me exhibetur." Die Hände (?), die diese Texte viermal griechisch (zum Teil mit lateinischer Übersetzung) abschrieben, gehörten offensichtlich dem Stab der Amanuenses der Hofbibliothek an; die Titelangabe zur zweiten Abschrift (*Antiquitas*, fol. *5ʳ) scheint von der Hand des Hugo Blotius zu stammen; am Ende der ersten Abschrift (mit Übersetzung; fol. *4ᵛ) ist von der Hand des Sebastian Tengnagel folgende Inhaltsangabe gegeben: *Nomina quorundam Patrum Synodi Nicaenae secundae, non autem primae, ut inscriptio prae se fert*. Die vorangehende Abschrift und Übersetzung müssen daher vor seiner Zeit geschrieben sein; bemerkenswert ist weiters, dass von einer Hand, die am Vorsatzblatt des Codex – d. h. des eigentlichen Kerns, an den die vier Abschriften von Lambeck hinzugebunden wurden – (fol. IIʳ) unter dem üblichen Besitzvermerk des Augerius Busbeck (*Augerius de Busbecke comparavit Constantinopoli*) und noch vor der von Lambeck vergebenen Signatur *Cod. Ms. Histor. Graec. 44* – diese Hand ist vermutlich mit einer der Abschriften identisch – eine Inhaltsangabe des Nucleus von Cod. hist. gr. 56 gegeben wird.

noch zu Sambucus' Lebzeiten erstellte Abschrift des Papyrus an der Hofbibliothek – seit Peter Lambeck in ÖNB, Cod. hist. gr. 56, eingebunden und einst im Aktenbündel der Sambuciana enthalten – dokumentiert[39], wobei allerdings die Namen auf dem Papyrus noch dem Nicaenum secundum zugewiesen wurden[40]:

> Ravennati in Ecclesia parochali olim reperta à Bartolomeo Bembo, avo P. Bembi, nunc Sambuci, 1553 Patavij ab Torquato Bembo abbate comparata, empta.
>
> Cod. hist. gr. 56, fol. *2^r

Prosopographisch hat sich der Verfasser der Notiz vom berühmten Pietro Bembo fehlleiten lassen (der *avus* wäre Nicolò), denn für Bartolomeo in Frage kommt viel eher ein Verwandter (Bruder?) des Vaters des Pietro, des Juristen und Sammlers Bernardo Bembo, der 1482–1483 in Ravenna die Funktion eines *podestà* und *capitano* der Serenissima ausübte (und aus dessen Fundus Ravennatische Papyri belegt sind)[41].

Wie Kollár detailliert ausgeführt hat, wurde der Inhalt des Papyrus nach Sambucus von einigen Rechtshistorikern veröffentlicht, und zwar von John Selden (1584–1654) im Rahmen seiner Eutychii Aegyptii, Patriarchae Orthodoxorum Alexandrini [...] Ecclesiae suae Origines (London: Richardus Bishopus 1642) im Anhang von *Nomina reliqua Patrum in Synodo Nicaena ex Charta Niliaca vetustissima Sambuci descripta*, allerdings auf der Basis einer Kopie der Abschrift in Wien[42]. Von ihm wurde der Text zum Teil verballhornt von Philippe Labbé und Gabriel Cossart[43], darauf basierend von Jean Hardouin[44], der das Fragment erstmals dem Constantinopolitanum tertium

---

[39] DE GREGORIO, KRESTEN, Papiro conciliare (s. Anm. 12), 346.
[40] DE GREGORIO, KRESTEN, Papiro conciliare (s. Anm. 12), 346 (fol. *1^r): *Ex vetustissima charta Niliaca aliquot nomina patrum Synodi Nicaenae, ut creditur, 2 reliqua* (2 durchgestrichen, dazu am Rand von der Hand Lambecks Korrektur *Imo Synodi Constantinopolitanae Tertiae, Oecumenicae autem sive Generalis Sextae* und Verweis auf den Commentarii).
[41] DE GREGORIO, KRESTEN, Papiro conciliare (s. Anm. 12), 346–349.
[42] DE GREGORIO, KRESTEN, Papiro conciliare (s. Anm. 12), 235 Anm. 6.
[43] Sacrosancta concilia ad Regiam editionem exacta II. Lutetiae Parisiorum: Societas Typographica Librorum Ecclesiasticorum 1671, coll. 54–55; siehe auch DE GREGORIO, KRESTEN, Papiro conciliare (s. Anm. 12), 236 Anm. 8.
[44] Conciliorum collectio Regia maxima, ad p. Philippi Labbei & p. Gabrielis Cossartii labores [...] haud modica accessione facta et emendationibus plurimis additis, vol. III. Paris: Typographia Regia 1714, coll. 1404 D 1–1405 E 1.

zuwies, sowie von Nicola Coleti[45] und schließlich von Giovanni Domenico Mansi[46] übernommen. Auch der bereits erwähnte Bibliothekspräfekt Peter Lambeck veröffentlichte den Text in seinen *Commentarii*[47] aus der fehlerhaften Abschrift zur Zeit (?) des Sambucus (Cod. hist. gr. 56). Die endgültige Zuweisung des Fragments zur 17. Sitzung erfolgte durch den Editor der kritischen Edition im Rahmen der Münchener *Acta Conciliorum Oecumenicorum*, Rudolf Riedinger[48].

In der Diskussion der Authentizitätsfrage der *Donatio Constantini* gab Sambucus die Position des Athener Bischofs ein neues Argument an die Hand, das die Macht des Papstes deutlich unterminieren sollte: Denn als Teilnehmer des *Quinisextum* (691) – ein Fehler des Sambucus! – rangiert dieser Bischof, der explizit als päpstlicher Legat unterzeichnete, an 22. Stelle nach der Zählung des Sambucus. Die entsprechende Stelle lautet:

> Iam vero, si haeres adhuc, legimus in trip(licibus) historiis LX annis post Constantinum Magnum: recens de religione Theodosii decretum, Senatum romanum non admisisse, ne animorum mutatione concordia solveretur. quod si est, cur asseras Papam Urbis Dominum iam a Constant(ino) aestimatum? Non parum me movet indicis cuiusdam apud me vetustas, qui in papyro arundinea | Trullianae Synodi nomina patrum, ipsorum, ut puto, manu rata, testataq(ue) continet, ubi XXII Ioan(nem) Ep(iscopu)m Athenien(sem): Roma adlegatum, non ubique, ut vultis, principe loco sedisse, colligitur: quod ipsum tamen Concilia vulgata dissimulant.
>
> Cod. 9534, fol. 9ʳ–9ᵛ

---

[45] Sacrosancta concilia ad Regiam editionem exacta [...] studio Philipp. Labbei & Gabr. Cossartii [...] II. Venetiis: Jo. Baptista Albrizzi & Hieronymus et Sebastianus Coleti 1728, coll. 59–60.

[46] Sacrorum conciliorum nova et amplissima collectio XI. Florentiae: Antonius Zatta 1756, coll. 693–697.

[47] Commentariorum de Augustissima Bibliotheca Caesarea Vindobonensi liber VIII. Vindobonae: Johannes Christophorus Cosmerovius 1679, 408–412. Der von Adam František Kollár besorgten (teils revidierten) Neuauflage (Vindobonae: Johannes Thomas Trattner 1782) wurden auch zwei Tafeln mit Kupferstichen (erstellt vom Scriptor der Hofbibliothek Adam Bartsch) beigegeben (zwischen coll. 864 und 865).

[48] Rudolf RIEDINGER, *Präsenz- und Subskriptionslisten des VI. oekumenischen Konzils (680/81) und der Papyrus Vind. G. 3*. München 1979 (Abhandlungen der Bayerischen Akademie der Wissenschaften, phil.-hist. Klasse, N. F. 85); DERS., *Acta Conciliorum Oecumenicorum, series 2, II: Concilium universale Constantinopolitanum tertium. 2. Concilii actiones XII–XVIII, epistulae, indices*. Berlin 1990.

Abb. 2: „Originalpapyrus" mit Unterschriftenliste der Konzilsteilnehmer am Constantinopolitanum tertium, 17. Sitzung (Wien, ÖNB, P. Vindob. G 3): Nennung des Bischofs Ioannes von Athen als päpstlichen Legaten (Nr. 20)

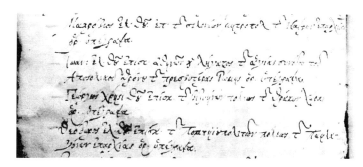

Abb. 3: 1. Abschrift der Unterschriftenliste der Konzilsteilnehmer am Constantinopolitanum tertium (Wien, ÖNB, Cod. hist. gr. 56, fol. *1v): Nennung des Bischofs Ioannes von Athen als päpstlichen Legaten (Nr. 20)

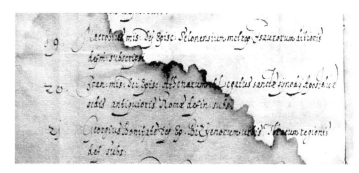

Abb. 4: 2. Abschrift der Unterschriftenliste der Konzilsteilnehmer am Constantinopolitanum tertium (Wien, ÖNB, Cod. hist. gr. 56, fol. *3v); Nennung des Bischofs Ioannes von Athen als päpstlichen Legaten (Nr. 20)

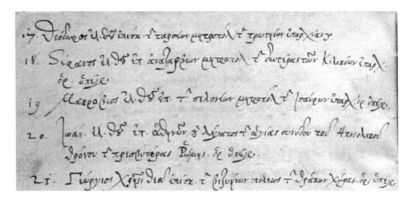

Abb. 5: 3. Abschrift der Unterschriftenliste der Konzilsteilnehmer am Constantinopolitanum tertium (Wien, ÖNB, Cod. hist. gr. 56, fol. *6ᵛ); Nennung des Bischofs Ioannes von Athen als päpstlichen Legaten (Nr. 20)

Wie aus der Stelle ersichtlich, war es der Rang des als Legat Roms signierenden Bischofs Ioannes von Athen, der Sambucus ganz besonders für seine romkritische Stellung interessierte[49]. Denn dieser unterzeichnete nach seiner Zählung an 22. Stelle des Fragments und damit in einer klar subordinierten Position, die einem Machtanspruch Roms zuwiderlaufen musste. Allerdings stimmt auch Sambucus' Zählung weder mit dem Original noch mit den Abschriften im Codex hist. gr. 56 überein: In letzteren ist Ioannes von Athen stets an 20. Stelle angeführt: 1. Abschrift, fol. 1ᵛ; 2. Abschrift (vor oder zur Zeit Sebastian Tengnagels erstellt, dessen Kurztitel am Ende [= äußeres Blatt] auf fol. 4ᵛ erhalten ist), fol. 3ᵛ (mit Randzählung); 3. Abschrift fol. 6ᵛ (mit Randzählung); 4. Abschrift fol. 9ᵛ (an 19. [!] Stelle).

---

[49] Zur Person siehe Ralph-Johannes LILIE, Claudia LUDWIG, Thomas PRATSCH, Ilse ROCHOW u. a., *Prosopographie der mittelbyzantinischen Zeit. Erste Abteilung (641–867)*. 2. Band: Georgios (# 2183) – Leon (# 4270), nach Vorarbeiten Friedhelm WINKELMANNS erstellt. Berlin, New York 2000, 195 (# 2710); der Bezug zu Rom ist hier damit erklärt, dass das Bistum des Bischofs dem Rom unterstehenden *Illyricum orientale* gehörte. Zu dieser Thematik vgl. ferner Heinz OHME, *Das Concilium Quinisextum und seine Bischofsliste. Studien zum Konstantinopeler Konzil von 692*. Berlin, New York 1990 (Arbeiten zur Kirchengeschichte 56), 222–234 (Die Vertreter der römischen Jurisdiktion).

DIE GRIECHISCHE VERSION DER KONSTANTINISCHEN SCHENKUNG

Als Beleg für die Echtheit der *Donatio Constantini* wurde von der romtreuen Seite auch die griechische Übersetzung[50] ins Treffen geführt, die man als den Ursprungstext vermutete[51], das geschah erstmals durch Lauro Quirini 1447. Diese Argumentationsstrategie verfolgten sodann im 16. Jahrhundert Bartolomeo Picerno[52] und Agostino Steuco[53]. Sambucus nahm dazu nun mit

---

[50] Zu den griechischen Versionen, die ab dem 12. Jahrhundert textlich fassbar sind: Enzo PETRUCCI, I rapporti tra le redazioni latine e greche del costituto di Costantino. *Bulletino dell'Istituto Storico Italiano per il Medio Evo e Archivio Muratoriano* 74 (1962), 45–160 (Nachdruck in: DERS., *Ecclesiologia e politica. Momenti di storia del papato medievale*. Introduzione di Ovidio Capitani. Rom 2001, 1–110); ferner Aleksej PAVLOV, Podložnaja darstvennaja gramota Konstantina Velikago pape Silvestru v polnom grečeskom i slavjanskom perevode. *Vizantijski Vremennik* 3 (1896) 59–80; Augusto GAUDENZI, Il constituto di Costantino. *Bolletino dell'Istituto Storico Italiano per il Medio Evo e Archivio Muratoriano* 39 (1919), 9–112; Roberto CESSI, Il Costituto di Costantino (Il testo), *Istituto veneto di scienze, lettere ed arti. Atti. Classe di scienze morali e lettere* 88 (1928), 915–1007; Helmut BOESE, Die Konstantinische Schenkung in den Verhandlungen des Florentiner Konzils. *Deutsches Archiv für Erforschung des Mittelalters* 21 (1965), 568–592; Werner OHNSORGE, Das Constitutum Constantini und seine Entstehung. In: DERS., *Konstantinopel und der Okzident. Gesammelte Aufsätze zur Geschichte der byzantinisch-abendländischen Beziehungen und des Kaisertums*. Darmstadt 1966, 93–162 (seine Version einer griechischen Konzept-Version aus dem 8. Jahrhundert ist mittlerweile widerlegt). Zum kulturellen Hintergrund in Byzanz siehe auch Paul J. ALEXANDER, The Donation of Constantine at Byzantium and its Earliest Use Against the Western Empire. In: DERS., *Religious and Political History and Thought in the Byzantine Empire*. London 1978, 11–26; Hans-Georg KRAUSE, Das Constitutum Constantini im Schisma von 1054. In: Hubert Mordek (Hg.), *Aus Kirche und Reich. Studien zu Theologie, Politik und Recht im Mittelalter. Festschrift für Friedrich Kempf zu seinem 75. Geburtstag und fünfzigjährigen Doktorjubiläum*. Sigmaringen 1983, 148–158; Dimiter G. ANGELOV, The Donation of Constantine and the Church in Late Byzantium. In: DERS., *Church and Society in Late Byzantium*. Kalamazoo 2009 (*Studies in Medieval Culture* 49), 91–157. Es handelt sich um insgesamt vier Versionen: von Theodoros Balsamon (ca. 1130/40–n. 1195; nur Text der *Donatio*); (anonyme) Kurzversion der Balsamon-Version im *Syntagma* des Matthaios Blastares (1335), von Demetrios Kydones (ca. 1369–1371; Vollversion mit *Confessio* und *Donatio*) und von dem griechischen Dominikaner und katholischen Erzbischof von Rhodos, Andreas Chrysoberges (1439 am Konzil von Florenz präsentiert, wahrscheinlich unter den byzantinischen Unionisten erstellt; nur *Donatio*).

[51] VIAN, *Donazione* (s. Anm. 70), 135–136.

[52] Seine lateinische Übersetzung der aufgefundenen griechischen Version findet sich etwa in Ulrich von Huttens Edition von Vallas Traktat (De donatione Constantini quid veri habeat, eruditorum quorundam iudicium, ut in versa pagella videbis [Straßburg: Andreas Cratander 1517]; neben Picernos lateinischer Übersetzung der griechischen Version mit den Stellungnahmen von Nicolaus von Kues und Antoninus archiepiscopus Florentinus) oder in der Ausgabe Basel: Andreas Cratander 1520 (VD 16 ZV 4645 und 4646) gemeinsam mit den Stellung-

einer griechischen Version aus seinem Besitz Stellung[54]. Den neuen Text veröffentlichte er als Anhang auf fol. 17ʳ–18ʳ. Schon in der Widmung nimmt er auf dieses außergewöhnliche Stück Bezug[55]:

> Adscripsi graecum Θέσπισμα Constantino tributum, quod nec annos nec caudam alitis superbae nec alia pleraque latine prodita contestatur.
> Cod. 9534, fol. 5ʳ

In der Abhandlung führt er gegen die romtreue Linie seine Gegenargumente vor; dabei nimmt er explizit zu Picerno Stellung; allerdings begründet sich der so betonte Unterschied schlicht in verschiedenen herangezogenen Versionen: Picerno hat auf einen der Codices Vaticani der vollständigen Kydones-Version – die auch für die slawischen Übersetzungen maßgeblich wurde – zurückgegriffen[56], Sambucus auf die Kurzfassung der Blastares-Version (die nur die *Donatio* enthält)[57]:

> Sed genus fuisse munificentiae, quo occidentis possessio sit episcopis relicta, diadema fuisse a vertice reiectum, ministerio servili Caesarem ad pedes sessoris abiectum, difficile de scriptoribus id ullis, nisi corruptis, unquam coegeris, qui cum omnes fere sacri fuerint, eiusmodi amplitudinem Sylvestro delatam minime reticuissent.
>
> Gratia ego fictum canonistarum theologorumque istud πρεσβεῖον[58] puto, ignorantia principum auctum, nec in vetustioribus manu exaratis codicibus invenitur.
>
> Inspexi, conquisivi ipse in Galliis, Belgis, Italia, Germania trecentorum annorum eius argumenti libros, ut idem facerent, non ociose monui, sed nuspiam haec prodiga largitio comparuit.

---

nahmen zur *Donatio* von Nikolaus von Kues, Lorenzo Valla, Ulrich von Hutten (Vorwort zu Vallas Edition), Antoninus archiepiscopus Florentinus und Paulus Hieronymus (Catthalanus).

[53] A. Steuchus Eugubinus, Contra Laurentium Vallam De falsa donatione Constantini libri duo. Lugduni: apud Sebastianum Gryphium 1547, 145–148. Vgl. Ronald K. DELPH, Valla Grammaticus, Agostino Steuco and the Donation of Constantine. Journal of the History of Ideas 57,1 (1996), 55–77.

[54] Die folgenden Daten sind VIAN, *Donazione* (s. Anm. 70), 91–167, entnommen.

[55] GERSTINGER, *Briefe* (s. Anm. 2), 122, 44–45.

[56] Zur Version siehe ANGELOV, Donation of Constantine (s. Anm. 50), 101–102.

[57] Zur Version siehe ANGELOV, Donation of Constantine (s. Anm. 50), 100–101; bei Blastares findet sich der Text in Stoicheion E, Kap. 11 (ed. bei Georgios A. RHALLES, Michael POTLES, Σύνταγμα τῶν θείων καὶ ἱερῶν κανόνων. Tom. 6. Athen 1859 [Nachdr. 1966, 1992], 261–262; überliefert auch in den *Epimetra* der *Hexabiblos* des Konstantinos Harmenopoulos [Gustav Ernst HEIMBACH, *Const. Harmenopuli Manuale legum sive Hexabiblos*. Leipzig 1851, 820–822]).

[58] Marginal der Lesevermerk von Sambucus: *Donatio dist. 96*.

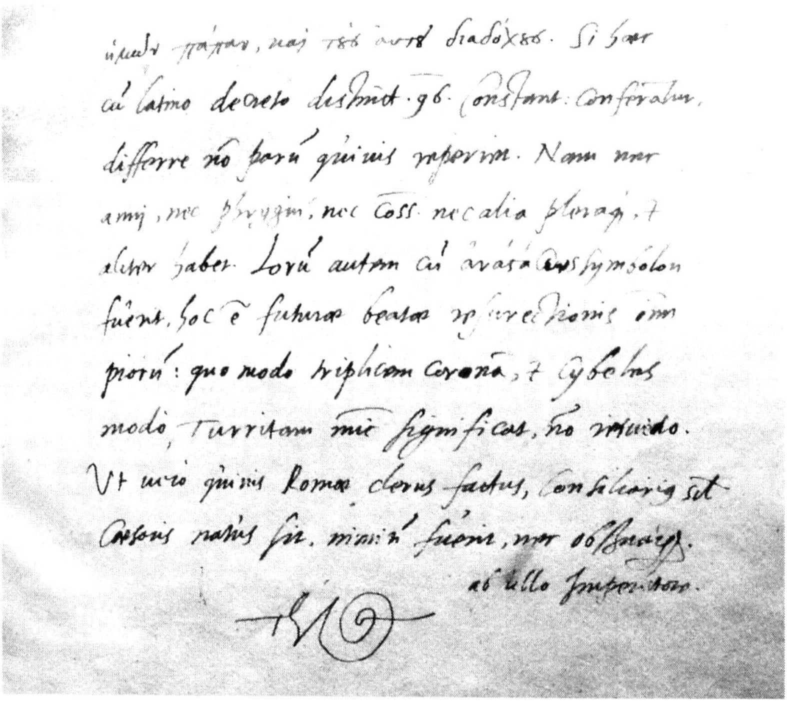

Abb. 6: Abschluss von Sambucus' Abhandlung zur *Donatio Constantini*
(Wien, Österreichische Nationalbibliothek, Cod. 9534, fol. 18r)

Fingit quidam Barptolomaeus [sic] Picernus[59], se graece eiusmodi πρωτεῖα reperisse, ad verbum translata, non discrepare ab canonistarum promulgatione, suspicari tamen quiddam de temporibus et quod ipsum et alii non suspitione, sed re ipsa consulumque[60] adscriptorum in latino ratione dudum convicere, | (8r) nec phrygium illud pavonicum nec alia pleraque eodem sensu habet.

Ipse ego eiusdem obscurae celebritatis graecum exemplum habeo[61]: inter prolationem[62] alicuius famelici graeci Florentino factam concilio, credo, sed non

---

[59] Marginal der Lesevermerk von Sambucus: *Ad. Iul. II.*
[60] Marginal der Lesevermerk von Sambucus: *Ca[s]siod. Coss.*
[61] Hs. noch nicht identifiziert.
[62] Marginal der Lesevermerk von Sambucus: *Graeca donat.*

tam est copiosum, nec annos habet definitos, nec confirmat verba pro bibliotheca[63] atrae tabellae rudibus literis inscripta, quae visuntur.

Quaeso, quis negarit, donationem romano latine potius quam graece factam[64] et consignatam? Si modo Theodoreto fides habenda est, Constantinum per interpretes libenter egisse et graecissare utcunque solitum? Cur non talium Jacobus de Voragine ille meminit, qui caeteroqui minima quaeque annotavit?

Omitto hic Vallae, et, si qui alii scripserant, argumenta et declamationes: an Constantinus, si facere voluisset, potuisset, si Sylvestro libuisset[65], cui auri peraeque prohibita est possessio, an acceptare licuisset, an iam tum Constant(inus) Christum recte cognorit: profecto regulam JURIS non dissimulabo: Nullum Imperatorem[66] suis privilegiis alii indulgentius communicatis, maiestati successorem derogare, et contra ius hominum agere posse: ne videlicet sibi quid ad interitum diminutione ista continua praeter ius et decorum accersant, siquidem AUGUSTI sint, non acceptorum profusi.

Cod. 9534, fol. 7ᵛ–8ʳ

Den Abschluss seines Traktats macht dann die Edition der so genannten Blastares-Version[67]; dazu hält Sambucus zusammenfassend als Kritikpunkt an der Authenitzität der *Donatio Constantini* fest:

Si haec cum latino decreto distinct. 96 Constant. conferantur, differre non parum quivis reperiret. Nam nec anni, nec phrygium, nec consules, nec alia pleraque et aliter habet. Lorum autem cum ἀναστάσεως (sic!) symbolon fuerit, hoc est futurae beatae resurectionis omnium piorum, quo modo triplicem coronam et Cybeles modo, turritam nunc significat, non invenio[68]. Ut vero quivis Romae clerus factus, consiliarius scilicet Caesaris natus sit, nimium fuerit, nec observatum[69] ab ullo imperatore.

Cod. 9534, fol. 18ʳ

---

[63] Marginal der Lesevermerk von Sambucus: *In Vatican*. Gemeint ist die *Sala di Costantino* im Vatikan (Musei Vaticani), die von Raffael-Schülern 1520–1524 geschaffen wurde.
[64] Marginal der Lesevermerk von Sambucus: *Epist. Const.*
[65] Marginal der Lesevermerk von Sambucus: *Dubia.*
[66] Marginal der Lesevermerk von Sambucus: *L. si qs. C. III.* (?)
[67] Dazu siehe ANGELOV, Donation of Constantine (s. Anm. 47), 100–101.
[68] *invenio* in Korrektur.
[69] Das Wort ist – wenn überhaupt richtig intendiert – mit ungewöhnlichen Abbreviaturen geschrieben: *ser = ss* ligiert, der Wortabschluss *-um* ist nur mehr als schwungvolles Schnörksel (ohne Bezug zu den Buchstaben) geschrieben. Die erkennbaren Buchstaben *obs + vat* legen die hier vertretene Lesung nahe.

APPENDIX:

DIE AUSEINANDERSETZUNG MIT DER KONSTANTINISCHEN SCHENKUNG IN DER RENAISSANCE

In der kritischen Auseinandersetzung mit der *Donatio Constantini* finden sich Stellungnahmen vor allem von Juristen und Kanonikern schon lange vor dem die folgende Diskussion bestimmenden Werk Lorenzo Vallas[70], so hat sich auch Dante im *Inferno, canto* 19, v. 115–117, und in *De Monarchia* damit auseinandergesetzt[71]. Mit Nicolaus von Kues am Konzil von Basel und vor allem dem ersten Werk, das nur dieser Thematik gewidmet war, Vallas *Declamatio*, begann eine öffentliche Debatte, die für die folgende Zeit prägend war. Dabei zeigt sich eine regelrechte Zäsur in der Rezeption, als im Zeitalter der Reformation das Werk 1506 in einer *Editio princeps* veröffentlicht wurde und in der Folge nicht nur mehrfach nachgedruckt, sondern auch in die Volkssprachen übersetzt wurde.

1433	Nicolaus von Kues zweifelt an der Echtheit der *Donatio* in seiner am Konzil von Basel am 7. November 1433 präsentierten Schrift *De concordantia catholica* (III 2).
1435/6	Leonardo Teronda (aus Verona), im Dienst der päpstlichen Kanzlei, verwirft die Echtheit der *Donatio* in zwei Schriften[72].
	Enea Silvio Piccolomini wechselt in seiner Stellungnahme vom Verteidiger der *Donatio* (1436) zum Kritiker im *Pentalogus* (1443) und im *Dialogus pro donatione Constantini*, von Piccolomini als *dialogorum quidam libellus*

---

[70] Aufgearbeitet in Giovanni Maria VIAN, *La donazione di Costantino*. Bologna 2004 (*L'identità italiana* 35), 91–128. Zu den bildlichen Darstellungen und dem Versuch der Propagierung des durch die Schenkung zugebilligten Machtanspruches siehe a. O., 145–147, und Jan L. DE JONG, The painted decoration of the Sala Regia in the Vatican. Intention and reception. In: Tristan Weddigen, Sible de Blaauw, Bram Kempers (eds.), *Functions and Decorations: Art and Ritual at the Vatican Palace in the Middle Ages and the Renaissance*. Vatikanstaat, Turnhout 2003, 153–168. Zu Vallas Werk siehe ferner Giovanni ANTONAZZI, *Lorenzo Valla e la polemica sulla Donazione di Costantino. Con testi inediti dei secoli XV–XVII*. Rom 1985 (*Uomini e Dottrine* 28).

[71] VIAN, *Donazione* (s. Anm. 70), 99–109.

[72] Franco GAETA, *Lorenzo Valla. Filologia e storia nell'umanesimo italiano*. Neapel 1955, 201–252; vgl. zur Person auch Giuseppe BILLANOVICH, Leonardo Teronda, umanista e curiale. *Italia medioevale e umanistica* I (1958), 379–381.

	[...] *de sompno quodam meo* bezeichnet (1453–1454); trotz Fälschungsbestätigung wird jedoch der päpstliche Machtanspruch legitimiert[73].
1440	Lorenzo Valla verfasst zwischen April und Mai 1440 im Konflikt zwischen Alfons V. von Aragon und Papst Eugen IV. das erste Werk, das nach Titel und Inhalt einzig der konstantinischen Schenkung gewidmet ist: *De falso credita et ementita Constantini donatione declamatio*.
1447	Der Venezianer Lauro Quirini zieht in seiner Widerlegung von Vallas Trakat die griechische Version zum Beweis der Authentizität heran (*Sanctio Constantini imperatoris de donatione a se facta Romano pontifici Silvestro eiusque successoribus*[74]).
ca. 1449	Reginald Pecock, Bischof von St. Asaph (1444), äußert sich kritisch zur Legende in seinem Werk *The Repressing Of Over Mich Wyting of the Clergie*.
n. 1464	Kritik an Vallas *Declamatio* durch Antonio Cortesi, tätig in der Kurienkanzlei und Verfasser des *Antivalla*[75], vor allem gegen Ton und Dreistigkeit Vallas.
1494	Editio princeps des *Constitutum Constantini* (*Bulla Constantini imperatoris qualiter fidem et baptismum Christi recepit et a lepra per beatum Silvestrum curatus fuit atque romanam ecclesiam dotavit et eam in multis privilegiavit, pape, episcopis et omnibus clericis in temporalibus copiose providit et multa privilegia dedit*; GW 07440; HAIN 13376).
1496	Prorömische Stellungnahme durch Pietro Capretto (Del Zochul, Edo), Verfasser von *Antidotum* (*Propositio qua quaeritur utrum quas terras ecclesia Romana papave possidet eas recte nec ne possideat adversus libellum eum quem Laurentius quidam Valla de ementita Constantini donatione, ut dicitur, inscripsit*; Februar 1496)[76], das auch den psychologischen Beweggründen Vallas nachgeht, und von *Apologia* (*In Laurentii Vallae famosum libellum quemdam Apologia*; 1. September 1496), eines fiktiven Dialogs zwischen Edo und Valla)[77].

---

[73] VIAN, *Donazione* (s. Anm. 70), 131–132.
[74] Ediert in Wolfram SETZ, *Lorenzo Vallas Schrift gegen die Konstantinische Schenkung*. Tübingen 1975 (*Bibliothek des Deutschen Historischen Instituts in Rom* 44), 118–120.
[75] Siehe dazu Giovanni ANTONAZZI, Lorenzo Valla e la donazione di Costantino con un testo inedito di Antonio Cortesi. *Rivista di storia della Chiesa in Italia* 4 (1950), 186–234; ANTONAZZI, *Polemica* (s. Anm. 70), 195–206.
[76] Text ediert bei ANTONAZZI, *Polemica* (s. Anm. 70), 213–244.
[77] Siehe Massimo MIGLIO, L'umanista Pietro Edo e la polemica sulla donazione di Costantino. *Bullettino dell'Istituto Storico Italiano per il Medio Evo e Archivio Muratoriano* 79 (1968), 167–232.

1505	Antonio de Ferrariis, Galateo, übermittelt an Papst Iulius II. eine griechische Version der *Donatio*[78]; Bartolomeo Picerno veröffentlicht in Rom bei Marcello Silber gegen Vallas *Declamatio* die griechische Version (EDIT 16 CNCE 17634: „non dopo il 1513").
1506	Editio princeps von Vallas *Declamatio*, gedruckt zu den Iden des März (Straßburg: Johann Grüninger; mit Beiträgen von Jodocus Badius und Sebastian Brant; VD 16 V 227).
1513	tschechische Übersetzung von Vallas *Declamatio* durch Gregorius Hruby (Gelenius), handschriftlich erhalten: *O neprávě uvěřeném a smyšleném Konstantinovu papeži nadáni* (Prag, Národní knihovná České republiky XVII.D.38, fol. 219v–267v)[79].
1517	Neudruck von Vallas *Declamatio* durch Ulrich von Hutten[80], es folgen weitere Nachdrucke mit großem Publikumsecho; Luther und Zwingli sind um 1520 begeistert von Vallas Schrift.
ca. 1522	französische Übersetzung von Vallas *Declamatio* (gedruckt in Paris [Pierre Vidoue?]: *Laurentz Valle, Poete et Orateur Romain, sur la Donation de Constantin Empereur*)[81].
ca. 1524	deutsche Übersetzung von Vallas *Declamatio* (gedruckt in Worms: *Des Edlen Römers Laurentii Vallensis Clagrede wider die erdicht unnd erlogene begabung so von dem Keyser Constantino der Römischen kirchen sol geschehen sein*; VD 16 ZV 15146).
1534	englische Übersetzung von Vallas *Declamatio* durch William Marshall (gedruckt in London bei Thomas Godfray: *A treatyse of the donation or gyfte and endowment of possessyons, gyven and graunted unto Sylvester pope of Rhome by Constantyne emperour of Rome & what truth is in the same graun thou mayst se and rede ye iugement of certayne great lerned men, whose names on the other page of this leafe done appere*).

---

[78] Siehe dazu Carlo VECCE, Antonio Galateo e la difesa della donazione di Costantino. *Aevum* 59 (1985), 353–360.

[79] Bořek NESKUDLA, Řehoř Hrubý z Jelení a takzvaný národní humanismus [Gregor Hruby aus Jelení und der sogenannte nationale Humanismus]. *Česká literatura* 62 (2014), 728–751.

[80] Anita TRANINGER, Fiktion, Fakt und Fälschung: Lorenzo Valla, Ulrich von Hutten und die Ambiguität der declamatio in der Renaissance. In: Ulrike Schneider, Anita Traninger (Hgg.), *Fiktionen des Faktischen in der Renaissance*. Stuttgart 2010 (Text und Kontext 32), 165–190.

[81] Bei Jonathan A. RIED, *King's Sister – Queen of Dissent: Marguerite of Navarre (1492–1549) and her Evangelical Network*, vol. 1, Leiden, Boston 2009, 371 Anm. 177, angegeben mit Alençon: Simon Du Bois 1529–1534?; beim Universal Short Title Catalogue (USTC) wird das Werk ebenso mit [Alençon: Simon du Bois 1530] angeführt <http://ustc.ac.uk/index.php/record/10459> (11. 8. 2015).

1537	Iohannes Cochlaeus' Antwort auf die deutsche Übersetzung von Vallas *Declamatio* (mit Vorwort Luthers) (*Von der Donation des Keysers Constantini, vnd von Bepstlichem gewalt, Grundtlicher bericht, aus alten bewerten Lerern vnd Historien, Auch etwas vom Laurentio Valla, vom Cypriano, vom Jreneo, Hierony. etc.*; [Leipzig: Nikolaus Wolrab]; [VD 16 C 4419]).
1544	Andrea Alciato tritt für die substantielle Gültigkeit der *Donatio* ein, auch wenn legendenhaft (Parergon iuris libri VII posteriores. Lyon: Sebastianus Gryphius 1544, p. 61 [VII 19]).
1546	italienische Übersetzung von Vallas *Declamatio* (*Trattato utile et degno d'esser letto da ogni persona, di Lorenzo Valla Gentil huomo Romano, doue si tratta della donatione, che uolgarmente si dice esser fatta da Costantino Magno Imperatore Romano, a Papa Siluestro*; gedruckt in [Basel] bei [Andreas Cratander Erben]; [VD 16 ZV 15147]; mit italienischem Schreiben des Ulrich von Hutten an Papst Leo X. vom 1. Dezember 1517).
1547	Agostino Steuco verfasst eine zweibändige Gegenschrift (*Contra Laurentium Vallam, De falsa Donatione Constantini. Libri Duo*) zu Valla und zieht die griechische Version heran (gedruckt in Lyon bei Sebastianus Gryphius)[82].
1554	Vallas Schrift im *Catalogo degli heretici* (Mailand, Venedig).
1559	Vallas Schrift im *Index librorum prohibitorum*.
1559/74	Von den Reformatoren wird Vallas Schrift in die Magdeburger Zenturien aufgenommen.

---

[82] *Atque decretum illud* [...] *sive ut Graecis vocari solet quasi oraculum*, θέσπισμα, *Constantini, per universam Graeciam circumferetur* (sic! für *circumfertur?*), *eius universas Graecorum bibliothecas plenas reperies, non una in bibliotheca palatina, quod quidam calumniatus est, delitescit. Ipsos Graecos voca testes, lustra quot sunt in Italia Graecae bibliothecae. Omnis Graecia pie, reverenterque assurgit huic edicto, ipsum adorat. Nec fuit tempus unquam, postquam ea sanxit Constantinus, quin fuerint semper ea pro verissimis habita, si rem altius perspicere cupiens ab ipsis imperatoribus aggrediaris, qui omnes unanimiter venerati sunt uti verissimum ac sanctissimum decretum illud. Ipsae synodi confirmaverunt, iidem ipsi Graeci, qui scriptis aliquid memoriae prodiderunt, id abunde testantur. Saepe ego percunctatus sum ex Graecis propter sparsam in homines a Laurentio dubitationem, quam fidem haberent huic decreto, nunquam non reperi eos constanter affirmare nullam esse super eo apud eos dubitationem, imo venerari, adorare. Atque eo usque venerationi fuit decretum illud vetustis imperatoribus, ut eum* (sic) *libros sacrorum canonum confici imperassent* (15–16). [...] *Haec confessio per omnem Graeciam circumfertur, omnia sacraria plena sunt eius etiam inimicis Graecis, qui semper Romanę maiestati invidissent assentientibus. Haec igitur primum falsas illas, ipsius e pectore natas, non e natura petitas Laurentii rationes coarguunt, quibus universum libellum suum superstruxit* (19–20).

Johannes Sambucus als Herausgeber und Verfasser von Herrscherserien

JOHANNES AMANN-BUBENIK (Waidhofen / Ybbs – Wien)

IN OPTATISSI-
mum Diui Cæsaris Fer-
DINANDI VIENNAM
REDITVM.

TE Iouis hic ales geminus, te, Maxime Cæsar,
    Fronde triumphali, tota Vienna capit.
Sidere fœlici te natum prædicat orbis:
    Tendit in occursum conscia turba nouum.
Vindice te cunctas pellemus fortiter iras,
    Regnaq; sperata non minuentur ope.
Induperatorum decus, ô Ferdnande, trophæis,
    Pace tua crescent gaudia nostra, bonis.
Gratamur reduci, quem pax comitatur, amorq;,
    Omnia sunt ausis læta futura tuis.
Non equidem vacua spe ducor, te fore solum,
    Cuius inoffensa concidat hostis ope.
Et quæ concussa est patria, vt lapsura putetur,
    Te vires subita sentiat illa die.
Deniq; tantus amor veri, fiducia constans,
    Nusquam dfsidium vt religionis eat.
Aurea sub te mox, Princeps, ô secla redibunt,
    Vltima nec primis deteriora manent.
Enses, agricolæ demptum vertentur in vsum,
    Vomer erit, gladius qui modo acutus erat.
Te metuent, cordi quibus est patrare nefanda,
    Sub teq; inuicto vesper, & ortus erunt.
Inspice tot lachrimas, discrimina, damna, precesq;,
    Imperij & socia vincito cuncta manu.
Insana rabie ceter furit ille Tyrannus,
    Qui verè Eumenidum sanguine cretus, adest.
Diuitias cogit, cælestia numina ridens,
    Afflictos proprij iuris & esse velit.

                                                    Huic

Begrüßungsgedicht für Ferdinand I. zur Rückkehr von der Kaiserproklamation.
Ioannes Sambucus, Obsidio Zigethiensis Ann. MDLVI. Viennae Austriae: excudebat Raphael Hofhalter 1558
(Wien, Universitätsbibliothek II 119.923)

Suscipe clementer tenuis munuscula Vatis,
Atque fove digna Principe dexter ope.
Sambucus, *Caesares Austrii*, ÖNB, Cod. 9534, fol. 23ʳ

Nach dem Vorbild der Epigrammserie *Caesares* des spätantiken Dichters Ausonius, der die römischen Kaiser ab Julius Caesar beschreibt, entstanden seit dem frühen 16. Jahrhundert zahlreiche Epigrammserien, die die römischen und römisch-deutschen Kaiser, Habsburger[1], aber auch andere Herrscher zum Gegenstand hatten[2]. Oft wurden diese Gedichtserien mit Holzschnitten (nach Münzen) oder Kupferstichen zu dem in der Renaissance beliebten Porträtbuch kombiniert, das bekannte Persönlichkeiten in Bild und Text darstellte[3]. Johannes Sambucus war sowohl Herausgeber als auch Verfasser von poetischen Herrscherserien.

---

[1] Johannes AMANN-BUBENIK, Kaiserserien und Habsburgergenealogien – Eine poetische Gattung. In: Manuel Baumbach (Hg.), *Tradita et Inventa. Beiträge zur Rezeption der Antike.* Heidelberg 2000 (*Bibliothek der Klassischen Altertumswissenschaften* Reihe 2, N.F. 106), 73–89; DERS., *Kaiserserien und Habsburger-Genealogien. Die Entwicklung einer Gattung poetischer Habsburgpanegyrik vom 16. bis zum 18. Jahrhundert.* Diss. Wien 2013 (hier bes. Kapitel 2: Die Habsburger Kaiserserie des Johannes Sambucus).

[2] Christopher A. UPTON, John Jonston and the Historical Epigram. In: Richard J. Schoeck (Hg.), *Acta Conventus Neo-Latini Bononiensis. Proceedings of the Fourth International Congress of Neo-Latin Studies. Bologna 26 August to 1 September 1979.* Binghamton, N.Y., 1985 (*Medieval and Renaissance Texts and Studies* 37), 638–644; Ulrich SCHLEGELMILCH, Successio Christianorum Bavariae Principum. Humanistische Fürstendichtung, politische Aussagen und Ergebnisse landesgeschichtlicher Forschung in den Herrscherepigrammen der „Trophaea Bavarica". In: Julius Oswald SJ, Rita Haub (Hgg.), *Jesuitica. Forschungen zur frühen Geschichte des Jesuitenordens in Bayern bis zur Aufhebung 1773.* München 2001 (*Zeitschrift für bayerische Landesgeschichte*, Beiheft 17, Reihe B), 255–330.

[3] Paul O. RAVE, Paolo Giovio und die Bildnisvitenbücher des Humanismus. *Jahrbuch der Berliner Museen* 1 (1959), 119–154; Pierre LAURENS, L'épigramme latine et le thème des hommes illustres au seizième siècle: ‚Icones' et ‚Imagines'. In: Raymond Chevallier (Hg.), *Influence de la Grèce et de Rome sur l'occident moderne. Actes du Colloque des 14, 15, 19 Décembre 1975.* Paris 1977 (*Caesarodunum* 12 bis), 123–132; auch in: Pierre LAURENS, *L'abeille dans l'ambre. Célébration de l'épigramme de l'époque alexandrine à la fin de la Renaissance.* Paris 1989 (*Collection d'études anciennes* 59), 419–429; Maria CYTOWSKA, Die Imagines in der neulateinischen Literatur des XVI. Jahrhunderts. In: *Antikerezeption, Antikeverhältnis, Antikebegegnung in Vergangenheit und Gegenwart. Eine Aufsatzsammlung.* Stendal 1983 (*Schriften der Winckelmann-Gesellschaft* 6), 187–195; Milan PELC, *Illustrium Imagines. Das Porträtbuch der Renaissance.* Leiden 2002 (*Studies in Medieval and Reformation Thought* 88).

SAMBUCUS ALS EDITOR

1552 edierte Sambucus eine Neuauflage von Johann Huttichs *Romanorum Principum effigies*[4] und widmete sie dem designierten böhmischen König und späteren Kaiser Maximilian II.[5] In der *Praefatio* empfiehlt er ihm seine von den Türken bedrohte Heimat, seine Eltern sowie sich selbst und verspricht für die Zukunft ein der Würde des Adressaten angemessenes Werk[6]. Dies ist als erster Versuch interpretiert worden[7], eine Position am kaiserlichen Hof zu erlangen. Die hier anklingenden Motive werden sich in späteren Werken wiederfinden.

1525 hatte der Humanist Johannes Huttich (1487–1544)[8] eine Serie von lateinischen Prosabeschreibungen der römischen und römisch-deutschen Kaiser von Julius Caesar bis Ferdinand I. zu Holzschnitten nach Münzbildnissen verfasst, die beim Straßburger Drucker Wolfgang Köpfel erschien[9]. 1526 folgten weitere Ausgaben auf Latein und Deutsch[10], von denen sich

---

[4] Romanorum Principum effigies: cum historiarum annotatione, olim ab Io. Hutichio confecta: nunc vero alicubi aucta et longe castigatiora opera Io. Sambuci Tirnaviensis Pannonii. Argentorati: apud Wolfium Cephalaeum 1552 (VD16 H 6475).

[5] *2ʳ *Maximiliano Regi Bohemiae Archiducique Austriae, Iohannes Sambucus Tirnaviensis Pannonius S.*

[6] *4ʳ [...] *quo inclinatis temporibus Ungariae succurras, labefactatas eius peneque depositas partes praesens subleves ac sustentes.* *4ᵛ [...] *per omnem fortunam oro et obsecro, parentes meos qui Tirnaviae degunt, meque una in clientelam ut recipias aliquam. sumus enim expositi quibusvis Thurca[rum] excursionibus, ac simul hunc libellum in quo Constantiae, Fortitudinis, Aequitatis reperies exempla, clementer excipito interim, dum aliquid ipse elucubrem, tua maiestate dignum, quodque cum tuis laudibus atque gloria coniunctum sit: ac etiam cumulate tuum animum gaudio adficiat.*

[7] Gábor ALMÁSI, *The uses of humanism. Johannes Sambucus (1531–1584), Andreas Dudith (1533–1589), and the republic of letters in East Central Europe*. Leiden 2010 (Brill's studies in intellectual history 185), 147f.

[8] Ferdinand W. E. ROTH, Johann Huttich (1487–1544). Euphorion 4 (1897), 772–789; Maria LANCKORONSKA, Des Johannes Huttichius Imperatorum Romanorum Libellus als Dokument des Glaubenskampfes. Gutenberg-Jahrbuch 1965, 262–270; Heinrich GRIMM, Huttichius. NDB 10 (1974), 105f.; Ilse GUENTHER, Johann Huttich. In: *Contemporaries of Erasmus. A biographical register of the Renaissance and Reformation* 2 (1986), 220f.; *Deutsche biographische Enzyklopädie* 5 (1997), 238.

[9] Imperatorum Romanorum Libellus. Una cum imaginibus, ad uiuam effigiem expressis. Argentinae: Wolfgangus Caephalius 1525 (VD16 H 6472).

[10] Imperatorum romanorum libellus una cum imaginibus ad vivam effigiem expressis. Argentinae: Wolfgangus Cephalaeus 1526 (VD16 H 6473); Römische Keyser abcontravegt, vom ersten Caio Julio an untz uff den jetzigen H. K. Carolum. Straßburg: bey Wolffen Köpffel 1526 (VD16 H 6477).

Huttich aber in der folgenden von 1534[11] distanzierte[12]. Dies mag erklären, warum Sambucus seine Edition als dritte Auflage[13] bezeichnen kann. Sambucus gibt an, dass er die Gedichtserien der humanistischen Autoren Georg Sabinus (1508–1560), Jakob Micyllus (1503–1558) und Caspar Ursinus Velius (ca. 1493–1539) hinzufügt[14] (außerdem die des Ausonius, die er nicht extra erwähnt). Allerdings hatte der Drucker Balthazar Arnoullet schon 1550 in Lyon Huttichs Kaiserserie[15] (mit dem Vorwort von 1534) mit den Epigrammen des Ausonius, Micyllus und Velius publiziert. Vorbild dafür dürften wiederum die *Icones Imperatorum* des Herausgebers Nikolaus Gerbel[16] gewesen sein, der Porträts der Kaiser mit den Tetrastichen des Ausonius und Micyllus und den Distichen des Velius kombinierte. Wirklich neu bei Sambucus ist also nur die Aufnahme der Gedichte des Sabinus, die als geschlossener Block auf die nach Kaisern geordneten Epigramme der anderen Autoren folgen.

SAMBUCUS ALS AUTOR

Im Jahre 1567 erschien eine Epigrammserie des Sambucus über die ungarischen Könige, die mit Attila beginnt[17]. Die 40 Epigramme umfassen teils

---

[11] Imperatorum et Caesarum Vitae, cum Imaginibus ad vivam effigiem expressis. Libellus auctus cum elencho et Iconiis consulum ab Authore. Argentorati: Wolfgangus Caephalaeus excussit 1534 (VD16 H 6474).

[12] Aa1ᵛ–Aa2ʳ *Editus sic libellus principio inauspicato et iterum minore librarii solertia quam primitus promissum fuerat et tertio authoris nomine penitus secluso insertis nonnullis ineptiis alibi ad questum prostitutum vidimus, foecit ut priores aeditiones resumeremus et illam quam vides summa castigatam diligentia publicaremus.*

[13] Romanorum Principum effigies (s. Anm. 4) *3ᵛ [...] *nunc tertio sub praelum* [...].

[14] *1ʳ *Quae tertiae, huic editioni accesserint versa pagina indicat;* *1ᵛ [...] *Trium poetarum. G. Sabini. Micylli, et Velii de imperatoribus Ro. versus.*

[15] Imperatorum et Caesarum vitae, cum Imaginibus ad vivam effigiem expressis. Huic aeditioni additi sunt cum Icunculis, et elencho, versus Ausonii, Mycilli, et Vellei poetarum paucis ingentem historiam complectentes. Lugduni: apud Balthazarem Arnolletum 1550; weitere Ausgabe: 1554.

[16] Icones Imperatorum, et breves vitae, atque rerum cuiusque gestarum indicationes: Ausonio, Iacobo Micyllo, Ursino Velio authoribus. Argentorati: apud Cratonem Mylium 1544 (VD16 G 1450).

[17] Reges Ungariae, ab an. Christi CDI. usque ad MDLXVII. Item Iani Pannonii Episcopi Quinqueccles. Eranemus nunc repertus. Viennae Austriae: excudebat Casparus Stainhofer

zwei, teils drei elegische Distichen, nur das letzte auf Maximilian II. ist sechs Distichen lang. Die Reihe lautet: Atila, Adalarius, Toxus, D. Stephanus, Petrus, Andreas cum Leventa, Andreas, Bela, Salomon, Geyssa, Ladislaus, Colimannus, Stephanus, Bela, Geyssa, Stephanus, Bela Filius, Emericus, Ladislaus II., Andreas II., Bela IIII., Stephanus IIII., Ladislaus III. Filius, Andreas III. Venetus, Carolus Robertus, Otho Bavarus, Carolus, Lodovicus, Carolus, Sigismundus, Albertus, Vladislaus Polonus, Ladislaus, Mathias, Ladislaus Polonus, Frider. III. + Maxim. I.,[18] Lodovicus, Ferdinandus, Ioan. Scepusius, Maximilianus II.[19]

Einige Monate später verfasste Sambucus eine Epigrammserie auf die Habsburgerkaiser, an die er eine überarbeitete Version der ungarischen Königsserie anschloss[20]. Neben kleineren Änderungen bei der Formulierung der Überschriften, die teilweise genauere Angaben bringen, enthält die Handschrift ein zusätzliches Epigramm (auf Geyssa, nach Toxus) und Ergänzungen bei folgenden Königen: Colimannus (8 statt 6 Verse), Stephanus Secund. (6 statt 4 Verse), Andreas II. Hierosolym. (8 statt 6 Verse), Bela Quartus (6 statt 4 Verse), Matthias Corvinus (10 statt 6 Verse), Ferdinandus Primus (8 statt 6 Verse), Maximilian. Secundus (16 statt 12 Verse).

Im Druck edierte Sambucus seine Königsserie noch zweimal in seinen Bonfini- und Werböczy-Ausgaben[21]. Diese folgen weitgehend dem Manuskript, nur die Gedichte auf Ferdinand I. und Maximilian II. umfassen 6 bzw.

1567 (nicht in VD16; ÖNB 46.S.44). Die Widmung an Franciscus Forgach ist mit *Viennae, kal. Febr. 1567* datiert.

[18] *Ein Gedicht auf beide Habsburger, im Druck fälschlicherweise Maxim. II.*

[19] Im Anschluss daran steht das hexametrische Gedicht *In eiusdem e comitiis Augustanis reditum LXVI. Congratulatio I. S. in vigilia Trinitatis.*

[20] *Caesares Austrii et Reges Ungariae ad MDLXVII. Cum brevi Chronologia authore Ioan. Sambuco Pan. Tirn. Ad poten. Invict. P. F. Aug. Vict. Thr. P. P. O. P. Maximil. II. D. S. S. Cl.* Viennae Austriae kal. Maii 1567, Wien, Österreichische Nationalbibliothek, Cod. 7284. Am Beginn steht ein neun Distichen langes Widmungsgedicht an den Kaiser. Nach der ungarischen Königsserie steht das hexametrische Gedicht (s. Anm. 19), es folgen Anmerkungen zu den Kaisern ab Friedrich III. (Geburtsdaten etc.) und zur Abstammung Maximilians mütterlicherseits.

[21] Antonii Bonfinii Rerum Ungaricarum decades quatuor cum dimidia. Basileae: ex officina Oporiniana 1568 (VD16 B 6593 und 6594); Tripartitum Opus Iuris Consuetudinarii Inclyti Regni Hungariae per spectabilem & Magnificum Dom. Stephanum de Werbewcz [István Werböczy], Personalis praesentiae regiae Maiestatis olim Locum tenentem accuratissime editum. Quarta Editio, cum Praefatione & Indice Ioan. Sambuci etc. Viennae: typis Blasii Eberi 1572 (VD16 W 1967).

14 Verse, die letztgenannte Edition hat als Schlussgedicht ein zusätzliches auf (den 1572 zum ungarischen König gekrönten) Rudolf II. (10 Verse).

Die Kaiserserie enthält Gedichte (bis auf zwei Ausnahmen Tetrastichen) auf folgende Herrscher: Rodolphus Habsp., Albertus Primus, Albertus Secund., Fridericus Tertius, Maximilian. Primus, Carolus Quintus (6 Verse), Ferdinand. Primus, Maximilianus Secundus (6 Verse).

Auch von dieser Serie gibt es eine zweite Fassung, die sich in einer ebenfalls Maximilian II. gewidmeten Handschrift findet, die in ihrem ersten Teil eine Schrift des Sambucus über die Konstantinische Schenkung enthält[22]. Wie die zweite Version der ungarischen Königsserie ist auch diese erweitert. Zwei Epigramme auf Friedrich den Schönen und Philipp den Schönen sind dazu gekommen, die ersten acht Epigramme umfassen jetzt je acht Verse, das auf Ferdinand I. zehn und das letzte Gedicht an den Widmungsträger sprengt mit seiner Länge von 36 Versen die Dimension der anderen überhaupt.

DIE GEDICHTE AN MAXIMILIAN II.[23]

Im Epigramm der Königsserie wird im ersten Vers (wie in dem der Kaiserserie) die Tugend des Kaisers gerühmt. Das zweite Distichon der ungarischen Serie vergleicht ihn mit Albrecht II.: Maximilian vereint wie Albrecht (als Herzog der fünfte seines Namens) drei Kronen auf seinem Haupt: die ungarische, böhmische und römische. Dann wird die Rettung Ungarns vor den Türken angesprochen und zum Sturm auf Byzanz gerufen (v. 5–8). Dazu wird der Beistand Christi erbeten. In der gedruckten Fassung von 1567 schließt das Epigramm mit dem Ruhm des Kaisers, der Himmel und Erde erfüllt, und der Rückkehr des goldenen Zeitalters.

Daran schließt Sambucus in der Manuskriptfassung vier weitere Verse, die sein eigenes Dichten betreffen. Das vorletzte Distichon, das sich auch in den späteren Druckfassungen findet, verspricht für die Zukunft ein episches Werk (in Hexametern: *pedibus fortibus*) über das unter Maximilian zu erwartende

---

[22] *Caess. Austrii X descripti per J. Sambucum* (1571), ÖNB, Cod. 9534, fol. 19ʳ–23ʳ. Vgl. Joseph CHMEL, *Die Handschriften der k.k. Hofbibliothek in Wien, im Interesse der Geschichte, besonders der österreichischen, verzeichnet und excerpirt.* Wien 1840/41, I (1840), 708–711 (hier sind u. a. das Rudolfepigramm und die letzten sechs Verse des Gedichts auf Maximilian II. zitiert).

[23] Texte s. Anhang.

goldene Zeitalter. Dass dies literarisches Spiel in alexandrinischer Manier ist, zeigt eine schon vorher versteckte Anspielung an Kallimachos. Vers 11 (*cantabitur orbi*) ist ein Anklang an dasjenige Distichon im Schlussgedicht von Ovids erstem Elegienbuch, wo dieser im Katalog der Dichter den Ahnherrn alexandrinischer Kleindichtung nennt: *Battiades semper toto cantabitur orbe* (Ovid, *am.* 1,15,13).

Im letzten Distichon der ungarischen Königsserie empfiehlt Sambucus sich und sein Werk seinem Herrn und bittet um seine Unterstützung.

Das erste Distichon des Schlussepigramms der Kaiserserie bringt in beiden Fassungen in jeweils variierter Form den Topos der Unmöglichkeit, den Kaiser angemessen zu rühmen. In der späteren Fassung ist der Pentameter zu einem Ovidzitat umformuliert:

> Scilicet imperii princeps statione relicta
> Imparibus legeres carmina facta modis?
>
> Ovid, *trist.* 2, 219–220

Ovid betont in seiner Verteidigungsschrift an Augustus, wie unpassend die Lektüre elegischer Dichtung, die er als törichtes Spiel bezeichnet[24], für den Herrscher ist, dessen Kräfte von Kriegen, u. a. in Pannonien[25], beansprucht sind. Daher ist es auch für Sambucus unangemessen, in elegischen Distichen die Taten Maximilians, der auch in Pannonien kämpfte, zu rühmen. Wie im Epigramm auf Maximilian in der ungarischen Königsserie betont er hier den Gegensatz seiner Kleindichtung zum Epos.

Daher (und weil die Türkengefahr noch immer nicht gebannt ist) besingt er auch nicht die Tugenden und Kriegstaten Maximilians (v. 1). Dass Sambucus in diesem Zusammenhang die Exildichtung Ovids zitiert, hat auch einen biographischen Grund. Wie Ovid befindet er sich ebenfalls in Verbannung von seiner Heimat, allerdings nicht zwangsweise im Osten bei den Skythen, sondern von den Skythen/Türken aus seiner östlichen Heimat „vertrieben". Seine Heimatstadt Trnava lag zwar nicht im türkisch besetzten Teil Ungarns, jedoch erzählt er in der Einleitung seiner Plautus-Edition[26], dass sein Vater von

---

[24] Ovid, *trist.* 2, 223 *lusibus* [...] *ineptis.*
[25] Ovid, *trist.* 2, 225 *nunc tibi Pannonia est, nunc Illyris ora domanda.*
[26] M. Accii [sic!] Plauti Comoediae viginti olim a Ioachimo Camerario emendatae nunc vero plusquam CC versibus, qui passim desiderabantur, ex VV.CC. additi suo quodammodo nitori restitutae, opera et diligentia Ioannis Sambuci Tirnaviensis Pannonii. Antverpiae: Ex

den Türken von seinen Besitzungen in Zamboc und Buda vertrieben worden war, was, wie Almási vermutet, möglicherweise eine fiktive Selbststilisierung sein könnte[27], aber gerade so unterstreicht das Ovidzitat das Bild, das er von sich zeichnen wollte.

Daran schließt sich (in der zweiten Fassung) ein Distichon, das die Furcht der Bösen vor dem Kaiser betont, die Niederlage von Aufrührern und die gottgleiche Verehrung des Kaisers in Ost und West darstellt.

Das zweite Distichon der ersten bzw. das dritte der zweiten Fassung stellt fest, der Kaiser sei schon als Knabe allen willkommen gewesen, und leitet daraus seinen Anspruch auf die Anerkennung seiner Herrschaft ab. Dabei stellt die überarbeitete Version geschickter die Parallele zwischen dem allen willkommenen Knaben und dem erwachsenen (v. 5 *adulti*) Kaiser her, für den dasselbe gelten müsste. Auch der Aspekt des Neides wird hier erst eingeführt (*invidiaque premat* gegenüber *imperiumque negat* in der ersten Version). Das Thema der Berufung zur Herrschaft und der Bedrohung derselben wird dann in sechs weiteren Versen (v. 7–12, Fassung 1571) ausgeführt: Schon in seiner Jugend vermochte er die Spanier mit Mäßigung zu lenken. Andererseits sei sein blühendes Leben oft hinterhältig bedroht worden. Der historische Hintergrund für diese Aussagen war der vergebliche Versuch Karls V., seinem Sohn Philipp die Nachfolge im Reich zu sichern: Maximilian war für die Protestanten schon als Jugendlicher wegen seiner offenkundigen Sympathien ein Hoffnungsträger. Trotzdem musste er im Heer Karls V. mit den Spaniern gegen den Schmalkaldischen Bund kämpfen und wurde anlässlich seiner Hochzeit mit Karls Tochter Maria nach Spanien geschickt, um Philipp die Möglichkeit zu verschaffen, in Deutschland Fuß zu fassen. Als Maximilian aus Spanien heimkehrte und nach einem Aufenthalt in Trient schwer erkrankte, glaubte er sogar, sein Gastgeber in der Konzilsstadt Kardinal Christoph Madruzzo habe ihn vergiftet, um sich bei Philipp beliebt zu machen[28].

Das dritte Distichon der ersten Fassung verbindet die rhetorische Frage nach der Unbesiegbarkeit des Kaisers mit dem Appell, endlich das Joch der

---

officina Christoph. Plantini 1566, A2ᵛ [Petrus Sambucus] *avitis sedibus ac bonis, quae ad oppidum Zamboc, ac ipsam Budam sita erant, eiectus* [...].

[27] ALMÁSI (s. Anm. 7), 145 mit Anm 4: „The story of the flight before the Turks and the reference to Buda was probably tailored for an Occidental readership".

[28] Viktor BIBL, *Maximilian II. Der rätselhafte Kaiser. Ein Zeitbild*. Hellerau bei Dresden 1929, 56–59; Paula SUTTER-FICHTNER, *Emperor Maximilian II*. New Haven, London 2001, 27.

Türken zu beseitigen. Dieses Herzensanliegen des ungarischen Autors wird in der erweiterten Fassung breit in 18 Versen ausgeführt. Der Anlass ist der eher unrühmliche, weil ergebnislose Kriegszug Maximilians gegen die Türken im Jahre 1566[29]. Während der für die Türken letztlich erfolgreichen Belagerung Szigets (Szigetvár) starb Sultan Süleyman, der jahrzehntelang Schrecken verbreitet hatte. Der Autor beklagt, dass die frühere Entsendung von Hilfstruppen den Fall der Festung verhindern hätte können und beschwört die Vertreibung des Tyrannen durch den Reichsadler und die Verbreitung von Frieden und Glauben über die ganze Welt. Insofern ist die Tatsache, dass Sambucus die Kriegstaten des Kaisers besingt, obwohl er am Beginn die Unangemessenheit des elegischen Versmaßes dafür betont hat, auch kein Widerspruch, da erst der zukünftige erfolgreiche Kriegszug die eines Epos würdigen Taten erhoffen lässt.

Das Gedicht schließt mit einer Sphragis des Autors (v. 31–36). Er bringt seine Verse dar, bittet um deren milde Aufnahme und verspricht dafür dem Kaiser und seiner Familie ewigen Ruhm. Diese Bitte erinnert mit wörtlichen Anklängen (*fove* [...] *Musa* [...] *recinat*) an das Ende des Gedichts der ungarischen Königsserie (*museo cantu* [...] *cani* [...] *foveat*), wo er ebenfalls seine Werke dem Kaiser empfiehlt.

Mit ähnlichen Worten (*Caesares Austrii* 1571, v. 33: *Suscipe clementer tenuis munuscula Vatis*) hatte er außerdem fast zwanzig Jahre zuvor seine Huttich-Ausgabe dem damaligen Thronfolger gewidmet:

> hunc libellum [...] clementer excipito interim, dum aliquid ipse elucubrem, tua maiestate dignum, quodque cum tuis laudibus atque gloria coniunctum sit: ac etiam cumulate tuum animum gaudio adficiat.
>
> *Romanorum Principum effigies* 1552, fol. *4ᵛ

Dieses Buch [...] nimm inzwischen milde an, bis ich selbst etwas ausarbeite, das deiner Majestät würdig ist, und das mit deinem Ruhm und deiner Ehre verbunden ist. Und es soll auch vollkommen dein Herz mit Freude erfüllen.

---

[29] V. 13ff.; vgl. BIBL (s. Anm. 28), 142–155; SUTTER-FICHTNER (s. Anm. 28), 128ff.; Eduard WERTHEIMER, Zur Geschichte des Türkenkrieges Maximilians II. 1565 und 1566. *Archiv für Österreichische Geschichte* 53 (1875), 43–101: Hier wird durch eine Depesche vom 5. September 1566 belegt, dass trotz kaiserlichen Befehls Hilfstruppen durch die Nachlässigkeit der Minister nicht rechtzeitig bei Sziget ankamen (87). Vgl. Gustav TURBA (Hg.), *Venetianische Depeschen vom Kaiserhofe (Dispacci di Germania)*. Bd. 3. Wien 1895, 346–349; hier 348.

Hat Sambucus mit seiner Kaiserserie jetzt also das versprochene Werk selbst (*ipse*) geschaffen, ein Werk, wie er es damals zwischenzeitlich (*interim*) nur als Kaiserserie anderer Autoren edieren konnte?

Sambucus bleibt den von ihm edierten Dichtern motivisch und strukturell verbunden. Wenn er in der ungarischen Königsserie Christus zum Schutz Maximilians herbeiruft (v. 9 *hunc* [...] *tuetor*), so tut er dies mit Worten, die an den ersten Vers von Micyllus' Epigramm auf Karl V. erinnern.

CAROLUS V.
Micyllus
Hunc si fata virum, si numina magna tuentur,
   Idem erit Eois Caesar, & Hesperiis.
Hoc perhibent veterum praesagia magna virorum,
   Hoc operum prae se facta priora ferunt.

Romanorum Principum effigies 1552, 180ʳ

Wenn diesen Mann das Geschick und die großen Götter beschützen, wird er Kaiser in Ost und West sein. Dies künden die großen Weissagungen alter Männer, dies offenbaren die früheren Taten seiner Unternehmungen.

Die *facta* des vierten Verses bei Micyllus wiederum scheinen ein Echo im ersten Vers des Maximiliangedichts der Kaiserserie zu haben. Die *numina magna* Micylls (v. 1) werden zu den *numina tanta* bei Sambucus im vierten Vers der zweiten Fassung der Kaiserserie, wo sich auch wie bei Micyllus (hier v. 2) das beliebte Motiv der Herrschaft der Kaiser in Ost und West findet, das ebenfalls bei den anderen beiden der von Sambucus in seiner Huttich-Ausgabe edierten zeitgenössischen Dichter, Caspar Ursinus Velius und Georg Sabinus, vorkommt[30]:

Velius
Carolus Hesperiis regnat, Fernandus Eois.
   Quam bene divisum est fratribus imperium.

Romanorum Principum effigies 1552, 180ʳ

Karl regiert im Westen, Ferdinand im Osten.
Wie gut ist die Herrschaft unter den Brüdern geteilt.

---

[30] Eine ausführliche Analyse dieses Motivs findet sich in: AMANN-BUBENIK 2013 (s. Anm. 1), 66–80.

FERDINANDUS

Hoc opus exegi florentibus integer annis,
   Bis duo cum natus lustra Sabinus eram;
Tempore quo Geticos rex Ferdinandus in hostes
   Arma, suo bellum fratre gerente tulit;
Unanimis cum quo regni moderatur habenas,   5
   Et grave terrarum sustinet orbis onus.
Vivite Semidei, concordes vivite fratres:
   Omnia sub vobis, vesper et ortus, erunt.
Vos metuat primus, vos ultimus horreat orbis:
   Vos, et si qua parum terra veretur, amet.   10

Romanorum Principum effigies 1552, 203ʳ

Dieses Werk habe ich, Sabinus, in der Blüte meiner Jahre, im Alter von 20 (d. h. 1528), vollbracht, als König Ferdinand gegen die getischen Feinde die Waffen trug, während sein Bruder (gegen Frankreich) Krieg führte. Mit ihm lenkt er einmütig die Zügel des Reichs (5) und trägt die schwere Last des Erdkreises. Lebt, Halbgötter, lebt, einträchtige Brüder, alles wird euer sein, West und Ost. Fürchten soll euch die Welt nah und fern, und wenn ein Land euch nicht fürchtet, soll es euch lieben (10).

Sambucus verwendet jedoch nicht die bei den drei Autoren vorkommenden Varianten des Motivs (*Hesperiis – Eois*[31], *vesper et ortus*[32]), sondern seine Wendung (*Ortus et occasus*) erinnert an eine Stelle im ersten Buch der *Metamorphosen*, wo sich Deucalion und Pyrrha nach der Sintflut allein auf der Erde wiederfinden, soweit sie sich dehnt von Osten nach Westen (*quasque vident occasus et ortus*, Ov. met. 1, 354). Die Sintflut steht bei Ovid im Zusammenhang mit dem Zeitaltermythos: Die Freveltaten der Menschen des eisernen Zeitalters veranlassten Jupiter, die Menschheit durch die Flut auszurotten und mit dem überlebenden Paar einen Neubeginn zu versuchen. Der Zeitaltermythos wird von Sambucus explizit im Gedicht der ungarischen Königsserie angesprochen, wo er mit Maximilian das Ende des eisernen Zeitalters und den Beginn des goldenen kommen sieht: *Ferrea nunc cessent, aurea saecla parat* (v. 12). Dies erinnert zugleich an Vergils vierte Ekloge, wo ebenfalls mit dem Ende des eisernen und dem Beginn des goldenen Zeitalters ein Neubeginn, symbolisiert durch die Geburt eines Knaben, verbunden ist.

---

[31] Vgl. Properz, *eleg.* 2, 3, 43f.; Ovid, *am.* 1, 15, 29.
[32] Vgl. Ovid, *ars* 3, 724; *Ib.* 38.

> Tu modo nascenti puero, quo ferrea primum
> Desinet ac toto surget gens aurea mundo,
> Casta fave Lucina:
>
> Vergil, ecl. 4, 8–10

Nicht ohne daran zu denken, wird Sambucus in der Kaiserserie Maximilian als *puer exoptatus* (v. 3 bzw. 5) bezeichnet haben.

Die Kombination des Motivs der Herrschaft bzw. der Verehrung eines Herrschers in Ost und West und der Furcht vor diesem (*te metuunt pravi*) übernimmt Sambucus ebenfalls vom Ferdinandgedicht des Sabinus (*vos metuat*[33]), allerdings verschiebt Sambucus den Akzent hier in Richtung der „Bösen", der Feinde, die sich vor Maximilian fürchten: Damit sind, wie in der Folge ausgeführt, natürlich vor allem die Türken gemeint.

Diese Motive finden sich schon in einem Gedicht an Ferdinand I. (*In optatissimum Divi Caesaris Ferdinandi Viennam reditum*, Abb. S. 270), das Sambucus in den Anhang seiner eigenen Prosabeschreibung der Belagerung von Sziget des Jahres 1556 stellte, die damals für die Türken noch nicht erfolgreich verlief[34]:

> Aurea sub te mox, Princeps, o secla redibunt,
>   Ultima nec primis deteriora manent.
> Enses agricolae demptum (demum?) vertentur in usum,
>   Vomer erit, gladius qui modo acutus erat.   20
> Te metuent, cordi quibus est patrare nefanda,
>   Sub teque invicto vesper, et ortus erunt.
>
> Obsidio Zigethiensis 1558, A5ᵛ

O, das goldene Zeitalter wird bald unter dir, Fürst, zurückkehren, das letzte, nicht schlechter als das erste, und es wird bleiben. Die Langschwerter werden endlich zum Gebrauch des Bauern umgewandelt[35], (20) zum Pflug wird, was gerade noch ein spitzes Schwert war. Dich werden die fürchten, die planen Frevlerisches auszuführen, und unter dir, der du unbesiegt bist, wird Westen und Osten sein.

---

[33] Vgl. Ovid, *fast.* I, 717f. *horreat Aeneadas et primus et ultimus orbis: / siqua parum Romam terra timebat, amet.*

[34] *Obsidio Zigethiensis Ann. MDLVI. descripta per Ioan. Sambucum Tirnavien. Pannonium.* Viennae Austriae: excudebat Raphael Hofhalter 1558 (VD16 S 1554), A5ᵛ.

[35] Das vom Druck gebotene *demptum* („zum Gebrauch des Bauern, der ihm im Krieg genommen war"?) ergibt wenig Sinn; angesichts der anderen Druckfehler bietet sich die Korrektur zu *demum* an.

Das strukturbildende, die Gedichtserie des Sambucus abschließende Element der Sphragis, der Selbstvorstellung mit der Nennung des eigenen Namens, und der Verweis auf das vorgelegte Werk findet sich wie die oben genannten anderen Elemente ebenfalls im Ferdinandgedicht des Sabinus:

> Hoc opus exegi[36] florentibus integer annis,
> Bis duo cum natus lustra Sabinus eram;

Sambucus jedoch betont stärker sein Klientenverhältnis zu Maximilian: *Suscipe clementer tenuis munuscula Vatis [...] Sambuci [...] clientis.* Die *munuscula* erinnern einerseits wieder an die vierte Ekloge Vergils, wo dem Knaben die Erde ihre Gaben darbringt (v. 18–20: *At tibi prima puer nullo munuscula cultu [...] tellus [...] fundet).* Der Versschluss *munuscula Vatis* zitiert aber auch den Beginn eines Gedichtes des Porcelio (Giannantonio de' Pandoni) an Janus Pannonius, das Sambucus 1569 ediert hatte[37]:

> Ad Ianum Pannonium Quinque Ecclesiarum Episcopum Porcellus Poeta
> Sume pater divine tui munuscula Vatis
>   Quae veniunt patriis aurea mala locis.
> [...]
> Munere sis liceat maiori dignus, et auro:
>
>   Ianus Pannonius, Opera 1569, 123ᵛ

Nimm, göttlicher Vater, die Geschenke deines Dichters, goldene Äpfel, die aus den väterlichen Gefilden kommen. [...] Magst du auch eines größeren Geschenks und Goldes würdig sein [...]

Darauf antwortet Janus Pannonius Porcelio, dass seine Gaben wertvoller seien als Gold und Edelsteine:

> Ianus Porcelio Poetae
> Misisti nobis et mala et carmina Vates,
> [...]
> Mala aurum superant, et vincunt carmina gemmas:
>   Aurum da et gemmas, deteriora dabis.
>
>   Ianus Pannonius, Opera 1569, 124ʳ

---

[36] Vgl. Ovid, *met.* 15, 871.
[37] Iani Pannonii Episcopi Quinqueeccles. illius antiquis vatibus comparandi, recentioribus certe anteponendi, quae uspiam reperiri adhuc potuerunt, omnia. Opera Ioannis Sambuci Cons. et Hist. Caesar. Viennae Austriae: ex officina Caspari Stainhoferi 1569 (VD16 ZV 24520), 123ᵛ.

Du hast uns, Dichter, Äpfel und Gedichte geschickt, [...]. Die Äpfel übertreffen Gold, die Gedichte besiegen Edelsteine: Gib Gold und Edelsteine, und du wirst Geringeres geben.

Welche Funktion haben also die *munuscula Vatis* bei Sambucus? Er bringt im Gegensatz zu Porcelio nur seine Dichtung dar, keine Früchte der Erde, er konzentriert sich auf die politische Botschaft. Einige Verse zuvor hat er ja schon ebenfalls mit einem Anklang an die vierte Ekloge prophezeit: *Pax et relligio totum fundentur* (ecl. 4, 20: *fundet*) *in orbem* (Vgl. *ecl.* 4, 17: *pacatum reget patriis virtutibus orbem*). Sambucus kann keine Früchte aus seiner väterlichen Heimat darbringen, weil er aus dieser vertrieben ist (wie so manche Hirten in den Eklogen Vergils).

Sambucus löst sein Versprechen aus der *Praefatio* der Huttichedition von 1552 insofern ein, als er eigene Werke darbringt, aber es sind noch keine epischen. So wie der Kaiser zwar Großes leistet, von Tag zu Tag mehr (*in dies plura*), so wachsen auch die Gedichte des Sambucus:

> Interea tu Macte animo, elabora, ut in dies de te plura narrari, atque in literas mitti possint, quae ad posterorum cognitionem transmittantur.
>
> *Romanorum Principum effigies* 1552 (s. Anm. 3), *4ᵛ

Inzwischen – gesegnet sei dein Mut – gib dir Mühe, damit von Tag zu Tag mehr von dir erzählt und der Schrift anvertraut werden kann, was der Kenntnis der Nachwelt überliefert werde.

Erst wenn die Türken vertrieben sind, wird Sambucus wirklich sein Versprechen[38] einlösen können, Würdiges zu dichten.

FUNKTIONEN UND INHALTE DER DICHTUNG DES SAMBUCUS

Janus Pannonius behandelt die Frage nach dem Wert der Dichtung. Die heutige Forschung stellt die Frage nach den Funktionen des Humanismus[39]. Almási nennt als einige Kernpunkte der zitierten *Praefatio* des Sambucus in seiner Huttich-Edition, die er als historisches Werk sah, den Wunsch als

---

[38] Versprechen dieser Art sind natürlich immer im Rahmen der alexandrinisch-römischen Recusatiotopik zu sehen. Vgl. Walter WIMMEL, *Kallimachos in Rom. Die Nachfolge seines apologetischen Dichtens in der Augusteerzeit*. Wiesbaden 1960 (*Hermes Einzelschriften* 16).

[39] Thomas MAISSEN, Gerrit WALTHER (Hgg.), *Funktionen des Humanismus. Studien zum Nutzen des Neuen in der humanistischen Kultur*. Göttingen 2006.

Klient angenommen zu werden und als ‚Pannonier' Maximilian daran zu erinnern, die Türken zu bekämpfen[40]. Von den vier thematischen Schwerpunkten, die Huber-Rebenich[41] bei den Funktionen der Dichtung im Humanismus unterscheidet, sind hier zwei zu nennen:

1) „Öffentlichkeitsarbeit und Meinungsbildung" – in dieser Kategorie finden sich die politischen Kernfunktionen panegyrischer Dichtung: Die Dichtung bringt Ruhm, Ansehen und Stabilität der Herrschaft, der Dichter hingegen profitiert durch das Mäzenatentum des Herrschers.

2) „Nationalgefühl und patriotische Gesinnung" – Nation sei hier im Sinne einer humanistischen (deutschen) Kulturnation zu verstehen, aber auch Türkenfeindschaft und Treue zum Kaiser spielen eine Rolle[42]. Leitfigur ist hier Conrad Celtis, der z. B. im ersten Gedicht seines ersten Odenbuchs unter Kaiser Friedrich III. die goldene Zeit mit der griechisch-römischen Kultur bei den deutschen Völkern wiederkehren sieht[43].

Bei Sambucus finden sich dieselben Elemente unter ungarisch ‚nationalen' Vorzeichen wieder, diese Harmonisierung war durch die Personalunion der Habsburger als Kaiser und ungarische Könige möglich. Das wiederholt formulierte Anliegen der Türkenabwehr lag außerdem im allgemeinen Interesse des Reichs, für Ungarn hatte es aber noch weitaus existentiellere Bedeutung.

Als Sambucus 1566 Hofhistoriograph wurde, war es seine erste große Aufgabe, das im ‚goldenen Zeitalter' Ungarns unter Matthias Corvinus entstandene Geschichtswerk des Antonio Bonfini, der den Einfluss Italiens und Deutschlands auf die ungarische Kultur betont[44], zu veröffentlichen und ihm

---

[40] S. Anm. 7, hier 147f.
[41] Gerlinde HUBER-REBENICH, Neue Funktionen der Dichtung im Humanismus? In: *Funktionen des Humanismus* (s. Anm. 39), 49–75.
[42] Vgl. Ulrich MUHLACK, Das Projekt der *Germania illustrata*. Ein Paradigma der Diffusion des Humanismus? In: Johannes Helmrath, Ulrich Muhlack, Gerrit Walther (Hgg.), *Diffusion des Humanismus. Studien zur nationalen Geschichtsschreibung europäischer Humanisten*. Göttingen 2002, 142–158, hier 148.
[43] Conradus Celtis Protucius, *Libri odarum quattuor. Liber epodon. Carmen saeculare.* Edidit Felicitas PINDTER. Leipzig 1937 (*Bibliotheca scriptorum medii recentisque aevorum. Saecula XV–XVI* 7), 1f. Vgl. Conrad Celtis, *Oden, Epoden, Jahrhundertlied. Libri odarum quattuor, cum epodo et saeculari carmine.* Übers. und hg. von Eckart SCHÄFER. Tübingen 2008 (*Neolatina* 16).
[44] László HAVAS, Sebestyén KISS, Die Geschichtskonzeption Antonio Bonfinis. In: *Diffusion des Humanismus* (s. Anm. 42), 281–307, hier 302.

dabei seine anti-habsburgische Schärfe zu nehmen[45]. Die ungarische Königsserie steht in engem Zusammenhang mit dieser Edition[46]. Mit dieser überträgt er das bewährte Modell der Kaiserserie auf die ungarische Geschichte und legitimiert so in poetischer Form den Anspruch der Habsburger auf den ungarischen Thron.

Dies und die Anspielung an die Gedichte mit Goldsymbolik an und von Janus Pannonius, der eine Leitfigur der Blütezeit der ungarischen Renaissance war und dessen Werk *Eranemus* Sambucus gemeinsam mit dem Erstdruck der Königsserie publizierte, unterstreichen die Erwartung einer Wiederkehr des goldenen Zeitalters, diesmal unter dem Habsburger Maximilian II.

Hier zeigt sich auch, wie wichtig für die Funktionen die Inhalte humanistischer Dichtung sind[47]. Die genannten Beispiele augusteischer Dichtung bieten dem Dichter die Möglichkeit, die Gegenwart zu deuten. Die Erfahrungen von Exil, Vertreibung, Krieg und der Zeitaltermythos mit der Hoffnung auf Frieden sind archetypische Modelle, die Sambucus für sich, sein Land und den Landesherrn fruchtbar macht.

---

[45] ALMÁSI (s. Anm. 7), 172ff.
[46] *Dum nova Bonfini* [...] *prodeat editio, versiculos* [...] *hosce rudes mitto* (Widmung an Franciscus Forgach): Reges Ungariae 1567 (s. Anm. 17), A1ᵛ.
[47] Vgl. Thomas MAISSEN, Schlußwort. Überlegungen zu Funktionen und Inhalt des Humanismus. In: *Funktionen des Humanismus* (s. Anm. 39), 396–402.

ANHANG: TEXTE ÜBER MAXIMILIAN II.

I. Aus der ungarischen Königsserie (Manuskriptfassung 1567):

MAXIMILIAN. SECUNDUS regnat in 4. ann.

Armipotens superat virtutibus, ore verendo,
    Asserit invicta regia sceptra fide.
Albertum praeter Quintum diadema quis umquam
    Mense triplex sexto vertice, quaeso, tulit?
Ungaricam redamat gentem, mirantur, honorant[48]   5
    Externi poscunt rite patrocinium.
Strenuus Europae decus hic reparabit, et usque[49]
    Byzantii ad muros saepe patebit iter.
Hunc fidum populo custodem Christe tuetor,[50]
    Semper inoffense iura ministret herus.   10
Laudibus implebit coelum, cantabitur orbi:
    Ferrea nunc cessent, aurea saecla parat.
Quae tempus dederit museo dicere cantu,
    Nam pedibus cupiunt fortibus illa cani.
Huic ego me domino commendo meosque labores,   15
    Ut foveat large nocte dieque precor.[51]

Caesares Austrii et Reges Ungariae, ÖNB, Cod. 7284, fol. 19ᵛ–20ʳ

II. Aus der Kaiserserie, 1. Fassung (1567)

Maximilianus Secundus.

Non ego laudabo virtutes, inclyta facta
    Nec possum verbis commemorare suis.
Tu cunctis fueras puer exoptatus amicus,
    Quis reicit fasces, imperiumque negat?
Auspiciis celebri quid non Victoria tradet?   5
    Tu Scythicum solus denique solve iugum.

Caesares Austrii et Reges Ungariae, ÖNB, Cod. 7284, fol. 5ᵛ

---

[48] Druckfassung 1567 (s. Anm. 17): *Ungaricam redamat gentem, hunc mirantur, honorant.*
[49] Druckfassung 1567 (s. Anm. 17), Bonfini- und Werböczy-Ausgabe (s. Anm 21): *Impiger Europae decus hic reparabit, et usque.*
[50] Druckfassung 1567 (s. Anm. 17): *Hunc populo fidum custodem Christe tuere.*
[51] V. 13–16 fehlen im Druck von 1567; v. 15–16 in der Bonfini- und Werböczy-Ausgabe.

I. Aus der ungarischen Königsserie (Manuskriptfassung 1567)

MAXIMILIAN II. im vierten Jahr seiner Regierung.

Tapfer obsiegt er mit seinen Tugenden, seinem ehrwürdigen Antlitz,
er behauptet mit unerschütterlicher Treue das Königsszepter.
Wer bitte, außer Albrecht V., trug jemals das dreifache Diadem
im sechsten Monat auf seinem Haupt?
Er erwidert die Liebe des ungarischen Volks, im Exil bewundern und ehren   5
sie ihn und fordern zu Recht Schutz.
Entschlossen wird er die Ehre Europas wiederherstellen, und bis hin zu
den Mauern von Byzanz wird der Weg oft frei sein.
Ihn bewahre, Christus, als treuen Wächter dem Volk.
Ungehindert soll er immer als Herr Recht sprechen.   10
Mit Lobpreisungen wird er den Himmel erfüllen, auf dem Erdkreis wird er
                                      besungen werden.
Das eiserne Zeitalter soll jetzt weichen, er bereitet das goldene vor,
die Zeit mag es geben, dieses Zeitalter im Musengesang zu verkünden,
denn es verlangt danach im starken Versmaß besungen zu werden.
Ihm als Herrn empfehle ich mich und meine Mühen   15
und bitte, dass er sie reichlich hege Tag und Nacht.

II. Aus der Kaiserserie, 1. Fassung (1567)

Maximilian II.

Ich werde nicht die Tugenden, die berühmten Taten loben,
nicht kann ich es mit gehörigen Worten erzählen.
Du warst als Knabe allen ein erwünschter Freund gewesen,
wer weist die Macht zurück und leugnet die Herrschaft?
Was wird Victoria dem durch Vorzeichen Berühmten nicht geben?   5
Beseitige du allein endlich das skythische Joch.

III. Aus der Kaiserserie, 2. Fassung (1571)

MAXIMILL. II.

Non ego cantabo virtutes, Martia facta
  Imparibus nequeunt illa vigere modis.
Te metuunt pravi, tot succubuere rebelles,
  Ortus et occasus numina tanta colit.
Tu fueras cunctis puer exoptatus, adulti   5
  Quis renuat fasces invidiaque premat?
Hesperios noras iuvenis moderamine Hiberos
  Et regere et socio continuisse gravi.
Praeterea quoties vita in discrimine florens
  Et fuit indignis illa petita dolis?   10
Erranti quoties venatibus improba turba
  Struxit hero extremas, proh scelus, insidias?
Quos equites nuper, pedites in Pannonis oras
  Duxisti, ut posses conseruisse manus?
Nempe tuis castris Solymanus cedere tentans   15
  Occidit, in dubio cetera turba fuit.
Ulterius nec sunt ausi infestare colonos,
  Finibus egressi disperiere fame.
Tertia vix reliqua est illis pars facta superstes,
  Complebunt numerum vix tria lustra suum.   20
O utinam potior, quod tu, comitatus inisset
  Consilium, Zygeth libera, tuta foret.
Sed nil negligitur curis, mora cuncta rependet,
  Victori veniet iam duplicatus honos.
Auspiciis celebri quid non eventa parabunt,   25
  Tu Scythici solves vincla repente iugi.
Lunatum vertat Iovis ales sede tyrannum,
  Conscia nec sacrum stella moratur opus.
Pax et relligio totum fundentur in orbem,
  Ulla nec offendet gens aliena tuos.   30
Hos ego versiculos cum Maiestatis honore,
  Imperii et dignis fascibus ecce fero.
Suscipe clementer tenuis munuscula Vatis,
  Atque fove digna Principe dexter ope.
Sic te, sicque tuos Sambuci Musa clientis   35
  Aeterna recinat posteritate Duces.

Caesares Austrii, ÖNB, Cod. 9534, fol. 21ᵛ–23ʳ

III. Aus der Kaiserserie, 2. Fassung (1571)
MAXIMILIAN II.
Nicht werde ich die Tugenden und Kriegstaten besingen,
diese können im ungleichen Versmaß nicht in ihrer Stärke zeigen.
Dich fürchten die Bösen, so viele Aufrührer unterlagen.
Ost und West verehrt eine so große Gottheit.
Du warst als Knabe allen erwünscht gewesen, 5
wer wird die Macht des Erwachsenen ablehnen und neidisch bedrängen?
Du wusstest als Jüngling mit Mäßigung die Iberer im Westen zu lenken
und mit dem schwierigen Gefährten im Zaum zu halten.
Wie oft war außerdem das blühende Leben in Gefahr
und durch unwürdige Arglist bedroht? 10
Wie oft bereitete die ruchlose Schar dem auf der Jagd herumschweifenden
Herrn, welch Verbrechen, einen lebensbedrohlichen Hinterhalt?
Welche Reiter hast du neulich, welche Fußtruppen nach Pannonien
geführt, um den Kampf beginnen zu können?
Freilich fiel Soliman beim Versuch in dein Lager einzudringen, 15
die übrige Schar war schwankend.
Weiter wagten sie die Siedler nicht zu belästigen.
Sie gingen aus ihrem Gebiet und starben an Hunger.
Kaum blieb ihnen ein Drittel über,
kaum werden 15 Jahre ihre Zahl wieder auffüllen. 20
Oh hätte doch der Hofstaat[52] eher denselben Entschluss wie du gefasst,
Sziget wäre frei und sicher.
Aber nichts wird von deiner Sorge vernachlässigt, die Zeit wird alles aufwiegen,
dem Sieger wird doppelte Ehre zuteil.
Was wird der Ausgang nicht dem durch Vorzeichen Berühmten bereiten, 25
du wirst sofort die Fesseln des skythischen Jochs lösen.
Jupiters Vogel möge den Tyrannen mit dem Halbmond aus seinem Sitz vertreiben,
und nicht hält der wissende Stern das heilige Werk auf.
Friede und Gottesfurcht werden sich über die ganze Welt ergießen,
und kein fremdes Volk wird die Deinen verletzen. 30
Siehe, diese Verslein mit der Ehre der Majestät
und der würdigen Macht des Reiches bringe ich dar.
Nimm milde an das Geschenk des geringen Dichters
und steh gnädig bei mit der eines Fürsten würdigen Macht.
So soll dich und deine Herzöge in ewiger Zukunft
die Muse deines Klienten Sambucus besingen. 35

---

[52] Vgl. Anm. 29.

Latein und Nationalsprachen im ersten Gespräch von Johannes Sambucus, *De imitatione Ciceroniana*

DANIEL ŠKOVIERA (Bratislava – Trnava)

EPITAPHIVM GENEROSI ADO-
lescentis Georgij Bonæ Transyluani, tan-
quam fratris, qui obijt M. D. LIX. ætatis
suæ XX. VI. Septemb.

Ὤλεθ' ἅπασ' ἀρετὴ πάτρας λιπόκοσμος ὁ Βῶνα,
 Θαῦμα χρισογενῶν τῶν φίλος ἔσκε Θεῶν.
Ἥρπασε τὖ᾽ ἴον πανδαμάτωρ μοῖρ᾽ οὐκ ἀέκοντος
 Αὐτοῦ ἐπ᾽ ἀίδιον, κὴ τριπόθητον ὄναρ.
Ὅν φίλοι, ὀρφανικὸς σὺν πᾶσιν ὀδύρετ᾽ οἶκος,
 Ἥ῾ Ἰητὴς κήπου φεῦξεν ὁδ᾽ ἀθερίη.
Τὴν σοφίαν μεγάλην, πραπίδας, κὴ τὰς μελεδῶνας
 Ἥ῾ μῖν λυσιπόνῳ θυμὸς ἐν ἡσυχίᾳ.
Εὐσεβέων ἥν παῖς ἀγαθὸς, πῇ κρείσσον᾽ ὁπηδεῖ,
 Ἀενάῳ συνέδρῳ νέκταει, καμβροσίᾳ.
Νείοθι ᾗ πέτρης τὸν ἀδωροδόκητον ἀκεσὴν
 Προσδέκετ᾽ κειτὴν, τῷ πλέον᾽ ὅσσ᾽ ἀνέφυ.

EPITAPHIUM GENEROSI ADOLESCENTIS GEORGII BONAE.
Johannes Sambucus, Emblemata et aliquot nummi antiqui operis.
Antverpiae: ex officina Christophori Plantini 1566, 197
(Wien, Universitätsbibliothek I 125.521)

Der gebürtige Tyrnauer Johannes Sambucus (1531–1584) war in der slowakischen Forschung lange abwesend. Es gab mehrere Ursachen für unsere beschämende Ignoranz, doch an erster Stelle stand meiner Meinung nach die Tatsache, dass die dezimierten geisteswissenschaftlichen Fächer in den Jahren nach dem Zweiten Weltkrieg und besonders nach der Machtübernahme durch die kommunistische Partei gezwungen waren, ihre ‚Verbindung mit dem Volk' zu demonstrieren. In der politischen Phraseologie war das Volk bekanntlich der Souverän und das Volkstümliche wurde forciert. Unsere Republik trug sogar die Bezeichnung ‚volksdemokratisch'. Der Aufbau des Sozialismus, jener Weg in die helle Zukunft, war als Kampf zwischen den Kräften des Fortschritts und denen der Reaktion inszeniert. Es existierte sogar eine Sprache des Fortschritts und Friedens und auf der anderen Seite die rückständige Sprache der Reaktion; die erste war das Russische, die andere Latein. Latein als Medium des elitären Kosmopolitismus und der Kirche war durch die Schulreform der endvierziger Jahre de facto abgeschafft. Die zwei klassischen Philologen an der Comenius Universität Bratislava, Miloslav Okál (1913–1997)[1] und Július Špaňár (1917–2007), waren mit der Verteidigung ihres wissenschaftlichen Faches völlig ausgelastet. Das Studium der Antike mussten sie mit ihrer Fortschrittlichkeit rechtfertigen; diese sollte durch Demokratie in der Staatsverwaltung, durch volkstümliche Elemente in Kunst und Literatur und besonders durch den Materialismus der antiken Philosophen verkörpert werden.

Die Tatsache, dass der Kosmopolit Johannes Sambucus lange Jahrzehnte außerhalb des Blickfeldes der slowakischen Philologen blieb, kann man nicht ohne den Kontext jener simplifizierten Ideen und der Öffentlichkeit servier-

---

[1] Daniel ŠKOVIERA, *Miloslav Okál. Prvý slovenský profesor klasickej filológie* [Miloslav Okál. Der erste slowakische Professor für Klassische Philologie]. Bratislava 2013, sowie die Beiträge im Sammelband Daniel ŠKOVIERA, Jana GRUSKOVÁ, Ľudmila BUZÁSSYOVÁ (Hgg.), *Klasický filológ Miloslav Okál* [Der klassische Philologe Miloslav Okál]. Bratislava 2014. Zur Situation der Klassischen Philologie unter dem Kommunismus auch Ľudmila BUZÁSSYOVÁ, Classical Philology in Slovakia during the Communist Period. In: György Karsai, Gábor Klaniczay, David Movrin, Elżbieta Olechowska (eds.), *Classics and Communism: Greek and Latin behind the Iron Curtain*. Ljubljana u. a. 2013, 129–140.

ten Klischees begreifen. Die erste und bis heute einzige slowakische Monographie über Sambucus erschien erst im Jahre 1975. Ihr Autor war kein Altphilologe, sondern ein Historiker. Anton Vantuch, Mitarbeiter des Historischen Instituts der Slowakischen Akademie der Wissenschaften, versuchte in seinem Buch *Johannes Sambucus. Leben und Werk eines Renaissance-Gelehrten*[2] ein komplexes Porträt seiner Persönlichkeit darzubieten. In seinem bisher unübertroffenen Werk sind auch Angaben über den Philologen Sambucus vorhanden. Anton Vantuch (1921–2001) hatte überhaupt ein bemerkenswert breites Feld von Interessen, und die slowakische Öffentlichkeit kennt ihn auch als Übersetzer französischer Fachliteratur und Belletristik[3]. Trotz seiner langjährigen Zusammenarbeit mit Hans Gerstinger, dem österreichischen Kenner der Persönlichkeit und des Werkes von Johannes Sambucus[4], musste er am Schluss seines Vorwortes beklagen, dass es ihm bei der Arbeit nicht möglich war, von den Wiener Archiven und Bibliotheken Gebrauch zu machen.

Unter den zeitgenössischen Literaturwissenschaftlern hat Zuzana Kákošová den bedeutendsten Beitrag zur Rückkehr von Sambucus in das slowakische Kulturbewusstsein geleistet. Die Dozentin an der Comenius Universität Bratislava, die sich auf die Geschichte der älteren slowakischen Literatur, das heißt auf das Schrifttum vor dem Jahre 1780, spezialisierte, konzentrierte sich auf den Dichter Sambucus. Die Ergebnisse ihrer Forschung fasste sie in der Studie *The Emblems of Ján Sambucus; an Interpretation of selected Emblems* (1995) zusammen[5]. In der erst kürzlich erschienenen Monographie *Lateinische humanistische Dichtung des 16. Jahrhunderts im Kontext der slowakischen Literatur*[6] finden sich weitere Forschungsresultate. Die zent-

---

[2] Anton VANTUCH, *Ján Sambucus. Život a dielo renesančného učenca* [Leben und Werk eines Renaissancegelehrten]. Bratislava 1975; deutsche Zusammenfassung: 243–246.

[3] Zu Biographie und Publikationen: Literárne informačné centrum. Informácie zo súčasnej slovenskej literatúry <http://www.litcentrum.sk/slovenski-spisovatelia/anton-vantuch> (19. 12. 2016).

[4] Zur Ausgabe Hans GERSTINGER, *Die Briefe des Johannes Sambucus, 1554–1584*. Wien 1968, trug Vantuch mit einem Anhang von insgesamt 28 Briefen bei: *Die Sambucusbriefe im Kreisarchiv von Trnava*, 325–356.

[5] *Graecolatina et Orientalia* 23–24 (1995), 85–93.

[6] Zuzana KÁKOŠOVÁ, *Latinská humanistická poézia 16. storočia v kontexte slovenskej literatúry* [Lateinische humanistische Dichtung des 16. Jahrhunderts im Kontext der slowakischen Literatur]. Bratislava 2010; englische Zusammenfassung 141.

rale Gestalt dieses Buches ist der lateinische Dichter Sambucus und das Verdienst ihrer Forschung kann man in folgenden vier Punkten formulieren: 1° Sambucus' Dichtung ist wirkliche Poesie; 2° sie ist formal fast vollkommen; 3° sie beinhaltet gewichtige Ideen; 4° sie ist europäisch orientiert, doch nicht abseits des damaligen ungarischen, bzw. geographisch gesehen, slowakischen Literaturlebens.

Zum Objekt des Forschungsinteresses der Philologen wurde Sambucus unmittelbar nach der Veröffentlichung der Vantuch-Monographie und zwar auf Initiative von Professor Okál[7]. Am Lehrstuhl für Klassische und Semitische Philologie an der Philosophischen Fakultät der Comenius-Universität wurden im akademischen Jahr 1977/78 zwei Diplomarbeiten präsentiert und verteidigt. Zuzana Šmatláková (verheiratet Kákošová) analysierte die Gedichtsammlung *Poemata*, Darina Hrubcová beschäftigte sich mit der Urfassung des Dialogs *De imitatione Ciceroniana*. Die heute bereits verlorengegangene maschinschriftliche Arbeit von Hrubcová war der erste und – man kann es nicht verschweigen – nicht ganz erfolgreiche Versuch, tiefer in die Bedeutungsstrukturen dieses anspruchsvollen Dialogs einzudringen.

Die Arbeit fand keine Fortsetzung, bis in der Editionsreihe *Bibliothek der slowakischen Literatur* (*Knižnica slovenskej literatúry*) im Jahre 2009 der Band *Lateinischer Humanismus*[8] erschien. Er beinhaltet die ins Slowakische übersetzten Werke von bedeutenden Humanistengelehrten, die in der Zeitspanne von 1480 bis 1580 tätig waren. Der Band bestätigte *ipso facto*, dass das lateinische Schrifttum in der slowakischen Literatur das Bürgerrecht genießen kann. Der Band *Lateinischer Humanismus*, der dreiundzwanzigste in der genannten Serie, enthält ausgewählte komplette Werke von acht Autoren, also nicht nur von einem. Der Text *De imitatione Ciceroniana* ist die einzige Ausnahme. Die Anthologie bietet nämlich nur die Übersetzung des ersten Dialogs. Widmen wir uns jetzt diesem Text.

Auch wenn wir den Text *De imitatione Ciceroniana* nur oberflächlich lesen, können wir klare und beabsichtigte Parallelen mit Ciceros Dialog *De oratore* nicht übersehen. Zuallererst wird die Ähnlichkeit durch die trichotomische

---

[7] Vgl. Iván LÁBAJ, Ján Sambucus v prácach Miloslava Okála. In: Škoviera, Grusková, Buzássyová, *Klasický filológ Miloslav Okál* (s. Anm. 1), 197–208.

[8] *Latinský humanizmus*. Auswahl und Nachwort von Daniel ŠKOVIERA. Übersetzung Jana Balegová, Ľudmila Buzássyová, Miloslav Okál, Daniel Škoviera. Bratislava 2008.

Makrostruktur der Erörterung signalisiert. Im ersten Gespräch wirft Sambucus die Frage auf, ob das Phänomen, nämlich das Imitieren, überhaupt existiert und ob es erforschbar ist; und nach einer positiven Antwort beschäftigt er sich mit den Beweggründen des Nachahmens und dessen Nützlichkeit. Der zweite Dialog thematisiert die Gattungen und die Wahl jener Gattung, die die größte Aufmerksamkeit verdient. Im dritten Dialog wird der Arbeitsplan eines Latinisten konkretisiert, der sich vornahm, die ausgewählten vorbildlichen Autoren nachzuahmen und mit ihnen den Wettbewerb aufzunehmen. Der vollkommene Imitator soll also dem vollkommenen Redner fast ebenbürtig sein[9].

Die Verbindung zu *De oratore* lässt sich auch auf der Ebene der Mikrostrukturen erkennen. Die Übernahme von Sentenzen wie z. B. *stilus est dicendi effector ac magister* (*De imitatione Ciceroniana* 4^r) nach *De oratore* I, 150 *Stilus optimus et praestantissimus dicendi effector ac magister* oder *omnium laude cumulatus orator* (*De imitatione Ciceroniana* 26^v = *De oratore* I, 20) zielte bestimmt auf einen solchen Effekt ab. Aus Ciceros Spruch *De oratore* 3, 178 *luna accessu et recessu solis lumen accipiat* („durch seine Annäherung und Entfernung empfängt der Mond das Licht der Sonne") entsteht zweifelsohne das poetische Bild, in dem Sambucus die Beziehung zwischen dem Schein des Mondes und dem der Sonne mit dem Nachahmen des gewählten Ideals vergleicht:

[…] qui summum et studiorum praecipuum suum ducem eum deligunt ac se Lunae assimilant, quae quo magis Soli appropinquat, etiamsi nobis non videatur, plus accipit luminis.

De imitatione Ciceroniana 1561, 21^v

[…] diejenigen, die ihn für den größten und wichtigsten Führer ihrer Studien wählen, werden dem Mond ähnlich; auch dieser nämlich – auch wenn es uns nicht so vorkommt – gewinnt umso mehr Licht, je mehr er sich der Sonne nähert.

---

[9] Im Folgenden wird nach der Erstausgabe zitiert: De imitatione Ciceroniana dialogi tres auctore Joan(ne) Sambuco Tirnaviense Pannonio. Parisiis: apud Aegidium Gobinum sub insigne Spei prope Collegium Cameracense 1561. Die Zweitausgabe erfolgte unter leicht geändertem Titel: Ioannis Sambuci Tirnaviens. De imitatione a Cicerone petenda dialogi tres, nunc recogniti et aucti. Antverpiae: excudebat Libertus Malcotius 1563; der Text wurde weitgehend revidiert, etwa um 30 % erweitert, öfters um griechische Zitate und antike Exempel bereichert, ohne jedoch die Argumentation geändert zu haben.

Dem Vergleich des Bildungsprozesses mit der Wirkung der Sonne auf die menschliche Haut liegt als Vorbild Ciceros ähnliches Bild zugrunde:

qui cum diu in sole versati sunt, et colorati, etiam si tecto recipiantur, quandam adustionis prae se ferunt notam.
Sambucus, *De imitatione Ciceroniana* 1561, 14ʳ

ut, cum in sole ambulem, etiam si ego aliam ob causam ambulem, fieri natura tamen, ut colorer, sic, cum istos libros ad Misenum – nam Romae vix licet – studiosius legerim, sentio illorum tactu orationem meam quasi colorari.
Cicero, *De oratore* 2, 60

Wie ich bei einem Spaziergang in der Sonne, auch wenn ich aus einem anderen Grunde spazieren gehe, trotzdem naturgemäß Farbe bekomme, so bekomme meine Rede, wie ich wahrnehme, dadurch dass ich diese Bücher bei Misenum – denn in Rom ist es mir kaum vergönnt – recht aufmerksam lese, durch die Auseinandersetzung mit ihnen gewissermaßen Farbe.[10]

Ciceronisch ist auch die Lokalisierung der Debatte in ein ungestörtes Milieu außerhalb der Stadt und zugleich in eine ungünstige politische Lage. In *De oratore* verläuft der Diskurs über den Meister der Rednerkunst in der Tuskulaner *villa* während der *ludi Romani* im September des Jahres 91 vor Chr., d. h. am Vorabend des Todes des Protagonisten Lucius Crassus und der Bürgerkriege. Sambucus führt das Gespräch am Fuße der malerischen Hügel unweit von Padua in einer höchst ungünstigen Zeit für seine Heimat, *tempore alienissimo patriae*. Was wollte der Verfasser durch diesen Ausdruck andeuten? Die politische Zersetzung infolge des innerungarischen Streites um den königlichen Thron zwischen Ferdinand und den Anhängern des Johann Sigismund Szapolyai (slowakisch Zápoľský)? Oder meinte er eher das militärische Vordringen der Türken, konkret die Belagerung der Burg Szigetvár im Jahre 1556, über die Sambucus ein Werk herausgab[11]? Man kann jedoch auch nicht ausschließen, dass die Parallele zu den Bürgerkriegen Roms den katholisch-protestantischen Zwist im Land darstellte.

De imitatione Ciceroniana hat selbstverständlich auch wichtige unterscheidende Determinanten. Auf den ersten Blick unterscheidet es sich vor allem

---

[10] Übersetzung nach: Marcus Tullius Cicero, De oratore / Über den Redner. Lateinisch – deutsch. Hg. und übers. von Theodor NÜßLEIN. Düsseldorf 2007, 157.
[11] Obsidio Zigethiensis An. MD.LVI. descripta. Viennae Austriae: excudebat Raphael Hofhalter 1558; VANTUCH (s. Anm. 1), 212. Zum tragischen Fall von Szigetvár kam es jedoch erst im September 1566.

durch die Anzahl der Gesprächsteilnehmer. In *De oratore* verteilt sich die Last des Exposés auf Lucius Crassus, Marcus Antonius Orator und Gaius Julius Caesar Strabo Vopiscus; in die Diskussion greifen auch Scaevola und Catulus ein, die Rolle der Schüler wird von Sulpicius und Cotta gespielt. Das Paduaner Gespräch wird dagegen auf zwei Akteure beschränkt, auf Sambucus und Georg Bona. Dabei wächst der Anteil des Lehrers Sambucus im Verlauf der Debatte bedeutend an und Bonas Repliken verlieren immer mehr an Umfang und Dynamik. Die dogmatischen Akzente des Dialogs *De imitatione Ciceroniana* werden dadurch auf Kosten der dialektischen verstärkt.

Was die Datierung betrifft, verlief das Gespräch zwischen Sambucus und Georg Bona – wenn es überhaupt je in dieser Form stattgefunden hatte – spätestens im Jahre 1556. Von Oktober 1553 an hatte Sambucus nämlich auf Aufforderung des neuen Graner Erzbischofs Nicolaus Olah die Funktion des *paedagogus* seines talentierten Neffen Georg Bona inne. Dabei studierte Sambucus Medizin in Padua und bereiste Italien. Seine erzieherisch-bildende Aufgabe beendete er im Sommer 1557, als Bona nach Ungarn zurückkehrte und am 3. September 1559 tragisch verstarb[12]. Der Dialog *De imitatione Ciceroniana* ist seinem Andenken gewidmet. Sambucus drückt seine Trauer über den Tod des begabten Jünglings in den ersten Zeilen des Vorwortes aus: quem [...] cum Georgio Bona [...] summoque luctu meo adolescente nuper extincto, sermonem[13] habueram („ein Gespräch, das ich mit dem vor kurzem zu meinem größten Leidwesen jung verstorbenen Georg Bona geführt hatte"). Das Vorwort ist am 22. Oktober 1559 in Padua datiert. An der endgültigen Redaktion des Dialogs arbeitete der Verfasser also schnell und intensiv. Die erste gedruckte Ausgabe erfolgte in Paris in der Druckerei von Ägidius Gorbinus im Jahre 1561, weitere folgten in Antwerpen 1563 und 1568.

Die Beziehung Latein versus Nationalsprachen stellt bei Sambucus kein Randphänomen dar; die Streitfrage wird auf mehr als 12 Seiten des ersten Dialogs erörtert, das heißt, sie nimmt etwa eine Hälfte des Textes ein. Das erste Thema ist die Frage, ob es nicht besser sei, Nationalsprachen statt einer degenerierten Form der lateinischen Sprache zu gebrauchen. Die De-

---

[12] VANTUCH (s. Anm. 1), 83. Dem Andenken seines geliebten Schülers erwies Sambucus Ehre durch eine besondere Rede, die er in Padua herausgab: Oratio in obitum generosi ac magnifici adolescentis Georgii Bona Transylvani. Patavii: Perchacinus 1560; VANTUCH 212.

[13] *Sermonem* fehlt im Druck von 1561.

batte wird von der Aussage des Lehrers initiiert, nämlich dass der Gebrauch eines entarteten Lateins oft seinen theoretischen Hintergrund hat: *in vitiosa et prava latini sermonis usurpatione [...] inest ars* (*De imitatione Ciceroniana* 6ᵛ). Die Aversion gegenüber einem kultivierten Latein entsteht seiner Meinung nach aus zwei Beweggründen. Der erste ist die übertriebene Liebe zu dem Seinigen, *nimius sui amor*, der zweite ist die intellektuelle Unfähigkeit, *vel potius ingenii frustratio*.

Dieses zweite Motiv erweist sich als das stärkere, indem das Wort *ars* im moralischen Kontext den negativen Begriff List bezeichnet. Die Gegner wollen Latein als bereits inhaltslos und tot beseitigen, damit sie dann umso leichter aus lateinischen Quellen entnommene Kenntnisse als originelle eigene vorlegen können. Sie wollen, dass das Lateinische, die Mutter, als lebloses, des jeweiligen Sachinhalts entledigtes und der Jahrhunderte lang dauernder Würde beraubtes Medium daliegen solle:

> vernaculam ita complectuntur, ut extinctam hanc matrem, unde pleraeque fluxerunt, velint adeoque rebus eam et dignitate, quam tot seculis obtinuit, exutam, vestigia scientiarum et furta sua ne ab imperitis agnoscantur, iacere cupiant.
>
> Sambucus, *De imitatione Ciceroniana* 1561, 6ᵛ
>
> sie verliebten sich so sehr in die Sprache ihres Volkes, dass sie sich wünschen, Latein, unsere Mutter, aus deren Quellen die meisten Sprachen hervorgehen, wäre bereits tot; sie sehnen sich danach, dass die lateinische Sprache als völlig inhaltslos und ihrer Würde, die sie im Laufe so vieler Jahrhunderte erlangt hatte, beraubt daliegen solle. Sie tun es, damit die Unwissenden nicht feststellen können, woher die Spuren der wissenschaftlichen Disziplinen kommen, und damit sie die Diebstähle nicht erkennen können.

Deshalb fordert Sambucus zur Verteidigung der lateinischen Sprache auf: *danda opera, ut eam defendamus* (6ᵛ). Sie muss vor den Menschen, die von intellektuellem (*ignari*) und moralischem (*iniusti*) Handicap gezeichnet sind, geschützt werden. Das ist die eindeutige Schlussfolgerung dieses Teils des Textes. Immerhin öffnet die lateinische Sprache die Tür zu tieferen wissenschaftlichen Kenntnissen, die auf der Arbeit mit Quellen beruht – *nec animus excelsus, nisi ortum videat, satis acquiescet* („der menschliche Geist, der eine erhabene Beschwingtheit hat, wird sich nie zufriedengeben, bis er seinen Ausgangspunkt sieht") – und hat eine unersetzbare Aufgabe bei der Gestaltung und Kultivierung des ästhetischen Gefühls:

enitetur semper Romana existetque elegantia, dum quas secum attulit opes in usu hominum versabuntur.

Sambucus, *De imitatione Ciceroniana* 1561, 6[v]

Die römische Eleganz wird immer leuchten und existieren, solange die Werte, die sie mit sich gebracht hat, den Menschen dienen werden.

Anschließend wiederholt Georg Bona mit anderen Worten die Einwände der Modernisten, die Latein als etwas Überwundenes und nicht mehr Aktuelles abschreiben wollen:

> Multi enim non solum non necessariam nostra aetate veterum illum splendorem cultumque dictionis, sed omnino inanem et modo non impium, nostra dignitate inferiorem arbitrantur: alios mores et vitam alia verba deposcere, postremo esse (sc. imitationem) impossibilem servilemque operam.

Sambucus, *De imitatione Ciceroniana* 1561, 7[r–v]

Viele sind nämlich zur Ansicht gelangt, dass heute, in der modernen Zeit, die antiken Autoren mit ihrem ganzen Prunk überflüssig sind. Auch die Pflege der lateinischen Spache selbst ist ihrer Meinung nach nicht nur etwas überaus Unnötiges, sondern sogar Unfruchtbares, und wenn schon nicht ausdrücklich gottlos, so doch unter unserer Würde. Eine andere Lebensweise und andere Sitten erforderten zugleich andere Worte. Als letztes Argument wird angegeben, dass die Nachahmung eine die menschlichen Fähigkeiten übersteigende, sklavenhafte Arbeit sei.

Der Lehrer Sambucus macht das Gewicht der angeführten Einwände nicht leichter: *dicunt quidem illi non omnino nihil*, er lässt sogar zu, dass diese wohlüberlegt und für das einfache Volk attraktiv sind (*argute ac populariter*). Er will diese jedoch nicht in vollem Umfang und direkt beantworten, damit er nicht in eine endlose Polemik verwickelt wird. Lieber weist er darauf hin, was die Nationalsprachen vom Lateinischen lernen können. Er argumentiert *per analogiam*: Die zeitgenössische Sprachkultur soll ihr Vorbild in Cicero, Antonius dem Redner und anderen Römern haben, die sich willig und erfolgreich die höher stehende Kultur der Griechen aneigneten und diese in ihrem großen Reich verbreiteten. Im Vergleich mit dem Römischen Imperium scheint die zeitgenössische Situation für das Lateinische sogar günstiger zu sein. Der *Orbis Christianus* hat nämlich eine größere Ausdehnung als das *Imperium Romanum*, und auch weit entfernte Länder schließen sich ihm nicht aus Angst, sondern aus Liebe an.

Das Problem der Wahl zwischen Latein und einer Nationalsprache bleibt aber weiterhin präsent und Georg Bona wiederholt die Behauptung der Opponenten, dass Latein heute nicht mehr fähig sei, die modernen Begriffe zu erfassen (8ʳ): *vix ad quasvis res praesertim recens inventas latinus sermo verba suffecerit* („kaum wird die lateinische Sprache genügend Wörter für alle Dinge finden und besonders für die nicht, die unlängst erfunden wurden").

Auch wenn es gelingen sollte, das Lateinische – wie es sich die Ciceronianer[14] wünschen – nach Ciceros Vorbild wieder zu beleben, wird es nicht reichen, Latein als erste Bildungssprache zu retten. Ihr Meister erfasste in seinen Schriften einfach nicht die ganze Realität des Lebens. Darüber hinaus gibt es neue Realien, die das althergebrachte Latein zwingen, komplizierte und oft nicht eindeutige Periphrasen zu verwenden: *res verborum caussa dissimulare aut obscure tractare* („Dinge unkenntlich machen oder unverständlich behandeln Wörtern zuliebe"). Diese Mühe ist dabei völlig überflüssig, die heimische Sprache erreichte ja bereits ein genügend hohes Niveau – wenn wir uns in der einheimischen Sprache auszeichnen; *cum vernacula excellamus* – so wird es eigentlich eine patriotische Pflicht, diese vor dem fremden Latein zu bevorzugen:

> Ita quisque nostrum patriam tueri nec indicio quodam priscae servitutis, neglecta propria (sc. lingua), nos deberemus externae adiungere.
>
> Sambucus, *De imitatione Ciceroniana* 1561, 8ʳ

So sollten wir, ein jeder von uns, der Sprache seiner Heimat Aufmerksamkeit widmen; wir sollten uns nicht mit der Sprache der Fremde verbünden und gewissermaßen gezeichnet mit dem Siegel der lang vergangenen Sklaverei die eigene Sprache vernachlässigen.

Die Verbindung von Pragmatismus mit dem befreiten Patriotismus will Sambucus nicht gefallen. Zuerst verwendet er ein schwächeres Argument gegen diese Verknüpfung. Er begründet es damit, dass die Menschen nicht nur notwendige Sachen nutzen, sondern auch andere, ja gerade diese Dinge

---

[14] Zum Ciceronianismus der Renaissance Tadeusz ZIELIŃSKI, *Cicero im Wandel der Jahrhunderte*. Leipzig ³1912, 179–191; neuere Literatur in Auswahl bei Jozef IJSEWIJN, *Companion to Neo-Latin Studies*. Vol. II: *Literary, linguistic, philological and editorial questions*. Leuven: University Press 1998, 418f.; vgl. auch Jörg ROBERT, Die Ciceronianismus-Debatte. In: Herbert Jaumann (Hg.), *Diskurse der Gelehrtenkultur in der Frühen Neuzeit. Ein Handbuch*. Berlin, New York 2010, 1–54.

sogar lieben und hochschätzen. Es geht ihnen hauptsächlich darum, dass sie nützlich sein sollten. Das zweite Gegenargument ist stärker. Der Autor gesteht, dass angesichts politischer Umwälzungen jede Sprache (insofern sie die Landessprache ist) in der Alltagskommunikation geeignet ist und Latein kein Recht hat, vor Deutsch oder Französisch bevorzugt zu werden:

> Usum in vita si spectemus, dum Imperia divinitus miscentur, augentur, transferuntur, quaevis lingua nobis, ut domestica, utilis fuerit, nec Latinam vel Germanicae vel Gallicae anteposuerim.
> Sambucus, *De imitatione Ciceroniana* 1561, 8^v

Wenn wir den Nutzen im Leben betrachten, so kann, da Herrschaftsverhältnisse nach dem Willen Gottes erschüttert, befördert oder übertragen werden, eine jedwede einheimische Sprache nützlich sein; darum würde ich Latein vor Deutsch oder Französisch nicht bevorzugen.

Worin soll also die spezifische Nützlichkeit des Lateinischen liegen? Sambucus antwortet mit Sätzen, die wir für programmatisch halten können. Aus der typischen Optik der Humanisten betont er den prinzipiellen Gegensatz zwischen den Sprachen. Die einen repräsentierten die Dunkelheit des Barbarentums, die anderen stehen für Weisheit und Beredsamkeit. Die Lateiner übernahmen diese von den Griechen, bereicherten sie und dem angehäuften Reichtum verliehen sie ihre Sprache als Medium. Deshalb halte sich Latein mit Recht das Privileg zugute, die wirkliche Sprache der Bildung und Literatur zu sein und die Nationalsprachen veredeln zu können:

> Nisi in caligine rerum et ignominiosa barbarie ingenia latere nostra velimus, ex imitatione latinam eloquentiam necessariam cum ad percipiendas, tum etiam tradendas res, imo vernaculam exornandam cogitare potes.
> Sambucus, *De imitatione Ciceroniana* 1561, 8^v

Wenn wir also nicht wollen, dass unser Verstand in Dunkel und die Schande der Barbarei gehüllt bleibt, kann man bedenken, dass die aus der Nachahmung gewonnene Eloquenz einerseits für die Aneignung der Sachkenntnisse, andererseits für ihre Überlieferung, und sogar für die Kultivierung der Beredsamkeit in der einheimischen Sprache notwendig sein wird.

Georg Bona hört das Lob auf die lateinische Sprache skeptisch an und spielt weiterhin die Rolle des Anwalts der Befürworter der modernen Sprachen, indem er ihre selbstbewussten Argumente übernimmt. Das erste stützt sich auf das Bildungsniveau: Die Zeitgenossen bleiben ja keineswegs hinter den Gelehrten des Altertums zurück. Im Gegenteil, zu den alten Kenntnissen fügten sie ihre neuen hinzu. Das zweite Argument operiert mit politischen Slogans: Die Freiheit muss Vorrang vor der Sklaverei, das Unsrige vor dem Fremden bekommen.

Da die *raison d'être* der ganzen Erörterung die Kultivierung des Lateinischen ist und der Weg dazu über die Nachahmung der antiken Vorbilder führt, äußert sich Sambucus zunächst kritisch über den zeitgenössischen Stand der lateinischen Sprache und drückt Unzufriedenheit mit dem durchschnittlichen, geläufigen und darüberhinaus regional zersplitterten Latein aus:

> *Quam latine loquantur, quam varia et copiosa cuiusque regionis lingua sit, quot partibus illa veteri posterior sit hodierna, quis paulo curiosior non videt?*
>
> Sambucus, De imitatione Ciceroniana 1561, 9^r

Wie sprechen sie lateinisch? Wie unterschiedlich ist das Latein von Land zu Land und wie reich ist ihr Wortschatz? Wie viele Gesichtspunkte gibt es, in denen die Ausdrucksfähigkeiten von heute hinter denen der Antike zurückbleiben? Existiert unter jenen, die sich für das Problem näher interessieren, überhaupt jemand, der den Unterschied nicht sehen würde?

Und welche Schlussfolgerung lässt sich daraus ziehen? Die heimischen Sprachen können nur einem heruntergekommenen Latein standhalten[15]. Die wirkliche Kraft der lateinischen Sprache beruht jedoch auf der unerreichbaren Eleganz seiner wahren, d. h. antiken Vorbilder:

> Quis Ciceronem quam Alanum, Livium quam germanice scripta chronica, Vergilium quam Baptistam Mantuanum [...] non malit?
>
> Sambucus, De imitatione Ciceroniana 1561, 9^r

Wer würde Cicero nicht lieber mögen als Alanus, Livius als deutsch geschriebene Kroniken, Vergil als Baptista Mantuanus?

Neben oder vielmehr gegenüber Cicero steht hier als vergleichbare Größe der Polyhistor aus dem 12. Jahrhundert Alanus ab Insulis, *doctor universalis*, dem Koryphäus der römischen Geschichtsschreibung ist die repräsentative Gattung der mittelalterlichen Historiographie gegenüber gestellt, dem Klassi-

---

[15] Zur Lage des gesprochenen Lateins in Ungarn vgl. István György TÓTH, Latinčina ako hovorená reč v Uhorsku v 17. a 18. storočí so zreteľom na Slovensko. [Latein als gesprochene Sprache in Ungarn im 17. und 18. Jahrhundert]. *Historický časopis* 44 (1996), Nr. 1, 102–113.

ker der römischen Poesie sein Karmeliter-Pendant vom Anfang des 16. Jahrhunderts, Baptista Mantuanus. Sambucus musste allerdings auch auf eine gewisse Abneigung gegen Cicero als Person reagieren. Dieser Widerwille äußerte sich auch in der Ablehnung seiner Sprache und seines Stils. Er verleugnet nicht, dass der historische Cicero menschliche Schwächen hatte, aber seinen Stil erklärt er für göttlich und der Imitation durchaus würdig:

> Ego vero si quae sunt in moribus vitia et naevi, non probo nec assumam; in oratione quia nihil casu, nihil extra artem positum est, observatione ac diligentia cur non divinam facultatem assecter?
>
> Sambucus, *De imitatione Ciceroniana* 1561, 9^r

Selbstverständlich billige ich, was mich betrifft, keine seiner Laster und Charaktermängel, noch weniger will ich sie übernehmen. In seiner Rede war jedoch nichts unbedacht verwendet, nichts steht außerhalb der Gesetze der Kunst. Warum sollte ich also nicht eifrig und mit Respekt in den Fußstapfen seiner göttlichen Fähigkeiten schreiten?

Wenn der Mensch an ephemeren körperlichen Genüssen Freude haben darf, umso mehr soll er die Reinheit und Schönheit der Sprache genießen. Diese bietet im höchsten Maß Cicero, deshalb wäre es vermessen, sein Latein abzulehnen:

> Numquam satis a mente eos constare, qui Latinam Ciceronis linguam prae aliis contemnunt, aio.
>
> Sambucus, *De imitatione Ciceroniana* 1561, 9^v

Ich behaupte, dass diejenigen, die andere Sprachen bevorzugend Ciceros Latein verachten, nie ganz bei Verstand waren.

Ganz logisch ist es dagegen, aus Cicero ein Vorbild des vollkommenen Latinisten zu machen: *latinissimi, hoc est Ciceroniani haberi volumus* (9^v).

Selbstverständlich ist nicht jeder, der sich für einen Anhänger Ciceros proklamiert, in der Tat ein Ciceronianer. Daher wird der Begriff *Ciceronianus* selbst zum Gegenstand einer Debatte. Sambucus charakterisiert vorerst kritisch und ironisch die zeitgenössischen Ciceronianer als eine geschlossene, quasi religiöse Gemeinschaft und Familie: *religio ista et quaedam familia*. Es reicht also nicht, ein kurzes Brieflein zu verfassen und sich dann gleich den Titel *Ciceronianus* anzumaßen.

Größeren Raum widmet Sambucus jedoch der Forderung, nicht irgendwelche, sondern nur bewährte Vorbilder nachzuahmen. Um eine lateinische

Rede für richtig und schön erklären zu können, genügt es nicht, wenn der Text grammatisch fehlerfrei ist. Die grammatischen Regeln müssen zwar berücksichtigt werden, aber in das Spiel um ein verständliches und elegantes Latein tritt als gleich gewichtiger Faktor der Usus ein:

> Praeceptiones grammaticorum abiiciendas minime censeo, nec tamen opinari debemus, idem esse Latinum et elegans, quod emendatum, quod grammaticum; idcirco illi (sc. Ciceroni) adhaerendum est.
> Sambucus, De imitatione Ciceroniana 1561, 10^r
> Die Lehrsätze der Grammatiker – davon bin ich überzeugt – darf man keinesfalls verwerfen. Wir sollten jedoch nicht zu der Annahme verleitet werden, dass das Fehlerlose und grammatikalisch Korrekte auch gutes, elegantes Latein ist. Deshalb sollte man sich an Cicero halten.

Der Usus schließt die grammatisch zwar akzeptablen, durch die Praxis jedoch nicht angenommenen Formulierungen (*grammaticus admittit, usus oratorum respuit*) aus. Diesen kann man sich in der lateinischen Sprache nur durch Beobachtung (*observatio*) aneignen, die die erste und unumgängliche Phase der Nachahmung darstellt.

Es ist zu wenig, im Lateinischen die Pannonismen, d. h. die ungarischen und slawischen Elemente zu vermeiden und ab und zu nach dem Muster der Zeitgenossen seine eigene Rede durch von Cicero ausgeliehene Floskeln zu verzieren; Bona ist sich dessen voll bewusst. Man muss von Ciceros Sprachgut durchdrungen sein. Das kann nur eine volle „Verdauung" seiner Kunst sichern:

> [...] ut confecta omnia in stomacho tuo et assimilata partibus, appositaque percipias.
> Sambucus, De imitatione Ciceroniana 1561, 10^v
> [...] ähnlich wie du alles, was du davor gekaut hast, im Magen verdauen und dies dann in die entsprechenden Teile des Organismus assimiliert und distribuiert aufnehmen musst.

Diese betrifft die Wortwahl, den Satzbau, die Struktur des Textes. Wer eloquent sein will, d. h. hundertprozentig lateinisch (*qui latinissime loquitur*) und ästhetisch vollkommen (*ornatissime scribit*, 10^v), muss in sich die erworbenen Kenntnisse durch Üben festigen.

Was für eine Rolle der Usus spielt, kann man laut Sambucus leichter in der eigenen Sprache feststellen, die wir im Unterschied zu Latein von Geburt an lernen:

> In vernacula quidem, et aliis pene nobiscum natis usu linguis soloecismos, κακοζηλίαν et id genus, consecutionem et συνθήκην facilius animadvertimus.
> Sambucus, *De imitatione Ciceroniana* 1561, 10ᵛ
> In unserer Nationalsprache und in anderen Sprachen, die im Prozess der praktischen Verwendung fast gleichzeitig mit uns geboren sind, bemerken wir gleich grammatische Unsensibilität, Nachäffen und ähnliche Missgriffe, und wir sind uns der Wortfolge und der konventionellen Bedeutung leichter bewusst.

Sambucus führt vier Arten von Fehlern an. Für einen Soloecismus hält man einen grammatischen Fehler, zum Beispiel falsche Kasus-Rektion. Die κακοζηλία[16] ist eine affektierte, ungeschickte Nachäffung. Die *consecutio* bezieht sich offensichtlich auf die Wortfolge und mit dem Begriff συνθήκη wird der konventionelle Charakter der Wörter als Zeichen bezeichnet[17]. Im Vergleich mit Latein ist die Schwäche der Nationalsprachen ihre unausgearbeitete Grammatik (*nec tanta ars*) und die Unterrichtsweise der Sprachen (*disciplina*).

Wie absurd es ist, den Usus der Sprache zu ignorieren, illustriert Sambucus an drei Beispielen. Das erste Beispiel ist deutsch und lautet:

> Ist mein frondtlich anlangen, wollet der alte Kundschofft nicht vergessen, und mir in der Sachen Zugefallen werden.
> Sambucus, *De imitatione Ciceroniana* 1561, 10ᵛ

Wenn dieselben Wörter in der falschen Reihenfolge stehen, d. h. so wie sie ein Italiener oder Ungar *minus peritus* verwenden würde, verliert der Text seinen Sinn. Ein Deutscher oder ein deutschsprechender Mensch versteht den Inhalt sehr schwer, bemerkt aber die Fehler sofort, die Aussprachefehler inbegriffen, und kann sich des Lachens nicht enthalten. Die lächerliche oder törichte (*ineptum*) Version lautet: *Ist anlangen mein frondtlich, wollet nicht der alte vergessen Kundtschofft, Zugefallen und mir werden in der Sachen.* Das Bei-

---

[16] Vgl. Quintilianus, *Institutio oratoria* II, 3, 9.
[17] Vgl. Jürgen TRABANT, *Mithridates im Paradies. Kleine Geschichte des Sprachdenkens.* München 2003, 30f.

spiel in Italienisch hat ebenfalls eine richtige und eine falsche Variante[18]. Nach den deutschen und italienischen Beispielen folgen vier Varianten eines stilistisch ausgefeilten, auch einer alltäglichen Situation entnommenen lateinischen Satzes:

> Quaeso, cras ad me pransum venias.
> Cras, quaeso, ad me, ut prandeas, venies.
> Ad me veniens, quaeso, prandebis cras.
> Pransum ad quaeso me cras venito.
>
> Sambucus, De imitatione Ciceroniana 1561, 11ᵛ

Jeder oberflächlich gebildete Zeitgenosse verwendet die vier Varianten als gleich geeignet und gleichwertig, ohne unter ihnen zu unterscheiden, *nos sine discrimine his uteremur, Latina probaremus*. Obwohl sie alle grammatisch zulässig sind, reicht das nicht und der Redner würde sich vor echten Römern blamieren, weil ihm das Gefühl für die Sprachsituation fehlte. Daraus erfolgt die allgemein gültige Lehre, dass man die Eigentümlichkeit einer jeden Sprache kennen und respektieren und die Eigenheiten der Muttersprache nicht in sie übertragen sollte:

> Adeo, Georgi, necessaria cuiusque linguae proprietas, et modi loquendi penitus cognoscendi, ne male quidvis ad nostram, ut fit, consuetudinem deflectamus.
>
> Sambucus, De imitatione Ciceroniana 1561, 11ᵛ

Insofern, mein lieber Georg, hat jede Sprache notwendigerweise ihren eigenen Charakter, und wir müssen unbedingt alle Ausdrucksweisen gründlich kennen, damit wir nichts, wie es geschieht, beliebig im Sinne unserer Gepflogenheiten entstellen.

Das bedeutet auf keinen Fall, dass die Sprachen gleichwertig sind. Sambucus bekennt sich zu einer Hierarchie der Sprachen. In dieser steht die Lateinische am höchsten, weil sie die Sprache der Wissenschaft und schönen Literatur ist. Mit ihr verbindet er deshalb eine ganze Reihe von positiven Attributen: *sapientia* („Weisheit"), *cultus dictionis* („Kultur des Sprechens"), *dignitas* („Würde"), *elegantia* („Feinheit"), *splendor* („Glanz"), *amplitudo* („Fülle"), *varietas* („Buntheit"). Nur Latein verdient die Liebe und Achtung als

---

[18] *De imitatione Ciceroniana* 1561, 11ʳ. Richtig: „Ho riposto alle partite, pero che non mi fido della vostra venuta qui." Falsch: „Alle partite ho risposto della venuta qui vostra, non mi pero che fido."

mater und Bewunderung als *aedificium magnifice fabricatum* („großzügig erbautes Gebäude"). Die lateinische Sprache ist *signum ab egregia natura et arte manans* („bildhauerisches Meisterwerk, das aus der erhabenen Natur und Kunst hervorgeht"). Ähnlich positiv sind die Epitheta, mit denen der Verfasser das Lateinische besingt. Die einen drücken sein ästhetisches Potential aus, z. B. *pulcher* („schön"), *affluens* („reichlich"), *elegans* („geschmackvoll"), *iocundus* („angenehm"), *concinnus* („kunstgerecht"), *ornatissimus* („zierlich"), andere hingegen sein hochentwickeltes Sprachsystem, z. B. *cultus* („gepflegt"), *egregius* („außerordentlich"), *laudatus* („löblich"), *purus* („rein").

Im Kontext der Nationalsprachen findet man solche Lobesworte kaum. Auch die *gratia* („Liebreiz"), die ab und zu das Italienische schmückt (11^r), geht leicht durch die obskure Platzierung der Wörter (*obscura collocatio*) und durch Ignorieren ihrer konventionellen Bedeutung (*ignoratio* συνθήκης) verloren. Im Vergleich mit den exemplifizierten Nationalsprachen hat Latein den einzigartigen Vorteil in der freien Wortfolge, in der feststehenden Semantik, in der Fähigkeit, Rhythmus in einen künstlerisch gestalteten Text bringen zu können[19]. Man kann der Bezeichnung der Nationalsprache als *lingua vernacula*, die Sambucus dreimal verwendete, eine deutlich pejorative Bedeutung nicht abstreiten. Das geht nicht nur aus der Ableitung des Wortes *verna* selbst hervor, weil ein *verna* ein im Haus geborener Sklave war, sondern auch aus seiner diminutiven Endung *-ulus*.

Es ist interessant, dass Sambucus dieselbe pejorative Endung auch im Zusammenhang mit den Griechen verwendete. Wer sind jedoch in den Augen unseres Humanisten jene *Graeculi, qui ut grammaticam inspexerunt, verba utcunque intelligunt, statim Orationes, poemata fundunt* (11^v), „Griechlein", die – kaum dass sie in die Grammatik schauten und schlecht und recht die Wörter verstanden – gleich Reden und Gedichte herausgeben? Das Wort *Graeculus* hat mehrmals auch Cicero im ersten Buch *De oratore* verwendet, der sonst die Verdienste der Griechen hochschätzte. Er konzentrierte in dem Wort typische negative Eigenschaften dieses Ethnikums, nämlich seine Streitsucht, Faulheit und Neigung zur Geschmacklosigkeit. Sambucus folgt darin Cicero

---

[19] Dem Rhythmus widmet Sambucus besondere Aufmerksamkeit im dritten Dialog (33^r–38^r). Z. B. 33^r *Ac ut aedificium comfabricatum et absolutum, ex partibus rationabiliter positis et convenientibus, velut dinumeratis et ubique aptis commendatur, ita oratio extremam quandam manum* ῥυθμοῖς *accipiat. Vox enim quamvis contenta et clamosa nihil afficit parumque significat, sed numerosa et verbis modificata instructaque movet ac docet.*

und betont, dass das Ziel seiner Kritik die Halbgebildeten sind. Sie trauen sich literarische Werke in einer Sprache, die sie nicht beherrschen, zu veröffentlichen. Solche Menschen würden der Redner Demosthenes und der Dichter Homer nicht für Griechen, sondern für Perser, Phryger, Skythen, Germanen halten. Ähnlich vermag ein Deutscher in Sambucus den Ungarn (*Ungarum me Germanus*) zu entdecken, der Italiener wiederum in jemandem mit Sicherheit den Rumänen (*aut certe Valachum Italus*), der Tscheche den Slowaken (*Sclavonem Boemus*), der Römer den Umbrer, der Toskaner den Lombarden.

Beherrschte Sambucus überhaupt das Slowakische und unterschied er es vom Tschechischen? Wir können mit Recht voraussetzen, dass er als sprachbegabter Junge das Slowakische seiner Geburtsstadt Tyrnau kannte[20] und sich seiner Verwandtschaft mit Tschechisch bewusst war. In der Familie herrschte jedoch offensichtlich Deutsch vor und bestimmt wurde auch Ungarisch gebraucht. Latein lernte er in den Schulen, in der Kirche und durch die Lektüre von Autoren, auf Latein verkehrte er mit den Gelehrten. Andere Sprachen eignete er sich im Verlauf seiner *peregrinatio academica* an. Sein gesamtes literarisches und wissenschaftliches Werk ist lateinisch, nur einige wenige Gedichte auf Griechisch (z. B. das *Epitaphium Georgii Bonae* in den *Emblemata*, Abb. S. 292) beweisen, dass er es in Übereinstimmung mit den damaligen Erfordernissen beherrschte.

Die Beziehung zu den Nationalsprachen spiegelt teilweise seine Korrespondenz wider, obwohl sie nicht vollständig erhalten blieb. Sambucus schrieb seine Briefe vorwiegend lateinisch. Von 193 veröffentlichten Briefen sind 172 lateinisch. Der einzige griechisch verfasste Brief war an einen der bedeutendsten deutschen Humanisten Joachim Camerarius den Älteren in Leipzig

---

[20] 1551 trat das Dekret von Ferdinand I. über die Paritätsverteilung der Ämter in der Stadtverwaltung unter Deutschen, Slowaken und Magyaren in Kraft, siehe Štefan KAZIMÍR, Trnava v rokoch 1526–1849. In: Jozef Šimončič, Jozef Watzka (Hgg.), Dejiny Trnavy [Geschichte von Tyrnau]. Bratislava 1988, 100; die Stadt- und Kapitelschule hatte neben ihrem Rektor zwei Magister, einen Deutschen und einen Slowaken, siehe Peter VAJCIK, Školstvo, študijné a školské poriadky na Slovensku v XVI. storočí [Schulwesen, Studien- und Schulordnungen in der Slowakei im 16. Jahrhundert]. Bratislava 1955, 75–77; Jarmila BENCOVÁ, Marian ZERVAN, Trnava v časoch humanizmu a renesancie: druhé Atény a malý Rím [Trnava in den Epochen von Humanismus und Renaissance: zweites Athen und kleines Rom]. In: Ivan Rusina et alii (Hgg.), Renesancia. Umenie medzi neskorou gotikou a barokom [Renaissance. Kunst zwischen Spätgotik und Barock]. Bratislava 2009, 133–141.

adressiert. Eine Äußerung der *captatio benevolentiae* war offensichtlich die Tatsache, dass er an den Kardinal Fulvio Orsini auf Italienisch schrieb, obwohl die Briefe größtenteils solche Angelegenheiten betrafen, die die humanistischen Gelehrten interessierten. Alle acht ungarischen Briefe aus den Jahren 1567 bis 1573 haben mit seinem Schwager Stephan Nyilas zu tun, der in Tyrnau lebte und im Lateinischen anscheinend nicht besonders gewandt war. In ihren Briefen werden fast ausschließlich Vermögensfragen besprochen. Von acht deutschen Briefen waren sieben aus den Jahren 1567–1574 an Johann Sommer, den Stadtrichter bzw. ehemaligen Stadtrichter von Tyrnau, adressiert, und diese beziehen sich auf Erb- oder Vermögensangelegenheiten.

Uns interessiert hier der deutsche Brief vom 26. April 1565: Sambucus, der sich damals in Wien aufhielt, adressierte ihn an die Wiener Hofkammerräte. Mit seinem Brief antwortete er prompt auf die Aufforderung des Kaiserhofes, die lateinische Version der Waldordnung vorzubereiten, die in Neusohl / Banská Bystrica auf Deutsch zusammengestellt worden war. Wie begründete unser höchst ambitionierter Humanist seine Ablehnung? Als ersten Grund gab er an, dass er das Deutsche nicht entsprechend beherrsche; als zweiten seine mangelnde Einsicht in die „montanistischen und agrarischen Termini". Bisher habe er Erfahrungen mit Cicero und Livius, jedoch nicht mit der montanistischen Terminologie gesammelt. Das wichtigste war das vierte Gegenargument: Auch wenn manche Termini bei Varro und anderen antiken Autoren auffindbar wären, würden sie die Zeitgenossen nicht mehr verstehen. Wenn der Übersetzer aber statt der Termini Periphrasen verwendete, würde sie jeder auf seine eigene Weise interpretieren. Für eine kompetente lateinische Übersetzung des Dokuments schlug er dem kaiserlichen Hof den Schemnitzer (Banská Štiavnica) Waldbürger und Humanisten Paulus Rubigallus (1520–1577?) vor, und dieser nahm sich der Aufgabe in der Tat an[21].

Natürlich fand man unter den Humanisten in Ungarn auch gegenüber den Nationalsprachen offenere Gelehrte als Sambucus. Der Preßburger Arzt Georg Purkircher (1530?–1577) war Sambucus' enger Freund. Purkircher begrüßte seine Hochzeit mit einer Parodie auf Ovids Geschichte des Py-

---

[21] GERSTINGER (s. Anm. 2), 69–71; Károly TAGÁNYI, *Magyar erdészeti oklevéltár I (1015–1745)*. Budapest 1896, 91–94, veröffentlichte die damit verbundenen Briefe.

ramus und Thisbe *Epithalamium metamorphoticum ad nuptias domini Joannis Sambuci* (1567)[22]. Er veröffentlichte 1567 in Wien eine zweisprachige Paraphrase des Psalms 79 *Deus, venerunt gentes,* und Sambucus trug zu der Ausgabe mit einem Kommendationsgedicht bei[23]. Die lateinische Version zeichnet sich durch ein technisch vollkommenes elegisches Distichon, durch eine typische Amplifikation der Vorlage und durch eine breite Applikation des *ornatus poetico-rhetoricus* aus, während der Stil ihres deutschen Pendants grundverschieden ist, beeinflusst von der Tradition der inbrünstigen Kirchenlieder. Die deutsche Paraphrase war an Katharina von Pernstein / Pernštejn gerichtet, die Gattin des Preßburger Gespans Eckhardt von Salm und zu Neuburg, die die lateinische Paraphrase offensichtlich nicht hätte genießen und schätzen können. Der Dedikationsbrief zusammen mit dieser biblischen Paraphrase ist übrigens der einzige auf Deutsch geschriebene Text von Purkircher, der erhalten blieb.

Noch vor ihm gliederte Leonard Stöckel (1510–1560), der berühmte Rektor der Bartfelder Lateinschule, deutsche Gedichte in sein Lehrbuch *Apophthegmata illustrium virorum* („Sprüche hervorragender Männer", gedruckt Breslau 1570) ein. Seine nicht ganz regelmäßigen gereimten jambischen Quaternare kommentierten, fassten zusammen oder aktualisierten den Sinn des jeweiligen Spruchs einer antiken Persönlichkeit. Der Rektor wünschte nämlich, dass die Eltern seiner Schüler aus den Sprüchen der antiken Persönlichkeiten eine Lehre ziehen könnten. Der Wunsch seine Mitbürger zu erziehen führte Stöckel dazu, dass er die lateinischen Schuldramen durch deutsche ersetzte. Sambucus jedoch interessierte sich wahrscheinlich für sein Werk nicht.

Trotz der späteren allmählichen Expansion der Nationalsprachen im Bereich der politischen Verwaltung, Kultur und des kirchlichen Lebens, hatte die Forderung, Latein als wichtigste Amtssprache des vielsprachigen Ungarn und besonders als eine ethnisch neutrale Sprache zu kultivieren, an Aktualität

---

[22] Georgius Purkircher, Opera quae supersunt omnia. Edidit Miloslaus OKÁL. Budapest 1988, 137–141.

[23] Psalmus LXXIX. Deus venerunt gentes etc. carmine redditus, pro Hungaria gravissime cum Turcis conflictante. Viennae Austriae: Casparus Stainhofer excudebat 1566; Der 79. Psalm dauids, Herr es sind Heyden in dein Erbe gefallen (etc.) in disen Kriegsleuffen wider den Türcken gantz nötig zu singen. Wien in Osterreich: durch Casparum Stainhofer.

kaum etwas eingebüßt[24]. So schrieb zum Beispiel der Jesuitenpater Gabriel Heveneschi aus dem südungarischen Városmiske, der in Wien, Győr und Tyrnau wirkte, sein Buch *Ungaricae sanctitatis indicia* (Tyrnau 1692) nur lateinisch, seine Übersetzung ins Ungarische überließ er jemandem anderen. Vielleicht ließ er sich auch durch die Ansichten seines Ordensbruders Melchior Inchofer (1585–1648) anregen, dessen Geschichte der heiligen Latinität, *Historia sacra Latinitatis* (Messina 1635, München 1638) die Schönheit, Würde und logische Genauigkeit der lateinischen Sprache hervorhob. Laut Inchofer wird Latein als Sprache unter den Lebenden in der ewigen Seligkeit dienen[25].

Kehren wir nun zu Sambucus' Werk *De imitatione Ciceroniana* zurück. Sein didaktisches Ziel ist zweifellos vorrangig: Der Lehrer Sambucus will aus Georg Bona einen perfekten Latinisten, also einen wahren Ciceronianer machen. Die polemischen Töne, die mit dem damaligen Ciceronianismus verbunden sind, kommen im Text nicht direkt zur Geltung. Wenn Sambucus diejenigen kritisiert, die lateinische Konversation unterrichten und ihre Schüler zwingen, ganze auswendig gelernte Verse und Sätze von Terenz und Plautus zu verwenden, lehnt er ihre Praxis als unnötiges Archaisieren und zugleich als ungeeignete Übertragung von metrisch bedingten Formeln in die Umgangssprache ab.

---

[24] Vgl. Jean BÉRANGER, Latin et langues vernaculaires dans la Hongrie du XVIIe siècle. *Revue historique* 252 (93) (1969), 5–28; 27. Wie aktuell diese Forderung im akademischen Milieu der Tyrnauer Universität im 18. Jahrhundert war und wie sie behandelt wurde, zeigte Nicol SIPEKIOVÁ in der Studienreihe: O uplatnení zásady rečovej elegancie v spise Syntaxis ornata [Über die Anwendung des Grundsatzes der sprachlichen Eleganz in der Schrift Syntaxis ornata]. *Sambucus* 1 (2005), 123–130; Puritas – cnosť latinského jazyka v spise Syntaxis ornata (1745) [Puritas – die Tugend der lateinischen Sprache in der Schrift Syntaxis ornata]. *Sambucus* 2 (2007), 201–209; Problematika prekladu frazeologizmov v učebnici latinskej štylistiky z 18. storočia [Die Problematik der phraseologisch korrekten Übersetzung in einem Lehrbuch der lateinischen Stilistik aus dem 18. Jahrhundert]. *Sambucus* 3 (2008), 150–167; Copia linguae Latinae – pramene jazykovej bohatosti [Copia linguae Latinae – Quellen des sprachlichen Reichtums]. *Sambucus* 6 (2010), 109–114.

[25] Die Grundangaben zu Inchoffer bringt Franz Heinrich REUSCH, Inchofer, Melchior. *Allgemeine deutsche Biographie* 14 (1881), 64f.; ausführlicher zu seinem Werk Marc LAUREYS, Latin as Language of the Blessed: Melchior Inchofer on the excellence and dignity of the Latin language. In: Eckhard Keßler, Heinrich C. Kuhn (Hgg.), *Germania Latina – Latinitas Teutonica*. München 2003 (*Humanistische Bibliothek. Texte und Abhandlungen*, Reihe I. Abhandlungen 54), 655–678. Die *Historiae sacrae Latinitatis libri VI* erschienen 1742 auch in Prag.

Wie wir gesehen haben, hatte Sambucus keine Lust, in die wenige Jahre zuvor noch sehr heftige Polemik zwischen den fundamentalistischen und gemäßigten Ciceronianern einzugreifen. Den Namen des gemäßigten Erasmus von Rotterdam erwähnt er nur ein einziges Mal und zwar im dritten Dialog, während er die Radikalen (Bembo, Nizolius) viel häufiger nennt, ohne sie strenger zu kritisieren. Die Ausdrücke, die er mit Ciceros Namen verbindet, sind klar und eindeutig: *unicus ex omnibus* („der Einzige unter vielen"), *numquam satis laudatus* („nie genug gepriesen"), *lux* („Licht"), *gratia* („Anmut"), *tantus princeps* („großer Fürst"), *divinus* (der Göttliche).[*]

---

[*] In slowakischer Sprache ist erschienen: Daniel ŠKOVIERA, Latinčina a národné jazyky v prvej verzii Sambucovho spisu De imitatione Ciceroniana. *Sambucus* 10 (2014), 84–98.

Sambucus on Ciceronianism

An overview focussing on the second dialogue of
De imitatione a Cicerone petenda

IVAN LÁBAJ (Bratislava)

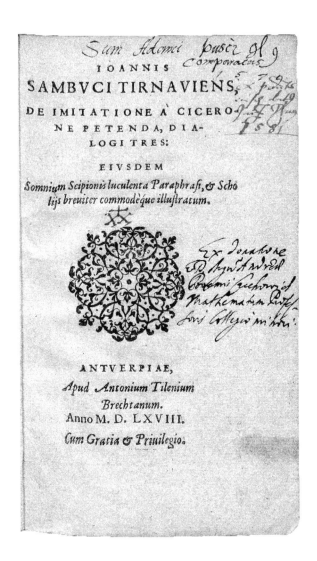

Title page of Ioannes Sambucus, De imitatione a Cicerone petenda.
Antverpiae: Apud Antonium Tilenium Brechtanum 1568
(Kraków, Biblioteka Jagiellońska, Gram. 1310)

Iohannes Sambucus (Zsámboky János, 1531–1584) was a well-known figure of the humanist movement in the central Danube area. Apart from his contributions as a collector and editor of numerous ancient Roman and Greek classics, he was also a court historiographer of Ferdinand I., Maximilian II. and Rudolf II., a doctor and a prolific writer[1]. Even though his most famous work is *Emblemata*, among his other works one can find not only poems but also historiographies, a number of letters, speeches, a handbook for writing letters, and a dialogue on Ciceronianism.

Ciceronianism[2], a tendency to define Cicero as the only model for correct Latin stylistics, reached its peak in the 16th century. One of the major promoters of the opinion that Cicero should be an example for all those who want to write good Latin was the Venetian scholar and cardinal Pietro Bembo (1470–1547). Humanists at the papal curia, considered experts in classical Latin, were devoted to this idea. Another scholar, a Dutch lawyer by the name Christophe de Longueil (1490–1522), spent a number of years in Rome among the Ciceronians and became a sharp critic of those authors who did not write Ciceronian Latin. On the other hand, the prince of the humanists himself, Erasmus of Rotterdam, criticized Ciceronianism and in his dialogue *Ciceronianus* (1528), he indirectly attacks Longueil.

---

[1] For a complete list of Sambucus' works see Anton VANTUCH, *Ján Sambucus. Život a dielo renesančného umelca*. Bratislava 1975, 211–213; for a partially incomplete collection of Sambucus' letters see Hans GERSTINGER (ed.), *Die Briefe des Johannes Sambucus (Zsamboky) 1554–1584. Mit einem Anhang: Die Sambucusbriefe im Kreisarchiv von Trnava von Anton Vantuch*. Wien 1968 (*Sitzungsberichte der Österreichische Akademie der Wissenschaften, philosophisch-historische Klasse* 255). Gábor Almási and Farkas Gábor Kiss prepared a monograph (as part of the *Europa Humanistica* series) collecting all of Sambucus' editions and containing all the prefaces: *Humanistes du bassin des Carpates*. II: *Johannes Sambucus*. Turnhout 2014.

[2] On Ciceronianism see the classic studies by Remigio SABBADINI, *Storia del Ciceronianismo* Turin 1885; Tadeusz ZIELINSKI, *Cicero im Wandel der Jahrhunderte*. Leipzig, Berlin ^{3}1912; Izora SCOTT, *Controversies over the Imitation of Cicero as a Model for Style and some Phases of their Influence on the Schools of the Renaissance*. New York 1910; John Edwyn SANDYS, *The History of Ciceronianism*. In: *Harvard Lectures on the Revival of Learning*. Cambridge 1905. From recent works see JoAnn DELLANEVA (ed.), *Ciceronian Controversies*. Cambridge 2007; Jörg ROBERT, *Die Ciceronianismus-Debatte*. In: Herbert Jaumann (ed.), *Diskurse der Gelehrtenkultur in der Frühen Neuzeit. Ein Handbuch*. Berlin, New York 2010, 1–54.

Erasmus humorously considers Ciceronianism a disease, which should be cured. Although he admired Cicero, he preferred those among the humanist authors who did not strictly imitate his style and chose a more eclectic style, for example Lorenzo Valla or Angelo Poliziano. Erasmus' main argument is that because the society has changed significantly since the antiquity, the language too has to adapt and change to be able to express new facts, especially the religious change from Roman paganism to Christianity.

In 1535, Étienne Dolet (1509–1546) published his response to Erasmus' work, entitled *Dialogus de imitatione Ciceroniana*, also called *Erasmianus*, in which he, on the contrary, defended Ciceronian Latin. In the same year, Mario Nizzoli (1498–1576) even published a dictionary of Ciceronian words. Despite the criticism, the phenomenon of Ciceronianism survived and its influence grew, mostly in the first half of the 16th century. Cicero continued to be an example, especially in teaching Latin. His works were used as textbooks, protestant pedagogues such as Melanchthon or Sturm, but also Catholic teachers and the Jesuits held on to Ciceronian standards.

Sambucus' contribution to the question of Ciceronianism is his work *De imitatione Ciceroniana dialogi tres* published in Paris in 1561 by Gilles Gourbin (Aegidius Gorbinus). It was published two more times, 1563 and 1568, with a slight change of the title to *De imitatione a Cicerone petenda dialogi tres*. Although Anton Vantuch stated[3] that these two editions were published by Christophe Plantin (1520–1589), each of the editions had in fact its own printer, the second one was published by the relatively unknown Libertus Malcotius[4], and the third and last edition was published by Antheunis Thielens[5] (ca. 1528–1598)[6].

Written as a dialogue between Sambucus and his pupil Georgius (György) Bona[7], nephew of Nicolaus Olahus, the Archbishop of Esztergom[8], De

---

[3] VANTUCH, *Ján Sambucus*, 212.
[4] See Anne ROUZET, *Dictionnaire des imprimeurs, libraires et éditeurs des XVe et XVIe siècles dans les limites géographiques de la Belgique actuelle*. Nieuwkoop 1975, 134.
[5] See ROUZET, *Dictionnaire*, 220.
[6] Károly SZABÓ, Árpád HELLEBRANDT, *Régi Magyar Könyvtár III*. Budapest 1896, no. 503 and 568. Vantuch, despite giving the wrong publisher, refers to the same entries in RMK.
[7] For four years (1553–1557), Sambucus was a preceptor of Bona and Nicolaus Istvánffy during their studies in Padua. Bona fell ill at his bother's *sponsalia* with Anna of the Frankopan family and died at the age of 20 in 1559 at Landsee. Sambucus then published several funerary poems, epigrams and speeches for him: Oratio, in obitum generosi ac

imitatione Ciceroniana belongs to the academic discussion about the place of Latin in science, literature and education. The contents of each part or dialogue are given right at the beginning[9]. The first dialogue deals with the question whether or not there is an imitation, whether it should be studied and whether the imitation is necessary and useful. The second dialogue, with the subtitle *Quid sit imitatio*, defines the genres of imitation, what they are and how many of them there are; and the last dialogue shows how one should lay out his work in competition with his samples, so his effort is not irrational.

Even though only two years passed between the publishing of the first two editions of *De imitatione Ciceroniana*, they greatly differ. First of all, there is an improvement in script; while the 1561 edition still uses a lot of abbreviations, the second edition greatly reduced them to just nasal syllabic abbreviations (e.g. *aliquādo*). However, even though the abbreviation reduction makes the text easier to read, the new edition introduces an increased number of commas and colons sometimes at the expense of the reader's effort to understand the meaning, especially if the new comma replaces the original full stop. Some mistakes of this kind, as well as other typographical errors, are corrected in the *errata* at the very end, others, however, are not.

As far as the content goes, Sambucus returned to this work after publishing, improved it and extended it considerably. Whereas the first edition has 101 pages, the second and third edition comes with 150 pages, which is composed of 50% of new text. And if we look at it at a scale of just the second dialogue, the extension from the first edition (30 pages) to the

---

magnifici adolescentis Georgii Bona Transylvani [...] Qui mortuus est, VI. Septemb. anni 1559. Padua: Gratiosus Perchacinus 1560, reprinted with letters from Paolo Manuzio, Piero Vettori, and Bona's teachers from Padua Francesco Robortello and Giovanni Faseolo in: Orationes duae funebres Ioan. Sambuci Tyrnaviensis Pannonii. Paris: Aegidius Gorbinus 1561 (published in *De imitatione Ciceroniana* 1561). See also the emblem *Epitaphium generosi adolescentis Georgii Bona Transylvani* (no. 228 in the 1564 edition of *Emblemata*) with epitaphs taken from *Orationes duae funebres*, out of which one is from Jacques Maniquet.

[8] Both Bona and Olahus came from a prominent family with ties to Wallachian and Hungarian high nobility. For Olahus' family tree, see Cristina NEAGU, *Servant of the Renaissance: The Poetry and Prose of Nicolaus Olahus*. Bern 2003, 373–376.

[9] De imitatione Ciceroniana [...]. Paris: Aegidius Gorbinus 1561, 4ª.

second one (a little less than 42) is approximately 30%[10]. Some parts or sentences of this dialogue are extended, others are completely new. There are new questions asked, longer responses given, and even Georgius Bona, whose role is to push the dialogue forward and help proving his teacher's point, has more space and can show his erudition. His highlight, so to say, is a moment when he speaks for almost three pages and even paraphrases Xenophon (*De imitatione a Cicerone petenda*, Ev^r), only to be silenced by a several pages long reply by his teacher.

We do not know when exactly this dialogue took place[11], however, the preface to Sambucus' collection *Poemata*, addressed to Bona and Istvánffy, provides a hint. In it, Sambucus writes that he is already preparing his *cogitationes De imitatione Ciceroniana*[12]. The preface is dated February 1, 1555 and because Sambucus left for Padua only in October 1553, we can assume the dialogue on the imitation of Cicero between himself and his pupil Bona took place in the year 1554. Sambucus could have been 22 or 23 years old and Bona 14 or 15. Although the idea of 14-year-old Bona paraphrasing Xenophon in Greek from memory is quite impressive, it is not uncommon considering Sambucus started studying Greek under Georg Rithaymer[13] at the University of Vienna at the age of 11.

At the beginning of the second dialogue, Sambucus explains imitation by paraphrasing a definition from *Rhetorica ad Herennium* I, 2, 3: *Imitatio est qua impellimur, cum diligenti ratione, ut aliorum similes in dicendo velimus esse* (*De imitatione a Cicerone petenda*, Cv^v). As Sambucus says, people are drawn to imitation by nature (*a natura*), but only their interest doesn't suffice. They need to learn the art (*ars*) as well as have enough diligence (*diligentia*). His pupil Bona expresses his concerns about the value of imitation quoting Horace (*ep*. I, 19, 19) and calling the imitators *servum pecus* (Cvii^r). Sambu-

---

[10] Since the editions have different sized pages, the comparison is based on the number of lines which are more or less equally long. The total number of lines is converted to pages with 30 lines per page. The third edition (1568) is identical to the second edition (1563).

[11] The preface only states it took place *tempore alienissimo patriae*. See *De imitatione a Cicerone petenda dialogi tres* [...]. Antwerp: Libertus Malcotius 1563, Aii^r.

[12] Johannes Sambucus, Poemata. Padua: Gratiosus Perchacinus 1555, Aii^v.

[13] Christian GASTGEBER, Griechischhumanismus an der Wiener Universität: Der erste *Professor linguae Graecae* Georg Rithaymer. *Zborník Filozofickej fakulty Univerzity Komenského, Graecolatina et Orientalia* 33/34 (2012), 83–110; 89.

cus teaches Bona that when imitating, one must use words moderately, the right *compositio* and *collocatio* of the words requires skill and practice. It is not hard to find the words to support a cause, the hard part is refining them (Cvii ᵛ).

The question arises: whom should we imitate, *quorum similes esse velimus* (Dʳ). Bona thinks imitating only one person can lead to imitating also his flaws (Dʳ)[14]. But Sambucus will show him *unum et solum Ciceronem Latinae linguae principem, vel potius aeque omnium linguarum summum et cumulatissimum esse oratorem* (Dᵛ). He tells Bona about Ciceronianism and how the matter of one true example of correct Latin is still unclear, citing Cicero's *Academics* (Diiʳᵛ)[15]. He says he draws from a speech he gave in Ingolstadt[16], which might have raised some negative reactions (Diiᵛ). He mentions Paolo Cortesi, Pietro Bembo, Guarino da Verona, Christophe de Longueil, Jacopo Sadoleto and Romolo Amaseo and the basic question that still troubled the minds of educated men: *unusne Cicero, an plures stylo usurpandi sint* (Diiiᵛ)? The argument of the Ciceronians was that Cicero has *excellentia tanti ingenii*, that his works contain all necessary parts of elegance as well as philosophy, and so he can be rightfully considered to be an author who excels above everyone (Diiiiᵛ). The anti-Ciceronians objected and claimed scholars should study all of the authors and collect their vocabulary from anywhere, so it perfectly represents reality, because the content (*res*) is more important than the form (*verba*)[17]. If the names of things are known, also the explanation of the words should be added[18], and the more elegant it is, the better. If Cicero did not write about some things, their explanation can be approached *transla-*

---

[14] Cf. Quint. *Inst. orat.* 10, 1, 25; Cic. *de Orat.* 2, 22, 90.
[15] Cic. *Acad.* 2, 41, 126 *ita cogimur dissensione sapientium dominum nostrum ignorare, quippe qui nesciamus soli an aetheri serviamus.*
[16] It's probably the speech we find in the catalogue of his library under the title *Oratio* [Ioannis] *Sambuci de Ciceroniana imitatione in 4° manus*[cripta] *solut*[a]. See Pál GULYÁS, *Sámboky János könyvtára.* Budapest 1941, no. 2583.
[17] Ibid. Divᵛ *rebus, non verbis aut ulli artificio captato inserviendum, facile ad res inventas verba sequi solere.* For a further discussion of the concept of *res* (the thing or the idea of something) and *verba* (the linguistic means used to refer to it), especially of the philosophical aspect of this concept, see Matthias WESSELER, *Die Einheit von Wort und Sache. Der Entwurf einer rhetorischen Philosophie bei Marius Nizolius.* München 1974.
[18] Ibid., Dvʳ *si vocabula rerum sunt notae*; Cf. Cic. *fin.* 5, 74 *nomina tamquam rerum notas.*

tione, circuitione, contrariis, similibus – methods that Cicero also used, including *figuratio* and *epithesis*.

Sambucus states that in his opinion the sum and main idea of Ciceronianism is that the words are not as important as the style, which one should take from Cicero[19]. In general, Sambucus considers Ciceronian every language which is pure, elegant, ornate, sound and pleasant[20].

Bona is a little uncertain in the question of imitating Cicero, so he presents nine arguments which sum up his concerns (Eiii^v–Eiiii^v). Among these are such problems as:

Cicero drew his style from not one but several authors;

Cicero took many things from other authors, so our imitation of him is not completely pure;

when we want to get an idea of a thing, it can be hardly done from one source, but more likely from more sources;

there is not only one, best, eloquence and other authors who strive to write *Romane et optime* should not be excluded.

Sambucus knows these arguments are not Bona's own (Ev^r *ista non domi tuae nata*) and that they represent the views of anti-Ciceronians. One by one he addresses single arguments more or less in the order in which they were presented (Ev^r–Fiii^v). He does not deny that Cicero took some things from others, but *arte ac virtute sua* he made it his own and characteristic for him. Even the Italians[21] and the French[22] enriched their languages with Cicero, so Sambucus does not consider a few foreign forms found in Cice-

---

[19] Ibid., Dvii^v *res et verba de melioribus, quae desideras, conquirito: artem et faciendi modum Ciceronis addas.*

[20] Ibid., Dviii^v *id ego solum Ciceronianum in quaqua lingua opinor, quod purum, elegans, quod ornatum, figuratum, illustre, optabile et sanum iocundumque sit.*

[21] Baldassare Castiglione (1478–1529) and his *Il cortegiano* (1528), which greatly borrows from Cicero's *De officiis* and especially *De oratore*. See Jennifer RICHARDS, Assumed Simplicity and the Critique of Nobility: Or, How Castiglione Read Cicero. *Renaissance Quarterly* 54, 2 (2001), 460–486. Sambucus must have studied Castiglione's work, *Il cortegiano* can be found twice in his library in editions from 1544 and 1552 (GULYÁS, *Sámboky János könyvtára*, no. 530 and 56).

[22] Sambucus mentions Sperone Speroni (1500–1588). He probably meant Speroni's dialogues, especially *Dialogo delle lingue* (1542), in which he defended vernacular languages against Latin.

ro a theft. In his youth, Cicero heard eleven orators and he picked various parts and forms from them, which he perfected in his own works. From what he had read, heard and seen, he created a general idea or form, which scholars later took over and from which the single forms or aspects can be easily understood. Cicero transformed various influences into his own style, as Sambucus explains using a common, and among the Ciceronians very well known, analogy of a bee that makes honey from different, yet in the final product still indistinctive flowers (Fiii^r *ut apes in mel varios, nec in melle tamen distinctos flores convertisse*)[23].

After convincing Bona that imitating a single author, preferably Cicero, is the right path, Sambucus answers one last question – if one should imitate also the composition of Cicero's rhetorical periods. The answer is clear; imitation must not lack any part. It is difficult and it requires commitment, art and exercise, but numbers, which represent the periodical structure, cannot be separated from speech (Fiiii^{rv}).

As a result of the expansion of the whole text, *De imitatione Ciceroniana* contains more Greek words and passages, although it can still be considered a rather small part of the dialogue. The first edition of the second dialogue contained precisely 21 words or phrases, out of which only one can be regarded as a direct quotation of a classical author – Aristotle. In the second edition, the amount of Greek is almost three times larger – 60 words or phrases. Of this number, 15 cases can be classified as quotations or paraphrases of classical authors with a couple of peculiarities.

When defining the imitation at the beginning of the dialogue, Sambucus names Latin words or synonyms for imitation and imitators and follows with Greek equivalents. These are μίμησις ("imitation"), μιμητική ("the power of imitating"), and ζῆλος ("emulation of someone"). Then there is also σύγκρισις ("comparison"), ὁμοιότης ("likeness") and ἀναλογία ("resemblance"). Some of the Greek forms are taken from the classical authors. Such is the expression παρέχειν μίμησιν, which Sambucus based in general on Aristotle's *Poetics*, or the phrase πρός τινα ἔχειν τὸν ζῆλον, which

---

[23] Seneca, *epist.* 84, 5–7. Cf. Petrarch, *Familiares* 23, 19; Giovanni Francesco Pico della Mirandola, *De imitatione* 16; Giovanni Battista Giraldi Cinzio, *Epistula super imitationem* 3. Jürgen von STACKELBERG, Das Bienengleichnis. Ein Beitrag zur Geschichte der literarischen Imitatio. *Romanische Forschungen* 68 (1956), 271–293.

can be found in different forms e. g. in Plutarch or in the *Encomium on Demosthenes* attributed to Lucian[24]. Also worth noting is the expression μίμημα δι' ἀπεργασίας ("a copy of work") and especially εἴδωλον ὅμοιον ("a similar image") and ἀπεικασμός ("representation"), the last two examples being both paraphrases of Xenophon's *Symposion*[25].

Later in the text (Cviii^r), there is a quote from Pindar, *Olymp.* 2, 87 κόρακες ὡς ἄκραντα γαρύετον Διὸς πρὸς ὄρνιχα θεῖον. Here, Sambucus talks directly about imitating Cicero and calls those who want to compete with Cicero himself "*crows that chatter vain things in strife against the divine bird of Zeus.*" Several pages later, there is another quote, this time from Xenophon's *Cynegeticus*, by which he attacks those writers who are "ignorant of philosophy and lack any serious thoughts" (Diii^v *ignari pilosophiae graviorumque cogitationum expertes*). Using Xenopohon's words[26], he says that "in their writings there are no opinions (or maxims) by which the young might be trained to virtue." And in another place in the text (Dviii^v), he continues on a similar subject. This time he chooses words from Euripides' *Hecuba* 294–295 λόγος γὰρ ἔκ τ' ἀδοξούντων ἰὼν κἀκ δοκούντων αὐτὸς οὐ ταὐτὸν σθένει. By saying "words are not as effective when spoken by a common man as they are when spoken by someone with a strong reputation", he stresses the fact that the words gain weight or importance on the one hand by knowledge and education, and on the other hand by the *gravitas* of the author.

This knowledge can be learned from Cicero, among others, by studying and imitating his style, but only closely and truly. Because as yet another quote, this time from Athenaeus' work *Deipnosophistai*, says: "treachery follows the uncertain."[27] A different kind of knowledge is knowing the proverbs, metaphors and expressions in certain language. As examples Sambucus quotes four Greek phrases: διελθεῖν ἀρετήν τινος τὰς ἀκοὰς τινῶν, ἀφικνεῖσθαι εἰς τὴν καρπογονίαν, ποιεῖσθαι τοὺς λόγους, and ἔννοιαν πρός τινα ἔχειν (Eviii^r). The second example is also a quote from Xenophon's *Symposium*[28]. Overall, it can be said that *Symposium* is by far Sambucus' favorite work

---

[24] Plut. *Per.* 2; Luc. *Dem. Enc.* 57.
[25] Xen. *Symp.* 4, 22, 1.
[26] Xen. *Cyn.* 13, 3–4 [...] ὅτι τὰ μὲν ῥήματα αὐτοὺς ἐζήτηται, γνῶμαι δὲ ὀρθῶς ἔχουσαι αἷς ἂν παιδεύοιντο οἱ νεώτεροι ἐπ' ἀρετὴν οὐδαμοῦ.
[27] Athen. *Deipn.* 15, 50, 18 τῷ γὰρ ἀφανῷ πᾶς ἕπεται δόλος.
[28] Xen. *Symp.* 2, 25.

to quote in this dialogue; there are at least four quotes and paraphrases in total. The third example (ποιεῖσθαι τοὺς λόγους) is a common phrase found also in Thucydides[29] or as a synonym for λέγειν in e. g. Plato[30] or Lysias[31]. With a little variation, the forth example (ἔννοιαν πρός τινα ἔχειν) can be found in Plato[32]. Furthermore, to prove the need of knowing certain expressions in a language, there are a few words in Attic Greek and their equivalents in Doric Greek (Eviii^r). The given Attic forms are πράττειν, δῆμος and ἄξονες κ' κύρβεις, and their Doric equivalents δρᾶν, κομή and ῥῆτραι.

One of the aforementioned Greek peculiarities in the second dialogue is bound to a passage from Xenophon's *Symposium* (4, 22). This passage, a dialogue between Socrates and Critobulus, was first quoted at the beginning, when Sambucus listed Greek words connected to imitation. Later, close to the end of the dialogue (Fiiii^r), he quotes the same passage again, this time the following sentence: ἡ ὄψις εὐφραίνειν δύναται, ἡ δὲ τοῦ εἰδώλου τέρψιν μὲν οὐ παρέχει, πόθον δὲ ἐμποιεῖ.

The only Greek quote appearing already in the first edition is from Aristotle's *Poetics*. Here Sambucus teaches Bona that our imitation must be consistent; and even if he imitates someone, who is inconsistent in his style, our imitation of him must be *inconsistently consistent*[33]. Expanding this thought further, Sambucus states that *quam artem quia non nulli aut contemnunt, aut non sentient, etiam aspernantur, et ut iudicant, ita loquuntur et scribunt, nihil gloriosum et insigne unquam assequuntur* (Fv^v). He follows with the last longer Greek passage in this dialogue, which is the second of the mentioned peculiarities; it is in fact a combination of two quotes from two different authors. The first part is a paraphrase of Pindar's tenth *Pythian ode* and by it Sambucus says that "different desires excited minds of different people."[34] The second part consists of a passage of Syrianus' *Commentary of*

---

[29] See for example Thuc. I, 128.
[30] Plat. *Pol.* 527a.
[31] Lys. 25, 2.
[32] Plat. *De leg.* 769e ἔννοιαν περί τι ἔχειν.
[33] Arist. *Poet.* 1454a ὁμαλῶς τὸ ἀνώμαλον δεῖ εἶναι.
[34] Ibid. καὶ γὰρ ἑτέροισιν ἑτέρων ἔρως ἔκνιξε φρένας. Cf. Pind. *Pyth.* 10, 59–60 καὶ γὰρ ἑτέροισιν ἑτέρων ἔρως ὑπέκνισε φρένας.

Hermogenes, in which Sambucus, together with Syrianus, concludes that "what kind of thinking, that kind of deeds"[35].

It is worth mentioning also shorter Greek fragments that can be found in various places in the text. The first of them refers to Plutarch and his opusculum Περὶ παίδων ἀγωγῆς (*On the education of children*), which Sambucus mentions directly in the text[36]. Here, Sambucus explains to Bona the importance of choosing the right model and compares it to the influence of parents on their children. He gives an example of the Lacedaemonians, who fined their king, when he married a woman of small stature and gave them hope not of kings but "kinglings" (Diiii').

Another Greek passage is a short paraphrase of a verse from the work of Pseudo-Phocylides. Sambucus illustrates the attitude of some people who search for something not commonly used by Cicero or Vergil and call it a theft (*furtum*), "for every idle man lives off thievish deeds,"[37] as Sambucus concludes humorously. Also, when defending Cicero's rhetorical periods as part of his imitation, Sambucus warns Bona of the consequences of not following Cicero's example. His work would be wrongly arranged (ἀνοικονόμητον), with the incorrect use of figures (ἀσχημάτιστον) and with the incorrect collocation of words (κακοσύνθετον). This warning originally comes from Quintilian[38].

Of some interest could be Greek words, more or less rarely used in the texts of classical authors. However, all can be found in Cicero's letters: ἀπροσδιόνυσον[39] and Ἑρμαθήνη[40] in letters to Atticus and κακοστόμαχος[41] in a letter addressed to Tiro. Since the words are not used in a direct

---

[35] *Syriani in Hermogenem commentaria*, 133, 26 καὶ οἷος λόγος, τοιαῦται καὶ αἱ πράξεις.
[36] *De imitatione a Cicerone petenda*, Diiii' *Atque laudo magnanimitatem Lacedaemoniorum, qui, ut meminit Plutarchus* Περὶ παίδων ἀγωγῆς, *regem suum Archidamum pecunia multarunt, quod adiuncta sibi nuptiis tenui et modico habitu brevique statura foemina spem non* βασιλεῶν, *sed* βασιλίδων *praebuisset.*
[37] Ibid., Eviii' πᾶς γὰρ ἀεργὸς ἀνὴρ ζώει κλοπίμων ἀπὸ ἔργων. Cf. Ps.-Phocyl. 154 πᾶς γὰρ ἀεργὸς ἀνὴρ ζώει κλοπίμων ἀπὸ χειρῶν.
[38] Quint. *Inst. orat.* 8, 3, 59. Sambucus uses incorrect forms Fiiii'/44': ἀνικονόμητον (corrected το ἀνοικονόμητων), ἀσχήματον, κακοσήνθετον.
[39] Ibid., Ev' ἀπροσδιόνυσα. Cf. Cic. *Att.* 16, 13, 1.
[40] Ibid., Evi' ἑρμαθηναῖς. Cf. Cic. *Att.* 1, 1, 5; 1, 4, 3. In both cases manuscripts of Cicero's text contain the word in Latin form, unlike Sambucus'.
[41] Ibid., F' κακόστομαχοι (sic). Cf. Cic. *Fam.* 16, 4, 1.

quote, one may assume that Sambucus wanted to show not only his excellent knowledge of Greek, but also his profound knowledge of Cicero, his works and, being a sympathizer of the Ciceronians, his vocabulary.

All previously mentioned Greek words, phrases and quotes are said by the author himself. However, his pupil Georgius Bona does not remain silent in this regard. Even though he is given significantly less space than the dominant Sambucus, he is still able to paraphrase Xenophon (and Sambucus' favorite *Symposium*)[42] in his longest speech when confronting Sambucus with the nine arguments of the anti-Ciceronians. Then again, close to the end of the dialogue, he slips some Greek into his words[43].

Lastly, there are more Greek words and expressions in the second dialogue of *De imitatione a Cicerone petenda*, but it is difficult to identify them because in some cases it is a word with a broader meaning (e. g. λόγος, καλός, ὕλη...), in other cases the expression is so modified, that it is hard to tell if it is originally from a classical author. Sambucus was very skilled in Greek, because he was able to easily support his ideas and statements with various quotes, often cleverly changed to fit his intentions. His Greek is not always flawless[44], but we can assume he quoted authors from memory, given the fact that every author or work he quoted can be found in his library, often in more than one edition.

In the question whether to use Latin or vernacular languages, Sambucus defends Latin as a unique way of preserving and transferring ideas, knowledge and aesthetic values[45]. He does not want to underestimate the national languages, because they are sufficient for our usual, daily needs. However, they do not suffice the mind which goes beyond the usual things[46]. He thinks classical languages teach people to think better, they uncover new relations;

---

[42] Ibid., Ev' γενεαλογεῖν τὴν συγγένειαν πρὸς Κικέρωνα. Cf. Xen. *Symp.* 4, 51, 4 γενεαλογοῦσι τὴν συγγένειαν.
[43] Ibid., Fiiii' *num imitabilem Ciceronem, quo ad omnem* σύνθεσιν *illam* ὀνομάτων *minutam dinumerationem dimensionemque syllabarum permittis?* When talking about the structure of Cicero's periods, the title of the work by Dionysius of Halicarnassus comes to mind – Περὶ συνθέσεως ὀνομάτων.
[44] There are some mistakes, be it a wrong accent or spiritus, sometimes even a spelling mistake. Almost all the mistakes are corrected in the errata, a couple of them is, however, ignored (e. g. κακόστομαχοι instead of κακοστόμαχοι).
[45] See the first dialogue of *De imitatione a Cicerone petenda*.
[46] VANTUCH, *Ján Sambucus* (n. 1), 97.

they are the source of knowledge. That is why they should be studied and cultivated. One should use all the knowledge the Greeks and Romans left us, so he could be even more productive and better than them. So, everyone who wants to use and cultivate his own mother language studies classical languages, so he can learn more, especially from Latin[47]. Although acknowledging the Latin origin of what are today referred to as Neo-Latin languages, Sambucus still considers the defense of Latin appropriate. He points out that although the knowledge of the authors who write in their national languages comes from Latin (thus what they do is imitate Latin), the multitude who are neither acquainted with Latin literature nor educated in philology regard all the treasures of Latin as solely the virtue of the vulgar and tend to neglect Latin as an incomprehensible scholarly language[48].

Sambucus sees every language as a living organism which cannot be damaged by putting in unnatural structures. When a student can handle Cicero, he can apply his Latin elsewhere because he has learnt to capture and define the topic and then organically add "spices" or "ornaments". That is how Erasmus taught it and especially Johannes Sturm, Sambucus' teacher[49].

In the Ciceronian debate, Sambucus can be associated with the camp of Ciceronians, although on the scale of devotion to Cicero, he ought to be placed in the middle – he is neither extreme, nor too liberal in the ways of following Cicero. The use of Tullius' style is necessary, in his view, because he is the principal author. Nevertheless, Sambucus does not define Cicero as the sole example, from which we must draw our inspiration; he does, however, say he is the best example. As for vocabulary, one does not necessarily have to restrain himself to one person's language[50]. After all, he considers Ciceronian all that which is elegant and pleasant.

---

[47] Ibid., 98.
[48] Imre TÉGLÁSY, János Zsámboky (Sambucus) and his theory of language. *Hungarian Studies* 10, 2 (1995), 245–246.
[49] VANTUCH, *Ján Sambucus*, 98; on Johannes Sturm and his relationship with Sambucus see Arnoud S. Q. VISSER, *Joannes Sambucus and the Learned Image. The Use of the Emblem in Late Renaissance Humanism.* Leiden 2005, 10–11; or VANTUCH, *Ján Sambucus* (n. 1), 65.
[50] See footnote 19. Cf. Johannes Sturm, De imitatione oratoria libri tres, cum scholiis eiusdem authoris, antea nunquam in lucem editi. Strasbourg: Bernhardus Iobinus 1576, D3ᵛ *Quae in Cicerone non sunt, aliunde sunt conquirenda.*

In conclusion, with *De imitatione a Cicerone petenda dialogi tres* Sambucus rejected the vehemence of the debate on Ciceronianism and offered a compromise placing himself in a middle ground between dogmatic Ciceronians and those who denied his absolute authority in Latin prose. He thinks imitation should be a process involving more than one author, and is more than only a matter of verbal expressions but also of deeper understanding of the imitated person[51]. Although primarily intended as a lecture for his pupil Georgius Bona, Sambucus' ideas are surprisingly mature and solid. Some contemporaries were impressed. For example, for the English humanist Gabriel Harvey it was Sambucus (and then Petrus Ramus) who opened his eyes to questions of imitation and made him start valuing content and thought more than words and language[52]. He then read Caesar, Varro, Sallust, Livy, Pliny and Columella, and found merits in all. He began to find imperfections in Cicero, though still he felt that Cicero was the chief model for imitation.[*]

---

[51] Gábor ALMÁSI, *The Uses of Humanism. Johannes Sambucus (1531–1584), Andreas Dudith (1533–1589), and the Republic of Letters in East Central Europe.* Leiden 2009, 228.
[52] G. C. Moore SMITH (ed.), *Gabriel Harvey's Marginalia.* Stratford-upon-Avon 1913, 14.
[*] This paper is published as a part of the project VEGA 1/0627/15 *Latinská humanistická literatúra na Slovensku v kontexte politickej propagandy* (Latin humanist literature in Slovakia in the context of a political propaganda). The part dealing with the Graeca is published in Slovak: Graeca v II. dialógu Sambucovho De imitatione a Cicerone petenda. *Sambucus* 12 (2017).

Machtsymbole und politisches Programm in den *Emblemata* des Johannes Sambucus

ZOLTÁN ERDÖS (Budapest)

Abb. 1a: *MATHIAE CORVINI SYMBOLUM, SYMBOLO IOANNIS REGIS AUCTUM*
aus: Johannes Sambucus, Emblemata. Antverpiae 1564, 161
(Hg. von Béla VARJAS. Budapest 1982)

D ie Gattung des Emblems, die sich um die Mitte des 16. Jahrhunderts in der europäischen Bildungsgeschichte entwickelte, ist eine bemerkenswerte Neuerung der Humanisten. Ein Emblem besteht aus folgenden Bestandteilen: einem Bild (*pictura*), einer Überschrift (*inscriptio*) und einem Epigramm (*subscriptio*). Seine Thematik wird meistens von einer mythologischen oder historischen Geschichte, einer moralischen oder wissenschaftlichen Problematik, einer gesellschaftlichen Erscheinung oder einem Naturphänomen bestimmt. Die Essenz eines Emblems lässt sich nicht immer allzu leicht deuten: Die Hinweise sind mehrfach zusammengesetzt, die antiken und zeitgenössischen Symbole verschmelzen oft miteinander[1].

Ein Emblem lädt dementsprechend den Betrachter zum gemeinsamen Spiel ein. Mit dieser Absicht stellte Johannes Sambucus die Erstausgabe seines Emblembuches im Jahre 1564 zusammen. Er schafft zwar keine systematische Moralistik, gibt aber mit den einzelnen Sinnbildern Ratschläge zum tugendhaften Leben; er tangiert Fragen der Poetik, der Rhetorik und der Medizin eher selten und vermeidet möglicherweise auch die zeitgeschichtlichen und politischen Probleme. Seine Bilder und Texte harmonieren fast immer miteinander[2], die Auslegung wird dadurch erleichtert. Es gibt aber einige seiner Embleme, die sich nur schwer enträtseln lassen. Eines der wenigen politisch orientierten Embleme verlangt zum Beispiel

---

[1] Johannes Sambucus, Emblemata. Antverpiae 1564. Hg. von Béla VARJAS. Einleitung: August BUCK. Budapest 1982 (*Bibliotheca Hungarica Antiqua* 11), 3–7; August BUCK, Einleitung, 16f.; 20. János ORBÁN, *Sámboky Jánosról*. Szeged 1916, 58f. Éva KNAPP, Irodalmi emblematika Magyarországon a XVI–XVIII. században [Emblematische Literatur in Ungarn im 16.–18. Jahrhundert]. Budapest 2003 (*Historia Litteraria* 14), 16–25; 31–39.

[2] Nach KNAPP (s. Anm. 1, 90f.) hielt Sambucus eine enge Beziehung zum Illustrator. Andere Forschungen weisen darauf hin, dass bei lediglich 9% der Embleme ein enger Zusammenhang zwischen Bild und Text besteht; die engste Zusammenarbeit zwischen Verfasser und Illustrator können wir nur in diesen Fällen vermuten. Solche Embleme, die Wappenbilder enthalten, wurden bestimmt mit Konsultation und Instruktion von Sambucus angefertigt. Arnoud VISSER, *Joannes Sambucus and the Learned Image: the Use of the Emblem in Late-Renaissance Humanism*. Leiden 2005 (*Brill's Studies in Intellectual History* 128), 225–240. Gábor ALMÁSI, *The Uses of Humanism. Johannes Sambucus (1431–1584), Andreas Dudith (1533–1589), and the Republic of Letters in East Central Europe*. Leiden, Boston 2009 (*Brill's Studies in Intellectual History* 185), 156f.

vom Betrachter deutliche Scharfsinnigkeit. Dem Titel *MATHIAE CORVINI SYMBOLUM, SYMBOLO IOANNIS REGIS AUCTUM* (Abb. 1) gemäß sieht man auf diesem Bild die vereinigten Wappen von König Matthias Hunyadi und Johann Szapolyai[3]; die *inscriptio* bestimmt also einen komplizierten Diskurs als Rahmen der Interpretation[4].

Im Zeitalter des doppelten Königtums zeichnete sich der antagonistische Gegensatz zweier politischer Gruppen scharf ab. Die Parteien von König Johann und Ferdinand I. leugneten gegenseitig das Existenzrecht der jeweils anderen Partei. Dabei titulierten sie sich gegenseitig als Staatsfeind oder Verräter, und in der Regel war dies noch eine milde Ausdrucksweise. Die Anhänger von König Johann sprachen darüber, dass einige Herren vom Satan angelogen zur Partei Ferdinands übertraten[5], die deutschen Bürger von Kaschau machten sogar ein lustiges Spektakel aus der Beleidigung des Wappens von Szapolyai[6]. Die auf politischen und moralischen Begriffen basierenden sprachlichen und bildlichen Botschaften dienten dazu, ein eigenes positives Ansehen zu schaffen und gleichzeitig dem Feind alle möglichen Mittel zur Legitimation zu entziehen[7]. An diesen Diskurs schloss Sambucus mit seinem Emblem an.

Auf der linken Seite des Bildes sehen wir das Wappentier der Familie Hunyadi, den Raben. Er hält eine Lyra und einen Schild mit dem Kopf von

---

[3] Sambucus (s. Anm. 1), 161f.

[4] Éva Gyulai ist der Meinung, dass das Emblem nur als Übernahme des Irrtums von Gabriele Simeoni entstanden sei. In seinem 1561 erschienenen Buch publizierte Simeoni das Wolf-Emblem fälschlicherweise als Symbol von Matthias Hunyadi. Die Sinnbilder von Sambucus entbehrten also jeder Bedeutung, die Struktur des Emblems sei zufallsartig. Éva GYULAI, Hunyadi Mátyás emblémái a 16–17. századi emblémáskönyvekben [Das Emblem des Matthias Hunyadi in den Emblembüchern des 16.-17. Jahrhunderts]. *Publicationes Universitatis Miskolcinensis. Sectio Philosophica* 14 (2009), 41–114; hier 84–86.

[5] Hieronymus Laski an Johannes de Tarnów, Klausenburg, 18. Okt. 1527. In: Mihály Sztárai, História Perényi Ferenc kiszabadulásáról [Geschichte der Befreiung von Ferenc Perényi]. Hg. von Imre TÉGLÁSY. Budapest 1985 (*Magyar ritkaságok*), 105.

[6] György Szerémi, Emlékirata Magyarország romlásáról 1484–1543 [Epistola de perdicione regni Hungarorum]. Hg. von Gusztáv WENZEL. Pest 1857 (*Monumenta Hungariae Historica. Scriptores*), 197.

[7] Reinhart KOSELLECK, Az asszimetrikus ellenfogalmak történeti-politikai szemantikája [Asymmetrische Gegenbegriffe in historisch-politischer Semantik]. In: Ders., Elmúlt jövő. A történeti idők szemantikája [Vergangene Zukunft. Zur Semantik geschichtlicher Zeiten]. 2003 (*Circus Maximus*), 241–298; hier 241–249.

Gorgo. In der Richtung des Raben schreitet ein Wolf (oder ein Hund), das Wappentier der Szapolyais, einher; sein Maul ist offen, die Brüste wulstig sind. Im Hintergrund des Bildes sieht man den Dreiberg, auf der mittleren und erhöhten Wölbung steht das Doppelkreuz, auf der linken etwas niedrigeren Wölbung ist eine Krone platziert. Vor dem Kreuz schwebt ein Band mit der Aufschrift SVA ALIENAQVE NVTRIT. Auf dem Rahmen entdeckt man eine Palette, ein Lineal und ein Senkblei. Oben in der Mitte sitzt eine Eule[8]. Das Epigramm preist die großen Taten des Königs Matthias und spricht am Ende Herzog Maximilian an und ermahnt ihn, an den nötigen europäischen Zusammenschluss gegen den Türken zu denken[9].

Wenn wir dieses Emblem vollständig verstehen möchten, müssen wir vorerst überblicken, in welchem Kontext und in welcher Bedeutung die einzelnen Symbole im politischen Diskurs des 16. Jahrhunderts stehen.

DAS STAATSWAPPEN

Am Ende des 15. Jahrhunderts begann man, die vier silbernen Streifen im ungarischen Staatswappen mit den vier größten Flüssen des Königreichs zu identifizieren; somit bekam das Wappen eine konkrete territoriale Bedeutung. 1496 identifizierte König Vladislav II. die auf dem slawonischen Wappen erscheinenden Wellenbalken mit den beiden Flüssen Drau und Sawe. Sechs Jahre später interpretierte eine Urkunde aus Kaschau die vier Streifen als Symbole der Flüssen Donau, Theiß, Drau und Sawe. Diesen Gedanken führte auch Werbőczy im *Tripartitum* weiter[10]. Der ungarische Gesandte Ladislaus de Macedonia zeugt in seiner 1522 vor dem deutschen Reichstag gehaltenen Rede ebenfalls von dieser Tradition[11]. Die vier silbernen Streifen stellten also sehr oft die territoriale Integrität des Landes dar. In der Deutung des Dreibergs erschien erst in der Mitte des 17. Jahrhunderts die Symbolik der drei höchsten Berge des Landes[12]. Zu Sambucus' Zeiten wurde ausschließlich den

---

[8] Der Illustrator benutzte zwar diesen Rahmen bei mehreren Bildern, es ist aber sicherlich kein Zufall, dass er auch bei diesem Emblem verwendet wurde.
[9] Sambucus (s. Anm. 1), 161–162.
[10] Iván BERTÉNYI, Magyar címerek [Ungarische Wappen]. *Rubicon* 20 (2009), 38–57; hier 43f.
[11] Janus Pannonius – Magyarországi humanisták [Janus Pannonius – Ungarische Humanisten]. Hg. von Tibor KLANICZAY. Budapest 1982 (*Magyar remekírók*), 905.
[12] BERTÉNYI (s. Anm. 10), 43f.

Streifen eine geographische Bedeutung zugeteilt, der Dreiberg kam selbständig nur sehr selten vor. Deshalb können wir das auf dem Emblem erscheinende Dreiberg-Motiv nicht als territoriales Symbol des Landes auffassen; wir müssen nach einer anderen Erklärung suchen.

Das Staatswappen verkörpert nicht nur die territoriale Integrität des Landes, sondern hängt auch mit der Geschichtsauffassung des Landes, mit den alten Rechten und Gewohnheiten des Volkes, und mit der Souveränität der Nation zusammen. So schreibt der Humanist Nicolaus Olahus in seinem Werk über König Attila[13]:

> Haec quatuor flumina, quae cum duplicata cruce alba e monte viridi enata insignia sunt Hungariae [...] De manu Athilae sanguinolenta et per illius impressa vestigia habemus insignia.
>
> Dies sind die vier Flüsse, die mit einem weißen Doppelkreuz, das aus einem grünen Berg herauswächst, das Wappen von Ungarn bilden. [...] Von den blutigen Händen Attilas und in seinen Fußstapfen schreitend besitzen wir unser Wappen.

DER WOLF

In der Repräsentation von König Johann bekam sein Wappentier, der Wolf, selbstverständlich die zentrale Rolle. Sein Familienwappen wurde dem Zeitgeist von König Matthias entsprechend meistens in der Mitte des Staatswappens, im Herzwappen platziert. Am Beispiel der ihm dedizierten Bücher sieht man, dass in seinem Wappen die Würde und – nach seiner Ehe – auch seine internationalen Beziehungen und die Anerkennung seiner politischen Person repräsentiert werden. In einer Ausgabe von Johannes Honterus aus dem Jahre 1539 erscheint zum Beispiel das Szapolyai-Wappen vereinigt mit dem Staatswappen und dem Wappen der Königin Isabella (Abb. 2)[14].

---

[13] Nicolaus Olahus, Hungaria – Athila. Ed. Colomannus EPERJESSY, Ladislaus JUHÁSZ. Budapest 1938 (Bibliotheca Scriptorum Medii Recentisque Aevorum. Saeculum XVI), 8.

[14] Éva GYULAI, Farkas vagy egyszarvú? Politika és presztízs megjelenése a Szapolyai-címer változataiban [Wolf oder Einhorn? Die Darstellung von Politik und Prestige auf den Varianten des Szapolyai-Wappens]. In: József Bessenyei, Zita Horváth, Péter Tóth (Hgg.), Tanulmányok Szapolyai Jánosról és a kora újkori Erdélyről [Studien über Johann Szapolyai und Siebenbürgen in der frühen Neuzeit]. Miskolc 2004 (Studia Miskolcinensia 5), 91–124; hier 118.

Abb. 2: Siegel des Königs Johann Szapolyai aus dem Jahre 1531
aus: GYULAI, s. Anm. 14, 118

Ähnlich große Bedeutung hatte der Wappengebrauch auf den meistverbreiteten Propagandamitteln, den Münzen. Auf den Geldstücken wurden seit Ende des 14. Jahrhunderts fast ausnahmslos die Figuren von Ladislaus dem Heiligen und der Jungfrau Maria, der *Patrona Hungariae*, abgebildet. Auch Ferdinand I. folgte dieser Tradition in den frühen Jahren seiner Regierung. Es war gerade Szapolyai, der damit brach: Er erhob sein eigenes Wappen zum zentralen Element seiner Münzen. Auf seinem dreifachen goldenen Forint aus dem Jahre 1527 (Abb. 3) – der aufgrund seines hohen Wertes eher eine Erinnerungsmedaille als wirkliches Zahlungsmittel sein konnte – ließ er auf die Vorderseite sein eigenes Porträt, auf die Rückseite sein Familienwappen prägen. Die beiden Hälften des Staatswappens wurden voneinander getrennt und verkleinert. In der Mitte fand der sichtbar größere Wolf seinen Platz[15].

---

[15] Ferenc SOÓS, A magyar fémpénzek feliratai és címerei [Die Inschriften und Wappen der ungarischen Münzen]. Budapest 1998, 102; GYULAI (s. Anm. 14), 99.

Machtsymbole und politisches Programm

Abb. 3: Dreifacher goldener Forint des Königs Johann aus dem Jahr 1527
aus: GYULAI, s. Anm. 14, 120

Den Wolf kann man auch in Paolo Giovios Impresensammlung finden. Das Bild wurde unter Mitwirkung von István Brodarics, der mit Giovio befreundet war, geschaffen. Auf der Imprese wurde die ursprünglich wachsende Figur des Wolfes zu einer vollständigen Figur und unverwechselbar in ein Muttertier verwandelt. Dabei ist die Annäherung an die kapitolinische Wölfin nicht zu verkennen. Damit wollte Giovio natürlich die positiven Attitüden Szapolyais zum Ausdruck bringen. Die Imprese erhielt auch eine Überschrift: *SUA ALIENAQUE PIGNORA NUTRIT*. Diese weist darauf hin, dass der König nicht nur seine treuen Anhänger ernährt, sondern auch seinen Gegnern vergibt und sie in seinen Dienst stellt (Abb. 4)[16]. Diese Abbildung erschien in mehreren Ausgaben, auch auf Spanisch und Französisch und diente unter anderem Sambucus als unmittelbare Quelle[17].

Auch der Gegner nutzte die in der Gestalt des Wolfes inhärenten Potentiale vielseitig und meisterhaft aus. Das Symbol wurde in einen negativen, dem ursprünglichen vollkommen gegenteiligen Kontext gestellt. Der Wolf, der in Szapolyais Repräsentation Mut, Ausdauer und seelenruhige Stärke verkörperte, wurde zum grausamen und blutdürstenden Untier verwandelt oder zum schwachen und schändlichen Hund degradiert. Die negativen Kon-

---

[16] Paolo Giovio, Dialogo dell'imprese militari et amorose. Lione: Appresso Gulielmo Roviglio 1559, 129. <https://archive.org/details/dialogomilitarie00giov> (12. 2. 2016).
[17] GYULAI (s. Anm. 14), 76–79.

Abb. 4: Imprese des Königs Johann Szapolyai aus: Paolo Giovio, Dialogo dell'imprese militari et amorose. Lione: Appresso Gulielmo Roviglio 1559, 129 (s. Anm. 16)

notationen wurden dadurch verstärkt, dass in der damaligen europäischen Kunst der Hund typischerweise in negativer Rolle, als Verkörperung der Gewalttätigkeit, von Wut und Treulosigkeit, oder sogar auch als Attribut von Judas gebraucht wurde[18].

Valentin Eck, der Schulmeister und spätere Bürgermeister von Bartfeld, nannte Szapolyai in seiner 1530 erschienenen Flugschrift einen fürchterlichen Bluthund, der das ganze Land bedrohe und die einst blühenden Städte Ungarns verwüste[19]. Es ist gut vorstellbar, dass der gelehrte Humanist damit auf das Bündnis mit den Türken und auf die damit hereinbrechenden Gefahren

---

[18] Simona COHEN, Animals as Disguised Symbols in Renaissance Art. Leiden, Boston 2008 (Brill's Studies in Intellectual History 169), 79–81; 185f.

[19] Ágnes RITOÓK-SZALAY, Politikai szatíra Magyarországon a XVI. században [Die politische Satire in Ungarn im 16. Jahrhundert]. Irodalomtörténeti Közlemények 75 (1971), 265–277; hier 267.

hinweisen wollte, denn die Türken wurden oft – meistens in deutschen Flugschriften – als Bluthunde bezeichnet und dargestellt[20]. Ein beliebtes Kommunikationsverfahren der Habsburger war, die Taten von Szapolyai mit den Aktionen der Türken zu vermischen. Nicolaus Olahus beklagt in einem Brief zum Beispiel die Leiden und Übeltaten, „*quas iamdiu et a Turcis Christiani nominis hostibus, et a Joanne Rege* [...] *perpessi sumus.*"[21]

In anderen Fällen verwendete man den Wolf nicht als abschreckendes Beispiel, sondern satirisch, indem der Wolf zum kleinen und harmlosen Hund herabgestuft wurde. Als Ferdinand im Sommer 1527 seinen Feldzug gegen König Johann startete, stellte sich die Stadt Kaschau an die Seite des „deutschen Königs". Ein Fest wurde organisiert, das *Te Deum* gesungen, und es wurde verboten, Szapolyai als König zu bezeichnen. Eine Gruppe der Bürger führte diese offizielle Zeremonie weiter:

> Interim armam suam super parietem aplicatam luppum retraxerunt et ad vnum canicullo ligauerunt cum straminibus, et insuper mingerunt cum vrinis suis et destercorauerant postea eum humana stercora. Et insuper incenderunt strameam super canem et dicebant blasfeman: ‚Ecce Rex canis; ecce Rex canis,' incessanter proclamabant.[22]

Mit der brutalen Lästerung des Wappens beleidigten die Bürger von Kaschau den König nicht nur in seiner Person, sondern entzogen ihm symbolisch sogar den Königstitel.

DER RABE

In den Streitigkeiten zwischen den zwei Königen erhielten die historischen Beweisführungen eine wichtige Rolle. Mit vielfältigen Mitteln wollte jede Königspartei die eigene Legitimität begründen, vor allem durch Aneignung des Erbes der Vorfahren. Neben der Gestalt Ludwigs II. wurden Johann Hunyadi und König Matthias die bedeutendsten Bezugspersonen.

---

[20] Magda HORVÁTH, A törökveszedelem a német közvéleményben [Die Türkengefahr in der deutschen öffentlichen Meinung]. Budapest 1937, 20–27.

[21] Nicolaus Olahus an Ferdinand I. Linz, 4. Feb. 1530. In: Oláh Miklós II. Lajos és Mária királyné titkára, utóbb magy. orsz. cancellár esztergomi érsek-primás és kir. helytartó levelezése [Die Korrespondenz von Nikolaus Oláh, Sekretär von Ludwig II. und Königin Maria, später Kanzler, Erzbischof von Gran und königlicher Statthalter]. Hg. von Arnold IPOLYI. Budapest 1875 (*Monumenta Hungariae Historica. Diplomataria*), 32.

[22] Szerémi (s. Anm. 6), 197.

Johann Szapolyai erklärte im Herbst 1527 ein Manifest an das ganze Land, in dem er erstmals über die Kontinuität zwischen König Matthias und sich selbst sprach. Demgemäß will er Matthias' großen Plan, den Krieg gegen die Türken, durchführen und siegreich beenden. Doch ebenso wie der große Vorfahre werde er bei diesem Werk durch den Habsburger behindert[23]. Johann war auch später um Ähnlichkeiten in seinem politischen Image bemüht. Er forcierte dies sogar in solchen Punkten, wo ihre tatsächlichen Taten erhebliche Unterschiede aufwiesen. Die Umstände der Wahl Johanns zum ungarischen König wurden eindeutig viel positiver dargestellt:

> non vi et mali metu, ut Matthias Rex [...] sed insignibus in Rempublicam meritis subnixus, jam ante quoque habitus suorum judicio Regno dignus, et Regni candidatus, desponsum sibi a Nobilitate unicum summae virtuti debitum praemium repeteret.[24]

> Er (sein Rechtsgrund) stütze sich nicht auf Gewalt und auf die Furcht des Bösen [...] wie König Matthias, sondern auf seine herausragenden Verdienste gegenüber dem Staat; nach der Meinung der Seinigen sei er schon vorher des Königstitels würdig und Kandidat für die Königswürde gewesen, er solle diesen ihm vom Adel versprochenen, einzigartigen, der höchsten Virtus geschuldeten Lohn erhalten.

Der Dichter Miklós Bogáti Fazekas versucht in seinem Gedicht über König Matthias das Türkenbündnis nachträglich zu erklären[25]: Matthias konnte dank guter internationaler Verhältnisse mehrmals gegen den Türken auftreten, doch Johann war gezwungen, mit dem Sultan Frieden zu schließen, um sein Land zu erhalten.

Die unmittelbare Verbindung mit den Hunyadis wurde auf ganz populäre Weise vorgestellt. István Szapolyai war ein Vertrauter von König Matthias, der auch zum Taufpaten des neugeborenen Johann gewählt wurde. Matthias prophezeite sogar, dass das Kind einst König von Ungarn sein werde[26] –

---

[23] Gábor BARTA, A törökös ideológia kezdetei Magyarországon [Die Anfänge pro-türkischer Ideologie in Ungarn]. *Keletkutatás* (1987) I, 8–19. hier 10f.

[24] Wolffgangi de Bethlen [...] Historia de rebus Transsylvanicis. Editio secunda. Tomus I. Cibinii: typis et sumptibus Martini Hochmeister 1782, 51f.

[25] István NEMESKÜRTY, *A magyar népnek, ki ezt olvassa. Az anyanyelvű magyar reneszánsz és barokk irodalom története 1533–1712* [Für das ungarische Volk, wer das liest. Geschichte der ungarischen Literatur im Zeitalter der Renaissance und des Barocks]. Budapest 1975, 165.

[26] Szerémi (s. Anm. 6), 46; 139. Farkas Bethlen, Erdély története, I. Übersetzt von András BODOR. Budapest, Kolozsvár 2000, 44.

durch die Verknüpfung der Vorhersage und der Person des großen Königs entstand ein anekdotenhaftes, leicht propagierbares Argument für die Seite Johanns. Auf ähnliche Weise ging auch Antonius Verantius vor, der sich ein paar Jahre später in seinem Lobgedicht auf die Geburt Johanns II. freut: *Nulla quidem nobis Matthiae a tempore magni / Illuxit melior, candidiorque dies*[27]. Auf persönlichen Kontakt konnte sich der Verfasser zwar nicht mehr berufen, er behauptete jedoch, dass das Kind das Lebenswerk von Matthias fortsetzen und erfüllen werde.

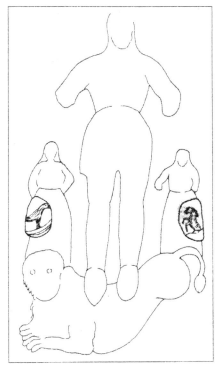

---

[27] Verancsics Antal összes munkái, XII. Hg. von László SZALAY, Gusztáv WENZEL. Budapest 1875 (*Monumenta Hungariae Historica. Scriptores* 32), 12.

Abb. 5ab: Deckplatte des Grabdenkmals von Johann Hunyadi, mit den Wappen der Familie Hunyadi und Szapolyai aus: Gábor BARTA, *Nándorfehérvár, 1456*. Budapest 1985, 307; schematische Darstellung aus: GYULAI, s. Anm. 14, 117.

Abb. 5cd: Szenen (Schlacht, Siegeszug ungarischer Soldaten mit türkischen Gefangenen) auf den Seiten des Grabdenkmals aus: BARTA, 157f.

König Johann konnte neben der textlichen Propaganda den Kult der Hunyadis auch mit bildlichen Mitteln pflegen und gleichzeitig die Kontinuität darstellen. Im Jahr 1533 ließ er das Grabdenkmal von Johann und Matthias Hunyadi errichten. Neben der Gestalt von Johann Hunyadi, gegenüber dem Wappen mit dem Raben, wurde das Wappen der Familie Szapolyai platziert. Das Epitaph verkündete darüber hinaus, die Szapolyais seien Nachfolger des

Hauses Hunyadi[28]. Die Person des christlichen Helden und die Kampfszenen darstellenden Reliefs wiesen eindeutig auf die antitürkischen Attitüden des Königs hin (Abb. 5a–d).

Der Kreis Ferdinands bestritt selbstverständlich Johanns Legitimität und versuchte gleichzeitig, diejenige Ferdinands mit positiven Argumenten zu begründen. Der Hofhistoriker Ursinus Velius erläuterte in seiner bei der Krönungsmesse Ferdinands gehaltenen Rede, dass König Matthias in der Gestalt Ferdinands wiedergeboren worden sei: Er werde das monumentale Werk des Königs, in erster Linie natürlich die antitürkischen Pläne, weiterführen[29]. Die Anhänger des habsburgischen Königs propagierten in weiten Kreisen der ungarischen Gesellschaft eine Variante der Legende über die Ermordung von König Matthias: Das Attentat sei unter der Leitung von István Szapolyai, dem Statthalter in Wien, geplant und durchgeführt worden. Die in dieser Zeit gestohlenen Schätze gingen nach dem Tode des Vaters in den Besitz von Johann Szapolyai über – symbolisch wurde er also Erbe der Ermordung des Königs[30].

DIE MÖGLICHEN INTERPRETATIONEN DES EMBLEMS

Aus der Überschrift des Emblems *MATHIAE CORVINI SYMBOLUM, SYMBOLO IOANNIS REGIS AUCTUM* geht hervor, dass auf dem Bild die vereinigten Wappenfiguren des Hauses Hunyadi und Szapolyai zu sehen sind. Es ist aber nicht eindeutig, in welcher Rolle der Wolf erscheint, und zu welchem Zweck die zwei Familienwappen und das Staatswappen vereinigt wurden.

Die erste und einfachste Interpretation wäre, dass der Wolf als Szapolyais Wappentier im negativen Kontext als Bluthund erscheint oder mindestens als Verbündeter des richtigen Bluthundes, der Türken. Er knurrt mit offenem

---

[28] GYULAI (s. Anm. 14), 97f.
[29] Mihály IMRE, „Magyarország panasza". A Querela Hungariae toposz a XVI–XVII. század irodalmában [„Die Klage Ungarns". Der Topos „Querela Hungariae" in der Literatur des 16.–17. Jahrhunderts]. Debrecen 1995 (*Csokonai Könyvtár* 5), 19.
[30] Henryk KRETSCHMAYR, Adalékok Szapolyai János király történetéhez [Zusätze zur Geschichte von Johann Szapolyai]. *Történelmi Tár* 26 (1903), I, 34–66. Hans Dernschwam, Erdély, Besztercebánya, Törökországi útinapló [Siebenbürgen, Banská Bystrica, Türkei – Reisetagebuch]. Hg. von Lajos TARDY. Budapest 1984 (*Bibliotheca Historica*) 112f.; RITOÓK-SZALAY (s. Anm. 19), 267.

Mund, bedroht das Land, und mit seinem erhobenen Bein will er möglicherweise das Erbe von Matthias zerdrücken. Nach dieser Gedankenfolge sollte die Aufschrift SUA ALIENAQUE NUTRIT nicht auf die Milde des Königs gegenüber seinen Feinden hinweisen, sondern sie bedeutet eher, dass Johann den Türken „ernähre" und ihnen Hilfe leiste. Diese Auslegung wird aber von der Darstellung des Wolfes überhaupt nicht unterstützt: Das Tier sieht nicht wie ein gefährlicher Bluthund, sondern eher wie ein friedliches Muttertier aus.

Die zweite Möglichkeit wäre, dass der Wolf gar nicht das Wappentier von Szapolyai darstelle; damit stimmen zwei Umstände überein. Erstens: im Gedicht ist König Johann nicht einmal erwähnt. Zweitens: Wenn wir den Wolf mit dem ungarischen Wappentier identifizierten, würde er sich in den Rahmen des antiken Symbolbestandes nicht einfügen können; die Lyra, der Schild mit dem Kopf der Gorgo und die Eule stammen gleicherweise aus der Antike, und auch der Rabe hat eine Beziehung zur klassischen Kultur dank der von Bonfini geschaffenen Genealogie. In der Gestalt des Tieres sollten wir also die Figur der Remus und Romulus ernährenden Wölfin, das Symbol des Römischen Reiches, erkennen. Dies wird sowohl von der Aufschrift als auch durch die sichtbar wulstigen Brüste unterstützt. Auf die Ernährung, Entwicklung des Landes, auf das hochberühmte Mäzenatentum des Königs verweisen die Lyra und die auf dem Rahmen des Bildes sichtbaren Symbole, die Sinnbilder des friedlichen Schaffens und einer guten Regierung. Aus dem Lebenswerk von Matthias kann natürlich das Image des christlichen Helden auch nicht wegbleiben: Der Rabe hält den Schild mit dem Kopf der Gorgo, dessen Anblick den Feind erstarren lässt. Man darf nicht übersehen, dass Rabe und Wolf in dieselbe Richtung blicken und nach dem gemeinsamen Feind spähen. Die Parallele zwischen der Gründung des Römischen Reiches und der Gründung der ungarischen Großmacht ist also unverkennbar.

Dieser Gedanke wird im Epigramm (Abb. 8) weitergeführt, indem der Verfasser zum Zusammenschluss gegen den Türken ermahnt und auf die Erfolge und die Tapferkeit des Königs Matthias hindeutet. Sambucus schloss sich dem pro-habsburgischen Diskurs an und stellte den Thronfolger Maximilian als Erben des großen Königs dar, der nicht nur ähnliche soldatische Tugenden aufwies, sondern auch im Mäzenatentum seinem Vorgänger nicht nachstand. Der Widmung des Buches und einem anderen Emblem entsprechend verfügen die Habsburger über alle Herrschertugenden, die zum Schutz und zur Erhaltung des Landes nötig sind[31]. Der Akt der Reichsgründung der kapitolinischen Wölfin verknüpft sich nicht nur mit Matthias und den ihm nachfolgenden ungarischen Königen, sondern auch mit den Habsburgern[32]. Die Parallele erscheint eindeutig: Der Rabe als Symbol des ungarischen Königreiches und die Wölfin verweisen auf die Habsburger, veranschaulichen die Rechtsgrundlagen ihrer Herrschaft und die verschiedenen Segmente ihrer historischen Berufung. Sie verkörpern nämlich die Erben des römischen Reiches und gleichzeitig die Erben des ungarischen Königtums. Damit sind sie verpflichtet, Einheit im Christentum zu schaffen und die christliche Welt vor den Barbaren und Heiden zu beschützen.

Diese Interpretation erscheint auf den ersten Blick kohärent und logisch, entpuppt sich aber bei genauerer Untersuchung eindeutig als falsch, da die Überschrift des Emblems außer Acht gelassen wurde. Neben dem Raben der Hunyadis sieht man den Wolf der Familie Szapolyai. Die Lösung wäre in diesem Fall, dass man in der Gestalt des Wolfes die kapitolinische Wölfin und zugleich das Wappentier von Szapolyai erkennen müsste. Durch die Gestalt der Wölfin erscheinen gleichzeitig zwei weltgeschichtliche Ereignisse: die Gründung des Römischen Reiches und die Behütung des von den Türken gefährdeten und angegriffenen Ungarn. Die intellektuellen Kreise in der Partei von Szapolyai beurteilten das Bündnis mit den Türken als unvermeidlichen Schritt zur Rettung des Landes. Diese Meinung artikulierte sich in den Schriften der protestantischen Dichter besonders konkret und intensiv, zum Beispiel in den Werken von András Farkas[33] und Miklós Bogáti Fazekas[34].

---

[31] Sambucus (s. Anm. 1), 9–12; 108f.; László VARGA, Sámboky (Sambucus) János filológiai és költői munkássága [Das philologische und poetische Lebenswerk von Johannes Sámboky (Sambucus)]. I. Debrecen 1963, 245–247; BUCK (s. Anm. 1), 33. – Über die Kontinuität zwischen Matthias und Maximilian: ORBÁN (s. Anm. 1), 30f.

[32] Auf dem ersten, Maximilian gewidmeten Emblem erscheint die kapitolinische Wölfin mit Remus und Romulus auf dem Familienwappen der Habsburger zwischen den Wappen und Symbolen der Territorien des Herrscherhauses. Sambucus (s. Anm. 1), 9.

[33] „Ah királ meglátá hogy ő nem bírhatja / Pogán törököknek temérdek sokaságát: / Bölcsen cselekedék, frigyet vélek vete, / Hogy csak épölhetne ah megnyomorodott ország." [„Der König sah, dass er die Übermacht der Türken nicht bewältigen kann: Er handelte wohlweislich, schloss ein Bündnis mit ihnen, damit das arme Land den Frieden genießen könnte."]. András Farkas, A zsidó és a magyar nemzetről [Über das ungarische und jüdische Volk]. In: Régi magyar költők tára [Sammlung alter ungarischer Dichter]. II. Hg. von Áron SZILÁDY. Budapest 1880.

[34] NEMESKÜRTY (s. Anm. 25), 165.

Es besteht natürlich kein Zweifel daran, dass das Ziel von Sambucus keineswegs die Legitimierung der Türkenfreundschaft oder das Propagieren der Politik von Szapolyai war. Für die ideale Herrscher-Dynastie hielt er natürlich die Habsburger und als die einzig mögliche Haltung gegenüber den Türken sah er den kompromisslosen Widerstand. In seinen Schriften erscheinen die Türken immer wieder als die Erbfeinde des Christentums, mit denen keine ehrenvolle Vereinbarung und kein Frieden vorstellbar ist. Diese Überzeugung vertrat er auch später als Hofhistoriker des Königs Maximilian[35], und dieselbe Geisteshaltung können wir sowohl an anderen Emblemen (z. B. *TIRNAVIAE PATRIAE MEAE ARMA*)[36] als auch in seinem Buch Arcus aliqout triumphales erkennen, mit dem er den Sieg bei Lepanto begrüßte[37].

Die zeitgeschichtlichen Ereignisse informieren uns darüber, aus welchem Grund das Szapolyai-Wappen in einer positiven Rolle erscheint und weshalb es mit dem Wappen der Familie Hunyadi (und mit dem Wappen der Habsburger, die als Nachkommen der Hunyadis angesehen wurden) vereinigt wurde. Sambucus schrieb mehrmals, wie sehr er Zwietracht und ständige Zwistigkeiten der Ungarn bedauere[38]. Deshalb konnte es für ihn äußerst erfreulich sein, dass 1563, als er noch an seinem Emblembuch arbeitete, Verhandlungen zwischen Ferdinand I. und Johann Sigismund, dem Sohn König Johanns, begannen. In seinem Antrag hat Johann Sigismund den Frieden angeboten, denn: *haec bella christianis funesta, communibus hostibus laeta esse, quando discordia christianorum satis superque aucti sint.* Im Gegenzug wollte er aber den Königstitel behalten (den seine Nachfolger nicht mehr erben durften). Gleichzeitig tauchte die Idee wieder auf, Johann Sigismund mit einer Schwes-

---

[35] Als Beilage zu seiner Ransanus-Ausgabe veröffentlichte er sein Werk über die Belagerung von Eger und Sziget. Die Beschreibung der Besetzung von Temesvár und Tokaj fügte er als Anhang zur Bonfini-Ausgabe hinzu. ALMÁSI (s. Anm. 2), 159f. – Moderne Ausgabe eines seiner historischen Werke: János Zsámboky, Sziget ostromának igen rövidre fogott és hű előadása, amint azt a király számára a napról napra történtek alapján följegyezték [Ganz kurze und wahrhaftige Beschreibung der Belagerung von Sziget, wie sie für den König Tag für Tag aufgezeichnet wurde]. Übersetzt von Gyöngyi M. Tihanyi. In: *Humanista történetírók* [Humanistische Geschichtsschreiber]. Hg. von Péter KULCSÁR. Budapest 1977 (*Magyar remekírók*), 402–410. – Die Forscher sind nicht einig, welche Rolle Sambucus als Historiker am Hof Maximilians zugeteilt wurde. ORBÁN (s. Anm. 1), 32; VISSER (s. Anm. 2), 19–26.
[36] Sambucus (s. Anm. 1) 167f.
[37] Johannes Sambucus, Arcus aliquot triumphales et monumenta victoriae classicae in honorem Jani Austriae. Antwerpiae: Plantin 1572.
[38] ORBÁN (s. Anm. 1) 15; 54–55.

ter Maximilians zu verheiraten, um das junge Bündnis zu stärken[39]. Die Verhandlungen kamen zwar sehr langsam voran, und wegen der Krönung des Thronfolgers Maximilian kam es erneuert zu Auseinandersetzungen mit den ungarischen Ständen[40], man konnte aber darauf hoffen, dass die zwei Herrscher mit vereinigten Kräften den längst erwarteten Krieg gegen den Türken starten. Diese Hoffnung widerspiegelt sich am Emblem: Sambucus ermutigte Maximilian zum Krieg mit dem Beispiel des Königs Matthias, und dabei – die Bedingungen der Siebenbürger akzeptierend – erteilte er auch für Johann Sigismund den Königstitel in der Überschrift des Emblems. Das Bild verkündet die Kooperation beider Landesteile: Es ist kein Zufall, dass der Rabe und der Wolf in dieselbe Richtung blicken – sie beobachten den gemeinsamen Feind, und planen einen aufeinander abgestimmten Auftritt.

Die Bedeutung des Wolfes steht der Gründungsgeschichte Roms, der kapitolinischen Wölfin, nahe: Sie symbolisiert nicht die Rettung des in äußerste Gefahr geratenen Landes durch das Türkenbündnis, sondern ganz im Gegenteil, die Vereinigung des gespaltenen Reiches und das Zusammenwirken gegen den gemeinsamen Feind. So erhalten der im Hintergrund platzierte Dreiberg und darauf auch das Doppelkreuz ihren Sinn. Das übergeordnete Ziel beider Herrscher ist es, die Sicherheit des Volkes, die alten Freiheitsrechte sowie Einheit und Souveränität des Landes zu bewahren.

Der Einheitsgedanke spielte eine bedeutende Rolle im Lebenswerk von Johannes Sambucus. Mehrmals ermahnte er den ungarischen Adel und die Intellektuellen beider Landesteile zur Vereinigung, und rief gegen die Streitigkeiten zwischen den Parteien der Habsburger und von Szapolyai auf. Er wurde damit beauftragt, ein Werk von Sebestyén Tinódi ins Lateinische zu übersetzen, dieses warnte den Adelsstand vor inneren Zwistigkeiten[41]. Sambucus

---

[39] Ghymesi Forgách Ferenc nagyváradi püspök magyar históriája 1540–1572 [Die ungarische Geschichte des Franz Forgach von Ghymes, Bischof von Großwardein]. Hg. von Fidél MAJER; Einleitung: Ferenc TOLDY. Pest 1866 (Monumenta Hungariae Historica. Scriptores 16), 250–252; 268f.

[40] Forgách (s. Anm. 39), 253–259. – Istvánffy Miklós magyarok dolgairól írt históriája, Tállyai Pál XVII. századi fordításában, I/2 [Geschichte des Nikolaus Istvánffy über die Taten der Ungarn, in der Übersetzung von Pál Tállyai aus dem 17. Jahrhundert]. Hg. von Péter BENITS. Budapest 2003, 309; 331–336.

[41] „Terek és magyar pártot ne báncsátok, / Mert Isten előtt ti nagy kárt vallotok" [„Beschimpft weder die türkische, noch die ungarische Partei, / sonst werdet ihr von Gott bestraft."].

Abb. 6: *VIRTUS UNITA VALET Ad principes Ungariae*
aus: Johannes Sambucus, Emblemata. Antverpiae 1564 / Budapest 1982, 70.

verurteilte diese Zwietracht zum Beispiel im Gedicht *De discordia*, in der Widmung seiner Janus Pannonius-Ausgabe und schließlich in der anlässlich des Todes von König Ferdinand geschriebenen Grabrede[42].

Dieser Gedanke kommt auch in den *Emblemata* mehrmals vor. Als Moralist erwartete Sambucus von den Bürgern, dass sie dem Vaterland bedingungslos dienen und jede Zwietracht untereinander vermeiden. Im Emblem *INTESTINAE SIMULTATES* stellt er bildhaft dar, welche Verwüstungen und Leiden die inneren Streitigkeiten mit sich bringen[43]. Ein anderes Emblem mit

---

Sebestyén Tinódi, Krónika. Hg. von István SUGÁR. Einleitung: Ferenc SZAKÁLY. Budapest 1984 (*Bibliotheca Historica*), 490; ORBÁN (s. Anm. 1), 18.
[42] VARGA (s. Anm. 31), 120; 125f.; 131.
[43] Sambucus (s. Anm. 1), 206.

Abb. 7: *VARII HOMINUM SENSUS Ad Franciscum Forgaz Episcop. Var.*
aus: Johannes Sambucus, Emblemata. Antverpiae 1564 / Budapest 1982, 65.

der Überschrift *VIRTUS UNITA VALET* (Abb. 6) ermahnt die Ungarn mit dem Beispiel der Hunyadis, dem Erbfeind gemeinsam furchtlos entgegenzutreten[44]:

> Huniadis memores, ac Regis quaeso Mathiae
>   Estote, ad quorum nomina Thurca tremit.
> Diversum ne vos studium disiungat iniquè,
>   Colligat in patriae vos amor unus opem.
>
> Sambucus, Emblemata 1564, 70

> An das Gedächtnis des großen Hunyadis und des Königs Matthias
>   erinnere ich euch; schon vor ihren Namen fürchtete sich der Türke.
> Zwietracht und Uneinigkeit darf euch nicht stören,
>   als Beihilfe binde euch die Vaterlandsliebe zusammen!

---

[44] VARGA (s. Anm. 31), 277–289; BUCK (s. Anm. 2), 19; VISSER (s. Anm. 2), 36.

Noch plastischer erscheint das Emblem *VARII HOMINUM SENSUS*, dessen *pictura* auseinander rollende Schädel darstellt, und in dessen *subscriptio* behauptet wird, es sei überhaupt nicht ungewöhnlich, dass sich entseelte Skelette zerstreuen, da auch die lebenden Menschen keinen gemeinsamen Weg gehen könnten (Abb. 7).

Die hoffnungsvollen Jahre vergingen schnell und ohne Erfolge. Der letztlich geschlossene Friedensvertrag mit Siebenbürgen wurde fast sofort gebrochen, und Maximilian II. beschloss, den Frieden mit den Türken zu verlängern. Als die Truppen von Johann Sigismund in Oberungarn siegreich vorstießen, verhandelten die Gesandten Maximilians in Istanbul über die Jahressteuer des Königs[45]. Die Hoffnung auf Übereinkunft zwischen den ungarischen Landesteilen und einen Zusammenschluss gegen die Türken, wie sie Sambucus in seinem Emblembuch beschleunigen wollte, löste sich bis September 1564 endgültig auf.

ZUSAMMENFASSUNG

Zeitgeschichte und Politik spielen in der Sambucus' Emblematik eine untergeordnete Rolle: Das Verhältnis des Einzelnen zur Öffentlichkeit behandeln weniger als 15% der Embleme. Der Verfasser beschäftigt sich meistens mit theoretischen Fragen, mit den Herrschertugenden, Regierungsformen und mit dem Verhältnis zwischen Recht und Moral. Die Anzahl der Embleme, welche die damals aktuellen Probleme behandeln, ist sehr gering. Trotzdem kann man im Buch ein kohärentes politisches Programm entdecken. Sambucus wollte mit seinem Werk eindeutig die Einheitsbestrebungen vorantreiben, sowohl auf politischer, als auch auf gesellschaftlicher Ebene.

In der Zeit des doppelten Königtums entstand ein breiter und vielfältiger politischer Diskurs, an dem mehrere Schichten der Gesellschaft, die Mitglieder der *respublica litteraria* und des königlichen Hofes, Adeligen und Bürger der freien königlichen Städte teilnahmen. Das lässt sich an der Verbreitung der einzelnen Argumente und Gedanken und an der Einheitlichkeit des Symbolgebrauchs abtasten. Die Symbolik des politischen Diskurses blieb auch nach Jahrzehnten lebendig, und zwar so stark, dass Sambucus die

---

[45] Forgách (s. Anm. 39), 273–276; Istvánffy (s. Anm. 40), 353–365.

einzelnen Zeichen als Elemente einer komplizierten Komposition, als Rätsel aufgeben konnte.

Der Verfasser konnte sich vieler in breiten Kreisen wohlbekannter, auch in der täglichen politischen Routine benutzter Symbole bedienen. Er stellte eine freie Kombination von Elementen der antiken Mythologie und der ungarischen Heraldik her und veränderte dabei nicht nur die Bedeutung der einzelnen Sinnbilder, sondern auch den ganzen ursprünglichen Kontext. Mit dieser komplexen Darstellung konnte er das System der asymmetrischen Gegenbegriffe lockern: Statt der heftigen Auseinandersetzungen argumentierte er für den Frieden.*

---

* Ich danke Josef Hervanek vielmals für seine unentbehrliche Hilfe beim Fertigstellen dieses Artikels.

Mathiæ Coruini Symbolum,
Symbolo Ioan. Regis auctum.

VT lupa non proprios, alienos sed quoque fœtus
Vbere nutriuit, Roma, tibi vnde duces:
Sic rex Mathias Hunnorum maximus author
  Dum superat cunctos, ingeniosa fouet.
Huius ad imperium concursus totius Orbis
  Et fuit inuicto principe dignus honos.
Vndique cogebat veterum monimenta, superstes
  Quo foret authorum fama, decensque labor.
Contudit indomitos vel solo nomine Thracas,

L   Et

Abb. 1b: *MATHIAE CORVINI SYMBOLUM, SYMBOLO IOANNIS REGIS AUCTUM*
aus: Johannes Sambucus, Emblemata. Antverpiae 1564, 161
(Hg. von Béla Varjas. Budapest 1982)

Et pauidos multo sanguine fudit humi.
Pannoniæ infestæ quis non metuebat habenas?
  Tum Venetum supplex factus & ipse leo est.
Gryphe nec inferior sacer & tunc coruus Apollo
  Est habitus, presso gutture suauè canens,
O vtinam in regnum qui successere, triumphos
  Conciperent animo, claraque facta ducis :
Sæua sed internis cesset discordia rebus,
  Et proceres concors sensus in arma vocet.
Quod nisi iam fiat te Maxmiliane tenente
  Iura, salus nulla est pòst reditura die.
Qui memor illius Geticum moliris in hostem
  Arma, nec impensis bibliotheca minor.
Quæ propter laudes repetet bene grata vetustas,
  Nec minor inceptis gloria semper erit.

Abb. 1c: *MATHIAE CORVINI SYMBOLUM, SYMBOLO IOANNIS REGIS AUCTUM*
aus: Johannes Sambucus, Emblemata. Antverpiae 1564, 162
(Hg. von Béla VARJAS. Budapest 1982)

Ganzheitliche Antikerezeption

Text und Bild im Werk des Johannes Sambucus

ELISABETH KLECKER (Wien)

Antiquitatis ſtudium.
Ad G. Schirletum.

OMNIA conſumit tempus, longamq́; ſenectam
Quid videt artifices quod peperere manus?
Imperio fatum eripuit monimenta, vetuſtas
Ne quid duraret, conficeretq́; ſitus.
Nunc Deus in frugem veterum virtute probatam
Vt vocet, en monſtrat marmora, Roma, tibi.
Effodiuntur opes irritamenta bonorum,
Nec poterit nummos vlla abolere dies.
Aerea teſtantur fuerint quibus aurea ſecla,
Multorumq́; monent quæ tacuere libri.

Abb. 1: *ANTIQUITATIS STUDIUM*. Emblemata et aliquot nummi antiqui operis. Antverpiae: ex officina Christophori Plantini 1566, 164 (Wien, Universitätsbibliothek I 125.521)

Multorumque monent quae tacuere libri
ANTIQUITATIS STUDIUM, Sambucus, *Emblemata.* Antverpiae 1564, 191

In seinem Emblem *ANTIQUITATIS STUDIUM* (Abb. 1) gibt Johannes Sambucus der geläufigen Klage über den Verfall von Monumenten bzw. Werken der bildenden Kunst und dem damit drohenden Vergessen eine überraschende Wendung: Setzten die antiken Dichter dem sicheren Untergang steinerner und eherner Denkmäler die Unvergänglichkeit literarischen Ruhms entgegen, so betrachtet Sambucus das Wiederauffinden antiker Marmormonumente, man könnte sagen: ‚archäologische Ausgrabungen' seiner Gegenwart, als gottgewollte Erinnerung an die Früchte einstiger Tugend. Und implizit widerspricht er der berühmtesten Ausformung des Topos von der Ewigkeit der Dichtung, Horazens *monumentum aere perennius* (c. 3, 30, 1): Gerade die kleinen metallenen Überreste der Antike seien es, die Zeugnis geben von dem, was Bücher verschweigen[1]. Mit Bezug auf die Metallsymbolik der Zeitalter pointiert ausgedrückt: Eherne Objekte künden von goldenen Zeiten.

> Omnia consumit tempus, longamque senectam
>   Quid videt artifices quod peperere manus?
> Imperio fatum eripuit monimenta, vetustas
>   Ne quid duraret, conficeretque situs.
> Nunc Deus in frugem veterum virtute probatam
>   Ut vocet en monstrat marmora, Roma, tibi.
> Effodiuntur opes irritamenta bonorum,
>   Nec poterit nummos ulla abolere dies.
> Aerea testantur fuerint quibus aurea secla,
>   Multorumque monent quae tacuere libri.

Alles verzehrt die Zeit. Was von den Werken, die Künstlerhand hervorgebracht hat, sieht ein hohes Alter? Das Schicksal hat dem römischen Reich die Monumente entrissen (und bewirkt), dass hohes Alter keinem Ding Bestand verleihe, son-

---

[1] Das Epigramm ist – dies vielleicht eine zusätzliche Pointe – Guglielmo Sirleto (1514–1585), seit 1554 Kustos der vatikanischen Bibliothek, gewidmet; Sambucus stand mit ihm in Briefkontakt: Hans GERSTINGER, *Die Briefe des Johannes Sambucus (Zsamboky) 1554–1584. Mit einem Anhang: Die Sambucusbriefe im Kreisarchiv von Trnava von Anton* VANTUCH. Wien 1968 (ÖAW, *Phil.-hist. Kl.,* Sitzungsberichte 255), 26f.

dern Moder alles vernichte[2]. Doch siehe, jetzt zeigt Gott dir, Rom, die Marmormäler, um dich zu den Früchten zu rufen, die alte Helden durch Tugend bewiesen haben. Es werden Schätze ausgegraben als Anreiz zum Guten, und kein Tag wird Münzen vernichten können. Dinge aus Erz bezeugen, für wen es goldene Jahrhunderte gab, und sie erinnern an vieles, was Bücher verschwiegen haben.

Eine derartige Hochschätzung dinglicher Quellen fügt sich gut zum Aufschwung antiquarischer Studien in der zweiten Hälfte des 16. Jahrhunderts[3], dennoch lässt die Gegenüberstellung von Büchern und Monumenten aus Marmor oder Erz vor dem Hintergrund der geläufigen Ewigkeitsansprüche der Dichter zunächst aufhorchen. Sie mag nicht zuletzt mit der Sammeltätigkeit des Humanisten zusammenhängen: Das Bemühen um besonders alte, d. h. dem Verfasser nahe, Handschriften zeigt Bewusstsein für die Instabilität des überlieferten Textes, sodass Münzen als verlässlichere, nicht durch Abschreiber gebrochene Quellen erscheinen mussten[4]. Und so ist für Sambucus, der sich durch zahlreiche Editionen (v. a. griechischer Autoren) um die Sicherung und Rekonstruktion antiker Texte bemühte, bezeugt, dass sich seine Sammeltätigkeit nicht nur auf Handschriften, sondern auch auf andere Trägermedien historischer Überlieferung erstreckte[5].

---

[2] Die Konstruktion mit *vetustas* und *situs* („durch langes Liegen entstandener Schmutz") als Subjekten ist nicht ganz glatt; *durare* scheint transitiv „Härte, Dauer verleihen". Die Übersetzung von Arnoud Visser auf der *Glasgow University Emblem website / French Emblems at Glasgow* <http://www.emblems.arts.gla.ac.uk/french/emblem.php?id=FSAb137> (23. 4. 2017) „Under his rule, destiny has snatched monuments away, so that antiquity cannot last longer, and form a structure" gibt wenig Sinn. Die französische Fassung der *Emblemata* (Les Emblemes du Signeur Jehan Sambucus. Traduits de Latin en François. Antwerpen: Plantin 1567) glättet: M7ᵛ / 190 „Pourtant l'antiquité entre tous honorable / Demeure avec le temps à jamais perdurable".

[3] Vgl. Margaret Daly DAVIS, *Archäologie der Antike. Aus den Beständen der Herzog August Bibliothek 1500–1700*. Wiesbaden 1994, sowie das Standardwerk Ingo HERKLOTZ, *Cassiano dal Pozzo und die Archäologie des 17. Jahrhunderts*. München 1999 (Römische Forschungen der Bibliotheca Hertziana 28).

[4] Zu Sambucus als Numismatiker: Maria RADNOTI-ALFÖLDI, Zu den frühen Illustrationen numismatischer Werke: die Emblemata des Johannes Sambucus 1531–1584. In: Rainer Albert, Rainer Kunz (Hgg.), *Wissenschaftsgeschichte der Numismatik. Beiträge zum 17. Deutschen Numismatikertag 3.–5. März 1995 in Hannover*. Speyer 1995, 71–95; Arnoud VISSER, *Joannes Sambucus and the Learned Image. The Use of the Emblem in Late Renaissance Humanism*. Leiden 2005 (Brill's Studies in Intellectual History 128), 45 mit weiterer Literatur.

[5] Ein Beispiel für einen zu Sambucus' Zeit außergewöhnlichen Überlieferungsträger bespricht Christian GASTGEBER in seinem Beitrag zu diesem Band.

VETERUM ALIQUOT AC RECENTIUM MEDICORUM PHILOSOPHORUMQUE ICONES

Wenn die Sicherung der Überlieferung bzw. der Umgang mit ihren Medien explizit Thema eines Emblems ist, liegt es nahe zu fragen, ob bzw. wie sich das Bewusstsein um die einander ergänzenden Medien der historischen Überlieferung in Sambucus' eigenem Schaffen auswirkte: Es ist wohl kein Zufall, dass sich in seinem Œuvre mehrere Bild-Text-Kombinationen finden.

Am Beginn von Sambucus' Publikationstätigkeit steht die beliebte Form des Porträtbuchs[6] in Gestalt einer erweiterten Neuauflage von Johann Huttichs Kaiserserie[7]. Ein späteres Werk des Typs *Illustrium imagines* ist Ärzten und Philosophen gewidmet: *Veterum aliquot ac recentium medicorum philosophorumq. Icones* (erstmals Antwerpen: Plantin 1574)[8]. Sambucus setzt damit nicht nur seiner Profession[9] ein Denkmal – die Reihe schließt mit Sambucus' eigenem Porträt –, sondern zeigt implizit literaturgeschichtliches Wissen um (nicht erhaltene) illustrierte Biographiensammlungen antiker Autoren[10], für die er quasi Rekonstruktion und Fortsetzung bis in die Gegenwart liefert. Die grundsätzliche Schwierigkeit, ein derartiges Werk zu realisieren, thematisiert Sambucus in der Widmungsvorrede: Aus der mangelnden Kenntnis antiker Bildüberlieferung resultiere die Praxis der Publikationsform, die oft aus Textquellen rekonstruierte Porträts präsentiere –

---

[6] Milan PELC, *Illustrium imagines. Das Porträtbuch der Renaissance*. Leiden 2002 (*Studies in medieval and reformation thought* 88).

[7] Romanorum Principum effigies cum historiarum annotatione, nunc aucta et longe castigatiora opera Jo. Sambuci. Ed. III. Argentorati: Cephaleaus 1551 (VD 16 H 6475). Vgl. den Beitrag von Johannes AMANN-BUBENIK in diesem Band.

[8] Benützt wurde das Faksimile der zweiten (um Kurzbiographien und Lobgedichte) erweiterten Auflage (Leiden: Ex officina Plantiniana Raphelengii 1603): Kísérő tanulmány a Zsámboky János (Joannes Sambucus) Veterum aliquot ac recentium medicorum philosophorumque Icones ex bibliotheca Johannis Sambuci; cum eiusdem ad singulas Elogiis, Lugduni Batavorum 1603 címü reprint kiadványhoz, írta VIDA Mária, KÁDÁR Zoltán, JANTSITS, Gabriella. Budapest 1985. Dazu die Beilage (in ungarischer, englischer und deutscher Sprache): Mária VIDA, János Zsámboky (Sambucus) 1531–1584 und die „Icones", 20–25. – Mit Fulvio Orsini, der 1580 Porträts von Philosophen und Schriftstellern aus seiner eigenen Sammlung publizierte, stand Sambucus in Briefkontakt: GERSTINGER, *Briefe* (s. Anm. 1), 28f.

[9] Sambucus hatte 1555 in Padua das Licentiat in Medizin erlangt: GERSTINGER, *Briefe* (s. Anm. 1), 14.

[10] Genannt seien Varro, *Hebdomades vel De imaginibus* (Gellius 3, 10) sowie eine illustrierte Sammlung von kurzen Elogia des Pomponius Atticus (Nepos, *Atticus* 18, 5).

wie es nach dem Zeugnis des älteren Plinius (*nat. hist.* 35, 9) und Aelians (*var. hist.* 13, 22) schon in der Antike für Homer geschehen sei. Er selbst habe sich bemüht, Bildquellen in Gestalt von Statuen, Gemälden, Münzen und Handschriften heranzuziehen:

> Ac scio multos hoc ipso argumento libellos hodie in vulgus produci: sed quod Plinius, & Aelianus de Homero fatebantur, idem censeo de multorum editionibus; Icones ad historiarum descriptiones penicillo informatas, non de protypis ectypa reddita. Quodsi in his quoque nostris eius aliquot generis deprehenderis, mihi id vitio non vertes; qui ista amicorum fide, ac testimonio, de statuis, signis tabellis, partim numis haud recentis memoriae, atque vetustissimorum codicum vestibulis comportarim.

> Ich weiß, dass heutzutage viele Bücher dieses Inhalts veröffentlicht werden: Was Plinius und Aelian für Homer eingestanden, das gilt meiner Einschätzung nach für die Editionen vieler. Die Porträts sind nach Beschreibungen in Geschichtsbüchern gebildet, nicht von Vorlagen abgenommen. Wenn du derartiges auch unter den unsrigen antriffst, laste es nicht mir als Fehler an, der ich diese Bilder nach dem vertrauenswürdigen Zeugnis von Freunden von Statuen, Bildwerken, Gemälden, zum Teil von alten Münzen und aus den Anfangsteilen der ältesten Codices zusammengetragen habe.

Eine wichtige Inspirationsquelle stellen die beiden Ärztebilder am Anfang des berühmten Wiener Dioskurides (Wien, Österreichische Nationalbibliothek, Cod. med. gr. 1; Abb. 3)[11] dar, auf die Sambucus mit *de* [...] *vetustissimorum codicum vestibulis* hinzuweisen scheint. Das erste, die Chirongruppe, ist im Epigramm für Xenokrates (Nr. 21, Abb. 2) genannt[12]:

> *Etsi qui fueris non affirmare licebat,*
>   *hoc lego quod plures nomine saepe viros*
> *te tamen herbarum gnarum vetus illa fuisse*
>   *prima Dioscuridis pagina nostra monet.*

Obwohl es nicht möglich war, deine Identität sicher zu bestimmen, weil ich von mehr als einem Mann dieses Namens lese, weist doch die erste Seite unserer alten Dioskurideshandschrift daraufhin, dass du kräuterkundig gewesen bist.

---

[11] Vgl. *Pedanius Dioscorides – Der Wiener Dioskurides: Codex medicus Graecus 1 der Österreichischen Nationalbibliothek.* Kommentar von Otto MAZAL. Graz 1998 (*Glanzlichter der Buchkunst* 8). Vgl. VIDA (s. Anm. 8), 27.

[12] Das Ärztebild im Dioskuridescodex wird als Xenokrates von Aphrodisias (M. 1. Jh. n. Chr.) identifiziert: MAZAL (s. Anm. 11), 18.

Abb. 2: Xenokrates (Nr. 21). Veterum aliquot ac recentium medicorum philosophorumque Icones. Leiden 1603 (reprint Budapest 1985, s. Anm. 8)

Abb. 3: Xenokrates aus der Chirongruppe des Cod. med. gr. 1.
(*Pedanius Dioscorides – Der Wiener Dioskurides*. Graz 1998, s. Anm. 11)

Ganzheitliche Antikerezeption

Mit dem Hinweis auf den Dioskuridescodex (der freilich nicht explizit als bildliche Quelle bezeichnet ist bzw. nur in Zusammenschau mit der Vorrede als solche kenntlich wird) verbindet sich wie im eingangs zitierten Emblem *ANTIQUITATIS STUDIUM* eine Aussage über die Unzulänglichkeit der Überlieferung: Die antiken Texte bieten mehrere Ärzte bzw. Gelehrte des Namens Xenokrates, das ‚Porträt' aus dem Ärztebild des Dioskurides lässt sich zwar keinem von ihnen sicher zuordnen, erlaubt aber, Pharmakologie als das Spezialgebiet des Abgebildeten zu bestimmen. Sambucus ist also bestrebt, Bild- und Textquellen zusammenzufügen und die Publikationsform des illustrierten Buchs bewusst zu einer ganzheitlichen Antikerezeption in Text und Bild zu nützen.

EMBLEMATA CUM ALIQUOT NUMMIS ANTIQUI OPERIS

Die bekannteste Bild-Textkombination im Œuvre des Johannes Sambucus sind zweifellos die *Emblemata*[13]: Wenn in diesen – wie in dem eingangs zitierten Emblem – antike Kunstwerke und Fundstücke thematisiert werden, entsprach dies einem der ‚Gattungstradition' der Emblematik inhärenten archäologischen Interesse: Ihr Archeget Andrea Alciato (1492–1550)[14] hatte nicht nur Nachdichtungen von ekphrastischen Epigrammen aus der griechischen Anthologie, die Werken der bildenden Kunst gewidmet sind, in seine Sammlungen aufgenommen, sondern sich an antiken Monumenten in Mailand inspiriert[15]; nicht zuletzt nützte er seine numismatischen Kennt-

---

[13] Zu den *Emblemata*: VISSER, *Joannes Sambucus* (s. Anm. 4) und die Kommentierung auf der *Glasgow University Emblem website* (s. Anm. 2). Zur Rezeption bei Geoffrey Whitney (ca. 1548–1601): Éva KNAPP, Gábor TÜSKÉS, *Emblematics in Hungary. A study of the history of symbolic representation in Renaissance and Baroque literature.* Tübingen 2003 (Frühe Neuzeit 86).

[14] Nach Pál GULYÁS, *A Zsámboky-könyvtár katalógusa (1587).* Szeged 1992 (Adattár XVI–XVIII. századi szellemi mozgalmaink történetéhez [Materialien zur Geschichte der Geistesströmungen in Ungarn im 16.–18. Jahrhundert] 12/2), Nr. 852 besaß Sambucus Alciatos *Emblemata* in der Ausgabe Paris: Jerome de Marnef 1561 (lateinisch mit der französischen Übertragung von Barthélemy Aneau). Siehe Alison ADAMS, Stephen RAWLES, Alison SAUNDERS, *A Bibliography of French Emblem Books of the Sixteenth and Seventeenth Centuries.* Genève 2002 (Travaux d'humanisme et Renaissance 331), Bd. 1, 7 F.041.

[15] Pierre LAURENS, Florence VUILLEUMIER, De l'archéologie à l'emblème: la genèse du *Liber Alciati. Revue de l'art* 101, 4 (1993), 86–95.

nisse[16]: Schon im *Emblematum liber* von 1531 zieht er für das Mailänder Wappen des ersten Emblems (*INSIGNIA DUCATUS MEDIOLANENSIS*) die Parallele zu Münzen Alexanders des Großen. In der zweiten Emblemserie (Venedig: Aldus 1546)[17] verwendet er im Emblem *RESPUBLICA LIBERATA* (26^r=$D2^r$) eine schon in der Antike berühmte Münze des Iunius Brutus[18]. In Sambucus' Fall lässt bereits das Titelblatt der *Emblemata* (Abb. 5) den Schluss zu, dass ihm daran gelegen war, die Antike über literarische Quellen hinaus in ‚authentischen' Bildern einzubeziehen: Der Holzschnittrahmen besteht aus Darstellungen der neun Musen mit ihren charakteristischen Attributen als Wiedergabe der von Quintus Pomponius Musa 67 v. Chr. geprägten Silberdenare, die die einzelnen Musen als Reversbilder zu einem Apollokopf als gleich bleibendem Avers zeigen[19]. Er verweist damit zunächst auf den Anhang, in dem mit separater Widmung an den Büchersammler und trésorier général Jean Grolier Holzschnitte von 23 Münzen aus Sambucus' eigener Sammlung abgebildet sind. Die Bedeutung erschöpft sich jedoch nicht in dieser ankündigenden Funktion: Mit dem Titelblatt korrespondiert ein eigenes Emblem, das das Spektrum der literarischen Gattungen bzw. musischen Künste auf die einzelnen namentlich genannten Musen aufteilt (Abb. 4):

MUSARUM, EX ANTIQUIS NUMIS Q. POMPONII, VERAE EFFIGIES,
& ETYMOLOGICA VIS. EX VIRGILIO
Clio gesta canens transactis tempora reddit.
Melpomene tragico proclamat maesta boatu.
Comica lasciuo gaudet sermone Thalia.
Dulciloquis calamos Euterpe flatibus urget.

---

[16] Zum Interesse am Revers als Quelle für Emblematik und Hieroglyphik: Stephane ROLET, D'étranges objets hiéroglyphiques. Les monnaies antiques dans les *Hieroglyphica* de Pierio Valeriano (1556). In: Wolfgang Harms, Dietmar Peil (Hgg.), *Polyvalenz und Multifunktionalität der Emblematik.* Akten des 5. Internationalen Kongresses der Society for Emblem Studies. Frankfurt am Main 2002 (*Mikrokosmos* 65), 813–844.

[17] Bartłomiej CZARSKI, Concerning Ancient Coins and Emblems: Some Notes on the Second Book of Alciato. In: Ingrid Hoepel, Simon McKeown (Hgg.), *Emblems and Impact. I: Von Zentrum und Peripherie der Emblematik.* Selected Proceedings of the 10th International Conference of the Society for Emblem Studies 27 July – 1 August 2014 Christian-Albrechts-Universität zu Kiel. Cambridge 2017, 393–418.

[18] Siehe S. 382 mit Anm. 60.

[19] Michael H. CRAWFORD, *Roman Republican Coinage.* Cambridge 1974; 410, 2–10; Arthur J. FRANK, Musa's Muses. The Muse Denarii of Quintus Pomponius Musa. *Journal of the Society of Ancient Numismatics* 11,4 (1980–81), 68–70.

Terpsichore affectus citharis mouet, imperat, auget.
Plectra gerens Erato saltat pede, carmine, vultu.
Carmina Calliope libris heroica mandat.
Urania coeli motus scrutatur & astra.
Signat cuncta manu, loquitur Polymnia gestu.
Mentis Apollineae vis has mouet undique Musas:
In medio residens complectitur omnia Phoebus.

Sambucus, *Emblemata* 1566, 103

Abb. 4: *MUSARUM, EX ANTIQUIS NUMIS Q. POMPONII, VERAE EFFIGIES.*
Emblemata et aliquot nummi antiqui operis. Antverpiae: ex officina Christophori
Plantini 1566, 103
(Wien, Universitätsbibliothek I 125.521)

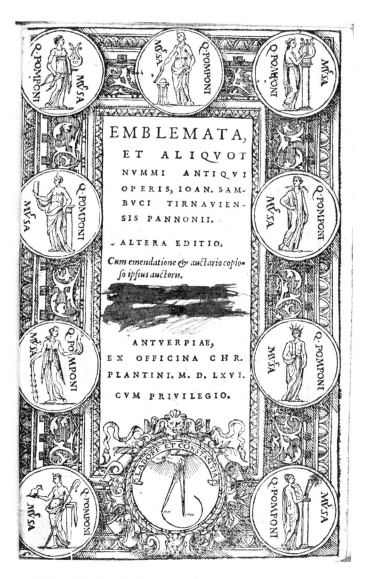

Abb. 5: Titelblatt. Emblemata et aliquot nummi antiqui operis. Antverpiae: ex officina Christophori Plantini 1566 (Wien, Universitätsbibliothek I 125.521)

Authentische Darstellungen der Musen nach den alten Münzen des
Q. Pomponius und ihre etymologische Bedeutung nach Vergil

Clio singt von Taten und verleiht der Vergangenheit Gegenwart.
Melpomene verkündet Trauriges mit tragischem Schall.
Die Muse der Komödie Thalia freut sich an lasziver Rede.
Mit süßtönendem Blasen bezwingt Euterpe die Rohrflöte.
Terpsichore erweckt mit der Kithara Leidenschaften, beherrscht und verstärkt sie.
Heroische Gedichte vertraut Kalliope Büchern an,
Urania erforscht die Bewegungen des Himmels und die Sterne.
Es bezeichnet alles mit der Hand und spricht mit Gesten Polymnia.
Die geistige Kraft Apolls bewegt allseits die Musen,
In der Mitte thronend umfasst Phoebus alles.

Die *inscriptio* des Emblems verweist also ausdrücklich auf die Münzbilder des Titelblatts, die Einzelbilder sind nun zu einer Parnassdarstellung in ‚Münzform' zusammengestellt. Für die Beschreibung bzw. Zuweisung der Attribute und Gattungen ist die höchste Autorität der lateinischen Dichtung bemüht: Der Text des Emblems gibt – ein durchaus ungewöhnlicher Fall[20] – im Wortlaut ein fälschlich Vergil zugeschriebenes Epigramm (*Anthologia Latina* 664 Riese[21]) wieder, das als üblicher Bestandteil der ‚*Appendix Vergiliana*' unter dem Titel *De Musarum inventis* auch in der von Sebastian Brant herausgegebenen ersten illustrierten Vergilausgabe (Strassburg: Grüninger 1502) enthalten und sogar mit einer Illustration versehen ist (Abb. 6)[22].

---

[20] Möglicherweise bot Alciatos Aufnahme von Übertragungen aus der griechischen Anthologie die Anregung für Sambucus. Sambucus weicht vom geläufigen Text (auch der Vergil-Ausgabe von 1502, s. Anm. 22) minimal ab: v. 8 *coeli* statt *poli motus*.

[21] Das Gedicht erscheint in der handschriftlichen Überlieferung unter *Nomina Musarum / Versus Catonis philosophi de novem Musis* und wurde auch Ausonius zugeschrieben. Vgl. Decimi Magni Ausonii Burdigalensis Opuscula. Rec. Rudolfus PEIPER. Lipsiae 1886, 412.

[22] Publii Virgilii Maronis Opera. Argentorati: ordinatione, elimatione ac relectione Sebastiani Brant operaque et impensa non mediocri Iohannis Grieninger 1502 (VD16 V 1332), IX bb^v–bb2^r; Digitalisat: <http://daten.digitale-sammlungen.de/~db/bsb00001879/images/> (10. 7. 2017). Zur Ausgabe und ihren Illustrationen: Bernd SCHNEIDER, Vergilius pictus – Sebastian Brants illustrierte Vergilausgabe von 1502 und ihre Nachwirkung. Ein Beitrag zur Vergilrezeption im deutschen Humanismus. *Wolfenbütteler Beiträge* 6 (1984), 202–262. Nikolaus HENKEL, Das Bild als Wissenssumme. Die Holzschnitte in Sebastian Brants Vergil-Ausgabe Straßburg 1502. In: Stephen Mossman, Nigel F. Palmer, Felix Heinzer (Hgg.), *Schreiben und Lesen in der Stadt. Literaturbetrieb im spätmittelalterlichen Straßburg.* Berlin 2012 (*Kulturtopographie des alemannischen Raums* 4), 379–410.

Abb. 6: *De Musarum inventis*. Publii Virgilii Maronis Opera. Strassburg: Grüninger 1502, IX bb^v
(München, Bayerische Staatsbibliothek Res/2 A.lat.a.292; s. Anm. 22)

Auf diese oder entsprechende Darstellungen in zeitgenössischer Tracht zielt wohl Sambucus und beansprucht für sich, das Bild der Musen anhand authentischer Überlieferung zu korrigieren[23]. Er führt damit an einer emblematischen Repräsentation von Dichtung geradezu programmatisch vor, wie literarische und bildliche Überlieferung komplementär zur Rekonstruktion der Antike zusammenwirken sollen. Dass er dabei in der sicher scheinenden literarischen Komponente getäuscht wurde, mag man als Ironie der (Literatur)Geschichte werten, das methodische Bemühen schmälert es nicht.

---

[23] Hinsichtlich der vorbildlichen Münzen hat er dabei unberücksichtigt gelassen, dass zur Serie des Pomponius Musa ein *HERCULES MUSARUM* gehörte. Hinsichtlich des Epigramms konnte er die in den letzten beiden Versen enthaltene Interpretation Apolls als Sonne und *mens mundi* (nach Cicero, *rep.* 6 = *Somnium Scipionis* 17), und damit Ursprung der schon von Macrobius mit den Musen verbundenen Sphärenharmonie, nicht bildlich umsetzen, sondern blieb bei der konventionellen Parnassdarstellung mit Pegasos. Vgl. Günter WILLE, *Musica Romana*. Amsterdam 1967, 623–630; Jean PÉPIN, Harmonie der Sphären. *Reallexikon für Antike und Christentum* 13 (1986), Sp. 593–618.

ARCUS ALIQUOT TRIUMPHALES

Wie sich Sambucus bei der ‚Rekonstruktion der Antike' um ein Zusammenführen mehrerer unterschiedlicher Überlieferungen bemühte, so bediente er sich der Kombinaton von Bild und Text auch für aktuelle Anlässe[24]. Wenn er im Emblem ANTIQUITATIS STUDIUM wiederentdeckten antiken Denkmälern protreptischen Wert zuerkennt, ist es nur konsequent, dass zeitgenössische Ruhmestaten ebensolche *monumenta* verdienen – zumindest virtuell auf Papier. Derartige papierene Siegeszeichen hat Sambucus mit den *Arcus aliquot triumphales* geschaffen, einer Huldigung für Juan de Austria (1547–1578), der in der Seeschlacht von Lepanto (7. Oktober 1571) den Oberbefehl über die Flotte der Heiligen Liga geführt hatte[25]. Das Werk ist mit Kupferstichen von Philips Galle[26] ausgestattet und wurde wie die *Emblemata* in Antwerpen gedruckt. Die Vorrede (Wien, 1. November 1571) ist an Don Juan gerichtet,

---

[24] Zur ungarischen Krönung Maximilians II. ließ er einen Einblattdruck in deutscher und lateinischer Version erscheinen, der den Krönungszug zeigt. Vgl. Leták Jána Sambuca s výjavom korunovácie Maximiliána II. v Bratislave [Flugblatt des Johannes Sambucus mit einer Szene der Krönung Maximilians II. in Bratislava]. In: Ivan Rusina a kol. (Hgg.), *Renesancia. Dejiny Slovenského výtvarného umenia. Katalóg výstavy* [Renaissance. Geschichte der bildenden Kunst in der Slowakei. Ausstellungskatalog]. Slovenská narodná galéria v Bratislave, 17 december 2009 – 28 marec 2010. Bratislava 2009, 39–40 (Kat.-Nr. II.1.11 II.1.12).

[25] *Arcus aliquot triumphal(es) et monumenta victor(iae) classicae, in honor(em) Invictissimi ac Illustriss. Iani Austriae, victoris non quieturi.* Antverpiae: apud Philippum Gallaeum 1572. Die bislang einzige Spezialuntersuchung Francisco Javier PIZARRO GÓMEZ, Entre la Emblemática y el arte efímero. A propósito del *Arcus aliquot triumphal. et monumenta victor. classicae* de Joannes Sambucus. *Norba Arte* 16 (1996), 153–170 <http://dialnet.unirioja.es/servlet/ articulo?codigo= 107517> (15. 9. 2009) beschränkt sich auf eine Beschreibung mit spanischer Übersetzung der Texte und gelegentlichen Hinweisen auf Emblematik, wobei dem Verfasser die Unvollständigkeit des ihm vorliegenden Exemplars entgangen ist (es fehlt Nr. 12). Vgl. Gábor ALMÁSI, *The Uses of Humanism. Johannes Sambucus (1531–1584), Andreas Dudith (1533–1589), and the republic of letters in East Central Europe.* Leiden, Boston 2009 (Brill's studies in intellectual history 185), 176–178. In slowakischer Sprache ist eine Kurzvorstellung erschienen: Elisabeth KLECKER, Emblematika. In: Ivan Rusina a kol. (Hgg.), *Renesancia: umenie medzi neskorou gotikou a barokom* [Renaissance. Kunst zwischen Spätgotik und Barock]. Bratislava 2009 (*Dejiny slovenského výtvarného umenia* [Geschichte der bildenden Kunst in der Slowakei]), 94–103.

[26] Philips Galle hatte sich 1571 in Antwerpen niedergelassen und arbeitete mit Plantin zusammen: Manfred SELLINK, Marjolein LEESBERG, Philips Galle. Rotterdam 2001 (*The new Hollstein Dutch & Flemish etchings, engravings and woodcuts, 1450–1700*), XLIV. Vgl. Karen Lee BOWEN, Dirk IMHOF, *Christopher Plantin and engraved book illustrations in sixteenth century Europe.* Cambridge 2008, 257.

Sambucus' unmittelbarer Adressat in Wien war jedoch Maximilian II.: Das Exemplar der Österreichischen Nationalbibliothek (66.C.31) trägt auf dem Titelblatt eine eigenhändige Widmung an den Kaiser (Abb. 7).
Sambucus musste aus eigener Anschauung bekannt sein, dass Kaiser Maximilian II. die europäische Allianz gegen die Osmanen, die Heilige Liga vom 25. Mai 1571, propagandistisch intensiv auszuwerten suchte und die Führungsrolle der spanischen Habsburger auf seine eigene imperiale Vorrangstellung bezog. Gelegenheit dazu bot die Hochzeit seines Bruders Karl von Innerösterreich Ende August 1571: Ein mythologisches tournois à thème, konzipiert wohl von Giovanni Battista Fonteo[27], realisiert von Giuseppe Arcimboldo, demonstrierte den universalen Machtanspruch des Kaisers als Oberhaupt der natürlichen wie kulturellen Ordnung Europas, ja der ganzen Welt: Der als Göttin von Hochzeit und Ehe erscheinenden Juno, die in ihrem Gefolge die Erdteile Asien, Afrika und Amerika mit sich führt, tritt Europa unterstützt von Italia, Hispania, Gallia und Germania mit den ihnen zugeordneten Jahreszeiten und Winden entgegen. Nach dem Sieg am 7. Oktober ließ sich dieses Programm ideal als Zusammenwirken des gesamten Kosmos gegen die Osmanen ausdeuten. Sambucus konnte also darauf vertrauen, dass ein Werk zur Feier der Seeschlacht von Lepanto auch in Wien beim Kaiser Beifall finden würde[28].

---

[27] Unter seinem Namen ist eine ausführliche, zum Teil poetische Dokumentation des Festes erhalten (Wien, Österreichische Nationalbibliothek, Cod. 12206). Ein Fonteius wird in Sambucus' Briefen erwähnt, es dürfte sich um den Dichter handeln, den wir damit in den Jahren 1573 bzw. 1575 in Rom im Kreis um Kardinal Sirleto und Fulvio Ursini sehen. Siehe GERSTINGER, Briefe (s. Anm. 1), 141f.; 182f.; 186f. Auf Parallelen von Sambucus' Arcus zu der von Fonteo gegebenen Ausdeutung des Turnierprogramms verweist Thomas DACOSTA KAUFMANN, Variations on the imperial theme in the age of Maximilian II and Rudolf II. New York 1978, 33–40. Vgl. Elisabeth KLECKER, Auster und Absburge. Ein „Habsburg-Mythos" des 16. Jahrhunderts. In: Bodo Guthmüller, Wilhelm Kühlmann (Hgg.), Renaissancekultur und Antike Mythologie. Tübingen 1999, 167–182.

[28] Almásis Vermutung, Sambucus habe sich mit dem Werk bei Maximilian II. als Designer für künftige Feste empfehlen wollen (ALMÁSI, Uses of Humanism, s. Anm. 25, 177), gewinnt an Wahrscheinlichkeit, wenn Giovanni Battista Fonteo nicht mehr zur Verfügung stand. Auch der Historiker Wolfgang Lazius war in die Gestaltung von ephemerer Architektur involviert: s. S. 373 mit Anm. 45–47.

ARCVS
ALIQVOT TRIVMPHAL·
ET MONIMENTA
VICTOR. CLASSICAE,

IN HONOR.

Inuictißimi ac Illustriß.

IANI AVSTRIAE,

VICTORIS NON QVIETVRI.

AVCTOR.

IOAN. SAMBVCO.

QVIBVS ADIECTVM EST
eiusdem argumenti Carmen Heroicum
PER HVGONEM FAVOLIVM.

ANTVERPIÆ.
Apud Philippum Gallæum.
M. D. LXXII.

MAXIMILLIANO. II. DNO, DNO SVO SEMPER
CLEMENTISSIO. d. Clientvl. Cos. Histor. p.

D. Joan. Sambucus ssp

Abb. 7: Widmung an Kaiser Maximilian II.
Arcus aliquot triumphales. Antverpiae 1572
(Wien, Österreichische Nationalbibliothek 66.C.31, nach KLECKER, Emblematika, Anm. 24, 96)

TROPHAEA NAVALIA

In Sambucus' Selbstbibliographie wird das Werk unter *Trophaea navalia* geführt[29], und in der Tat enthält es nicht nur die im Titel angekündigten Triumphbögen. Unter den insgesamt 16 symbolischen Darstellungen sind diese zwar in der Mehrzahl (Nr. 2, 3, 5, 6, 9–12, 14, 15), daneben werden aber weitere Siegeszeichen präsentiert: ein Waffentropaion (Nr. 7), ein (Schand-) Grabmal für die Besiegten (Nr. 8) und zwei Siegessäulen (Nr. 13 und 16); am Anfang steht ein Monument mit Widmung auf einem zentralen Inschriftenfeld. Nur Nr. 4 fällt aus dieser Reihe, indem kein Siegeszeichen, sondern eine Szene ohne architektonischen Rahmen ins Bild gesetzt wird: Der Meeresgott geht mit dem Dreizack gegen einen rücklings im Wasser treibenden Osmanen vor (Abb. 22). Dies entspricht dem Revers einer Gedenkmedaille, die mit der Legende *VENI ET VICI* eine weitere Unternehmung Don Juans, seinen Sieg von Tunis (Oktober 1573), feiert (Abb. 24)[30]. Auch wenn die Medaille zu einem späteren Anlass entstand, ist festzuhalten, dass die Abbildung einer Gedächtnismünze zum Konzept von Sambucus' Schrift, nämlich der graphischen Wiedergabe unterschiedlicher Siegeszeichen, gut gepasst hätte.

Die einzelnen *arcus* bzw. *trophaea* sind so präsentiert, dass jeweils recto der Kupferstich zu stehen kommt, auf der gegenüberliegenden Versoseite ein Prosatext, der als Widmung(sinschrift) zu verstehen ist. Es folgen zwei Oden des Sambucus[31], weiters eine Prosarede, Sambucus' Aufruf, den Sieg zur völligen Vernichtung der Osmanen zu nützen (*Exhortatiuncula Sambuci*,

---

[29] Gedeon BORSA, James E. WALSH, Eine gedruckte Selbstbibliographie von Johannes Sambucus. *Magyar Könyvszemle* 81 (1965) 2, 129–133.

[30] Giovanni Melon, datiert 1573. Abgebildet bei: Karl DOMANIG, Porträtmedaillen des Erzhauses Österreich von Kaiser Friedrich III. bis Kaiser Franz II. aus der Medaillensammlung des Allerhöchsten Kaiserhauses; Taf. in Lichtdr. von Max Jaffé. Wien 1896, 70; sowie im Katalog: Kaiser Karl V. 1500–1558. Macht und Ohnmacht Europas. 2000, 366; und auch CoinArchives <http://www.coinarchives.com/w/results.php?results=100&search=melon> (13. 7. 2017). Zu Giovanni Vincenzo Melone / Melon siehe Leonard FORRER, *Biographical Dictionary of Medallists, Coin-, Gem- and Seal-Engravers, Mint-Masters etc. Ancient and modern, with refrences to their works*. London 1909, Bd. 4, 17–19.

[31] Im Widmungsexemplar für Kaiser Maximilian II. (Wien, Österreichische Nationalbibliothek 66.C.31) hat Sambucus seine Verfasserschaft für beide Oden mit *SAMB.* ausgewiesen.

ad victoriam epirotico mari paratam Idibus Xbris) sowie ein episches Lobgedicht des Mediziners und Literaten Hugo Favolius (1523–1585)[32].

Unter den Erwähnungen des Werks in Sambucus' Briefen verdient die Kurzcharakteristik als *libellus inscriptionibus antiquis et triumphalibus, ut ait ille, vermiculatus* Beachtung[33]: Sie zitiert einen antiken Vergleich von Redeteilen mit Mosaiksteinchen einer „verschlungenen Einlegearbeit" (*emblema vermiculatum*), beschreibt damit ein Werk, in dem sich symbolische Bilder und Texte quasi mosaikartig verbinden, und charakterisiert es, da Zeitgenossen mit *emblema* eine von Alciato ausgehende Tradition verbanden, als ein im weitesten Sinn ‚emblematisches'[34]. In der Tat rezipiert Sambucus, wie zu zeigen sein wird, Vorbilder aus dem Bereich der Emblematik bzw. nützt mit Numismatik und Hieroglyphik dieselben Quellen.

Bereits der Titel verweist auf ein antikes Propagandamedium, das Bild- und Schriftträger zugleich ist und darüber hinaus eine aktive räumliche Erfassung anregt: Ein Triumphbogen bildet eine Sichtachse und fordert zum Durchschreiten auf, zu einer performativen Nutzung etwa bei einem Festzug. Es ist gerade dieser Aspekt, den Sambucus auch in der Zweidimensionalität einzufangen sucht, indem er die Bogenöffnung ausfüllt: In Nr. 10 (Abb. 22) wird der Blick auf den von Juan/Janus geschlossenen Janustempel gelenkt, auf dem eine Inschrift den Anlass in einem Wortspiel (*Ianus Ianum clusit*) kommemoriert. Wie hier der Sieg zusätzlich auf dem Tempeldach im Bild eines Storchs, der eine Schlange frisst[35], illustriert wird, so schaffen auch die anderen Tri-

---

[32] Biographie und Werkverzeichis bei: Elly COCKX-INDESTEGE, Bibliotheca Belgica 227ᵉ–228ᵉ livraisons. Brussels 1963. Hugo Favolius arbeitete als Textdichter mit Philipps Galle zusammen: Ilja M. VELDMAN, Philips Galle: een inventieve prentontwerper. *Oud Holland* 105 (1991), Nr. 4, 262–290.

[33] Brief an Pietro Vettori vom 1. 12. 1571: GERSTINGER, Briefe (s. Anm. 1), Nr. 49.

[34] Es handelt sich um ein bei Cicero (*Orator* 149; *De oratore* 3, 171) überliefertes Fragment des Satirikers Lucilius: fr. 84 MARX *quam lepide lexis compostae ut tesserulae omnes / arte pavimento atque emblemate vermiculato* („Wie anmutig sind seine Phrasen zusammengefügt! Wie alle Steinwürfelchen auf dem Estrich im kunstvoll eingelegten Mosaik." Übersetzung nach: Marcus Tullius Cicero, De oratore – Über den Redner. Lateinisch – deutsch. Hg. und übers. von Theodor NÜSSLEIN. Düsseldorf 2007).

[35] Nach der *Declaratio: Ciconia pia anguem, id est Ianus molestias devorat*. Der Storch gilt in der zeitgenössischen Hieroglyphik als Symbol der Pietas (Pierio Valeriano, *Hieroglyphica* 17, 1 mit Bezug auf Münzen Hadrians), darüberhinaus als Bild für den guten Feldherrn: Nach Plinius, *nat. hist.* 10, 62 genießen Störche als Schlangenvertilger in Thessalien beson-

umphbögen einen architektonischen Rahmen für Darstellungen, die man als narrativ im weitesten Sinn – das Geschehen von 1571 mit historischen und mythologischen Paradigmen erfassend – bezeichnen könnte. In der Bogenöffnung agieren mythologisch-allegorische Gestalten: Jupiters Adler mit dem Blitzbündel (Nr. 5), die den Bogen durchschreitende geflügelte Victoria (Nr. 11; Abb. 9), die auf einem Hirsch der Mondgöttin Diana reitende und die Unterwerfung des (türkischen Halb-)Mondes anzeigende Sonne der göttlichen Wahrheit (Nr. 12)[36]. Schließlich wird auf der Meeresfläche hinter dem vorletzten Bogen (Nr. 14; Abb. 8) eine reduzierte, zugleich allegorisch überhöhte Darstellung der Schlacht sichtbar: ein von den Tugenden gerudertes Schiff, auf dessen Bug *Labor* – Don Juan als Verkörperung der Bemühungen der Christenheit – die Fahrt nach dem Gestirn der Vorsehung ausrichtet.

Es entstehen symbolische Gesamtkompositionen, die auf die europäische Allianz und den Türkensieg hin auszulegen sind. Dies geschieht in der einleitenden, zum Verständnis unentbehrlichen *Brevis picturae declaratio*, in der Bild für Bild aufgeschlüsselt wird.

MONUMENTE AUS PAPIER

Als Inspirationsquelle für die Triumphalarchitektur konnten antike Monumente dienen, von denen Publikationen vorlagen: So dürfte etwa die erste der beiden Siegessäulen (Nr. 13) nach der Trajanssäule in der *Urbis Romae topographia* des Giovanni Bartolomeo Marliani (1488–1566) gestaltet sein (Abb. 11)[37]. Sambucus selbst beschäftigte sich 1581 mit der 1565 aufgefundenen Inschrift der *Columna rostrata* des Duilius[38]. Angesichts seiner Affinität zur Numismatik nicht zu vergessen sind Architekturdarstellungen auf Münzen, wie sie noch im Barock – etwa von Johann Bernhard Fischer von Erlach in seiner *Historischen Architektur* – zur Rekonstruktion gerade von

---

deren Schutz; dies wird von Pierio Valeriano im Kapitel *Hostis profligatus* (*Hieroglyphica* 17, 11) aufgegriffen.

[36] Nach der *Declaratio*: *Sol hoc est veritas Christiana*. Die Inschrift VIRTVTE ET IVSTIC: PART. spricht jedoch dafür, dass beim Betrachten des Bogens auch *Mal*. 4, 2 *orietur vobis timentibus nomen meum sol iustitiae* evoziert werden soll.

[37] Urbis Romae topographia. Cum adjectis urbis atque insignium in ea aedificiorum descriptionibus. Romae: Valer. Doricus et Aloisius fratres 1544, 93.

[38] GERSTINGER, *Briefe* (s. Anm. 1), 255f.

Triumphbögen (Buch 2, Tafel V) genützt wurden[39]. In erster Linie aber war für die Konzeption eines derartigen Werks Festarchitektur mit heraldischen Symbolen, allegorischen Gestalten und (oft aus klassischen Autoren übernommenen) Inschriften vorbildlich, wie sie in Festschriften (zum Teil mit Illustrationen) dokumentiert wurde[40].

Publikationen liegen schon für mehrere Einzüge Karls V. vor[41]: Sambucus könnte die 1549 in Gent und Antwerpen errichteten Triumphtore gekannt haben, die zudem Beschreibungen der zum Anlass errichteten Schaubühnen mit mythologisch-allegorischen Szenen bieten[42]; diese lassen sich gut mit den Darstellungen in den Bogenöffnungen der *Arcus* vergleichen. Weiters ist nicht auszuschließen, dass Sambucus Jacques Androuet Ducerceau, *Quinque et viginti exempla arcuum* (Orléans 1549)[43] einsehen konnte, auch wenn das Werk nicht unter seinen Büchern nachzuweisen ist. Sambucus hatte sich

---

[39] Vgl. George KUNOTH, *Die historische Architektur Fischers von Erlach*. Düsseldorf 1956, 67–69.

[40] Schwer zu beurteilen ist, ob die Ehrenpforte Maximilians I. eine Anregung für Sambucus darstellen konnte.

[41] Marion PHILIPP, *Ehrenpforten für Karl V. Festdekorationen als Medien politischer Kommunikation*. Heidelberg 2010; vgl. auch Roy STRONG: *Feste der Renaissance, 1450–1650. Kunst als Instrument der Macht*. Freiburg, Würzburg 1991, 136–173; Fernando CHECA CREMADES, *Carlos V. La imagen del poder en el renacimiento*. Madrid 1999, 196–224.

[42] *Brevis descriptio eorum quae a S. P. Q. Gand. Philippo Austri. [...] exhibita fuere Gandavi III. Id. Jul. a. 1549.* Gandavi: Cornelius Manilius 1549. Für Sambucus ist nicht uninteressant, dass bei den Inschriften der Bögen auf sprachliche Variation (Hebräisch, Griechisch, Lateinisch, Niederländisch) gesetzt wurde. Abbildungen bei: Hugo SOLY, *Karl V. (1500–1558) und seine Zeit*. Köln 2003, 216f. Cornelis Graphaeus (Schrijvers), *Spectaculorum in susceptione Philippi Hispan. Princ. a. 1549 Antverpia aeditorum mirificus apparatus*. Antverpiae: typis aegidii Disthemii 1550. Zu nennen sind ferner: Giovanni-Alberto Albicante, *Trattato del'intrar in Milano di Carlo V*. Mediolani: Andreas Carolus 1541 und ein nicht illustrierter Wiener Druck über die Triumphtore, mit denen Karl V. nach dem erfolgreichen Tunisunternehmen – also einem ‚Türkensieg' – in Messina und Neapel empfangen wurde: *De insigni adventu Caroli V. Caesaris semper Augusti ad primarias opulentissimas civitates Messanam et Neapolim et arcubus triumphalibus [...] positis*. Viennae Pannoniae: in aedibus Ioannis Singrenii 1536. Keines der genannten Werke ist jedoch bisher im Besitz des Sambucus nachgewiesen.

[43] Frédérique LEMERLE, Jacques Androuet du Cerceau et les antiquités. *Journal de la Renaissance* 2 (2004), 135–144; Monique CHATENET, Entrée de Henri II et de Catherine de Médicis à Orléans: Les arcs de triomphe éphémères de Jacques Androuet du Cerceau. In: Hanns Hubach u. a. (Hgg.), *Reibungspunkte. Ordnung und Umbruch in Architektur und Kunst. Festschrift für Hubertus Günther*. Petersberg 2008, 27–32; Hubertus GÜNTHER, Du Cerceau et l'Antiquité. In: Jean Guillaume, Peter Fuhring (Hgg.), *Jacques Androuet du Cerceau*. Paris 2010, 75–90.

vom März 1560 bis zum Spätsommer 1561 in Paris aufgehalten und blieb u. a. mit Henricus Stephanus auch von Wien aus in Kontakt[44]. Mit größter Wahrscheinlichkeit aber kannte Sambucus die zur Rückkehr Maximilians II. von der Kaiserkrönung in Wien errichteten, von Wolfgang Lazius konzipierten und poetisch beschriebenen[45] Triumphtore – zumindest aus der erst 1566 erschienenen illustrierten Publikation in deutscher Sprache[46].

In zeitlich unmittelbarer Nähe liegt das schon genannte Hochzeitsfest vom August 1571: Im Druck der deutschen Festbeschreibung durch Heinrich Wirre/Wirrich, die sich vor allem auf die heraldische Repräsentation der Teilnehmer konzentriert, werden neben einzelnen Kostümen auch eine Victoria auf einer Siegessäule und die vier an eine Säule gefesselten Laster, also wohl Aufbauten der Festdekoration, wiedergegeben[47].

---

[44] Endre BACH, *Un humaniste hongrois en France. Jean Sambucus et ses relations littéraires (1551–1584)*. Szeged 1932 (*Études françaises* 5), 20–24 sowie 51f.

[45] Ad eundem invictiss. et sacratis. Caesarem incolumem ab inauguratione Romani Bohemique regnorum in patriam ditionemque suam redeuntem, Wolfgangi Lazii Viennen. medici, Caesarii historici ac consiliarii gymnasiique superintendentis et primarii carmen congratulatorium cum explicat. arcuum triumphalium quos obsequii ergo resp. Viennen. constituerat ipso consultore. [...]. Viennae Austriae: excudebat Raphael Hoffhalter 1563; Epitome solenniorum quae in auspicatum adventum invictiss. ac sacratiss. Rom. Caesaris D. N. Maximiliani, Bohemiae regis et archiducis Austriae [...] respub. Viennen. omnia obsequii ergo supplex [...]. Viennae Austriae: excudebat Michael Zimmerman 1563 (VD16 E 1842). Den Hinweis verdanke ich Martin Čičo / SNG Bratislava.

[46] Gründtliche und khurtze beschreibung des alten vnnd jungen Zugs welche beede zur Einbeleittung [...] Kaiser Maximiliani des Anndern [...] wie Ire Röm. Kays. Mt. etc. sampt derselben geliebsten Gemahl vnd Kindern von der Crönung von Franckfurt zu Wienn den 16. Martij im 63. Jar ankhomen daselbst seind angerichtet worden, sambt aller schönen vnd zierlichen Ehrenporten Prunnen vnd anderer Solenniteten warhsfftigen angehaenckten Contrarnfactu. Wienn in Österreich: bey Caspar Stainhofer 1566 (VD16 S 8519). Vgl. Werner KAYSER, Melchior Lorichs' Ehrenpforten und Weinbrunnen zum Einzug Kaiser Maxyimilians II. in Wien, insbesondere die Ehrenpforte beim Waaghaus. *Philobiblon* 23 (1979), 279–295; Josef WÜNSCH, Der Einzug Kaiser Maximilians II. in Wien 1563. *Berichte und Mitteilungen des Altertums-Vereines zu Wien* 46/47 (1914), 9–34.

[47] Ordenliche Beschreibung des Christlichen, Hochlöblichen vnd Fürstlichen Beylags oder Hochzeit, so da gehalten ist worden durch den Durchleuchtigsten [...] Herrn Carolen, Ertzhertzog zu Österreich [...] mit dem Hochgebornen Fräwlein Maria, geborne Hertzogin zu Bayrn, den XXVI. Augusti in der Kayserlichen Statt Wienn / [...] in Teutsche Carmina gestelt [...] Durch Heinrichen Wirrich. Wienn: Blasius Eber 1571.

Inschriften als Bildelemente

Wie gebaute Triumphalarchitektur tragen Sambucus' graphische *Arcus* Inschriften, etwa die Weiheinschriften *Neptuno Ithacibero* (Nr. 2), *Nicatori Atlantico in praedam* (Nr. 6), ΕΝΑΡΗΦΟΡΩ ΜΕΓΙΣΤΩ (Nr. 7) und *Domitori As(iae) et Africae* (Nr. 12). Aber auch wenn kein typisches Inschriftenformular vorliegt, kann die Position der am Baukörper angebrachten Kurztexte aussagekräftig sein: Wenn das Vergilzitat *VIVIDA VIRTUS* (Aen. 5, 754) in Nr. 2 auf den Säulenbasen angebracht ist, soll *virtus* als Grundlage und Voraussetzung für den Sieg charakterisiert werden.

Konsequent durchgehalten ist die inschriftliche Anbringung nicht; häufiger sind Texte im freien Raum positioniert und kommentieren – zum Teil als Zitate aus der klassischen Literatur und der Bibel[48] – Dekorationselemente oder Gestalten in der Bogenöffnung. Der Psalmvers 68 (69), 10 *Zelus domus tuae* (*comedit me*) erklärt durch seine Position das auf dem Siegesmonument brennende Opferfeuer (Nr. 1). Der Niederschlag in der Bogenöffnung von Nr. 9 (Abb. 23) wird direkt darunter mit *QUID EST HOC* als Mannaregen (Ex 16, 15) identifiziert, während *NUMQUAM MARCESCENT* als Kommentar zu den gewählten immergrünen Pflanzen, die nach der *Declaratio* (*laurus et hedera, perpetua Iani victoriae memoria*) für die unvergängliche Erinnerung an den Sieg stehen, am Bogen selbst angebracht ist. Griechische Zitate (z. B. Euripides, fr. 353 ΟΥΔΕΙΣ ΣΤΡΑΤΕΥΣΑΣ ΑΔΙΚΑ ΣΩΣ ΗΛΘΕΝ ΠΑΛΙΝ; Nr. 15[49]) dienen der Variation und verweisen bereits mit ihrem Schriftbild auf die (postulierte) Bedeutung des Siegs für Griechenland.

Die ins Bild integrierten Texte haben also zwei Dimensionen: Sie haben einerseits Bildqualität[50] und interagieren mit anderen Bildelementen, ander-

---

[48] Weitere Zitate: Nr. 4 *victrices incitat ira manus* nach Prop. 3, 22, 22 *victrices temperat ira manus*; Nr. 6 *Sub iuga quot gentes captivis regibus ibunt* nach Claudian 22 (*De consulatu Stilichonis*), 2, 311 *Sub iuga quo gentes captivis regibus egi*.

[49] Tragicorum Graecorum Fragmenta. Bd. 5: Euripides. Hg. von Richard Kannicht. Göttingen 2004, 396. Das Zitat ist bei Stobaeus 4,13,13 überliefert. Zu Sambucus' Beschäftigung mit Stobaeus vgl. Gábor Almási, Gábor Farkas Kiss, *Humanistes du bassin des Carpates*. II: *Johannes Sambucus*. Turnhout 2014 (*Europa humanistica* 14), LXII und 192–201.

[50] Darüber hinaus sind Planetensymbole (Nr. 13) verwendet. – „Schriftbildlichkeit" ist Gegenstand neuerer interdisziplinärer Forschung: Sybille Krämer, Die Schrift als Hybrid aus Sprache und Bild. Thesen über die Schriftbildlichkeit unter Berücksichtigung von Diagrammatik und Kartographie. In: Torsten Hoffmann, Gabriele Rippl (Hgg.), *Bilder. Ein (neues) Leitmedium?* Göttingen 2006, 79–92; Dies., „Schriftbildlichkeit" oder Über eine

seits müssen sie als Texte mit intertextuellen Bezügen verstanden werden. Der Bogen Nr. 14 (Abb. 8) zeigt die Verflechtung beider Aspekte besonders deutlich: Die im Schiff mitfahrenden Gestalten werden durch den ins Bild integrierten Text als Tugenden INDUSTRIA, FORTITUDO, CONSIL(ium), CELERITAS identifiziert, sodass sich die Darstellung als Allegorie der Schlacht von Lepanto interpretieren lässt; es sind eben jene Qualitäten, die Don Juan zum Sieg verhalfen. Berücksichtigt man dazu die Declaratio (Comites, et remiges sunt quattuor in imperatore summo Virtutes, de quibus Cicero; Industria, Fortitudo, Consilium, Celeritas), die diese Beischrift als Zitat aus Ciceros Rede De imperio Cn. Pompei (für den Oberbefehl des Gnaeus Pompeius im Dritten Mithridatischen Krieg) erklärt[51], so ergibt sich zusätzlich eine historische Dimension, eine Gleichsetzung Don Juans mit einem der bedeutendsten Feldherrn der Antike.

Ähnlich funktionieren drei V in Nr. 11 (Abb. 9): Sie sind wieder in Gestalt eines V angeordnet und flankieren Victoria im Torbogen. Zugleich sind sie nach der Declaratio (Venimus, Vidimus, Vicimus, ut Iul. Caesar de Britannis) als Abkürzung für das berühmte Caesar-Dictum Veni, vidi, vici – das nach Sueton beim Triumphzug zur Schau getragen wurde![52] – zu lesen.

(fast) vergessene Dimension von Schrift. In: Horst Bredekamp, Sybille Krämer (Hgg.), *Bild, Schrift, Zahl*. München 2003, 157–176. Michael ROTH (Hg.), *Schrift als Bild*. Unter Mitarbeit von Nadine Rottau, mit weiteren Beiträgen von Beate Braun-Niehr und Jürgen Geiß, Ausstellung Schrift als Bild Kupferstichkabinett, Staatliche Museen zu Berlin Kulturforum Potsdamer Platz 29. Oktober 2010 – 23. Jänner 2011, Berlin 2010.

[51] *De imperio* 29 *Neque enim illae sunt solae virtutes imperatoriae, quae volgo existimantur, labor in negotiis, fortitudo in periculis, industria in agendo, celeritas in conficiendo, consilium in providendo: quae tanta sunt in hoc uno, quanta in omnibus reliquis imperatoribus, quos aut vidimus aut audivimus, non fuerunt* („Denn nicht nur die Vorzüge machen den Feldherrn, die jedermann für erforderlich hält: angestrengte Tätigkeit im Dienst, Beherztheit in Gefahren, Rührigkeit beim Handeln, Raschheit bei der Ausführung, Weitblick bei der Planung. All dies besitzt der eine Pompeius in einem Maße, wie es alle anderen Feldherrn, die wir sahen oder von denen wir hörten, nicht besessen haben." Übersetzung nach: Marcus Tullius Cicero, Die politischen Reden. Lateinisch – deutsch. Bd. 1. Hg., übers. und erl. von Manfred FUHRMANN. München 1993).

[52] *Divus Iulius* 37, 2 *Pontico triumpho inter pompae fercula trium verborum praetulit titulum VENI : VIDI : VICI*. Das Dictum über den Sieg bei Zela über Pharnakes II. (47 v. Chr.; vgl. Plutarch, *Caesar* 50, 3) wird von Sambucus auf die Britannienexpedition bezogen. Mit seiner Verwendung liegt wieder eine Parallele zur bereits genannten Medaille vor: s. S. 369 mit Anm. 30.

Abb. 8: *VIRTUTI CHRISTIANAE* (Nr. 14). Arcus aliquot triumphales. Antverpiae 1572.
(Wien, Österreichische Nationalbibliothek 66.C.31)

Abb. 9: *TEMERITAS GETHICA* (Nr. 11). Arcus aliquot triumphales. Antverpiae 1572.
(Wien, Österreichische Nationalbibliothek 66.C.31,
nach KLECKER, Emblematika, s. Anm. 25, 97)

Nicht zuletzt sind die synoptisch zu den Tafeln gesetzten Kurztexte in ihrer Formatierung auf eine visuelle Erfassung als Textbilder berechnet. Selbst wenn keine spezifisch epigraphische Schrift gewählt ist, erscheinen sie auf der sonst leeren Blattfläche als ‚Inschriften'. Der Form der Weiheinschrift entspricht die mehrheitliche Formulierung im Dativ: NEPTVN(o) VLTOR(i) (Nr. 4); IOVI SOSPITI (Nr. 5); FVLMINI BETHICO IANO AVSTRIAE (Nr. 6); AEQUORIS OMNIPOTENTI (Nr. 9); PRINCIPI IVVENT(vtis) ET AVREI SAECVLI (Nr. 10); VIRTVTI CHRISTIANAE (Nr. 14); GENIO VICTORIS libidinum Barbararum; Iterum triumphanti IANO (Nr. 16). Ganz aus Widmungsdativen ist die Textseite zur ersten Siegessäule (Nr. 13) aufgebaut – wodurch sich eine kolumnenartige Textformation als Pendant zur gegenüberliegenden Architekturdarstellung ergibt (Abb. 10ab). Auch für das Schandgrabmal der Besiegten (Nr. 8) spiegelt das Layout des Textes die architektonische Form (Abb. 12ab).

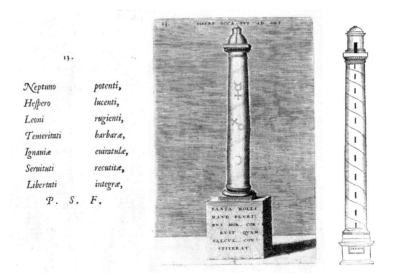

Abb. 10ab: Siegessäule Nr. 13. Arcus aliquot triumphales. Antverpiae 1572.
(Wien, Österreichische Nationalbibliothek 66.C.31)
Abb. 11: Trajanssäule. Giovanni Bartolomeo Marliani, Urbis Romae topographia.
Romae: Valer. Doricus et Aloisius fratres 1544, 93
(Wien, Universitätsbibliothek II 185.517)

8.

CENOTAPH. BARBB.

IN
QVEM-
CVMQVE
RECIDAT: NI-
SI PERFIDIA IN-
FLATA COMES INFOE-
LICIS DOLORIS, IN-
FAMIA ORBIS, RIDICVLI
MVRES EX ELEPHANTIS
SVBITO FACTI SCYTHÆ, HIC
COELO POEN. LVERE.

H. M. H. R. S.

Abb. 12ab: *CENOTAPH(ium) BARB(arorum)* (Nr. 8). Arcus aliquot triumphales. Antverpiae 1572 (Wien, Österreichische Nationalbibliothek 66.C.31)

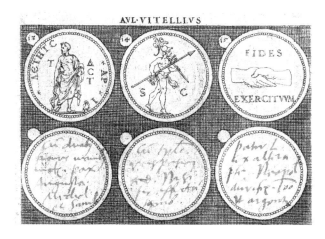

Abb. 13: Ergänzungen des Johannes Sambucus in: Omnium Caesarum verissimae imagines. [Venedig] Vico 1554 (Wien, Österreichische Nationalbibliothek 44.G.49)

Ganzheitliche Antikerezeption

Abb. 14: Besitzvermerk des Johannes Sambucus. Omnium Caesarum verissimae imagines. [Venedig] Vico 1554
(Wien, Österreichische Nationalbibliothek 44.G.49)

Münzen und Embleme

Der Bildschmuck der Bögen stammt in erster Linie von Münzen – vermittelt durch zeitgenössische Publikationen. Nachdem römische Münzen im Humanismus zunächst in erster Linie als authentische (Kaiser-)Porträts rezipiert worden waren[53], wandte sich die Aufmerksamkeit im Lauf des 16. Jahrhunderts immer mehr den Reversbildern als Zeugnissen politischer Propaganda zu. Es entstanden illustrierte Publikationen wie die 1548 vom venezianischen Sammler Antonio Zantani und dem Künstler Enea Vico veröffentlichte, die die ersten zwölf Kaiser von Caesar bis Domitian erfasste, also jene, für die Suetons Biographien vorliegen[54]. Sambucus besaß ein Exemplar der lateinischen Fassung von 1554 (Wien, Österreichische Nationalbibliothek 44.G.49), das er annotierte (Abb. 13; 14)[55]. So bestand auch bei den im Anhang zu seinen *Emblemata* publizierten seltenen Münzen aus seiner eigenen Sammlung die Rarität in den Reversbildern, und dieselbe Ausrichtung zeigt der Publikationsplan des Wolfgang Lazius, *Commentariorum vetustorum numismatum specimen exile*[56]. Derartige Zusammenstellungen bildeten aber zugleich Repertorien politischer Ikonographie, wie sie in zeitgenössischer Kunst zum Einsatz kommen konnte[57].

---

[53] Annegrit SCHMITT, Zur Wiederbelebung der Antike im Trecento. Petrarcas Rom-Idee in ihrer Wirkung auf die Paduaner Malerei: Die methodische Einbeziehung des römischen Münzbildnisses in die Ikonographie Berühmter Männer. *Mitteilungen des Kunsthistorischen Instituts Florenz* 18 (1974), 167–218. John CUNNALY, *Images of the Illustrious. The Numismatic Presence in the Renaissance*. Princeton 1999.

[54] Le imagini con tutti riversi trovati et le vita de gli imperatori tratte dalle medaglie et dalle historie de gli antichi. Libro primo. [Venedig] 1548; Edith LEMBURG-RUPPELT, *Enea Vico, ein Künstler-Antiquar des 16. Jahrhunderts*. Diss. Berlin 1988; DIES., Der systematische Ausbau der Numismatik im Werk Enea Vicos (1523–1567). In: Reiner Albert, Reiner Cunz (Hgg.), *Wissenschaftsgeschichte der Numismatik*. Speyer 1995, 49–70; Giulio BODON, *Enea Vico fra memoria e miraggio della classicità*. Roma 1997. Vgl. PELC (s. Anm. 6), Nr. 171 und 172.

[55] Omnium Caesarum verissimae Imagines ex antiquis numismatis desumptae. Addita Perbrevi Cvivsqve Vitae Descriptione, Ac Diligenti Eorvm, Qvae Reperiri Potvervnt Nvmismatvm, Aversae Partis Delineatione Libri Primi Ed. Altera. [Venedig] Vico 1554. Im folgenden wird daher diese Ausgabe für Münzbilder herangezogen.

[56] Commentariorum vetustorum numismatum maximi scilicet operis et IV sectionibus multarum rerum publicarum cum Asiam, Aphricam et Europam antiquitatis historiam [...] comprehendentis specimen. Viennae Austriae: excudebat Michael Zimmermann 1558 (VD16 L 847; Wien, Österreichische Nationalbibliothek 57.C.11).

[57] Münzen wurden auch für tatsächlich errichtete ephemere Architektur herangezogen: Vgl. Peter BERGHAUS, Numismatische Bezüge der Pompa ntroitus des Caspar Gevaerts, Ant-

In den *Arcus triumphales* finden römische Münzen auf unterschiedlicher Ebene Verwendung: Explizit vermerkt ist der Bezug bereits für den ersten Bogen (Nr. 2), bei dem Münzbilder als heraldische Symbole dienen: Nach der *declaratio* tragen „die Seitenteile die Wappen der befreiten Küstenregionen nach antiken Münzen" (*latera habent ex Numis vetustis regionum litoralium insignia liberatarum*)[58]. Nach Münzen sind auf dem einleitenden Siegesmonument sakrale Gerätschaften (*lituus, urceolus*; z. B. Zantani / Vico, *Vespasianus, ex argento* 5[59]) abgebildet, wohl um den Anteil des Papstes als sakrale Autorität zu würdigen, während Spanien und Venedig heraldisch repräsentiert sind. An Münzbildern orientiert sich die im Waffentropaion (Nr. 7) verwendete Prora mit Rammsporn (z. B. Zantani / Vico, *Vespasianus, ex argento* 39). Der geschlossene Janustempel, der durch den Bogen Nr. 10 sichtbar wird, ist von einem Sesterz Neros genommen (Zantani / Vico, *Domitius Nero, ex aere* 17; Abb. 18)[60]. Für die Darstellung der an den Torpfeiler von Nr. 9 (Abb. 21) gelehnten, sitzenden Kybele mit Mauerkrone verweist Sambucus in der *Declaratio* auf Hadrian; es könnten Münzen der spätantoninischen Zeit gemeint sein[61]. Besonders reich an numismatischen Bezügen ist der Bogen Nr. 15 (Abb. 12), der nach der *Declaratio* die Befreiung von der Türkengefahr und die heilbringende Wirkung des auf Frömmigkeit und Mut beruhenden Siegs für Griechenland und die Kontinente Asien und Afrika thematisiert.

---

werpen 1643. In: Christian Dekesel, Thomas Stäcker (Hgg.), *Europäische numismatische Literatur im 17. Jahrhundert.* Wiesbaden 2005 (*Wolfenbütteler Arbeiten zur Barockforschung* 42), 193–210.

[58] Vergleichbar ist die Verwendung auf der Griechenlandkarte des Wolfgang Lazius: *Commentariorum rerum Graecarum libri II.* Viennae: Raphael Hoffhalter, Michael Zimmermann s. a. [1558] (Wien, Universitätsbibliothek III 302.215 ES). Vgl. Petra SVATEK, Wolfgang Lazius und seine Commentarii rerum Graecarum unter besonderer Berücksichtigung der beiden Griechenlandkarten. In: Elisabeth Klecker, Christian Gastgeber (Hgg.), *Johannes Cuspinianus (1473–1529). Ein Wiener Humanist und sein Werk im Kontext.* Wien 2012 (*Singularia Vindobonensia* 2), 287–306.

[59] Innerhalb jedes Kaisers werden die Prägungen jeweils nach Gold, Silber und Kupfer geordnet durchnummeriert; entsprechend werden sie im folgenden zitiert.

[60] Frank BUBEL, PACE POPVLI ROMANI TERRA MARIQUE PARTA IANUM CLVSIT. Zum Datum der Schließung des Janus-Tempels durch Nero. *Rheinisches Museum für Philologie* 141 (1998), 410–412.

[61] Vgl. Erika SIMON, Kybele. *Lexicon ikonographicum mythologiae classicae* 8.1 (1997), 744–767; hier 761 Nr. 108.

Abb. 15a: *LIBERTATI RELIGIONE ET ARMIS RECUPERATAE* (Nr. 15). Arcus aliquot triumphales. Antverpiae 1572.
(Wien, Österreichische Nationalbibliothek 66.C.31, nach KLECKER, Emblematika, s. Anm. 25, 97)

Cruce et sica, id est, Pileus libertatis Religione et armis constitit, ocioque aliquo parto alvearia apum abundant. Galea vero curulibus id est domesticis sellis imposita. Serpens gyrosus longam salutem publicam in ara, id est, Pietate, et animo significat. Ad quam conferunt se suaque vovent, Graecia, Asia et Africa.

Auf Kreuz und Dolch, d. h. auf Religion und Waffen ruht die Freiheitsmütze, und wenn Frieden geschaffen ist, sind die Bienenhäuser voll. Der Helm ist auf kurulischen Stühlen, d. h. Stühlen des Friedens abgelegt. Die gewundene Schlange bedeutet, dass lange Wohlfahrt für den Staat auf dem Altar, d. h. auf Frömmigkeit und Mut, beruht. Zu diesem Altar begeben sich Griechenland, Asien und Afrika und weihen sich und ihren Besitz.

Sowohl am Bogen angebrachte Dekorationselemente als auch die Figurengruppe in der Bogenöffnung sind von Münzen inspiriert. Die auf einem Denar Hadrians abgebildete Frauengestalt mit *patera*, die eine sich vom Altar erhebende Schlange nährt[62], wird von Sambucus erweitert zu einer Dreiergruppe der Personifikationen Griechenlands, Asien und Afrikas, die am Altar der Salus (mit der Weiheinschrift *SALUTI PUBLICAE*) das Dankopfer für ihre Befreiung darbringen.

Von einer berühmten Münze, die schon Alciato für ein Emblem herangezogen hatte (*RESPUBLICA LIBERATA*, erstmals Venedig 1546, 26ʳ/D2ʳ), stammt der *pileus libertatis*, die Kopfbedeckung des freigelassenen Sklaven, der als Bekrönung über den Torbogen gestülpt ist. Iunius Brutus hatte auf dem Revers einer Münze mit seinem Porträt die Ermordung Caesars mit dem *pileus* zwischen zwei nach unten gekehrten Dolchen als Befreiung Roms vom Tyrannen proklamiert (Abb. 16)[63]. Alciato (?), jedenfalls aber der Illustrator des Drucks von 1546 hatte den *pileus* in Unkenntnis der bildlichen Überlieferung als Galero dargestellt (Abb. 17); eine ‚korrekte' Wiedergabe nach der Münze

---

[62] Vincenzo SALADINO, Salus. *Lexicon iconographicum mythologiae classicae* 7 (1994), 656–661; hier 658 Nr. 30, 31. Für Karl V. war die Darstellung der Salus bereits 1546 auf einer Medaille von Leone Leoni aufgegriffen worden: CHECA CREMADES, *Carlos V.* (s. Anm. 41), 279, fig. 161B.

[63] Cassius Dio 47, 25, 3 ἐς τὰ νομίσματα ἃ ἐκόπτετο εἰκόνα τε αὐτοῦ καὶ πιλίον ξιφίδιά τε δύο ἐνετύπου, δηλῶν ἔκ τε τούτου καὶ διὰ τῶν γραμμάτων ὅτι τὴν πατρίδα μετὰ τοῦ Κασσίου ἠλευθερωκὼς εἴη. Edward Allen SYDENHAM, *Historical references on coins of the Roman Empire from Augustus to Gallienus.* Chicago 1969, 1301. Vgl. Herbert A. CAHN, EIDibus MARtiis. *Numismatica e antichità classiche* 18 (1989), 211–233. CRAWFORD, RRC (s. Anm. 19), 508/3. Vgl. Libertas: The Coins of Brutus. In: Michelle O'REILLY, Kenneth SHEEDY, The Coins of Julius Caesar. *Macquarie University. Australian Centre for Ancient Numismatic Studies* <http://www.humanities.mq.edu.au/acans/caesar/CivilWars_Libertas.htm> (3. 6. 2017).

bietet erst die Ausgabe Padua 1621[64]. Der Triumphbogen bei Sambucus zeigt dagegen den *pileus* wie auf der Münze, hat deren Reversbild jedoch quasi zerlegt, indem statt der zwei Dolche flankierend auf den Torpfeilern ein Kreuz und ein aufgerichtetes Schwert (die *declaratio* spricht von *sica* „Dolch") als ‚Befreiungsinstrumente' angebracht sind. Da nun aber nicht das in sich geschlossene Münzbild abgebildet ist, übernimmt der Text der *declaratio* die Funktion, die Zusammengehörigkeit der drei Elemente, und damit den Bezug auf die antike Münze (und das Emblem Alciatos) abzusichern.

Abb. 16: Münze des Iunius Brutus.
(Macquarie University, W. L. Gale Collection of Roman Republican Coins, s. Anm. 63)

Abb. 17: *RESPUBLICA LIBERATA*. Alciato, Emblematum libellus. Venetiis: Aldus 1546, 26ʳ / D2ʳ (Glasgow University Library, Stirling Maxwell Collection, s. Anm. 64)

Eine ähnliche Aufspaltung im Bild und Zusammenführung im erklärenden Text zeigt sich im mittleren Bereich des Bogens: Sieht man den Bienenkorb am linken Pfeiler und den rechts auf einer – auf Münzen vorkommenden und so bei Zantani / Vico für Titus, *ex argento* 7, dokumentierten (Abb. 19) – *sella curulis* abgelegten Helm zusammen, ergibt sich eines der bekanntesten Embleme Alciatos *EX BELLO PAX* (*Emblematum liber* 1531, C3ᵛ; Abb. 18). Dies entspricht der Deutung in der schon zitierten *Declaratio*.

---

[64] Die einfachste Vergleichsmöglichkeit der Ausgaben bietet die Internetseite *Glasgow University Emblem Website / Alciato at Glasgow* <http://www.emblems.arts.gla.ac.uk/alciato/index.php> (3. 6. 2017).

Abb. 15bc: *LIBERTATI RELIGIONE ET ARMIS RECUPERATAE* (Nr. 15), Details
Abb. 18: *Ex bello pax.* Emblemata Andreae Alciati. Lugduni: apud Gulielmum Rovillium 1548 (Wien, Universitätsbibliothek I 24.401)
Abb. 19: *Titus, ex argento* 7. Omnium Caesarum verissimae imagines antiquis numismatis desumptae. [Venedig] Vico 1554 (Wien, Universitätsbibliothek I 178.102)

Gerade dieses Nebeneinander an einem Bogen zeigt aber auch die unterschiedliche Wertigkeit von Referenzen auf Emblem und Münze: Reversbilder von Münzen sind mit historischem Geschehen verknüpft; über das allgemeine Deutungspotential einer symbolischen Darstellung hinaus evozieren sie historische Ereignisse bzw. deren Interpretation, ‚Geschichtsbilder' also, wie sie freilich nicht zuletzt auf literarischen Texten basieren. Ganz besonders ist dies bei der Wiedergabe von Münzen des Augustus der Fall. So stammt der Janustempel in Nr. 10 (Abb. 22) zwar von einer neronischen Münze, von der mit *clusit* auch die Legende anzitiert ist (Zantani / Vico, *Domitius Nero, ex aere* 17; Abb. 20), der Bezug auf die weit berühmteren Schließungen unter Augustus ist jedoch schon in der *declaratio* gesichert: *Templum Iani per eum nostro tempore contra Thurcas clausum, ut per Augustum et Neronem.* Auch für die Kombination von Steuerruder und Weltkugel als Bekrönung des Bogens *AEQUORIS OMNIPOTENTI* (Nr. 9; Abb. 23) bezieht sich Sambucus auf ein Münzbild (Zantani / Vico, *Divus Augustus, ex aere* 39; Abb. 21) und nennt in der *declaratio* explizit die Schlacht bei Actium (2. Sept. 31 v. Chr.): *orbis cum temone ut Actiaca victoria.* Auf den Sieg über Kleopatra bezieht sich eine Münze mit dem Reversbild eines Krokodils und der Legende *AEGYPTO CAPTA* (Zantani / Vico, *Divus Augustus, ex argento* 41), von der das Krokodil des ersten eigentlichen Bogens (Nr. 2) übernommen ist. Schließlich stammt auch die Beischrift zu Nr. 4 *COL(ligavit) NEMO* (Abb. 24) von einer Münze des

Augustus (Zantani/Vico, *Divus Augustus, ex aere* 43; Abb. 25), auf der sie ein an eine Palme gefesseltes Krokodil kommentierte: Octavian sei mit der Eroberung Ägyptens bislang Unerreichtes gelungen. Bereits Claude Paradin hatte die Münze für seine *Devises heroïques* (ab der zweiten, erweiterten Auflage 1557) herangezogen und auf die Inbesitznahme Ägyptens in der Folge des Siegs von Actium gedeutet worden[65]. Sambucus akzentuiert in der *Declaratio* freilich anders, auf die Heilige Liga: *nemo colligavit, hoc est, adhuc tam firme Christianos nemo, ac Papa, conduxit*. Die Schlacht von Actium war freilich nicht allein aufgrund der relativen geographischen Nähe (Actium liegt etwas weiter nördlich als Lepanto) ein geeigneter historischer Referenzpunkt[66], sondern auch aufgrund der augusteischen Propaganda, die den Verlierer Marcus Antonius und seine Verbündete Kleopatra als orientalische, unrömische Herrscher diffamierte und sich daher leicht mit Klischees aus der antiosmanischen Propaganda engführen ließ. So rufen die Münzbilder (deren Augustusbezug durch die *Declaratio* festgeschrieben wird) beim gebildeten Publikum ein geläufiges Paradigma des Siegers über orientalische Tyrannis auf, das als solches in erster Linie literarisch durch die augusteische Dichtung konstituiert wird – nicht zuletzt durch ein literarisches Bildwerk: die Schildbeschreibung im achten Buch von Vergils *Aeneis* (8, 626–728; bes. 671–713).

Abb. 20: *Domitius Nero, ex aere* 17. Omnium Caesarum verissimae imagines antiquis numismatis desumptae. [Venedig] Vico 1554 (Wien, Universitätsbibliothek I 178.102)
Abb. 21: *Divus Augustus, ex aere* 39. Omnium Caesarum verissimae imagines antiquis numismatis desumptae. [Venedig] Vico 1554 (Wien, Universitätsbibliothek I 178.102)

---

[65] Claude Paradin, Devises heroïques. A Lion: par Ian de Tournes et Guillaume Gazeau 1557, 68. Sambucus besaß ein Exemplar der lateinischen Fassung: Heroica M. Clavdii Paradini [...] & D. Gabrielis Symeonis Symbola [...]. Antverpiae: Plantin 1562; hier 86 / 41ᵛ. Siehe GULYÁS (s. Anm. 14), Nr. 1093.
[66] David QUINT, *Epic and Empire. Politics and generic form from Virgil to Milton*. Princeton 1992, 49 Appendix 2: Actium and Lepanto.

Abb. 22: *PRINCIPI IVVENT(vtis) ET AVREI SAECVLI* (Nr. 15). Arcus aliquot triumphales.
Antverpiae 1572
(Wien, Österreichische Nationalbibliothek 66.C.31,
nach KLECKER, Emblematika, Anm. 23)

Abb. 23: *AEQUORIS OMNIPOTENTI* (Nr. 9). Arcus aliquot triumphales. Antverpiae 1572.
(Wien, Österreichische Nationalbibliothek 66.C.31, nach Klecker, Emblematika, s. Anm. 24, 96)

Abb. 24: *NEPTVN(o) VLTOR(i)* (Nr. 4). Arcus aliquot triumphales. Antverpiae 1572.
(Wien, Österreichische Nationalbibliothek 66.C.31)

Abb. 25: *Divus Augustus, ex aere* 43. Omnium Caesarum verissimae imagines antiquis numismatis desumptae. [Venedig] Vico 1554 (Wien, Universitätsbibliothek I 178.102)

Abb. 26: Giovanni Melone, Medaille auf den Tunissieg des Don Juan 1573 (CoinArchives, s. Anm. 30)

INTERMEDIALITÄT UND AUTORSCHAFT

Für die Verbindung von Text und Bild im Emblem sind in der deutschsprachigen Forschung die Termini Bimedialität und Synmedialität[67], zuletzt auch Intermedialität in Gebrauch gekommen[68]. Für Sambucus' *Emblemata* – eine Ausnahme bildet das bereits vorgestellte Musenemblem – gilt jedoch wie für die des Archegeten Alciato, dass sie auch ohne *picturae* als Gedichtsammlung bestehen könnten. In den *Arcus aliquot triumphales* sind Bild und Text dagegen zu einer unauflöslichen Einheit verschmolzen, ihre Wirkung lebt von der Interaktion von Schrift und Bild: Die *Arcus* bieten Schrift im Bild, Schrift als Bild. Schrift dient als Textmedium für Erklärungen und Kommentare zu Bildern, für Zitate, die intertextuelle Bezüge herstellen, auf ‚Geschichtsbilder' verweisen. Dies leisten aber auch Bild-Zitate von Münzen, die historischen Ereignissen zugeordnet werden und damit deren Darstellung in der Textüberlieferung evozieren. Zugleich spielt das Werk mit dem ständigen Verweis auf dreidimensionale Medien politischer Propaganda. Sieht man Intermedialität gegeben, wo Charakteristika eines Mediums mit den Mitteln eines anderen zum Ausdruck gebracht werden, wo in Hinblick auf ein konzeptuelles Ganzes Mediendifferenzen berücksichtigt und Mediengrenzen überschritten werden[69], so scheint die Anwendung der modernen Begrifflichkeit von Intermedialität gerechtfertigt, um das Raffinement von Sambucus' Huldigung adäquat zu beschreiben[70].

---

[67] Rüdiger ZYMNER, Das Emblem als offenes Kunstwerk. In: Wolfgang Harms, Dietmar Peil (Hgg.), *Polyvalenz und Multifunktionalität der Emblematik. Akten des 5. Internationalen Kongresses der Society for Emblem Studies.* Frankfurt am Main 2002 (Mikrokosmos 65), Bd. I, 9–24: „synmediale Gattung".

[68] Vgl. z. B. Johannes KÖHLER, Christian SCHNEIDER (Hgg.), *Das Emblem im Widerspiel von Intermedialität und Synmedialität.* Hildesheim 2007 (Philosophische Texte und Studien 89).

[69] Irina O. RAJEWSKY, Intermedialität >light<? In: Roger Lüdeke, Erika Greber (Hgg.), *Medium Literatur. Beiträge zu einer Medientheorie der Literaturwissenschaft.* Göttingen 2004 (Münchener Universitätsschriften. Münchener Komparatistische Studien 5), 27–77; bes. 39: „Es werden […] Elemente und/oder Strukturen eines anderen, konventionell als distinkt wahrgenommenen Mediums mit den eigenen, medienspezifischen Mitteln thematisiert, evoziert oder simuliert". Jürgen E. MÜLLER, Intermedialität als poetologisches und medientheoretisches Konzept. Einige Reflexionen zu dessen Geschichte. In: Jörg Helbig (Hg.), *Intermedialität. Theorie und Praxis eines interdisziplinären Forschungsgebiets.* Berlin 1998, 31–40.

[70] Vgl. auch Werner WOLFF, Intermedialität: Ein weites Feld und eine Herausforderung für die Literaturwissenschaft. In: Herbert Foltinek, Christoph Leitgeb (Hgg.), *Literaturwissenschaft: intermedial – interdisziplinär.* Wien 2002 (Veröffentlichungen der Kommission für Litera-

Die Konzeption eines derartigen Werks erforderte, dass der Autor Einfluss auf die graphische Gestaltung nehmen konnte, also neben dem Text auch wesentlichen Anteil an der Bilderfindung hatte. Abgesehen von Architektur und Dekoration der Bögen war die Position von Texten im Bild zu bestimmen, mussten die Textelemente als Bildtexte bzw. Textbilder konzipiert werden. Da Sambucus lange vor dem Erscheinen des Drucks die Möglichkeit ins Auge fasst, das Werk Hugo Blotius bekannt zu machen (in einem Brief vom 29. Dezember 1571[71]), muss er zumindest sehr genaue, über die *Declaratio* hinausgehende Beschreibungen, wohl Skizzen, zur Hand gehabt haben – aus den Textpartien allein ließe sich kein befriedigender Eindruck von der Komposition gewinnen. Derartige Materialien müssen auch nach Antwerpen geschickt worden sein, da Sambucus ebenso wenig wie im Falle der *Emblemata* vor Ort war, um den Produktionsprozess zu überwachen[72]. Der Bezug auf Münzen erhielt damit auch einen sehr pragmatischen Aspekt: Sie konnten als Möglichkeit dienen, die bildliche Realisierung zumindest in wichtigen ikonographischen Details zu steuern. Leicht konnte Sambucus für die Produktion entsprechende – auch in Antwerpen verfügbare – Vorlagen benennen, um die Korrektheit der Darstellung, ihre Wiedererkennbarkeit und damit ihren Erfolg als antikisierende Huldigung zu gewährleisten.

APPENDIX

Während Sambucus' Bemühen um die handschriftliche Überlieferung antiker und byzantinischer Texte seit langem gewürdigt wird, hat sein Interesse an antiken Bildquellen und deren Einsatz in seinen eigenen Werken noch wenig Aufmerksamkeit und Resonanz gefunden. Hier sei daher abschließend ein unerwartetes Beispiel für die Rezeption der bereits vorgestellten Ärztebilder (*Veterum aliquot ac recentium medicorum philosophorumque Icones*) gebracht.

---

turwissenschaft 22), 163–192, hier 164f. Joachim PAECH, Intermedialität. Mediales Differential und transformative Figurationen. In: Jörg HELBIG (Hg.), *Intermedialität. Theorie und Praxis eines interdisziplinären Forschungsgebiets*. Berlin 1998, 14–30; hier 15.

[71] GERSTINGER, *Briefe* (s. Anm. 1), Nr. 52.

[72] Zu den Holzschnitten der *Emblemata*: Werner WATERSCHOOT, Lucas d'Heere und Johannes Sambucus. In: Alison Adams, Anthony John Harper (eds.), The Emblem in Renaissance and Baroque Europe. Selected Papers of the Glasgow Internatonal Emblem Conference. Leiden 1992, 45–52.

Als für das Bildprogramm des neu erbauten Hauptgebäudes der Universität Wien bedeutende Vertreter der Wissenschaften ausgewählt wurden, war unter den Repräsentanten der Medizin Aretaios von Kappadokien (ca. 80–138 n. Chr.), der mit der ersten exakten Beschreibung der Zuckerkrankheit das spezielle Interesse der zeitgenössischen medizinischen Forschung traf (Abb. 25)[73]: Als authentisches Porträt fand der Stich der *Icones* (Nr. 11; Abb. 26) Verwendung[74].

Abb. 27: Aretaeus, Porträtmedaillon am Hauptgebäude der Universität Wien

---

[73] Konstantinos LAIOS, Marianna KARAMANOU, Zenia SARIDAKI, George ANDROUTSOS, Aretaeus of Cappadocia and the first description of Diabetes. *Hormones* 11, 1 (2012), 109–113 <http://www.hormones.gr/760/article/article.html> (22. 6. 2017). Vivian NUTTON, Aretaios. *Der Neue Pauly. Enzyklopädie der Antike.* Bd. 1: A–Ari. Stuttgart, Weimar 1996, 1051f.

[74] Vgl. Julia RÜDIGER, Begegnung mit dem steinernen Autor. Die Gelehrten an der Fassade der Wiener Universität. In: Herbert Bannert, Elisabeth Klecker (Hgg.), *Autorschaft. Konzeptionen – Transformationen – Diskussionen.* Wien 2013 (*Singularia Vindobonensia* 3), 223–246. Vgl. DIES., *Die monumentale Universität. Funktioneller Bau und repräsentative Ausstattung des Hauptgebäudes der Universität Wien.* Wien [u.a.] 2015.

Tu breuis, obscurus, nec vocula pondere priua,
   Gloria Cappadocum proximus Hippocrati es.
Goupylus à tineis seruat, te Crassus honorus
   Induit Ausonia veste: legére diu.

Abb. 28: Aretaeus (Nr. 11). Veterum aliquot ac recentium medicorum philosophorumque Icones. Leiden 1603 (reprint Budapest 1985, s. Anm. 8)

Abbildungsnachweis

© *Alciato at Glasgow* (Glasgow University Library, Stirling Maxwell Collection) <http://www.emblems.arts.gla.ac.uk/alciato/index.php> (3. 6. 2017): S. 387, Abb. 17.

© Gábor BARTA, *Nándorfehérvár, 1456.* Budapest 1985: S. 342, Abb. 5a; S. 343, Abb. 5cd.

© Budapest, Országos Széchényi Könyvtár, Sammlung Alte Drucke, Apponyi M.130: S. 16, Abb. 1; App. H. 432: S. 216, Abb. 1; S. 232, Abb. 2+3.

© CoinArchives <http://www.coinarchives.com/> (3. 6. 2017): S. 392, Abb. 26.

© Paolo Giovio, Dialogo dell'imprese militari et amorose. Lione: Appresso Gulielmo Roviglio 1559, 129 <https://archive.org/details/dialogomilitarie00giov> (12. 2. 2016): S. 339, Abb. 4.

© Éva GYULAI, Farkas vagy egyszarvú? Politika és presztízs megjelenése a Szapolyai-címer változataiban [Wolf oder Einhorn? Die Darstellung von Politik und Prestige auf den Varianten des Szapolyai-Wappens]. In: József Bessenyei, Zita Horváth, Péter Tóth (Hgg.), *Tanulmányok Szapolyai Jánosról és a kora újkori Erdélyről* [Studien über Johann Szapolyai und Siebenbürgen in der frühen Neuzeit]. Miskolc 2004 (*Studia Miskolcinensia* 5), 91–124: S. 337, Abb. 2; S. 338, Abb. 3; S. 342, Abb. 5b

© Elisabeth KLECKER, Emblematika. In: Ivan Rusina a kol. (Hgg.), *Renesancia. Umenie medzi neskorou gotikou a barokom* [Renaissance. Kunst zwischen Spätgotik und Barock]. Bratislava 2009 (*Dejiny slovenského výtvarného umenia* [Geschichte der bildenden Kunst in der Slowakei]), 94–103: S. 370, Abb. 7; S. 379, Abb. 9; S. 385, Abb. 15; S. 388, Abb. 15bc; 390, Abb. 22; 391, Abb. 23.

© Elisabeth KLECKER: S. 6, Abb. 1; S. 395, Abb. 27.

© Kraków, Biblioteka Jagiellońska, Gram. 1310: S. 316.

© *Pedanius Dioscorides – Der Wiener Dioskurides: Codex medicus Graecus 1 der Österreichischen Nationalbibliothek.* Kommentar von Otto MAZAL. Graz 1998 (*Glanzlichter der Buchkunst* 8): S. 361, Abb. 3.

© Michelle O'REILLY, Kenneth SHEEDY, The Coins of Julius Caesar. Macquarie University, W. L. Gale Collection of Roman Republican Coins / Australian Centre for Ancient Numismatic Studies <http://www.humanities.mq.edu.au/acans/caesar/CivilWars_Libertas.htm> (3. 6. 2017): S. 387, Abb. 16.

© Johannes Sambucus, Emblemata. Antverpiae 1564 / Reprint. Hg. von Béla VARJAS. Budapest 1982: S. 332, Abb. 1a; S. 349, Abb. 6; S. 350, Abb. 7; S. 353, Abb. 1b; S. 354, Abb. 1c.

© Johannes Sambucus, Veterum aliquot ac recentium medicorum philosophorumque Icones ex bibliotheca Johannis Sambuci; cum eiusdem ad singulas Elogiis. Lugduni Batavorum 1603 / reprint Budapest 1985: S. 361, Abb. 2; S. 396, Abb. 28

© Wien, Bibliothek des Dominikanerkonvents, Sign. 8884: S. 130, Abb. 1; Sign. 12630: S. 139, Abb. 2; Sign. 14731: S. 141, Abb. 3.

© München, Bayerische Staatsbibliothek: Publii Virgilii Maronis Opera. Strassburg: Grüninger 1502, IX bb^v, Res/2 A.lat.a.292: <http://daten.digitale-sammlungen.de/~db/bsb00001879/images/> (3. 6. 2017): S. 367, Abb. 6.

© Wien, Österreichische Nationalbibliothek: P. Vindob. G 3: S. 259, Abb. 2; Cod. 9534, fol. 1^r: S. 242, Abb. 1; S. 263, Abb. 6; Cod. hist. gr. 10, fol. 1^r: S. 146; Cod. hist. gr. 56: S. 259, Abb. 3+4; S. 260, Abb. 5; Cod. phil. gr. 45: S. 182, Abb. 5; 44.G.49: S. 381, Abb. 13; S. 382, Abb. 14; 66.C.31: S. 378, Abb. 8; S. 380, Abb. 10; S. 381, Abb. 12ab; S. 392, Abb. 24.

© Wien, Universität Wien, Universitätsbibliothek: I 24.401: S. 388, Abb. 18; I 125.521: S. 13, Abb. 3; S. 206, Abb. 1; S. 209, Abb. 2; S. 292; S. 356, Abb. 1; S. 364, Abb. 4; S. 365, Abb. 5; I 161.822: S. 38; S. 83; I 178.102: S. 388, Abb. 19; S. 389, Abb. 20+21; S. 392, Abb. 25; I 240.480: S. 123; I 249.157: S. 162, Abb. 1; S. 171, Abb. 2; S. 174, Abb. 3; S. 214, Abb. 3; II 57.452: S. 35, Abb. 3; S. 100; II 119.923: S. 270; II 138.230: S. 176, Abb. 4; II 185.517: S. 380, Abb. 11; II 251.737: S. 96; II 256.737: S. 9, Abb. 2.

Inhalt

Elisabeth KLECKER
    Neue Forschungen zu Johannes Sambucus.
    Vorwort 5

Géza PÁLFFY
    Aus einer königlichen Freistadt Ungarns in die
    kaiserliche Residenzstadt Wien.
    Das Königreich Ungarn zur Zeit des Johannes Sambucus 15

Gábor ALMÁSI – Gábor Farkas KISS
    In search of Sambucus.
    His philology, publications and friends 37

Sonja REISNER
    Ein Bücherfund aus der Bibliothek des
    Johannes Sambucus 129

Jana GRUSKOVÁ
    Unwissentliche Vermittlung griechischen Kulturerbes.
    Palimpseste aus dem Besitz des Johannes Sambucus 145

Herbert BANNERT
    Die *editio princeps* der *Dionysiaka* des Nonnos
    von Panopolis *ex bibliotheca Ioannis Sambuci* 161

Herbert BANNERT
    Johannes Sambucus und seine Hunde
    Bombo und Madel 205

Gyula MAYER
    Die Janus-Pannonius-Edition und das fragmentarische
    Brandolini-Manuskript von János Zsámboky............................. 215

Christian GASTGEBER
    Johannes Sambucus und die *Donatio Constantini* 241

Johannes AMANN-BUBENIK
    Johannes Sambucus als Herausgeber und Verfasser
    von Herrscherserien 269

Daniel ŠKOVIERA
    Latein und Nationalsprachen im ersten Gespräch von
    Johannes Sambucus, *De imitatione Ciceroniana* 291

Ivan LÁBAJ
    Sambucus on Ciceronianism.
    An overview focussing on the second dialogue of
    De imitatione a Cicerone petenda 315

Zoltán ERDÖS
    Machtsymbole und politisches Programm
    in den *Emblemata* des Johannes Sambucus 331

Elisabeth KLECKER
    Ganzheitliche Antikerezeption.
    Text und Bild im Werk des Johannes Sambucus 355

Abbildungsnachweis 397